COGNITIVE PSYCHOLOGY

Dedicated to Jeff, Connor, Daphne, and Cleo, and the rest of my family, especially to Nan for always wanting a signed copy.

—DMM

Dedicated to Adena, Charlie, and Isabel for their understanding and patience while I spent many afternoons, nights, and weekends away from them while writing.

—JCC

SAGE was founded in 1965 by Sara Miller McCune to support the dissemination of usable knowledge by publishing innovative and high-quality research and teaching content. Today, we publish more than 750 journals, including those of more than 300 learned societies, more than 800 new books per year, and a growing range of library products including archives, data, case studies, reports, conference highlights, and video. SAGE remains majority-owned by our founder, and after Sara's lifetime will become owned by a charitable trust that secures our continued independence.

Los Angeles | London | Washington DC | New Delhi | Singapore | Boston

COGNITIVE PSYCHOLOGY

THEORY, PROCESS, AND METHODOLOGY

Dawn M. McBride
Illinois State University

J. Cooper Cutting
Illinois State University

Los Angeles | London | New Delhi
Singapore | Washington DC | Boston

Los Angeles | London | New Delhi
Singapore | Washington DC | Boston

FOR INFORMATION:

SAGE Publications, Inc.
2455 Teller Road
Thousand Oaks, California 91320
E-mail: order@sagepub.com

SAGE Publications Ltd.
1 Oliver's Yard
55 City Road
London EC1Y 1SP
United Kingdom

SAGE Publications India Pvt. Ltd.
B 1/I 1 Mohan Cooperative Industrial Area
Mathura Road, New Delhi 110 044
India

SAGE Publications Asia-Pacific Pte. Ltd.
3 Church Street
#10-04 Samsung Hub
Singapore 049483

Executive Editor: Reid Hester
Associate Editor: Nathan Davidson
Associate Digital Content Editor: Lucy Berbeo
Editorial Assistant: Morgan McCardell
Production Editor: Jane Haenel
Copy Editor: Mark Bast
Typesetter: C&M Digitals (P) Ltd.
Proofreader: Kate Macomber Stern
Indexer: Karen Wiley
Designer: Janet Kiesel
Marketing Manager: Shari Countryman

Detailed Contents photo credits: Chapter 1: National Institute of Mental Health; Chapter 2: ©iStockphoto.com/annedde; Chapter 3: Jim Arbogast/Digital Vision/Thinkstock; Chapter 4: Jupiterimages/Creatas/Thinkstock; Chapter 5: ©iStockphoto.com/Renphoto; Chapter 6: David De Lossy/Photodisc/Thinkstock; Chapter 7: ©iStockphoto.com/peepo; Chapter 8: ©iStockphoto.com/GoodLifeStudio; Chapter 9: ©iStockphoto.com/Nadezhda1906; Chapter 10: ©iStockphoto.com/VikramRaghuvanshi; Chapter 11: ©iStockphoto.com/azndc; Chapter 12: ©iStockphoto.com/andresr

Printed in the United States of America

Library of Congress Cataloging-in-Publication Data

McBride, Dawn M.

Cognitive psychology : theory, process, and methodology / Dawn M. McBride and J. Cooper Cutting, Illinois State University.

pages cm
Includes bibliographical references and index.

ISBN 978-1-4522-8879-6 (pbk. : alk. paper)

1. Cognitive psychology. I. Cutting, J. Cooper. II. Title.

BF201.M37 2016
153—dc23 2014045585

This book is printed on acid-free paper.

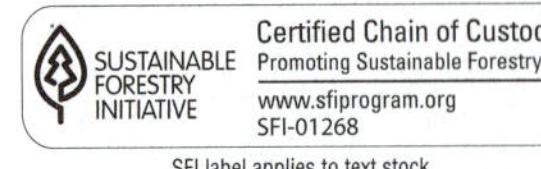

15 16 17 18 19 10 9 8 7 6 5 4 3 2 1

Brief Contents

Preface xvii
Acknowledgments xix
About the Authors xxi

Chapter 1 • Introduction to Cognitive Psychology 1
Chapter 2 • Cognitive Neuroscience 21
Chapter 3 • Perception 43
Chapter 4 • Attention 69
Chapter 5 • Memory Structures and Processes 95
Chapter 6 • Long-Term Memory: Influences on Retrieval 127
Chapter 7 • Memory Errors 151
Chapter 8 • Imagery 181
Chapter 9 • Language 203
Chapter 10 • Concepts and Knowledge 239
Chapter 11 • Problem Solving 267
Chapter 12 • Reasoning and Decision Making 297

Glossary 329
References 333
Author Index 349
Subject Index 357

Detailed Contents

Preface xvii

Acknowledgments xix

About the Authors xxi

Chapter 1 • Introduction to Cognitive Psychology 1

Introduction: Cognition and Shopping 2

What Is Cognitive Psychology? 2

Development of Cognitive Psychology 3

Current Approaches to the Study of Cognition 5

Representationalism 5

Embodied Cognition 6

Biological Perspective 6

Research in Cognitive Psychology 7

The Scientific Method 7

Research Methodologies 8

Case Studies 8

Correlational Studies 9

Experimental Studies 10

Commonly Used Measures Within Cognitive Psychology 12

Accuracy 13

Response Time 13

Beyond Accuracy and Response Time 14

Thinking About Research 15

Chapter Review 16

Summary 16

Chapter Quiz 17

Key Terms 18

Stop and Think Answers 18

Chapter 2 • Cognitive Neuroscience 21

Introduction: Knowledge From Cognitive Deficits 22

Clinical Case Studies in Cognitive Neuroscience 22

Structure of the Nervous System 25

The Neuron 25

The Brain 27

Measures in Cognitive Neuroscience 28

Single-Cell Recording 29

Electroencephalography (EEG) 29

Magnetoencephalography (MEG) 31
Electrical Stimulation/Inhibition of Neurons 31
Brain Imaging Techniques 32
Magnetic Resonance Imaging (MRI) 32
Positron Emission Tomography (PET) 32
Functional Magnetic Resonance Imaging (fMRI) 32
Recording Activity in the Living Brain 33
Can All Mental Processes Be Explained in Terms of Brain Activity? 36
Thinking About Research **37**
Chapter Review 39
Summary 39
Chapter Quiz 39
Key Terms 40
Stop and Think Answers 40

Chapter 3 • Perception 43

Introduction: Perception in Everyday Tasks 44
Sensory Systems: How Sensations Become Perceptions 44
Approaches to the Study of Perception 46
Computational Approaches 46
Ponzo Illusion Activity 49
Visual Perspective Illusion Activity 49
Top-Down Processing Activity 49
Gestalt Approaches 50
Triangle and Circle Activity 50
Similarity Activity 51
Proximity Activity 51
Principle of Pragnanz Activity 52
What Do You See Activity 53
Figure Ground Activity 53
Configural Superiority Activity 53
Perception/Action Approaches 54
Walking Through a Room Activity 55
Comparison of Approaches to Perception: Motion Perception 60
Thinking About Research **62**
Chapter Review 64
Summary 64
Chapter Quiz 65
Key Terms 65
Stop and Think Answers 65

Chapter 4 • Attention 69

Introduction: How We Pay Attention 70
Views of Attention 71
Attention as an Information Filter 71
Attention as a Limited Resource 74
Attention as a Spotlight 74
Attention as a Mental Capacity 76
Attention as a Feature Binder 77
Visual Search Activity 79
How Attention Affects Our Perceptions 80
The Gorilla in the Room: Inattentional Blindness 81
Asking Directions Activity 81
Noticing Changes Activity 81
Incompatibilities Tax Attention: The Simon Effect 81
Simon Effect Activity 82
Effects of Automatic Processes on Attention: The Stroop Task 83
Stroop Effect Activity 83
Automatic and Controlled Processing: A Cognitive Dichotomy 84
Thinking About Research 88
Chapter Review 90
Summary 90
Chapter Quiz 91
Key Terms 91
Stop and Think Answers 91

Chapter 5 • Memory Structures and Processes 95

Introduction: The Pervasiveness of Memory 96
Memory as Structure or Process 96
Encoding, Storage, and Retrieval 97
Modal Model of Memory 97
Sensory Memory 99
Short-Term Memory (STM) 101
Memory Span Activity 102
Capacity of STM 102
Duration of STM 103
Long-Term Memory (LTM) 105
Types of LTM Memories 106
The Working-Memory (WM) System 107
Baddeley's Model 108
Visuospatial Sketchpad 108
Phonological Loop 110

Word Length Effect Activity 111
Episodic Buffer 112
Central Executive 113
Beyond Baddeley's Model 114
Retrieval From Long-Term Memory 114
Recall Tasks 115
Recognition Tasks 115
Comparing Recall and Recognition Tasks 116
Implicit-Memory Tasks 117
Prospective-Memory Tasks 117
Memory Overview 119
Thinking About Research **119**
Chapter Review 120
Summary 120
Chapter Quiz 121
Key Terms 122
Stop and Think Answers 122

Chapter 6 • Long-Term Memory: Influences on Retrieval 127

Introduction: Superior Memory 128
Why We Forget 128
Encoding Effects 130
Levels of Processing 131
Levels of Processing Effect Activity 131
Spacing Effects 132
Serial Position Curve 133
Retrieval Effects 135
The Testing Effect 135
Using the Testing Effect 136
Encoding-Retrieval Interactions 137
Environmental Context Effects 137
Mood-Dependent Effects 139
Transfer-Appropriate Processing 140
Summary of Encoding-Retrieval Interactions 142
Mnemonics 143
Image Mnemonic Activity 143
Method of Loci Activity 144
Superior Autobiographical Memory 144
Thinking About Research **145**
Chapter Review 147
Summary 147
Chapter Quiz 147

Key Terms 148
Stop and Think Answers 148

Chapter 7 • Memory Errors 151

Introduction: The Inaccuracy of Memory 152
The Seven "Sins" of Memory 153
Error #1 Transience 154
Error #2 Absentmindedness 154
Error #3 Blocking 154
Error #4 Source Misattribution 155
Error #5 Suggestibility 155
Error #6 Bias 156
Error #7 Persistence 156
Summary 156
The Reconstructive Nature of Memory 157
Bartlett's Studies 157
Identify the Task Activity 158
Schemata and Scripts 158
Memory Errors in the Laboratory 160
The DRM Procedure 160
False Memory Activity 160
Eyewitness Memory Studies 164
Applications of Eyewitness Memory Research 167
Summary and Conclusions 168
Clinical Memory Failures—Amnesia 169
Types of Amnesia 169
Amnesia and Implicit Memory 170
Amnesia in Alzheimer's Disease 172
Amnesia in Childhood 173
Thinking About Research 174
Chapter Review 175
Summary 175
Chapter Quiz 176
Key Terms 177
Stop and Think Answers 177

Chapter 8 • Imagery 181

Introduction: Visual Imagery in Everyday Life 182
Mental Images and Cognition 182
The Debate on Propositional and Spatial Representations 183
Imagery and Memory 186
Imagery and Memory Activity 186

The Picture Superiority Effect 186
The Concreteness Effect 187
The Bizarreness Effect 188
Bizarreness Effect Activity 188
Imagery and Mnemonics 189
The Dark Side of Imagery 190
Imagery in Problem Solving and Wayfinding 190
Pick a Card Activity 190
Imagery in Problem Solving 191
Pulley System Problem Activity 191
Imagery in Wayfinding 193
Nonvisual Imagery 193
Imagery and Simulation 196
Thinking About Research 197
Chapter Review 198
Summary 198
Chapter Quiz 199
Key Terms 199
Stop and Think Answers 199

Chapter 9 • Language 203

Introduction: A Simple Conversation 204
What Is Language? 205
Structure of Language 205
Language Form: Phonology and Orthography 205
Morphology: Language Interface of Form, Syntax, and Semantics 206
Syntax (Grammar) 206
Semantics (Meaning) 208
Pragmatics (Using Language) 208
Listening for Nonliteral Meaning Activity 208
How Do We Process Language? 209
Language Comprehension 210
Listening for Ambiguity Activity 210
Language Perception 211
Using Top-Down Information Activity 212
Lexical Recognition and Access 213
Interpreting Sentences: Syntactic Analysis 215
Interpreting Syntax Activity 215
Beyond the Sentence: Texts and Discourse 217
Language Production 220
Making Mistakes: Speech Errors 221

Listening to Speech Activity 221
Separation of Semantics, Syntax, and Form 222
Dialogue: Production and Comprehension Together 225
Acquiring Language 226
Typical Language Development 226
Nature or Nurture: Mechanisms for Learning Words and Syntax 228
Human Language and Animal Communication 230
Comparing Human Language to Animal Communication 230
Attempts to Teach Animals Human Language 231
Thinking About Research 232
Chapter Review 233
Summary 233
Chapter Quiz 234
Key Terms 235
Stop and Think Answers 235

Chapter 10 • Concepts and Knowledge 239

Introduction: Game Night 240
What Are Concepts? 241
The Classical Approach: Concepts as Definitions 241
Theoretical Problems With Definitions as Concepts 241
What Is a Chair? Activity 241
Empirical Problems With Definitions as Concepts 242
Birds Activity 242
Alternative Approaches to Concepts 244
Prototype Approach 244
Exemplar Approach 246
Concepts Based on World Knowledge Approach 249
Other Alternative Approaches to Concepts 252
Organizing Our Concepts 252
Conceptual Hierarchies 252
Basic-Level Concepts 253
Basic Concepts Activity 253
Organizational Approaches 254
Stored-Network Approaches 254
Feature Comparisons Approaches 255
Neuroscience-Inspired Approaches 255
Summary of Conceptual Organization 256
Using Concepts: Beyond Categorization 257
Category Induction 258
Stereotypes 258
Expertise 259
Conceptual Combination 260

The Future of Research and Theory of Concepts 260
Thinking About Research **261**
Chapter Review 263
Summary 263
Chapter Quiz 263
Key Terms 264
Stop and Think Answers 264

Chapter 11 • Problem Solving 267

Introduction: Problem Solving in Daily Life 268
Recognizing and Identifying a Problem 268
Defining and Representing Problems 270
Moving Pennies Activity 270
Dominos and a Chessboard Activity 270
Functional Fixedness 272
Two Strings Problem Activity 272
Developing Solutions to Problems: Approaches and Strategies 273
Sudoku Activity 273
Associationist Approach: Trial-and-Error Strategy 274
Gestalt Approaches 274
Insight 275
9-Dot Problem Activity 275
Mental Set 276
Cups and Water Problem Activity 276
Analogical Transfer 277
Radiation Problem Activity 277
Summary 279
Problem Solving as Problem Space Searches 280
Means-Ends Strategy 281
Hill-Climbing Strategy 282
Working-Backward Strategy 282
Summary of Approaches and Strategies 283
Allocating Mental Resources for Solving the Problem 283
Matchstick Math Activity 285
Expertise 286
Experts Versus Novices 287
Perception and Attention 287
Memory 287
Better Strategies 287
Becoming a Better Problem Solver 288
Thinking About Research **289**
Chapter Review 291
Summary 291

Chapter Quiz 292
Key Terms 293
Stop and Think Answers 293

Chapter 12 • Reasoning and Decision Making 297
Introduction: A Night at the Movies 298
Deductive Reasoning 299
Syllogistic Reasoning 299
Syllogisms Activity 299
Conditional Reasoning 300
Conditional Arguments Activity 301
Wason 4-Card Task Activity 302
Adapted Wason 4-Card Task Activity 303
Deductive-Reasoning Approaches 304
Conclusion Interpretation Approaches 304
Representation-Explanation Approaches 304
Surface Approaches 307
Combining These Approaches: Dual-Process Framework Approach 308
Inductive Reasoning 309
Types of Inductive Reasoning 309
Analogical Reasoning 309
Category Induction 309
Causal Reasoning 310
Hypothesis Testing 311
Hypothesis Testing Activity 311
Counterfactual Thinking 312
Everyday Reasoning 312
Making Decisions 313
A General Model of Decision Making 314
Ideal Decision Making: A Normative Model 315
Heuristics and Biases 315
Representativeness Bias 315
Tom's Job Activity 315
Availability Bias 317
Framing Bias 317
Descriptive Decision-Making Approaches 318
Prospect Theory 319
Dual-Process Framework 319
Future Advances in Theories of Reasoning and Decision Making 320
Thinking About Research 322
Chapter Review 324
Summary 324

Chapter Quiz 325
Key Terms 325
Stop and Think Answers 326

Glossary 329
References 333
Author Index 349
Subject Index 357

Preface

We are pleased to present *Cognitive Psychology: Theory, Process, and Methodology* to aid students in their learning about this field. We want to share our love of cognitive psychology with students learning about this exciting area of psychology.

Our main goal in writing this text is to engage students in the topics through *connections to everyday situations* they might encounter (each chapter begins with one of these real-world situations or stories) and with a student-friendly and personal writing style. However, we also focused on methodology in this field as a way to allow students to gain the researcher's perspective in studying these topics and to understand how such research aids in evaluating theoretical perspectives on cognitive psychology, which are constantly changing as new data are collected. To illustrate the different methodologies, we have chosen a mix of classic studies and more recent findings in the areas covered in each chapter.

Each chapter is written to be encapsulated, such that instructors can choose to cover topics in the order they wish. We also worked to show connections between the different topics (as well as to other fields of study such as social psychology, philosophy, linguistics, and biology) within the chapters to show students the large overlap between the mental processes studied in cognitive psychology.

Chapter 2, "Cognitive Neuroscience," is presented early in the text to provide students with necessary background on the methods used in this subfield and the biological mechanisms the methods rely on for measurement. This chapter follows an introductory chapter (Chapter 1) covering general research methodology in cognitive psychology that helps students better understand the studies presented in the chapters. Neuroscience studies are then embedded within the chapters, where they provide evidence for different theoretical and conceptual descriptions of the cognitive processes discussed in each chapter.

Each chapter ends with a *Thinking About Research* activity that provides a description of a current study in that area of cognitive psychology from the journal *Psychological Science*. Descriptions are summary versions of the subsections of the published studies to help scaffold student learning of journal article reading skills. The full reference for each article is provided (with the full text of the article available on the text's SAGE edge website) to allow instructors to assign and/or discuss the article in their courses. Each Thinking About Research section also includes *critical thinking questions* to help students connect the study to the topic of the chapter and think about the design (and reasons for the design) used in the study.

Chapters include *Stop and Think* sections to help students pause and consider the information they have just read. Some questions are designed to help students do a quick review of the material to gauge their learning. Other questions are designed to help them think critically about the material and connect it to their own lives. Answers are provided for these questions at the end of each chapter.

The text can also be paired with an Interactive eBook that contains carefully placed links to lab exercises and demonstrations, with follow-up questions to help students make connections between the methods of study presented in the text and the suggested exercises. The exercises and related assessment are also available via the book's SAGE edge website, described in more detail below. Look for the following icons accompanied by labels in the margins of the print book that signal when you can visit the SAGE edge website to find additional resources:

Watch a video clip with an example or demonstration of the concept.

Listen to a clip from a news story or podcast about the concept.

Read a SAGE journal article demonstrating research on the concept.

Visit a website with more information, an interactive exercise, or a demonstration related to the concept.

In addition, activities that students can do on their own as they read are embedded within the chapters. Those activities are listed in the table of contents, and they are marked with an icon (pictured here) in the book margins so that instructors can find them easily in the chapters if they want to use them as in-class demonstrations as well.

We hope you enjoy reading *Cognitive Psychology* as much as we enjoyed writing it!

Dawn M. McBride

J. Cooper Cutting

Ancillaries

SAGE edge offers a robust online environment featuring an impressive array of tools and resources for review, study, and further exploration, keeping both instructors and students on the cutting edge of teaching and learning. Go to **edge.sagepub.com/mcbridecp** to access the companion site.

SAGE edge for Instructors

SAGE edge for Instructors, a password-protected instructor resource site, supports teaching by making it easy to integrate quality content and create a rich learning environment for students. The following chapter-specific assets are available on the teaching site:

- **Test banks** provide a diverse range of questions as well as the opportunity to edit any question and/or insert personalized questions to effectively assess students' progress and understanding.
- **Lecture notes** summarize key concepts by chapter to assist in the preparation of lectures and class discussions.
- **Sample course syllabi** for semester and quarter courses provide suggested models for structuring a course.
- Editable, chapter-specific **PowerPoint slides** offer complete flexibility for creating a multimedia presentation for the course.
- Lively and stimulating **ideas for class assignments** can be used in class to reinforce active learning. The creative assignments apply to individual or group projects.
- Chapter-specific **discussion questions** help launch classroom interaction by prompting students to engage with the material and by reinforcing important content.
- A **Course cartridge** provides easy LMS integration.

SAGE edge for Students

SAGE edge for Students provides a personalized approach to help students accomplish their coursework goals in an easy-to-use learning environment. The open-access study site includes the following:

- A customized online **action plan** includes tips and feedback on progress through the course and materials, allowing students to individualize their learning experience.
- **Learning objectives** reinforce the most important material.
- Mobile-friendly practice **quizzes** allow for independent assessment by students of their mastery of course material.
- Mobile-friendly **eFlashcards** strengthen understanding of key terms and concepts.
- **Interactive exercises** and meaningful web links make it easy to mine internet resources, further explore topics, and answer critical thinking questions.
- **Multimedia content** includes audio and video resources that appeal to students with different learning styles.
- EXCLUSIVE! Access to full-text **SAGE journal articles** that have been carefully selected to support and expand on the concepts presented in each chapter.

Acknowledgments

We'd like to acknowledge a number of important people who helped in many ways in the writing of this text and helped improve it from its initial drafts. First are Jeff Wagman and Adena Meyers. Jeff read some chapters and both Jeff and Adena offered feedback and provided essential support during the project. In addition, our family, friends, and colleagues provided support and helpful feedback during the writing process. In particular, Marla Reese-Weber and Corinne Zimmerman provided helpful discussion while we worked on this text. Several reviewers also provided valuable suggestions that greatly improved the quality of the text. At SAGE, we'd like to thank Reid Hester for his valuable assistance in getting this project approved, keeping it going, and providing important discussion of issues that arose. Nathan Davidson and Lucy Berbeo also provided much appreciated support and feedback about the text. Dawn also thanks the students at Illinois State University who have taken her PSY 253 course and influenced her teaching of this material. All the individuals named here contributed in important ways to the production of this text and have our sincere thanks and gratitude.

SAGE Publications gratefully acknowledges the following reviewers:

Lise Abrams, University of Florida

Elizabeth Arnott-Hill, Chicago State University

Caroline A. Arout, The College of Staten Island of The City University of New York

George M. Diekhoff, Midwestern State University

Susan E. Dutch, Westfield State University

Dr. Jane E. Dwyer, Rivier University

Sara Finley, Pacific Lutheran University

Kathleen A. Flannery, Saint Anselm College

Alexandra K. Frazer, Muhlenberg College

Kelly M. Goedert, Seton Hall University

Tina L. Jameson, Bridgewater State University

Jerwen Jou, University of Texas – Pan American

Todd A. Kahan, Bates College

Jeff Kellogg, Marian University

Melissa K. Kelly, Millsaps College

Adam Krawitz, University of Victoria

William Langston, Middle Tennessee State University

Sara J. Margolin, The College at Brockport, State University of New York

Lisa M. Maxfield, California State University, Long Beach

Glenn E. Meyer, Trinity University

Michaela Porubanova, SUNY, Farmingdale

Jianjian Qin, California State University, Sacramento

Hiroko Sotozaki, Western Illinois University

Melissa S. Terlecki, Cabrini College

Silvana M. R. Watson, Old Dominion University

About the Authors

Dawn M. McBride is a professor of psychology at Illinois State University. Her research interests include automatic forms of memory, false memory, prospective memory, and forgetting. She has taught courses in introductory psychology, statistics, research methods, cognition and learning, human memory, and a graduate course in experimental design. She is a recipient of the Illinois State University Teaching Initiative Award. Her out-of-work interests include spending time with her family, traveling, watching Philadelphia (her place of birth) sports teams, learning new languages (currently, Japanese) and reading British murder mysteries. She earned her PhD in cognitive psychology from the University of California, Irvine, and her BA from the University of California, Los Angeles.

J. Cooper Cutting (PhD, cognitive psychology, University of Illinois, Urbana-Champaign) is associate professor of psychology at Illinois State University. Dr. Cutting's research interests are in psycholinguistics, primarily with a focus on the production of language. A central theme of his research is how different types of information interact during language use. He has examined this issue in the context of lexical access, within-sentence agreement processes, figurative language production, and pragmatics. He teaches courses in research methods, statistics, cognitive psychology, computer applications in psychology, human memory, psycholinguistics, and sensation and perception.

Glow Images, Inc/Glow/Getty Images

Introduction to Cognitive Psychology

Questions to Consider

- What is cognitive psychology? How did it develop as a field?
- How have psychologists approached the study of cognition?
- What types of research methods are useful in the study of cognition?
- What behaviors do psychologists observe to study cognition?

Introduction: Cognition and Shopping

Crash Course: Cognitive Psychology

Last night as I wandered into the kitchen I noticed that the lighting looked dim. As I looked up, I realized that three light bulbs had burned out. Furthermore, I noticed that they were each a different type of bulb. So I jumped into the car and headed to the grocery store for more light bulbs. I wandered into the store, grabbed a cart, and headed down the aisle. "While here," I thought to myself, "I may as well pick up some other things that we need." As I passed through the cereal aisle I tried to decide which brand to get. I noticed a brightly colored sign announcing "Buy 2, get 50% off" for Fruity O's. While my daughter likes that brand, I decide that I really don't want two boxes of it, so instead I buy one box and another of Raisin Flakes. Next up are bread, milk, butter, swiss cheese, and orange juice. Since this is the store that I usually shop at I wander through quickly, checking things off from my mental list. At the checkout counter I'm asked, "Paper or plastic?" and I hesitate while I realize that I have left my reusable bags in the trunk of the car and then reply, "Plastic, please." After paying, I exit the store, drive home, unload, and put away the groceries. Afterward, I sit down at the kitchen table and notice how dim it is. I suddenly realize that I had forgotten the very thing I ran out to the store to get: light bulbs.

What Is Cognitive Psychology?

In the shopping story you just read, cognition is involved in many of the tasks described. In fact, cognition is used in most of the tasks that people do every day, from ordinary tasks like grocery shopping to more complex tasks like deciding what to major in or studying for a difficult exam. You may have related the preceding story to things that have happened to you: walking upstairs in your house and then forgetting why you went up there, making a decision about whether an offered deal will really save you money, trying to remember things you have to do or things you need to buy. Cognition is involved in so many things we do that it is difficult to come up with events in our lives that do not involve cognition. In fact, just thinking about what cognitive psychology is involves cognition. As a simple answer, cognition involves thinking and other mental processes. However, as a student of psychology, you probably already know that few questions in psychology have simple answers, and the question of "What is cognitive psychology?" is no exception. A more complete answer to this question is that cognitive psychology includes the following:

- Our perception of the world around us through our senses and how we interpret the sensations brought in by our senses (e.g., noticing that the lights are dim in your kitchen)
- The attentional processes that allow us to focus on a particular stimulus in our environment (e.g., a brightly colored sign catching our attention in a grocery store)
- How our memory operates to allow us to remember episodes, information, and intentions when we attempt to retrieve them (e.g., remembering—or not remembering—to buy light bulbs at the store)
- Our language processes that help us communicate our thoughts and ideas with others (e.g., being able to read the advertisement for the cereal or understanding the cashier's question of "Paper or plastic?")

Profile: Endel Tulving

- The processes that contribute to our decision making, both helpful and hindering (e.g., trying to decide if the "Buy 2, get 50% off" deal is going to save you money or be a healthy choice)
- The brain activity that controls all of the processes described so far

This may seem like a long list, but it only touches briefly on the major areas of cognitive psychology studied in this field. Current research in cognitive psychology also bridges cognition with other areas of psychology, philosophy, linguistics, cognitive science, and neuroscience. For example, some cognitive psychologists are interested in the role of consciousness in our cognitive processes and how much conscious choice we actually have in our behaviors. Others are considering how brain function might affect our social interactions and be involved in social dysfunction such as autism spectrum disorders. Thus, cognitive psychology is broad and overlaps with many other fields (e.g., social psychology, biological psychology, philosophy), both inside and outside of psychology.

Development of Cognitive Psychology

In some form, cognitive psychology has been a field of study for thousands of years. Early philosophers asked questions about cognition that are still viable today. For example, Aristotle suggested an early metaphor for the mind to explain how memory processes work. He proposed that our memory is like a wax tablet with memories formed in the tablet like molds in hot wax. The durability of the memory depended on different factors in the same way that the durability of molds in wax are variable—if the wax is heated, the form can become distorted or disappear. As you will read later in this chapter and in Chapters 5, 6, and 7, memory researchers still seek models of memory in current research.

Limits of the Mind

As scientific methods were developed in other fields (e.g., physics, biology, chemistry), researchers began to apply these methods to the study of the mind. Wilhelm Wundt (one of the first psychologists) studied conscious experience through introspective methods that involved systematic self-reports of a person's thoughts. In this way, some early psychologists studied how people perceived sounds, colors, and other sensory experiences. Others (e.g., Fechner, Helmholtz) studied perception using psychophysical methods with a goal of developing laws of perception. Another early psychologist, Ebbinghaus, studied the processes of memory by testing his own memory extensively to determine the savings in relearning that can be gained from previous exposures to information. He measured the decline in his memory performance over time and thus mapped out the forgetting curve that researchers still find in current studies of memory performance over time (see Chapter 6 for further discussion of the forgetting curve).

In the early to mid-twentieth century, the study of cognition fell out of favor in psychology with the rise in popularity of the **behaviorist** perspective. Behaviorists argued that introspective methods, such as the methods used by Wundt, were biased by the perspective of the subject. How did the researcher know that the mental processes of the mind were consciously accessible and could be verbally reported in an accurate way? Instead, behaviorists focused on behaviors they could directly observe, with the thought processes behind the behaviors of less interest. However, in the mid-twentieth century, with the development of information-processing approaches to studying the mind and behavior, cognitive psychology as a field took hold and has been a driving force in psychology ever since. An important influence in this change was an attack on the behaviorist approach to language learning by the linguist Noam Chomsky. An important behaviorist, B. F. Skinner, had proposed that language learning occurs through conditioning processes (Skinner, 1957). In other words, language development occurred

Cognitive Revolution

Behaviorist: one who adheres to the perspective in psychology that focuses on observable behaviors

Andrew Rusk/CC-BY-2.0

Photo 1.1 Noam Chomsky, an early proponent of cognitive psychology

through the imitation of speakers around a child and the feedback (reinforced orpunished) the child's speech elicited. Chomsky (1959) presented a strong counter to this proposal, the centerpiece of which pointed out that children produce language that has never been produced around them or reinforced (e.g., original sentences never heard before, incorrect grammar). Instead, Chomsky suggested that children have the mental capacity to learn the rules of the language(s) spoken around them without explicit feedback on the language they produce. In other words, language abilities result from cognitive processes inherent to humans. From Chomsky's argument, psychologists began to realize that the study of cognitive processes is an important part of understanding behavior—that understanding the processes behind the overt behaviors would advance our understanding of the mind and behavior in important ways. However, behaviorism did influence the way we study cognitive processes today. Its focus on the experimental examination of behavior shaped the way researchers approach the study of mental processes. Experimentation is still the focus, but cognitive psychologists examine the behaviors resulting from the mental processes being studied.

Another influential development in the return to cognitive psychology research was the invention of the computer. Computers presented an information-processing model as a way of thinking about cognitive processes. In this new metaphor for the mind, the brain could be thought of as a biological computer, capable of storing large amounts of information and acting to alter that information as learning takes place. Cognitive processes were the "software" that processed the information (with the brain as the "hardware"). The information-processing model helped psychologists think about cognition in a new way, which spurred research on how information is stored in our minds and how that information is acted on as we encounter new information related to what is already stored. This model also provided a universal language to allow researchers to discuss the processes of the mind and their connection to the brain.

A milestone in the development of cognitive psychology as a coherent field of study was a book by Ulric Neisser (1967) that tied together various topics, such as memory, perception, attention, and language, as a unified field. Neisser coined the term *cognitive psychology* for the topics you are studying in this course, and he is widely viewed as the father of the field due to this contribution. Throughout his career, Neisser conducted research in different areas of cognitive psychology with a focus on cognition in everyday behaviors.

Sandra Condry/Cornell Department of Psychology

Photo 1.2 Ulric Neisser, an important figure in the development of cognitive psychology

Despite his important contribution, the field of cognitive psychology differs somewhat from the topics Neisser discussed in his book. The topics you see in this text are broader in scope than those Neisser started with when he first described cognitive psychology. For example, in each chapter of this text you will find discussion of work in neuroscience that examines the biological underpinnings of cognitive processes. Cognitive neuroscience has become one of the most influential areas of cognitive psychology. This topic is introduced in Chapter 2 and comes up throughout the book, as research in this area informs theory about different cognitive processes. This area of cognitive psychology brings together the different topics in the other chapters of the text under the biological approach to the study of cognition. In addition, a more holistic approach to memory is now taken by researchers than what was presented in Neisser's book. He discussed memory by modality of information (e.g., "visual memory," "active verbal memory") instead of as one connected topic. In fact, the study of memory has become a large part of the study of cognition in the decades that followed the publication of Neisser's book. A glance at the table of contents of this text shows three chapters (Chapters 5–7) devoted to memory, and this topic is touched on in additional chapters as it connects with other topics (e.g., concepts, imagery). Finally, cognitive psychology is not an isolated field. It has important connections to other fields such as social psychology, philosophy, biology, and the law. You will see some of these connections illustrated in the chapters as we discuss the mental processes that make up the field.

Stop and Think

1.1. List four cognitive processes studied by cognitive psychologists.

1.2. What three events influenced the development of cognitive psychology?

1.3. From the description of the types of processes studied in cognitive psychology, what processes do you think were involved in generating your response to the two previous questions?

Current Approaches to the Study of Cognition

In the past few decades, cognitive psychology has risen as a major field of study in psychology, with a large number of researchers investigating questions about cognition and its relation to everyday experiences. Current research takes a number of approaches to understanding cognition. We discuss a few of the most influential approaches to allow you to better understand why researchers have focused on some of the research questions we discuss later in this text. These approaches represent some of the ways that researchers think about how cognition works, which in turn influences the way they design research studies to investigate these processes.

Representationalism

A popular perspective in cognition is to consider information from the world as being represented in some form in our minds. For example, we might store the concept of *armadillo* in various ways. We could represent armadillo as an exemplar of the category of animals or in interconnections with related animals. We might also represent it as a concept with characteristic features (e.g., mammal, hard shell, digs). The basic aspect of the **representationalist** approach is that knowledge about the world is represented in our minds such that cognitive processes can "operate" on the representations. If we read about armadillos or see a documentary about them, we might change or add to this stored information as we learn more about armadillos than we previously knew.

Photo 1.3 Armadillo

In early representationalist models (Rumelhart & Norman, 1988), information was thought to be stored as symbols that could be operated on in the way that mathematical variable symbols (e.g., *2* and *II* are both symbols used to represent the concept of two) are operated on (we can manipulate these symbols using operations such as addition or multiplication). This allowed researchers to study the operations as processes of cognition. For example, models of perception relied on feature detectors that stored information about features encountered in the world (e.g., lines, curves, colors). We can identify objects when our feature system identifies particular features that we know to be a part of an object. If we detect perpendicular edges in an object, then the feature system can rule out objects with rounded edges and narrow identification down to objects with sharper edges. In this way, the features we see are stored as feature symbols in our minds. As knowledge of cognition has advanced, these symbol systems have become more complex in representing the knowledge stored in our minds.

The representationalist approach arose from the computer and information-processing models of cognition. Information is stored in computers in the form of 0's and 1's that form chains of "off" and "on" signals. This is similar to the way that neurons either fire or do not fire at any given time. In this way, the computer model is analogous to how the brain functions. Seeing this similarity, some cognitive and

Representationalist: one who adheres to the perspective in psychology that concepts can be represented in the mind

physiological psychologists have considered information as being represented in the mind through the "on" and "off" firing patterns of groups of neurons. This allows researchers to think of information as being stored in the mind and available for processing as we interpret, analyze, and alter this information in our thinking.

The representationalist perspective connects well with the biological perspective (see later in this section), as it provides a model of cognition in sync with the physiological processes that occur in the brain. However, the primary model for representationalism is the computer metaphor for the mind. The language of computers is typically evoked in describing the representations found in the mind. For example, concepts are often described as storage nodes of information in a hierarchical network (see Chapter 10 for further discussion of concepts). Thus, this approach has a different origin and conceptual structure than the biological approach described shortly.

Embodied Cognition

Embodied Cognition

Another approach to the study of cognition views our cognitive processes as providing a means of interacting with the world around us. In this view, our visual sense doesn't simply create representations of objects and scenes from the world for us to interpret and process. Instead, it provides information about the world that allows us to do things in that world, such as walking through a doorway or catching a ball. In other words, our cognitive processes have evolved to allow us to interact with the world (objects, people, conversations) and should be studied according to the purpose they serve. As such, our motions and interactions with objects in the world will influence our cognition. Researchers who adhere to the **embodied cognition** perspective examine cognition as an interaction between humans (and other animals) and their environment. Studies from this area, for example, have shown that memory of a text is better when people act it out compared with other learning strategies, like rereading the text (Scott, Harris, & Rothe, 2001), that people will look at the space on an empty screen when recalling information previously presented at that location on the screen (Richardson & Spivey, 2000), and that when people are asked to wear shoulder pads, those with experience wearing shoulder pads to play American football pass through a small open space in a different way than those without experience playing the sport (Higuchi et al., 2011). These results show that our memory, language, and perception processes depend on our interactions with the world around us. More about this perspective is discussed in each of the topical chapters where this approach has been applied.

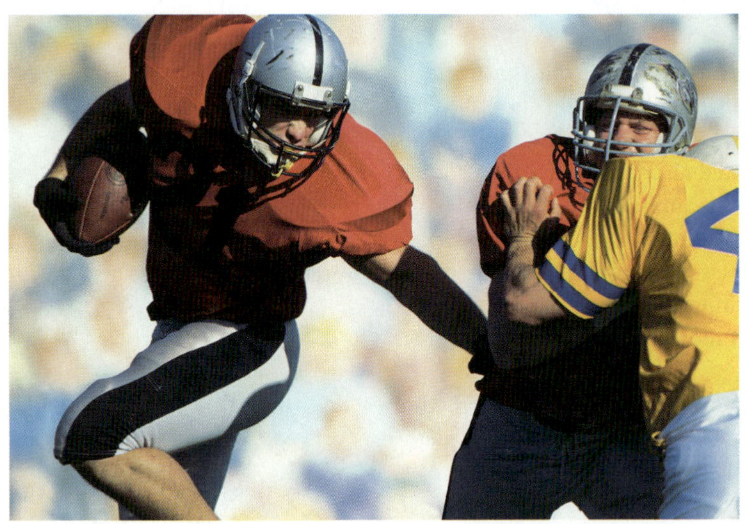

Photo 1.4 Researchers who adhere to the embodied cognition approach believe that perception serves as a process to aid interaction with the environment.

Embodied cognition: a perspective in psychology that cognition serves for bodily interaction with the environment

Biological perspective: perspective in psychology that describes cognition according to the mechanisms of the brain

Biological Perspective

We have already had some discussion of the role biology plays in the study of cognition as we have considered the area of cognitive neuroscience and its connection to the representationalist approach. However, some researchers have considered a **biological perspective** behind cognition beyond just the specific brain activity associated with different cognitive processes. These researchers build theories of cognition using a different metaphor for the mind, one not based on a computer but rather on how the brain works. In other words, they propose theories based not on the manipulation of symbols but rather on networks of connections loosely analogous to networks of neurons. For example, in attempting to model how our memory system learns new information, researchers have considered the way in which neurons are connected in networks in the brain and simulated such networks in models of memory (McClelland, 1999). Models of this sort, known as connectionist models, have also been developed to explain how we identify language through individual features of letters and spoken words. Thus, our knowledge of the biological architecture of the brain and the neurological functioning of the brain has guided researchers in their attempts to better understand how different cognitive processes work.

Stop and Think

1.4. How are the representationalist and biological approaches connected?

1.5. What does embodied cognition mean?

1.6. In what ways are the biological features of the brain important in the study of cognition?

1.7. Given what you know so far about cognitive psychology, which of the approaches described in this section do you think you would follow as a researcher in psychology? Why?

Brain Bugs

Research in Cognitive Psychology

One thing is clear from the preceding review of the historical and theoretical perspectives: the field of cognitive psychology relies heavily on research and more broadly on observations of behavior. Throughout this text you will review research used to develop many of the major theories within cognitive psychology. The following sections briefly review some basics of the scientific method and different research methodologies, and the chapter ends with a review of measurements commonly used in the discipline.

The Scientific Method

The **scientific method** is grounded on four core principles: empiricism, determinism, testability, and parsimony. **Empiricism** is the principle that the key to understanding new things is through systematic observation. In the case of cognitive psychology, the "things" that we want to know are the mental processes that underlie human behavior. This is tricky for most cognitive psychologists because it is difficult to directly observe mental processes. Sometimes there are observable outcomes of these processes that are readily measured (e.g., remembering or forgetting to do something, buying cereal, selecting plastic bags). However, often these outcomes are assumed to be the result of a string of different mental processes. As a result, much of cognitive psychological theory is based on clever indirect measurements of these processes. **Determinism** is the principle that behaviors have underlying causes and that "understanding" involves identification of what these causes are and how they are related to the behavior of interest. The set of these cause and effect relationships between variables (the "causes" and the "behaviors" that they influence) are what make up theories of behavior. **Testability** is the principle that theories must be stated in ways that allow them to be evaluated through observation. In many respects, the scientific process is a competitive one in which the predictions of different theories are like players pitted against each other and research studies are the playing field. Research consists of systematically collecting observations designed to test the

Scientific method: a method of gaining knowledge in a field that relies on observations of phenomena and which allows for tests of hypotheses about those phenomena

Empiricism: the principle that the key to understanding new things is through systematic observation

Determinism: the principle that behaviors have underlying causes and that understanding involves identification of what these causes are and how they are related to the behavior of interest

Testability: the principle that theories must be stated in ways that allow them to be evaluated through observation

Monkey Business Images/Shutterstock

Photo 1.5 How we make decisions in our daily lives depends on a variety of different variables.

predictions of multiple theories, ruling some out, and leaving only those consistent with the data left standing. **Parsimony** is a kind of tiebreaker in this competition. It is the principle to prefer the simple explanations over more complex ones. If there are two or more theories left standing (accounting for the same amount of data), then adopting the least complex one is preferred (at least until further data are collected that refute the simpler theory).

Consider once again the shopping story with which we started the chapter. This story includes many behaviors that we (as cognitive psychologists) may wish to understand. Let's focus on one of them: deciding whether to take the "buy 2, get 50% off" deal. Our behavior of interest here is how one makes this and other similar decisions. In the context of research, the behavior of interest is typically referred to as the **dependent** (or response) **variable**. Having identified what we want to explain, the next step is to identify what and how different variables might affect this dependent variable. The variable you have control over and can control and manipulate is known as the **independent** (or explanatory) **variable**. The set of variables and how they are related to each other is what constitutes our theory. For this example there may be many relevant variables, but for our purposes here let's keep it simple and just pick two: the nature of the deal being offered ("buy 2, get 50% off") and the starting price of the product. Suppose our theory says that people make their decisions based on how they frame their potential gains and losses (e.g., Thaler, 1985; Sinha & Smith, 2000). In other words, the shopper's decision may depend on whether he or she is thinking about the deal as either a gain or a reduced loss. How the deal is presented may have an impact on how shoppers view the deal. Consider three ways of presenting what is essentially the same deal: "50% off," "buy one, get one free," and "buy 2, get 50% off" (so if you buy two boxes with an initial price of $1 each, you'll pay only $1 total with all three deals; see Figure 1.1). The first case frames the deal in terms of price savings (a reduced loss), the second in terms of getting extra product (a gain), and the third is a mixture of the two. With a starting price of $1, consumers may view the potential of gaining an extra product as most important. However, if the starting price of the product is larger (e.g., $5), then consumers may change their decision-making processes in favor of reduced losses. These last statements amount to predictions or hypotheses made by the theory. The next step is to design research studies to test the predictions derived from the theory.

Crash Course: Psychological Research

Good Methods

Research Methodologies

While following chapters describe research and theories across a broad spectrum of behaviors, the methods used can generally be classified into three approaches: case studies, correlational studies, and experimental studies.

Case Studies

A **case study** focuses on intensive analyses of a single individual or more broadly on a single observation unit (e.g., the unit of analysis for the research could be on a couple or on a single institution). Often, the focus of case studies is on unique individuals who display characteristics outside of what is considered the norm. Henry Molaison ("H. M.") was one of the most studied individuals of all time. In 1953, to relieve his severe epileptic seizures, H. M. had brain surgery to remove parts of his medial temporal lobe. Following the surgery it was revealed that H.M. had lost the ability to remember events of his life that occurred after his surgery (anterograde amnesia). H. M. was the subject of

Parsimony: the principle of preferring simple explanations over more complex ones

Dependent variable: the behavior that is measured in a research study

Independent variable: a factor in an experiment that is manipulated by the researcher (e.g., randomly assigning subjects to a group in the experiment)

Case study: a research study that focuses on intensive analyses of a single individual or more broadly on a single observation unit

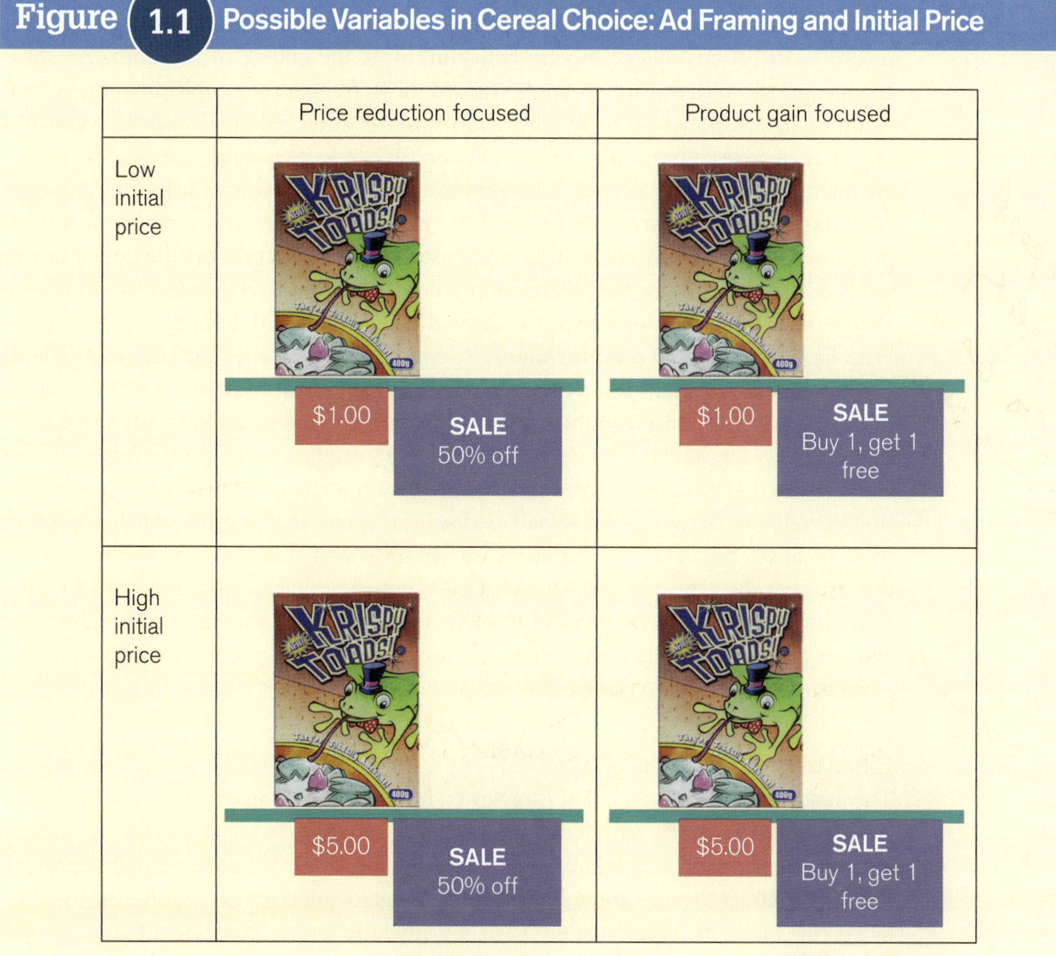

Photo from Hemera Technologies/PhotoObjects.net/Thinkstock

intense observation from 1957 to his death in 2008 (Squire, 2009). Theories of how memory is organized are largely based on this work.

Returning to our shopping and decision-making example, you may decide to make a case study of somebody who identifies himself as an "extreme couponer." To investigate his decision-making processes you systematically observe his behavior over a long period, using a variety of ways to collect the observations. For example, you may directly observe him while he shops, ask him to keep detailed records of his shopping behaviors, and ask him to "think out loud" as he engages in his shopping-related decision processes. The advantage of a case study is the sheer amount of intensive observations that may be collected and examined. This allows the researcher to identify many of the variables that may be relevant and to speculate about the relationships between these variables. The major disadvantage of this approach is that it centers on describing and explaining the behavior of a single, often unique, exemplar. As a result, it is often difficult to make broad generalizations of the results to other individuals.

Correlational Studies

A **correlational study** allows one to systematically observe groups, recording the frequency and/or intensity of many variables at once. These observations may include indirect measures such as self-report (i.e., asking the participant to report about his or her own behaviors). The key feature of this method is that researchers are attempting to

Correlational study: a research study that examines relationships between measured variables

collect the observations with minimal impact on the variables of interest. So in our shopping story we might set up a camera in cereal aisles of fifteen grocery stores and record video of customers' buying behaviors over the course of a month. As stores change prices and deals, we might record how frequently people buy the cereal. Additionally, we may wish to systematically observe other potentially relevant variables (e.g., size of boxes, time of day, gender of people). Not surprisingly, correlational studies are often analyzed using correlational procedures. Suppose in our example the researchers found a negative correlation between the price of cereal and the amount consumers purchased. This negative correlation simply states that as prices drop, the rate of buying tends to increase (a positive correlation would describe a relationship in which the change in the variables moves in the same direction rather than opposite directions). Data like these may be used for theory testing. For example, if our particular theory predicts a negative relationship between price (an explanatory variable) and the amount of buying (our response variable), then these data may be considered support for the theory. However, had the result been a positive correlation (or no correlation), that could be used as evidence against the theory. It is important to remember that evidence of a correlation between two variables does not mean that the relationship between them is causal. Because the researchers are just observing things as they naturally occur, determining the causal relationships between variables is extremely difficult. So while correlational studies have the advantage(s) of allowing the observation of many variables at once, within relatively natural contexts, one should not make cause and effect generalizations based on these methods.

Experimental Studies

The majority of the research that is reviewed in this text uses an experimental approach. An **experimental study** is designed to simplify the contexts surrounding the behavior of interest, allowing for focused investigation of the impact of a relatively small set of variables. In contrast to correlational studies, experiments intentionally involve the manipulation of variables. Manipulated variables include both independent and control variables. Let's consider a simple example. Suppose that you want to know whether people prefer the taste of cane sugar or a sugar substitute that you developed. You design an experiment in which you ask two groups of people to taste one of the types of sweetener and then rate how much they like the taste. Then you compare the ratings of the two groups (see Figure 1.1). In this example, the behavior of interest (our dependent variable) is taste, as measured by their ratings. The independent variable is which sweetener is presented to each group. However, how something tastes is complex, with many different variables influencing it (e.g., whether in food or drink, what smells are present, how the food looks). To keep your observations focused on the sweetener, you may also manipulate these other variables by keeping them constant for everybody in both groups (e.g., use lemon cookies baked using the same recipe with the only difference being what kind of sweetener was used). The logic of doing this is to try to ensure that the only difference between the two groups is the independent variable. Thus, if a difference in the dependent variable is found between the two groups, the most likely explanation for this difference is the manipulated independent variable.

Researchers often include more than one independent variable in an experiment to allow for efficiency in examining multiple variables at once but also to be able to see how these variables interact to affect the dependent variable. For example, a perception researcher might be interested in how much sweetener should be added to a cola product to optimize flavor. He or she might manipulate the amount of sweetener and ask people to rate how much they like the cola. But suppose that the amount of sodium in the cola influences how the sweetener affects the taste such that more sweetener tastes better with less sodium, but less sweetener tastes better with more sodium. The only way a researcher will be able to determine this is to manipulate *both* sweetener and sodium

Experimental study: a research study that examines causal relationships between variables in the same study. The researcher can then compare whether the high sweetener/low sodium condition is preferred to the low sweetener/high sodium condition and choose the best one for the cola product to optimize flavor. This is known as a factorial design, because multiple independent variables are combined factorially to create conditions that involve levels of each independent variable.

Earlier we described a hypothetical correlational study to examine our decision making in shopping behavior. Imagine designing an experiment to look at the same issues. From the theory outlined earlier, we may predict that the framing (focusing on reduced price or increased product) and price of items will have an impact on the decision making of shoppers. To examine this experimentally we randomly assign people to one of four groups (see Figure 1.1). We manipulate two different independent variables. To examine the impact of the framing variable we provide two of the groups with products labeled "50% off" (emphasizing reducing price) and the other two groups with products labeled "buy one, get one free" (emphasizing gaining product). To examine the pricing variable, the products in one group will be given an initial price of $1, and the other group will get items priced at $5.

Types of Research Studies

For our dependent variable, each participant will be asked to consider the "sale" and rate how likely he or she is to buy two boxes of the product. This experimental design allows us to examine three separate effects. We can examine the effect on purchasing decisions of the initial price variable and the effect of framing the deal variable separately. However, the design also allows us to examine how these two variables interact with one another. For example, consider the fictional set of data presented in Figure 1.2. We can see that the overall effect of framing was that participants had a higher likelihood of buying two boxes with the 50 percent off deal than the buy one, get one free deal. The overall effect of pricing was that participants were more likely to buy two boxes when the initial price was low. The final graph shows how these two variables interact with each other to form a more complex relationship. Here it becomes apparent that the framing effect really only has an impact when the initial price is high, with participants much more likely to buy two boxes with the 50 percent off deal than the buy one, get one free deal. However, when the initial price was low, there was no difference in likelihood between the two framing conditions.

Figure 1.2 Fictional Data From Framing and Pricing Experiment

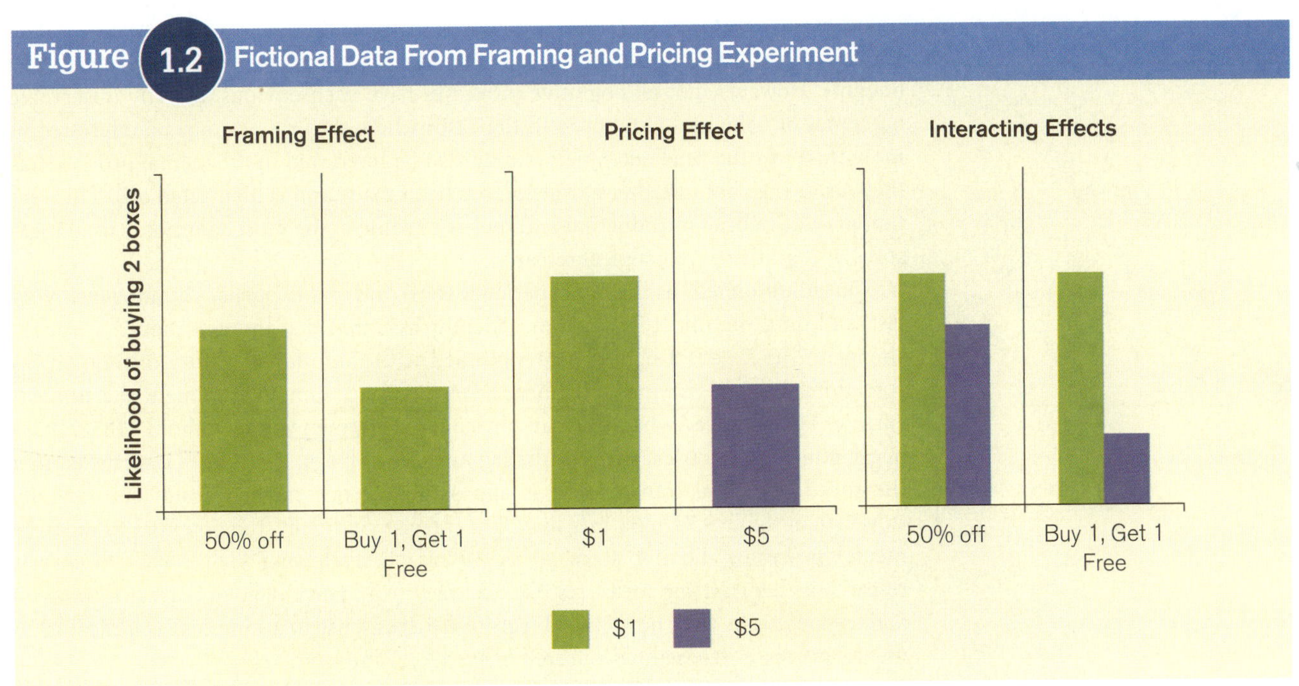

By virtue of experimental control and the explicit manipulation of independent variables, researchers can be more confident about testing cause and effect relationships between variables. This is the biggest advantage of using experimental approaches. However, this advantage comes at the cost of an ability to generalize to other contexts (external validity). Because the experiment is explicitly designed to simplify the context surrounding the behavior of interest, it opens the door to the potential that the results are applicable only to those simplified contexts. In other words, one must be careful in generalizing the conclusions drawn from experiments to the more complex, naturally occurring contexts in which the behavior normally occurs.

Stop and Think

1.8. What core principles is the scientific method founded on?

1.9. What are the main differences between case study, correlational, and experimental designs?

1.10. What are the main advantages and disadvantages of the different approaches?

1.11. Consider one of the other behaviors described in the shopping example. Identify potential variables that may impact that behavior and design a research study to examine how those variables are related.

Sometimes a complete experimental design isn't possible because we may not be in a position to truly manipulate the independent variable. For example, suppose we think that men and women may differ with respect to their shopping decision-making behaviors. So we design an experiment like the one described earlier but add gender as an additional variable. In this example, gender is a quasi-independent variable. This is because we are not actually able to manipulate our participants' gender (i.e., we can't randomly assign some people to the male condition and others to the female condition). Because gender is a preexisting characteristic, it should be treated like an explanatory variable in a correlational design. As a result, when interpreting any of the results that involve the gender variable, one needs to be appropriately conservative about making casual claims.

Commonly Used Measures Within Cognitive Psychology

In most of the examples given, the behavior of interest allowed us to observe how different variables influenced the outcome of the decision processes (how much cereal they bought). However, not all cognitive processes have such obvious, directly observable outcomes or behaviors. And even in the cases where they do, we may be interested in more than just the final outcome; we may also be interested in the mental processes as they occur (i.e., not just after a decision has been made and is then acted on). This section provides a brief introduction and review of some of the most commonly used measures in cognitive psychological research.

Our intuition tells us that we experience the world as it happens. Thinking feels very fast, and until the mid 1850s, it was generally assumed that thought moved at speeds similar to the speed of light. That, combined with the internal nature of thought (as something that goes on inside the head), led most to assume that thought was unmeasurable. That changed when German physiologist Herman von Helmholtz (1850/1853) began attaching electrical wires to the leg muscles of frogs. His studies established that the speed of neural transmission is approximately one meter/second (substantially slower than the 299,792,458 m/s that light travels). Suddenly, the potential to measure mental processes did not seem so out of reach. Following Helmholtz's discovery, researchers began using measures like accuracy (e.g., percentage of correct responses) and response time (e.g., how fast subjects make a response to a stimulus) as indicators of mental processes (sometimes referred to as mental chronometry).

Accuracy

Accuracy measurements are common in research designs in which there are right and wrong responses. For example, when probing how we comprehend language, participants may be asked questions about facts from a passage they read (e.g., in the shopping story, "How many light bulbs were burned out?" "What brand of cereal did I end up buying?"). In a reasoning task, researchers may measure how often participants arrive at the correct solution to a target problem as a function of how similar it is to example problems. Research examining the nature of memory has a long tradition of using accuracy as a measure of mental processing. Without looking back, make a list of all of the details that you can recall from our shopping example. After you've made your list, go back and compare your list with the story itself. How many details did you remember? How many details did you leave out? Memory researchers have been using questions like these, about the quantity of correctly remembered details or items, for over 150 years to investigate factors that influence memory (e.g., what kinds of things you are memorizing, the time between learning and testing, what sort of rehearsal you use when trying to memorize things).

However, accuracy isn't always just about how many items you can correctly recall; it can also be about the number and kinds of errors you make. Frederic Bartlett (1932) reported a series of experiments he conducted in which he presented British students with a brief Native American Indian folk tale and later tested their memories for details from the story. Bartlett discovered that their memories were dramatically influenced by their own cultural experiences and stereotypes. This was primarily evidenced by the memory distortion errors his participants made. Consider, too, the case of eyewitness testimony. When witnesses are asked to recall details of an event, some of the details they "remember" are often not accurate. Research examining how and why people have these "false memories" has greatly shaped our theories explaining how memory works.

Response Time

Simple Reaction Time Test

Choice Reaction Time Test

Another widely used method to examine cognitive processes is to measure how long it takes to respond to a stimulus. One of the earliest and most influential set of experiments was conducted by Franciscus Donders (1969/1868). Donders developed a reaction time technique called the subtractive method to examine cognitive processing. His technique combined two measurements from two slightly different tasks. In the first task (simple reaction time procedure), he measured the time it took for a person to respond to a simple stimulus (e.g., push the button when you see a light). The second task was similar, but instead of having a single button to press, there were multiple lights and buttons. If the left light came on, the person would press the left button and if the right light came on, then the right button (choice reaction time procedure). Having multiple lights and buttons required the same set of processes needed in the simple reaction time procedure but also required discrimination (left or right light) and decision (left or right button) processes. Donders's methodology assumes that components of mental processes are strictly discrete and serial. That is, each stage operates separately and in sequence. With these assumptions, one may subtract the reaction times of the first task from the reaction times of the second task, leaving a measurement of the time required to perform discrimination and choice.

In the years since Donders's experiments, reaction time procedures have become more sophisticated. Not all of the underlying assumptions of his task have turned out to be true. However, the same basic underlying logic that mental processes are measureable is still present in the bulk of cognitive psychology research. Consider two popular paradigms currently used in cognitive psychology laboratories: priming and eye movement studies.

Priming tasks are pervasive within the field of cognitive psychology (typing "priming" into the search field of an article database yields thousands of articles). In a typical

Paradigm-Driven Research

Functional Approach

priming task, participants respond to a series of stimuli (e.g., "Press the right button if the string of letters is a real word. Press the left button if the string of letters is not a real word."). Embedded within the list of stimuli are sets of paired trials, the first of which is called the "prime" and the second the "target." Researchers are typically interested in how quickly participants respond to the target stimuli when it follows a related prime (compared to when it follows an unrelated prime). For example, suppose the target is the word DOCTOR and it is preceded by either the word NURSE (related) or BREAD (unrelated). Typically, participants would respond faster to DOCTOR when NURSE precedes it than when it is preceded by BREAD (Meyer & Schvaneveldt, 1971). Following a logic similar to that proposed by Donders, this difference in reaction time between the two conditions is thought to reflect cognitive processing differences.

After reading the previous examples you might have the impression that all reaction time studies focus on button pressing. That isn't the case. Throughout this textbook you'll see a wide variety of reaction time measurements involving other behaviors (e.g., naming times, reaching times, recognition judgments). Recently, monitoring eye movements has become an extremely popular behavioral measurement in cognitive psychology. Our eyes are constantly jumping around, moving from one fixation (keeping still with one thing in focus for 200–350 milliseconds) to another. The fundamental assumption with this methodology is that there is a tight coupling between the eyes and the mind. In other words, we think about what we look at, and how long we look at something reflects underlying mental processing. Initial interest in using eye movements to measure cognition focused on attempts to understand the processes involved in reading. However, recent technological advancements have led to an explosion of the use of eye movements to address research questions across a wide range of cognitive psychology subdomains (e.g., spoken language comprehension, language production, attention and visual search, scene perception). Similar to their work with the button-pressing method discussed earlier, researchers typically compare how long participants fixate on stimuli from different experimental conditions to test their theories.

Beyond Accuracy and Response Time

While much of the research that you will read about in the following chapters reports dependent variables using either response time or accuracy alone, many other measures are used as well. Think of your own experiences. When you try to do something very quickly, your error rate increases; as a task gets harder, your performance may get slower and you make more errors. Some research focuses on this tight tradeoff between speed and accuracy (e.g., Kahana & Loftus, 1999; Meyer, Osman, Irwin, & Yantis, 1988). Other research focuses not on the time taken to initiate a response but rather on other characteristics (e.g., duration, velocity, direction of movement) of response (e.g., Abrams & Balota, 1991).

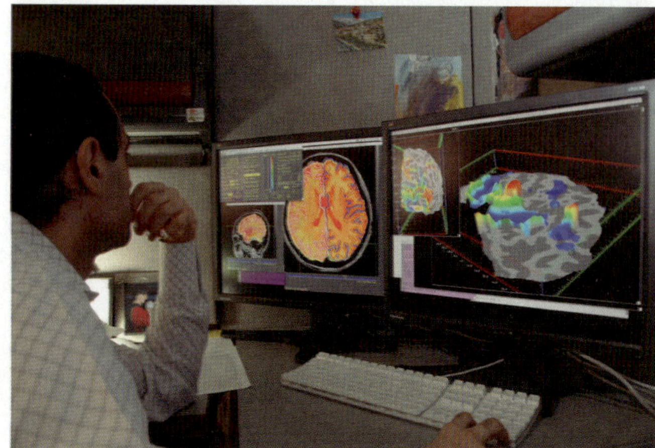

National Institute of Mental Health

Photo 1.6 A researcher checking fMRI images.

Within the rapidly growing field of cognitive neuroscience, recent technological advances in brain imaging techniques have led to the development of brain visualization measures. For example, using methods like electroencephalography (EEG) and functional magnetic resonance imaging (fMRI) researchers are able to "watch" the neural activity of the brain while it is processing information. We describe some of these procedures in greater detail in Chapter 2. Often these new techniques are combined with the old standbys of accuracy and response time to gain new insights into the nature of mental processing (e.g., Posner, 2005).

One thing to keep in mind with nearly all of these measures is that they are indirect measurements. Regardless of whether we are examining response times (e.g., to push a button, read a sentence, or stare at an object), accuracy measures (e.g., how often we arrive at the correct solution to a problem or remember 100 percent of a list), or brain activity within a particular region, in all cases we are measuring something we assume to be correlated with the cognitive processes, not the processes themselves. Given this, you should always critically evaluate the assumed connection between the behavior measured and cognitive process being tested.

Stop and Think

1.12. What are two commonly used dependent measures in cognitive psychology?

1.13. Briefly explain the logic used in Donders's subtractive method.

1.14. Think back to the shopping story that started the chapter. Suppose that you were interested in studying how the shopper understood the bagger's question "Paper or plastic?" How might you design a study to investigate this issue?

THINKING ABOUT RESEARCH

As you read the following summary of a research study in psychology, think about the following questions:

1. Which approach to the study of cognition is being used in this study?
2. What type of research design are the researchers using in this study?
3. What is the independent variable in this study?
4. What is the dependent variable in this study?

Study Reference

Proffitt, D. R., Stefanucci, J., Banton, T., & Epstein, W. (2003). The role of effort in perceiving distance. *Psychological Science, 14*, 106–112.

Note: Experiment 1 of this study is described here.

Purpose of the study: The purpose of the study was to examine the effect of physical effort on distance judgments. It was hypothesized that wearing a heavy backpack would increase judgments of distance compared with not wearing a backpack. This hypothesis is consistent with the view that our perceptual processes operate in reference to bodily movements in the environment.

Method of the study: Subjects were randomly assigned to one of two groups: the backpack group or the no backpack group. Subjects in the backpack group wore a backpack during the study that held weights equivalent to 1/6 to 1/5 of their reported body weight. Subjects in the no backpack group did not wear a backpack during the study. All subjects then judged the distance between themselves and construction cones placed at various distances in a field in front of them. Distance in feet and inches was recorded from each subject on each judgment trial. All subjects completed 12 practice trials and then 12 test trials.

Results of the study: Distance judgments from the 12 test trials were analyzed. All subjects underestimated the distances to the cones. However, subjects in the backpack group gave higher mean estimates of distance than subjects in the no backpack group. The results of the study are presented in Figure 1.3.

Conclusions of the study: The results of the study supported the hypothesis that wearing a heavy backpack increases estimates of distance. These results support the view that distance perception depends on an interaction between one's body and the environment.

(Continued)

(Continued)

Figure 1.3 Mean Distance Estimates as a Function of Target Distance and Group

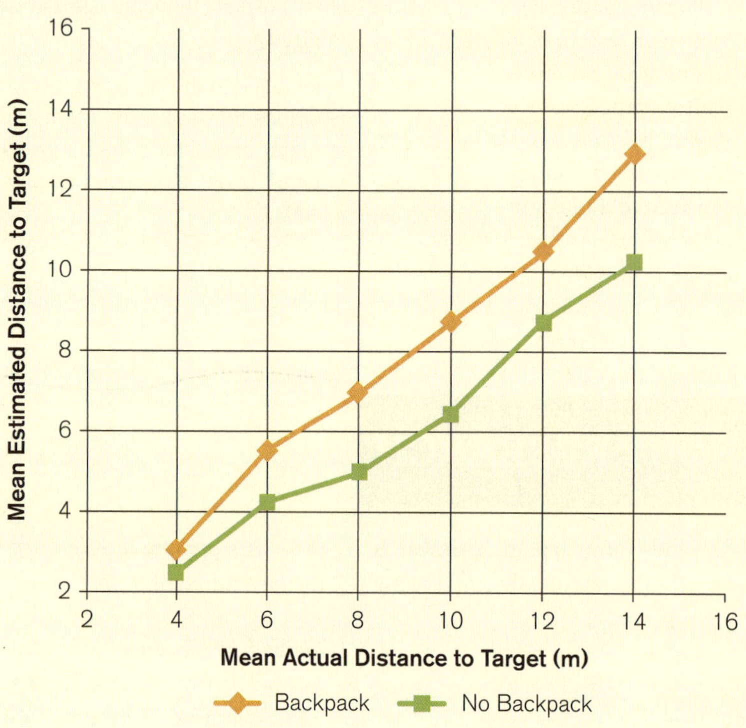

SOURCE: Adapted from Proffitt, D. R., Stefanucci, J., Banton, T., & Epstein, W. (2003). The role of effort in perceiving distance. *Psychological Science*, 14, 106–112.

CHAPTER REVIEW

Summary

- **What is cognitive psychology? How did it develop as a field?**

Cognitive psychology is the study of how our minds receive, store, and use information. This includes theory and research about perception, attention, memory, language use, decision making, and problem solving. The roots of the discipline may be traced to philosophy and physiology before the twentieth century. However, modern cognitive psychology primarily developed since the mid-twentieth century. This was in part a reaction to the behaviorist tradition within psychology but also is a reflection of developments within other disciplines, including biology, linguistics, and computer science.

- **How have psychologists approached the study of cognition?**

Explanations of cognitive processes have been developed within three general approaches: representationalist, embodied, and biologically motivated. Representationalist theories of cognition generally view the mind as a symbolic processor, similar to a computer. In these views, information is conceptualized as abstract representations that may be acted on by mental operations. Embodied approaches envision the mind as something situated within a body and an environmental context. These approaches examine cognition as interactions between individuals and their environment. Biologically motivated approaches to cognition focus on theories based on neurologically inspired elements.

- **What types of research methods are useful in the study of cognition?**

Three main types of research designs are employed in research in cognition: (1) case studies that focus on the behaviors of a distinct individual or group, (2) correlational studies that examine relationships between sets of dependent (or response) variables, and (3) experiments that test causal relationships between variables through the manipulation of independent variables and control of the conditions under which the dependent (or response) variables are measured. Researchers may also use quasi-independent variables (group subjects based on a particular characteristic such as gender or age) to compare groups for the dependent variable when manipulation of a variable is not possible.

- **What behaviors do psychologists observe to study cognition?**

There is a range of behaviors studied by cognitive psychologists. A common measure is accuracy for a task (such as memory or perceptual judgments). Another common measure is the speed to complete a task (such as identify a word or solve a problem). There are also behaviors specific to an area of cognitive psychology (such as measurement of brain activity in cognitive neuroscience).

Chapter Quiz

1. Enter the letter for the approach to the study of cognition next to its corresponding definition below:
   (a) Representationalism
   (b) Embodied cognition
   (c) Biologically motivated models

   ___ describe cognitive processes in a similar fashion to the physiological functioning of the brain
   ___ describe cognitive processes as operating on knowledge concepts represented in our minds
   ___ describe cognitive processes as the interplay between the body and the environment

2. Which core principle of the scientific method involves the identification of the underlying causes of behavior?
   (a) empiricism
   (b) determinism
   (c) parsimony
   (d) testability

3. Which core principle of the scientific method involves the assumption that simpler explanations of behavior are preferred?
   (a) empiricism
   (b) determinism
   (c) parsimony
   (d) testability

Use the following study description to answer questions 4 through 7:

> A researcher is interested in examining the relationship between one's actual memory abilities and one's perception of how good his or her memory abilities are. Subjects in this study are given a study list of words and asked to remember these words after a short delay. They are also given a questionnaire and asked how good the subject thinks his or her memory is, where a high score means the subject thinks he or she has high memory abilities. The researcher finds a small but positive relationship between the memory test scores and the questionnaire scores.

4. What type of research design is used in this study?
   (a) experiment
   (b) case study
   (c) correlational study

5. Explain how you know which research design is being used.

6. Which of the following are dependent (response) variables in this study? (Choose all that apply)
   (a) the delay between the study list and the memory test
   (b) the score on the questionnaire
   (c) the score on the memory test
   (d) the number of words in the study list

7. The results indicated a positive relationship between the variables that were measured. Explain what this means.

8. In what way does an experiment differ from other research designs?

9. The measure used by researchers that indicates the speed with which someone completes a task is known as
   (a) accuracy.
   (b) reaction time.
   (c) self-report.
   (d) an independent variable.

10. What are two "metaphors of the mind" that have influenced the development of theories of cognition?

11. What are two developments that led to a rapid expansion of the field of cognitive psychology after the mid-twentieth century?

12. Describe Donders's experiments and explain how they propose to measure cognitive processes.

Key Terms

Behaviorist 3
Biological perspective 6
Case study 8
Correlational study 9
Dependent variable 8
Determinism 7
Embodied cognition 6
Empiricism 7
Experimental study 10
Independent variable 8
Parsimony 8
Representationalist 5
Scientific method 7
Testability 7

Stop and Think Answers

1.1. List four cognitive processes studied by cognitive psychologists.

Processes involved in understanding and using information are studied by cognitive psychologists. These generally include attention, memory, perception, language, concept formation, imagery, and judgment and decision making. These processes include the neurobiological processes involved.

1.2. What three events influenced the development of the field of cognitive psychology?

The three main influences on the development of cognitive psychology as a unified field are (1) Chomsky's arguments against a behaviorist description of language development, (2) the development of computer technology models of information processing, and (3) the publication of Ulric Neisser's book tying together different topics of study under the field of cognitive psychology.

1.3. From the description of the types of processes studied in cognitive psychology, what processes do you think were involved in generating your response to the two previous questions?

Many answers are possible here, but some involve memory of the information, perception of the writing on the page, attention to the individual words in the sentence, and interpretation of the language in the writing.

1.4. How are the representationalist and biological approaches connected?

The representationalist approach proposes that information is represented symbolically in the mind. The biological approach suggests a physiological means of representing information in the brain.

1.5. What does embodied cognition mean?

The embodied cognition approach assumes that cognition serves the purpose of allowing us to interact bodily in the world and developed around the structure of the human body for that purpose.

1.6. In what ways are the biological features of the brain important in the study of cognition?

The activity of neurons provides a physical structure and mechanism for cognitive processes to take place in the mind. Features of neuron processing are considered when current models of cognition are developed.

1.7. Given what you know so far about cognitive psychology, which of the approaches described in this section do you think you would follow as a researcher in psychology? Why?

Answers will vary.

1.8. What core principles is the scientific method founded on?

The core principles are determinism, empiricism, parsimony, and testability. Determinism is the assumption that events in the world have identifiable causes. Empiricism is the assumption that those causes can be understood through observation of the world. Parsimony is the assumption that simpler causes are more likely to be true. Testability is the assumption that theories about causes can be tested through observation of the world.

1.9. What are the main differences between case study, correlational, and experimental designs?

In a case study, researchers are interested in learning about different aspects of the behavior of an individual or group. In a correlational study, researchers are interested in learning about relationships between measured variables. In an experiment, researchers are interested in learning about a cause and effect relationship between variables to test hypotheses about the causes of behaviors.

1.10. What are the main advantages and disadvantages of the different approaches?

Case studies allow for thorough study of a unique individual or group, but they do not allow for tests of causal relationships, and the results may not generalize beyond the individual or group being studied. Correlational studies allow study of behaviors of large groups of individuals but do not allow researchers to fully test the cause of those behaviors. Experiments allow for tests of causal relationships but due to control of extraneous factors may not generalize to real-life behaviors.

1.11. Consider one of the other behaviors described in the shopping example. Identify potential variables that may impact that behavior and design a research study to examine how those variables are related.

Answers will vary.

1.12. What are two commonly used dependent measures in cognitive psychology?

Two commonly used dependent measures in cognitive psychology are accuracy and reaction time.

1.13. Briefly explain the logic used in Donders's subtractive method.

Donders compared reaction times in two situations: one in which subjects are asked to press a single button when a light comes on and one in which subjects must choose between two buttons to press depending on which side (right or left) the light appears on. In the first situation, the reaction time includes the motor processes involved in pressing a button at a specific time. In the second situation, the reaction time involves everything from the first situation *plus* the decision-making process needed to decide which button to press. By subtracting the first reaction time from the second, what is left is the time it takes to decide which button to press—in other words, the time it takes to "think."

1.14. Think back to the shopping story that started the chapter. Suppose that you were interested in studying how the shopper understood the bagger's question "Paper or plastic?" How might you design a study to investigate this issue?

Answers will vary.

Student Study Site

Sharpen your skills with SAGE edge at **edge.sagepub.com/mcbridecp**

SAGE edge for students provides a personalized approach to help you accomplish your coursework goals in an easy-to-use learning environment.

Go to edge.sagepub.com/mcbridecp for additional exercises and web resources. Select Chapter 1, Introduction to Cognitive Psychology, for chapter-specific resources. All of the links listed in the margins of this chapter are accessible via this site.

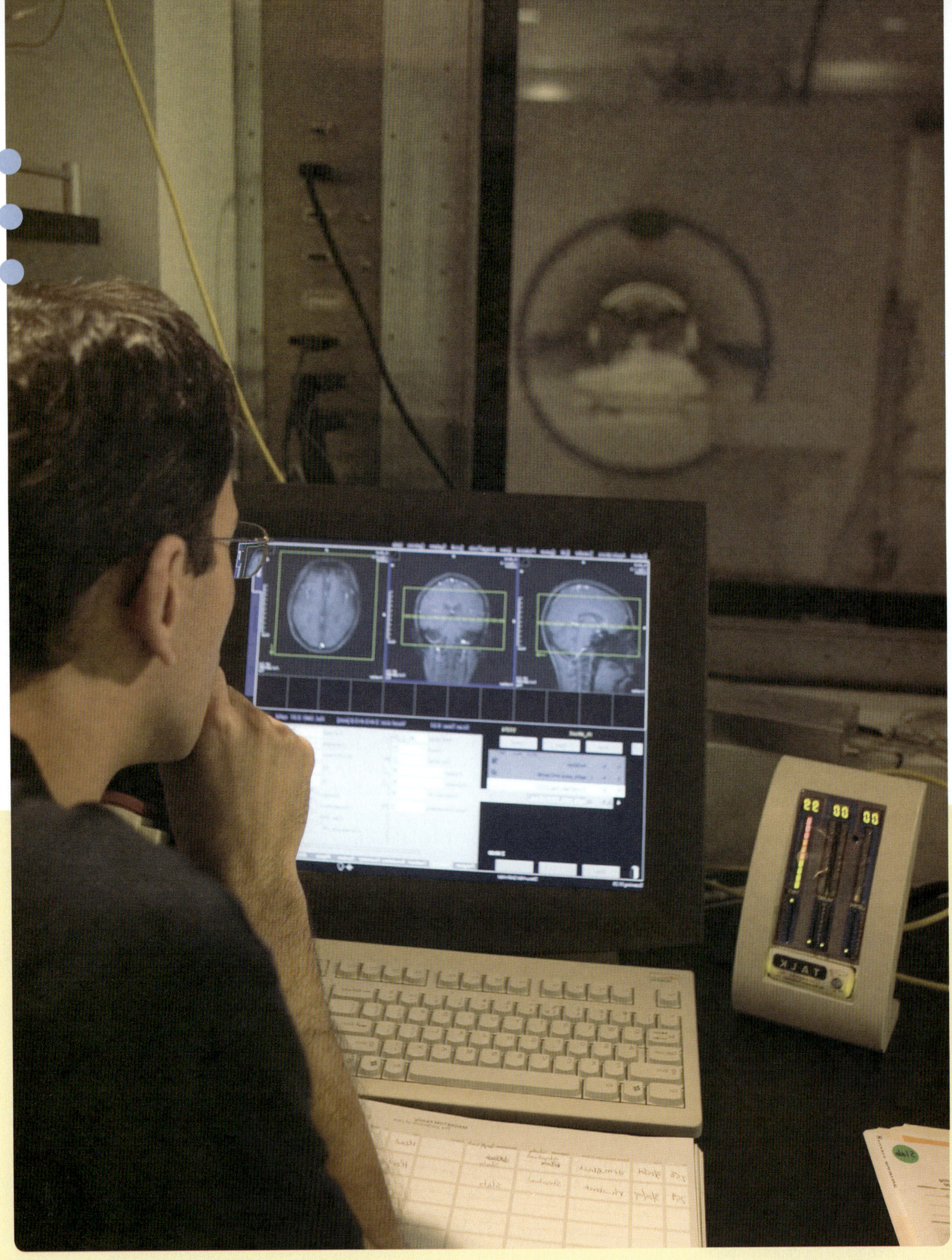

Mark Harmel/Science Source

Cognitive Neuroscience

Questions to Consider

- How is the examination of brain activity involved in the study of cognition?
- How do case studies of individuals with cognitive deficits inform us about the connection between cognition and brain function?
- What can be learned about cognition through measurements of neuron activity in the brain?
- Can all behavior be explained in terms of brain activity?

Introduction: Knowledge From Cognitive Deficits

Imagine that you are a neurologist focusing on cognitive deficits in your patients. You see several patients in a day. One is an older woman who is having some memory problems. Another patient is a man who can identify which words on a page represent animals but cannot distinguish between an elephant and a horse or identify that a tiger is an animal that has stripes. Another patient is a veteran who lost a leg in the Iraq War but still feels pain where the leg should be. A fourth patient can understand and follow verbal instructions but cannot produce verbal speech.

As you further examine each one of these patients, you realize that they illustrate the connection between brain function and cognitive abilities. The first patient is tested with some cognitive tasks, including remembering words and numbers for a short time. She shows lower functioning on these tasks compared with typical scores of nonclinical individuals, and you conclude that she may be showing the first signs of Alzheimer's disease. The second patient is one you have seen in your office several times before. He has Pick's disease, a disorder where fine-grained conceptual knowledge is gradually lost due to deterioration of the neurons that help us retrieve general knowledge. The veteran is suffering from a condition known as phantom limb syndrome, where a patient has perceptions of feeling from a limb that has been removed. The last patient is suffering from Broca's aphasia, a language disorder where comprehension abilities are spared but production abilities show a deficit.

What can we learn about the connection between brain activity and cognitive abilities from examining these patients? In fact, we can learn quite a lot. The first neuroscientists relied on such patients to learn about brain function and how it relates to different cognitive processes. When a patient showed a particular deficit, neuroscientists would identify the area of the brain that was damaged (either by learning about the patient's disease or accident and/or by examining his or her brain after the patient's death) to begin mapping out the functions of specific brain areas. From such studies, we were able to learn quite a lot about how the brain contributes to cognition. However, in more recent years, new brain recording techniques allow researchers to examine brain activity in cases where there is no deficit and to more precisely pinpoint the affected areas in cases where a patient shows a deficit. In this chapter, we consider how cognitive neuroscientists study brain function and review some of the important case studies of clinical patients that helped us learn about brain function. In upcoming chapters, we discuss more current studies in cognitive neuroscience that are contributing knowledge about brain function connected to attention, perception, memory, and language abilities.

Clinical Case Studies in Cognitive Neuroscience

As just described, neuroscientists have learned a lot about which brain areas contribute to different cognitive abilities through the examination of clinical patients. Such studies continue to contribute to our knowledge in this area. In this section we review some clinical case studies to show how these studies have contributed to the field of cognitive neuroscience and discuss the advantages and disadvantages of the case study.

One of the first clinical cases to contribute knowledge about brain function was that of Phineas Gage (Harlow, 1993/1868). Gage was a railroad foreman in the mid-1800s. While on the job, a blasting cap drove a metal rod into his left eye, up through the frontal lobe of his brain and out the top of his skull (see Figure 2.1). Gage survived the accident and lived for several more years, but his personality and cognitive abilities were altered from the way he was before the accident. He was less able to control his emotions, and his decision-making abilities suffered. He was no longer able to serve as a foreman because he lacked the cognitive control needed for this role. From this clinical case, we learned that the frontal lobe is important in emotional regulation and decision making.

Figure 2.1 Phineas Gage's Brain

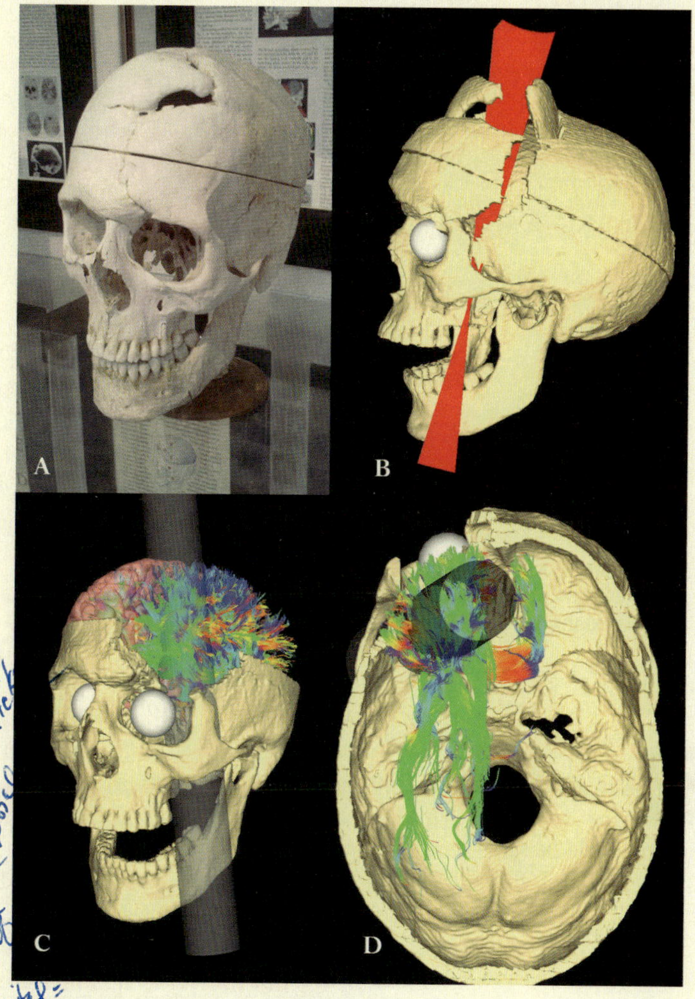

The area of damage to Phineas Gage's brain can be identified by examination of the path of the rod that went through his head.

SOURCE: Van Horn, J.D., Irimia, A., Torgerson, C.M., Chambers, M.C., Kikinis, R., et al. (2012) Mapping Connectivity Damage in the Case of Phineas Gage. PLoS ONE 7(5): e37454. doi:10.1371/journal.pone.0037454

Other clinical studies have helped researchers localize language functions in the frontal and temporal lobes of the brain (Rorden & Karnath, 2004). A patient named Tan was studied by Paul Broca in the late 1800s. Tan had been unable to speak for many years ("tan" was one of the only sounds he could produce). After Tan's death, Broca examined Tan's brain and found damage to the left frontal lobe, near the front of the temporal lobe (see Figure 2.2). This location was named Broca's area, and damage to this area causes Broca's aphasia, a disorder where a person has difficulty producing speech. Near this time, another important brain area for language was identified by Karl Wernicke. This area is in the left temporal lobe close to the front of the occipital lobe and is known as Wernicke's area (see Figure 2.2). Damage to Wernicke's area causes a deficit in language comprehension and meaningful language production. A person with Wernicke's aphasia can speak, but his or her speech is meaningless. The person produces what is known as a "word salad," where the speech is fluent but incomprehensible. For Broca and Wernicke, clinical case studies aided in their development of this early knowledge about the brain areas responsible for language abilities.

A more recent case study illustrates the role of brain function in a more specific skill: object identification. Oliver Sacks (1990) described a patient he saw who had difficulty in distinguishing between living and nonliving objects. For example, the patient mistook parking meters for children and furniture for people. However, the patient was an academic in the field of music and had little difficulty with other cognitive abilities. He could even identify objects by touch and describe them in detail. His deficit only occurred in visual recognition of the objects. This condition is known as object agnosia, the inability to correctly recognize objects. Patients

Case Study: Phineas Gage

Phrenology and Modern Neuroscience

Figure 2.2 Broca's and Wernicke's Areas

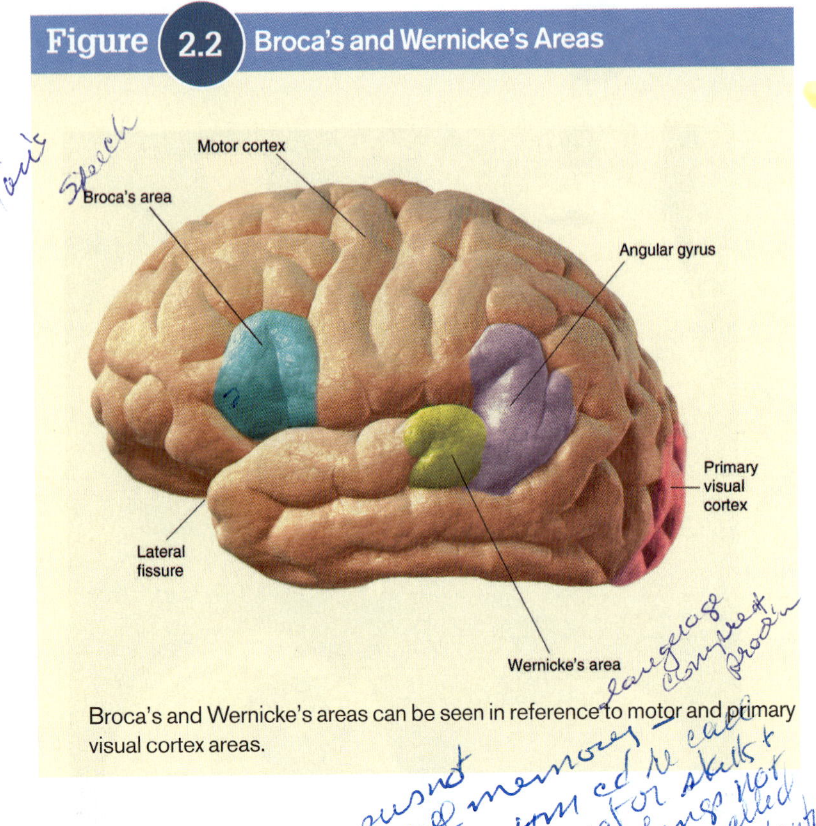

Broca's and Wernicke's areas can be seen in reference to motor and primary visual cortex areas.

with object agnosia typically have damage in the inferior (lower) temporal cortex, suggesting that the deficit is related to language abilities.

Knowledge about localization of memory function has also been gained from clinical case studies. As discussed in the previous chapter, one of the most well-known of these cases is that of H. M., a man who suffered from a form of amnesia where he could remember his life before the damage occurred but could not remember episodes of his life that occurred after the damage (Hilts, 1996). H. M.'s brain lesion was caused by a surgical procedure he received early in his life to help diminish the severity of epileptic seizures from which he was suffering. During the surgery, a brain area known as the hippocampus was damaged. After the surgery, H. M. seemed to have lost the ability to form new memories. He would meet new people but would not remember them a few minutes later when they came back into his room. He did not remember world events that occurred after the time of his surgery. It seemed as if the timeline of his life stopped at the point of his surgery. From H. M.'s case, researchers learned about the importance of the role of the hippocampus in memory abilities, but they also learned that the hippocampus is not necessary for forming and retrieving all types of memories. H. M. showed the ability to improve on tasks requiring motor skills, indicating that he could still retain new information and retrieve implicitly (i.e., without intention). Thus, H. M.'s case taught us that the hippocampus is not important for all types of memory formation and retrieval but is important for intentional retrieval of memories.

Probe the Brain Exercise

Clinical case studies have revealed important connections between brain function and cognitive abilities. They provide clues to the brain areas most important for different types of cognitive tasks as we examine the damage areas in these patients. However, one disadvantage of using case studies in neuroscience is that the brain damage is not controlled by researchers and the damage may be spread across multiple brain areas. Thus, it may be difficult for researchers to determine the specific brain areas connected to the cognitive deficits seen in the patients. In addition, because the brain damage is not controlled by the researchers, they are limited to those damaged brain areas in patients available to study. Current neuroscience brain recording techniques provide a means to both more precisely identify the brain areas most active during different tasks and to examine the brain areas they are most interested in studying. Thus, these newer techniques have helped us overcome the disadvantages present in clinical case studies to further add to the knowledge gained in these studies. In the next sections, we describe some of the techniques cognitive neuroscientists have employed in recent research.

Make Up Your Mind

Stop and Think

2.1. Explain why controlled experiments cannot always be conducted to determine how different types of brain damage cause cognitive deficits.

2.2. Describe some of the limitations of using the clinical case study method in cognitive neuroscience.

Structure of the Nervous System

Clinical case studies are still used as a method of study in cognitive neuroscience research. However, advances in technology have also allowed researchers to record the brain activity present in clinical and nonclinical subjects to test hypotheses about what kind of activity and what activity location should be present under different task conditions. The specifics of how these recording techniques work rely on some understanding of the brain and the nervous system, so we review the relevant physiology in this next section before we introduce the most common brain recording techniques used in cognitive neuroscience research.

The Neuron

The brain is composed of billions of microscopic **neuron** cells forming the basic structure seen in Figure 2.3. Neuron activity is both chemical and electrical. Chemicals called neurotransmitters are first brought into the cell by the **dendrites** at the top end of the neuron. These neurotransmitters provide signals to the cell that are either excitatory (i.e., more likely to fire) or inhibitory (i.e., less likely to fire). The cell body of the neuron takes in these chemical signals from the dendrites and determines if there is enough of an excitatory signal to allow the neuron to fire. If so, an action potential occurs that creates an electrical signal that travels down the neuron's **axon**. This electrical signal is detected in some of the brain recording techniques used by researchers. Once the electrical signal reaches the end of the axon, the terminal buttons release neurotransmitters into the **synapse** to be collected by other neurons nearby. Then the process begins again.

The Remarkable Neuron

Neuron: the basic cell of the brain

Dendrites: extensions from neurons that receive chemical messages (neurotransmitters) from other neurons

Axon: an extension from the neuron nucleus where an electrical impulse in the neuron occurs

Synapse: a space between neurons where neurotransmitters are released and received

The process of the action potential is what creates the electrical signal in the neuron when it fires. This activity occurs within the axon of the cell. Before the neuron fires, the inside of the axon contains a resting state negative charge due to the division of ions in the fluid inside and outside the cell (see Figure 2.4). The action potential redistributes these ions through channels in the axon's membrane that control the flow of potassium (K^+), sodium (Na^+), and chlorine (Cl^-) ions in and out of the cell. When the excitatory signal comes down the axon from the cell body, the axon opens specific channels in the axon membrane to allow sodium to flow into the axon, producing a positive charge inside the cell. The channels open quickly in sequence from the top of the axon (at the axon hillock) near the cell body down to the end near the terminals that contain the neurotransmitter (see Figure 2.5). This positive charge can be detected and recorded by electrodes that are either placed inside the cell or on top of the scalp, as we see shortly in the discussion of brain recording techniques. Once the action potential is complete, other channels open in the axon membrane to allow potassium (K^+) to flow out of the cell and the sodium channels close. This redistributes the ions back to the resting negative state inside the axon. The excitatory message then reaches the terminals and a neurotransmitter is released into the synapse (see Figure 2.6).

Figure 2.3 A Neuron

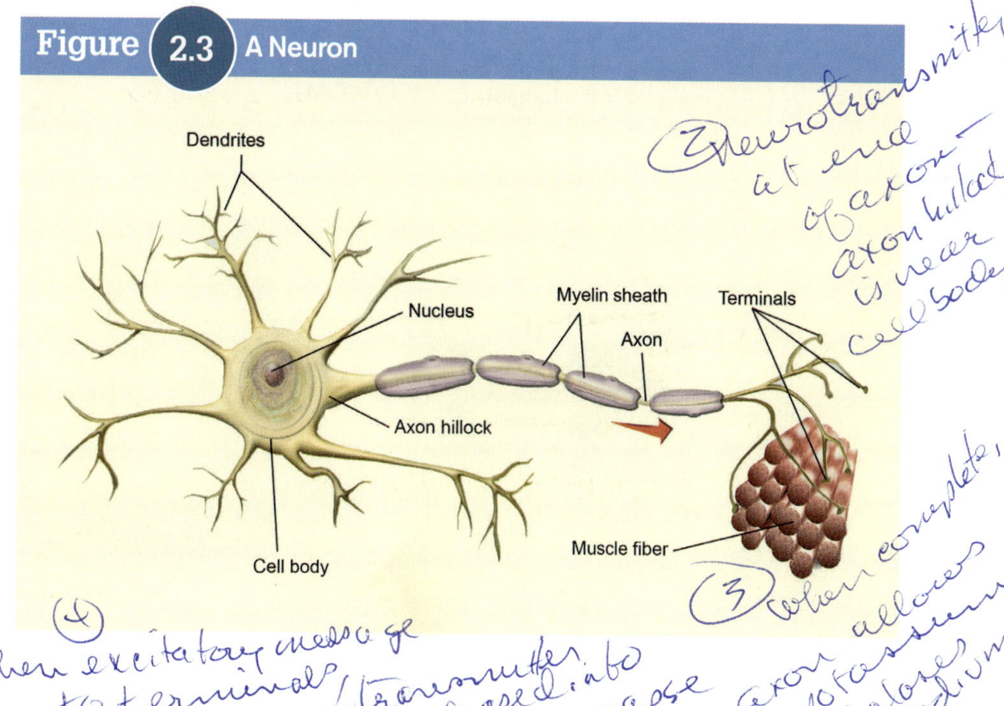

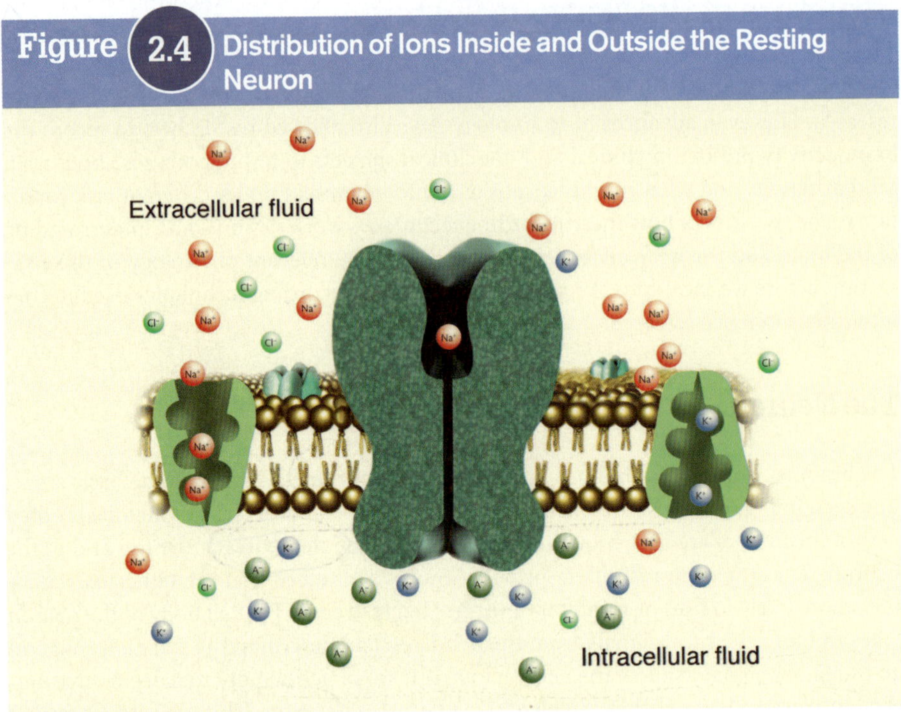

Figure 2.4 Distribution of Ions Inside and Outside the Resting Neuron

Figure 2.5 Ions' Movement and Voltages During and After an Action Potential

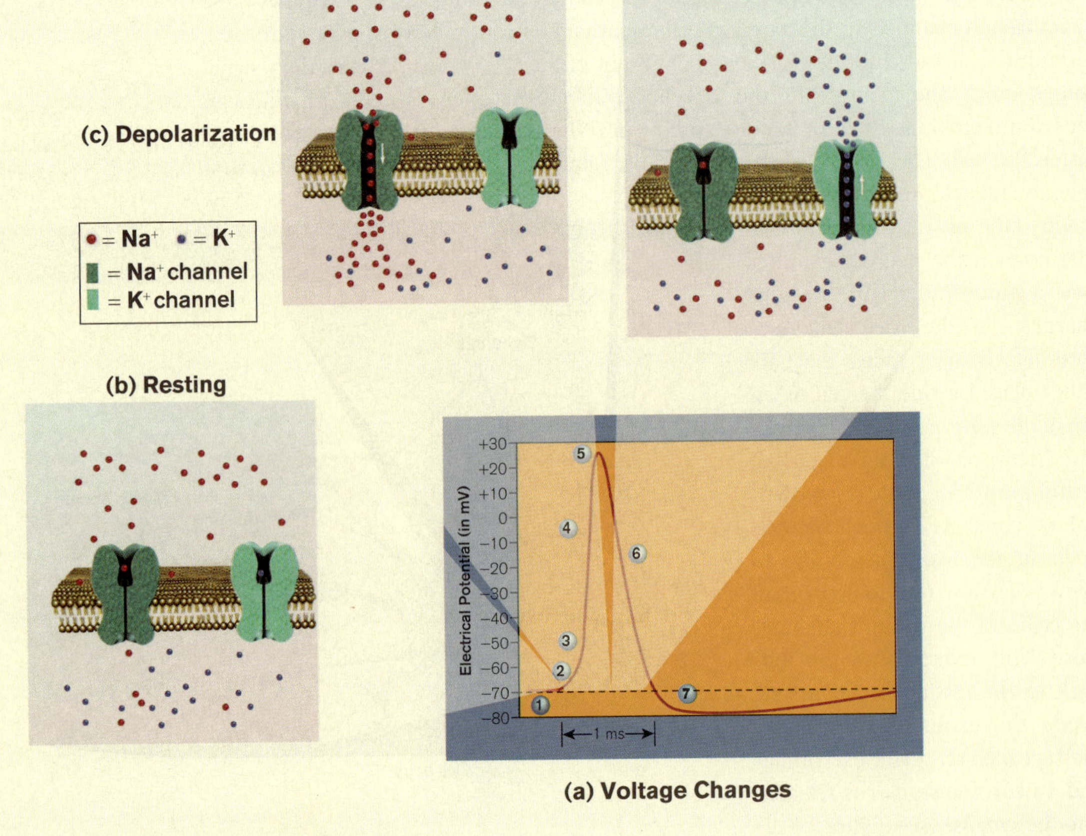

The synapse is the small gap between neurons in the brain. Each neuron is connected to other neurons in an organized network that allows the pattern of firing in the network to translate into specific thoughts or behaviors. This is how information is processed and stored in the brain: through the pattern of firing across multiple neurons within the network (i.e., specific neurons being active or not active or firing at different rates) and types of connections (excitatory or inhibitory) across the neurons connected in each network.

Figure 2.6 Release of Neurotransmitter by the Presynaptic Neuron Into the Synapse

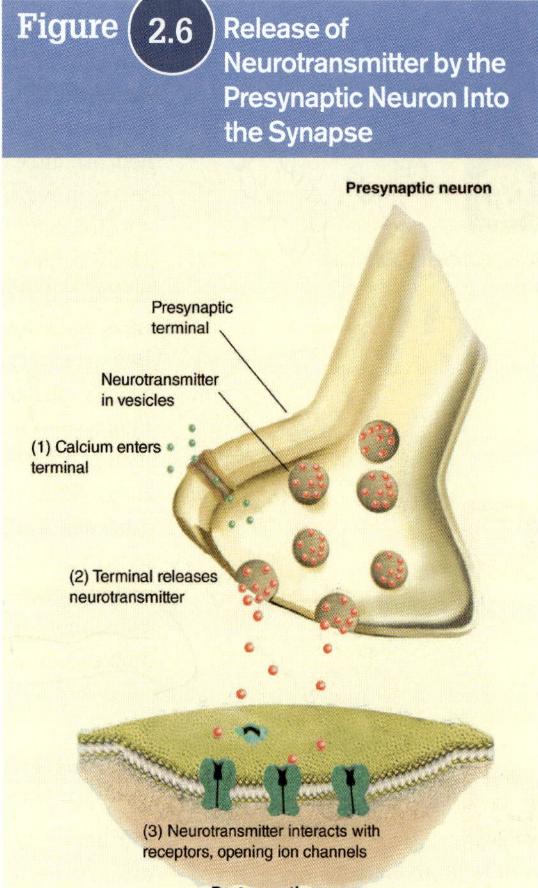

The Brain

The brain is composed of the networks described in the previous section, which are organized according to their cognitive functions. This is known as localization of function. Many of the clinical cases reviewed in the previous section provided the initial information we have about localization and lateralization (i.e., the two hemispheres of the brain contribute to different types of tasks) of brain function through the deficits present in different areas of brain damage. Looking at the kind of task deficits these patients exhibited helped researchers to identify brain areas (i.e., the damaged areas) that were important for completing those tasks. These early studies suggested that different areas of the brain specialized in different functions. Figure 2.7 shows the four lobes of the brain and functions that are localized in those brain areas. Recent research in cognitive neuroscience has used this knowledge gained in early case studies to focus on different areas of the brain as researchers examine the functioning in different

Figure 2.7 Diagram of the Four Lobes of the Brain and Functions Lateralized in These Areas

Frontal lobe (reasoning)

Parietal lobe (sensation and movement)

Occipital lobe (vision)

Temporal lobe (language)

Graphic from © iStockphoto.com/Ciawitaly

The Brain's Inner Workings

The Tell-Tale Brain

Brain Atlas Exercise

cognitive tasks. The newer brain recording techniques described in the next sections have allowed researchers to go beyond the basic knowledge of localization and lateralization of function to map out more specific brain areas and to piece together full neural systems (i.e., a collection of brain areas organized in pathways) that are involved in different tasks. We explore some of the most recent research in cognitive neuroscience throughout the subsequent chapters that cover different cognitive processes in further detail.

Neuroimaging Exercise

However, more recent research has suggested that despite the general feature of localization of function, many complex cognitive tasks (e.g., memory retrieval, object identification) are a function of distributed processing in the brain. In other words, brain areas work together in systems to process different kinds of information. This idea is supported by research in different areas of study. For example, a series of brain areas has been implicated in explicit memory retrieval (i.e., intentionally retrieving a memory). This system seems to be separate from more automatic or unintentional uses of memory, such as those relied on when we perform a skill or task we know how to do (Squire, 2004). Pulvermüller (2010a) also describes neural circuits for lexical and semantic processes underlying language abilities as "distributed neural assemblies reaching into sensory and motor systems of the cortex" (p. 167). In other words, the processing of spelling, grammar, and meaning of words is distributed across several areas of the brain. Thus, there is localization of function for cognitive processes, but for most functions multiple areas are organized into processing systems for different cognitive abilities.

Tools in Cognitive Neuroscience

Measures in Cognitive Neuroscience

How Neurons Shaped Civilization

In Chapter 1, we described the biological perspective on the study of cognition. Using this approach, researchers attempt to connect brain activity with cognitive processes they observe along with some of the other behavioral measures (e.g., accuracy, reaction time). For example, cognitive neuroscientists have investigated how brain activity differs for accurate and false memories (e.g., Düzel, Yonelinas, Mangun, Heinz, & Tulving, 1997), which areas of the brain are involved in language production and comprehension (e.g., Gernsbacher & Kaschak, 2003), and whether visual areas of the brain are involved in imagery (e.g., Kosslyn et al., 1993).

Figure 2.8 Recording Electrical Activity in a Neuron

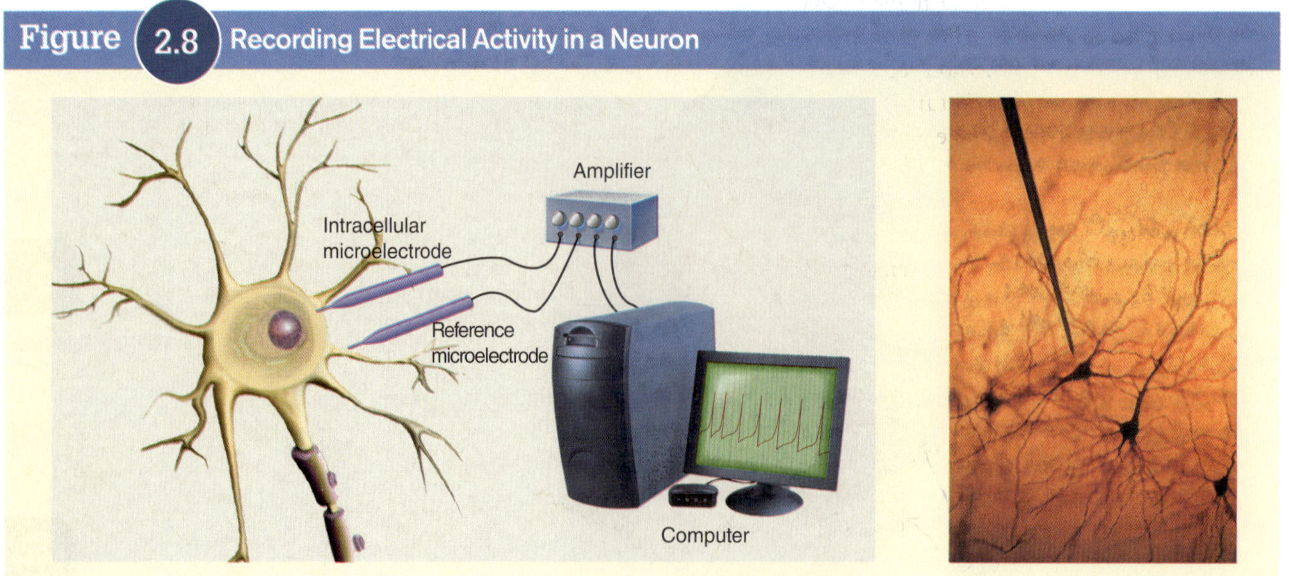

Photo at right courtesy of Bob Jacobs

Advances in technology have allowed researchers to record different types of brain activity. Some techniques are more invasive and are typically only performed with laboratory animals (e.g., single-cell recordings), but many of the brain imaging techniques in use today are able to record brain activity in humans as they perform various cognitive tasks. However, all of the techniques rely on activity of the neuronal cells in the brain.

Figure 2.9 Stereotaxic Instrument Used in Single-Cell Recordings

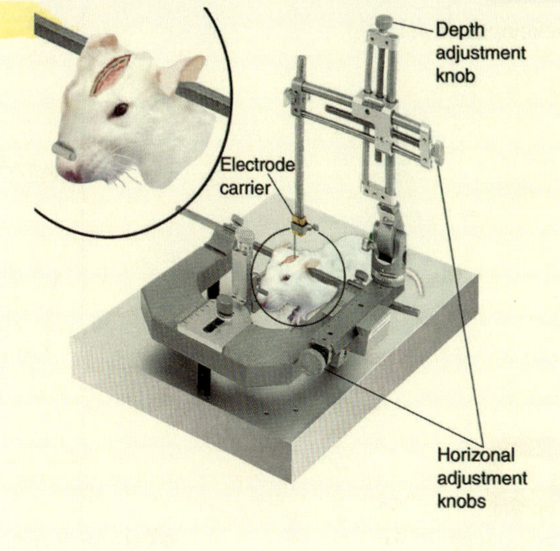

Single-Cell Recording

A technique available to record the electrical signals from neurons is **single-cell recording**. In this technique a tiny recording needle is inserted into a neuron in an area of the brain the researcher is interested in (see Figure 2.8). However, this technique requires surgical insertion of the needle and bonding to the head to keep the needle steady (see Figure 2.9). Thus, this technique is typically used in research with laboratory animals. Such recordings have contributed important information about cognition. For example, using single-cell recordings from monkeys, Rizzolatti, Fadiga, Gallese, and Fogassi (1996) discovered a new type of neuron they called a mirror neuron. This neuron fired both when the monkeys picked up an object and when the monkeys were watching the researchers or other monkeys perform that action. In other words, these neurons were active when motor actions were performed and when the monkeys were just watching a motor action they knew how to perform. Since this discovery, researchers have suggested that mirror neurons may play a role in many sorts of social cognitions, including understanding others' actions, imitation of others' actions, and facilitation of language through gestures (Rizzolatti & Craighero, 2004). Other work using single-cell recordings has shown that neuronal cell responses can be extremely specific. For example, Quiroga, Reddy, Kreiman, Koch, and Fried (2005) found neurons in the hippocampus (known to be involved in memory functioning) that were selectively responsive to photos of celebrities such as Jennifer Aniston and Halle Berry (in recordings from epilepsy patients undergoing treatment). These results are consistent with the idea that neurons serve as feature detectors (see Chapter 3 for more discussion of feature detection); in this case, the features are specific faces. These neurons have been called "grandmother cells" (Gross, 2002) because they suggest that we might even have a neuron (or set of neurons) that selectively responds to the face of our grandmother (assuming we have met her before).

Single-cell recording: a brain activity recording technique that records activity from a single neuron or small group of neurons in the brain

Electroencephalography (EEG): a brain recording technique that records the activity of large sections of neurons from different areas of the scalp

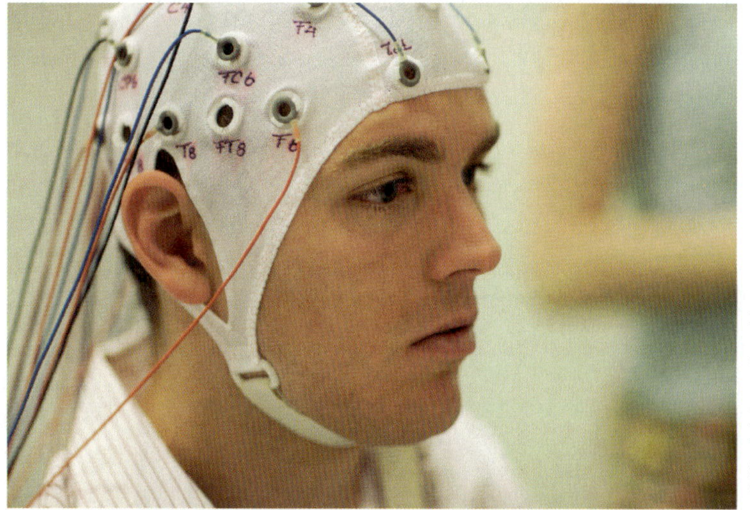

Photo 2.1 In recording an EEG, a scalp cap with electrodes in different locations on the head is worn by the participant.

Electroencephalography (EEG)

Another technique that records the electrical signals from neurons is **electroencephalography** or **EEG**. When recording an EEG, a set of electrodes is placed on the head (see Photo 2.1) to record the electrical signals from groups of neurons in different areas of the

Development of EEG

Figure 2.10 Sample EEG Recording

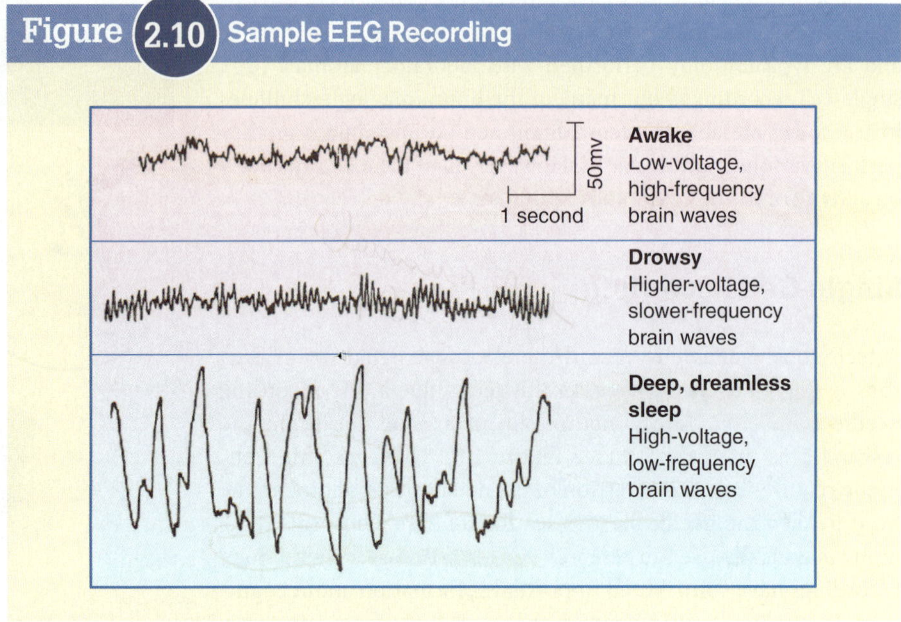

ERPs and EEG

SOURCE: From *Current Concepts: The Sleep Disorders*, by P. Hauri, 1982, Kalamazoo, MI: Upjohn.

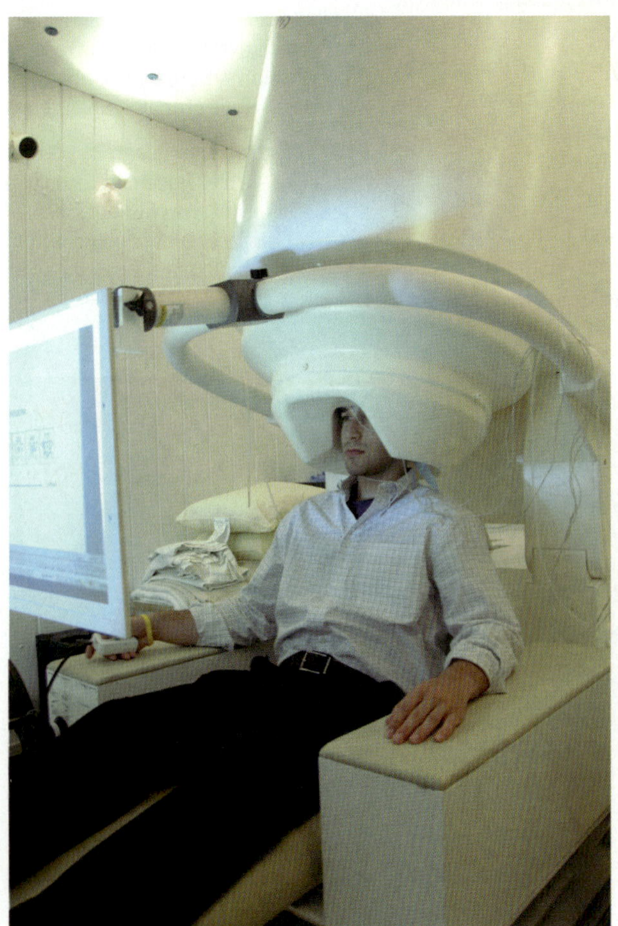

National Institute of Mental Health

Photo 2.2 A person receiving a MEG scan.

brain. Because the electrodes are recording from outside the skull, it is the activity of the neurons closest to the skull (primarily neurons in the outer cortex) that is being recorded. The activity is recorded over time to detect changes (positive or negative) in the electrical signals (see Figure 2.10). Researchers can use EEG recordings to examine an event-related potential (ERP), which is a change in activity related to a specific event like the presentation of a stimulus. In that way, they can determine if there is an effect of that stimulus presentation on neuron activity and in what general area of the brain the effect occurs. Electrical activity patterns can be overlaid onto a map of the brain to show the general location on the cortex of the different levels of electrical activity.

An example of EEG/ERP research is provided by Düzel et al. (1997). These researchers recorded ERPs during recognition judgments for studied words. Although voltage for different scalp areas differed based on the type of judgment subjects made (i.e., did they "remember" having studied the word, or did they just "know" they had studied the word?), voltage recordings were similar for items the subjects correctly remembered and for items subjects falsely remembered having studied (i.e., items they recognized as studied in the memory test but that were not studied in the list). The electrical activity recorded in the ERP showed that similar activity occurs for true and false memories, but that the activity differs depending on the strength of the memory based on the type of response ("remember" or "know") the subjects gave.

Figure 2.11 Transcranial Magnetic Stimulation (TMS)

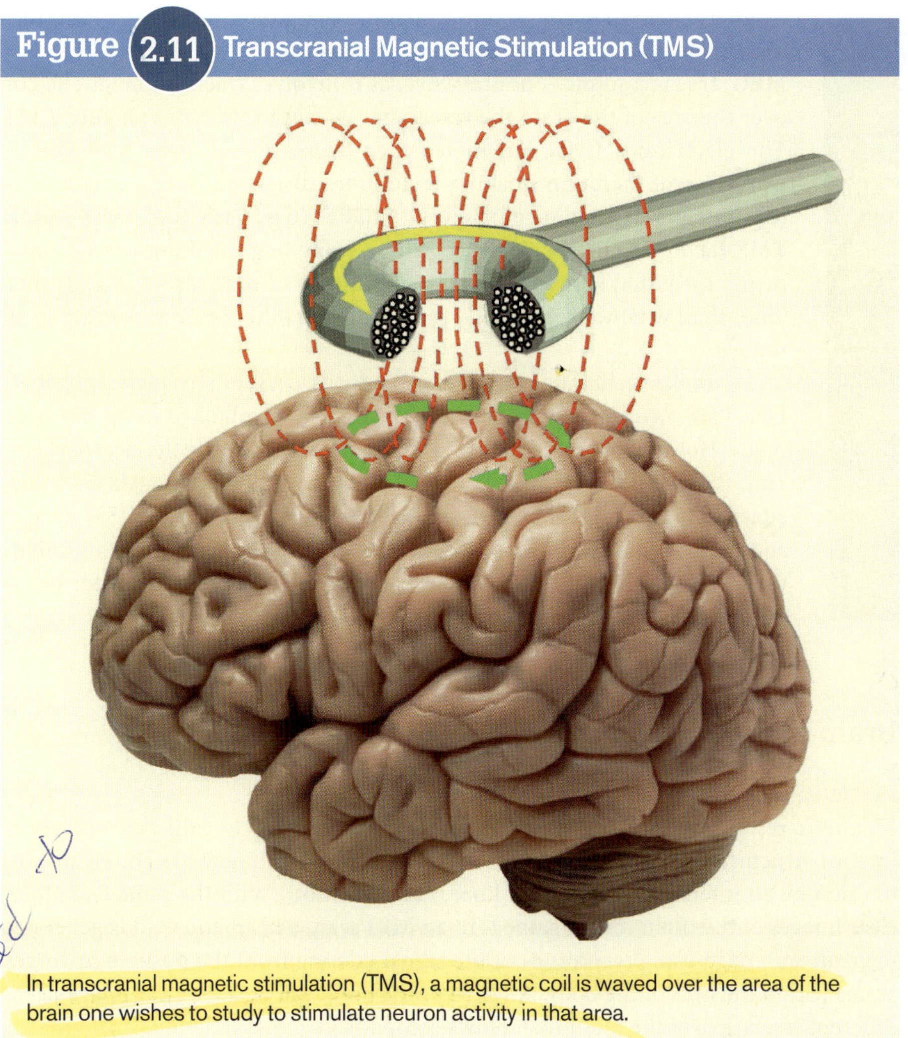

In transcranial magnetic stimulation (TMS), a magnetic coil is waved over the area of the brain one wishes to study to stimulate neuron activity in that area.

SOURCE: Courtesy of Eric Wassermann, M.D., Behavioral Neurology Unit, National Institute of Neurological Disorders and Stroke.

Magnetoencephalography (MEG)

MEG Technique

Another newer technique that records electrical signals from neurons in the brain is **magnetoencephalography (MEG)**. Instead of electrodes placed on the head as for an EEG, MEG involves placing the head in or near an electrical scanner that can detect electrical activity with better location accuracy than EEG. As with EEG recordings, MEG recordings can occur during a task such that changes in activity can be detected that correspond to the presentation of cognitive stimuli. However, as with EEG, MEG is limited to recordings on the outer cortex and cannot provide a good measure of activity occurring below the cortex.

Magnetoencephalography (MEG): a brain recording technique that records activity of large sections of neurons from different areas of the scalp using a large magnet that is placed over the head

Electrical Stimulation/ Inhibition of Neurons

Transcranial magnetic stimulation (TMS): a method of temporarily stimulating or suppressing neurons using a magnetic field

Another newer technique that also relies on the electrical activity in the brain involves **transcranial magnetic stimulation (TMS)**. With TMS, researchers use a

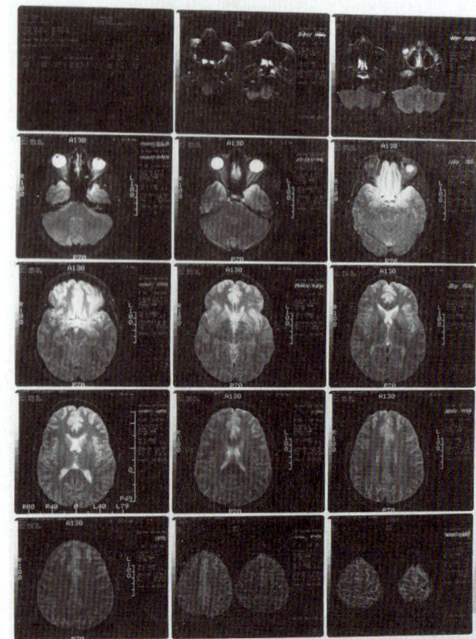

Thomas Northcut/Photodisc/Thinkstock

Photo 2.3 Images from an MRI of the brain.

magnetic field to excite or inhibit neuron activity to investigate functioning in specific areas or processing systems of the brain. Like EEG and MEG, this technique is noninvasive, as it involves tracing a magnetic coil over the area of the brain the researcher wishes to study (see Figure 2.11). The electrical activity (an increase or decrease) can then be recorded using one of the brain imaging techniques discussed in the next section (e.g., magnetic resonance imaging). Studies (e.g., Sach et al., 2007) using TMS have shown that some cognitive tasks (e.g., making spatial judgments for visual stimuli) use a broader range of brain areas (e.g., frontal lobe) than what was previously thought using other brain recording techniques.

A similar technique is **transcranial direct current stimulation (tDCS)**. Like TMS, neuron activity can either be excited or inhibited using this technique. However, where TMS uses a magnetic field to create the electrical current, tDCS delivers a small electric current to the brain through electrodes attached to the scalp. Thus, it is also a noninvasive technique. tDCS is cheaper and easier to use than TMS but produces a weaker effect on neuron activity than TMS. Both of these techniques are becoming more popular for use in cognitive neuroscience research.

Brain Imaging Techniques

Mind and Brain

fMRI

Magnetic Resonance Imaging (MRI)

Magnetic resonance imaging (MRI) is often used medically to gain clear images of interior structures of the body. Perhaps you or someone you know has gotten an MRI to examine an internal injury (e.g., a knee, hand, or foot). With the same technique, clear images of the brain can be gained. In an MRI scan, a magnetic field is generated to create an image using recordings of the signal coming from the positive hydrogen atoms within the cells of the body. An MRI of the brain can create a clear image of the different structures of the brain that allows comparison across individuals and identification of damage or the presence of tumors (see Photo 2.3).

Positron Emission Tomography (PET)

Using **positron emission tomography (PET)**, researchers can measure the blood flow to different areas of the brain. Blood flows in greater volume to more active areas of the brain; thus, the measure of the blood flow will indicate the areas of the brain most active during a cognitive task. Blood flow is detected through the ingestion of a small amount of a radioactive substance. The radioactive substance is then absorbed into the blood and flows to the brain as blood is needed in active areas. The radioactivity in the blood is then measured in a PET scan to determine which areas of the brain are more active than others during a task. The recording of the radioactivity is then overlaid onto a map of the brain to examine which areas are the most and least active. In a PET scan, color indicates the level of activity occurring in different areas. Photo 2.4 shows a PET scan of brains for two individuals: one who has taken cocaine and one who has not. The most active areas of the brain are colored in red (followed by yellow and then green with the least amount of activity in blue). In this figure, it is clear that there is less activity globally for individuals who have cocaine in their system than for individuals who do not (control).

Functional Magnetic Resonance Imaging (fMRI)

A newer technique related to MRI is **functional magnetic resonance imaging (fMRI)**. fMRI is a technique that records brain activity with a scan of the magnetic properties of the blood flowing through the brain. Similar to PET, fMRI shows blood

Transcranial direct current stimulation (tDCS): a method of temporarily stimulating or suppressing neurons using an electrical current

Magnetic resonance imaging (MRI): a technique to image the internal portions of the body using the magnetic fields present in the cells

Positron emission tomography (PET): a technique that images neuron activity in the brain through radioactive markers in the bloodstream

Functional magnetic resonance imaging (fMRI): an MRI technique that images brain activity during a task

flow activity to specific areas of the brain with more active areas shown in brighter colors on the scan. fMRI relies on a subtraction method, where activity recorded before the task (called the baseline recording, which is a control condition in this type of study) is subtracted from the activity recorded during the task. What is left is the activity present only during the tasks.

Like an MRI, an fMRI requires that the participant be placed in a magnetic scanner during the task. Typically, a mirror is positioned in the scanner for the participant to view the stimuli presented. fMRI is often preferred by researchers conducting brain scans because they are able to view brain activity during a task (unlike MRI) and there is no potentially harmful radioactive substance that needs to be ingested by the participant (unlike PET). Figure 2.12 shows images from fMRI scans for a participant performing different language tasks. As can be seen, different areas of the brain are most active during the different tasks.

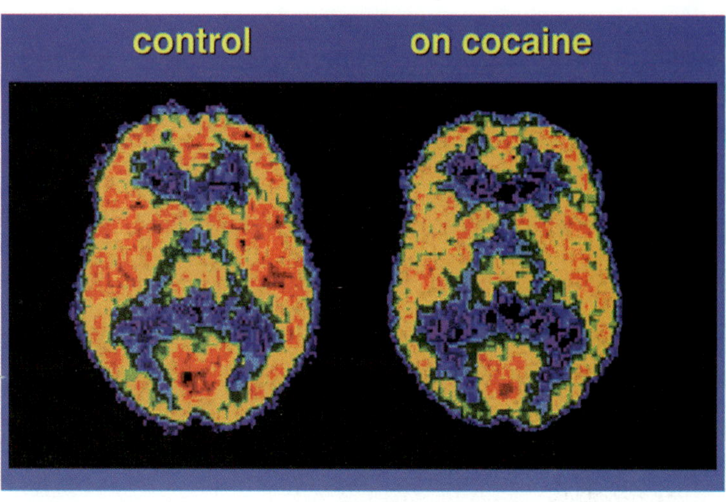

http://www.drugabuse.gov/

Photo 2.4 A PET scan. The areas in red are the most active, those in blue are least active.

Recording Activity in the Living Brain

Neuroimaging

Throughout this text, we discuss studies that have used the brain recording techniques described in this chapter to illustrate the connection between brain function and the cognitive processes discussed. Here we highlight two of these studies to illustrate the use

Figure 2.12 Images From fMRI Scans of the Brain Taken During the Different Language Tasks Identified in the Scan

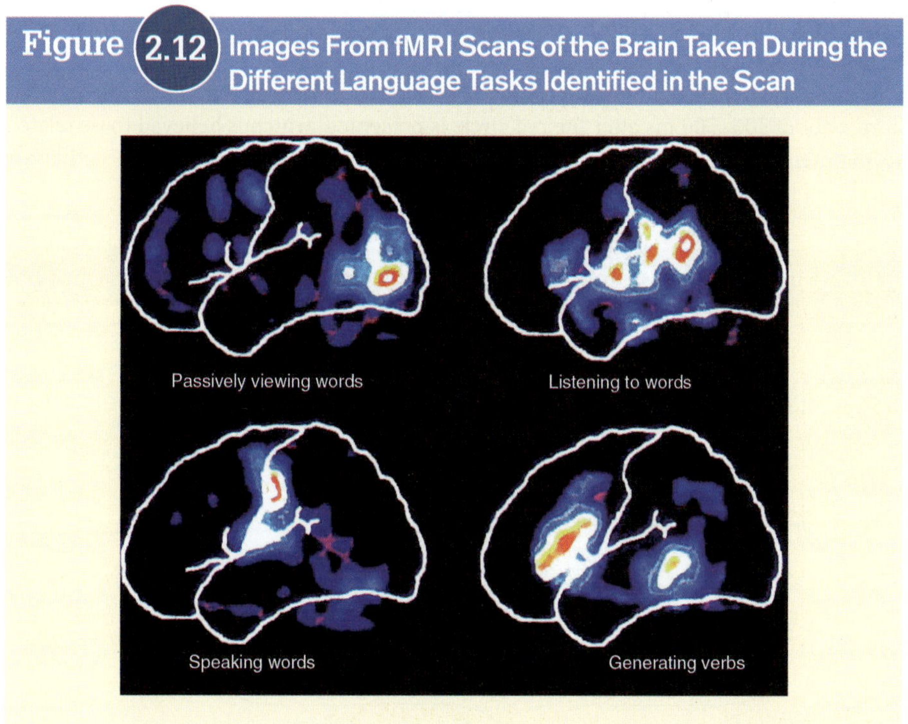

SOURCE: Adapted from Petersen, S. E., Fox, P. T., Posner, M. I., Mintun, M., & Raichle, M. E. (1988). Positron emission tomographic studies of the cortical anatomy of single-word processing. *Nature, 333*, 585–589.

Stop and Think

2.3. What type of neuron activity is recorded in single-cell, EEG, and MEG recordings?

2.4. What type of brain activity is detected in PET and fMRI scans? Why is an fMRI scan preferred to a PET scan in most cases?

2.5. In general, what has been learned about the organization of brain activity using cognitive neuroscience techniques?

2.6. Does research connecting brain activity with cognitive task performance gain causal information or merely correlational information? Explain your answer.

of these techniques in cognitive neuroscience as a field, and then in further chapters, we discuss some of the most recent studies in cognitive neuroscience in perception, attention, memory, and language.

Two categories of brain recording techniques were described earlier in this chapter: recordings of electrical activity of neurons (single neurons or larger groups of neurons) and brain imaging techniques. Each technique has contributed important knowledge about the connections between cognition and brain function. For example, many EEG studies have shown the areas of the cortex most active during specific tasks. When EEG recordings are connected to specific stimulus presentations, as in ERP, this activity can be examined across stimulus conditions to make comparisons as tests of theoretical hypotheses.

In an example of this type of study, Barron, Riby, Greer, and Smallwood (2011) used ERP recordings to examine the factors that contribute to mind wandering (i.e., thinking about things other than the current task you are working on). Do you ever start thinking about something going on in your life (e.g., an argument with your boyfriend, girlfriend, or spouse or an assignment that is due at the end of the week) while you are reading this text? If so, then you have experienced the type of mind wandering that Barron et al. studied. These researchers recorded EEGs during a task where subjects were asked to respond to a rare target event (a red circle appearing) that occurred in a series of presented stimuli (green and blue squares). However, the nontarget stimuli were presented with different proportions. Green squares were presented often and blue squares were presented as infrequently as the red circles. This type of stimulus presentation was used to see if the blue squares would capture the subjects' attention even if they were not asked to respond to them (see Figure 2.13).

In this task, past studies have shown an increase in neuron activity in the parietal cortex about 300–500 ms after the red circle is presented, which is believed to be related to maintenance of the stimulus in memory. Further, a similar increase in activity is

Figure 2.13 Stimuli Used in the Barron et al. (2011) Study

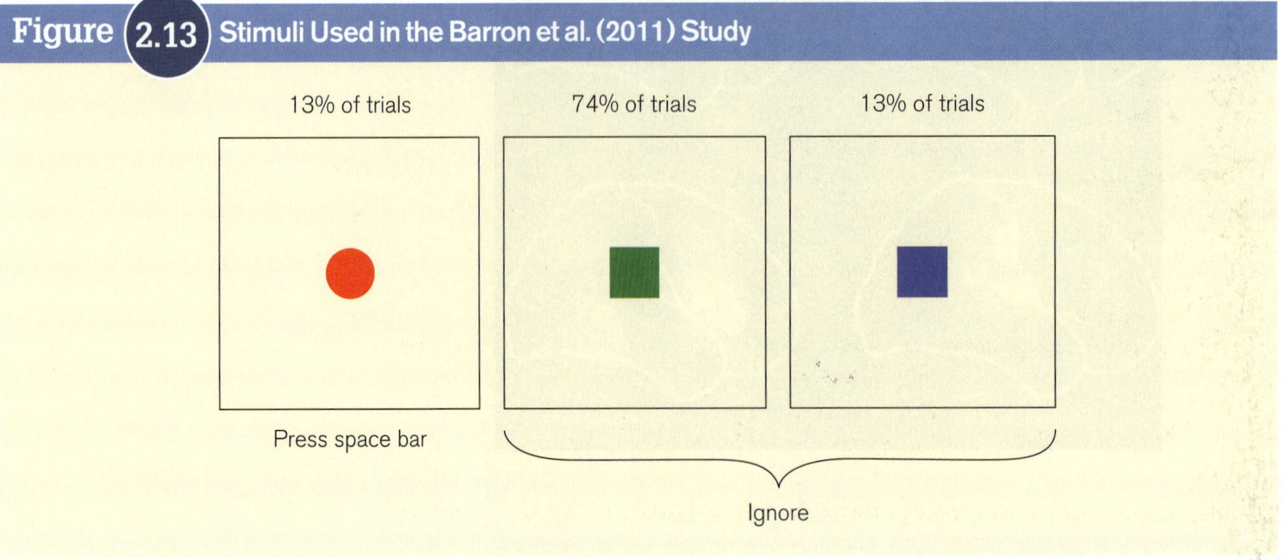

shown in the frontal lobe if the blue square (that requires no response) is presented. The activity in the frontal lobe that occurs with this distracting rare event is believed to be due to attention being paid to this stimulus because it occurs infrequently in the trials.

In the Barron et al. (2011) study, subjects also completed a survey at the end of the trials to gauge the amount of mind wandering that occurred during the task. Subjects were separated into groups: high, medium, and low mind wandering. The study was designed to investigate different theories about how mind wandering occurs for those who reported off-task thoughts during the task (i.e., the high mind wandering group). For example, mind wandering might happen because something distracts the person from his or her main task. If so, subjects in the high group should show greater brain activity in the frontal cortex area when the distracting blue squares are presented. Alternatively, mind wandering might be due to subjects completely disengaging from the task and focusing attention on other thoughts. If so, subjects in the high group should show lower brain activity in both the frontal and parietal cortex when the target and nontarget rare events (red circles and blue squares) are shown, because they are not attending well to any of the stimuli in the task. The results of the Barron et al. (2011) study showed that subjects with high levels of mind wandering had lower levels of brain activity in response to both the red circles and blue squares, supporting the idea that subjects were not attending to the task while their mind was wandering. The researchers concluded from these data that suppression of the external events (i.e., not paying attention to the rare events, regardless of whether a response is required) contributes to mind wandering. This study shows how EEG/ERP studies can be used to test theories about cognitive processes.

Brain imaging techniques are also frequently used in cognitive neuroscience studies. An example of this type of study was done by Segaert, Menenti, Weber, Petersson, and Hagoort (2012) to investigate the link in processing between language production and comprehension. The similarities and differences between language comprehension and production has been a topic of interest in the past few decades within language research as researchers in this area develop and test theories of how these processes occur (see Chapter 9 for more discussion of language comprehension and production processes). Segaert et al. (2012) used fMRI recordings to test the idea that the same brain areas are active during syntactic processing (i.e., understanding how words fit together grammatically in sentences) in both language comprehension and production. Subjects were asked to complete a task of either comprehending a sentence or producing a sentence when a verb and a picture were presented. The color of the verb (green or gray) indicated whether a comprehension trial or a production trial was used. fMRI scans of the subjects' brains were taken during the task. The researchers examined the change in brain activity when the same syntactic structure of sentences was repeated in the trials to see if adaptation to the structure (i.e., lowered brain activity) would be seen. They then compared the adaptation effects across the comprehension and production trials to see if adaptation was similar across speaking and listening trials. Results showed adaptation to the repeated syntactic structure of the sentences in both comprehension and production trials. In addition, the same level of adaptation was found in both speaking and listening trials. The researchers concluded that the same brain activity contributes to syntactic processing in both comprehension and production of language.

Cognitive Neuroscience of Episodic Memory

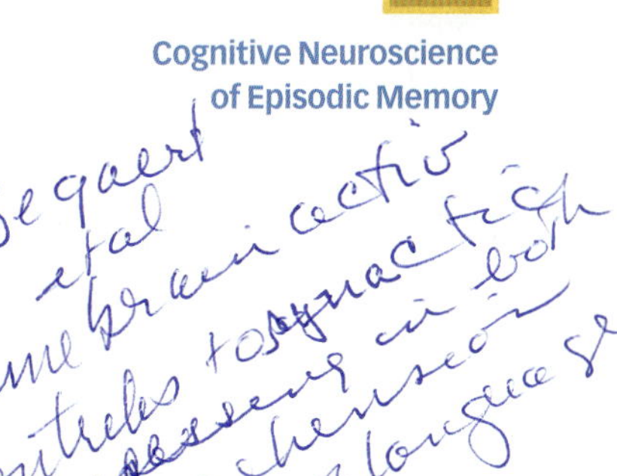

The newest brain recording technologies have allowed cognitive neuroscientists to gain important knowledge about the connection between brain function and cognitive processes. As an example from language research suggests (Pulvermüller, 2010b), four key questions can be answered from cognitive neuroscience research: (1) where the brain activity occurs during specific cognitive tasks, (2) when the brain activity occurs during a task (e.g., at stimulus presentation or after a delay when processing has begun), (3) how the brain activity occurs (e.g., in specific networks of brain areas), and (4) why brain activity occurs (i.e., testing hypotheses about how the processing occurs in

Stop and Think

2.7. How has the use of brain recording techniques allowed researchers to test causal relationships between brain activity and cognitive functions?

2.8. Suppose that you were interested in learning about the brain areas involved in memory processing. You are specifically interested in testing whether the retrieval of accurate and false memories relies on the same underlying processes in brain function. Describe a study using one of the brain recording techniques described in this chapter that would test this question.

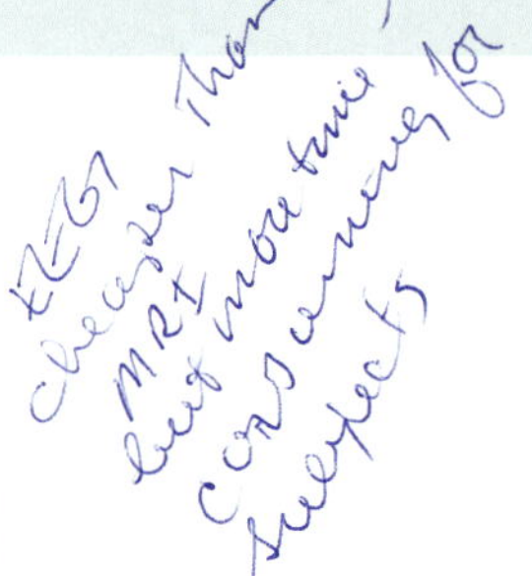

particular cognitive tasks). Thus, there is a great advantage in using brain recording techniques in cognitive neuroscience research to learn about these specific aspects of cognitive functioning. However, some disadvantages exist as well. One disadvantage is that not all cognitive tasks are easily adapted to the brain recording techniques. The neuroscientific study of insight (i.e., that "aha" moment when you suddenly realize how to solve a problem; see Chapter 11), for example, has been difficult to conduct because it is hard to predict when insight will occur for a specific problem. Luo and Knoblich (2007) describe the difficulties in using fMRI and EEG techniques to study the process of insight and some of their methods to adapt insight studies to brain recording techniques. Another disadvantage is the limited availability of brain scan technology. Because MRI machines are expensive and also serve as a medical tool, it can be difficult for researchers to obtain time available for use of these devices. EEG machines and technology are relatively cheaper and more readily available for research, but this can be a time-consuming procedure for subject participation. Thus, although these recording techniques represent significant advances in our ability to connect cognitive function with brain activity, they are not without drawbacks.

The Cognitive Atlas Project

Can All Mental Processes Be Explained in Terms of Brain Activity?

Brain Porn

One question researchers have begun to ask is whether all behavior can be explained in terms of brain activity. Although we do not yet know the answer to this question, some interesting studies have begun to explore it. For example, Libet (1985) describes studies of EEG brain activity showing that about half a second before someone is aware that he or she will perform an intentional action (e.g., pressing a button in an experiment), the brain signals that it is preparing to perform that action. Libet argued this evidence suggests that our choices (at least simple ones like button presses) are determined unconsciously by the brain before we are consciously aware of making such choices. More recently, Schurger, Sitt, and Dehaene (2012) have argued that the activity seen in the brain before these choices are consciously made indicates readiness to make a choice rather than the actual choice itself. The debate on this question continues, but conscious choices are one area where researchers are investigating whether brain activity can define behavior.

Another area where progress has been made in investigating how brain activity translates into specific behaviors is in patterns of activity related to identification of simple objects. For example, some studies have shown that a unique pattern of brain activity accompanies the identification of objects such as faces and houses (Grill-Spector, 2008). In fact, researcher Marcel Just and his colleagues (Mitchell et al., 2008) have been developing a "mind reading" program that can identify a word a person is looking at simply from the pattern of brain activity seen in an fMRI scan of the person's brain.

What Brain Scans Reveal

The research highlighted here is promising in making specific connections between predictable brain activity and cognitive behavior. However, one criticism is that the behaviors being examined are too simple (e.g., choosing to press a button, looking at a word). It may be much more difficult, and maybe impossible, to make such precise connections between brain activity and more complex behaviors such as driving, having a conversation, and imagining yourself in a situation you have never been in. Thus, the question of whether all behavior can be connected to specific brain activity is yet unanswered.

An alternate idea is that the mind and body (i.e., the brain) are separate and distinct entities. In other words, the mind exists and functions separate from the functioning of the brain. This idea has been debated by philosophers for over a century and is called the mind-body problem. Dualists believe that the mind exists separately from the brain—that the mind is our conscious self and is not reducible to brain function. In contrast is the view presented earlier—that the mind is defined by brain function and cannot be separated from brain activity. The research presented here represents some cognitive neuroscience support for this view, but this question is still typically discussed at a philosophical level, given the current state of the field.

Stop and Think

2.9. Suppose research determined that specific brain activity is present when someone is lying and not present when the person is telling the truth. Do you think this knowledge could be used to develop a foolproof lie detector? Why or why not?

THINKING ABOUT RESEARCH

As you read the following summary of a research study in psychology, think about the following questions:

1. Explain how this study used recordings of brain activity to test a theoretical description of a cognitive process.
2. What was the primary manipulated variable in this experiment? (Hint: Review the Research Methodologies section in Chapter 1 for help in answering this question.)
3. Do you think the researchers would have achieved similar results if they had used EEG instead of fMRI in this study? Why or why not?
4. Explain why it was important for the researchers to show that subjects were slower in performing the nonfocal than the focal prospective memory task.

Study Reference

McDaniel, M. A., LaMontagne, P., Beck, S. M., Scullin, M. K., & Braver, T. S. (2013). Dissociable neural routes to successful prospective memory. *Psychological Science*, *24*, 1791–1800.

Purpose of the study: The researchers investigated brain activity associated with prospective memory, which is remembering to perform a future task (e.g., taking medicine after dinner, stopping at the store on the way home to buy milk). The researchers tested two theoretical perspectives used to describe how prospective memory operates. One perspective suggests that when there is a future task we are trying to remember, remembering the task always uses cognitive attentional resources. The other perspective suggests that in some cases, prospective memory can be performed after a spontaneous retrieval of the task that does not consume cognitive resources in the remembering period. To test these two perspectives, the researchers compared two prospective memory tasks, one that should consume cognitive resources to retrieve and one that (according to the second perspective) would not consume cognitive resources to retrieve because spontaneous retrieval could be used. If the second perspective on prospective memory is correct, different brain activity in the two types of tasks is predicted.

Method of the study: Subjects in the study performed one of two types of prospective memory tasks. The prospective memory tasks were given within the context of

(Continued)

(Continued)

Figure 2.14 Activity Compared for the Focal and Nonfocal Prospective Memory Tasks From fMRI Scans in the McDaniel et al. (2013) Study

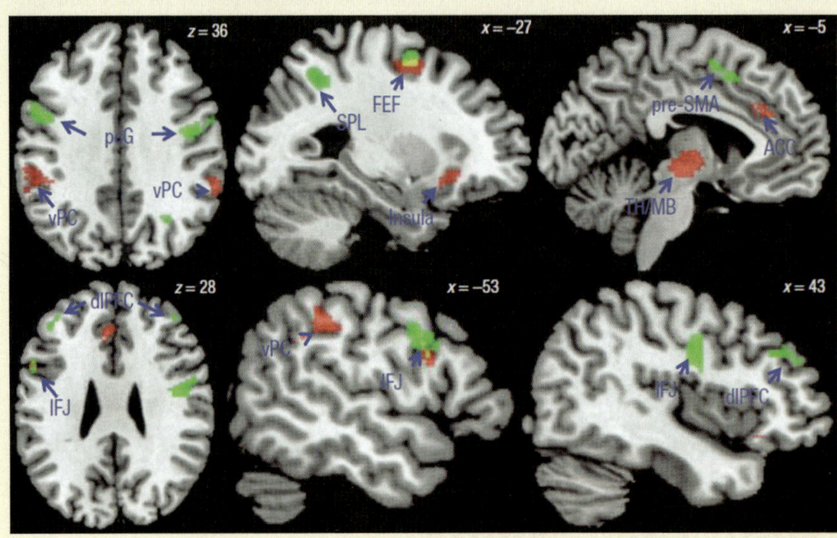

SOURCE: Figure 1, McDaniel, M. A., LaMontagne, P., Beck, S. M., Scullin, M. K., & Braver, T. S. (2013). Dissociable neural routes to successful prospective memory. *Psychological Science*, 24, 1791–1800.

an ongoing task of category judgments (e.g., Is GREEN a COLOR? Is a GRAPE a type of FURNITURE?). All subjects completed the same ongoing task where an item appeared with a category on the computer screen, and subjects were asked to decide if the item belonged in the category given. However, different groups of subjects were given different prospective memory tasks to perform during the category task. One task, called a nonfocal task, has been shown in studies to require cognitive resources to retrieve (resulting in a slowing down in ongoing task performance). In this task, subjects were asked to respond if they saw the syllable *tor* in any of the category tasks. Looking for the syllable would require extra attention, because subjects do not need to notice the syllables of the words in order to complete the category task. The other type of prospective memory task, called a focal task, has been shown in studies to sometimes rely on spontaneous retrieval where no slowing down in ongoing task performance was seen. In this task subjects were asked to respond when they saw the word *table* in the category task. During the completion of the tasks, subjects' brain activity was measured using fMRI scans.

Results of the study: The results showed two important findings of the study. First, subjects slowed down in the category task more when they completed the nonfocal prospective memory task than when they performed the focal prospective memory task, supporting previous findings that the nonfocal task requires more attentional resources than the focal task. The second primary finding was that brain activity differed in the two types of prospective memory tasks. In the nonfocal task, the researchers found activity in the prefrontal cortex area of the brain that was not present in the focal task. See Figure 2.14 for a comparison of the brain activity seen in the fMRI scans for the focal and nonfocal conditions.

Conclusions of the study: From the recordings of brain activity seen in this study, the researchers concluded that some prospective memory tasks do not require cognitive resources to retrieve because no activity was seen in the prefrontal cortex area for the focal task, whereas this activity was present in the nonfocal task. The primary conclusion from this study was that brain activity supports the idea that prospective memory tasks do not always require additional attentional resources.

CHAPTER REVIEW

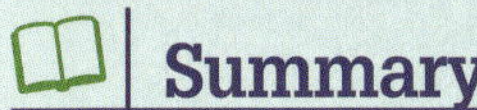

Summary

- **How is the examination of brain activity involved in the study of cognition?**

  A number of brain activity recording techniques are used by cognitive neuroscientists to better understand how brain activity is tied to cognition. All rely in some way on neuron activity, with some (single-cell recordings, EEG) measuring the electrical signals from neurons and others (PET, fMRI) recording images of neuron activity in larger areas of the brain.

- **How do case studies of individuals with cognitive deficits inform us about the connection between cognition and brain function?**

  Individuals who have suffered a brain lesion can help us connect cognitive deficits to specific areas of the brain. By examining the area(s) of the lesion and which cognitive deficits the individuals have, researchers can make hypotheses about the primary function of different areas of the brain. Much of the early knowledge of localization of function in the brain came from such clinical case studies.

- **What can be learned about cognition through measurements of neuron activity in the brain?**

  Like clinical case studies, researchers can connect specific brain areas with cognitive abilities. However, measurements of brain activity also allow researchers to provide better tests of hypotheses about brain function because experiments can be conducted with brain activity as the dependent measures.

- **Can all behavior be explained in terms of brain activity?**

  Some studies suggest that it can, at least for simple behaviors. However, the answer to this question is not yet known.

Chapter Quiz

1. Which brain recording technique(s) is (are) often limited to laboratory animals because it requires insertion of a recording needle into the brain?
   (a) PET scan
   (b) EEG/ERP
   (c) fMRI
   (d) single-cell recording
   (e) both (a) and (b)
2. Which brain recording technique(s) measures a change in blood flow to different areas of the brain?
   (a) PET scan
   (b) EEG/ERP
   (c) fMRI
   (d) single-cell recording
   (e) both (a) and (b)
3. What is meant by localization and lateralization of brain function?
4. Describe some disadvantages of using clinical case studies to connect brain function and cognition.
5. From Phineas Gage, researchers learned that the ____________ lobe of the brain is important for reasoning abilities and control of emotion.
   (a) frontal
   (b) parietal
   (c) temporal
   (d) occipital
6. In which lobe of the brain is visual information primarily processed?
   (a) frontal
   (b) parietal
   (c) temporal
   (d) occipital
7. In what ways is the single-cell recording technique different from other brain recording techniques?
8. How do brain recording techniques allow for experiments that cannot be done with clinical case study patients?

9. When EEG recordings are connected to the timing of the presentation of a stimulus, it is called ____________________.

10. The MEG technique provides better ____________ than EEG.

Key Terms

Axon 25
Dendrites 25
Electroencephalography (EEG) 29
Functional magnetic resonance imaging (fMRI) 32
Magnetic resonance imaging (MRI) 32
Magnetoencephalography (MEG) 31
Neuron 25
Positron emission tomography (PET) 32
Single-cell recording 29
Synapse 25
Transcranial direct current stimulation (tDCS) 32
Transcranial magnetic stimulation (TMS) 31

Stop and Think Answers

2.1. Explain why controlled experiments cannot always be conducted to determine how different types of brain damage cause cognitive deficits.

In order to conduct an experiment of this type, one would need control over the brain damage that occurs. This would be unethical in humans. However, animal models can provide some information about how brain damage affects behavior; thus, experiments are possible to conduct with animal subjects.

2.2. Describe some of the limitations of using the clinical case study method in cognitive neuroscience.

Because the brain damage is not controlled in these cases, it can be difficult to connect deficits with a specific brain region. It is also difficult to provide good tests of hypotheses about how brain function affects cognitive abilities.

2.3. What type of neuron activity is recorded in single-cell, EEG, and MEG recordings?

Electrical activity from a single neuron or multiple neurons is recorded with these techniques.

2.4. What type of brain activity is detected in PET and fMRI scans? Why is an fMRI scan preferred to a PET scan in most cases?

Blood flow to active regions of the brain is recorded in these techniques. fMRI scans are typically preferred because they are less invasive than PET scans. The subject or patient does not need to ingest anything to conduct an fMRI scan.

2.5. In general, what has been learned about the organization of brain activity using cognitive neuroscience techniques?

Research has uncovered the localization of function in the brain, and how different areas are specialized for different tasks.

2.6. Does research connecting brain activity with cognitive task performance gain causal information or merely correlational information? Explain your answer.

This knowledge is primarily correlational due to measurement of the relationship between two measured variables (brain activity and cognitive performance on a task). However, some causal information can be gained by manipulating the cognitive task the subject performs to examine how this affects brain activity being measured.

2.7. How has the use of brain recording techniques allowed researchers to test causal relationships between brain activity and cognitive functions?

Brain recording techniques allow for the measurement of brain activity during the manipulation of cognitive tasks.

2.8. Suppose that you were interested in learning about the brain areas involved in memory processing. You are specifically interested in testing whether the retrieval of accurate and false memories relies on the same underlying processes in brain function. Describe a study using one of the brain recording techniques described in this chapter that would test this question.

Answers will vary, but the key is to measure brain activity during the retrieval of accurate and false memories to compare these situations. Chapter 7 provides some discussion of how false memories can be created experimentally for such studies.

2.9. Suppose research determined that specific brain activity is present when someone is lying and not present when the person is telling the truth. Do you think this knowledge could be used to develop a foolproof lie detector? Why or why not?

Answers will vary.

Student Study Site

Sharpen your skills with SAGE edge at **edge.sagepub.com/mcbridecp**

SAGE edge for students provides a personalized approach to help you accomplish your coursework goals in an easy-to-use learning environment.

Go to edge.sagepub.com/mcbridecp for additional exercises and web resources. Select Chapter 2, Cognitive Neuroscience, for chapter-specific resources. All of the links listed in the margins of this chapter are accessible via this site.

Perception

Questions to Consider

- What is perception?
- How do our sensory systems affect our perception of the world?
- Do we control our perceptions or can we perceive automatically?
- Why do we sometimes perceive things incorrectly?
- What does it mean for something to be "more than the sum of its parts"?
- How does perception aid in action?
- What is the purpose of perception?

Introduction: Perception in Everyday Tasks

Everyday Perception

Have you ever walked across your campus at a busy time, say when classes have just gotten out and students are pouring out of the buildings and trying to get to their next class or the food court to eat lunch? Think about what is involved when you work your way through a busy crowd on your way somewhere. You have to look at what is around you to avoid running into other people or objects in your path. You have to listen to what is around you to avoid objects that you may not be able to see (e.g., moving out of the path of a grounds truck driving across the quad behind you). You have to judge distances between people to make sure you can fit between them if you are moving more quickly than they are or if they are moving toward you. You have to identify landmarks to make sure you are taking the correct path to your destination. In addition to these perceptions that are relevant to your task, you are perceiving many other things that are irrelevant to your task: the conversation of the people walking behind you, the smell of the guy who just walked by who has not showered in a while, how cold the temperature feels on your skin, the taste of the candy bar you are eating as you walk.

Test Your Perceptions

In this scenario, you may recognize that your five senses are clearly involved in bringing in information from the world around you but that there is more going on in your cognition than just receiving sensory input from the world. You are interpreting the information, deciding what is relevant and irrelevant to your task and relying on your other cognitive abilities to aid your perception and complete your task. For example, you are using memory to remember your path, language abilities to distinguish language from other sounds and to understand the conversations around you, and problem-solving abilities to determine where you can fit through the crowd. In this chapter, we discuss the aspects of perception present in this scenario: how they work together to help you interpret the information around you and how perception is tied to your action goals in moving around in the world. This chapter focuses on visual perception, as this is the sense the majority of research has focused on and the visual nature of this text allows for easier illustration of visual examples.

Sensory Systems: How Sensations Become Perceptions

As you might guess from reading through the previous scenario, the starting place for our perceptions is the sensations we bring in from the outside world. Our sense organs—ears, eyes, nose, tongue, and skin—all begin the process of perception for us, sometimes unintentionally. Often, we are simply sensing the world without intending to hear, see, or feel, but our sense organs work automatically to bring in the sensations from our environment. For example, do you sometimes work or study with background music on? The music continues to play with the sound waves continuously hitting your ears, but you do not always "hear" it if you are not paying attention to it or thinking about it. If you stop reading for a moment and listen or look around you, you will likely see and hear things that you did not notice were there until you paid attention to them (we discuss the role of attention in cognition more in Chapter 4). Yet those stimuli are being sensed by your sense organs, even if you are not currently perceiving them.

The sense organs make up the first part of our sensory systems. A **sensory system** processes the sensations coming into each sense organ that allows us to understand and interpret the sensations we receive. If a hot stimulus comes near our skin, we can very quickly perceive that sensation as "too hot" and move away from the heat source before we are burned. Within each sense organ, receptor cells receive the environmental stimuli: sound waves, light waves, pressure on the skin, or chemicals in food or the air. The receptor cells do the job of turning the environmental stimuli into neural signals the brain can receive and interpret. The receptor cells then send this information to the appropriate area of the brain through a nerve cell that connects to the neurons in different brain areas.

Figure 3.1 illustrates the four parts of a sensory system for the visual sense system: (1) sense organ—the eye, (2) receptor cells—the rods and cones in the retina, (3) nerve conduit to the brain—optic nerve, and (4) brain area where the information is being processed—occipital lobe of the brain (with extensions to other areas to connect with other cognitive processes). This sensory system structure is followed in the other sense systems as well with ears, nose, tongue, and skin as the sense organs. Each of these sense organs contains receptor cells of different sorts that convert the stimulus energy (e.g., air waves and pressure, chemicals in the air and food, temperature and pressure from stimuli) received by the sense organ into neural signals to be sent to the brain for processing. As described in Chapter 2, different brain areas are specialized for different functions. Thus, auditory sensory information is primarily processed in the temporal lobe, tactile sensory information is processed in the parietal cortex, gustatory sensory information is processed in the insular cortex at the junction of the frontal, temporal, and parietal lobes, and olfactory sensory information is processed in the olfactory bulb near the temporal lobe and then sent to several connected areas of the brain.

Find Your Blind Spot Demonstration

Sensory system: a system that receives and processes input from stimuli in the environment

Figure 3.1 Diagram of the Visual Sensory System Showing the Four Parts of the System

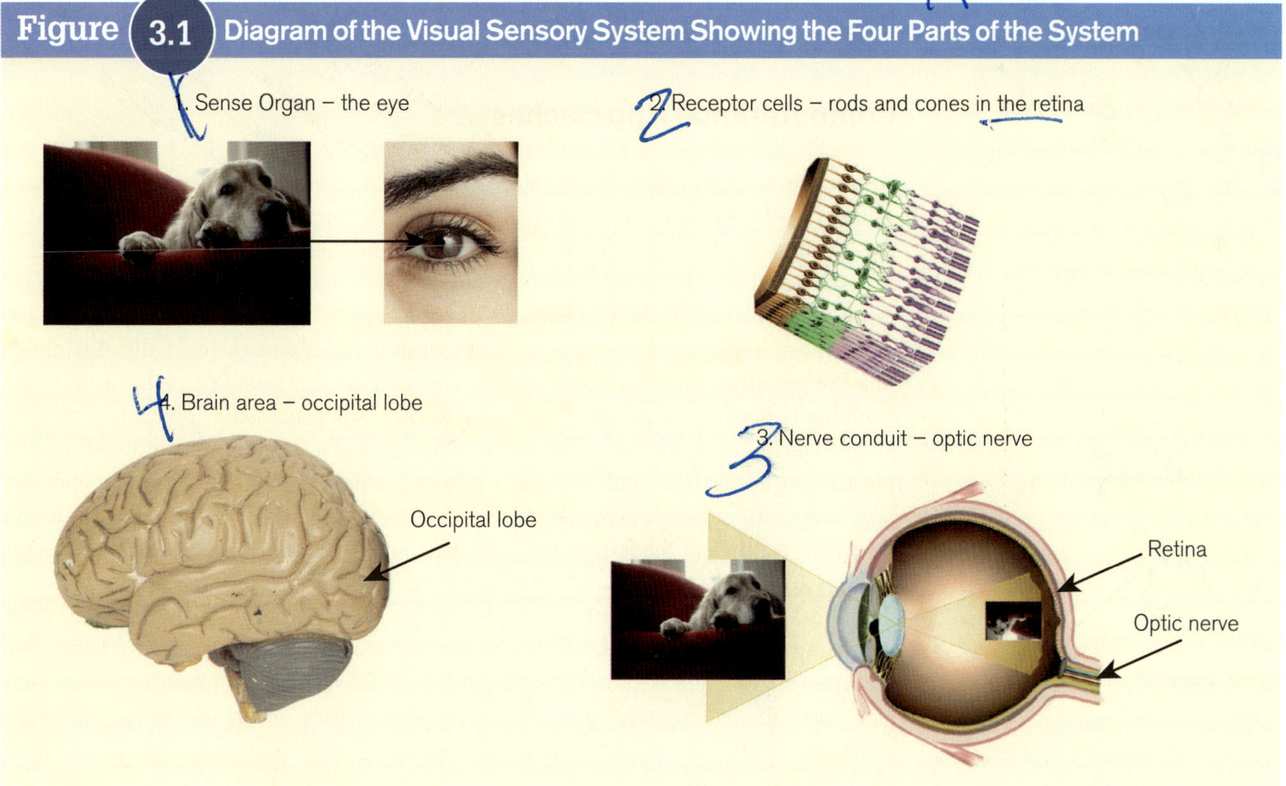

SOURCES: Photo of dog: Janie Airey/Digital Vision/Thinkstock; photo of eye: Christopher Robbins/Photodisc/Thinkstock; photo of brain: Hemera Technologies/PhotoObjects.net/Thinkstock.

Stop and Think

3.1. Describe the four parts of a sensory system.

3.2. What is the role of receptor cells in perception?

3.3. What are the advantages to having a perceptual system that has automatic input of all environmental stimuli but only consciously processes a small portion of those stimuli?

3.4. Can you think of a situation where your perception of your environment did not match the reality of the environment? Why do you think that error occurred?

The primary job of the sensory system then is to receive stimulus energy from the environmental stimulus and to recode that stimulus, called the **distal stimulus**, into something the brain can interpret and process. This is just the start of our perceptual process, however. Once the distal stimulus has been represented in our minds, it becomes a **proximal stimulus**. This representation process is proposed to occur for all types of sensory information. The brain then processes the proximal stimuli in an attempt to interpret and act on the distal stimuli you are encountering in the world. The rest of this chapter focuses on the cognitive process of perception.

Approaches to the Study of Perception

Crash Course: Perception

Given the different roles of perception in our lives, researchers have approached the study of perception in different ways to better understand how perception operates in each of these roles. Each approach considers a different way that stimuli are processed in the brain. In the computational approach, researchers consider how different cues in the stimuli can be used to interpret the environment. In the Gestalt approach, researchers have considered how organizational principles of the world allow us to interpret the stimuli in our environment. In the perception-action approach, researchers consider the goals of action achieved through more direct perception. Each of these approaches has aided in our understanding of the processes of perception and how they work together to interpret the world around us.

Computational Approaches

Psychologists first used a computational approach to study our perceptions. In fact, some of the first psychologists studied perception through this approach in the field of psychophysics, where the goal was to discover fundamental knowledge of perception that showed us the scope and limits of our perceptual abilities. This approach to perception considers how we use features of objects and scenes to interpret and understand them. The features or cues in the environment help us turn the distal stimulus into the proximal stimulus in our minds. One process that aids in creating a proximal stimulus is bottom-up processing. Using **bottom-up processing**, perception is conducted starting with the most basic units or features of a stimulus and adding the parts together to understand and identify a coherent whole object. For example, consider how bottom-up processing might allow us to identify the words on this page. We might start with features of the letters, the lines and curves that make up each letter, use the features to identify letters, and then combine letters to identify the separate words. Figure 3.2 illustrates how bottom-up processing might work to perceive the word *safe* in a feature detection model, where features of the letters are first identified and then that information is passed on through a hierarchical system that identifies more complex forms of written language at each level. The features of the individual letters are combined to identify each letter, and then the letters are combined to identify the word. This bottom-up process can work for verbal language as well: phonemes of the language can be detected and activate words that contain those sounds (see Chapter 9 for more discussion of bottom-up processing in language).

Distal stimulus: stimulus in the environment

Proximal stimulus: stimulus as it is represented in the mind

Bottom-up processing: understanding the environment through basic feature identification and processing

Bottom-up processing as described in feature detection models received early physiological support. Using the single-cell recording technique described in Chapter 2,

Figure 3.2 An Example of Bottom-Up Processing That Would Allow Perception of the Word *Safe*

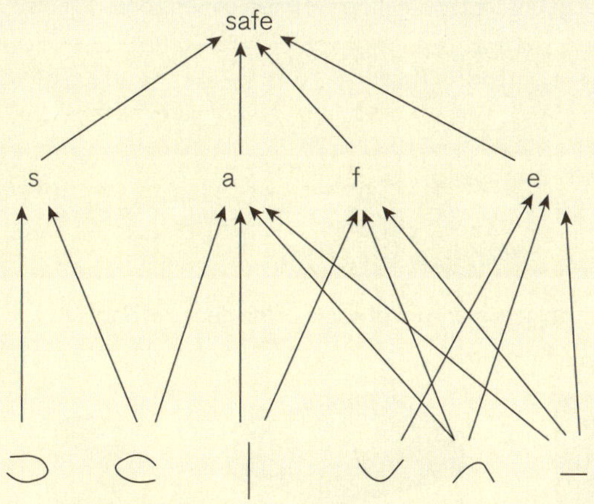

Basic features of letters are detected by the visual system. Then this information goes through a hierarchy of letters and then words from the bottom up to eventually identify words.

researchers Hubel and Weisel (1959) identified neurons in the visual cortex that are selectively activated by features in the environment. They recorded the activity from neurons in the striate cortex (an area in the occipital lobe) of cats as different shapes of light were presented to their retinas. Recordings from the neurons showed that some cells were active to horizontal bars, others to vertical bars, and still others to diagonal bars of one orientation (see Figure 3.3). These results suggest that feature detection is done at the neuron level and is consistent with how the visual cortex functions. Others (e.g., Bullock, 1961) suggested that feature detection specialization in the brain also exists for other sensory systems, such as the auditory system.

Feature Detection

Another example of bottom-up processing from the computational approach is a theory about object recognition based on features of the objects called geons. Geons are the basic three-dimensional pieces of objects, such as cylinders, cones, and blocks (see Figure 3.4 for examples of geons and some objects that can be created from them). Biederman (1987) proposed that we identify objects by first identifying the geons that make up the object. We then match the geons we perceive against representations of objects stored in memory to identify the whole object. He showed that we can easily identify objects from different angles and objects that are occluded based on the geons. This is similar to the feature detection model described in Figure 3.2 for perceiving words; however, in Biederman's object recognition model, the features are three-dimensional geons instead of the two-dimensional lines and shapes seen in Figure 3.2.

One process the computational approach to perception has focused on is the use of basic cues in the environment as a means of interpreting the stimuli with which we are presented. For example, cues in visual stimuli help us estimate objects' size and distance. See Photos 3.1 and 3.2 here for illustrations of the use of these cues. In Photo 3.1, we can use the linear perspective of the

Figure 3.3 Neuron Activity for Lines at Different Orientations in Hubel and Weisel's (1959) Study

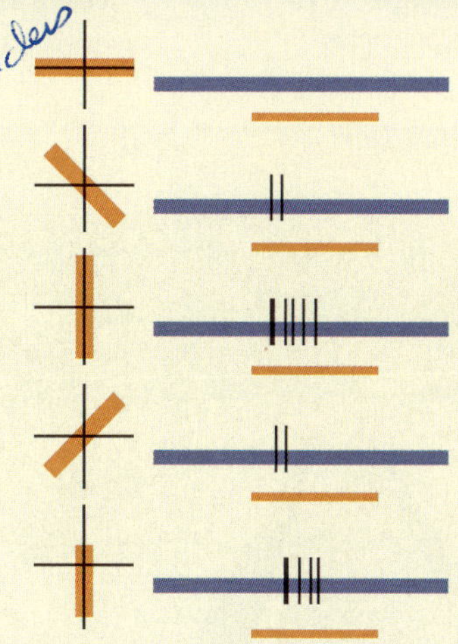

SOURCE: Figure 3, "Receptive Fields of Single Neurons in the Cat's Striate Cortex," by D. H. Hubel and T. N. Wiesel, 1959, *Journal of Physiology, 148*, pp. 574–591. © 1959 by The Physiology Society. Reprinted with permission from John Wiley & Sons, Inc.

Object Recognition

Eye Tricks

Color Games

Illusions and V1 Size

Light From Above Demonstration

Top-down processing: understanding the environment through global knowledge of the environment and its principles

Figure 3.4 Geons

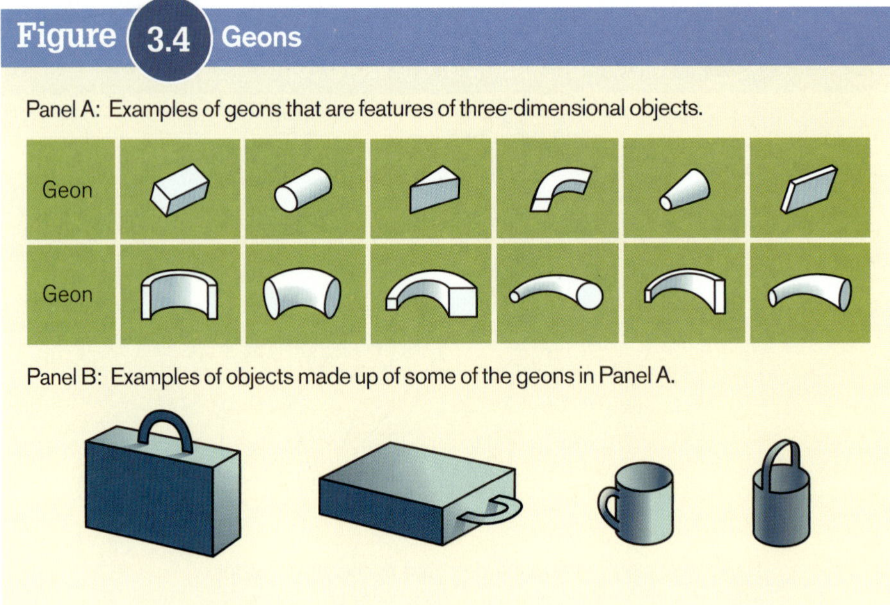

Panel A: Examples of geons that are features of three-dimensional objects.
Geon
Geon
Panel B: Examples of objects made up of some of the geons in Panel A.

SOURCE: Galotti, K. M. (2014). *Cognitive psychology in and out of the laboratory* (5th ed.). Thousand Oaks, CA: Sage.

tracks to help determine the distance of the two signs in the photo. The tracks seem to converge (i.e., get closer together) higher up in the photo. This implies that the tracks go off into the distance in a three-dimensional environment. We can also use the size of the image of an object on our retina to help us determine the object's distance. In the photo on the right, we perceive that the woman is closer to us than the buildings, partly because the image of the woman imposed on our retina is larger than the image of the buildings. However, we also need to use some knowledge about the objects to make these judgments. Knowing that the woman is not as tall as the building can help us judge the objects' distance as well. In Photo 3.2, the size is similar for the images of the woman and the tallest building. Thus, we use additional knowledge we have about the objects to determine that the building must be farther away because at the same distance, the building should have a larger retinal image size.

Using knowledge of the objects is an example of **top-down processing**. When we perceive objects using our knowledge of the world, we use top-down processing. Thus, although

NA/AbleStock.com/Thinkstock

Photo 3.1 Train tracks showing a linear perspective for the distance of the two signs.

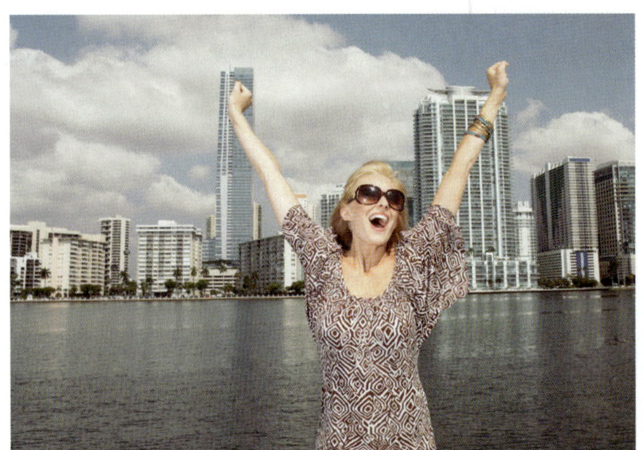
Jim Arbogast/Digital Vision/Thinkstock

Photo 3.2 The woman in front of these buildings shows how the distance of objects can be determined from retinal image size and knowledge about the objects.

we are using basic feature cues in the environment to perceive, we also rely on our knowledge of the world to interpret those cues. In some cases, our interpretation of these cues can be incorrect, creating an incorrect interpretation of an object. In other words, the proximal stimulus in our mind does not provide an accurate representation of the distal stimulus in the environment. This can be seen in some common illusions. In fact, these illusions seem to occur because we are interpreting the cues in a consistent way across stimuli.

Train track photo: NA/AbleStock.com/Thinkstock

Photo 3.3 Illustration of the Ponzo illusion: the cat on the bottom looks smaller due to the linear perspective of the train tracks.

Consider the Ponzo illusion. In Photo 3.3, two cats are placed on the tracks from Photo 3.1. Which cat looks larger? Most people perceive the cat near the top of the photo as larger. This is because in the photo it looks like it is farther away at a point where the tracks are closer together, but, in fact, the images of the two cats are exactly the same size (measure them to see!). Because the images of the two cats in the photo are the same size, they create retinal images that are also the same size. Thus, retinal image is not the only cue we use to determine the size and distance of objects. This type of illusion is interesting to perceptual researchers because it shows how we use the linear perspective cues in the scene to misinterpret the size of the objects on the tracks. However, in many cases, the linear perspective gives us an accurate depiction of the objects' distance, as it does in Photo 3.1 when we judge the distance of the two signs and the trees in the scene. The illusion shows that we use the linear perspective cues present in the environment to perceive the distance of objects.

Confuse Your Illusion

Ponzo Illusion Activity

Visual Perspective Illusion Activity

Top-Down Processing Activity

Neuropsychologists have recently studied the relationship between brain function and organization and the perception of illusions. For example, Schwarzkopf, Song, and Rees (2011) examined the relationship between the strength of the Ponzo illusion seen in Photo 3.3 and the size of the primary visual cortex area in the occipital lobe known as V1. They found a positive correlation such that the subjects with larger V1 areas also showed stronger illusions (i.e., the subjects reported a larger size difference between the two objects in the image that were actually the same size).

Even though we use other cues to help determine size and distance of stimuli, retinal image size is an important cue for our interpretation of objects' size and distance. Try this yourself: Hold two objects of the same length (e.g., two pencils) in front of you with one object held right in front of your face and the other object held out at arm's length. You can easily see that you perceive the object held at arm's length as farther away. Figure 3.5 shows how two pencils held at different distances create different-sized

Figure 3.5 Retinal Image Size

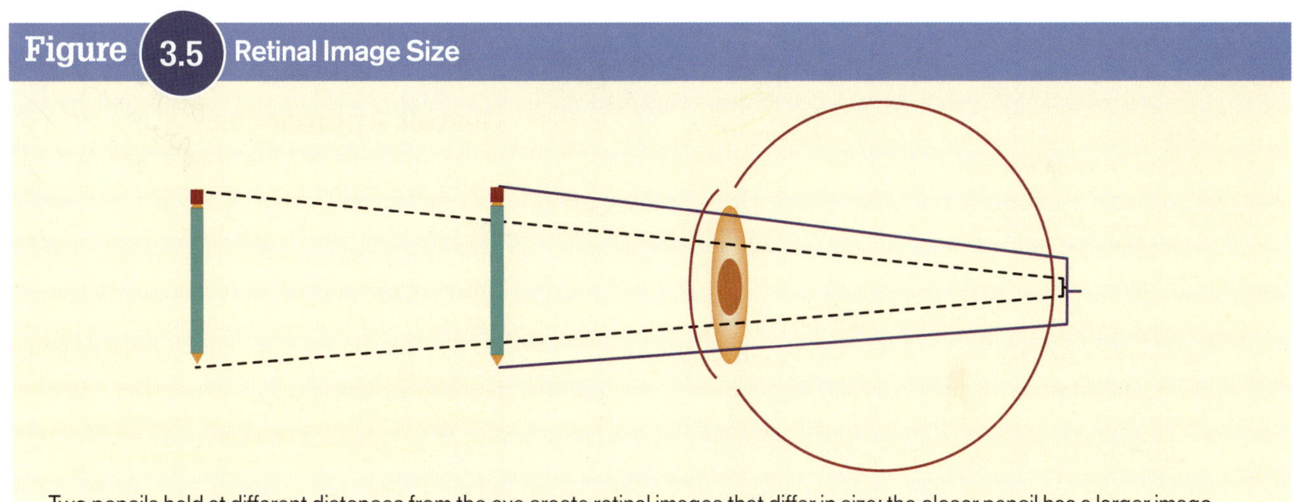

Two pencils held at different distances from the eye create retinal images that differ in size; the closer pencil has a larger image.

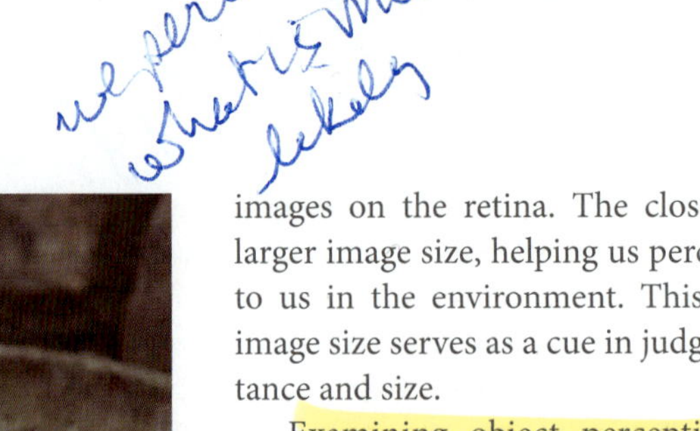

BananaStock/BananaStock/Thinkstock

Photo 3.4 This cat lying in a pot illustrates how we make unconscious inferences about objects to perceive the environment.

images on the retina. The closer pencil has a larger image size, helping us perceive it as closer to us in the environment. This is how retinal image size serves as a cue in judging objects' distance and size.

Examining object perception using cues such as linear perspective and retinal image size led to the **theory of unconscious inference** proposed by one of the first perceptual psychologists, Hermann von Helmholtz. The theory of unconscious inference suggests that we make unconscious inferences about the world when we perceive it. In other words, we use our top-down processing unconsciously to perceive and interpret the environment. Consider the objects in Photo 3.4. How would you describe these objects? Most people would say something like "A cat is lying in a pot." However, the entire cat is not actually visible in this picture. Thus, it is possible that only a portion of a cat is there and the rest of the cat is missing. But since that is an unlikely scenario, we interpret the scene as a whole cat in a pot with some of the cat hidden from view. This illustrates the likelihood principle that is part of the theory of unconscious inference. We perceive the object that is most likely in the scene when we view it, even if there are other possible interpretations of the scene.

Theory of unconscious inference: the idea that we make unconscious inferences about the world when we perceive it

Gestalt psychology: a perspective in psychology that focuses on how organizational principles allow us to perceive and understand the environment

In summary, the computational approach to perception focuses on cues in the environment as a means of perceiving and interpreting stimuli. Both bottom-up and top-down processing contribute to object and scene interpretations. Cues such as linear perspective and retinal image size help us determine the size and distance of objects in the environment. However, those cues can be incorrectly interpreted and create errors in our perceptions in certain situations. But the errors are simply a by-product of a perceptual system that works by means of processing these cues in consistent ways. We will encounter another example of how our normal cognitive processes can inadvertently create errors in Chapter 7 when we consider memory errors.

Stop and Think

3.5. Explain what it means to interpret scenes based on cues present in those scenes.

3.6. In what way do illusions illustrate the normal processes of perception?

3.7. You see a light approaching on the road at night. According to the likelihood principle, which of the following are you most likely to perceive: (a) a deer crossing the road wearing a headlight, (b) a UFO, or (c) an approaching car? Explain your answer.

3.8. In the scene in Photo 3.4, describe some cues you can use to determine that the front of the pot is closer to you than the cat.

3.9. People report a "moon illusion" such that the full moon appears larger when it is lower in the sky and close to the horizon than when it is high in the sky and above us. Using what you learned about the use of cues in this section, why do you think the moon illusion occurs?

Gestalt Approaches

Take a look at the scene in Figure 3.6. What do you see there? Most people perceive a triangle with the points overlaid on top of circles. However, consider what is actually in the figure: Are there any triangles or circles in the figure? No, so why do we see these shapes? The **Gestalt psychology** approach to perception suggests that interpretation of a scene involves applying principles of how the world is organized. In other words, top-down processing is a key component of Gestalt approaches to perception. According to the Gestalt approach, perception occurs through applying a set of organizational principles that follow physical processes of the natural world. In applying these organizational principles, our perception of a scene is "more than the sum of its parts." Table 3.1 summarizes some of the first organizational principles proposed by Gestaltists (see Wagemans et al., 2012, for a more complete listing of principles), and each of these is described with illustrative examples.

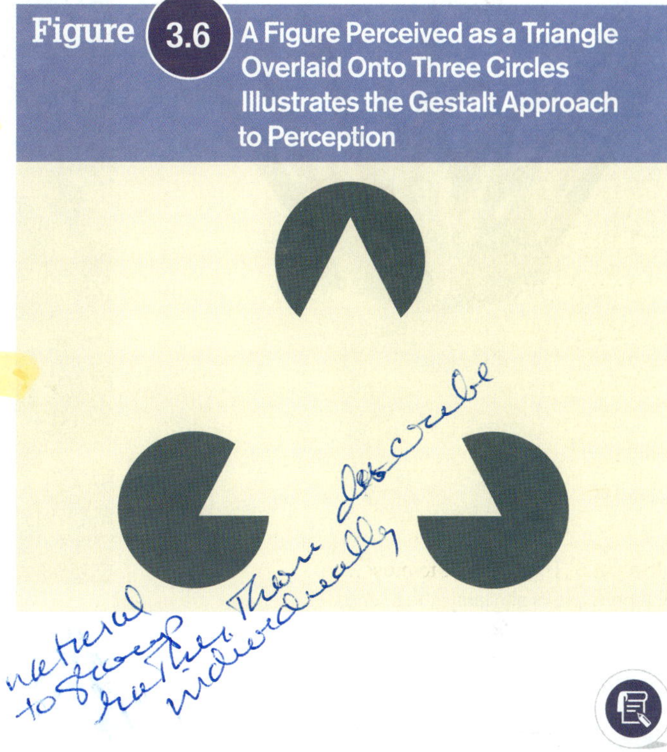

Figure 3.6 A Figure Perceived as a Triangle Overlaid Onto Three Circles Illustrates the Gestalt Approach to Perception

1. Similarity. The first organizational principle of perception is similarity. We tend to group objects or features of a scene based on their similarity. Consider Photo 3.5: Describe what you see in this figure. Did you say something like "a number of pencils, a few pens, and scissors in a cup"? If you did, you illustrated the principle of similarity: You organized like objects together and described the figure according to these similarities. This is more natural and common than describing each individual object in the cup on its own or grouping objects that are not similar.

Similarity Activity

2. Proximity. Another organizational principle of perception is proximity. We tend to group objects or features of a scene based on their proximity to one another. How would you describe the scene in Photo 3.6? Do you see two girls talking on a bench while other people walk by, shopping in the background? This is a common organization described for a scene like this. We tend to group the people close to one another in the scene together as we describe and interpret it. For example, we're likely to assume the girls on the bench are having one conversation, while the people in the background are having their own conversation. Proximity can also help us distinguish between the objects in a scene and the background of a scene. We discuss

Proximity Activity

Triangle and Circle Activity

Gestalt Principles of Perception

Table 3.1 Some Organizational Principles of Gestalt Perception

Principle	Description
1. Similarity	Objects are grouped according to their similarity.
2. Proximity	Objects are grouped according to their proximity in a scene.
3. Good continuation	Objects are perceived as continuous in cases where it is expected that they would continue.
4. Closure	Objects are perceived as whole even in cases where parts are occluded or missing.
5. Pragnanz (simplicity)	Objects are perceived in the simplest way possible.

Ryan McVay/Photodisc/Thinkstock

Photo 3.5 This figure illustrates the principle of similarity; the scene is typically described with similar objects grouped.

Maria Teijeiro/Digital Vision/Thinkstock

Photo 3.6 This scene illustrates the principle of proximity; we organize the scene into sets of people based on their proximity to one another.

Principle of Pragnanz Activity

Principle of Pragnanz: an organizational principle that allows for the simplest interpretation of the environment

further the separation of foreground and background in the environment later in this section.

3. Good continuation. Good continuation refers to our understanding that objects continue, even if parts of them are occluded. Photo 3.4 with the cat in the pot illustrates this principle. We interpret the scene as an entire cat lying in the pot, even though we can only see a portion of the cat in the photo. Photo 3.7 illustrates good continuation as well. We tend to see this figure as a woman holding two ends of single rope, rather than holding two separate pieces of rope, even though we cannot see the entire rope. We have the same interpretation for any line that has an object occluding a portion of it.

Figure 3.7 Due to the Principle of Closure, We View This Object as a Circle, Even Though It Is Not Complete

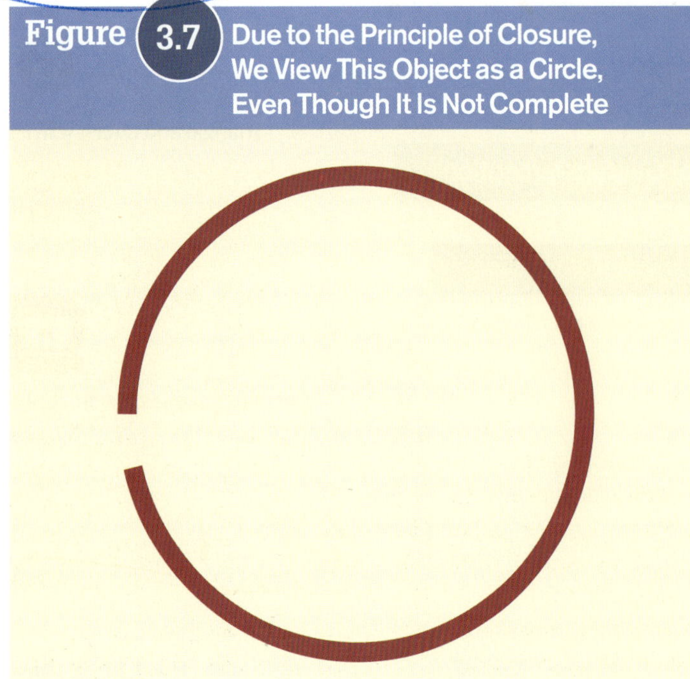

4. Closure. The principle of closure allows us to view incomplete objects as a whole. For example, we see the object in Figure 3.7 as a circle, even though it is missing a small piece. In fact, closure contributes to perceiving a triangle in Figure 3.6. We perceive the complete triangle with angles on the circles even though the sides of the triangle are not filled in completely.

5. Principle of Pragnanz. The **principle of Pragnanz** (also called the law of good figure or law of simplicity) suggests that we perceive scenes as simply as possible. *Pragnanz* is a German term meaning concise or succinct. Thus, this principle proposes that we view scenes in the most concise way possible, with a simple interpretation (thus, the law of simplicity). The first four principles can be viewed as specifics of the principle of Pragnanz. They each provide a specific way that we organize a scene more simply.

Consider the scene in Photo 3.8. According to the principle of Pragnanz, we organize the scene according to the simplest interpretation. What other organizational principles help you perceive this scene? Do you perceive a complete boy in the pile of leaves, even though part of him is occluded, due to good continuation? Do you perceive a pile of leaves because you grouped the leaves together as similar objects?

Now consider a more difficult perceptual task: How many horses do you see in Photo 3.9? The similar coloring of the horses and the background make this a difficult task (i.e., the principle of similarity works against our perception of the horses here), but because of the organizing principles of perception, we can detect horses in this scene. We see continuation of the outlines of the horses that are occluded to perceive them as a complete horse. We view a group of horses that are in proximity to one another in the scene. If you look carefully, you may be able to view five different horses in this scene.

Jupiterimages/Pixland/Thinkstock

Photo 3.7 This photo illustrates the principle of good continuation; we see the line as a single rope held at both ends instead of as two separate ropes.

Finally, consider Photo 3.10. What do you see in this photo? Do you see a white vase or do you see two blue faces? It is possible to see both of these in the figure, depending on which color you assign to the background, white or blue. With a blue background, you see the white vase. With a white background, you see two blue faces. This occurs because of the figure-ground organization within a scene and is consistent with Gestalt principles. We simplify the scene by assigning a color to the background that allows us to see the objects. By organizing the figure in terms of similarity of color, we can perceive different objects. This also occurs in Photo 3.9. We can perceive the horses in this figure by organizing some patches of brown and white as belonging to the background and some patches of brown and white as belonging to the horses. However, this is what makes the horses harder to see. We have a figure-ground problem in the horse scene because the figure and background are so similar. In Photo 3.10, the figures and background are much more distinct, allowing us to separate them more easily as we view either the vase or the faces.

What Do You See Activity

Figure Ground Activity

Configural Superiority Activity

Pomerantz and Portillo (2012) describe research that supports use of the organizing principles from the Gestalt approach in perception. Such studies have shown that larger arrays of stimuli containing basic feature elements and more complex stimuli are easier to perceive than smaller basic arrays and stimuli shown to subjects. This is called the configural superiority effect. To illustrate the effect, consider two situations where you are attempting to find a target stimulus that is different from the others in an array of stimuli. Examine the three arrays shown in Figure 3.8. The first array (A) shows lines all slanted in the same direction except one. You may notice the line that is different, but it probably does not "pop out" of the array easily. Now suppose we add the stimuli in Array B to Array A. This results in the more complex array (that is, more of a "whole") seen in Array C. How easily can you detect the line slanted in the opposite direction in this more complex array? For most people it pops out at them and they very quickly detect it in the array.

Is there evidence for corresponding brain activity to perceptual processes as described in the Gestalt approach? Recent studies in neuropsychology suggest there is. Some studies using the EEG recording technique (see Chapter 2 for a review of brain activity recording techniques) have shown that when subjects view figures such as the one shown in Figure 3.6, there is evidence that the features of the object perceived along with features detected in other modalities (e.g., sounds) are bound together in the occipital-temporal cortex of the brain (Fiebelkorn, Foxe, Schwartz, & Molholm, 2010). Other studies using fMRI have found similar evidence of feature binding in the parietal cortex for Gestalt figures (Zaretskaya, Anstis, & Bartels, 2013). Thus, neuroscientists are exploring how the organizational principles proposed in the Gestalt approach correspond to brain activity that connects the features of stimuli in the environment.

Photo 3.8 This complex scene illustrates several Gestalt principles. How many can you identify?

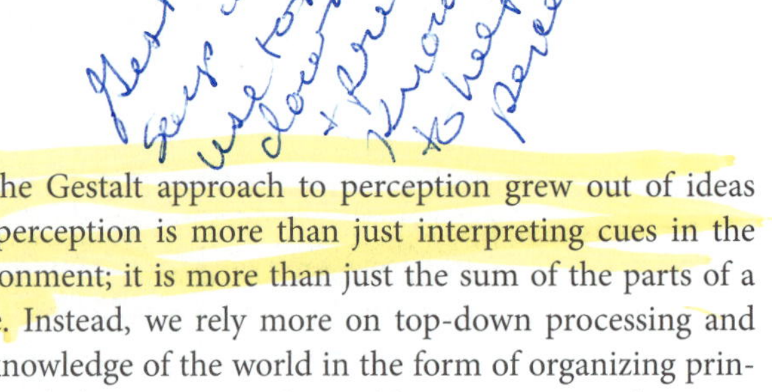

Pintos ©Bev Doolittle, The Greenwich Workshop, Inc.

Photo 3.9 This photo further illustrates Gestalt principles of similarity, closure, and Pragnanz. How many horses do you see?

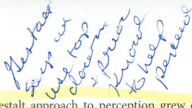

The Gestalt approach to perception grew out of ideas that perception is more than just interpreting cues in the environment; it is more than just the sum of the parts of a scene. Instead, we rely more on top-down processing and our knowledge of the world in the form of organizing principles to help us perceive the world. Even in cases where perception is more difficult (as in Photo 3.9), these organizational principles can help us view objects in a scene that may be hard to perceive.

Perception/Action Approaches

Where computational and Gestalt approaches focus more on the "what" of perception, perception/action approaches focus more on the "what for" aspect of perception. What are the possible **affordances** of this environment (i.e., possible behaviors in a given environment)? Can I pass through that space? Can I use this stick to hammer in that nail? If I jump over this gap, will I make it without falling? According to these approaches, perception and action are intricately linked. One must consider them together to understand each one. Because the perception/action approach examines perception according to how it aids in performing behaviors, it is consistent with the embodied cognition approach described in Chapter 1.

Ecological Approach: Harry Heft

Ecological Approach: Michael Turvey

This approach has its roots in ecological psychology, first suggested by James Gibson (1979) as an alternative to representationalist approaches to perception. The computational approach describes perception to some degree as relying on representations of the world, with a proximal stimulus created in our minds to represent the distal stimulus in the environment. Thus, the focus is on how we interpret stimuli in the environment and the processes responsible for those interpretations. With the ecological approach, Gibson suggested that information about the world is available in the detectable patterns in the environment such that we directly perceive without first transforming a distal stimulus into a proximal stimulus. From this approach, the focus in studies of perception should be on how we perform goal-directed behaviors (Fajen, Riley, & Turvey, 2009). For example, how are we able to avoid bumping into objects when we move around in the environment?

Photo 3.10 Do you see a blue vase or two white faces? This drawing illustrates the figure-ground organization of scenes.

Affordances: behaviors that are possible in a given environment

For the past few decades, researchers following the ecological view have focused on this question in perceptual research: How do we perform goal-directed perceptual behaviors? Optic flow was one of the first concepts to be studied in this research. If you drive a car (or ride in one), consider what you experience as you move through the environment. Objects in the environment that are closer to you seem to pass by faster than objects that are farther away, even though you are moving and they are not. This is an example of optic flow. It is the movement pattern generated by objects at different distances as you move past them. Photo 3.11 shows the optic flow that might be experienced from a moving vehicle. The girl on the bike is closer so she would appear to move more quickly than the bridge railing and houses in the distance. Optic flow is an important part of our perception of the environment. According to the perception/action approach, we perceive objects' distance based on the optic flow, not from first representing the object in our minds based on its retinal image size.

Figure 3.8 These Arrays Help Illustrate the Gestalt Idea of "Whole" Stimulus Processing at Work

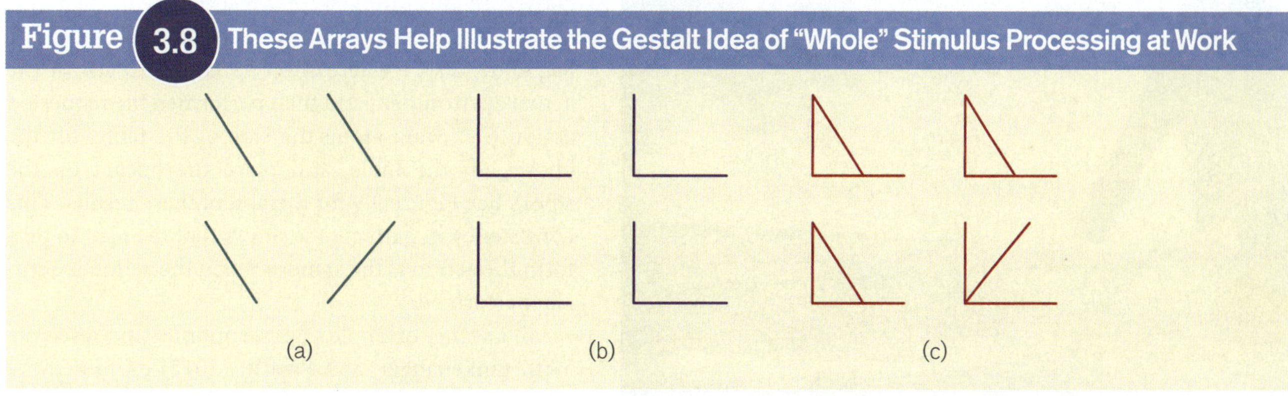

SOURCE: Adapted from Pomerantz, J. R., & Portillo, M. C. (2011). Grouping and emergent features in vision: Toward a theory of basic Gestalts. *Journal of Experimental Psychology: Human Perception and Performance, 37*(5), 1331–1349.

The perception/action approach is broader than the ecological view of perception. In some perception/action approaches, actions are an important part of the process of perception, but perceiving an object may still involve representations of that object in the mind. Thus, perception/action approaches often blend elements of the ecological view and the representationalist view. For example, the perception of a chair may result from knowing that a chair can be used to sit or stand on because that is what you are currently looking for in your environment, but you can still identify the object as a chair if someone asks you what the object is.

Stop and Think

3.10. How does the Gestalt approach to perception differ from the computational approach to perception?

3.11. How is top-down processing involved in the Gestalt approach to perception?

3.12. Look around your environment and describe some examples of good continuation in the objects around you.

3.13. Consider the moon illusion described in Stop and Think 3.9. Would the Gestalt approach to perception explain this illusion differently than the computational approach? Why or why not?

Research with a perception/action approach has considered how perception and action are tied together. Consider the following scenario: You are shown the room setup that appears in Photo 3.12a. Given this room configuration, would you prefer to (1) walk to the left of the table, pick up the bucket with your right hand, and place the bucket on the near stool, or (2) walk to the right side of the table, pick up the bucket with your left hand, and place the bucket on the far stool? How about the room setup in Photo 3.12b or in Photo 3.12c? Would you choose the same path or change your path? These were scenarios faced by subjects in a study by David Rosenbaum (2012). In this task, the reaction time to choose a path was recorded for different scenarios to determine if people simulated the paths in their minds one by one (i.e., sequential processing) before choosing the shorter path or if they considered all the paths at once (i.e., parallel processing) and chose the shorter path more quickly. Their reaction time data showed that the time it took to choose a path was a function of the difference in length of the two paths, supporting the suggestion that both paths are considered at once (i.e., parallel processing of path possibilities). Reaction times did not increase with the overall lengths of the paths, which is contrary to what is predicted if subjects simulate each path one at a time before choosing the shortest path. In other words, if reaction times increased based on the total length of the two paths, this would mean the decision takes as long as it takes to first mentally travel the length of one path and then mentally travel the length of the second path. Rosenbaum also showed that the paths

Walking Through a Room Activity

Ryan McVay/Photodisc/Thinkstock

Photo 3.11 An illustration of optic flow; less blurry objects are closer.

chosen in this study were consistent with data collected in a previous study (Rosenbaum, Brach, & Semenov, 2011) where subjects chose a path in the actual environment and then performed the requested action (i.e., walk along the side of the table, lift the bucket off the table, and place the bucket on the stool). See Figure 3.9 for a graph of these results. This consistency in path choice shows that the plan to perform the action is the same as when the action is actually performed.

In another example of perception/action research, Witt, Linkenauger, and Proffitt (2012) examined the effect of a perceptual illusion on putting performance in golf. These researchers asked subjects to perform golf putts to a hole with projected surrounding circles. This was done in the context of a perceptual illusion: Larger circles around the hole make the hole appear smaller than if the hole is surrounded by smaller circles (see Figure 3.10). This is known as the Ebbinghaus illusion. When subjects saw the hole surrounded by larger circles, as in Figure 3.10 (a), their putting performance was worse than when they saw the hole surrounded by smaller circles, as in Figure 3.10 (b). These results are shown in the graph in Figure 3.11. Witt et al.'s (2012) study showed the important connection between sports performance and perception. Another study by two of these researchers (Witt & Proffitt, 2005) also showed that softball players with higher batting averages judged the size of the ball as larger when they were shown images of balls and asked to choose the correct size of the softball, further illustrating the link between perception and action.

Interactions of Perception and Action

Research in this area has also shown that judgments about the environment can be influenced by our current body perspective, even when no action was planned. Malek and Wagman (2008) asked subjects to judge whether they could stand upright on an inclined surface either while wearing a weighted backpack on their back or on their front. Wearing the backpack on their back pulled the subjects' center of mass backward, whereas wearing the backpack on their front pulled the subjects' center of mass forward. If one stands on an inclined surface, having your center of mass pulled backward makes it more difficult to stand on the surface, but having your center of mass pulled forward makes it easier to stand on the surface. Malek and Wagman (2008) asked if this difference in backpack position would affect perceptual judgments of affordances (i.e., possibilities for standing behavior) even though the subjects did not have to actually stand on the surface. They found results consistent with a perception/action perspective: When wearing the backpack on their front, subjects judged they could stand on higher-angled surfaces than when they wore the backpack on their backs. These results suggest that perception is influenced by possible actions, even when those actions do not actually need to be performed.

Is there brain activity evidence for a connection between perception and action? The answer is controversial. There is evidence that different brain areas are responsible for recognition of an object and the location of an object (Milner & Goodale, 2008). Since the location of an object is more important for actions related to that object, if these two functions are separate and independent, this might suggest that perception and action are also separate. The "what" brain pathway responsible for recognition of an object is located in the lower occipital lobe and leads to the temporal lobe where language functions are controlled. This is known as the **ventral pathway** (or ventral stream) because it is on the underside of the cortex. The "where" brain pathway responsible for locating an object is in the upper occipital

Ventral pathway: the pathway in the brain that processes "what" information about the environment

lobe and leads to the parietal lobe where the motor cortex resides. This is known as the **dorsal pathway** (or dorsal stream) because it is on the top of the cortex (think of a dorsal fin on a shark to help you remember where this is located). See Figure 3.12 for the location of these pathways in the brain.

The controversy here comes from the mixed evidence in studies attempting to dissociate ventral and dorsal pathway functions. For example, Ganel, Tanzer, and Goodale (2008) reported that although subjects showed the Ponzo illusion (see Photo 3.3) in their size judgments of objects, their reaching behaviors were not affected by the illusion. However, as described earlier, Witt et al. (2012) showed that the Ebbinghaus size illusion affected subjects' golf performance. Thus, studies have produced data both in support of a dissociation between perception and action (i.e., showing that a variable affects one behavior but does not affect other behaviors) and in contradiction to such a dissociation. One possibility is that some actions have stronger links with perception than others. For example, many of the studies showing dissociations between the ventral and dorsal pathway functions involved reaching and/or grasping behaviors, behaviors that require real-time location information for objects. In addition, McIntosh and Lashley (2008) showed that expected object size affected reaching behaviors, indicating a link between perception and action, but Borchers, Christensen, Ziegler, and Himelbach (2010) showed that this effect only occurred when the objects being reached for were familiar to the subjects after long-term use (e.g., objects they used in everyday life). Thus, different types of action behaviors may vary in the strength of their connection to visual perception.

Photos 3.12a, b, & c Room setups shown in the Rosenbaum (2012) study. Which path would you choose?

SOURCE: Figure 1, Rosenbaum, D. A. (2012). The tiger on your tail: Choosing between temporally extended behaviors. *Psychological Science, 23,* 855–860.

A neuropsychological finding that provides stronger support for the link between perception and action is the discovery of mirror neurons (first described in Chapter 2). Mirror neurons were discovered in a study by Rizzolatti, Fadiga, Gallese, and Fogassi (1996). These researchers were recording activity from neurons in an area of the brain known as F5 in the premotor cortex that contains neurons involved in sensation and movement in the hands. Neuron activity was recorded using the single-cell recording technique (see Chapter 2) on monkey subjects. These subjects were trained to reach into a box and grasp an object. Neurons in the F5 area were active during this grasping task. However, the researchers also showed that these neurons were active when hand movements related to grasping were performed by the researchers while the monkey watched (e.g., grasping an object, placing an object on a surface). These neurons were not active when the researchers performed other movements not related to grasping the object (e.g., picking up the object with a tool). Rizzolatti et al. (1996) called these neurons mirror neurons because they were active both for tasks the monkeys knew how to do and when they saw those actions performed by others. In other words, mirror neurons seem to be specialized for the connection between perception and action of known movements.

Dorsal pathway: the pathway in the brain that processes "where" information about the environment

Figure 3.9 Results From the Rosenbaum, Brach, and Semenov (2011) Study

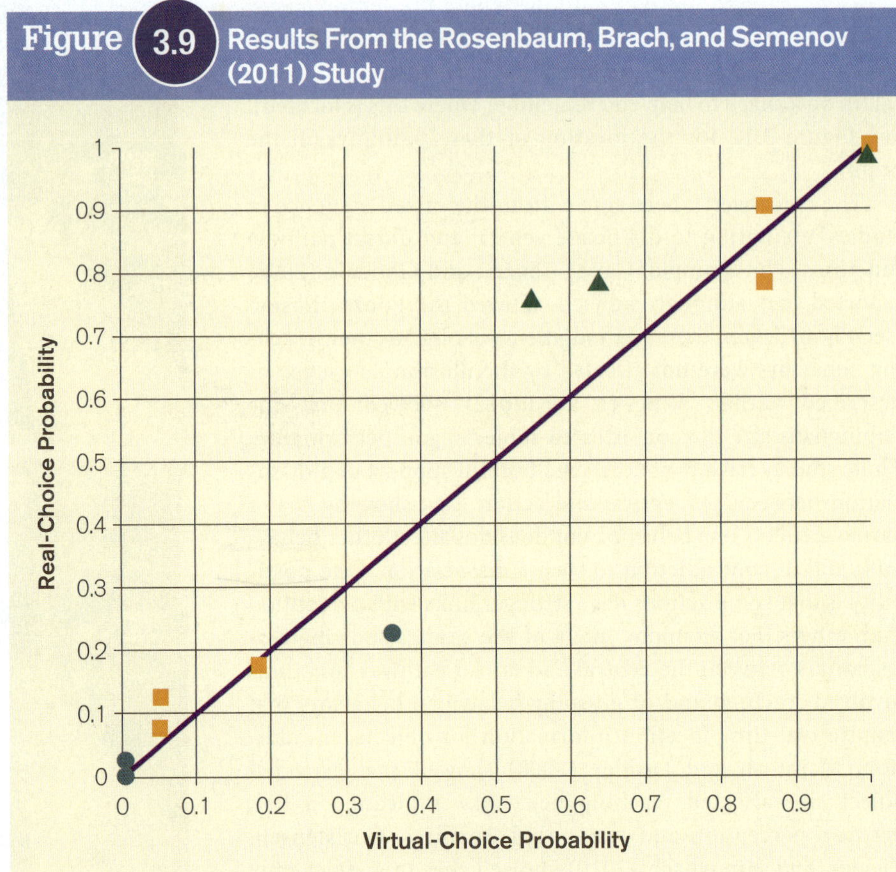

This graph shows the probability of choosing the left path in the virtual task (x-axis) in the Rosenbaum (2012) study compared with the probability of choosing the left path in the actual performed (real-choice) task (y-axis) in the Rosenbaum, Brach, and Semenov (2011) study.

Figure 3.10 The Ebbinghaus Illusion

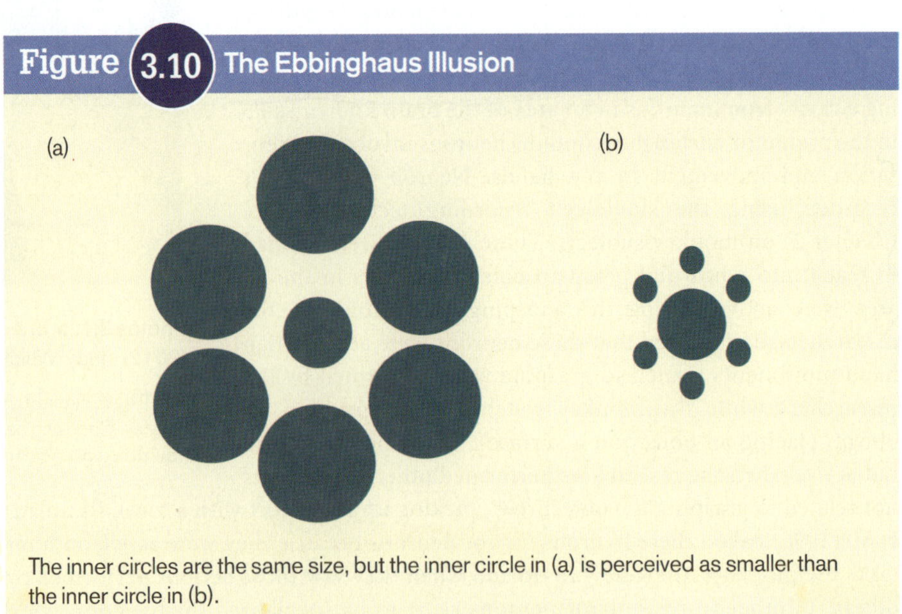

The inner circles are the same size, but the inner circle in (a) is perceived as smaller than the inner circle in (b).

SOURCE: Figure 1 excerpt, Witt, J. K., Linkenauger, S. A., & Proffitt, D. R. (2012). Get me out of this slump! Visual illusions improve sports performance. *Psychological Science, 23*, 397–399.

Figure 3.11 Results From the Witt et al. (2012) Study

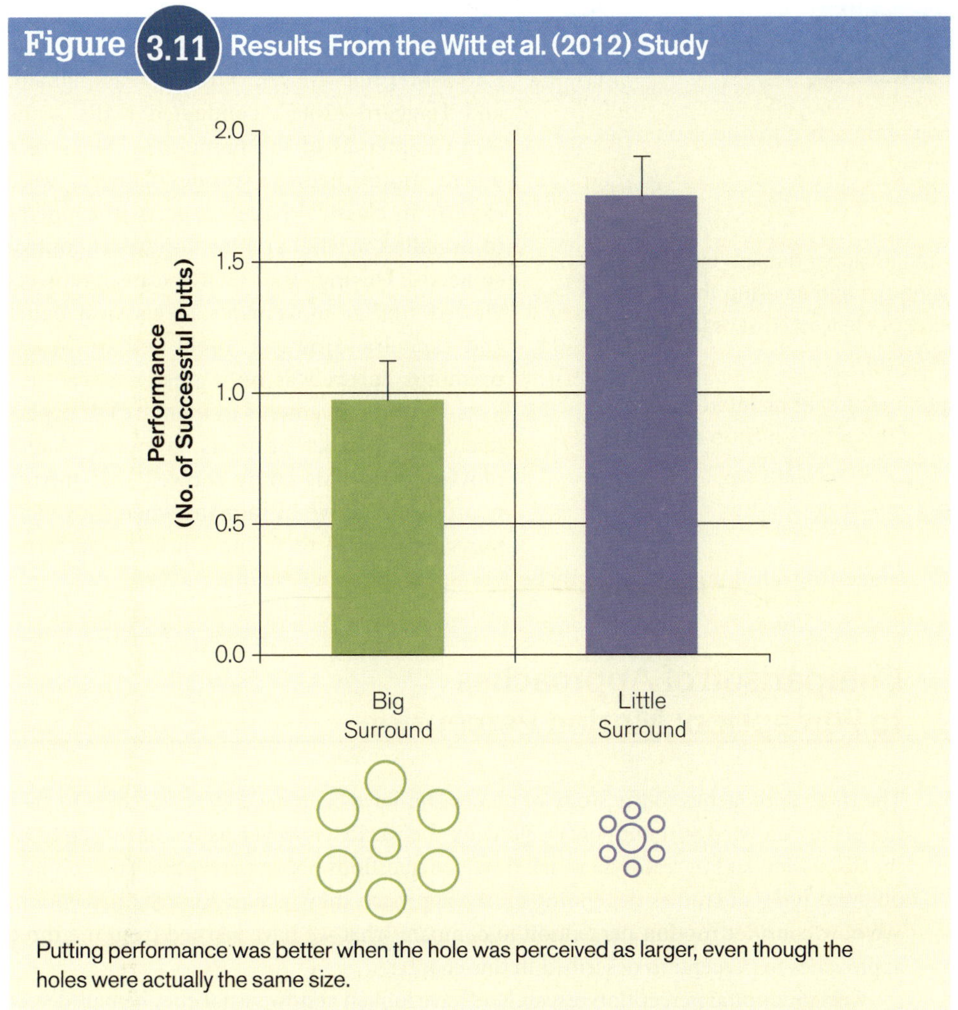

Putting performance was better when the hole was perceived as larger, even though the holes were actually the same size.

SOURCE: Figure 1 excerpt, Witt, J. K., Linkenauger, S. A., & Proffitt, D. R. (2012). Get me out of this slump! Visual illusions improve sports performance. *Psychological Science, 23*, 397–399.

Figure 3.12 Location of Dorsal and Ventral Visual Streams in the Brain

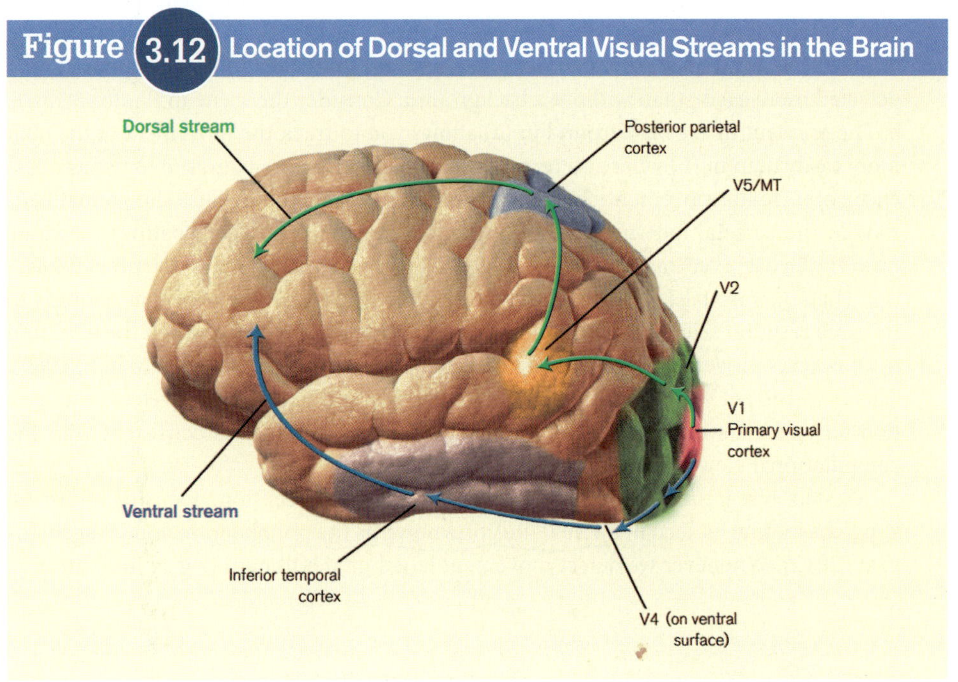

Stop and Think

3.14. How do perception/action approaches to cognition differ from computational approaches?

3.15. What is an affordance?

3.16. I am looking at the lilac tree in bloom outside my window. I immediately imagine going out and smelling the flowers. Explain how my perception of the lilac flowers fits a perception/action approach.

3.17. Would a perception/action researcher be interested in explaining the moon illusion described in Stop and Think 3.9? Why or why not?

More recent studies have shown mirror neuron function in humans. For example, Calvo-Merino, Glaser, Grèzes, Passingham, and Haggard (2005) conducted fMRI scans (see Chapter 2) of the premotor cortex areas where motor neurons reside. Subjects were experts in classical ballet, experts in capoeira (a Brazilian martial art), or nonexpert control subjects. During the fMRI scans, subjects viewed similar movements in classical ballet and capoeira. However, brain activity in the premotor cortex was only greater when subjects viewed movements in their area of expertise (e.g., ballet experts viewing ballet movements). This study showed that mirror neurons are active in humans when they view movements that they know how to perform, suggesting a link in brain activity between perception and action.

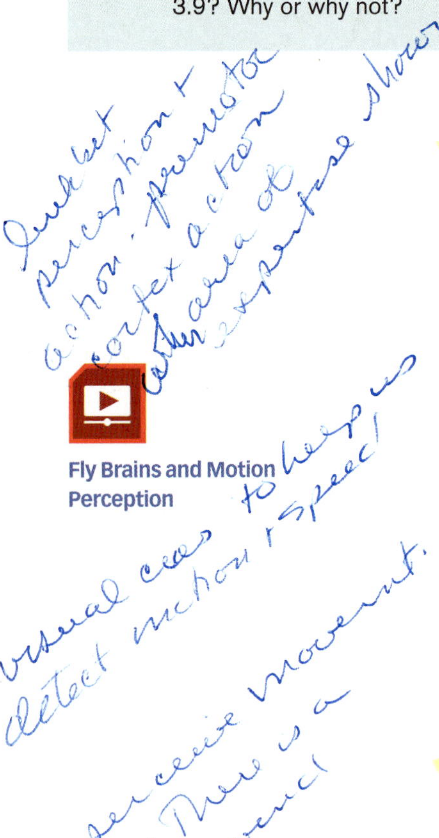

Fly Brains and Motion Perception

Comparison of Approaches to Perception: Motion Perception

The three approaches to the study of perception have been used by researchers to gain important knowledge about how we perceive the world. However, as you have seen from the discussion so far, researchers ask different questions about perception and conduct different types of studies depending on the approach they take in studying perception. We now consider motion perception to compare what we have learned from the three approaches to perception described in this chapter.

Computational perception researchers have looked at how visual cues help us detect motion and the speed of motion in the environment. Changes occurring in the retinal images over time are one cue. Although retinal images are constantly moving, even for stationary objects, due to the constant movement of our eyes across a scene, retinal images that move more than others over time can indicate movement of the objects creating those retinal images. Further, cues in the scene can aid in detecting movement of objects. If an object moves across a background in a scene, the movement can be detected more easily than without a background. Consider the scene in Photos 3.13a & b. The gradient in the background in (a) allows you to track the movement of the man more easily than in (b) where there are no landmarks in the background to use as reference points to his movement. Finally, research in neuropsychology has shown that neurons in the parietal lobe near the occipital lobe make up a "when" pathway separate from the "what" (ventral) and "where" (dorsal) pathways described in the previous section (Batteli, Pascual-Leone, & Cavanagh, 2007). Studies have shown that neurons in this area respond selectively to motion stimuli and are highly active when the direction of an object's movement is accurately detected (Newsome, Britten, & Movshon, 1989). This is consistent with the idea of feature detection and neurons with selective activation for specific stimuli described earlier in the chapter, which is consistent with the computational view of perception.

Gestalt researchers have also examined motion perception, focusing more on apparent motion as seen in a visual illusion known as the phi phenomenon (Wagemans et al., 2012). Whenever we detect movement in a digital billboard (e.g., a Jumbotron at

Thomas Northcut/Photodisc/Thinkstock

Comstock/Stockbyte/Thinkstock

Photos 3.13a & b In the scene in (a), we can use the lines of the fence in the background to perceive the movement of the man more easily than in (b) where the background does not contain these cues.

a football game), we are actually seeing light pixels flashing on and off or changing colors in a specific pattern rather than anything actually moving. This is why the movement is called "apparent"—the lights seem to show objects moving, but in reality nothing is actually moving in space. The phi phenomenon shows that we organize the stimuli moving on and off as moving in the way we know objects move in a scene. A classic example of the phi phenomenon is seen at railroad crossings. The next time you are stopped at a track with a crossing train, look at the blinking red lights on the sign. They appear to hop back and forth on the sign, but this is simply caused by two red lights blinking on and off with opposite timing.

Motion Aftereffect Demonstration

In an example of research on apparent motion, Oyama, Simizu, and Tozawa (1999) examined how the principles of proximity and similarity influence apparent motion effects. Proximity and similarity were manipulated in apparent motion and perceptual grouping displays to determine which of these organizational principles is most important in perceiving apparent motion. Their results suggested that similarity was the more important element because they found that changes in similarity of color, size, and other factors influenced both perceptual grouping and apparent motion perception. Thus, research on Gestalt principles is contributing to our understanding of these kinds of motion effects.

The perception/action approach considers movement in terms of goals for our own action. When an outfielder views the movement of a fly ball and adjusts his action

Stop and Think

3.18. Reconsider the scenario presented at the beginning of the chapter where you are walking across your crowded campus. How would each of the three approaches describe perception in this situation?

Curveballs

behaviors to catch the ball, he is showing the type of behaviors that perception/action researchers are interested in studying. An example of this type of research was conducted by Shaffer, Krauchunas, Eddy, and McBeath (2004). These researchers examined the movements of dogs catching flying Frisbees. Small video cameras were attached to the dogs' heads while they completed the task of catching the Frisbees. The researchers then analyzed the video data from the dogs. They found that the dogs worked to catch the Frisbees by matching their movements to the speed and trajectory of the Frisbees to keep the Frisbees in sight; as the Frisbees came closer, the dogs were able to close the gap to catch them. Other research has shown that humans use similar control mechanisms in completing tasks such as catching a fly ball or controlling an aircraft (McBeath, Shaffer, & Kaiser, 1995). The study of optic flow described earlier also provides an example of the perception/action approach to motion perception. Beall and Loomis (1997) showed that aircraft pilots use optic flow in the environment to guide their landings.

The perception of motion likely involves a combination of processes. Thus, multiple approaches to the study of motion perception can aid in creating a full understanding of how it is accomplished. The three approaches described in this chapter have each contributed information about how these processes operate in humans and other animals. In this way, these approaches continue to guide perceptual researchers as they explore all areas of perception.

THINKING ABOUT RESEARCH

As you read the following summary of a research study in psychology, think about the following questions:

1. Which of the three approaches to the study of perception do you think this study most adheres to?
2. What was the primary manipulated variable in this experiment? (Hint: Review the Research Methodologies section in Chapter 1 for help in answering this question.)
3. From this study, is there evidence of bottom-up and/or top-down processing in scene categorization? Explain your answer.
4. Of the results described, which are most informative about the research question in this study? Explain your answer.

Study Reference

Malcolm, G. L., Nuthmann, A., & Schyns, P. G. (2014). Beyond gist: Strategic and incremental information accumulation for scene categorization. *Psychological Science, 25*, 1087–1097.

Purpose of the study: Researchers investigated how we categorize complex scenes. Previous studies have shown that understanding the gist (i.e., basic meaning) of a scene occurs very quickly. Malcolm et al. (2014) were specifically interested in whether we use detailed information of a scene in quickly interpreting that scene. They showed common scenes (e.g., restaurant, pool) in a blurred state to subjects. However, the subjects could choose to focus on a part of the scene to help them understand it. Subjects were asked to view the scene and choose the category it belonged

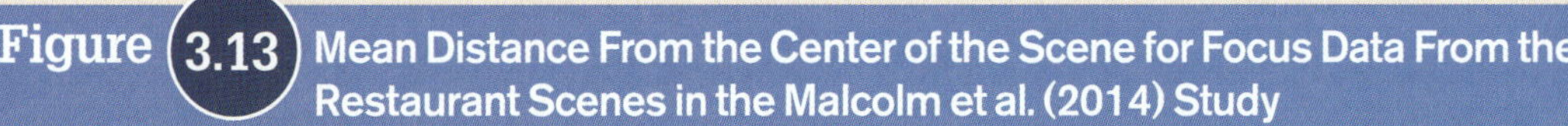

Figure 3.13 Mean Distance From the Center of the Scene for Focus Data From the Restaurant Scenes in the Malcolm et al. (2014) Study

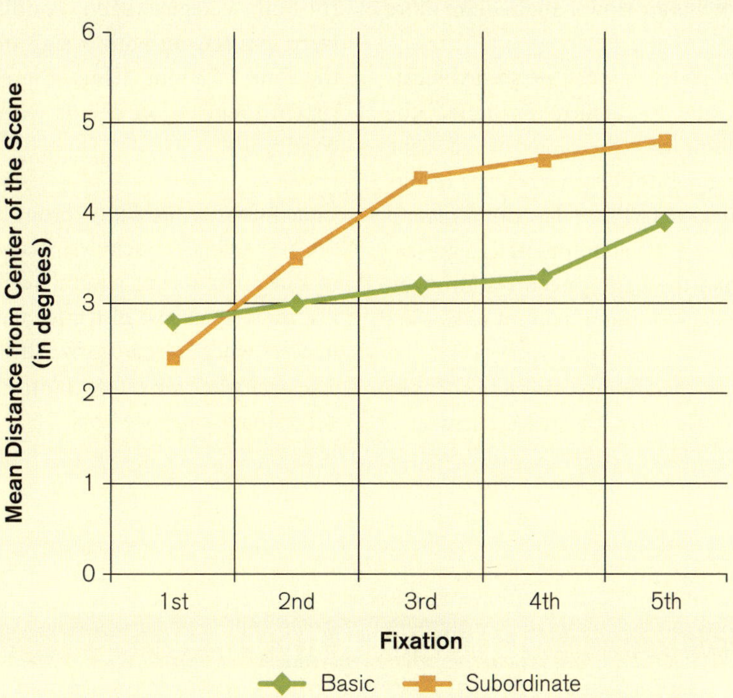

to. The area of the subjects' focus in the scene provided the primary test of the research question. If subjects showed no consistency across scenes in their focus, this would indicate that the specifics of the scenes did not aid in categorization of the scene. However, if subjects focused on consistent aspects of the scenes, this would indicate that those details of the scene were important in the categorization process.

Method of the study: Twenty-eight subjects participated in the experiment, each viewing 32 scenes. Each of the scenes belonged to one of the following four basic categories: pool, restaurant, classroom, or road. For each category, the scene belonged to a subcategory (e.g., restaurant: diner, pub, fine-dining establishment, cafeteria). Half of the subjects were asked to categorize the scene according to one of the four basic categories. The other half of the subjects were asked to categorize the scene according to a subordinate of that basic category (e.g., choose one: diner, pub, fine-dining establishment, or cafeteria).

The scenes were filtered such that they were blurred. Subjects viewed the scenes through an eye-tracking apparatus that recorded the location of their eyes' fixation. When subjects focused on a location, that location in the scene was focused such that it could be viewed clearly. The scenes were presented randomly (blocked by basic category for the subjects who completed the task for subordinate categories). Scenes were shown until subjects pressed a button with their category choice or until 15 seconds had passed, whichever came first. Reaction time to respond was also recorded.

Results of the study: Reaction time data showed that subjects were significantly faster at categorizing scenes at the basic level (e.g., restaurant) than at the subordinate level (e.g., pub). Eye fixation data showed that subjects made

(Continued)

(Continued)

more fixations in the subordinate condition than in the basic category condition. These results suggest that subordinate category judgments are slower and require more details of the scene.

To examine fixation pattern across the scene by categorization condition, the researchers examined the distance of the focus point from the center of the scene for the first five focusing points of each trial. The results showed that subjects fixated farther from the center of the scene when completing the subordinate categorization (e.g., pub) task than the basic categorization (e.g., restaurant) task. These data for the restaurant scenes are shown in Figure 3.13.

To examine whether specific objects were focused on during the task consistently, the researchers also considered the number of fixations per object compared to the total number of fixations in the scene. In both categorization conditions, specific objects were focused on with a significant proportion out of the total fixations. Thus, there was evidence of consistent focusing on details within the scenes for both conditions.

Conclusions of the study: From the results of this study, the researchers concluded that details of the scene aid in categorization of natural scenes. This shows that we use more than just gist information to interpret scenes in cases where we categorize the scene at a basic category level and when we categorize the scene at a more detailed subordinate category level.

CHAPTER REVIEW

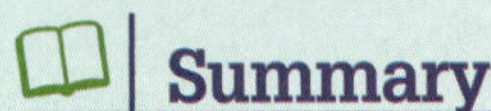

Summary

- **What is perception?**

  Perception is the cognitive processes through which we interpret the stimuli in the world around us.

- **How do our sensory systems affect our perception of the world?**

  Sensory systems do the job of turning sensations into perceptions that help us understand what we are encountering in the world. Sensory systems do the job of turning stimulus energy into neural signals that can be processed in the brain.

- **Do we control our perceptions or can we perceive automatically?**

  In some cases perception happens automatically, without our control (e.g., in experiencing perceptual illusions), but there are situations where we control perception (e.g., in perceiving a way to accomplish a behavioral goal).

- **Why do we sometimes perceive things incorrectly?**

  Perceptual illusions occur through the natural processes of perception. In fact, they help illustrate the way that perception typically occurs in cases where illusions do not result.

- **What does it mean for something to be more than the sum of its parts?**

  The Gestalt idea of perceiving the whole is proposed as a contrast to the computational approach where the parts are added together to achieve perception of the whole stimulus (e.g., as in feature detection models and encoding of geons). In the Gestalt approach, perception is viewed as a process that organizes stimuli into a coherent whole based on top-down processing in the form of organizing principles.

- **How does perception aid in action?**

  According to the perception/action approach, perception is conducted as a means to achieve goal-directed behaviors. Thus, perception and action are intricately tied together.

- **What is the purpose of perception?**

  The purpose of perception is to interpret the world around us. However, the means by which this occurs is varied and described in different ways by the different approaches researchers take in studying perception.

Chapter Quiz

1. Which of the three approaches to perception would describe perception of an object in terms of the geons that make up the object?
   (a) Gestalt
   (b) computational
   (c) perception/action
2. Which of the three approaches to perception would describe perception of a doorway in terms of whether it can be walked through?
   (a) Gestalt
   (b) computational
   (c) perception/action
3. Which of the three approaches to perception would describe perception of a tree as more than the addition of its branches, leaves, roots, and flowers?
   (a) Gestalt
   (b) computational
   (c) perception/action
4. Which of the following parts of a sensory system is responsible for transforming stimulus energy into neural signals?
   (a) sense organ
   (b) brain areas
   (c) receptor cells
   (d) nerve conduit
5. In which lobe of the brain is visual information first processed?
   (a) parietal
   (b) frontal
   (c) temporal
   (d) occipital
6. Two objects appear in a scene: an elephant and a mouse. The mouse is much closer than the elephant. Explain how you might know that the mouse is closer from cues in the scene.
7. Regarding question 6, what aspects of the scene would be of interest to a perception/action researcher?
8. According to the perception/action approach, explain how the perception of the gap in my backyard fence would differ between the rabbit in my backyard and me.
9. Look around the room you are in and describe your perception in terms of the Gestalt principles of proximity, similarity, and closure.
10. Explain the difference in processing of visual stimuli that occurs in the ventral and dorsal brain pathways.
11. In what way does the discovery of mirror neurons support the connection between perception and action?
12. How might mirror neurons be useful in social perception?
13. The ____________ visual pathway extends into motor cortex, whereas the ____________ visual pathway extends into the temporal lobe where language is processed.
14. The information in the environment about movement where farther objects appear to be passing by more slowly than closer objects is called ______________.
15. Perception of the taste of food begins in the __________.

Key Terms

Affordances 54
Bottom-up processing 46
Distal stimulus 46
Dorsal pathway 57
Gestalt psychology 50
Principle of Pragnanz 52
Proximal stimulus 46
Sensory system 45
Theory of unconscious inference 50
Top-down processing 48
Ventral pathway 56

Stop and Think Answers

3.1. Describe the four parts of a sensory system.

The four parts of a sensory system are: (1) sense organ (eyes, ears, nose, tongue, skin), (2) receptor cells in each sense organ that receive stimulus energy and convert it to neural signals, (3) nerve conduit that carries the neural signal from the sense organ to the brain, and (4) brain area(s) that processes the neural signals received from the sense organ.

3.2. What is the role of receptor cells in perception?

The receptor cells serve the important role of converting stimulus energy (e.g., light, sound waves) to neural signals that can be received and processed by the brain.

3.3. What are the advantages to having a perceptual system that has automatic input of all environmental stimuli but only consciously processes a small portion of those stimuli?

Answers will vary, but a primary advantage is that we can focus our attention on (or attention can be captured by) any stimuli in the environment because all are being received. Thus, we have the ability to consciously process any stimulus in our environment.

3.4. Can you think of a situation where your perception of your environment did not match the reality of the environment? Why do you think that error occurred?

Answers will vary based on personal experiences. The illusions described in the chapter provide some examples of these errors.

3.5. Explain what it means to interpret scenes based on cues present in those scenes.

This describes the computational approach to the study of perception. Cues in the stimuli such as basic features, linear perspective, and retinal size help us interpret the size and distance of objects in the environment and also help us identify those objects.

3.6. In what way do illusions illustrate the normal processes of perception?

Because we use cues to interpret stimuli, those cues can sometimes lead to an inaccurate interpretation when they conflict with or are not an accurate representation of the environment.

3.7. You see a light approaching on the road at night. According to the likelihood principle, which of the following are you most likely to perceive: (a) a deer crossing the road wearing a headlight, (b) a UFO, or (c) an approaching car? Explain your answer.

In this situation, the most likely object causing this stimulus is (c) an approaching car. The likelihood principle states that we interpret stimuli based on the most likely event.

3.8. In the scene in Photo 3.4, describe some cues you can use to determine that the front of the pot is closer to you than the cat.

The retinal image size of the pot is larger than the retinal image of the cat. The cat is also higher in the photo; thus, linear perspective may help us determine that it is farther away.

3.9. People report a "moon illusion" such that the full moon appears larger when it is lower in the sky and close to the horizon than when it is high in the sky and above us. Using what you learned about the use of cues in this section, why do you think the moon illusion occurs?

One possible explanation of this illusion is that we misinterpret the size of the moon based on the comparison of retinal images of objects near the horizon (e.g., buildings and trees that can be seen along with the moon when it is low in the sky). When the moon is high in the sky, there are typically no other objects to compare it with. However, the explanation of the moon illusion is still debated within research in perception so there is no one right answer to this question.

3.10. How does the Gestalt approach to perception differ from the computational approach to perception?

The Gestalt approach to perception focuses almost entirely on top-down processing in the form of organizational principles of the world that we use to interpret stimuli in the environment. Adding cues or features together, as in the computational approach, is seen as providing an incomplete perception of objects and scenes.

3.11. How is top-down processing involved in the Gestalt approach to perception?

Top-down processing is involved in the use of knowledge about how the world is organized. We use this knowledge to mentally organize scenes (e.g., by proximity, similarity).

3.12. Look around your environment and describe some examples of good continuation in the objects around you.

Answers will vary.

3.13. Consider the moon illusion described in Stop and Think 3.9. Would the Gestalt approach to perception explain this illusion differently than the computational approach? Why or why not?

The Gestalt approach would provide a different explanation of this illusion because it would not consider cues such as retinal image size to explain the illusion.

3.14. How do perception/action approaches to cognition differ from computational approaches?

Perception/action approaches consider perception as a means to achieve behavioral action goals.

3.15. What is an affordance?

An affordance is a possibility for behaviors in a given environment.

3.16. I am looking at the lilac tree in bloom outside my window. I immediately imagine going out and smelling the flowers. Explain how my perception of the lilac flowers fits a perception/action approach.

Answers will vary but should include some description of an action goal (e.g., smelling the flowers).

3.17. Would a perception/action researcher be interested in explaining the moon illusion described in Stop and Think 3.9? Why or why not?

A perception/action researcher would only be interested in this illusion in terms of any behaviors it might influence.

3.18. Reconsider the scenario presented at the beginning of the chapter where you are walking across your crowded campus. How would each of the three approaches describe perception in this situation?

Answers will vary.

Student Study Site

Sharpen your skills with SAGE edge at **edge.sagepub.com/mcbridecp**

SAGE edge for students provides a personalized approach to help you accomplish your coursework goals in an easy-to-use learning environment.

Go to edge.sagepub.com/mcbridecp for additional exercises and web resources. Select Chapter 3, Perception, for chapter-specific resources. All of the links listed in the margins of this chapter are accessible via this site.

Attention

Questions to Consider

- When somebody tells you to "pay attention" what does he or she mean? How do we define attention?
- What descriptions of attention have helped researchers study attention?
- How do researchers study what someone is and is not paying attention to?
- What factors in the environment have been found to influence our attention abilities?
- How does our automatic processing affect what we pay attention to?

Introduction: How We Pay Attention

How We Pay Attention

Imagine that you are at a crowded party. Suppose you are looking for your friend Brandon, who wears a stocking cap and has a bushy beard. As you scan the crowd you see lots of hats and some beards, and eventually you see your friend talking to a girl with blond hair. After making your way through the noisy crowd you chat with him and his date. When you get over to them, you immediately notice the new nose ring Brandon has gotten since you last saw him. You listen to them talk for a while and can follow most of the conversation, but it is difficult with the noise of the music and all of the other conversations going on. Suddenly you hear your name mentioned across the room. You glance over to where you heard your name and another friend is telling some people about the trip the two of you took to go skiing last weekend. When you turn back around, Brandon is still talking about the movie he saw last week and you realize you didn't miss any important parts of the conversation. You continue listening to him talk about the movie. The woman standing next to him starts to talk about a movie coming out next week she wants to see and you realize that she has red hair and is not the same person who was there when you walked up. While your attention was diverted across the room, Brandon's date had walked off to get another drink and a new person had joined the conversation, but you hadn't even noticed!

Familiarity and Speech Perception

William James (1842–1910), one of the first American psychologists, said, "Every one knows what attention is. It is the taking possession by the mind, in clear and vivid form, of one out of what seem several simultaneously possible objects or trains of thought" (1890, p. 403). However, the idea that "everyone knows what attention is" does not mean that attention is not difficult to define such that it can be studied in research. It seems to be one of those concepts where you "know it when you see it," but you have trouble coming up with a clear definition. One of the reasons for this is that attention is involved in almost all aspects of cognitive processes (e.g., perception, memory, language, problem solving). The scenario just described illustrates several aspects of attention: focused attention on the conversation while attempting to filter out other sounds around you, the capture of your attention by your name spoken across the room, and the failure of your attention in noticing that a different person was standing nearby when your attention came back to the conversation. James's statement implies that attention has a clear conscious element—we pay attention to something by choosing something in the environment to hold in our current consciousness to the exclusion of other things in the environment. This could mean focusing on the words of the text and ignoring the sounds (e.g., background music) and other sights (e.g., the surface your book is lying on or the other things on your computer screen) in your current environment. Alternatively, you could begin to think about your plans for tonight even as you read, focusing your attention on your thoughts instead of on what you are reading (necessitating a rereading of the last paragraph). In this chapter, we consider the different ways that cognitive researchers have described attention and how it operates and some of the aspects of attention researchers have studied.

Views of Attention

As researchers have attempted to define attention as a cognitive process, several metaphors have arisen to aid in the description of what attention is (Fernandez-Duque & Johnson, 1999). Attention has been described as a filter of information, as a spotlight focused on an aspect of the environment, and as glue that binds features of the environment together. In this section, we consider each of these descriptions of attention and what they have contributed to our understanding of this complex cognitive process.

Anatomy of Attentional Networks

Attention as an Information Filter

One idea of how attention operates as a cognitive process is as a filter of information. In other words, attention works to filter out the irrelevant stimuli in the environment such that the only aspect(s) of the environment left in our consciousness is what we choose to pay attention to. According to Broadbent (1958), a researcher who used this description of attention in his model, our attention is limited by the amount of information we can focus on at a particular time. This occurs due to our attention process paring down the vast amount of information in the environment to just a small amount we can focus on. Thus, there is a "bottleneck" in our processing that filters out everything except the information we are attending to (see Figure 4.1). The filter acts as an early processor of the information to only let in what is relevant to one's current task or focus.

Theories of Selective Attention

Some support for the filter model of attention comes from research using what is known as a **shadowing task**. In this task, subjects are asked to repeat a message played over headphones to one ear. During this task, a competing message is played to the other ear such that subjects must focus their attention on the target message they have been

Shadowing task: a research procedure where subjects are asked to repeat (i.e., shadow) a message heard over headphones

Figure 4.1 Attention as an Information Filter With Limited Capacity

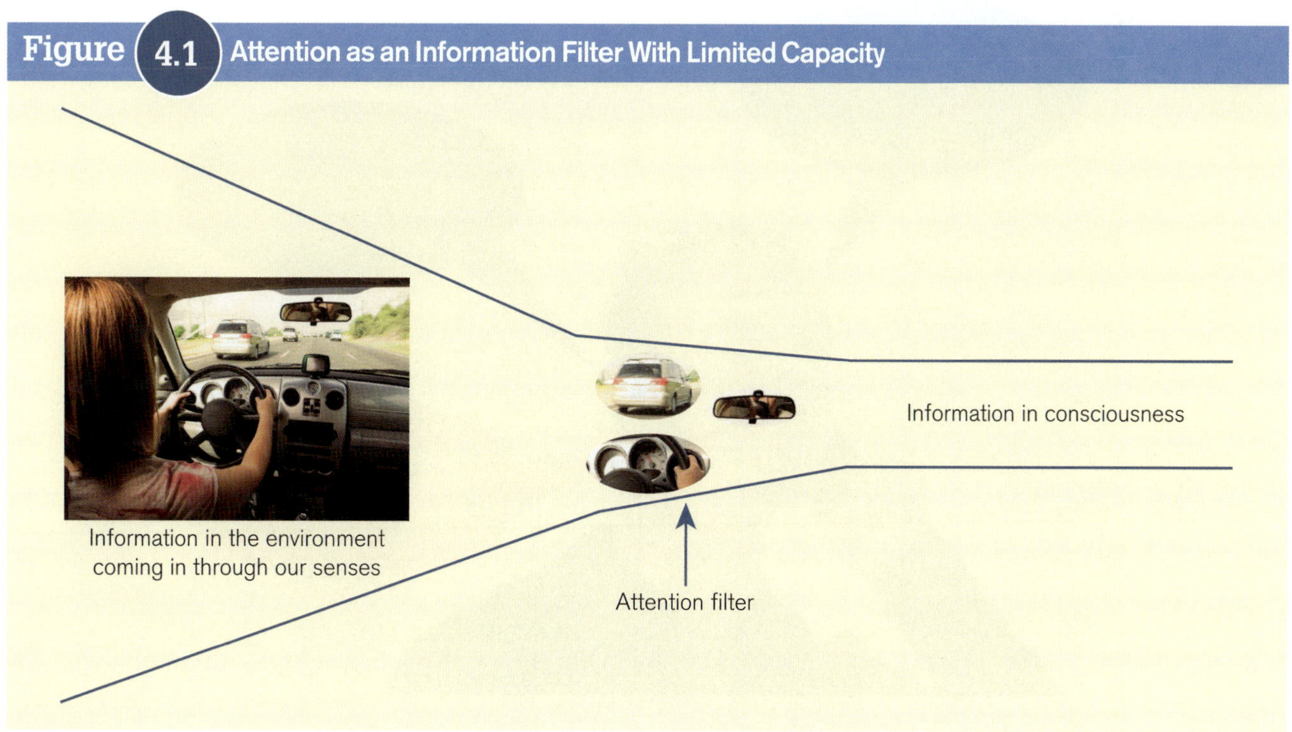

Photo from Jupiterimages/Creatas/Thinkstock.

asked to repeat. Research (e.g., Cherry, 1953) has shown that subjects can complete this task quite well. When subjects are asked what they heard in the competing message, they often cannot accurately report the content of that message, supporting the idea that it was filtered out during the shadowing task.

Cocktail Party Effect

However, this does not mean that the competing information is not being processed at all. If a salient stimulus is played in the nonattended ear (e.g., the subject's name), some subjects are able to switch their attention to the other message during the task, as occurred in our party scenario at the beginning of the chapter. This is known as the **cocktail party effect**, and research has shown that about a third of subjects will detect their name in the nonattended message (Moray, 1959; Wood & Cowan, 1995). The cocktail party effect suggests that more salient (i.e., important) information can get through the filter to capture attention.

Cocktail party effect: an effect of attention where one's focus changes abruptly due to a salient stimulus (such as one's name) in the environment

Conway, Cowan, and Bunting (2001) investigated the factors that contribute to the cocktail party effect in subjects. What causes some people to detect their name in the unattended message? Subjects were asked to repeat a message played over headphones in their right ear, while ignoring the competing message played in their left ear (see Figure 4.2). For all subjects, their first name was inserted into the message played in their left ear. A posttest questionnaire examined whether subjects detected their name in the nonshadowed message. Subjects also completed a task where they had to verify the accuracy (responding with yes or no) of mathematical equations while also remembering words presented with the equations. This type of task tests a subject's ability to keep track of several pieces of information at once and is known as a working memory task (see Chapter 5 for more discussion of working memory). The score on this task

Figure 4.2 An Example of the Shadowing Task From the Conway et al. (2001) Study

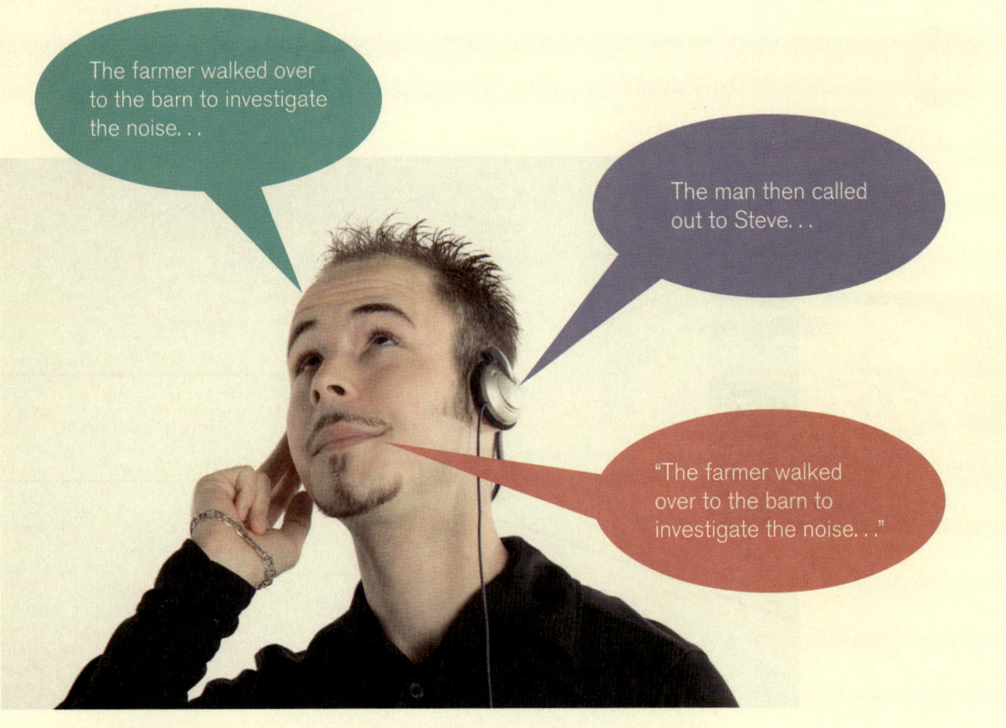

Photo from Jupiterimages/liquidlibrary/Thinkstock.

indicates the capacity of one's working memory abilities. Thus, the researchers hypothesized that the score on this task would be related to the subjects' ability to filter out the competing message in their left ear during the shadowing task. Subjects were grouped according to their score on the working memory task into high- and low-score groups. Results of the study showed that more of the low-score subjects (65%) noticed their name in the competing message than the high-score subjects (20%). These results support the researchers' hypothesis that individual differences in filtering abilities influence the cocktail effect.

Other research suggests that the salience of the message in the competing ear is not the only factor in switching attention. Treisman (1960, 1961, 1964) showed that subjects report information from the competing message in a shadowing task when the information is meaningfully related to the information in the attended-to message. For example, if a sentence is separated such that alternating words are presented to different ears, the subject will sometimes report the full sentence. In other words, if "BLACK/runs/MEOWS/funny" is presented to the right (attended) ear and "march/CAT/clock/LOUDLY" is presented to the competing left ear, subjects will sometimes report the capitalized words as part of a meaningful sentence: BLACK CAT MEOWS LOUDLY. This suggests that information in the competing channel is not being completely filtered out. Thus, either the filter could occur early in the perceiving process (as suggested by Broadbent's filter model), but be only a partial filter, or attention could act as a full filter but occur later in the perceiving process such that most or all of the information is being processed to some degree before the relevant information for one's attention has been selected (Fernandez-Duque & Johnson, 1999).

Treisman (1960) suggested a modified filter model of the first type: An early process partial filter allows some information to pass through but only after it has been attenuated (i.e., decreased in importance according to the relevance of the information). This is as if some of the information (e.g., information in the competing message in a shadowing task) is being passed through the filter but at a lower volume than the most relevant information (e.g., information in the attended-to message). This is known as the attenuation theory of attention. Figure 4.3 illustrates how this might work for the CAT example described earlier. The attenuator filters the incoming information such that it allows the attended message to come through at full strength, but the meaning-related parts of the competing message come through at lower strength because they are in the less relevant message for the shadowing task. Treisman also proposed a second stage of processing in the form of a dictionary unit where information is stored with a threshold value. The lower the threshold, the more likely the information is attended to. Thus, information with a low threshold, such as important information like one's name or meaning-related information to the attended-to information, can reach one's consciousness, even if it comes through the attenuator with a low strength (see Figure 4.3). Treisman (Treisman & Gelade, 1980) later revised her ideas about how attentional processes work (see the Attention as a Feature Binder section that follows), but her attenuation theory shows how models of cognitive processes go through revision when new results suggest that the original model is not quite right.

Stop and Think

4.1. Attention is an important process for many cognitive tasks. Describe some ways that attention is important in the tasks you perform as a student.

4.2. Describe how Treisman's attenuation model would explain how you can study with background music playing without it interfering with your task. How would this model describe your ability to hear your text alert on your phone without losing concentration in your studying?

4.3. Can you think of other ways to describe attention processes besides the filter metaphor? (Continue reading for some ideas.)

Figure 4.3 Treisman's (1960) Attenuation Theory of Attention

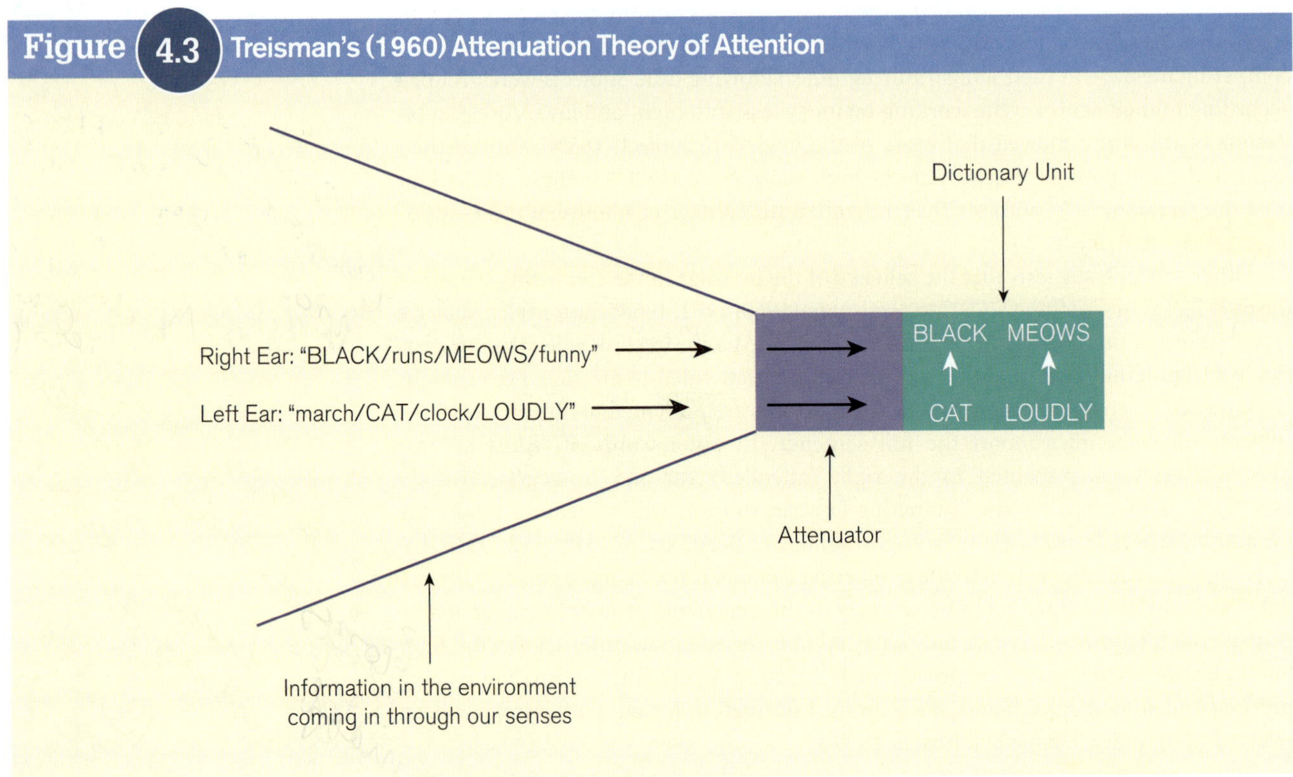

Juggling Multiple Tasks

Attention as a Limited Resource

Some models of attention have focused on its description as a limited resource. In this section we describe how attention has been examined as a spotlight focusing on different information in the environment and as a mental resource available for a task.

Attention as a Spotlight

A popular description of attention among researchers is as a spotlight. In this model, attention is viewed as the spotlight of our consciousness that is focused on some aspect of the environment that currently has our attention. The spotlight can be moved around the environment as our attention shifts to different things, either intentionally or automatically as something salient captures our attention (e.g., if something moves or is brightly colored). This description led researchers to consider what people focus their attention on in the environment and to develop methods that aided in that goal. For example, in some studies researchers have measured where one's gaze is directed in a display of stimuli. In other studies, how easily a target stimulus can be detected is measured.

Consequences of Multitasking

Some support for a spotlight description of attention comes from studies showing that shifts of attention affect the speed with which a task is performed. Such studies have shown that the reaction time to complete a task (e.g., respond when the number 7 appears) is linearly related to the distance from the position where one's attention is currently focused. In an example of this type of study, LaBerge (1983) asked subjects to complete one of two tasks on each trial: categorize a five-letter word or respond if the number 7 appears on the screen. The categorization task in the letter condition (i.e., decide if the center letter of the word is a letter from A to G) was designed to focus subjects' attention on the center of the screen. The target number 7 or nontarget stimuli (T or Z) were then presented either at the center of the screen or in positions where the other letters in the word appeared on other trials (i.e., to the left or right of the center of the screen). Figure 4.4 illustrates this condition of the experiment. Reaction times to respond to the 7 increased linearly as the 7 appeared farther from the center of the screen. See Figure 4.5 for the results from LaBerge's study. These results indicate that attention moves from the center of the screen to the target in the same way that a spotlight would be moved around in space to focus on different aspects of the environment. However, despite this evidence for an analog spotlight model, results from other studies (e.g., LaBerge & Brown, 1986; LaBerge, Carlson, Williams, & Bunney, 1997) have

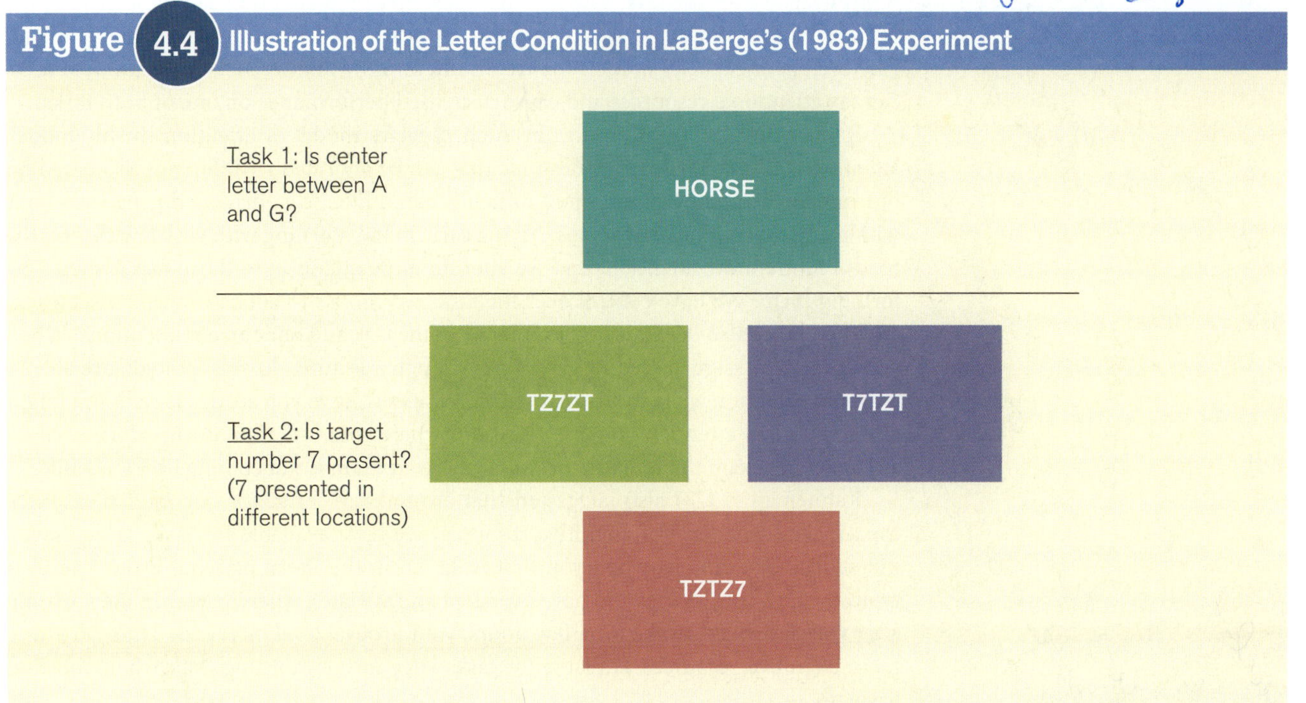

Figure 4.4 Illustration of the Letter Condition in LaBerge's (1983) Experiment

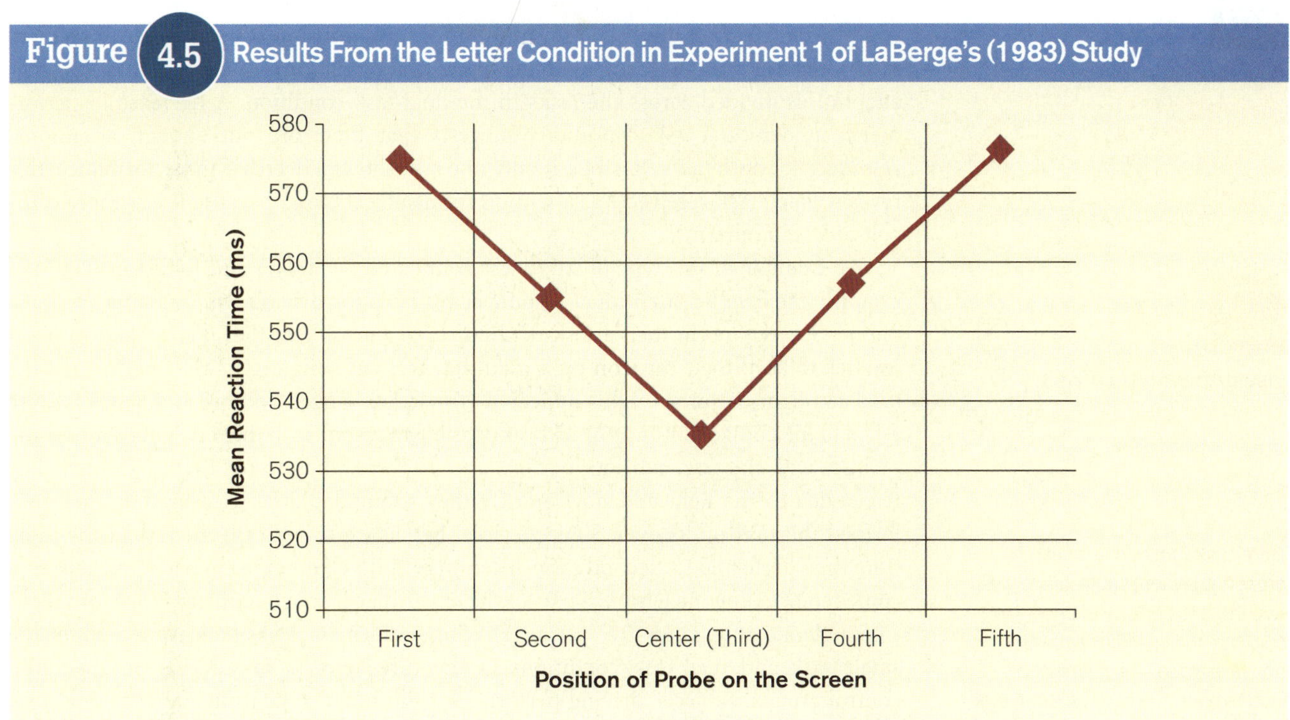

Figure 4.5 Results From the Letter Condition in Experiment 1 of LaBerge's (1983) Study

suggested that attention may be more distributed as a preparatory process for selective attention to focus on a specific location.

Attention as a Mental Capacity

Additional descriptions of attention as a limited resource are present in capacity models of attention. According to this type of model, attention has a limited capacity due to the limited amount of cognitive resources available for a task. Thus, attention depends on the amount of mental effort required for a task in relation to the cognitive resources currently available for the task. The spotlight description of attention can be seen as a type of capacity model because attentional resources are limited by the size of the spotlight. However, later capacity models focused more on how interference from multiple tasks can tax attentional resources and cause decreased performance on one or both tasks.

Kahneman (1973) proposed one such capacity model of attention. In his model, attention is a limited cognitive resource that can be allocated to different tasks based on our intentions. Tasks that are more difficult than others (e.g., driving during rush hour with many cars on the road versus driving early in the morning with very few cars on the road) require more attention, and we allocate more attention to those tasks when performing them. We have control over the tasks we choose to allocate more resources to, and this choice also depends on our interest in the task and our current intentions. When you are doing assigned reading or sitting through a lecture, do you find you are able to pay more attention when topics that are more interesting to you are discussed? You might also focus more attention on review sessions where your intention is to perform well on an upcoming exam than on other classes where an exam is not coming up for a while.

Kahneman (1973) also suggested that arousal can influence our mental resource capacity (i.e., the level of cognitive resources we have available for tasks at any given moment). For example, when you first wake up in the morning, your arousal level is typically fairly low (unless you have overslept and are late), whereas later in the morning after you have been awake for a few hours, your arousal level increases. Thus, you have more cognitive resources available for tasks later in the morning than when you first wake up.

Dual Task Experiment

The description of attention proposed in Kahneman's model is supported by studies using the divided-attention or **dual-task method**. In these studies, subjects are asked to complete two tasks at once (dual-task condition) to compare with performance on these tasks when they are performed alone (single-task condition). In other words, subjects' attention is divided across the tasks in the dual-task condition. A decrease in performance under dual-task conditions suggests that there are not enough attentional resources for both tasks. Further, if only one task shows a decrease in performance, this reveals which task received less attention from subjects (e.g., because it was more difficult or less important).

Visual Attention in Driving

Dual-task method: a research procedure where subjects are given two tasks to perform at once—to compare with performance on one task alone—to examine interference due to the second task

An example of this type of study was conducted by Strayer and Johnston (2001) to examine the level of attentional resources available for driving while talking on a cell phone. Subjects performed a task to simulate driving where they were asked to use a joystick to keep their car icon on a road they were moving on. As they performed the task, red lights or green lights appeared (the icon changed colors), and subjects were asked to hit a brake button as quickly as possible in response to the red lights. After some practice with the task, subjects' performance in responding to red lights (whether they responded to the light and how quickly they responded) was measured as they performed this task on its own. Subjects were then asked to perform the task at the same time they performed a second task: listen to a radio channel of their choice, talk to a confederate (someone who was part of the experiment) on a handheld phone, or talk to a confederate on a hands-free phone. Driving performance was then compared for the single task and dual-task conditions in the three groups of subjects. In the radio control groups, subjects' driving performance did not change from single to dual-task

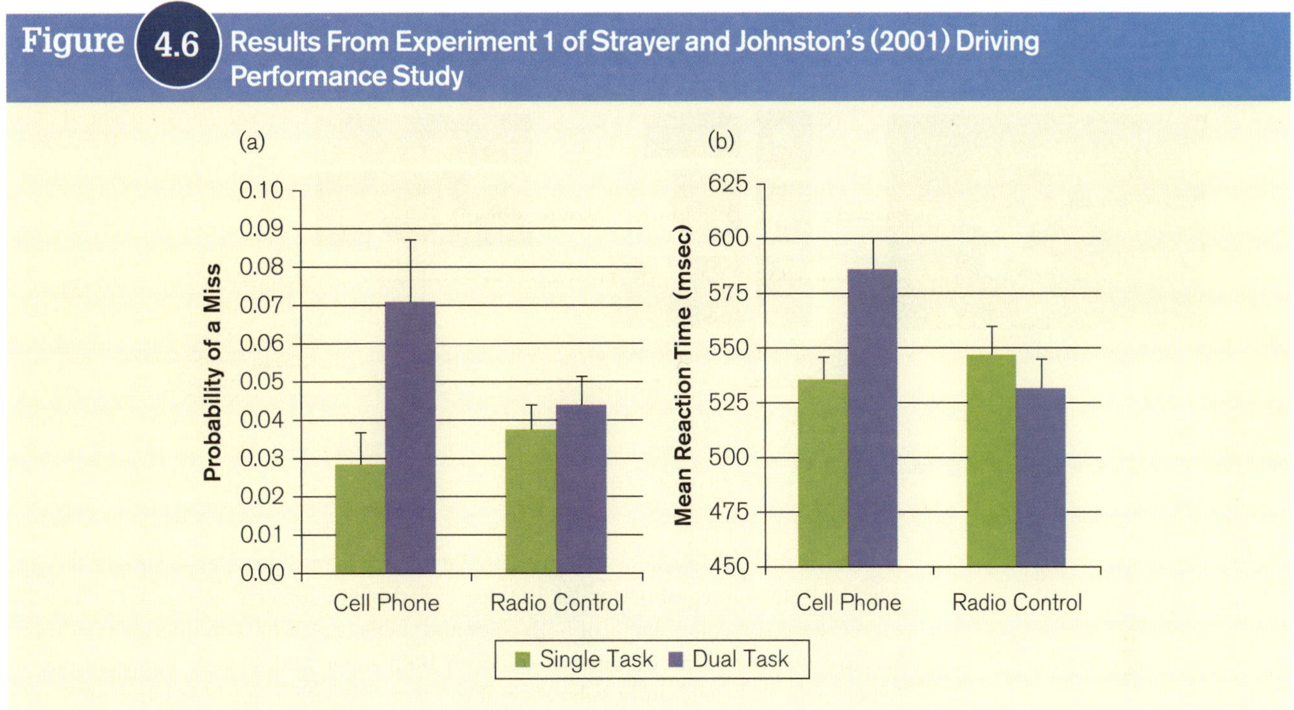

Figure 4.6 Results From Experiment 1 of Strayer and Johnston's (2001) Driving Performance Study

SOURCE: Figure 1, Strayer, D. L., & Johnston, W. A. (2001). Driven to distraction: Dual-task studies of simulated driving and conversing on a cellular telephone. *Psychological Science, 12*, 462–466.

conditions. However, in both cell phone groups, subjects missed more red lights and responded more slowly to red lights when they talked on the phone while driving. These results are shown in Figure 4.6. Studies like Strayer and Johnston's help identify situations where cognitive resources are not sufficient for good performance of the intended tasks and show that our attentional resources are limited.

Attention as a Feature Binder

As described in the Attention as an Information Filter section earlier in this chapter, Anne Treisman refined her ideas about attention into what she called the feature-integration theory of attention (Treisman & Gelade, 1980; Treisman, Sykes, & Gelade, 1977). In this model of attention, separate stages of processing contribute to focused attention. The first stage is an automatic identification and processing of the features within a scene in the environment. These features could be the colors, shapes, or brightness present in the scene. Because this processing occurs automatically, we are typically not aware of the identification of these features, and this stage occurs before attention processes kick in. The second stage in the model involves conscious, focused attention to combine the features of the scene and allows us to understand and think about what we are focused on in the scene. In this stage, attention is viewed as the glue that binds the features of the objects together. Figure 4.7 illustrates the stages of this model.

Stop and Think

4.4. What does it mean that attention is a "limited mental resource"?

4.5. Can you think of situations in your own life where attempting to complete multiple tasks at once showed the limits of your attention abilities?

4.6. The results of the Strayer and Johnston study showed that driving abilities are inhibited when subjects talked on the phone. What do these results mean for new laws requiring "hands free" cell phone use while driving?

Figure 4.7 Treisman's Feature-Integration Model

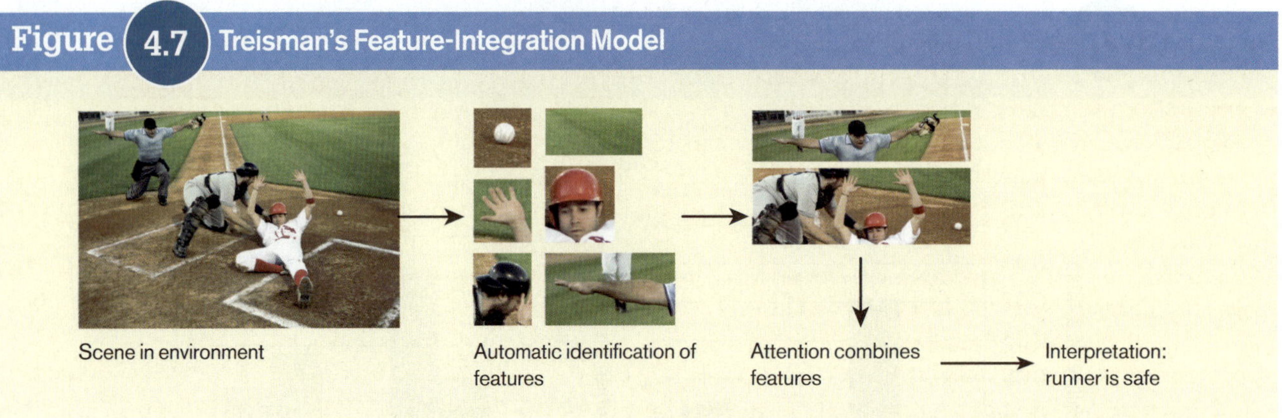

Photo from Donald Miralle/Digital Vision/Thinkstock

Treisman and Gelade (1980) presented evidence from several experiments to support the feature-integration model. In these experiments, subjects were asked to identify a target based on color, shape, or both color and shape (called the conjunction condition, because it involved a conjunction between both color and shape). For example, in Experiment 1 of their study, subjects had to identify whether any blue letter, an *S*, or a green *T* was present in the display (see Figure 4.8 for examples of these conditions). Reaction time to detect the target was measured. When the target differed by only one feature from the distractors (blue letter or an *S*), subjects very quickly detected the target

Figure 4.8 Conditions in Treisman and Gelade's (1980) Experiment 1

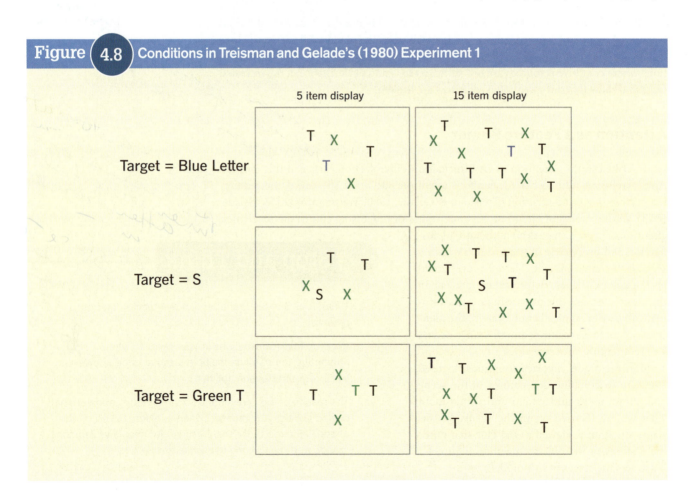

5 item display
15 item display

Target = Blue Letter
T X T T X
T T X X T T X T T T X X T X X

Target = S
T T X S X
X T T X X T T S T X X T X X T

Target = Green T
X T T T X
T T X X X X T T T X T T X T

in all displays, regardless of how many items were in the display. However, when they had to detect a conjunction target (a green *T*), subjects were slower as the number of distractors increased. In other words, the blue letter and the *S* seemed to pop out of the display easily because there was only one feature difference with the distractors, but subjects had to search for the conjunction target based on both features and it took longer to search with more items to search through. The search was harder when two features differed between the target and distractors, illustrating the importance of the features in attending to the target.

Consider the six displays in Figure 4.8. How easy is it to find the blue *T* in the top two displays compared with the green *T* in the bottom two displays? Many people report that the blue *T* in the first displays and the brown *S* in the middle displays seem to pop out of the rest of the distractors and are easily detected. This illustrates a concept known as attention capture. It shows how our attention can be easily attracted to something that is different from the rest of a scene (in Figure 4.8 by one important feature). This was seen in the chapter-opening party scenario when you noticed Brandon's new nose ring. It seemed to pop out at you and capture your attention because it was something you had not expected to see. The attention capture phenomenon illustrated by this example and in Figure 4.8 provides support for the feature-integration model of attention. The more features that must be integrated in using attention to search for an object in a scene, the more difficult and slow the search is.

Visual Search Activity

Visual Search Demonstration

The feature-integration model is also consistent with current knowledge of brain function in processing features of scenes. As described in Chapter 3, different sensory systems are designed to receive and process different types of sensory input from the environment. Due to localization of function in the brain (see Chapter 2), information from different modalities (e.g., visual, auditory, tactile) is processed in different brain areas. Further, as described in Chapter 3, recent cognitive neuroscience studies (e.g., Fiebelkorn, Foxe, Schwartz, & Molholm, 2010; Zaretskaya, Anstis, & Bartels, 2013) have shown evidence of feature binding in the occipital and parietal cortex areas of the brain. For example, single-cell recording studies have provided evidence for feature integration based on features presented to the visual fields in each eye (Baars, 2007). Feature areas of the visual cortex respond to the features presented to both eyes' visual fields, but activation only occurs for the consciously attended features in the temporal cortex where conscious identification takes place.

Neural Basis of Selective Attention

Attention and Visual Perception

Further evidence for feature integration was presented by Zaretskaya et al. (2013). These researchers conducted fMRI scans during a task in which subjects identified whether the display illustrated movement of local features of the display or global features of the display. Local feature movement was created by moving each of four dots on a screen within its quadrant of the screen. Global feature movement was created by

Figure 4.9 Displays Used in the Zaretskaya et al. (2013) Study

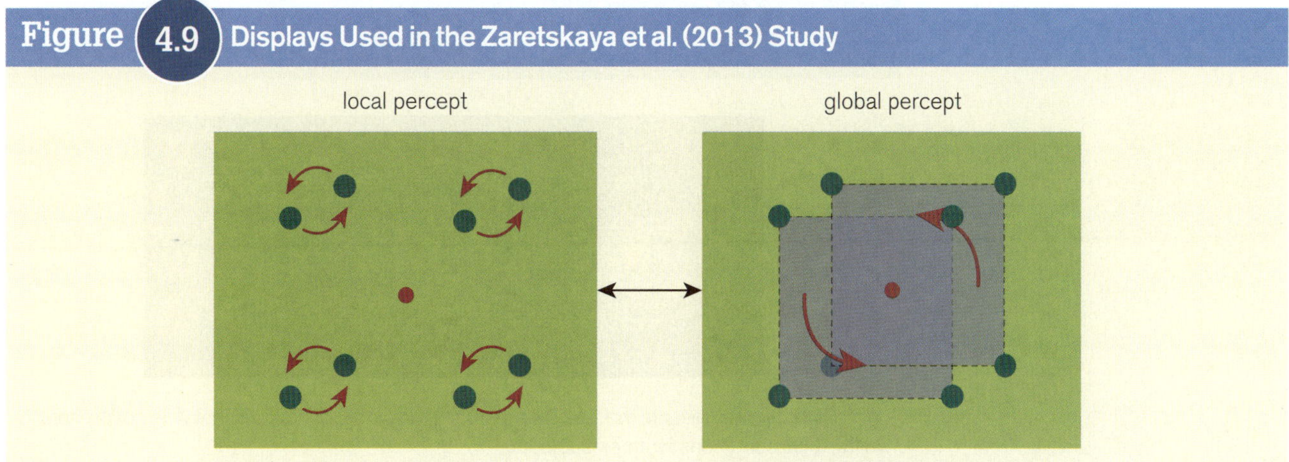

SOURCE: Figure 1, Zaretskaya, N., Anstis, S., & Bartels, A. (2013). Parietal cortex mediates conscious perception of illusory Gestalt. *Journal of Neuroscience, 33*, 523–531.

Stop and Think

4.7. Identify some features that are likely relevant for focusing attention on a particular object (e.g., a picture, a clock) in your current environment.

4.8. How do the two stages of the feature-integration model of attention differ?

4.9. Imagine you are focusing your attention on a person in a crowd. For each of the three models of attention–filter model, spotlight model, feature-integration model–explain how this task would work.

moving each of the four dots across a larger area of the screen. Figure 4.9 shows the displays used in the task. Subjects fixated on the red dot in the center of the screen for each trial. They were then asked to identify whether they saw local or global movement in each display by pressing one of two buttons. The researchers examined the brain activity that accompanied each type of display (see Figure 4.10) and found that activity in the right parietal cortex was present in the global condition that was not present in the local condition. These results indicate that distinctive brain activity is present when features of a display are bound together to view a global percept. Thus, this model of attention is consistent with the results of current studies examining the connection between attentional processes and brain function.

How Attention Affects Our Perceptions

The Science of Magic

So far in this chapter we have discussed the way that attention has been defined and studied based on those definitions. Throughout these research studies, interesting effects of how we use our attention have been discovered. Specifically, researchers have identified several ways that attention influences our perception of the environment. We have discussed some of these concepts already: the attention capture phenomenon where objects pop out of a scene, the cocktail party effect where salient or important stimuli attract our attention automatically, and the limitations of our attention abilities in attempting multiple tasks at once in dual-task situations. In this section, we explore some additional effects of attention that have come from research in this area: detecting changes in the environment, attentional boosts to performance based on congruencies between targets and responses, and deficits in our attention due to interference from automatic processing.

Figure 4.10 Brain Activity Data From Zaretskaya et al.'s (2013) Study

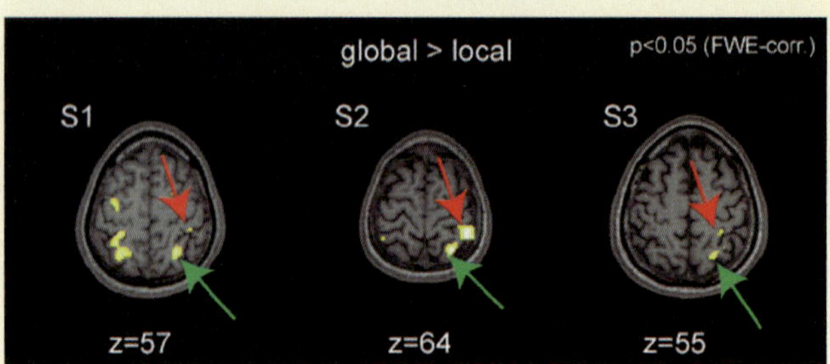

Activity shown represents the activity present in the global conditions that was not present in the local conditions for three subjects.

SOURCE: Figure 2, Zaretskaya, N., Anstis, S., & Bartels, A. (2013). Parietal cortex mediates conscious perception of illusory Gestalt. *Journal of Neuroscience, 33*, 523–531.

The Gorilla in the Room: Inattentional Blindness

The Invisible Gorilla

Some now classic experiments have shown our inability to notice a major change in our environment due to attention focused on other aspects of the environment. Daniel Simons (e.g., Simons & Chabris, 1999; Simons & Levin, 1998) illustrated this phenomenon in some interesting studies, illustrating that many subjects do not notice major changes in the environment such as a change in the person asking a question or a gorilla dancing across the scene.

Interview: Christopher Chabris

Imagine that you are walking across the quad at your school and someone stops to ask you where the student union building is (see Photo 4.1). While you are giving the person directions, some students walk between you and this person carrying a large art project that blocks your view of the person. You stop and wait for them to walk by and then continue giving directions. If the person you were talking to had been replaced by someone else when your view was blocked, would you notice? This is a similar situation to the one described in the opening party scenario, where you did not notice that a different person had joined your conversation while your attention was diverted when you heard your name across the room. Most people think they would notice, but Simons's research has shown that many do not. Simons and Levin (1998) created the situation just described in their study. After the unsuspecting subject finished giving directions, the researcher informed the subject that they were conducting a study and asked the subject if he or she noticed anything unusual when the object passed between them. In Experiment 1, only 7 of the 15 subjects noticed the change, and in Experiment 2, only 4 of the 12 subjects noticed the change.

Asking Directions Activity

Try this for yourself. Take the test for selective attention on Daniel Simons's website (www.simonslab.com/videos.html). Did you notice the change? This phenomenon has been called **inattentional** or **change blindness** because people fail to notice a change in the scene through lack of attention. One possibility is that the subjects have their attention focused on other aspects of the scene, keeping them from noticing the change. An example of this lack of attention is seen in the scenario from Simons and Chabris's (1999) study. In their study, subjects were shown a video of people passing a basketball (like the video on Simons's website). Some people wore white shirts and others wore black shirts. Subjects were asked to count the number of passes made by one of the teams (black shirts or white shirts). However, while the passing task was going on, either a person wearing a gorilla suit or a person carrying an open umbrella walked through the scene. At the end of the video, subjects were asked to write down their count for the number of passes. Then they were asked if they noticed anything unusual in the video. If they failed to report the gorilla or umbrella, they were explicitly asked if they saw these in the video. Overall, about half of the subjects did not notice the gorilla or umbrella. This number was actually lower (56%) for people who did not notice the gorilla, even though this event seems more unusual and more likely to capture attention. These studies show that not all salient events will capture our attention in a scene.

Noticing Changes Activity

Jupiterimages/BananaStock/Thinkstock

Photo 4.1 Would you notice if the person you were giving directions to changed to a different person when your view was blocked?

Incompatibilities Tax Attention: The Simon Effect

Have you ever used the roller ball on a computer mouse (or track pad) to make the text on the screen move down? Or played a game where you moved the joystick down to go faster and up to go slower? With practice, you likely were able to do these tasks, but it was

Inattentional blindness (also change blindness): failure to notice a change in the environment

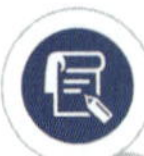

Simon Effect Activity

probably harder to do the first time you played because the action and the response were not consistent. These examples illustrate the decrement to attention that occurs when a task and response are incompatible.

This effect was first shown by Richard Simon (1969; Simon & Rudell, 1967; Simon & Wolf, 1963). The task was fairly simple: Subjects were asked to press a key on the left side when they saw or heard a target and a key on the right side when they saw or heard a different target. For example, they might press the left key when they heard the word *left* over headphones and the right key when they heard the word *right* over headphones (Simon & Rudell, 1967). Results showed, however, that subjects' reaction time to complete this simple task was affected by the location of presentation. Subjects were much slower when the word *right* was presented in the left ear and when the word *left* was presented in the right ear. In another example of the task, Nicoletti and Umiltá (1989) asked subjects to press the right key when a square was presented and a left key when a circle was presented. The objects appeared in one of six boxes on the screen, three to the left of the center fixation and three to the right of the center fixation (see Figure 4.11). Subjects were faster when the object appeared on the side of the screen that was consistent with the key press, with larger distances from center showing slower reaction times. These results are shown in Figure 4.12. The objects appearing on the right of the screen were overall more quickly responded to with the right key, and the objects appearing on the left side of the screen were more quickly responded to with the left key. This effect weakened as objects appeared farther from the center of the screen. These results illustrate the Simon effect.

Simon effect: interference in response due to inconsistency between the response and the stimulus

The **Simon effect** is proposed to occur due to one of two mechanisms (Hommel, 1993). The first mechanism, known as the attentional-movement hypothesis, suggests that the shift in attention to a target on the left or the right of one's attentional focus biases one to want to respond on the side of the attention shift (left or right). Thus, a response on the other side from the target must overcome this bias, requiring extra time. The other mechanism regarding how the Simon effect occurs is similar but suggests that the bias in response side is due to a correspondence to an object of reference in the

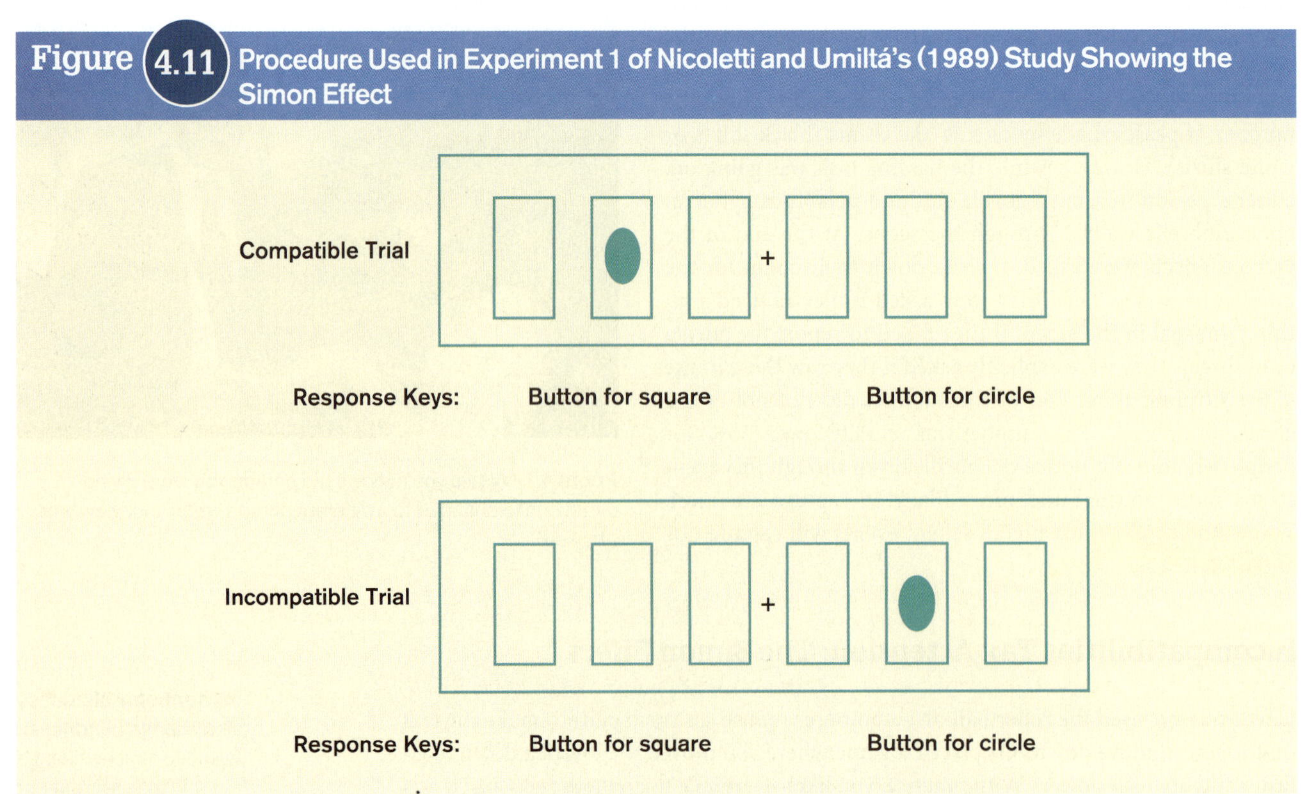

Figure 4.11 Procedure Used in Experiment 1 of Nicoletti and Umiltá's (1989) Study Showing the Simon Effect

Figure 4.12 Results From Experiment 1 of Nicoletti and Umiltá's (1989) Study

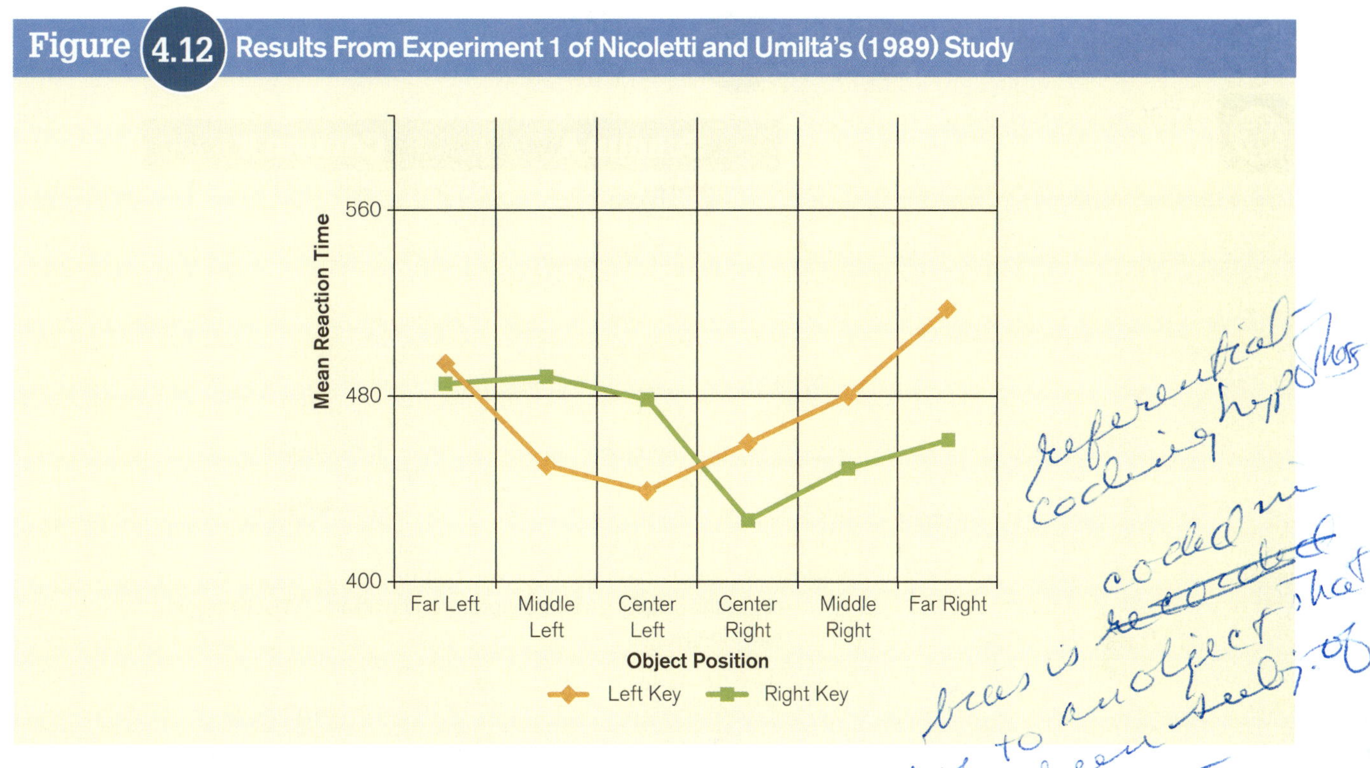

scene, rather than the current focus of attention. In other words, the bias to respond on one side or the other is coded in reference to an object in the scene that one has attended to. This is known as the referential-coding hypothesis. Hommel (1993) conducted experiments that provided support for the referential-coding hypothesis but acknowledged that this hypothesis needed further development to more precisely define how the coding occurs.

Effects of Automatic Processes on Attention: The Stroop Task

A well-known task that measures one's ability to inhibit automatic processes and focus attention on a conflicting task is the **Stroop task**. In Stroop's (1935) original study, subjects were asked to name the color of blocks or words on a page under different conditions. Try this for yourself: Time how long it takes you to name the color of print of the words in Column A of Figure 4.13. Then compare this time with how long it takes you to name the color of the print of the words in Column B. Which took longer? For most people Column B takes much longer. What do you notice about the difference between the words in the columns? In Column A, it is generally easier to name the color because the color is consistent with the word itself, facilitating the naming of the color. In Column B, the print color and the words are inconsistent, interfering with your ability to name the color. This interference occurs even though you are not asked to read the words because reading is an automatic process once you know how to read. It is a task you have had a lot of practice with. You cannot help but read the words as you are attempting to name the print color and the processing of what that word is can either aid in your color naming task (as in Column A) or interfere with your color naming task (as in Column B).

Stroop Effect Activity

Stroop (1935) also included a control condition that did not involve reading as a comparison to the condition where reading interferes with the color naming task. In this condition, subjects simply named the color of blocks presented to them. This is an easy task, requiring little attention. However, compared with this task, naming the color of the words in Column B of Figure 4.13 is quite difficult and requires more attention.

Stroop task: a research procedure where subjects are asked to name the color of printed words where some words are color words that conflict with the print color showing interference in the naming task

Stroop Test Demonstration

Figure 4.13 Example of the Stroop Task

Column A	Column B
brown	black
green	purple
blue	red
orange	blue
yellow	green
purple	yellow
red	orange
black	brown

Name the color of ink for the words in each column. Which column takes longer?

Stop and Think

4.10. Can you think of any instances from your own life where the Simon effect impairs your performance on a task?

4.11. The Stroop task shows that once we have learned this skill well, reading is an automatic process. Can you think of any other cognitive processes you use that are likely automatic for you?

4.12. The party scenario at the beginning of the chapter illustrated a simple example of change blindness (i.e., not noticing a change in the scene). Have you ever experienced change blindness in your environment? What factors contributed to your failure to notice the change?

Stroop also found that with practice, subjects got better at the task: They could name the color of ink faster in the interference condition after completing the task several times. The Stroop task shows that some cognitive processes require very little attention and are considered automatic processes. Reading in a native language is one of those processes. Tasks that we have less practice with (such as color naming) require more effort and attention because they are controlled processes that are not performed automatically. If I presented color words to you in Spanish (e.g., rojo, azul, verde) and you do not know the Spanish language (or are not very good at reading it), you would be able to perform the color naming task almost as easily as the subjects naming the color of the blocks because reading Spanish is not an automatic process for you. We consider automatic processes and their effect on attention further in the next section of the chapter.

Flanker Compatibility Task

Automatic and Controlled Processing: A Cognitive Dichotomy

Automatic processing: processing that is not controlled and does not tax cognitive resources

Controlled processing: processing due to an intention that consumes cognitive resources

The Stroop task in the previous section illustrates an example of an automatic cognitive process. **Automatic processing** and **controlled processing** are important parts of cognitive abilities, and the distinction seems to be important for completing cognitive tasks in an efficient manner. We have already seen an example of this dichotomy in this chapter: the automatic preattentive stage versus the attention binding stage of Treisman's feature-integration model. Because tasks that are automatic require little attention, they do not tax our cognitive resources in the way that controlled tasks do. Thus, how a process becomes automatic has been a topic of interest to cognitive psychologists.

Practice seems to be a factor in turning a controlled task into an automatic one. This is seen in the Stroop task. Children begin to show Stroop task interference effects from reading the words when they have had sufficient practice reading their native language (Schiller, 1966), and reading ability has been shown to be related to Stroop interference effects (Cox et al., 1997). Another common task that shows automaticity with practice is driving ability. Although driving can require attention in cases where it is more difficult (e.g., in heavy traffic or in unfamiliar cities), many people report that driving typically requires little attention once enough practice with this task has been achieved. However, that does not mean that performance is always good. Have you ever driven somewhere you did not intend to go (e.g., to work or school when you were on your way somewhere else)? Many people report this experience when they are focusing their attention on something else (e.g., their thoughts or a phone conversation). Because your driving route to places you typically go, like work or school, is well-practiced, you can drive it without much attention, even if that is not where you wanted to go! The Strayer and Johnston (2001) study described earlier in this chapter also illustrates this point: Driving can be done while doing another task that requires attention, such as talking on the phone, but performance can be impaired when attention is needed in the driving task (e.g., noticing a red light or a person in the road).

Schneider and Shiffrin (1977) provided an important examination of differences in automatic and controlled processing in attention tasks. They defined an automatic process as one that is initiated from specific input (internal or external) and activated without control or attention. Controlled processes, on the other hand, are activated based on one's intentions and require attentional resources. They argued that visual search tasks (e.g., looking for your friend Brandon at the party) rely on both controlled and automatic processes. They developed a task that allowed the use of controlled and automatic processes to be shown in different conditions. In this task, subjects were first asked to memorize one or more items as the targets they were looking for. Different items were targets on different trials. Then a series of displays was presented very quickly in which the subjects had to look for the target(s) among distractors. This is similar to retrieving an image of your friend Brandon from memory and then searching among the people at the party for him (where other party guests are distractors). The subject was asked to respond with one key if he or she saw a target and a different key if he or she did not see a target. Figure 4.14 illustrates the task procedure.

Two conditions were included in the experiments to compare processing types (see Figure 4.14). The first condition, called the consistent mapping condition, always involved distractors of a different type from the targets (i.e., letter targets and number distractors or number targets and letter distractors). This was predicted to be an easy condition for target detection because the distractors were always of a different type and to show performance improvement with practice. The other condition was called the varied mapping condition and involved targets and distractors of the same type (i.e., letter targets and distractors or number targets and distractors). This condition was predicted to be more difficult. The researchers also manipulated the number of targets subjects had to remember, the number of distractors shown in each display, and the amount of time each display was shown to examine how these factors affected performance in each of the conditions.

Just considering the data for correct responses in detecting targets (known as hits in target detection tasks), results from Schneider and Shiffrin's first experiment indicated that the consistent mapping condition was generally easier than the varied mapping condition (see Figure 4.15). Hit rates were higher in the consistent mapping condition

Figure 4.14 Procedure and Conditions From Schneider and Shiffrin's (1977) Experiments

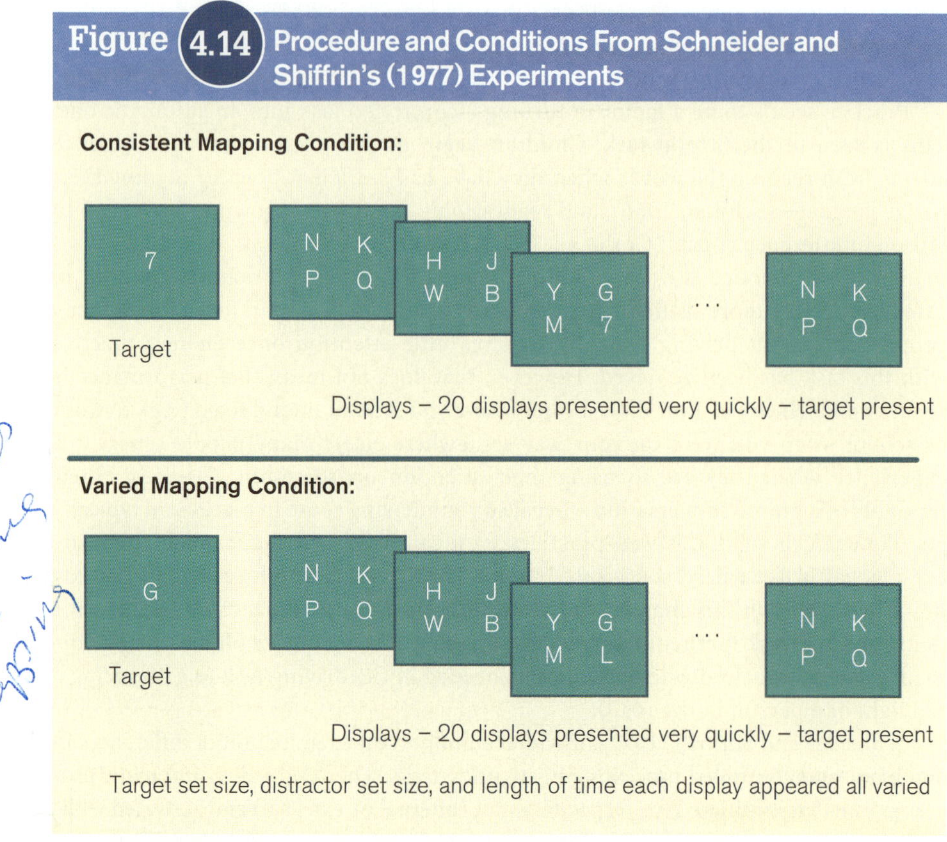

overall, and subjects required less time looking at the displays to reach this high performance in detecting targets (see the difference in timing across the two panels for the conditions). This suggests that the consistent mapping conditions were easier and may have relied more on automatic processing than the varied mapping conditions. Another interesting result was that the target set size and distractor set size factors reduced performance much more as set size increased in the varied mapping conditions than in the consistent mapping conditions (see the spread of the lines in the second panel compared to the first panel). This also suggests that more controlled processing is needed in the varied mapping condition because these factors should not affect performance on an automatic task. Schneider and Shiffrin concluded that subjects were doing controlled searches for the targets in the varied mapping conditions, which were required because the distractors were similar. They based this conclusion on the results showing that as distractor and target set sizes increase, subjects need longer display times and generally show lower performance in the varied conditions. These results were not seen in the consistent mapping conditions (the lines are all similar for different distractor and target set sizes), indicating that subjects did not need to conduct a controlled search in these conditions. Instead, it is more likely that the target popped out of the display that contained it, especially at longer display times. This suggests that the type of pop-out described earlier in the chapter for attention capture in Treisman and Gelade's (1980) experiments is an automatic process, consistent with the preattentive first stage of the feature-integration model.

In additional experiments, Shiffrin and Schneider (1977) explored how performance for the consistent mapping conditions changed with practice. However, consonant letters were used for both targets and distractors with items for each chosen from either the first half of the alphabet (B-L) or the second half of the alphabet (Q-Z). Performance with one mapping (e.g., B to L for targets and Q to Z for distractors) was

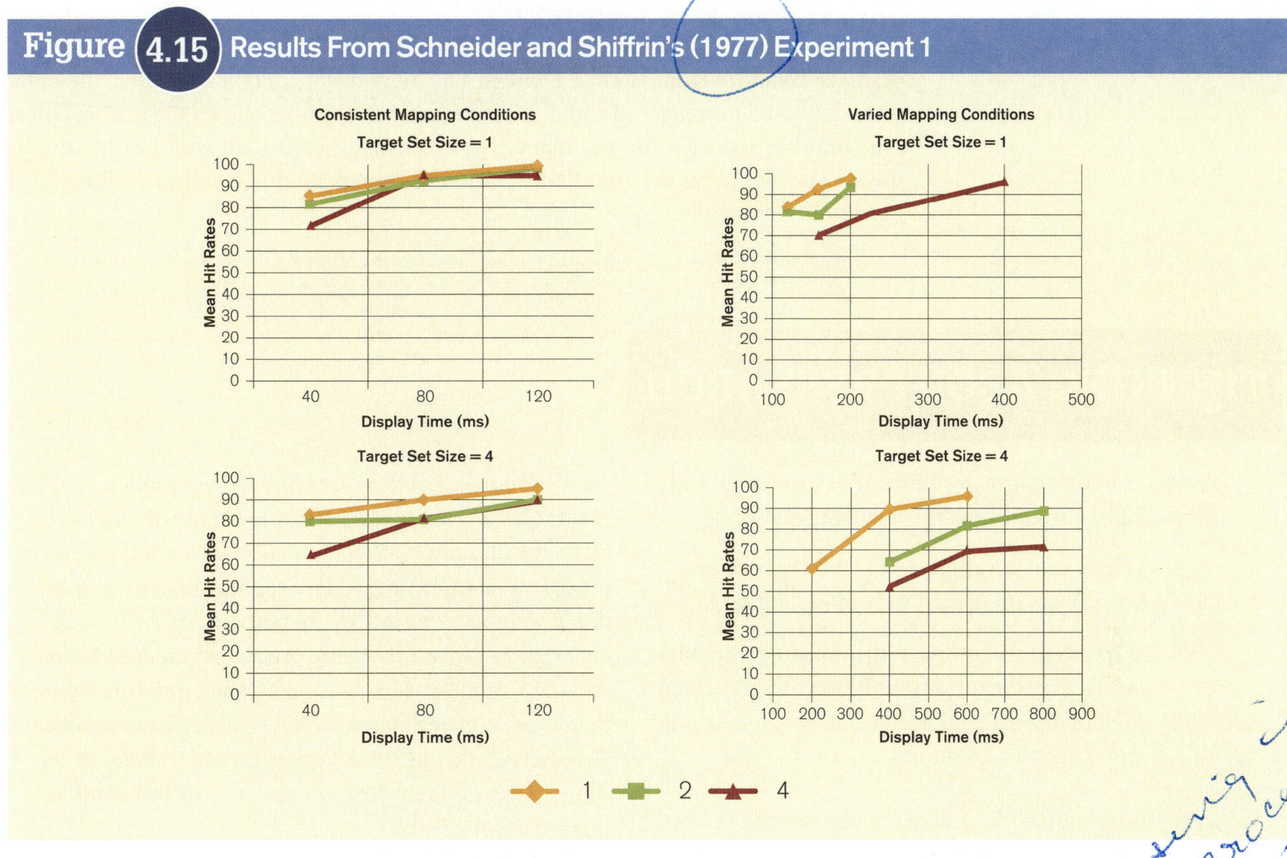

Figure 4.15 Results From Schneider and Shiffrin's (1977) Experiment 1

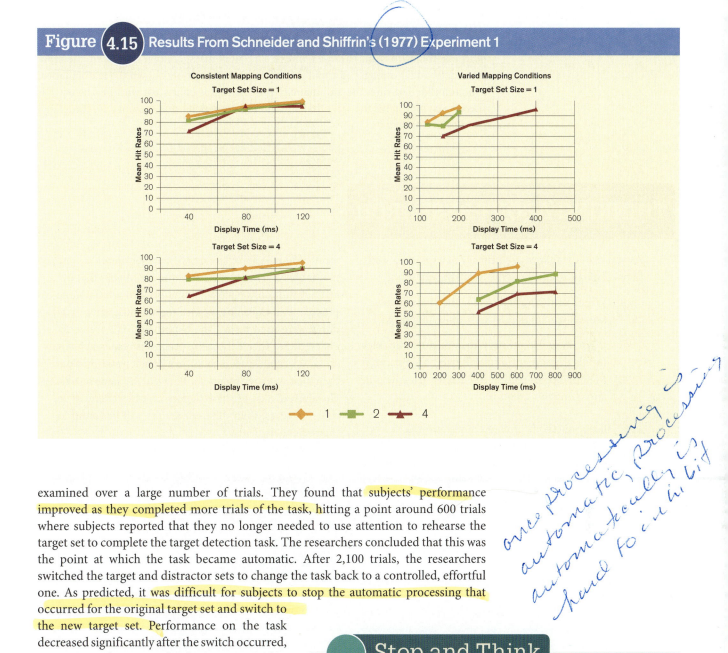

examined over a large number of trials. They found that subjects' performance improved as they completed more trials of the task, hitting a point around 600 trials where subjects reported that they no longer needed to use attention to rehearse the target set to complete the target detection task. The researchers concluded that this was the point at which the task became automatic. After 2,100 trials, the researchers switched the target and distractor sets to change the task back to a controlled, effortful one. As predicted, it was difficult for subjects to stop the automatic processing that occurred for the original target set and switch to the new target set. Performance on the task decreased significantly after the switch occurred, supporting the researchers' suggestion that automatic processing is difficult to inhibit.

Schneider and Shiffrin's (1977) model was important in defining and supporting the use of both controlled and automatic processing in attention tasks. Other researchers have employed these concepts in more recent theories of how controlled attentional processes become automatic. For example, Logan (1988, 1990, 1992) has suggested what he calls an instance theory of automaticity. According to Logan's theory, automaticity occurs through the encoding and retrieval of multiple experiences (i.e., instances) with a task. Controlled attention is required initially for the encoding and

Stop and Think

4.13. In Stop and Think 4.11, you considered some tasks that were automatic for you. How long (i.e., how much practice) did it take for you to go from controlled processing to automatic processing in these tasks? Is that length of time comparable to the time it took Shiffrin and Schneider's (1977) subjects to move to automatic processing in the target detection task? Why or why not?

4.14. In what way is a cognitive system designed to transfer tasks from controlled to automatic processing adaptive?

4.15. In what way is automaticity involved in Logan's instance theory?

retrieval of information about the task in memory, but over time, with many separate experiences of a task stored in memory, retrieval of the information about that task occurs automatically in that task context. The more instances that are stored, the more information that is retrieved about the task. Logan has further shown the mathematical function that describes the automaticity process that is consistent with his theory. His theory also highlights the ways that attention, automaticity, and memory are integrated in cognitive processes.

THINKING ABOUT RESEARCH

As you read the following summary of a research study in psychology, think about the following questions:

1. Which of the metaphors for the study of attention do you think this study most adheres to?
2. What were the primary manipulated variables in this experiment? (Hint: Review the Research Methodologies section in Chapter 1 for help in answering this question.)
3. Can you think of an example from your own life where direct eye gaze captured your attention? How does that situation relate to the procedure used in the following study?
4. Given the discussion of attention in this chapter, why do you think eye gaze and motion in particular capture our attention?

Study Reference

Böckler, A., van der Wel, P. R. D., & Welsh, T. N. (2014). Catching eyes: Effects of social and nonsocial cues on attention capture. *Psychological Science*, *25*, 720–727.

Purpose of the study: This study focused on the attention capture effects of eye contact and motion in our environment. Both eye contact and motion have been shown to capture attention in humans, but it is unclear if these aspects of the environment capture attention by the same process or different processes. The researchers of this study investigated this question by asking subjects to perform a target identification task within an array of four faces where eye contact and motion were manipulated. This study tested the hypothesis that eye contact and motion attract attention through the same process. Two experiments with slightly different procedures were used to test the hypothesis. The researchers predicted that if the same process is responsible for attention capture from both eye contact and motion, then the two experiments should yield the same results. However, if each of these factors captures attention in different ways, then different results will be found in the two experiments.

Method of the study: Subjects were asked to perform a task where they identified which target letter (*H* or *S*) appeared on the forehead of faces with either a direct gaze (eye contact) or an averted gaze (no eye contact). Four faces were shown in each display, two with direct gaze and two with averted gaze. Motion was included in the displays such that two of the faces changed gaze condition between the eye fixation screen (where 8's appeared on all foreheads) and the target screen (where letters appeared on the foreheads, one of which was the target letter). In Experiment 1, the gaze change occurred at the same time the letters appeared on the screen. However, in Experiment 2, the letters appeared 900 ms after the gaze change occurred. This timing difference allowed the researchers to test the primary hypothesis, because previous studies have shown that a delay between the cues affects eye gaze and motion attention capture in different ways. Thus, if one process is responsible for both types of attention capture, no difference in results should be seen in Experiments 1 and 2.

Results of the study: Accuracy (in the form of errors) and speed of target detection were analyzed in this study. In Experiment 1, performance was best (fastest and fewest errors) when the target appeared on the forehead of the face with a change to a direct gaze (i.e., eye contact). Thus, both eye contact and motion captured attention in Experiment 1. However, in Experiment 2, direct gaze showed better performance than averted gaze, but motion (i.e., change in gaze) reduced performance. See Figures 4.16 and 4.17 for the results of Experiments 1 and 2, respectively.

Conclusions of the study: The researchers had predicted that if the same process is responsible for attention capture by eye contact and motion, the results in Experiments 1 and 2 should be similar. However, although target detection performance was best in Experiment 1 with the direct gaze and motion condition, this result was not seen in Experiment 2 when the target appeared 900 ms after the motion occurred. Thus, the researchers' prediction was not supported. From these results, they concluded that direct eye contact and motion attract attention in different ways.

Figure 4.16 Results From Böckler et al.'s (2014) Experiment 1

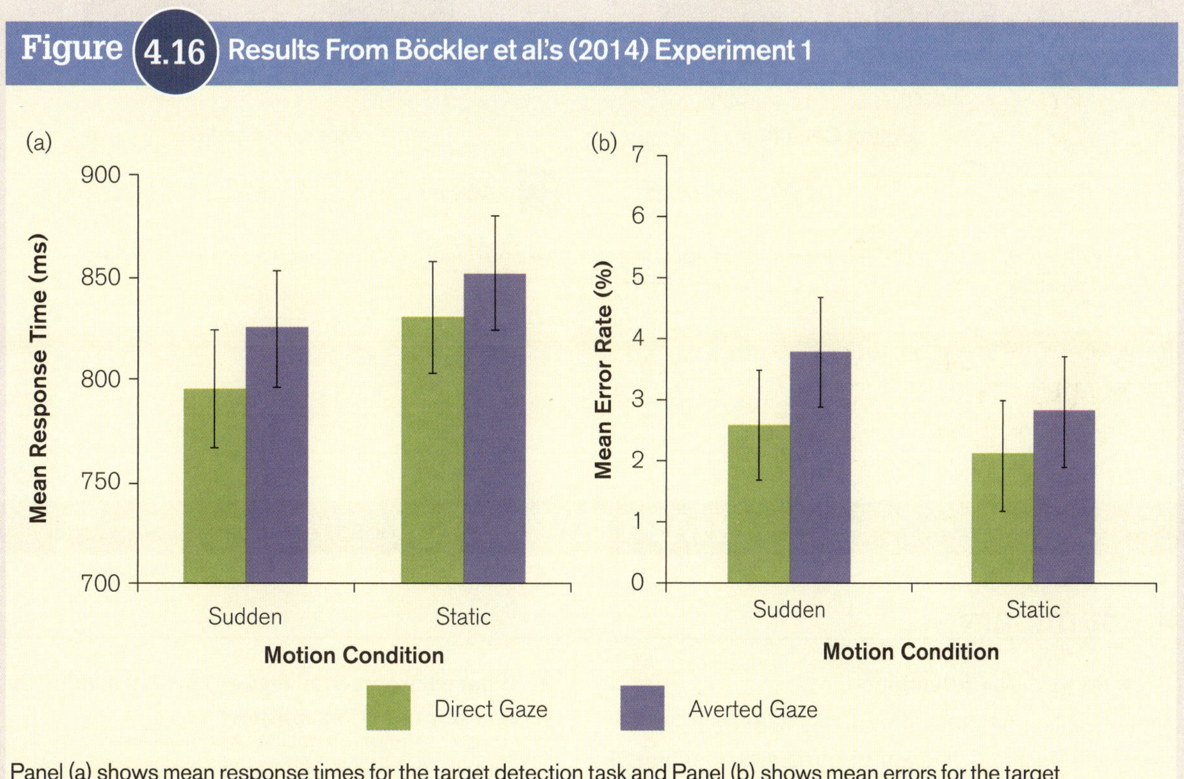

Panel (a) shows mean response times for the target detection task and Panel (b) shows mean errors for the target detection task.

SOURCE: Figure 2, Böckler, A., van der Wel, P. R. D., & Welsh, T. N. (2014). Catching eyes: Effects of social and nonsocial cues on attention capture. *Psychological Science, 25*, 720–727.

(Continued)

(Continued)

Figure 4.17 Results From Böckler et al.'s (2014) Experiment 2

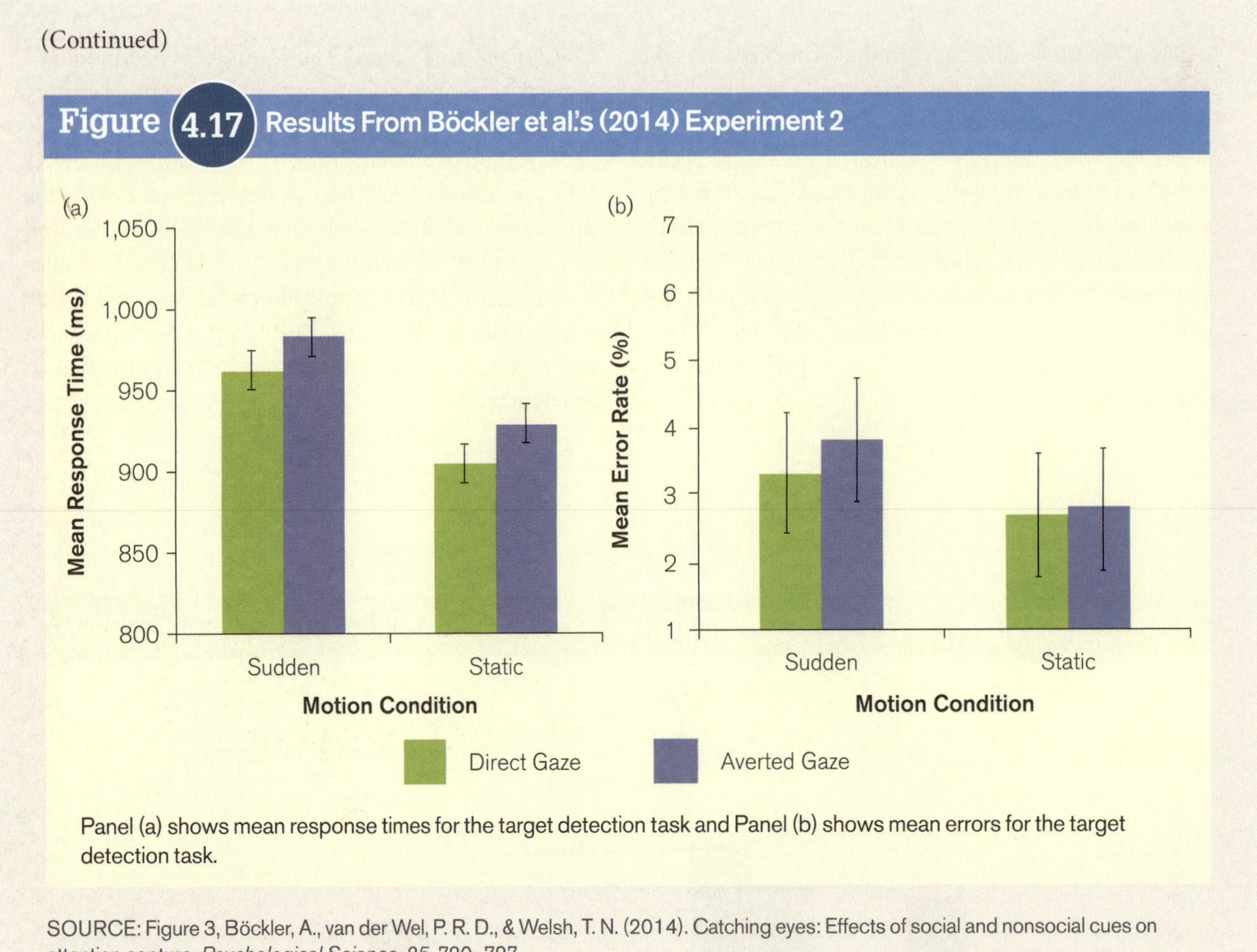

Panel (a) shows mean response times for the target detection task and Panel (b) shows mean errors for the target detection task.

SOURCE: Figure 3, Böckler, A., van der Wel, P. R. D., & Welsh, T. N. (2014). Catching eyes: Effects of social and nonsocial cues on attention capture. *Psychological Science, 25*, 720–727.

CHAPTER REVIEW

Summary

- **How do we define attention?**

  Attention can be difficult to define because it overlaps with many other cognitive processes. One proposed definition is the focus of our consciousness to the exclusion of other things.

- **What descriptions of attention have helped researchers study attention?**

  Attention has been described as a filter, a spotlight, a limited mental capacity, and as feature glue.

- **How do researchers study what someone is and is not paying attention to?**

  There are multiple methods described in this chapter. One task involves a target search to determine the ease of this task and the amount of attention it requires. Another method involves two tasks with interference on these tasks measured as someone performs them together versus separately.

- **What environmental factors have been found to influence our attention abilities?**

  The current limits on mental resources influence our attention abilities. Arousal states can affect the capacity of our mental resources. The difficulty of a task and our interest in a task can also affect our attention abilities.

- **How does our automatic processing affect what we pay attention to?**

  Automatic processing can interfere with an attentional task, as it does in the Stroop task. However, according to Treisman's model and Schneider and Shiffrin's model, automatic processing can also aid in cognitive tasks by either preparing our attention or requiring less attention as tasks become more automatic.

Chapter Quiz

1. Enter the letter for the description of attention next to its corresponding definition below.
   (a) Spotlight model
   (b) Feature-integration model
   (c) Filter model
   (d) Attenuation model
   ___ attention excludes irrelevant stimuli to allow one to focus on the relevant aspects of the environment
   ___ attention binds aspects of a scene together to identify objects
   ___ attention is the focus of consciousness and can be moved around in the environment
   ___ attention reduces the strength of irrelevant stimuli in the environment
2. Not noticing a change in the environment from moment to moment is called
   (a) selective attention.
   (b) inattentional blindness.
   (c) attention capture.
   (d) visual search.
3. In Treisman and Gelade's (1980) experiments on visual search for a target, the targets in the ____________ condition seemed to pop out of the displays.
   (a) single-feature
   (b) conjunction-feature
   (c) change blindness
   (d) color
4. In a study, subjects are asked to perform an arithmetic task while also attempting to remember lists of words for later recall. The researchers in this study compared the performance on the memory task with and without the accompanying arithmetic task to determine if the arithmetic task interferes with one's performance on the memory task. This study used the ____________ methodology to study attention abilities.
   (a) visual search
   (b) conjunction search
   (c) inattentional blindness
   (d) dual-task
5. Describe the similar aspects in Tresiman's feature-integration model and Schneider and Shiffrin's (1977) description of attention.
6. Suppose you were a researcher who wanted to study attention capture of warning signals in aircraft that occur when pilots are focused on another task (e.g., landing a plane). Describe how you might design such a study using methodologies described in this chapter.
7. Based on the work of Daniel Simons, explain how it is possible that you did not notice that a different person was now part of your conversation in the party scene described at the beginning of the chapter.
8. Explain how tasks that initially require controlled attention can become automatic.
9. Schneider and Shiffrin's (1977) experiments showed that when the targets and distractors were ____________, the task became automatic for the subjects.
   (a) of different types
   (b) of the same types
   (c) were all numbers
   (d) were all letters

Key Terms

Automatic processing 84
Cocktail party effect 72
Controlled processing 84
Dual-task method 76
Inattentional blindness (also change blindness) 81
Shadowing task 71
Simon effect 82
Stroop task 83

Stop and Think Answers

4.1. Attention is an important process for many cognitive tasks. Describe some ways that attention is important in the tasks you perform as a student.

Answers will vary, but some key aspects of attention involve focusing on a task, searching for an object in a scene, and having your attention captured by important things in the environment.

4.2. Describe how Treisman's attenuation model would explain how you can study with background music playing without it interfering with your task. How would this model describe your ability to hear your text alert on your phone without losing concentration in your studying?

The attenuation model suggests that the strength of less relevant stimuli (such as background music) is reduced as it passes through the filter such that less attention is paid to it. However, information does make it through, and stimuli that have a low threshold in the dictionary unit (like the important sound of your text alert) can capture attention.

4.3. Can you think of other ways to describe attention processes besides the filter metaphor?

Answers will vary, but some other ideas proposed are as a spotlight of consciousness and as glue to bind features.

4.4. What does it mean that attention is a "limited mental resource"?

This means that our available cognitive resources for paying attention have a particular level at any given moment such that if we divide them across tasks requiring attention, performance on the tasks can suffer.

4.5. Can you think of situations in your own life where attempting to complete multiple tasks at once showed the limits of your attention abilities?

Answers will vary.

4.6. The results of the Strayer and Johnston study showed that driving abilities are inhibited when subjects talked on the phone. What do these results mean for new laws requiring "hands free" cell phone use while driving?

Because the "hands free" and handheld cell phone groups both showed equally lowered performance in the study, these results suggest that requiring hands-free phone devices will not be sufficient to keep people from having lowered driving performance while talking on a cell phone.

4.7. Identify some features that are likely relevant for focusing attention on a particular object (e.g., a picture, a clock) in your current environment.

Answers will vary but could be features like size, shape, or color.

4.8. How do the two stages of the feature-integration model of attention differ?

The first stage is an automatic processing stage that does not require attention in identifying features in a scene. The second stage is a controlled processing stage requiring attention that binds features together to allow for object identification and scene understanding.

4.9. Imagine you are focusing your attention on a person in a crowd. For each of the three models of attention—filter model, spotlight model, feature-integration model—explain how this task would work.

The filter model suggests you filter out all the other people to focus on the relevant person. The spotlight model suggests you move your "spotlight" of attention around the crowd and then focus it on the relevant person once he or she is identified. The feature-integration model suggests that the features of the people in the crowd are automatically processed and you bind those features together with your attention to identify the individuals in the crowd to find the relevant person.

4.10. Can you think of any instances from your own life where the Simon effect impairs your performance on a task?

Answers will vary.

4.11. The Stroop task shows that once we have learned this skill well, reading is an automatic process. Can you think of any other cognitive processes you use that are likely automatic for you?

Answers will vary, but they will be well-practiced tasks like addition and multiplication or puzzle solving or game playing if one has a lot of experience with a particular puzzle or game (e.g., a video game).

4.12. The party scenario at the beginning of the chapter illustrated a simple example of change blindness (i.e., not noticing a change in the scene). Have you ever experienced change blindness in your environment? What factors contributed to your failure to notice the change?

Answers will vary.

4.13. In Stop and Think 4.11, you considered some tasks that were automatic for you. How long (i.e., how much practice) did it take for you to go from controlled processing to automatic processing in

these tasks? Is that length of time comparable to the time it took Shiffrin and Schneider's (1977) subjects to move to automatic processing in the target detection task? Why or why not?**

Answers will vary.

4.14. In what way is a cognitive system designed to transfer tasks from controlled to automatic processing adaptive?

This is a more efficient system because more mental resources are available for controlled tasks when automatic processes take over for other tasks.

4.15. In what way is automaticity involved in Logan's instance theory?

Logan suggested that after many experiences/ instances with a task, the information about that task is retrieved automatically when one is placed in the task context.

Student Study Site

Sharpen your skills with SAGE edge at **edge.sagepub.com/mcbridecp**

SAGE edge for students provides a personalized approach to help you accomplish your coursework goals in an easy-to-use learning environment.

Go to edge.sagepub.com/mcbridecp for additional exercises and web resources. Select Chapter 4, Attention, for chapter-specific resources. All of the links listed in the margins of this chapter are accessible via this site.

Bruno Boissonnet/Photo Researchers, Inc.

Memory Structures and Processes

Questions to Consider

- Is memory a process, a structure, or a system?
- How many types of memories are there?
- Are there differences in the ways we store and retrieve memories based on how old the memories are?
- What kind of memory helps us to focus on a task?
- How does our memory influence us unintentionally?
- What are the limits of our memory?

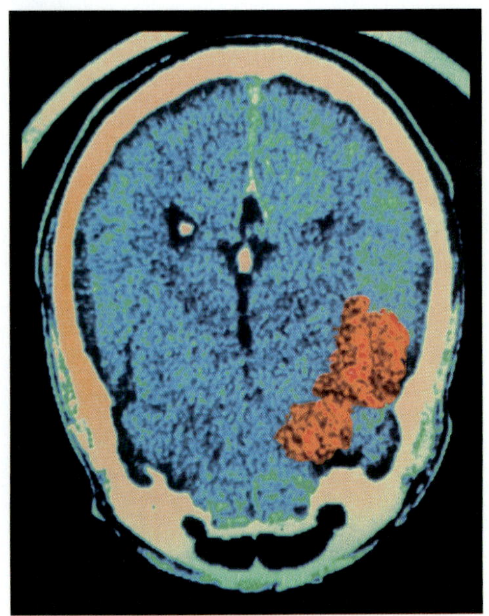

Airelle-Joubert/Science Source

Photo 5.1 Brain with encephalitis.

Introduction: The Pervasiveness of Memory

Memory is pervasive. It is important for so many things we do in our everyday lives that it is difficult to think of something humans do that doesn't involve memory. To better understand its importance, imagine trying to do your everyday tasks without memory. When you first wake up in the morning you know whether you need to jump out of bed and hurry to get ready to leave or whether you can lounge in bed for a while because you remember what you have to do that day and what time your first task of the day begins. Without memory, you would not know what you needed to do that day. In fact, you would not know who you are, where you are, or what you are supposed to be doing at any given moment. It would be like waking up disoriented every minute.

There are, in fact, individuals who must live their lives without the aid of certain kinds of memory. An extreme case is the story of Clive Wearing, a man in the United Kingdom who suffered a brain injury due to an illness from encephalitis (see Photo 5.1). From the illness, the area of his brain known as the hippocampus and the surrounding brain tissue were damaged. The hippocampus is a brain structure that is very important in storing and retrieving memories. Due to this damage, Clive lost the ability to know what was going on around him for more than about a minute at a time. He described his life as if he were just waking up every moment. He has to continuously figure out what is going on around him. Imagine having the experience of suddenly becoming consciously aware of yourself and your surroundings, but everyone else around you is acting normally and not paying any attention to your wakening. It is like waking up from being in a coma for many years and yet no one is standing around you explaining what has happened. You have to try to figure it out for yourself with no context or knowledge of what has occurred in the previous few moments. Imagine how frustrating this would be! Interestingly, Clive retains his musical abilities (e.g., playing the piano), at which he was an expert before his illness. This illustrates one of the important differences in types of memories: those about episodes in one's life, known as episodic memories, and those about skills we have developed over time, known as procedural memories. We talk more about each of these types of memories in this chapter, in addition to other types of memory such as memory for general knowledge and facts (semantic memories), memory about one's self (autobiographical memory), and memory for tasks we intend to perform in the future (prospective memory). Memory deficits, including amnesia, are discussed further in Chapter 6.

What Is a Memory?

Crash Course: Memory

Living Without Memory

Memory as Structure or Process

Memory can be thought of in many different ways. As described in Chapter 1, Aristotle thought of memory as similar to a wax tablet that can be molded, melted, and remolded over time. Memory can also be thought of as a filing system for information organized in different ways (e.g., all the animals are stored together, all the colors are stored together), depending on how it is encoded and how it is retrieved. Both of these ideas

How Memory Works

view memory as a "thing," as a storage unit or structure where information is held. However, memory can also be thought of as a collection of interdependent processes. In other words, rather than thinking of memory as a thing, memory is thought of more as "remembering," and researchers who adhere to this view of memory focus more on how and when remembering occurs, rather than as a storage structure or unit. Structure and process views of memory have both been important in how researchers studied memory, and you will see examples of both views as we consider some of the types of memory researchers have investigated in this chapter.

Encoding, Storage, and Retrieval

Three important processes in memory are encoding, storage, and retrieval. **Encoding** is the process by which information enters our memory. It is sometimes a fairly active process, such as you reading this text or quizzing yourself to try to remember the material you are leaning in a course. It can also be a less active process when information is encoded without one intending to remember it. However, in order for information to be encoded, attention to the information is often required (see Chapter 4). **Storage** is the process by which information is kept in memory. Connecting with one's preexisting knowledge seems to be important in the retrieval process, as information seems to be stored with related concepts (see Figure 5.1). However, there is no single place in the brain where an individual memory is kept. Instead, the storage of memories seems to be distributed across multiple brain areas. Specific brain areas (e.g., the hippocampus) are involved in pulling the pieces of a memory back together when it is retrieved. Like encoding, the **retrieval** process can be intentional, such as when you attempt to remember what you had for breakfast last Thursday or the name of the instructor of your course, or unintentional, such as when you suddenly remember the correct answer to an exam question at 3:00 a.m. the day after you took your exam. Figure 5.1 summarizes the processes of encoding, storage, and retrieval.

How Our Brains Make Memories

Cognitive neuroscience studies show that these three processes are controlled by different brain areas (Moscovitch, Chein, Talmi, & Cohn, 2007). Let's consider the process of encoding, storing, and retrieving a scene from my office that is occurring as I type: my dog, Daphne, lying in her bed. Encoding of the visual information of the scene takes place initially in my visual cortex in the occipital lobe. From there, the visual information is processed in my medial temporal lobe, where the visual information binds to other sensory information from other areas of the cortex (e.g., the sound of her snoring as she sleeps, the concept knowledge I have about dogs). The binding of the information stored in these different cortical areas will aid in putting those pieces back together later when I want to remember the scene. When I turn back around to my computer and attempt to recall the scene of Daphne in my mind, the area of my visual cortex where the visual information of that memory is stored becomes active, along with the sound of her snoring stored in the temporal cortex that this information was bound to when it was stored. With help from the medial temporal lobe area (especially the hippocampus) these different areas that were bound together when the memory was stored will each become reactivated to allow me to retrieve the encoded memory.

Information Processing Model

Modal Model of Memory

In addition to the descriptions of memory we have already discussed, memory has also been classified according to duration: sensory memories, short-term memories, and long-term memories that describe very brief memories, fairly brief memories, and

Encoding: the process of inputting information into memory

Storage: the process of storing information in memory

Retrieval: the process of outputting information from memory

Figure 5.1 Encoding, Storage, and Retrieval

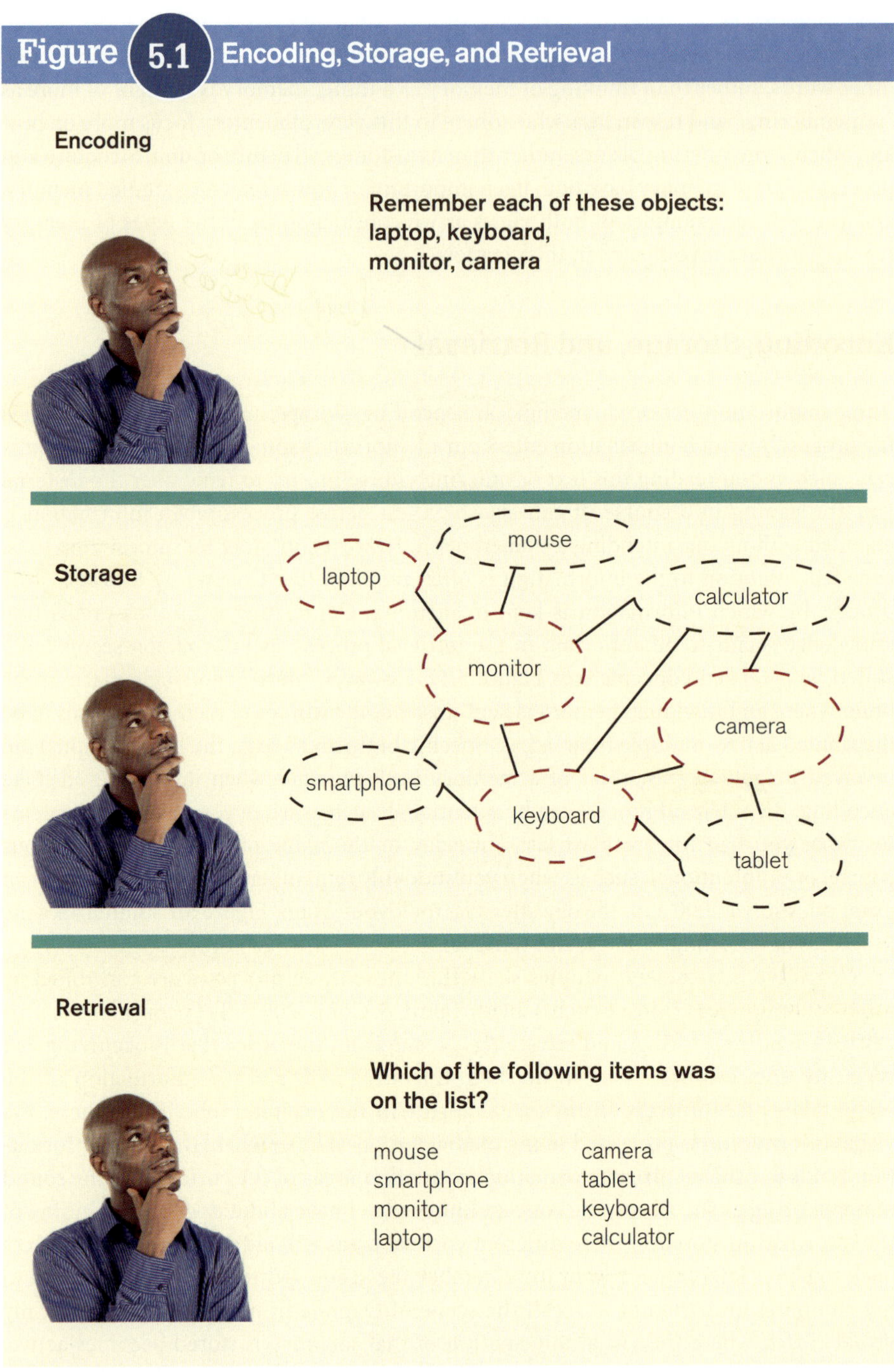

Photo from BananaStock/BananaStock/Thinkstock

longer-held memories, respectively. An early model of memory known as the modal model of memory (Atkinson & Shiffrin, 1968) describes these types of memories along with hypothetical structures that hold memories for different lengths of time. Figure 5.2 illustrates the modal model of memory with information coming in through our senses into sensory memory, being passed on to short-term memory when attention is given to the information, and finally being stored in long-term memory if the information is processed in connection with other knowledge already stored there. Each of these three types of memories is described, along with the methods researchers have used to study them.

Figure 5.2 Atkinson and Shiffrin's (1968) Modal Model of Memory

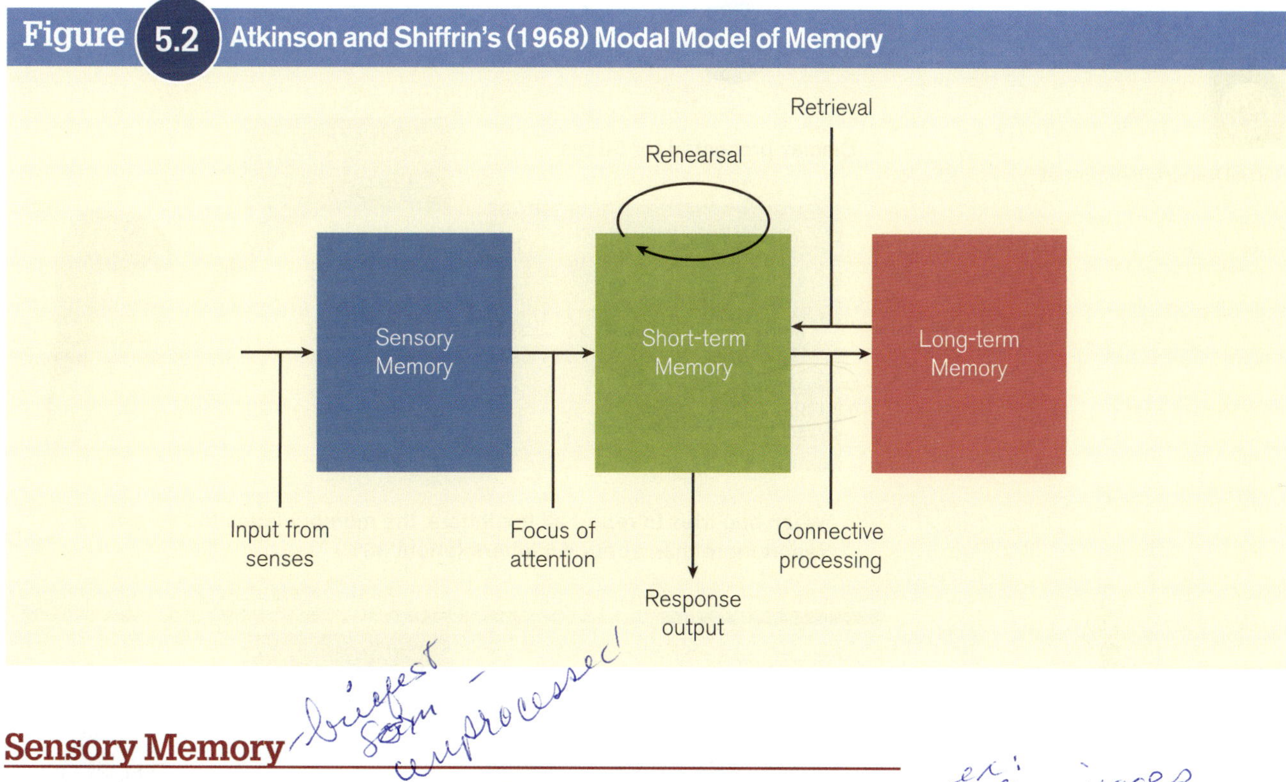

Sensory Memory

Sensory memory is the briefest form of memory. It includes memories of raw, unprocessed sensory information. If you focus your eyes on a bright scene (e.g., looking out the window) and then close your eyes, you will see a brief afterimage of the scene that fades very quickly. This is a sensory memory. It is a visual representation of the scene that exists in its sensory form and is lost from memory within a second or two. Sensory memories can be stored for very brief periods of time for each of our senses, but these memories have been very difficult for researchers to measure because of their brief duration. These memories are short enough that subjects in research studies typically do not have time to report their retrieval from sensory memory before the memory has disappeared. How then do we know about the capacity and duration of these memories?

Stop and Think

5.1. Describe the three primary processes of memory.

5.2. List the three hypothetical storage structures of memory from the shortest to the longest storage.

5.3. Consider different ways in which you encode information you learn in class (e.g., visually, aurally). How effective do you think each of these encoding processes is for storing information in long-term memory?

One of the first studies of visual sensory memory (also known as iconic memory) to help answer this question was conducted by George Sperling (1960). To allow subjects in his study to report enough of the memory to measure sensory memory capacity and duration, he asked them to report on a portion of what was presented to them. This method is known as the **partial-report method** because subjects are only asked for a partial report of what was presented. Figure 5.3 illustrates how the method was used in Sperling's study. In this study, subjects were presented with arrays of letters for a very brief time (only 50 ms in one experiment) and then asked to report just one row of letters according to a tone (low for first row, medium for middle row, and high for top row). Based on how many letters subjects could report for that one row, he estimated how many they would have been able to report from the whole array if there had been enough time to do so before they faded from sensory memory. Thus, if

Sensory memory: the very short-term memory storage of unprocessed sensory

Partial-report method: a research procedure where subjects are asked to report only a portion of the information presented

Partial Report Experiment

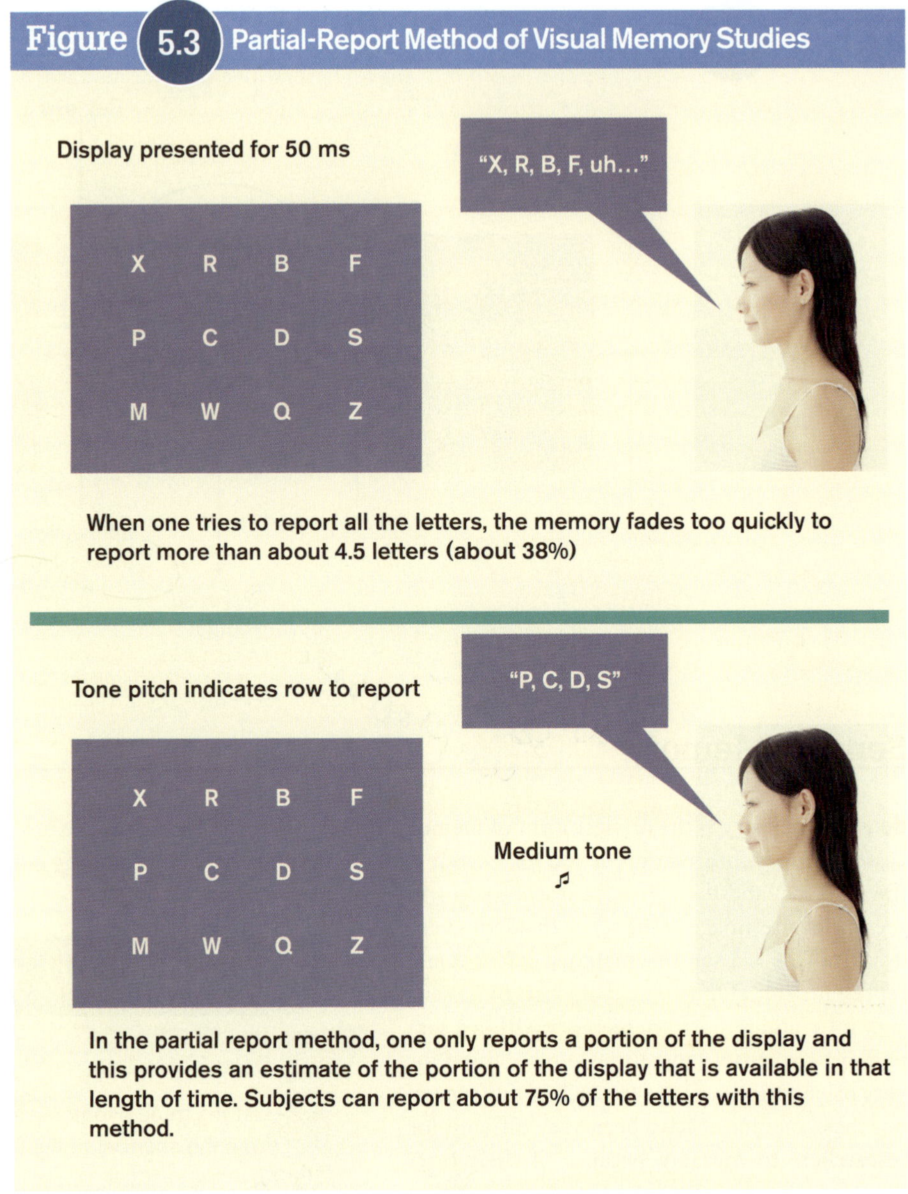
Display presented for 50 ms
"X, R, B, F, uh..."
X R B F
P C D S
M W Q Z
When one tries to report all the letters, the memory fades too quickly to report more than about 4.5 letters (about 38%)
Tone pitch indicates row to report
"P, C, D, S"
X R B F
P C D S
M W Q Z
Medium tone
In the partial report method, one only reports a portion of the display and this provides an estimate of the portion of the display that is available in that length of time. Subjects can report about 75% of the letters with this method.

Figure 5.3 Partial-Report Method of Visual Memory Studies

SOURCE: Based on Sperling's (1960) study design. Photo from Digital Vision/Digital Vision/Thinkstock

subjects could report an average of three of the four letters in the row, then 75 percent (3/4) of the letters were available to them at the time they were asked to report them. With no delay between the end of the display and the instruction tone, subjects could remember and report an average of about 75 percent of the letters in the row they were asked to report. When asked to report all the letters (not just one row), subjects could only accurately report about four letters on average regardless of how many letters they were shown (e.g., if shown twelve letters, this is only about 33 percent of the letters in the whole array). With the partial-report method, Sperling showed that the capacity of the visual sensory memory is fairly large and much larger than had been measured previously. In subsequent experiments, Sperling systematically delayed the presentation of the tone to measure the duration of sensory memories. In these experiments, he learned that visual sensory memories are held for about one second. After this length of time, memory performance from a partial report declines to the level equal to the performance seen when subjects were asked to report the whole array (about four letters).

After the Sperling (1960) study showed that visual sensory memories last about one second, other researchers examined the duration of sensory memory for nonvisual senses. For example, studies using the partial-report method that focused on auditory sensory memory (also known as echoic memory) reported that these memories could last as long as four seconds (e.g., Darwin, Turvey, & Crowder, 1974). Studies of tactile sensory memory (e.g., Sinclair & Burton, 1996) suggest that these memories last as long as five seconds. However, from the researcher's perspective, it can be difficult to determine if subjects are reporting sensory memories involving unprocessed sensory stimulation or short-term memories that have been processed to some degree. In other words, where does sensory memory end and short-term memory begin? Because of this issue, it is unclear if the longer estimates for auditory and tactile sensory memory reflect sensory or short-term memories. In addition, the majority of research in sensory memory has focused on visual and auditory senses. Thus, little is known about sensory memory for the other senses.

More recently, researchers have attempted to better understand how information is lost from sensory memory. One proposal is that there are two stages of sensory memory storage of different durations (Cowan, 1988). In the first stage, the raw, unprocessed perceptual information is stored, and in the second stage, the perceptual information connects with information stored in long-term memory that allows for interpretation of the stimuli. This description of sensory memory can explain the difference in results across the different sensory modalities: The duration of one second for visual sensory memory reported by Sperling (1960) represents the first stage of sensory memory, whereas the longer durations reported for auditory and tactile sensory memory represent the second stage of sensory memory.

Stop and Think

5.4. Explain how the partial-report method allows researchers to more accurately estimate the capacity of sensory memory than a whole-report method.

5.5. According to the research in this area, what is the duration of sensory memories?

5.6. Research in sensory memory for senses other than vision and audition is scarce. Imagine that you are researching olfactory (sense of smell) sensory memory to contribute to the gap in the research in this area. Describe a study you might design using the partial-report method to study olfactory sensory memory. What are some of the limitations of this method for this type of sensory memory?

Recent research in cognitive neuroscience has been providing new information about how sensory memory operates. For example, studies by Lu, Williamson, and Kaufman (1992a, 1992b) have shown that the decay of auditory sensory memory corresponds to decay in activity in specific areas of the brain responsible for processing auditory information (e.g., auditory cortex). Lu, Neuse, Madigan, and Dosher (2005) have also shown that visual sensory memories in individuals with mild cognitive impairments (such as those shown by individuals with early stage Alzheimer's disease) decay faster than comparison individuals without these impairments. These studies suggest that there may be a link between the experience of a sensory memory and specific neural activity. Thus, research in sensory memory using methods from neuroscience is providing important new information about how these memories are formed and experienced and how to define a sensory memory.

Short-Term Memory (STM)

What were you just thinking about before you started reading this section? This memory is probably one stored in what is known as your short-term memory. **Short-term**

Short-term memory: the short-term storage of memory with minimal processing that is forgotten quickly without elaborative processing

memory (STM) is an intermediate memory storage that begins processing of perceptual information transferred from sensory memory. Information that becomes the focus of attention moves from sensory memory to STM. Clive Wearing, the amnesic described in the introductory section of this chapter, can hold memories in his STM for a short time, but once his attention moves on, those memories are lost. The term *working memory* is also used to describe the system that controls the processing and activation of the information held in STM (Nairne & Neath, 2013). We discuss the working-memory system later in this chapter because it was not a part of the original modal model of memory shown in Figure 5.2 and has its own model and research support.

Visual Short-Term Memory

Information in STM can be held for a short time if it remains in the focus of attention (e.g., by rehearsing the information), but in order to store information for a longer period of time, the information must be transferred to long-term memory (e.g., by connecting the information to other information already stored in long-term memory). Processing of the information also affects the capacity of STM. When information is organized according to its meaning, more items can be stored in STM.

Consider this example: Look at the following numbers for a minute or so. Then close your eyes and try to recall them in order:

Memory Span Activity

1 9 9 0 4 1 1 9 1 1 1 4 9 2 2 0 1 5

How many could you remember? Most people can remember about five to nine items stored in STM. Now, let's try that again. This time when you look at the numbers, try to see if you can group them in some meaningful ways (e.g., as years or important numbers to call on your phone). Close your eyes and try to recall the numbers again. If you did not notice some meaningful organization the first time you studied them, you should have been able to increase your recall on the second try. In fact, if you were able to find important meaning in all of the numbers, you may have remembered all eighteen of them. This organizational processing likely more than doubled your initial recall level. The process of organizing information into fewer meaningful units is called **chunking**. You may have chunked the numbers together as 1990, 411, 911, 1492, 2015, leaving you with only five items to remember.

Chunking Demonstration

Capacity of STM

This example illustrates the capacity of STM for most people: about five to nine items. This was famously shown by Miller (1956) in a study titled "The Magical Number Seven, Plus or Minus Two" that represents the average capacity of STM. Chunking works with other types of information as well. Letters can be grouped as words and words can be grouped as sentences to hold more items in STM. Miller measured STM capacity in a particular way. His seven-plus-or-minus-two number is based on the average number of items his subjects could recall accurately in order 50 percent of the time. This is known as the span of STM and has been used by numerous researchers to measure the capacity of STM for different types of information. There are some limits on the span of STM based on the type of information being stored, however. For example, span is smaller for words with more syllables (e.g., *hippopotamus*) than for words with fewer syllables (e.g., *horse*) (Simon, 1974). More recent research also suggests that STM span may be closer to three to five chunks in some cases and that limits on our attention (i.e., information in our attentional focus at a given time) are linked to the number of chunks that can be successfully stored in STM (Cowan, 2001). Thus, the capacity of STM can depend on factors like the type of information and our attentional limits.

Short-Term Memory Experiment

Chunking: a process of organizing information that allows more items to be stored in memory

Duration of STM

In fact, our attention limits the duration of STM storage as well. Information enters STM when we focus our attention on specific information in our sensory memory. It disappears from STM when our attention moves on to the next thing we are thinking about. Thus, memories are held in STM for as long as our attention lasts. If we intentionally hold information in our focus of attention for a longer than usual period of time, we can increase how long that information stays in STM. This typically occurs through active rehearsal, which means repeating the information within our mind. This is represented by the curved arrow in Figure 5.2, showing that information can be recycled in STM through rehearsal. To illustrate this, suppose that you have stopped at the store to get a few items on a list you have stored on your phone. Your phone's battery is dying so you take a quick glance at the list containing soda, chips, milk, bread, and cereal just before your phone's battery dies. To remember the items as you go through the store, you may say the list to yourself (maybe just in your head, maybe not) over and over until you have all of the items in your basket. Then you can focus on paying for the groceries and retrieving the PIN of your ATM card. Once you focus on your payment, the list will likely be lost from STM, but because you have already gotten your items, the rehearsal has served its purpose.

Without rehearsal, the duration of STM is set by the typical time your attention stays focused on the information. But this attention can be given to information in degrees (as anyone who has worked on two tasks at once can attest). Thus, information is lost from STM gradually, rather than instantaneously. This was shown using a method originally developed by J. Brown (1958) and Peterson and Peterson (1959). In this method (see Figure 5.4), subjects are asked to remember a short sequence of letters, such as GRX. Meaningless strings of letters are used to prevent meaningful processing that might transfer the information to long-term memory. After hearing the letters, subjects are asked to complete a verbal interference task that typically involves counting down from a starting number (such as 576) by threes (e.g., 573, 570, 567). Counting is done for a variable amount of time to manipulate the delay time for recalling the letters. Peterson and Peterson (1959) had subjects count for three to eighteen seconds. A different string of letters was presented on each trial and then subjects counted for a set period of time within this range. They were then asked to recall the letters. Recall rates declined to near zero for delays of eighteen seconds, suggesting that information in STM is forgotten within this time frame. Figure 5.4 shows the results of the study across this range of delays.

Peterson and Peterson (1959) suggested that information decays from STM within eighteen seconds, as shown at the top of Figure 5.5. However, later studies have shown that another factor is more likely the cause of forgetting from STM: interference. When new information replaces old information in a memory store, this is known as **retroactive interference**. This occurs when new information effectively kicks old information out of STM (see middle of Figure 5.5). Numerous studies have shown that retroactive interference occurs for information stored in STM. In fact, Waugh and Norman (1965) showed that the counting task in the Peterson and Peterson (1959) study likely interfered with the letter strings stored in STM causing them to be forgotten. This is likely due to the way information is stored in STM. Encoding makes use of the different features of information (verbal, visual, meaning) to store that information in STM, but verbal features seem to be most important. Many studies have shown that subjects make more errors in STM retrieval based on similar verbal information than on other features of the information (e.g., confusing BAKE and RAKE from a list of words) (e.g., Conrad, 1964; Hanson, 1990; Healy, 1974) and show higher recall for information that has a verbal feature than for information that does not have a verbal feature (e.g., Zhang & Simon, 1985). However, there is also evidence that visual and semantic (i.e., meaning-based,

Retroactive interference: when new information interferes with the storage or retrieval of old information

Figure 5.4 STM Studies

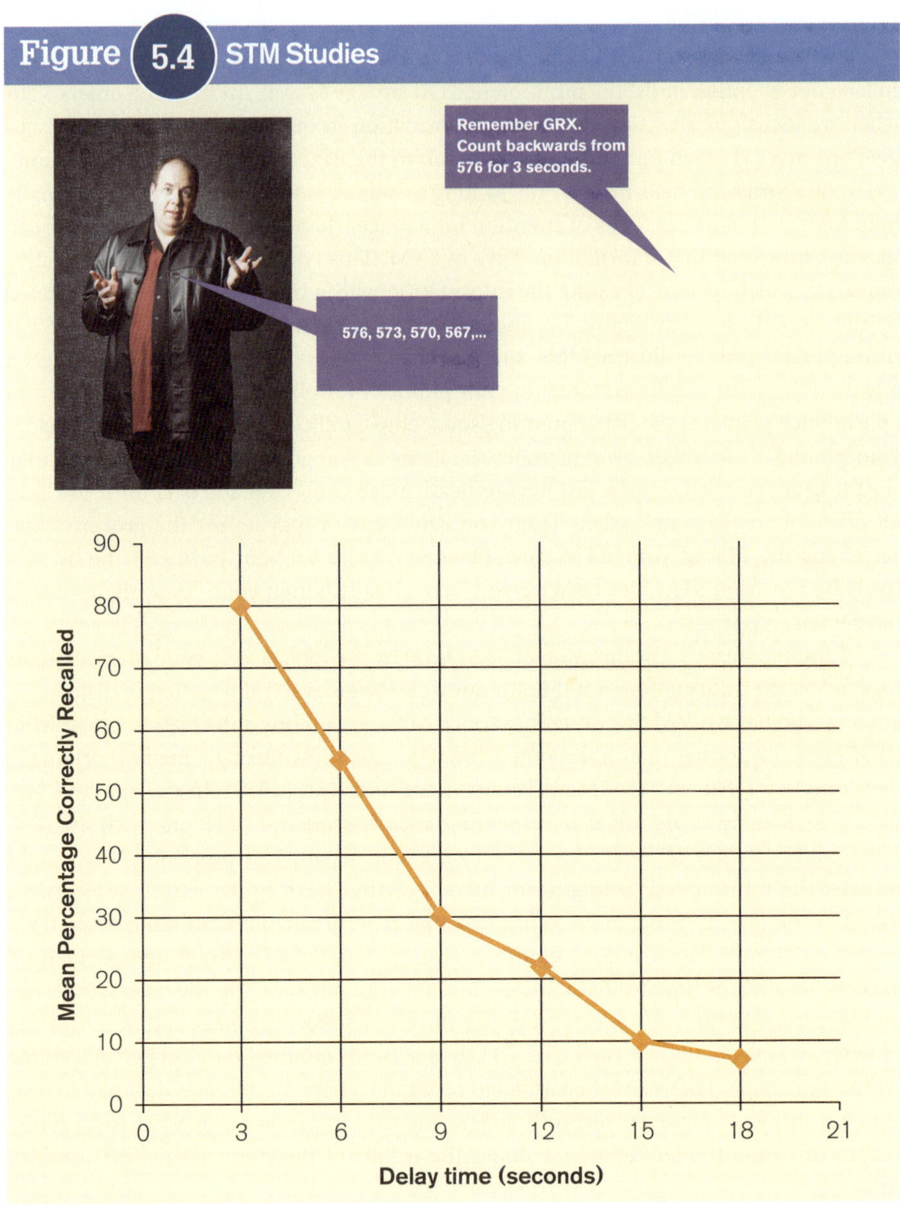

SOURCE: From Peterson & Peterson (1959), Experiment 1. Photo from Jupiterimages/Photos.com/Thinkstock

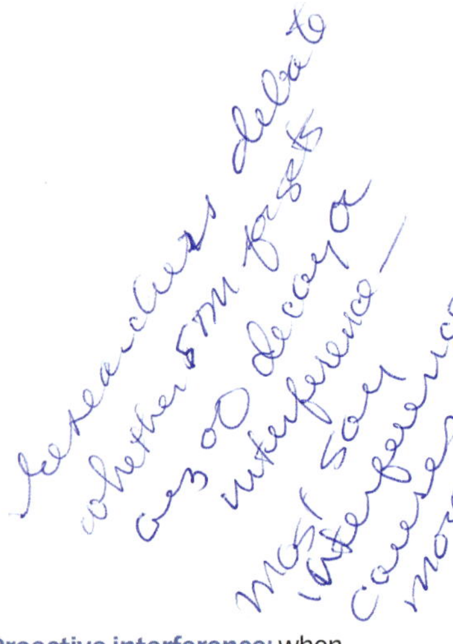

such as the connection between the items RAKE, LEAVES, and AUTUMN) features are also stored in STM (Brooks, 1968; Wickens, 1970). Feature coding in STM is discussed further in the section on working memory later in this chapter.

Proactive interference has also been shown to cause forgetting from STM (see bottom of Figure 5.5). This type of interference occurs when the old information already stored in STM keeps new information from being stored. Keppel and Underwood (1962) showed that in the Peterson and Peterson (1959) study, regardless of delay to recall, letter strings studied first had an advantage over letter strings studied later. This result suggests that proactive interference occurred such that early items in the list kept new information from being fully stored in STM, giving the early list items an advantage.

Proactive interference: when old information interferes with the storage or retrieval of new information

Today, researchers still debate the cause of forgetting from STM: decay or interference. Nairne and Neath (2013) suggest evidence for both processes to some extent with decay responsible for a small amount of forgetting and interference responsible for

Figure 5.5 Decay Versus Interference

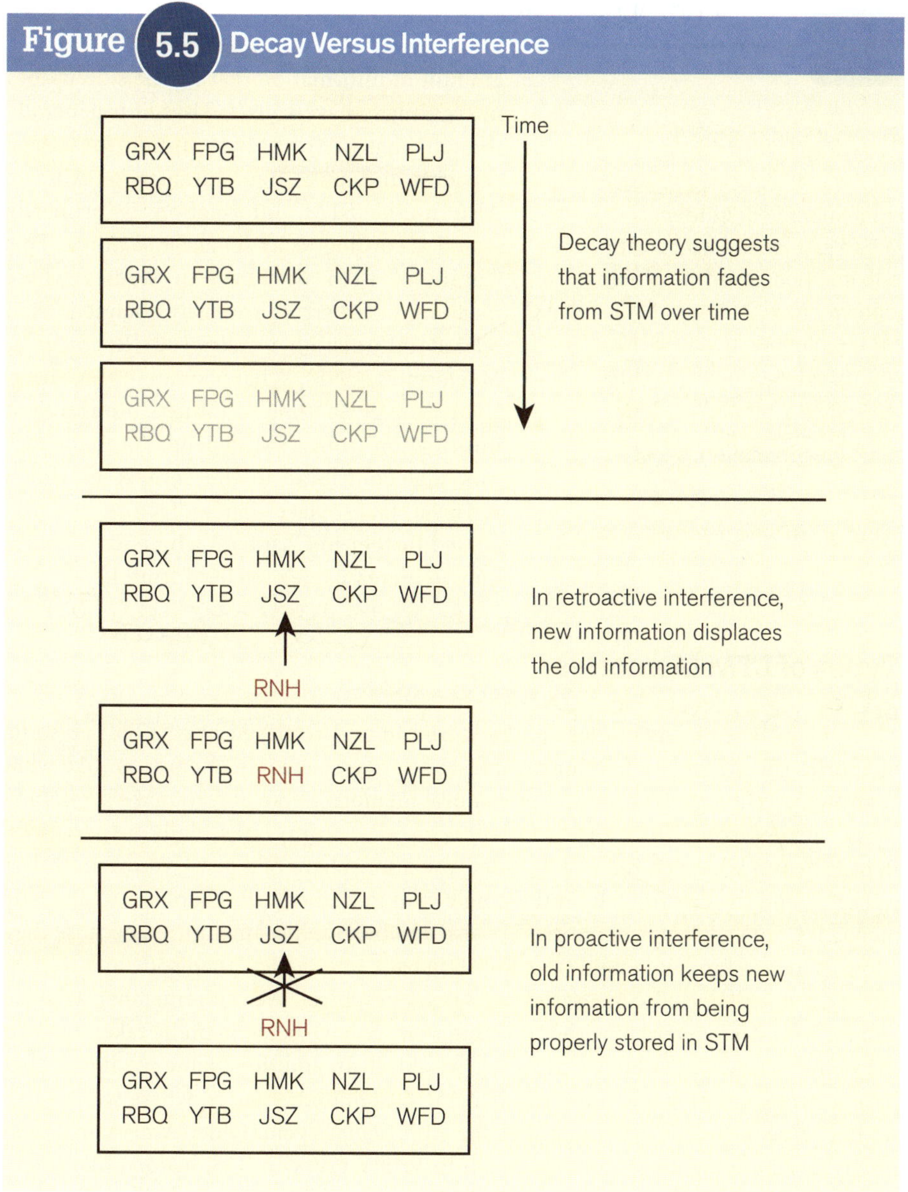

most of the forgetting that occurs. They also suggest that interference comes in the form of temporal confusion: In order to recall items from a list just presented, you have to remember that it was on the most recent list and not on a list further in the past. Some studies (e.g., Neath & Knoedler, 1994; Turvey, Brick, & Osborn, 1970) have shown that changing the delay during the task can either decrease or increase recall, depending on whether the change in delay makes the items less or more temporally distinctive (Nairne & Neath, 2013). Thus, the cause of forgetting from STM is a topic still under investigation.

Long-Term Memory (LTM)

What did you have for breakfast yesterday? If you can recall this information, it is likely stored in your **long-term memory** (LTM). Unlike sensory and short-term memory, LTM appears to be an unlimited store of information. Studies (e.g., Bahrick,

Long-term memory: long-term (i.e., lifetime) storage of memory after some elaborative processing has occurred

Stop and Think

5.7. What is the capacity of STM? What can one do to increase this capacity?

5.8. Suppose you were trying to remember your student nine-digit ID number that you had just looked up on your web account in order to give to someone over the phone. Your cell signal is not very good where your computer is located so you need to hold the number in your STM until you can make the call and report your number. How would you accomplish this task using your STM?

5.9. What is the most likely cause when information is lost from STM?

5.10. Describe some situations in your life in which you rely on your STM.

1984) have shown that not only can we store information across our lifetimes in LTM, the amount of information that can be stored does not appear to have a limit. Thus, it is generally thought that LTM has both unlimited storage capacity and unlimited duration of storage. Also unlike STM, information is primarily stored according to its semantic features. This feature of LTM is shown in studies where meaning-based errors are easily obtained when related information is retrieved (Roediger & McDermott, 1995). What one can retrieve from LTM at a given time *is* limited. Retrieval of information from LTM depends on many factors that contribute to the context in which retrieval takes place. These factors are discussed further in Chapter 6 where we consider how to increase one's retrieval from LTM.

Types of LTM Memories

Episodic Memory Experiment

Three main types of memories can be stored in and retrieved from LTM: episodic memories (like what you had for breakfast yesterday), semantic memories (like what cognitive psychology means), and procedural memories (like how to make scrambled eggs). An **episodic memory** involves episodes from one's daily experiences. Remembering what you did last Tuesday, the atmosphere of a party you went to last weekend, and the day you fell off the jungle gym in elementary school are all episodic memories. Some episodic memories are also autobiographical memories, because they allow us to do a kind of mental time traveling back to a particular episode in our lives. However, not all episodic memories are autobiographical. We can remember what we had for breakfast yesterday without feeling as if we have been mentally taken back to the point in time yesterday when we ate breakfast. In addition, some memories that have a strong emotional content can become flashbulb memories, where we feel like we have frozen time in our memories for a particular event. Older Americans often report flashbulb memories for significant historical events in U.S. history, like where they were when they heard that President Kennedy had been shot and killed. You may have a flashbulb memory for when you heard about a significant event in your country's history (e.g., the Boston Marathon terrorist bombings in 2013, the 2011 earthquake in Japan, or the 2005 London bus and Underground bombings). Although flashbulb memories seem very accurate to us, studies have shown that they can be as inaccurate as other episodic memories (Talarico & Rubin, 2003). Thus, even flashbulb and autobiographical memories can contain errors. Memory errors are discussed further in Chapter 7.

A **semantic memory** involves general knowledge we have but does not contain information about the time and place we learned that knowledge. You may know that Earth is the third closest planet to the sun, but you probably do not remember the day and place you learned that fact. Semantic memories contribute to many of our other cognitive abilities such as language (see Chapter 9) and concept formation (see Chapter 10). They also seem to be important in the formation of some types of false memories (see Chapter 7). The key difference between episodic and semantic memories is that episodic memories contain contextual information (e.g., time, place, mood) about the formation of the memory, whereas semantic memories do not contain this contextual information.

Episodic memory: memory for a specific episode or experience in one's life

Semantic memory: memory for facts or knowledge

A **procedural memory** involves "how to" instructions for skills and tasks. Knowing how to ride a bike or drive a car involves procedural memories once that skill is learned and can be performed somewhat automatically. These memories can be retrieved without us even intending to remember anything. Our abilities just seem to "flow" as we perform a task we know how to do, without much effort in retrieving the procedural steps. In fact, even amnesic individuals who lack the ability to intentionally retrieve episodic and semantic memories show retrieval of procedural memories (Warrington & Weiskrantz, 1970). For example, Clive Wearing, described in the introduction to this chapter, lost the ability to retrieve episodic and semantic memories (e.g., he could not remember where he was or why he was there), but he could still play the piano because his procedural memories could still be retrieved. We further discuss procedural memory later in this chapter and describe how it may be different from other types of memory at a neuropsychological level in Chapter 7.

Stop and Think

5.11. In what ways does LTM differ from STM?

5.12. Describe a memory of your own that fits each of the three types of LTM memory described in the previous section.

5.13. Can you think of a memory of your own that you would describe as a flashbulb memory? How confident are you that your memory for this event is accurate?

Brain function supports the distinction between these types of memory (Moscovitch et al., 2007). As described earlier in this chapter, episodic memories (such as the scene of my dog, Daphne, lying in my office) are retrieved using the medial temporal lobe (MTL) areas, including the hippocampus, to pull back together the perceptual pieces of the memory from the cortical areas in which they are stored. However, semantic memory retrieval also relies on the MTL area, but the area activated by knowledge retrieval can depend on the type of knowledge being retrieved. Information seems to be stored in the area related to its use. For example, retrieval of motor information (e.g., a dog can run) will activate areas near the visual cortex areas that detect motion in the environment. The prefrontal cortex also seems to be more involved in retrieval of semantic than episodic memories. Procedural memories are thought to be retrieved using a different memory system altogether due to the abilities amnesics with MTL damage show in retrieving these types of memories. H. M., described in a famous case study in Chapter 2, was able to show improvement on procedural skills, even though he had no episodic memory for performing the tasks related to those skills in the past. Instead, procedural memories rely on the basal ganglia and its connections to the frontal lobe for retrieval.

n-Back Memory Test

The Working-Memory (WM) System

The description of the structure of memory as storage units based on the duration of storage that we have discussed so far in this chapter is one way of describing memory. However, there are other approaches to describing memory. For example, some (e.g., Squire, 2004) have described memory as a set of systems responsible for the encoding, storage, and retrieval of information. **Working memory** is one system that has been proposed for the control of memories that one encodes in, stores in, and retrieves from STM. You can think of STM as a fairly passive storage unit for information held over a short period of time. Working memory can be thought of as the system that controls the flow of information in and out of STM, keeping important information active in STM when it is needed and using the information to control the output from STM. In other words, the term *working memory* describes the system that controls the memories we are currently "working on" or "operating on" in our minds. As an example of the role of working memory in our lives, consider this scenario: You are biking down a busy

Working Memory: Theories, Models, and Controversies

Procedural memory: memory for a skill or procedure

Working memory: processing a unit of information that is the current focus of attention

Photo 5.2 The working-memory system controls our memories over the short term and our current focus of attention to allow us to perform complex tasks.

walking path through your town. As you approach an intersection of the path and a busy street, you see another biker approaching from the opposite direction. There is also a person in front of you walking a dog that is on a leash but is rambunctious and veering across the path in an unpredictable manner. You also hear a nearby siren from the street you are approaching, but you do not see an emergency vehicle in the portion of the street you can see. To successfully navigate this scene, you need to be able to briefly store each piece of relevant information by focusing your attention on different parts of the scene and then processing the information such that you can anticipate where objects will be as you proceed on your bike. In this scenario, your working memory is controlling the input of visual and auditory information, coordinating that information to help you decide which way to steer your bike and where you should focus your attention at any given moment to achieve this task without crashing or being hit by cars passing in the street. If you think back to the way short-term memory was described earlier, with information coming in from sensory memory when it is the focus of attention and then either transferring on to long-term memory or being replaced by new information, this description does not seem complex enough to handle the bike-riding scenario. A more complex description of memory is needed to account for such behaviors.

Mind Wandering and Working Memory

Working Memory Capacity Demonstration

Baddeley's Model

Baddeley (Baddeley, 1992, 2000; Baddeley & Hitch, 1974) proposed the most prominent model of working memory. One thing that sets this model of working memory apart from the short-term memory store we described earlier in the chapter is that it contains multiple storage subsystems for different types of information. It also proposes the existence of a central executive subsystem that controls the flow of information between the other storage subsystems and long-term memory and decides where one's attention will be at any given moment. The primary storage subsystems in working memory are the visuospatial sketchpad and the phonological loop that hold visual and auditory information, respectively. In a newer version of the model, Baddeley (2000) added a fourth component that he called the episodic buffer, which acts as a temporary episodic storage subsystem and as a connection between working and long-term memory. Figure 5.6 illustrates his model of working memory.

Visual Working Memory

Visuospatial Sketchpad

The **visuospatial sketchpad** is responsible for the storage of visual information in working memory. It acts as a type of dry-erase board for visual and spatial information that can be written on, stored for a brief time, erased, and rewritten on. However, as we will see in the description of studies that support the existence of the sketchpad, the information stored there can be moved around in the sketchpad and analyzed like a three-dimensional model. Much of the evidence for a separate subsystem for visuospatial information comes from studies where subjects are asked to perform two tasks at once.

Visuospatial sketchpad: the part of the working-memory system that holds visual and spatial codes of information

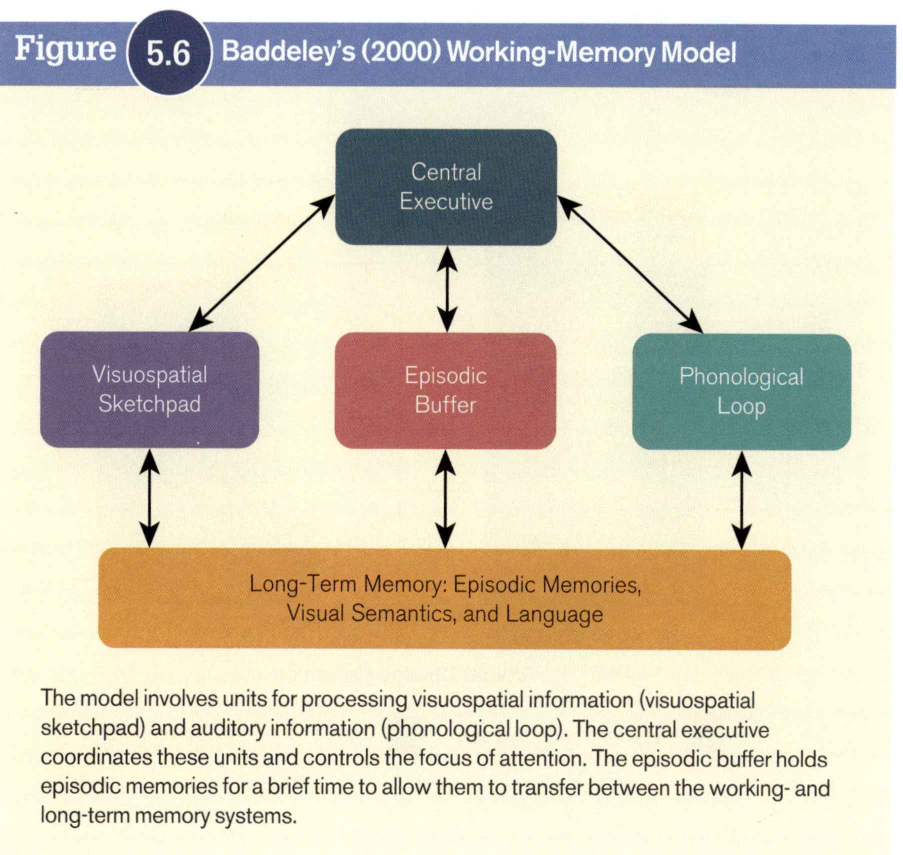

Figure 5.6 Baddeley's (2000) Working-Memory Model

The model involves units for processing visuospatial information (visuospatial sketchpad) and auditory information (phonological loop). The central executive coordinates these units and controls the focus of attention. The episodic buffer holds episodic memories for a brief time to allow them to transfer between the working- and long-term memory systems.

The researchers then look for interference in the tasks, depending on the type of tasks the subjects are asked to perform (e.g., two visuospatial tasks, versus one visuospatial and one verbal task). In other words, if lower task performance (i.e., more interference) is seen when both tasks involve the same type of information (two visual tasks) than when the two tasks involve different types of information (one visual task and one auditory task), then these results provide evidence that the working-memory system includes different subsystems for visual and auditory information.

Brain Concentration Game

As an example of this type of study, we examine the methods used by Quinn and McConnell (1996) in their study. They asked subjects to remember a list of words either by verbally rehearsing the words (in their heads) or by forming a visual image of the words. While subjects were learning the words, they were also presented with a changing visual display (seemingly random visual block patterns) or no visual display. When the visual display was present, subjects who were told to visually imagine the words remembered fewer of the words than subjects who were told to verbally rehearse them. When no visual display was present, there was no effect on learning instruction. Figure 5.7 illustrates these results for the learning task and visual display conditions. These results showed that when irrelevant visual information is displayed during a visual learning task, subjects cannot perform the task as well as when they are doing a verbal learning task or when no irrelevant visual information is displayed. These results and others like them (e.g., Baddeley, 1998) show that when two tasks both rely on brief visual storage of information, they interfere with one another, supporting the notion of a separate storage subsystem in working memory for visuospatial information that has a limited capacity.

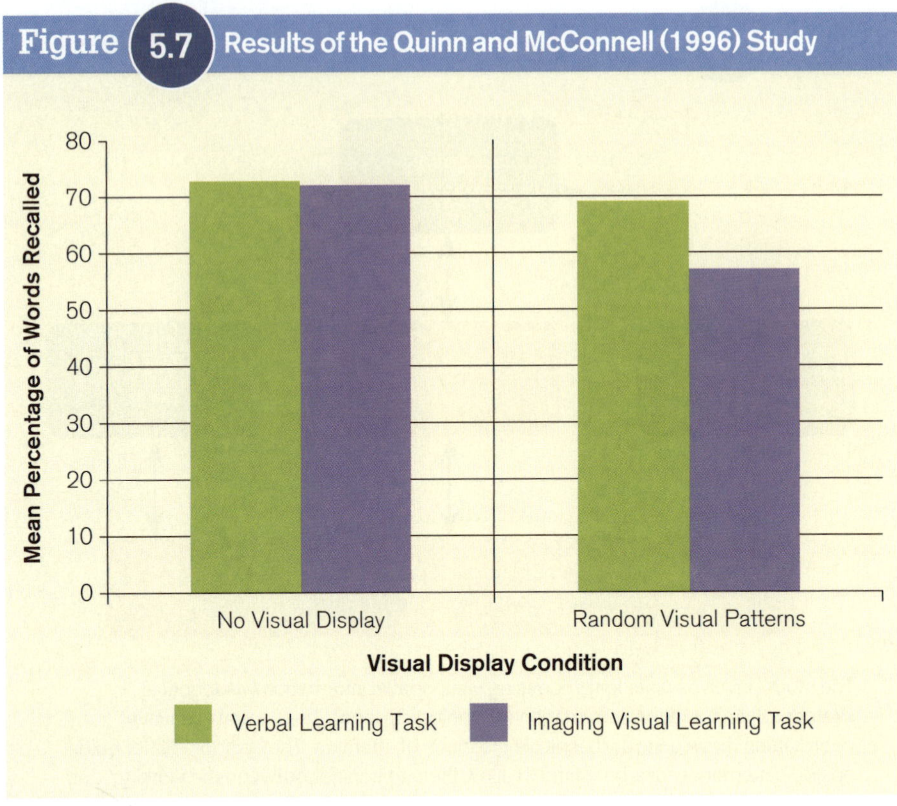

Mental Rotation Experiment

Other studies supporting the visuospatial sketchpad have shown that visuospatial figures can be manipulated mentally. For example, Shepard and Metzler (1971) asked subjects to judge whether two three-dimensional objects were the same or different (see Figure 5.8). The objects were rotated in space to different degrees. The researchers showed that the degree of rotation affected the time it took subjects to make the judgments (i.e., reaction time), such that each increment in degree of rotation increased the reaction time by the same amount. In other words, subjects were creating an image of the objects in the sketchpad subsystem of working memory and rotating those objects within the sketchpad to determine what they would look like when rotated to the same orientation as the comparison object. The more they had to rotate them mentally, the longer it took them to make their judgment. This is exactly the sort of task the visuospatial sketchpad is proposed to be useful for, and these results suggest that this subsystem of working memory is able to hold and manipulate this type of information.

Phonological Loop

Phonological loop: the part of the working-memory system that holds auditory codes of information

The **phonological loop** is proposed to operate much like the visuospatial sketchpad but as a storage subsystem for verbal information. Verbal information is stored in a loop in this subsystem and then is replaced by new verbal information as it comes in. An articulatory control process in this subsystem allows rehearsal of the information to hold the information in the loop for a longer period of time. As described earlier for short-term memory, verbal codes seem to be the dominant method of storing information for a short period of time; thus, the phonological loop has been the most heavily studied portion of the working-memory model. We have already described some evidence for the phonological loop in discussing short-term memory earlier in this chapter: More errors occur when recalling items that sound alike (e.g., *C* and *T*) than when recalling items that do not sound alike (e.g., *C* and *X*). This result occurs even when the items are presented visually because it is assumed that visual information involving language is automatically translated into verbal codes in working memory and stored in the phonological loop. Similar verbal codes (i.e., items that sound alike) can then become mixed up when recalling information stored in the phonological loop. This is known as the phonological similarity effect (Baddeley, 1998).

In addition to the phonological similarity effect, studies have shown that having subjects repeat a word or phrase out loud while they learn a list reduces recall for those items. This is an effect known as articulatory suppression: articulatory rehearsal of items is suppressed by the articulation of the irrelevant, repeated word. With both the repeated word and the items to be remembered stored in the phonological loop, it becomes overloaded and recall for the studied items is reduced. The list information cannot be rehearsed in the loop while it is also producing a verbal response. Studies by Peterson and Johnson (1971) and Baddeley, Lewis, and Vallar (1984) have shown these results for lists of letters and words, respectively.

The word length effect also supports the dominance of verbal coding in working memory and the existence of the phonological loop. The word length effect is seen when longer words (e.g., words with more syllables) show lower recall rates than shorter words.

Try this for yourself: Read over the following list of words. Then cover them up and try to recall them.

> help, train, dream, gift, fight, blow, drive, brain, kite

How many could you remember? Probably about four to six of them, right? Now try a list with the same number of words.

> helicopter, university, happily, hippopotamus, flowering, computer, fortify, opportunity, grocery

If you remembered fewer of the words in the second list, then you have illustrated the word length effect.

Figure 5.8 Objects Used in the Shepard and Metzler (1971) Mental Rotation Study

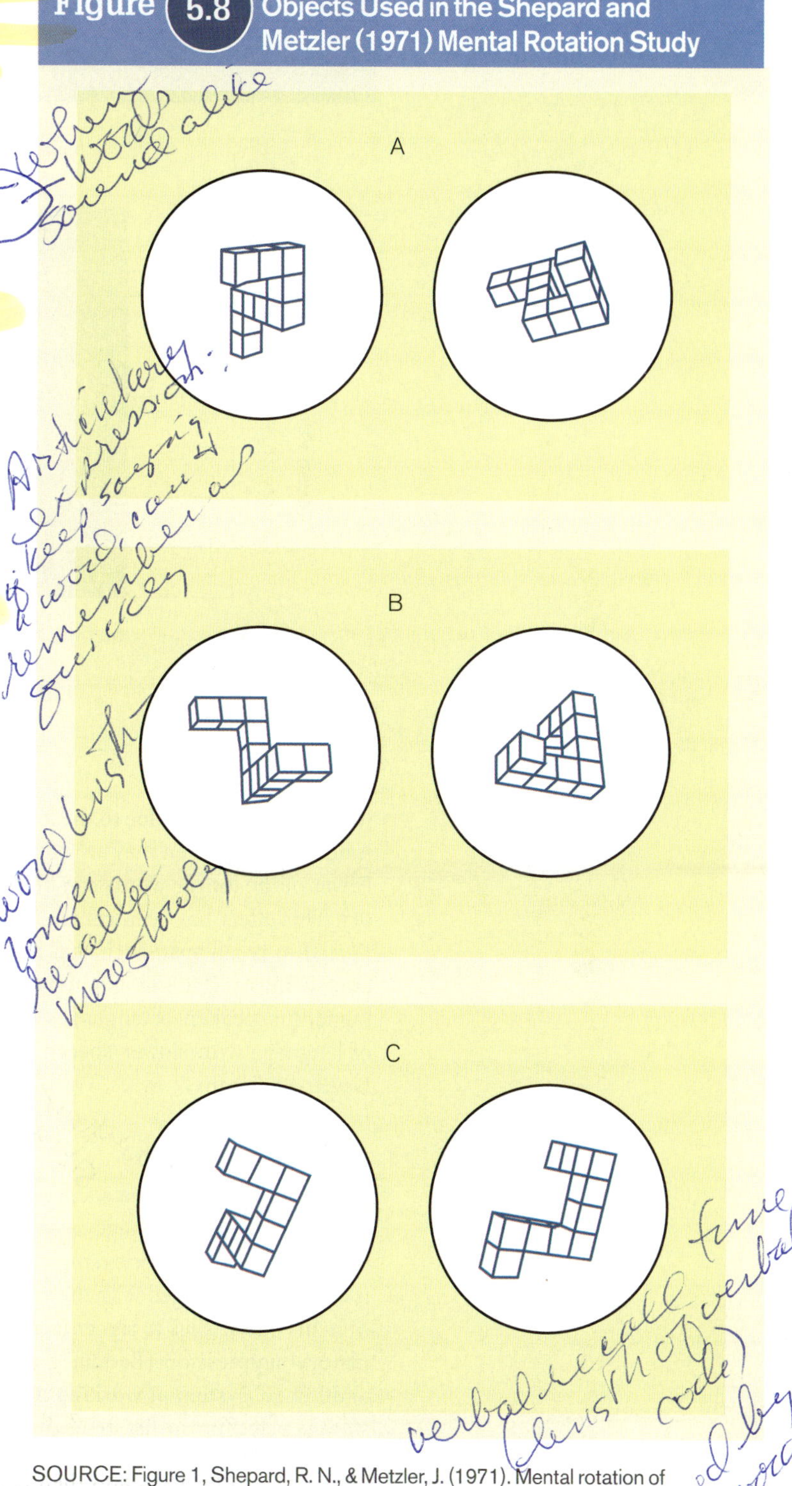

SOURCE: Figure 1, Shepard, R. N., & Metzler, J. (1971). Mental rotation of three-dimensional objects. *Science, 171*, 701–703.

Baddeley, Thompson, and Buchanan (1975) showed this effect in their study comparing short-term recall for words with one syllable compared with words with five syllables. When the list contained five words, the lists with one-syllable words showed recall rates of almost 80 percent; however, the lists with five-syllable words showed recall rates of only about 30 percent. Figure 5.9 illustrates these results. Baddeley and his colleagues interpreted the results of their experiments as an indication that the time it takes to read a word verbally (i.e., the length of its verbal code) affects its recall. In other words, the

Word Length Effect Activity

Figure 5.9 Results From Experiment 1 of Baddeley, Thompson, and Buchanan's (1975) Study for List Length of Five Items

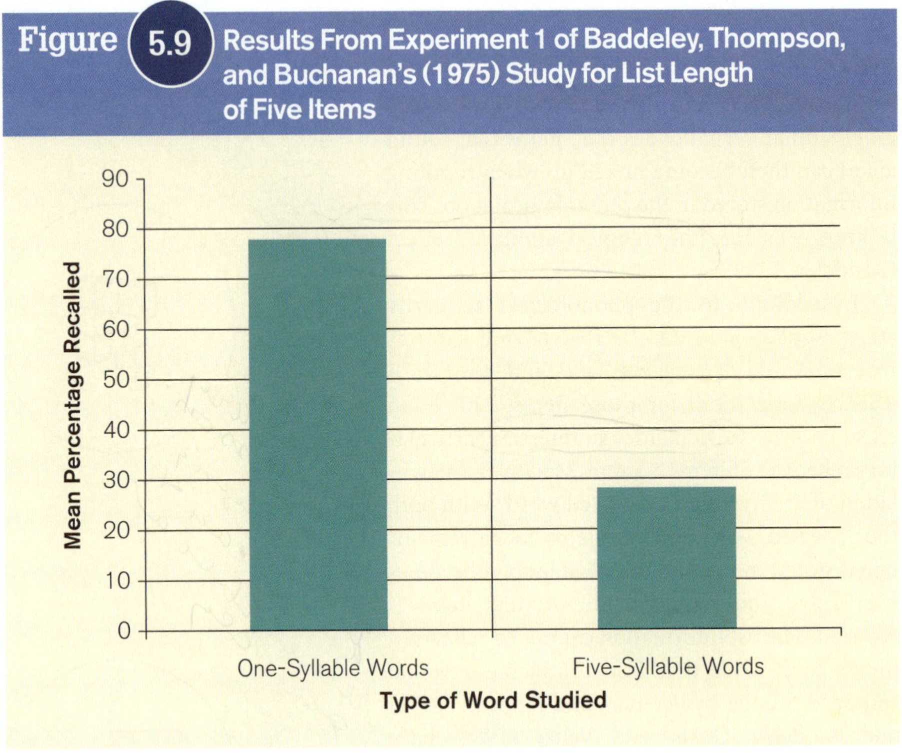

word length effect is due to the longer words being forgotten more quickly because more time is passing when they are rehearsed in the phonological loop than for shorter words. Fewer of the longer words can be rehearsed before they are lost from short-term memory. This effect has been generalized to show that the length of time it takes to speak is related to recall span such that adults have a faster speech rate and higher recall span than children (Hulme, Thompson, Muir, & Lawrence, 1984). Further, recall span is higher for speakers of languages with faster speech rates (e.g., Chinese) than for speakers of language with slower speech rates (e.g., Arabic or Welsh) (Ellis & Hennelly, 1980; Naveh-Benjamin & Ayres, 1986).

Episodic Buffer

The **episodic buffer** is a subsystem of working memory proposed by Baddeley (2000) to handle the brief storage of episodic memories when the loop and/or sketchpad are otherwise engaged. For example, when performing articulatory suppression, one's loop is completely engaged with the verbal repetition task and is unable to verbally store a list of items one wishes to remember. Yet recall of a list is not drastically impaired by articulatory suppression (Baddeley et al., 1984). Thus, the list items are being stored in another subsystem of working memory. Researchers have ruled out the sketchpad as a storage place for the list items during this task (Nairne & Neath, 2013); thus, a different storage subsystem is needed. Baddeley suggested that the episodic buffer serves in this role by briefly storing episodic memories with visual and verbal codes integrated from the other two storage subsystems. In other words, it can bind information with different codes (verbal, visual, semantic) to hold the combined information temporarily. It also serves as a link between working memory and long-term memory, allowing information stored in long-term memory to be used in the storage and retrieval of information in short-term memory.

Episodic buffer: the part of the working-memory system that holds episodic memories as an overflow for the phonological loop and visuospatial sketchpad

Because it is the newest subsystem in the working-memory model, the episodic buffer and its functions have been tested by fewer studies than the other subsystems. The

Figure 5.10 Results From Experiment 3 in Baddeley, Hitch, and Allen (2009)

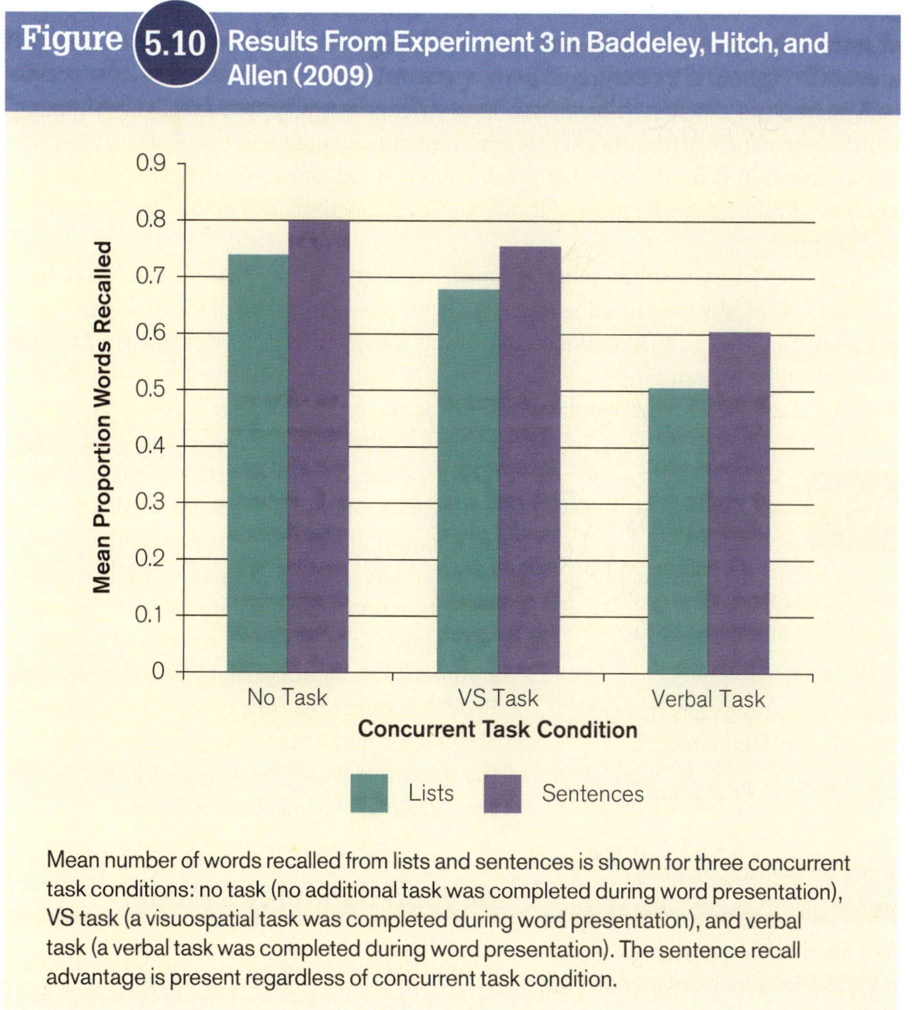

Mean number of words recalled from lists and sentences is shown for three concurrent task conditions: no task (no additional task was completed during word presentation), VS task (a visuospatial task was completed during word presentation), and verbal task (a verbal task was completed during word presentation). The sentence recall advantage is present regardless of concurrent task condition.

studies that have examined the episodic buffer have primarily focused on its binding function. Baddeley's work (e.g., Baddeley, Hitch, & Allen, 2009) has shown that short-term memory for sentences is better than short-term memory for lists of words, indicating a role for binding of words using language knowledge and semantic information that increases the overall recall of words in sentences. Further, this effect did not depend on the amount of attention (based on verbal or visual interference) available for the tasks (see Figure 5.10 for their results). Thus, binding of features seems to occur automatically without requiring resources from the central executive and does not rely on the visuospatial sketchpad or phonological loop. Although Baddeley and his colleagues have begun testing the functions of the episodic buffer in recent studies (see Baddeley, 2012), it is clear that further work is needed to more fully describe the role of this subsystem in working memory.

Central Executive

If there is a manager of the working-memory system, it is the **central executive**. The central executive is the subsystem of working memory that controls the flow of information between the three storage subsystems described earlier, the flow of information between the episodic buffer and long-term memory, and which part of the system is the

Central executive: the part of the working-memory system that controls the flow of information within the system and into long-term memory

current focus of attention. In the biking example that opened this section, the central executive would be responsible for focusing your attention on the most important object and feature of that object at each moment as you move through the scene. This subsystem does not store information as do the other subsystems. Instead, it controls which information in the other subsystems is in our current focus of attention. However, as our attention is limited in what it can handle at any one time, the central executive also has a limited capacity in what it can control at any time. It is limited by the limits of our attention.

Compared to the other subsystems of working memory, less research has been devoted specifically to examining the central executive subsystem of the Baddeley model due to its function as an attentional processing subsystem. However, numerous models of attention have been proposed (see Chapter 4) that could describe the functioning of the central executive component of working memory. For example, Baddeley (1998) has suggested that Norman and Shallice's (1986) model of the control of action that includes a supervisory attentional system could describe the functioning of the central executive. In this model, many tasks are proposed to rely on automatic functioning (e.g., routines) with the supervisory attentional system coming in to play when automatic functioning is not sufficient for a task. Baddeley argues that this model of attention can account for performance in tasks where the central executive would be expected to play a role (e.g., driving, playing chess, reading).

Stop and Think

5.14. Describe the four subsystems of Baddeley's model of working memory. Which subsystem controls our focus of attention?

5.15. Which storage subsystem seems to be dominant in terms of features of information stored in working memory?

5.16. What role does the episodic buffer serve in working memory?

5.17. Describe two other perspectives on working memory besides the Baddeley model.

5.18. Describe some tasks from your life that involve your working memory. How might the working-memory model described earlier be involved in these tasks?

Beyond Baddeley's Model

Although Baddeley's is the most popular model for working memory and has been tested more than other models, some researchers have suggested other ways to conceptualize working memory. For example, Cowan (1999) has suggested that instead of being a separate system of memory as Baddeley's model proposes, working memory is simply the part of long-term memory that is currently activated in our attention. In other words, long-term memory is the main memory system with working memory operating on a portion of long-term memory currently active in our attention. Another approach to describing working memory is through neurobiology. Jonides and colleagues (2008) examined the neural activity that accompanies the encoding, storage, and retrieval of information over the short term, with an emphasis on brain activity that occurs when information is the focus of attention and binding the features of the information when it is stored. The researchers rely on studies using the techniques of cognitive neuroscience (see Chapter 2) to support their approach to working memory. Thus, the study of working memory is being conducted from multiple perspectives.

Retrieval From Long-Term Memory

Up to this point in our descriptions of memory, we have focused primarily on the encoding and storage of information. We have not yet discussed different means of retrieval from memory, although the studies described earlier in this chapter illustrated some of the types of tasks researchers have relied on to measure memory retrieval. Here we focus more specifically on memory retrieval tasks. How do researchers measure memory retrieval? The answer depends on the type of retrieval they are interested in. Are they measuring intentional retrieval or unintentional retrieval? This is one important distinction. Are they interested in memory retrieval using cues or without the help of cues? Whether the retrieval task includes cues to guide retrieval is another distinction between retrieval tasks. We focus first on some standard intentional-retrieval tasks (also called explicit-memory tasks) designed to measure episodic and semantic memories: free recall, cued recall, and recognition. Then we describe some unintentional retrieval tasks known as implicit memory tasks that were designed to measure procedural memories. Finally, we consider a common form of everyday memory task: retrieving an intention to complete a future task (e.g., remembering to stop at the grocery store on the way home from work, remembering to take medication after you eat dinner) known as prospective memory.

Recall Tasks

Recall tasks are intentional-retrieval tasks that either provide specific cues to aid retrieval (cued recall tasks) or do not provide specific cues, as in free-recall tasks. In free-recall tasks, one is asked to retrieve information without any additional context for the information. In a standard episodic-memory experiment, this typically involves having subjects study a list of items and then (after some delay) asking them to recall the items without any additional information. Free-recall tasks can also be used for retrieval of semantic memories. When you complete a short-answer question for an exam, you are typically completing a free-recall task. If someone asks you, "What is the capital of Romania?" you are being asked to free recall a semantic memory that you may be able to retrieve if at some point in the past you have learned that the capital of Romania is Bucharest. If you'd been asked, "What is the capital of Romania? It starts with a B," this would be a cued recall task because the first letter that is given serves as a cue for remembering the correct city name. Different kinds of information can be given as cues in a cued-recall task. In the previous example, the starting letter serves as a cue. But suppose instead you are asked to retrieve a list of words that you studied such as *lemon*, *banana*, *soda*, *vodka*, *pineapple*, *orange*, *water*, *wine*. In this case, you are asked to retrieve episodic memories, but the cued-recall task could ask you to first recall all the drinks and then recall all the fruits. The cues in this test are the categories of the items being retrieved. Thus, there are many ways to construct a cued-recall task.

Recognition Tasks

Unlike recall tasks, in recognition tasks one is not asked to generate any information. Instead, one is asked to verify whether information has been experienced before. When you see the face of someone you know you have met before across a room of strangers, you are recognizing that the face is one you know, whereas the other faces in the room are ones you do not know. When you take a multiple-choice exam, you are completing a recognition test, because you are presented with the correct answer among other choices and you need to "recognize" which answer provided is the correct one. In a standard recognition task in a memory study, subjects are asked to study a set of items. They are then given a list of items (typically one at a time) with some items that were on the list and some that were not on the list. Subjects are asked to judge whether each item was on the list (an "old" item) or not on the list (a "new" item). This is known as a yes-no recognition test. In another variant of this type of test, subjects are presented with two items at a time, one old item and one new item, and their task is to choose the item that is old.

This is known as a two-alternative forced-choice test. Subjects may also be asked about how the items "feel" to them when judging the items. For example, they may be asked to rate their confidence in their judgment (e.g., on a 1 to 5 scale). Or for items they judge to be old, they may be asked about whether they "remember" the item (i.e., they can remember details about the item such as position in the list or perceptual details) or if they just "know" the item was on the list (i.e., they cannot retrieve the details of its presentation, but they are sure the item was on the list).

Comparing Recall and Recognition Tasks

The likelihood of intentionally retrieving an episodic memory sometimes depends on the type of retrieval task that is given: recall or recognition. In fact, researchers have found that in some cases, retrieval in different conditions is heavily influenced by the retrieval task used. For example, Eagle and Leiter (1964) showed that recall and recognition are affected in different ways by subjects' knowledge of the upcoming memory test when items are studied. In their study, different groups of subjects were given different instructions when they studied the list. Half of the subjects were told they would need to remember the words for a memory test. In other words, they performed an intentional learning task. The other half of the subjects were given a task to perform on the list items (e.g., classify them by parts of speech) and was not informed about the later memory test. They performed an incidental learning task. The results in this experiment showed that recall was higher for the intentional study condition than for the incidental study condition. However, recognition was better for items studied in the incidental study condition than the intentional study condition (i.e., they found an interaction between study condition and type of test). These results showed that knowing about the upcoming memory test helped when that test was a recall test but hurt when the test was a recognition test (see Figure 5.11). A similar effect was shown when common (e.g., boat) and uncommon (e.g., feat) words were studied. Common words were more likely to be

Figure 5.11 Results From Eagle and Leiter's (1964) Study

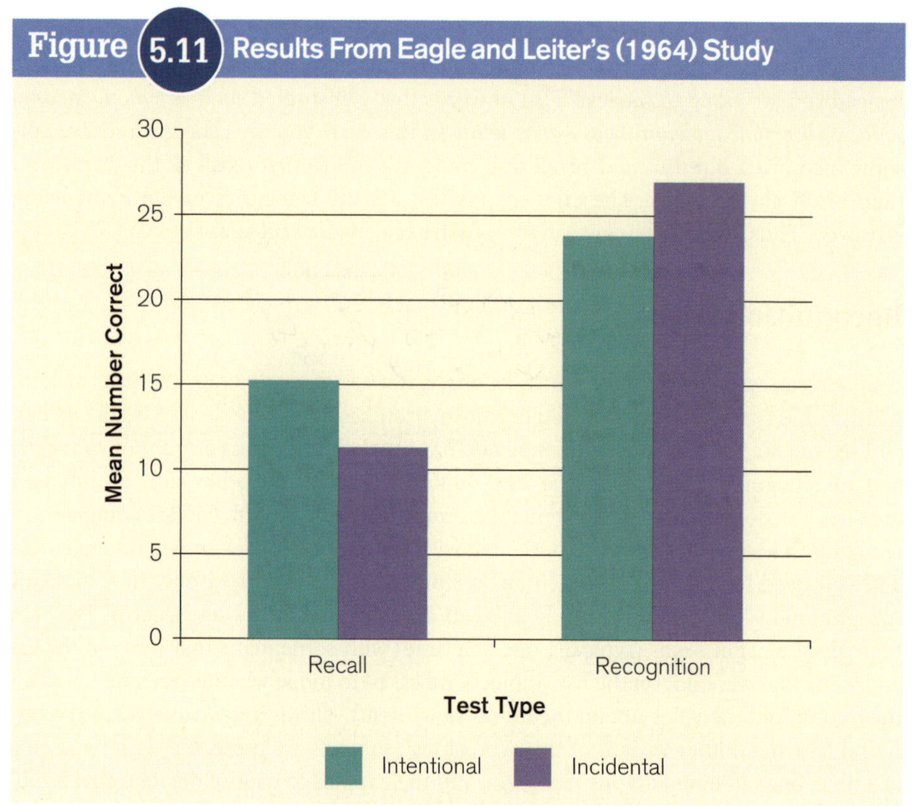

recalled, but uncommon words were more likely to be recognized (Kinsbourne & George, 1974). Thus, the retrieval test used to measure memory can influence one's ability to remember. Implicit memory tests illustrate this point even further.

Implicit Memory Tasks

Implicit and Explicit Memory

How does our memory influence our behavior without us intending it to or (in some cases) without us even knowing it is influencing us? Can we be "primed" to respond a certain way to a task based on a previous experience? This type of memory retrieval seems quite different from the recall and recognition retrieval tasks described earlier because the retrieval is not intentional as it is in those tasks. Consider this example: Suppose you are walking across campus and you pass someone who looks familiar to you. You were not likely looking at each face you passed, thinking about whether you knew them. Instead, you retrieved the memory of the person's face unintentionally (which may have then prompted explicit retrieval of meeting him or her at a party last weekend). The experience of meeting that person before prompted the feeling of familiarity with the person's face using implicit memory when you passed him or her on campus. **Implicit memory** tasks are designed to measure memory without intentional retrieval. Implicit-memory tasks typically involve a cue, as in the cued-recall tasks described earlier, or identification, as in the recognition tasks described earlier, but no instruction to retrieve a memory is given as it is in explicit memory tasks. Instead, subjects are asked to complete a task that makes no reference to a previously studied episode. Subjects may be asked to complete word stems (e.g., *app-*) with the first word they think of that starts with those letters (e.g., *apple*) in a stem completion task, or they may be asked to identify words or pictures that are flashed very briefly on a computer screen in a perceptual-identification task. The key is that some of the stems or items in these tasks correspond to items presented earlier in the experiment. Implicit memory is measured in these tasks by the advantage (e.g., completion rates, speed of identification) shown for studied items compared with unstudied items. In other words, having studied some items earlier makes one more likely to complete stems with those items or likely to identify them more quickly. Other forms of implicit-memory tests involve conceptual cues, such as categories or semantic knowledge questions where category exemplars or the answers to the questions have been presented as studied items.

Implicit Memory Exercise

An interesting example of an implicit task was used in research by Larry Jacoby and colleagues (Jacoby, Woloshyn, & Kelley, 1989). They presented both famous and nonfamous names for subjects to study. They then asked subjects to identify famous names among a list of famous and nonfamous names; some were famous and nonfamous names that had been presented in the study list, and some were new famous and nonfamous names. Their results showed that having seen the nonfamous names in the study list made the subjects more likely to call them famous later on, showing that their implicit memory of the names they had studied influenced their judgments of fame. In other words, names became "famous" simply because they had been studied previously and retrieved unintentionally. We discuss additional examples of implicit tests in Chapter 7 and connect implicit memory more to neurological functions in that chapter.

Prospective Memory Tasks

Have you ever forgotten to take medication that you were supposed to take at a certain time? Or forgotten to turn in an assignment even though you had it completed on time? These examples represent failure of another type of LTM retrieval: prospective memory.

Implicit memory: procedural memory that alters performance based on previous experiences

Prospective Memory

Prospective memory refers to remembering to perform a task at some point in the future. Tasks like remembering to stop at the store on your way home to buy milk, call your mother on her birthday, or take medication at 9:00 p.m. every night are prospective memory tasks. You likely rely on your prospective memory abilities often in completing academic tasks such as remembering to study for an upcoming exam, remembering to register for courses at a certain time, and remembering to hand in a paper on the day it is due. At this point, it is unclear how much prospective memory differs from the other forms of memory we have already discussed. It is an intentional task but requires that one remember the intention to perform the task. Thus, accurate retrieval of an intention depends on how that retrieval is initiated. This can occur through cues in our environment. For example, seeing a picture of someone blowing out candles on a cake in a TV commercial might cue your retrieval of your intention to call your mother on her birthday. Or the sight of the store on your route home can cue your retrieval of your intention to stop and buy milk. This type of prospective memory task is known as an event-based task because some type of event (e.g., seeing the commercial or the store) cues the retrieval of the task you intend to perform. Another type of prospective memory is time based in that you intend to perform that task at a specific time in the future. For example, taking medication at 9:00 p.m. is a time-based task and involves monitoring of the time in some way to perform it accurately. You might happen to glance at a clock near 9:00 p.m. or notice that a 9:00 p.m. TV show is starting to cue you to the time that aids in your retrieval of the task (i.e., taking your medicine). There is some evidence that event-based tasks are easier to remember (Sellen, Louie, Harris, & Wilkins, 1997), but this question is still being investigated.

Stop and Think

5.19. Describe the primary difference between recall and recognition tasks.

5.20. In what way do implicit memory tasks measure memory without intention?

5.21. How do prospective memory tasks differ from other forms of intentional retrieval?

5.22. Provide an example of each of the following memory tasks from your life: free recall, cued recall, recognition, implicit memory, prospective memory.

Prospective memory tasks have been studied by researchers in two ways: as they occur in everyday life (e.g., remembering to call someone at a specific time) and as they occur in laboratory tasks (e.g., remembering to press a key when one sees a specific word in a task). In both cases, the prospective-memory tasks are designed to simulate typical prospective-memory tasks that people perform in their everyday lives (e.g., remembering to call your mother on her birthday). To allow more control over the factors that can influence prospective memory performance, Einstein and McDaniel (1990) developed a frequently used laboratory procedure to study prospective memory tasks. In this lab-based method, a prospective memory task is embedded within an ongoing task to simulate the remembering of a prospective memory task within the typical tasks of everyday life. The prospective memory tasks given in studies employing Einstein and McDaniel's methodology typically involve asking subjects to make a certain response (e.g., press the 5 key) when they encounter a specific word (e.g., *rabbit*) or specific type of word (e.g., animals). The subjects are then asked to perform an ongoing task (e.g., rate the pleasantness of words or decide if a string of letters is a word) while they attempt to remember the prospective memory task. Using this methodology, researchers are exploring questions about how prospective memory works, such as: How much attention is needed to perform the prospective memory task? (e.g., Einstein et al., 2005); Does prospective-memory performance decline with age? (e.g., Kvavilashvili, Kornbrot, Mash, Cockburn, & Milne, 2009); and What are the effects of delay on prospective memory performance? (e.g., McBride, Beckner, & Abney, 2011).

Prospective memory: memory for future intentions

Memory Overview

How We Remember

We discussed the processes of encoding, storage, and retrieval from memory and the approaches researchers have taken in their study of these processes. In this discussion, we identified several forms of memory. However, there is no clear agreement yet on how many types of memory there are. Some of the forms of memory described in this chapter are similar enough to one another that they may not represent distinct forms of memory. One way to distinguish different forms of memory is to determine the brain systems responsible for them. We discuss this approach further in Chapter 7 in the section on amnesia. It is also possible that researchers have yet to identify additional forms of memory that are distinct from the forms we discussed.

We focused on the types of tasks that measure different types of memory retrieval. Researchers have used these tasks to examine different ways of retrieving information from memory. Models of retrieval have also been developed as a way to describe the process of retrieval that occurs in these tasks. Some models propose a single retrieval mechanism from memory for all forms of memory, whereas other models focus on a specific type of memory and the processes involved in retrieval for a certain type of task. Thus, the process (or processes) of retrieval is an ongoing topic of study for memory researchers. In Chapter 6, we focus further on the factors that affect retrieval from long-term memory.

THINKING ABOUT RESEARCH

As you read the following summary of a research study in psychology, think about the following questions:

1. What type of memory is being measured in this study?
2. What type of research design are the researchers using in this study? Explain your answer. (Hint: Review the Research Methodologies section in Chapter 1 for help in answering this question and Question 3.)
3. What are some possible controls the researchers likely included in this study? Why are these controls important?
4. What are some practical implications of the results of this study?

Study Reference

Scullin, M. K., & McDaniel, M. A. (2010). Remembering to execute a goal: Sleep on it! *Psychological Science, 21*, 1028–1035.

Purpose of the study: In this study, the researchers examined the effect of sleep on memory for future intentions. Many previous studies have shown a positive effect of sleep on memory for a list of items. In the current study, this work was extended to memory for remembering to press a key during a cognitive task when specific words appeared in the task. The purpose of the study was to compare performance on the key press task for subjects who had slept and subjects who had not slept in the time between the instruction for the key press task and when they had to remember to complete the task.

Method of the study: Undergraduate students completed a series of cognitive tasks in this study across two sessions. At Session 1, all subjects practiced completing a living/nonliving judgment task (Is this item alive or not?), a lexical decision task (Is this item a word or not?), and a categorization task (Does this item fit in the category shown?). Subjects were then asked to press the Q key if they saw the words *table* or *horse* in the rest of the experiment. Session 1 took place at either 9:00 a.m. or 9:00 p.m. In a long-delay condition, Session 2 took place 12

(Continued)

(Continued)

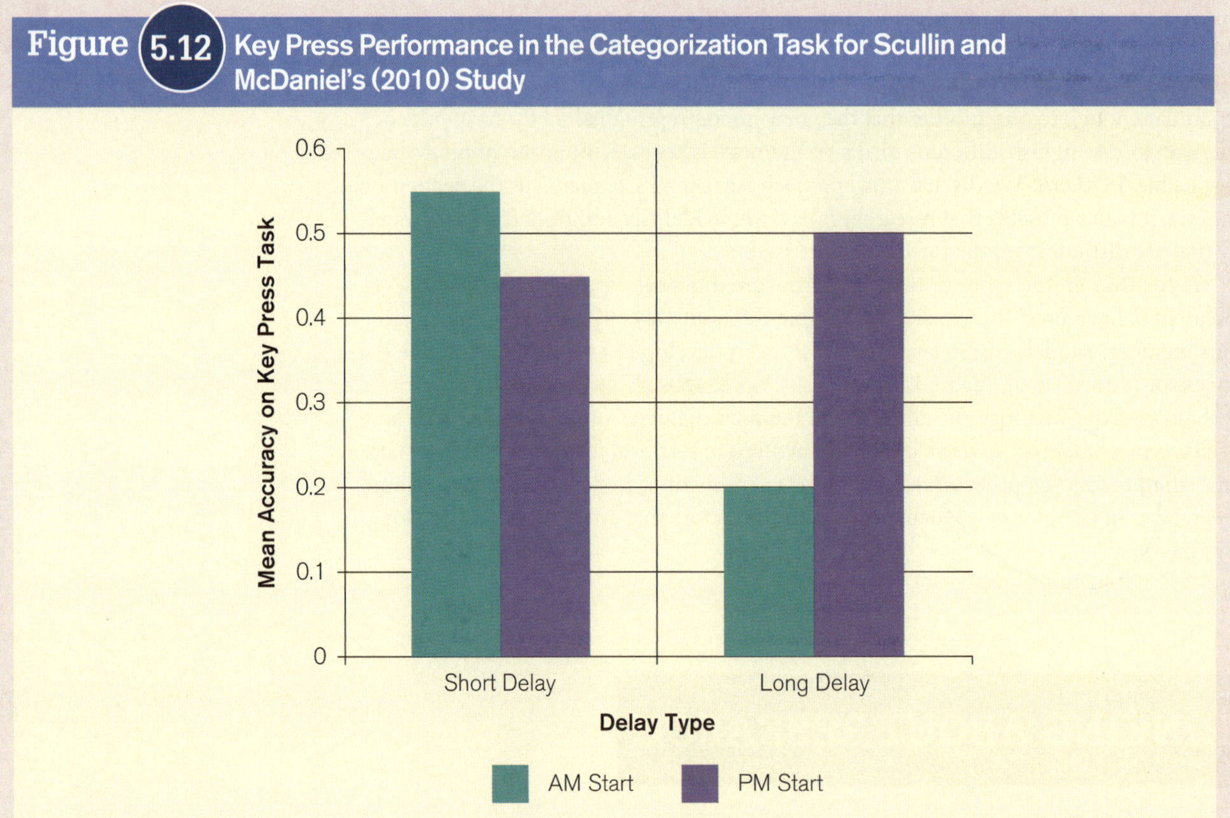

Figure 5.12 Key Press Performance in the Categorization Task for Scullin and McDaniel's (2010) Study

hours after Session 1. Thus, half the subjects slept before completing Session 2 and half did not sleep before completing Session 2. To examine the effect of time of day, a short-delay condition was also run at both 9:00 a.m. and 9:00 p.m., where Session 2 took place only a few minutes after Session 1 ended.

Results of the study: The results of the study indicated that sleep only aided performance in the *Q* key press task when *table* or *horse* appeared in the categorization task. No difference was seen between subjects who slept and had not slept in the other two tasks for the long-delay conditions. In addition, the short-delay conditions showed similar performance regardless of time of day of the sessions. The results for the categorization task are displayed in Figure 5.12.

Conclusions of the study: The researchers concluded that sleep aids in performance of certain types of tasks intended for the future. These results are similar to those found in previous studies for memory of a list of items.

CHAPTER REVIEW

Summary

- **Is memory a process, a structure, or a system?**

  Memory has been thought of as both a process and a structure. Researchers have viewed memory in terms of processes (encoding, storage, and retrieval), structural storage units (sensory, short-term, and long-term memory), and systems (working-memory system with multiple subsystems).

- **How many different types of memory are there?**

  There is no clear answer to this question, as it is unclear which types of memory are distinct from other types. However, researchers have attempted to identify several different types of memory: memory based on duration (short-term vs. long-term memory), memory based on content (episodic, semantic, and procedural memory), memory based on retrieval task (recall and recognition), memory based on reference to the self (autobiographical memory), memory based on vivid details and emotional context (flashbulb memory), memory based on intentionality of retrieval (explicit vs. implicit memory), and memory for future tasks (prospective memory).

- **Are there differences in the ways we store and retrieve memories based on how old the memories are?**

  Yes. There are important differences in memories we store for the short term and memories stored over the long term. The main distinction between these types of memories is the duration of storage: less than a minute for short-term memories and a lifetime for long-term memories. In addition, short-term memories seem to be coded primarily with verbal codes, and long-term memories seem to be coded primarily with semantic codes. Finally, the capacity of short-term memory seems to be limited (about five to nine chunks of information), whereas long-term memory seems to have an unlimited capacity.

- **What kind of memory helps us to focus on a task?**

  Working memory involves information about a task currently in our focus of attention. Thus, it aids in the completion of tasks we are currently attending to, while also helping us keep track of other things in our environment and ignore things that are irrelevant.

- **How does our memory influence us unintentionally?**

  Implicit-memory retrieval involves unintentional retrieval of information. Implicit memory can be based on episodes (such as a study list) or procedures (such as a skill like driving a car).

- **What are the limits of our memory?**

  In some cases, the limits of memory are based on our limits of attention in terms of what we can encode effectively and focus on for appropriate cues for retrieval. Over the short term, our attention limits influence what we can focus on in working memory (or store in STM). Over the long term, we seem to be able to store unlimited amounts of information, but we are limited in what we can retrieve at any given time.

Chapter Quiz

1. Enter the letter for the memory term next to the example below that illustrates that form of memory.
   (a) semantic memory
   (b) episodic memory
   (c) procedural memory
   (d) prospective memory
   (e) flashbulb memory
   ___ you have a vivid memory of where you were and what you were doing when you heard about a devastating earthquake in Russia
   ___ after years without practice you pick up a golf club and make an excellent drive
   ___ you know that the capital city of China is Beijing
   ___ you remember on Tuesday to go to a doctor appointment at 10:00 a.m.
   ___ you remember the time you went with your friends to the movies to see *The Hunger Games*
2. Which memory storage unit in the modal model of memory holds information for a second or two as raw sensory information?
   (a) working memory
   (b) long-term memory
   (c) short-term memory
   (d) sensory memory
3. Which subsystem of the working-memory system controls the focus of attention?
   (a) the episodic buffer
   (b) the central executive
   (c) the phonological loop
   (d) the visuospatial sketchpad
4. Which subsystem of the working-memory system allows for rehearsal of information held for the short term?
   (a) the episodic buffer
   (b) the central executive
   (c) the phonological loop
   (d) the visuospatial sketchpad
5. Which of the following is an example of prospective memory?

(a) remembering what you had for breakfast yesterday
(b) remembering how to make breakfast
(c) remembering to have breakfast before you leave the house
(d) remembering what the word *breakfast* means

6. Describe the types of memory errors one is likely to make if one studies and recalls the following list—happy, game, honey, trust, lame, bee—
   (a) when recall occurs after thirty seconds.
   (b) when recall occurs after twenty-four hours.

7. (a) Describe a recall task you performed yesterday.
   (b) Describe a recognition task you performed yesterday.

8. Provide examples of both proactive and retroactive interference.

Key Terms

Central executive 113
Chunking 102
Encoding 97
Episodic buffer 112
Episodic memory 106
Implicit memory 117
Long-term memory 105
Partial-report method 99
Phonological loop 110
Proactive interference 104
Procedural memory 107
Prospective memory 118
Retrieval 97
Retroactive interference 103
Semantic memory 106
Sensory memory 99
Short-term memory 101
Storage 97
Visuospatial sketchpad 108
Working memory 107

Stop and Think Answers

5.1. Describe the three primary processes of memory.

Encoding is the process of getting information into memory. Storage is the process by which information is held in memory. Retrieval is the process by which information is remembered.

5.2. List the three hypothetical storage structures of memory from the shortest to the longest storage.

Shortest: sensory memory; intermediate: short-term memory; longest: long-term memory

5.3. Consider different ways in which you encode information you learn in class (e.g., visually, aurally). How effective do you think each of these encoding processes is for storing information in long-term memory?

Answers will vary.

5.4. Explain how the partial-report method allows researchers to more accurately estimate the capacity of sensory memory than a whole-report method.

The partial-report method allows for a report of a smaller amount of information than the whole set of stimuli presented. Because information is lost from sensory memory so quickly, it is difficult for one to report what is stored in sensory memory before it is lost. The partial-report method allows researchers to estimate how much information is stored before it is lost by extrapolating from the part the subject is asked to report to the whole set of stimuli presented.

5.5. According to the research in this area, what is the duration of sensory memories?

The duration of sensory memory is believed to be about one second for visual information and a little longer (about four seconds) for auditory information. However, due to the differences in how these modes of stimuli are presented, it is difficult to know if there is a different duration for visual and auditory information or if the differences found in research are caused by this confounding factor.

5.6. Research in sensory memory for senses other than vision and audition is scarce. Imagine that you are researching olfactory (sense of smell) sensory memory to contribute to the gap in the research in this area. Describe a study you might design using the partial-report method to study olfactory sensory memory. What are some of the limitations of this method for this type of sensory memory?

Answers will vary, but the limiting factor is allowing subjects to report the information stored in sensory memory before it is lost. It is difficult to apply the partial report to other senses, which is one reason there has been less research done on the other senses.

5.7. What is the capacity of STM? What can one do to increase this capacity?

The capacity of STM seems to be about five to nine chunks of information. The capacity can be increased with chunking (i.e., organizing the information into fewer units according to meaning). For example, more letters can be stored in STM if they are chunked into words when they are encoded.

5.8. Suppose you were trying to remember your student nine-digit ID number that you had just looked up on your web account in order to give to someone over the phone. Your cell signal is not very good where your computer is located so you need to hold the number in your STM until you can make the call and report your number. How would you accomplish this task using your STM?

Answers will vary. Based on results from studies using the Brown-Peterson method, information can be stored in STM for about twenty seconds. You can increase the duration of storage of information in STM by rehearsing the information to keep it in your focus of attention.

5.9. What is the most likely cause when information is lost from STM?

Interference is the most likely cause (either proactive or retroactive interference).

5.10. Describe some situations in your life in which you rely on your STM.

Answers will vary.

5.11. In what ways does LTM differ from STM?

Storage duration and capacity in LTM appears to be unlimited, whereas it is clearly limited in STM. In addition, the primary mode of storage of information in LTM seems to be the meaning of the information, whereas verbal coding is the dominant storage mode in STM.

5.12. Describe a memory of your own that fits each of the three types of LTM memory described in the previous section.

Answers will vary. Episodic memories are for episodes, semantic memories are for facts and knowledge, and procedural memories are for skills memories.

5.13. Can you think of a memory of your own that you would describe as a flashbulb memory? How confident are you that your memory for this event is accurate?

Answers will vary, but they should describe memories that are highly vivid and about significant events.

5.14. Describe the four subsystems of Baddeley's model of working memory. Which subsystem controls our focus of attention?

The phonological loop (verbal information) and visuospatial sketchpad (visual information) serve as storage units of information in working memory. The episodic buffer stores episodic information and connects with LTM. The central executive acts as the control system to determine what our attention is currently focused on.

5.15. Which storage subsystem seems to be dominant in terms of features of information stored in working memory?

The phonological loop appears to be the dominant subsystem for storing information.

5.16. What role does the episodic buffer serve in working memory?

The episodic buffer stores episodic information and connects with LTM.

5.17. Describe two other perspectives on working memory besides the Baddeley model.

Other perspectives include describing working memory as the activated portion of LTM and describing working memory through the brain activity that accompanies encoding, storage, and retrieval of memories in the short term.

5.18. Describe some tasks from your life that involve your working memory. How might the working-memory model described earlier be involved in these tasks?

Anything that involves attention will qualify for working memory. Answers will vary.

5.19. Describe the primary difference between recall and recognition tasks.

In recall tasks, one attempts to retrieve information without any additional cues or with some cues connected with the information to help guide one's retrieval. In recognition tasks, one is presented with information that one must judge in terms of whether one has studied it or not.

5.20. In what way do implicit memory tasks measure memory without intention?

In implicit-memory tasks, subjects are given a task related to a study episode but with no instruction to retrieve the study episode.

5.21. How do prospective memory tasks differ from other forms of intentional retrieval?

Prospective-memory tasks involve remembering to complete a task in the future. The person retrieving the task must put himself or herself into a retrieval mode at the appropriate time to retrieve the task, instead of having someone else (e.g., an instruction from a researcher) initiate retrieval.

5.22. Provide an example of each of the following memory tasks from your life: free recall, cued recall, recognition, implicit memory, prospective memory.

Answers will vary.

Student Study Site

Sharpen your skills with SAGE edge at **edge.sagepub.com/mcbridecp**

SAGE edge for students provides a personalized approach to help you accomplish your coursework goals in an easy-to-use learning environment.

Go to edge.sagepub.com/mcbridecp for additional exercises and web resources. Select Chapter 5, Memory Structures and Processes, for chapter-specific resources. All of the links listed in the margins of this chapter are accessible via this site.

QUARTZ

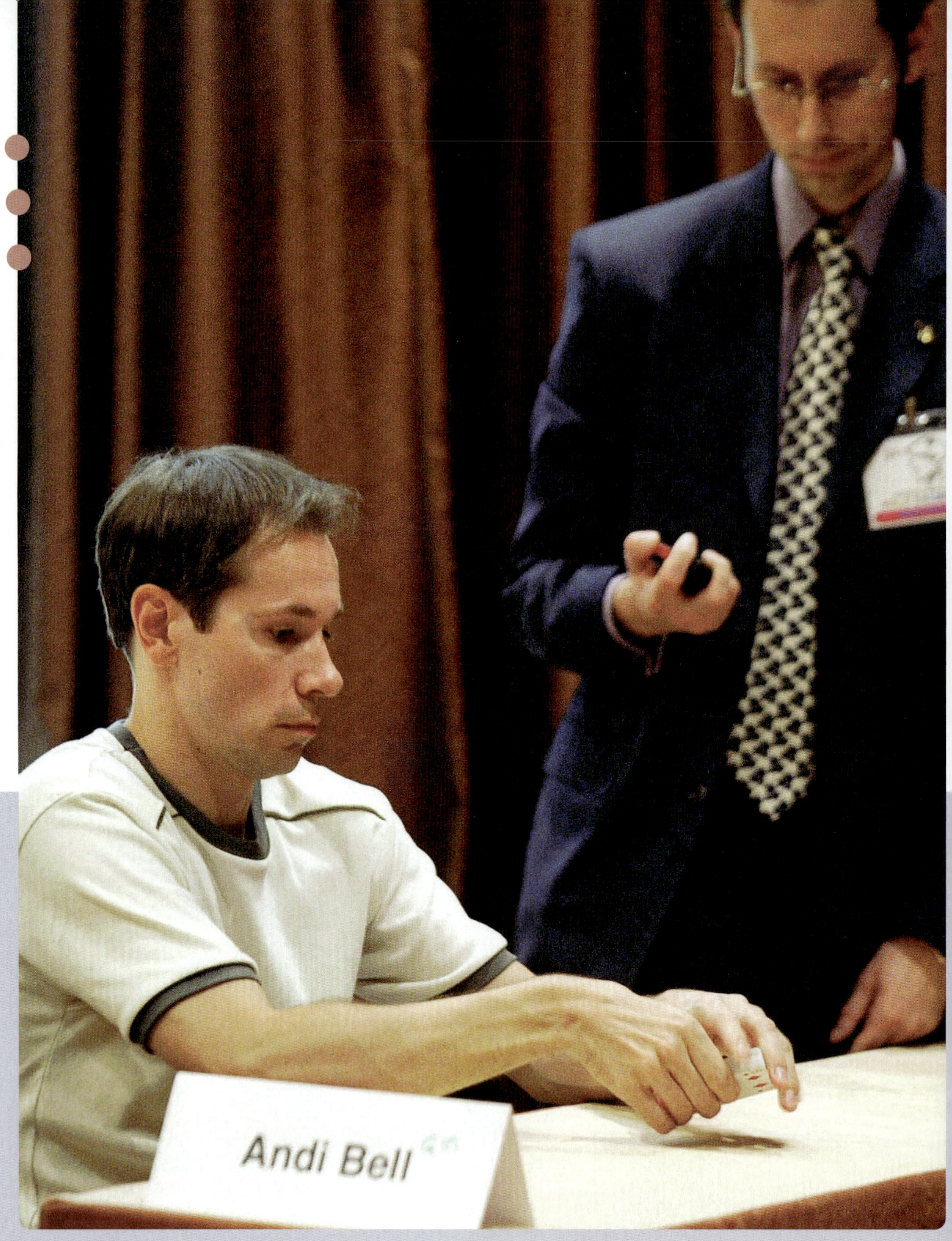

JIMIN LAI/Staff/Getty Images

Long-Term Memory

Influences on Retrieval

Questions to Consider

- Why does forgetting occur and what can you do to prevent it?
- Which methods of encoding information are effective in increasing retrieval from long-term memory?
- Which methods of retrieving information are effective in increasing memory performance?
- In what ways do encoding and retrieval interact to affect long-term memory?
- What are some simple methods you can use to increase retrieval from long-term memory?
- How effective are mnemonics in increasing long-term memory retrieval?
- Does photographic memory exist?

Introduction: Superior Memory

Imagine that you could remember everything you ever experienced, everything you ever read, and everything you ever learned. Does that sound like the kind of memory you would want? You would probably score higher on exams in your courses, but you would also remember the pain of every bad event from your life, remember lots of useless knowledge that you do not care about, and would not be able to revise your older memories based on new experiences. Our memory is not designed to work perfectly because it does not need to in order for it to help us make it through our lives. However, it is designed to remember things that are important to us if we do the right things to help strengthen those memories. That is what this chapter is about: factors that affect retrieval from long-term memory and how we can use those factors to our advantage in improving our memories.

Memory Athletics

Joshua Foer: Feats of Memory

Although no one's memory is perfect, there are individuals who have learned to train their memories such that they can perform extraordinary feats of memory. Andi Bell, who is the 1998, 2002, and 2003 World Memory Champion, can recall the order of playing cards in ten shuffled decks after only twenty minutes of study time. He can achieve the same perfect recall for a single deck of cards with less than two minutes of study time. How do individuals like Andi Bell accomplish such amazing memory tasks? Do they have a photographic memory such that the cards are stored as pictures in their minds? The answer is no. Memory champions like Andi Bell instead work hard to train their memories using mnemonic techniques that take advantage of the way our memories work to remember extraordinary amounts of information. These techniques have been used by humans throughout our history to help us remember important information. For example, ancient Romans used mnemonics to help them remember speeches. These skills were so important that those most respected in society for their intellect were those who had the best memory skills. However, anyone willing to work to develop them can learn to use them. Joshua Foer eloquently describes how they work, along with his story of using these techniques to win the 2006 U.S. Memory Championship, in his book Moonwalking with Einstein *(2011). But what if you do not wish to put in the amount of effort required to win a memory championship, and you simply want to better remember some of the techniques you are trying to learn for this course? In this chapter, we examine some simple techniques you can use to aid your retrieval from long-term memory (these tools are bolded in the text to draw your attention to them as memory aids you might find useful) as we describe some of the important factors that influence memory.*

Why We Forget

The Upside of Forgetting

Why do we forget things? Why aren't we able to retrieve important information when we need it? The process of forgetting has been studied for as long as there has been a field of experimental psychology. Forgetting is a natural process that occurs when information is unable to be retrieved from memory. The inability to retrieve information generally seems to increase as the time since the information was learned increases. Ebbinghaus (1885) first showed that forgetting follows a typical pattern where a lot of information is forgotten very quickly after study, but then the rate of loss slows as the length of time

Figure 6.1 The Classic Forgetting Function

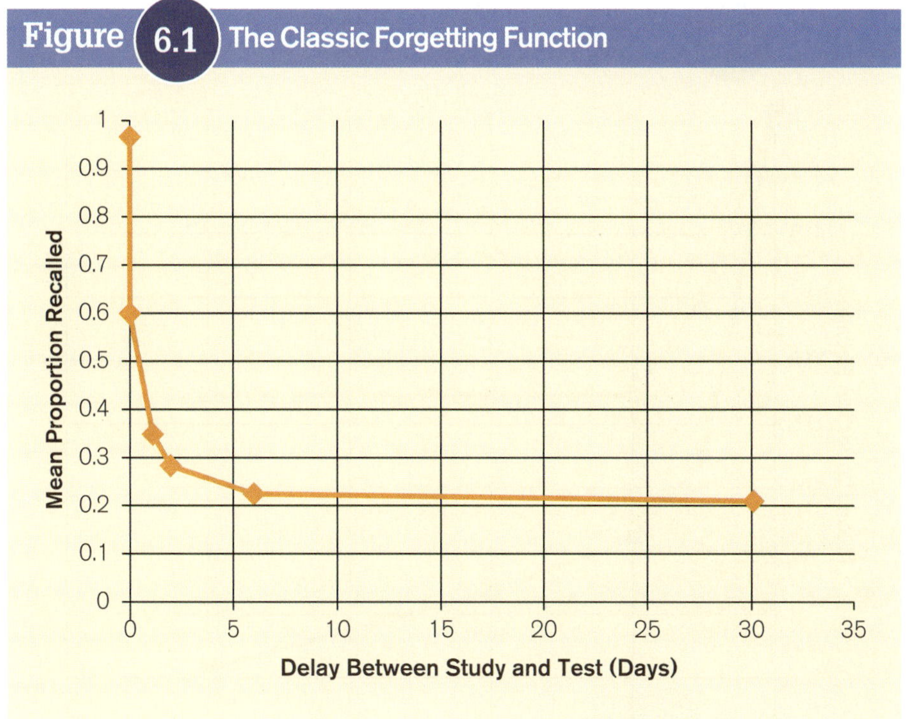

since study increases. Figure 6.1 illustrates this classic pattern. This pattern of forgetting has held up over many studies in the time since Ebbinghaus's experiments.

Early in the study of memory, researchers suggested that memories simply decay over time, the way the colors in a printed photograph fade over time. However, this idea does not describe the mechanism by which information is lost from memory, and its popularity as a cause of forgetting has decreased over the decades of memory research (Wixted, 2004). One mechanism by which forgetting does seem to occur is interference. Interference occurs when other information prevents the retrieval of the target information (see Chapter 5 for further discussion of interference). For example, if you learned that the capital of Brazil is Brasilia and then later learned that the largest city in Brazil is São Paulo, you might have interference when you attempt to retrieve the name of the capital of Brazil and mistakenly retrieve São Paulo. However, interference can occur even if you do not retrieve any city name in this case. The vast amount of information you encounter in your daily life can serve as interference in preventing retrieval from memory.

Is Forgetting Caused by Inhibition?

Another proposed cause of forgetting is lack of consolidation. **Consolidation** is a neural process by which memories are strengthened and more permanently stored in the brain. Initially, memory storage relies on a brain structure called the hippocampus, long known for its importance in memory functioning. However, over time, memories are stored elsewhere in the cortical areas of the brain, allowing for more permanent storage (McGaugh, 2000). This is the process of systems consolidation and can take days, weeks, or months to complete (Wixted, 2010). However, a second type of consolidation occurs on a shorter time scale: synaptic consolidation. Synaptic consolidation occurs within and across neurons, the individual cells that make up the tissue in the brain. Sleep seems to be important in aiding the consolidation process (Stickgold, Hobson, Fosse, & Fosse, 2001); thus, sleeping between a study episode and testing will aid long-term memory. This has been shown in numerous studies where subjects are asked to learn some information, followed by half of the subjects being asked to sleep while the other half stay awake. After the same delay, both sets of subjects are tested on the learned

Consolidation: neural process by which memories are strengthened and more permanently stored in the brain

Figure 6.2 Results From Jenkins and Dallenbach's (1924) Study

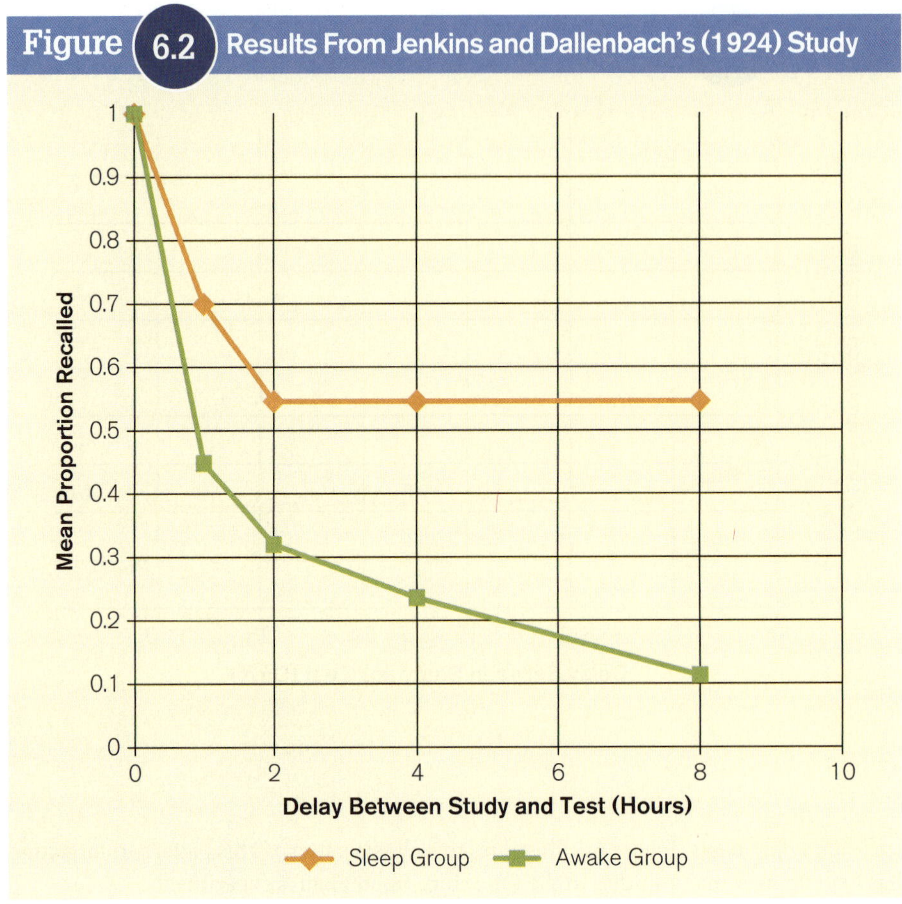

Crash Course: Remembering and Forgetting

information. The group that slept generally shows less forgetting than the group that did not sleep. See Figure 6.2 for results from the classic study by Jenkins and Dallenbach (1924) with this design.

Stop and Think

6.1. Why does forgetting occur?

6.2. How do systems consolidation and synaptic consolidation differ?

6.3. What is one way you can increase your retrieval from long-term memory as you study for an upcoming exam?

Wixted (2010) has argued that both interference and consolidation failures contribute to forgetting. Thus, one way to increase retrieval from long-term memory (and improve memory performance) is to facilitate consolidation (e.g., by sleeping after studying) and prevent interference as much as possible. In other words, **sleeping between the study and test of information you want to remember will help you retrieve that information from long-term memory**. Many additional factors aid in efforts to improve your memory, and we discuss each of these in this chapter along with their effects on long-term memory retrieval.

Interference Experiment

Modifying Memories

Encoding Effects

Of the three main processes of memory—encoding, storage, and retrieval (see Chapter 5 for more description of these processes)—encoding and retrieval are the processes most under our control, and therefore, these processes can be conducted in ways that help us remember information. We begin with a discussion of encoding processes (i.e., how we process information coming into our memory system) to highlight encoding techniques that aid in retrieval from long-term memory. In general, the more active and effortful encoding processes are, the better we remember. But how do we make these processes "active and effortful"?

Levels of Processing

Levels of Processing Effect Activity

In the 1970s, researchers discovered something interesting about memory performance: The "deeper" information was encoded, the better it was remembered. To illustrate this principle, consider this example.

For the following words, note whether each word is in capital letters (yes or no):

TREE	fork
BIRD	DEER
nail	FISH
moon	baby
HILL	card

Now cover up the words and count backward by threes from sixty to zero. When you get to zero, try to recall all of the words. How did you do? Count how many words you got right. Now, let's try it again with a different task. For the following words, note whether each word represents a living thing (yes or no):

pail	pole
girl	kite
well	toad
bear	lamp
goat	crab

Now cover up the words and count backward by threes from sixty to zero. When you get to zero, try to recall all of the words. How did you do on this list? Count how many words you got right. (Hold on to your recall lists from this example; we will come back to these data in the Serial Position Curve section of this chapter.) Did you remember the words better on the first list or the second list? Most people remember more words on the second list where they are deciding if each item is a living thing because it involves "deeper" encoding of the words.

Depth of encoding in this case means processing of the meaning of the information (also called **elaborative encoding**). For example, Craik and Tulving (1975) had subjects study words (e.g., SHARK) while answering different questions about the words. Some questions involved fairly **shallow processing** (e.g., Is the word in capital letters?). Other questions involved a moderate level of processing (e.g., Does the word rhyme with PARK?). And other questions involved **deep processing** (e.g., Is the word a type of FISH?) that required the subjects to consider the meaning of the words. Craik and Tulving (1975) showed that as the depth of processing at encoding increased, memory performance on a later recognition test increased. Figure 6.3 illustrates their results. Studies like this one helped show the now classic **level-of-processing effect** in memory: **Encoding information according to its meaning aids long-term memory**.

Elaborative encoding: processing of information according to its meaning to allow for longer storage in memory

Shallow processing: encoding information according to its surface features

Deep processing: encoding information according to its meaning

Level-of-processing effect: an effect showing better memory for information encoded with deep processing than with shallow processing

Figure 6.3 Results From Craik and Tulving's (1975) Experiment 1

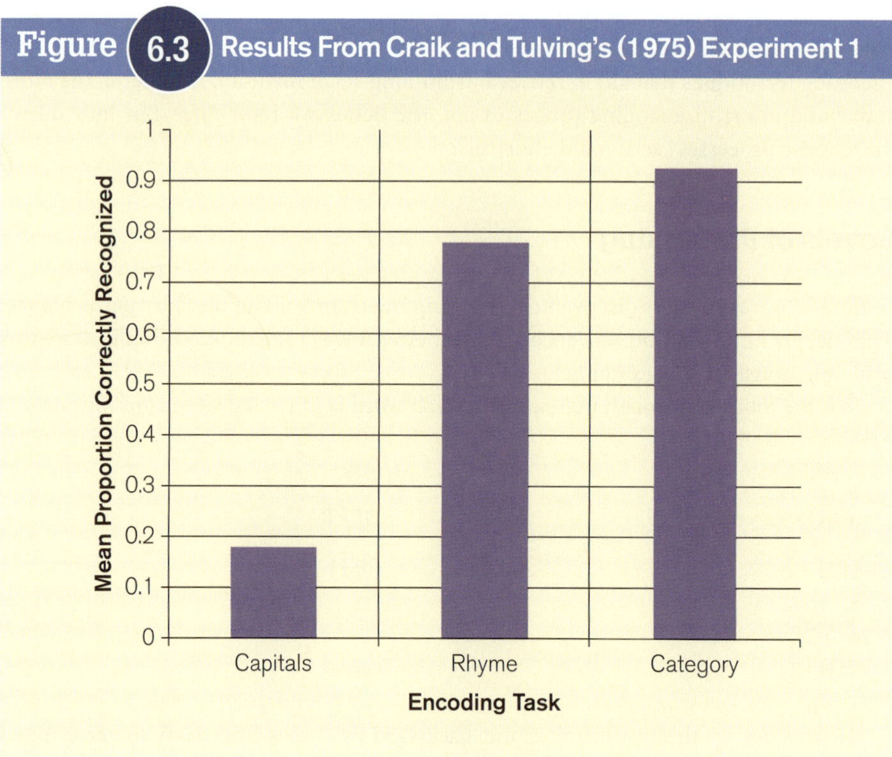

The level-of-processing effect seems to work because long-term memory is organized primarily according to the meaning of information (for example, see Figure 5.1). Thus, information that is encoded according to meaning connects better with knowledge already stored in long-term memory, making it easier to retrieve that information later on. One issue, however, with this encoding technique is that an exact definition of depth has never been fully described. Clearly, meaning is important, but what type of meaning is most important? Is a categorization task (e.g., Is this word a FISH?) deeper or shallower than a sentence completion task (e.g., Does the word fit in this sentence: "He ate the _________ for dinner last night."?) or than a living/nonliving judgment (e.g., Is a SHARK a living thing?)? How do we know how "deep" encoding is? Researchers have not been able to clearly answer these questions. In addition, it seems that the type of retrieval used in remembering the information is also important in defining which encoding tasks are best (see the Encoding-Retrieval Interactions section later in this chapter). Thus, using deep encoding techniques may only aid memory in certain situations.

Spacing Effects

When you have a big exam coming up, how do you study for it? Do you study for a couple of hours each day for several days before the exam or study all day the day before the exam? Research in memory (e.g., Melton, 1970) has shown that the first study plan often results in better memory than the second study plan. This is called the **spacing effect**. This result holds even when the total amount of study time is equivalent across the two study plans. In other words, studying for one hour every day for the week before an exam (a total of seven study hours) should result in better memory for the material than studying for seven hours the day before the exam (see Figure 6.4). This result represents the difference between spaced and massed encoding repetitions: **Spaced repetitions result in better memory than massed repetitions.**

Spacing effect: an effect showing better memory when information is studied in smaller units over time instead of all at once, as in cramming

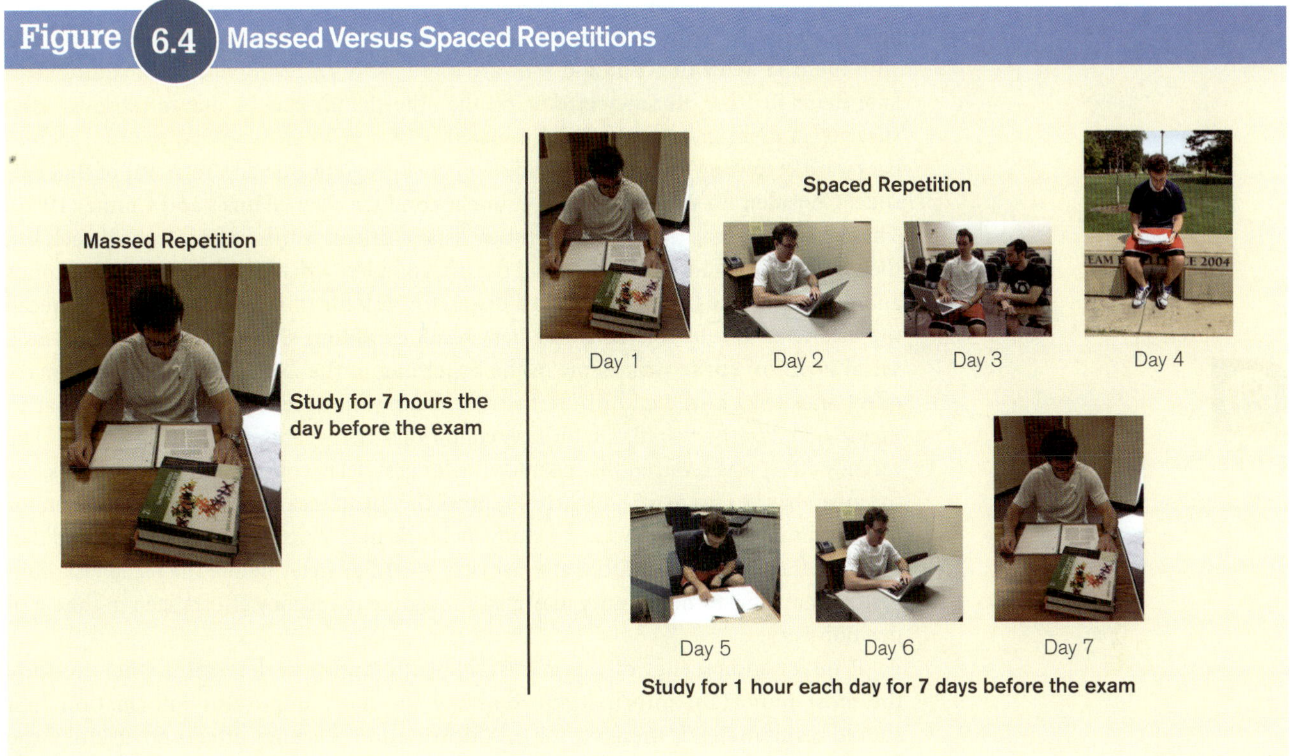

Figure 6.4 Massed Versus Spaced Repetitions

One reason studying over time is typically better than cramming is that multiple study episodes provide more varied retrieval cues (i.e., pieces of the circumstances that existed when information was encoded, such as things in the environment or thoughts you had about the information) that can be useful when information is retrieved from long-term memory. If you study at different times, you are likely changing some of the circumstances that exist during study, such as your environment, your mood, your thoughts during study, and perhaps even your study technique. All of this contextual information is stored with the material you are studying. When you attempt to retrieve the information, these contextual cues can help you connect to information you are trying to remember. This process is described further in the Encoding-Retrieval Interactions section.

Serial Position Curve

Memory research has shown that the first information encoded and the last information encoded tend to be remembered better than information encoded in the middle. This has generally been shown in encoding lists of items (e.g., words). For example, words studied at the start of a list and words studied at the end of a list are the ones most likely to be retrieved from memory. When the first information encoded shows a memory advantage, this is known as a **primacy effect**. When the last information encoded shows a memory advantage, this is known as a **recency effect**. Look back at the recall data you created for the demonstration in the Levels of Processing section. Were you able to recall most of the items from the beginning of the lists? If so, you have illustrated the primacy effect. How about the items at the end of the lists? Did you recall most of those? If so, you have illustrated the recency effect. However, the recency effect may have been weakened in this example because you did the backward counting after each list that may have wiped out this effect.

Primacy effect: an effect in memory showing the best memory for information encoded first

Recency effect: an effect in memory showing the best memory for information encoded last

Primacy effects are quite strong and seem to be due to the greater likelihood of storage in long-term memory for information studied first. There is nothing to interfere with the first items of a list, and they are more likely receiving deeper encoding than later items in a list. Recency effects, on the other hand, may be due to retrieval from short-term memory and can be eliminated with a delay or intervening task (such as backward counting) between the end of an encoding episode and retrieval of that episode. Consider, for example, an experiment conducted by Glanzer and Cunitz (1966). These researchers asked subjects to study lists of fifteen words. After study of each list, they were asked to immediately recall the list, complete a distractor task for ten seconds and then recall the list, or complete a distractor task for thirty seconds and then recall the list. Their results for the immediate recall condition showed what is known as a **serial position curve** with items in the beginning of the lists illustrating the primacy effect and items at the end of the lists illustrating the recency effect (see blue bar in Figure 6.5). For the two distractor task conditions, the recency effect was reduced. The recency effect was reduced the most for the longest delay condition (thirty seconds, see the green bar in Figure 6.5). Figure 6.5 shows the mean recall results by list position for these three conditions. However, a study by Bjork and Whitten (1974) also showed that recency effects can be produced after a distractor-filled delay before the recall task, suggesting that long-term memory may also contribute to recency effects seen in the serial position curve.

Serial Position Experiment

Primacy and recency effects are useful in attempting to determine when to study the most important information. Studying the most important information first should result in better memory for this information. Recency effects are useful if the

Figure 6.5 Results From Experiment 2 of Glanzer and Cunitz's (1966) Study Showing the Serial Position Curves

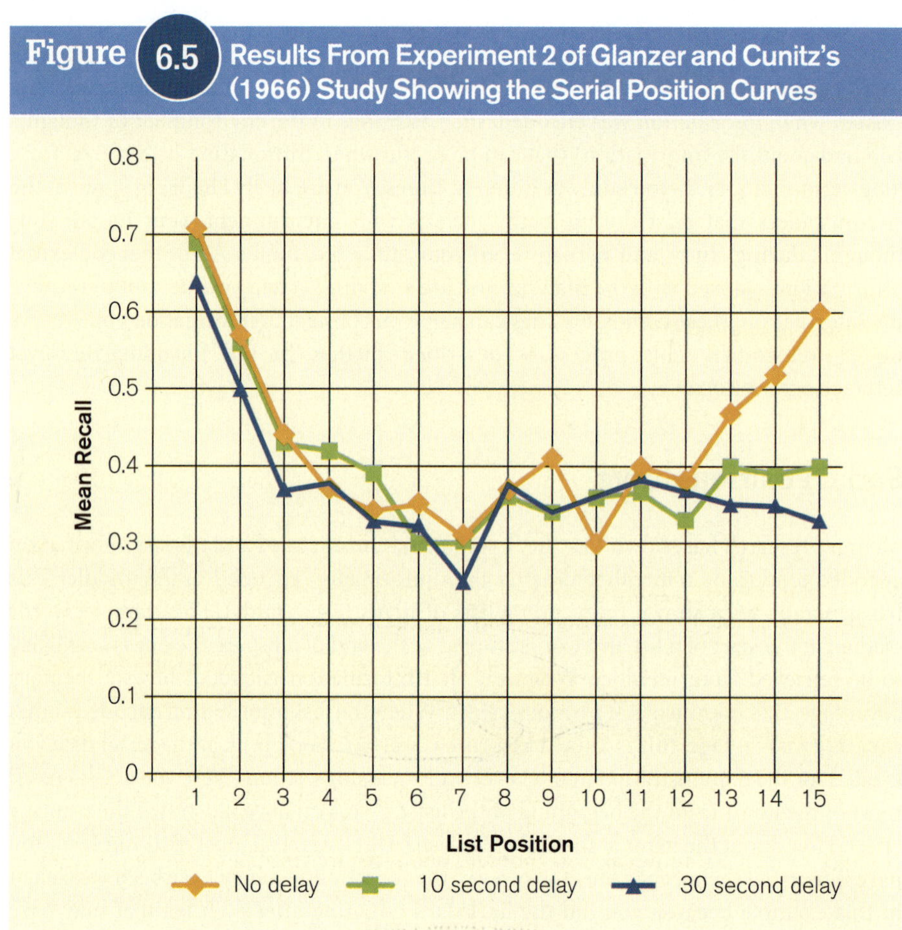

Serial position curve: an effect in memory showing the best memory for information encoded at the beginning and end of an encoding session

test will occur after only a very short delay (e.g., looking over your notes right before the test is handed out). In summary, **the first information encoded will show the best memory. The last information encoded will show a memory advantage primarily if the delay between encoding and retrieval is very short.**

Stop and Think

6.4. Describe three methods of encoding that can increase retrieval from long-term memory.

6.5. What is a serial position curve?

6.6. Describe two ways of studying information that would qualify as deep encoding.

6.7. Based on what you have learned in this section, in what ways can your study techniques for your courses be improved?

Retrieval Effects

In many cases, retrieval from long-term memory depends on what occurs at retrieval. Retrieval practice that comes after study and before the final test can affect retrieval. In addition, the way retrieval practice is used can affect memory performance. Each of these factors is discussed in this section.

Storage and Retrieval

The Testing Effect

What techniques do you use to study for exams? Do you read over your notes? Reread the assigned readings? Highlight important concepts in the text or in your notes? Take the practice quizzes in your text or on the online learning site? If you are like most students, then you probably reread your notes and/or the text and highlight important concepts (Roediger & Pyc, 2012). However, of these techniques, recent research has shown that taking the practice quizzes is the most effective way to improve later retrieval because it provides retrieval practice. This effect is known as the **testing effect**. **Reviewing information by means of an intervening test aids later retrieval.** For some time, researchers have suggested that retrieving information from memory strengthens those memories (e.g., Bjork & Bjork, 1992). However, a series of studies has shown just how effective retrieval practice can be in increasing later retrieval from long-term memory. In one of the first of these studies, Roediger and Karpicke (2006a) asked subjects to read two passages (one about the sun and the other about sea otters). For one of the passages, the subjects were asked to reread the passage for seven minutes, and for the other passage, the subjects were asked to recall the information in the passage for seven minutes to provide retrieval practice. They were then asked to complete a final recall test of the information in the passage (regardless of which task they did after the first reading) either five minutes later, two days later, or one week later. Their results, shown in Figure 6.6, clearly show that for the longer delays (two days and one week), subjects remembered much more of the information when they recalled the passage after the first reading than when they simply reread the passage after the first reading.

The testing effect has been the topic of a number of memory studies in recent years. One possible reason for the effect suggested is the depth of encoding involved in the additional recall task (Roediger & Karpicke, 2006b). Because the intervening recall task involves more effortful processing than simply rereading the passage, the testing effect could be due to the deeper additional encoding that takes place in the recall task. However, additional mechanisms for the testing effect have also been proposed. For example, retrieval practice may strengthen memories by strengthening the connection between the cues for retrieval (e.g., thoughts about the material) and the information to be retrieved (Karpicke & Blunt, 2011). As yet, researchers do not know if one or more of these mechanisms are the primary underlying cause(s) of the testing effect. It is clear,

Testing effect: an effect in memory showing better memory for information that has been tested in the retention interval as compared with other encoding of the information

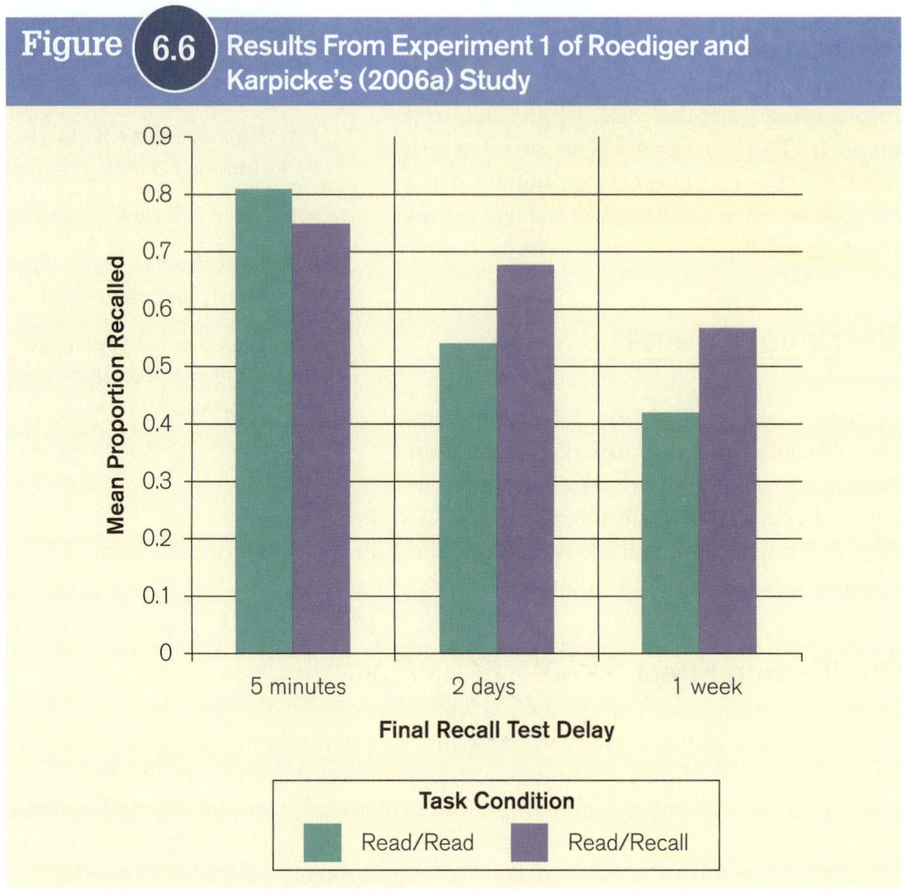

though, that practicing retrieving information is an effective means of increasing the likelihood of retrieving that information in the future.

Using the Testing Effect

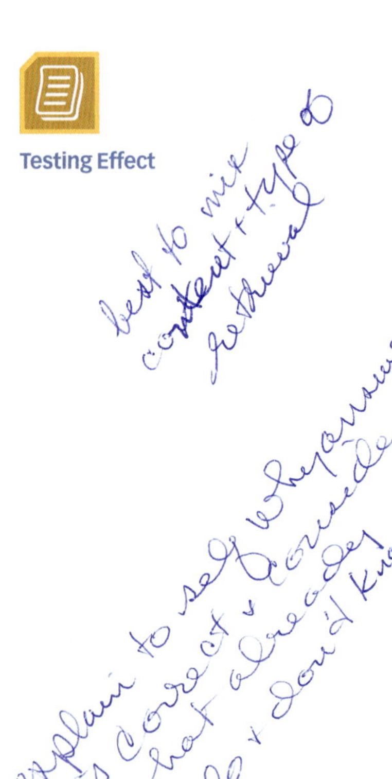

Testing Effect

From the previous section, it is clear that retrieval practice aids long-term memory as long as the retention interval is long enough. However, the way retrieval practice is used as a learning tool can influence its effectiveness. One method ties back to a concept discussed with encoding effects: spaced practice. The other method relates to the type of retrieval practice that occurs: using explanatory questioning.

With regard to spacing retrieval practice, Roediger and Pyc (2012) summarize research showing that long-term memory is better when retrieval practice is mixed in content and type than if one topic is practiced in large blocks of problems. In other words, the best way to use retrieval practice as an aid to memory is to interweave practice of different topics and types of material. Thus, if you are preparing for multiple exams in the future (as most students are throughout the semester), it is best to do some retrieval practice of each topic at each of your study sessions to maximize the effects of that retrieval practice.

In addition, the type of retrieval practice you do can influence its effectiveness. According to the research summarized by Roediger and Pyc (2012), learning that involves processing known as explanatory questioning will be most effective. This type of learning involves the student considering why an answer is correct (explaining it to oneself) and considering what the student already knows and does not know. For example, if you were to attempt to recall all of the techniques to improve memory performance discussed so far in this chapter and you could only recall three of them, it would be helpful to consider to yourself (1) why the techniques work (i.e., how they increase retrieval from long-term memory) and (2) which techniques you did not recall so that you can study those techniques again before your next retrieval attempt. Thus, if you incorporate retrieval practice into your study techniques, you should consider the type of retrieval practice you do. Mixing the topics in each study session, doing an active analysis of why answers are correct or incorrect, and considering which material you could not correctly retrieve will be most effective in increasing your later retrieval of that information for an exam. You should also consider the type of test you will be taking (e.g., multiple choice, short answer) because encoding and retrieval can interact to affect long-term memory, as we discuss in the next section.

Stop and Think

6.8. What is retrieval practice? What effect does it have on long-term memory?

6.9. Which study-test delays show a memory advantage due to retrieval practice?

6.10. What types of retrieval practice are the most effective? Which of the encoding effects described in the Encoding Effects section do you think may be involved in the more effective retrieval practice techniques?

Encoding-Retrieval Interactions

The interaction between encoding and retrieval processes has been a topic of numerous research studies in memory in recent decades (e.g., Meier & Graf, 2000; Mulligan, 2012; Roediger, 1990). Based on the results of these studies, it is clear that **matching the circumstances of encoding and retrieval aids memory**. This phenomenon is known as the **encoding specificity principle**. These circumstances can involve the stimuli in the environment; one's mood, thoughts about the information, and physiological state; and processing type. We now consider three examples of this phenomenon: environmental effects, mood effects, and processing effects.

Environmental Context Effects

Studies of memory in the past few decades have shown that a match in environment between study and test aids memory. Godden and Baddeley (1975) conducted one of the classic studies showing this effect with divers. This subject sample (see Figure 6.7) allowed for two study conditions, underwater or above water, and two test conditions, underwater or above water. Thus, half of the subjects heard a list of words underwater while diving and half heard a list of words above water after diving. Then half of each of these groups (underwater study, above-water study) were tested in each environment (underwater test, above-water test). Overall, no effects of study condition or test condition alone were found on recall performance. In other words, being underwater did not reduce recall. However, the study and test conditions interacted such that there were different results when the study and test conditions matched and when they did not match. Figure 6.8 shows these results. Memory performance was higher when the study and test conditions matched (i.e., underwater study and test, above-water study and test) than when they did not match (i.e., underwater study and above-water test, above-water study and underwater test). These results show the importance of matching the environment of study and test.

What do these results mean for you and your study habits? These results suggest that a match in environment between your study locations and your testing locations will provide the best condition for memory retrieval. If you are not tested with music playing, then you should not study with music playing. If you are tested in a large,

Encoding specificity principle: the idea that memory is best when the circumstances of encoding and retrieval are matched

Figure 6.7 Divers Participated in Godden and Baddeley's (1975) Study With Study and Test Taking Place Above Water or Underwater

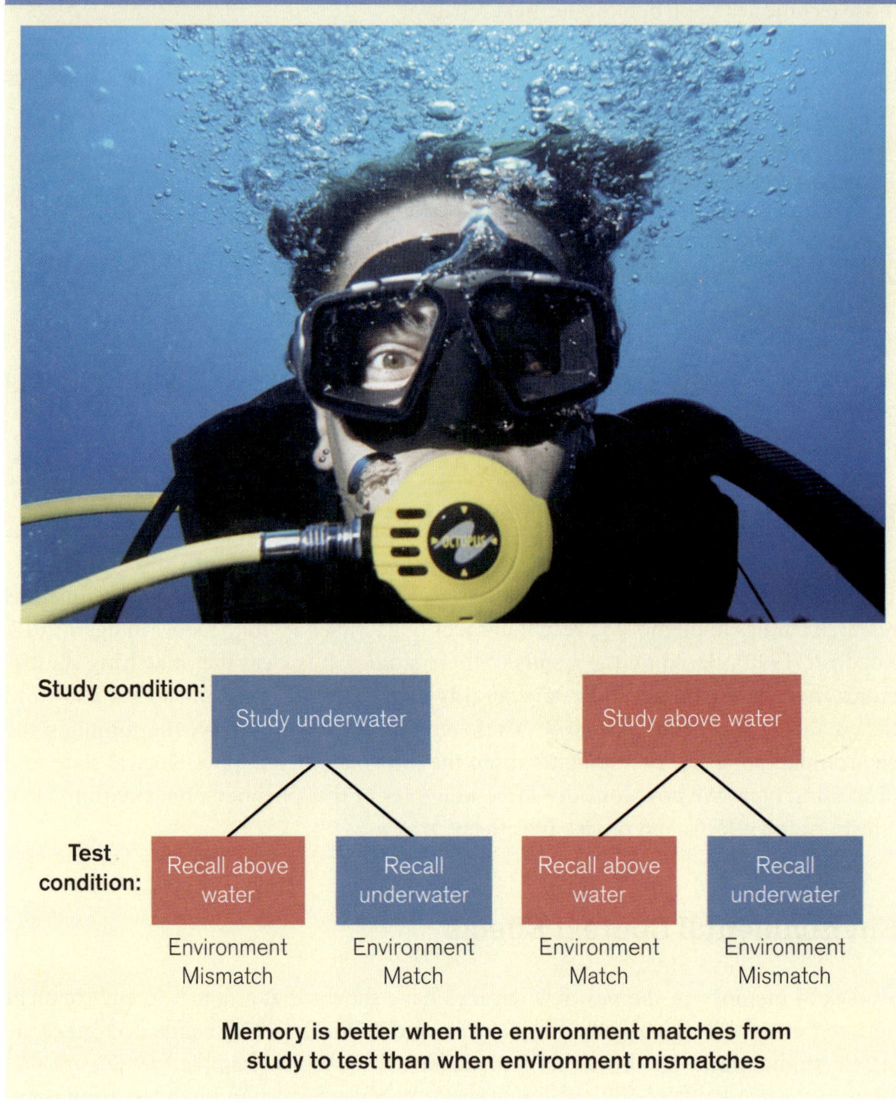

Photo from David De Lossy/Photodisc/Thinkstock

quiet room, then you should study in a large, quiet room. In fact, studying in your classroom will provide the best match in environment, and luckily, this is where your first learning of the material takes place (in the classroom your class is in), so you are already getting some advantage from this environmental match when you attend class.

Some studies (e.g., Isarida, Isarida, & Sakai, 2012) have shown that other contextual cues (e.g., how meaningful the information is) can reduce the effects of environmental matches between study and test on memory. Because other types of context provide better cues for retrieval, the environmental cues become less important. However, given the number of studies showing environmental-context match effects in both recall and recognition (see Smith & Vela, 2001), matching the environment from study to test may help you when other contextual cues fail to aid your retrieval of information you need during an exam.

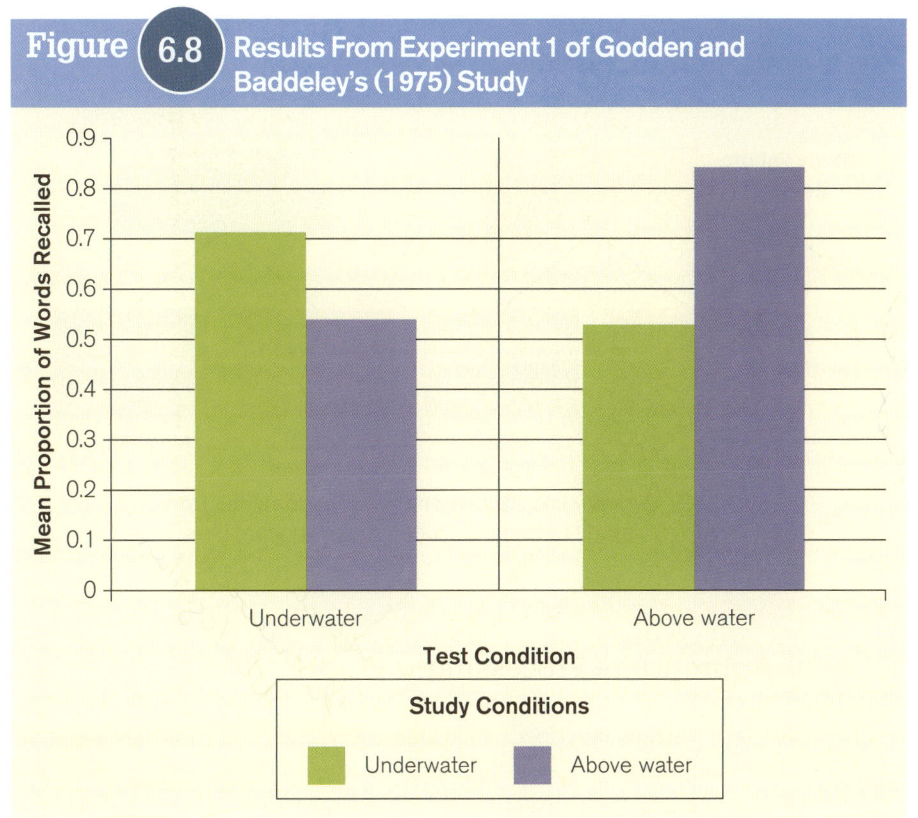

Figure 6.8 Results From Experiment 1 of Godden and Baddeley's (1975) Study

Mood-Dependent Effects

Just as a match in environment between study and test can aid memory, so can a match in mood between study and test. Numerous research studies support this idea (Eich, 1995). One research method used in investigating such effects involves the induction of a particular mood in subjects (e.g., happy mood or sad mood). This is often accomplished by playing a "happy" or "sad" piece of music or having subjects read sentences that are either on positive or negative topics. The mood induction is used both at study and at test so that matches and mismatches in mood between study and test can be compared (as in the match and mismatch of the environments in the Godden & Baddeley, 1975, study). Figure 6.9 illustrates this procedure. The findings from many of these studies show that a match in mood from study to test results in better memory for studied information than when mood at study and test are different. This means that it is helpful to be somewhat anxious while you study for a test if you will be anxious while you are taking the test.

In many cases, it may be difficult for students to match a mood during study for a test and the taking of that test. Study sessions often take place in quiet, calm environments, whereas students are often anxious while taking a test with other anxious students around them. However, before you become discouraged that the mood-dependent effect may not work for you, consider that many studies have failed to find the mood-dependent effect, especially when the test involves recognition memory. In addition, Eich (1995) suggested that in order for mood-dependent effects to occur, a strong and stable mood (e.g., a mood that can be clearly identified with a specific valence and arousal level and that does not quickly fade or change) must be present at both study and test, along with active encoding (e.g., deep processing) of information. Thus, this effect may work to your advantage only if you use the deep and active encoding strategies described in this chapter and if your moods tend to be stable and similar across study and testing situations. The effect also might only aid your memory when you are completing recall tests (e.g., short-answer tests).

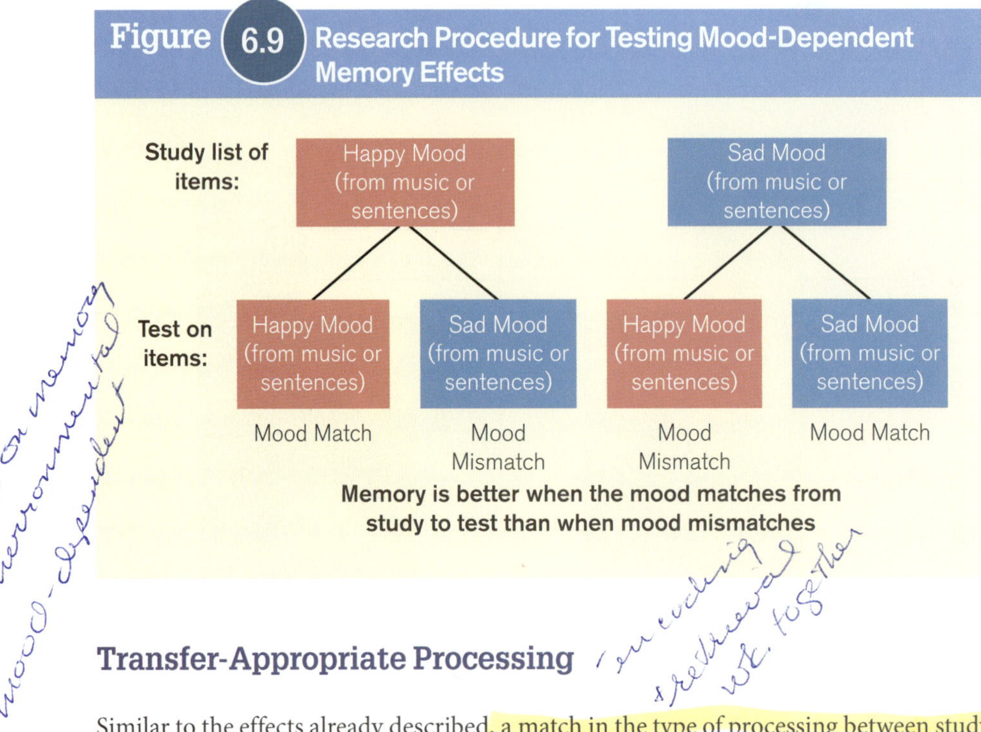

Figure 6.9 Research Procedure for Testing Mood-Dependent Memory Effects

Transfer-Appropriate Processing

Memory Encoding and Retrieval

Similar to the effects already described, a match in the type of processing between study and test will also aid memory. This match in processing is called transfer-appropriate processing and seems to have a stronger effect on memory than either environmental or mood-dependent effects. In other words, unlike depth-of-processing effects where encoding is the only influencing factor on memory performance, in **transfer-appropriate processing** effects, both encoding and retrieval together influence memory performance. Transfer-appropriate processing effects were shown in research by Morris, Bransford, and Franks (1977). They varied level of processing at study: Subjects performed a sentence completion task (deep processing) or a rhyming task (shallow processing). They were then given either a typical recognition test ("Was this a studied item—yes or no?") or a rhyming recognition test ("Does this item rhyme with a studied item—yes or no?"). The results of the study are shown in Figure 6.10. When subjects studied the items with meaning-based (deep) processing, standard recognition, which relies on such processing, resulted in higher memory scores. However, when subjects studied the items with rhyme-based processing, the rhyming recognition test resulted in higher memory scores.

Transfer-appropriate processing effects have been shown in a number of studies using different types of processing. Roediger (1990) described studies extending this effect to different types of explicit cued-recall tasks (recall tests where cues are given to aid intentional retrieval of studied items) and implicit-memory tasks (tests relying on unintentional retrieval of studied items; see Chapter 5 for more description of cued-recall and implicit-memory tasks). The type of test (explicit and implicit) did not affect results very much, but a match in processing between study and test resulted in better memory. For example, in Blaxton's (1989) study, subjects studied items by either reading them as they were presented (e.g., *cold*) or generating them from words that had the opposite meaning (e.g., hot – ?). In other words, the study task involved a visual presentation of the words that did not involve automatic processing of meaning (saying the words out loud) or the meaning of the words with no visual presentation of the words (generating opposites). Memory depended both on study task and type of test. For tests that involved the visual form of the studied items like recalling them from cues of similar looking words (e.g., *cost*) or solving word fragments (e.g., c_l_), the read study task resulted in better memory. But for tests that involved the meaning of the studied items

Transfer-appropriate processing: an effect in memory showing that matches in processing between encoding and retrieval improve memory

Figure 6.10 Results From Morris et al.'s (1977) Experiment 1

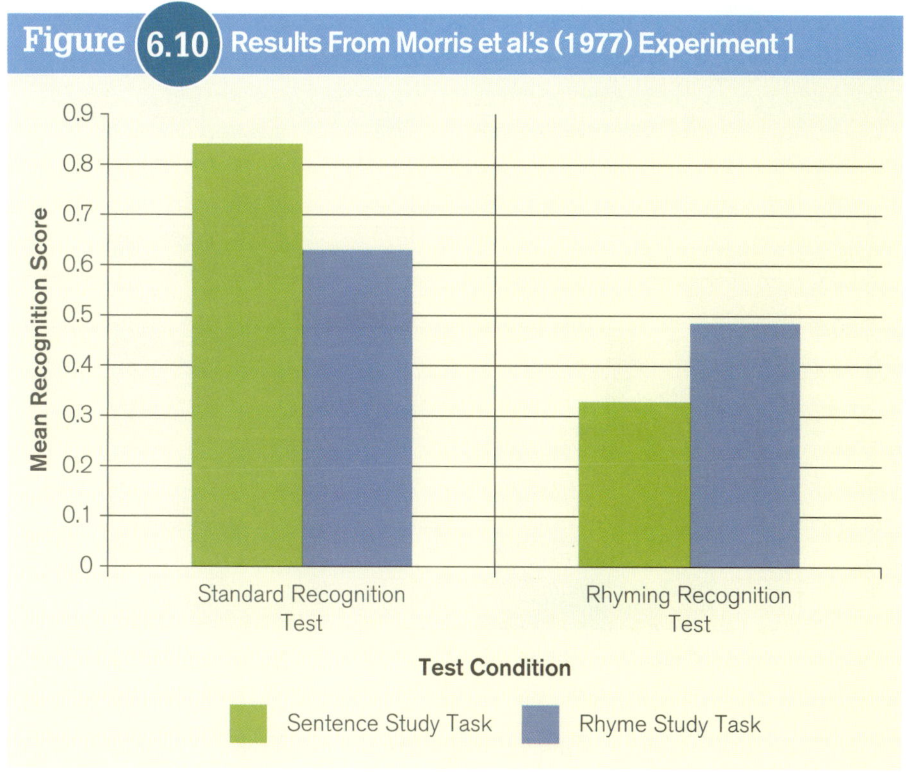

like free recall and answering general knowledge questions (e.g., What type of environment do penguins live in?), the generation study task resulted in better memory. These results show that the processing match between study and test is important, regardless of the type of memory test used for retrieval.

Even more recently, researchers examining prospective memory (remembering to perform a future task; see Chapter 5 for further description) have shown that transfer-appropriate processing can influence accuracy in performing this type of memory task. In one such study, Meier and Graf (2000) used two different types of prospective-memory tasks: respond when you see an animal word as a meaning-based prospective memory task, and respond when you see a word with three e's as a visual form prospective memory task. In addition, two different ongoing tasks were used in which the prospective-memory task was embedded (decide if words represent natural or fabricated things as a meaning-based ongoing task and decide how many enclosed spaces are included in the letters of the word as a visual-form ongoing task). They found that subjects remembered to respond to the prospective-memory cue words (animals or words with three e's) more often if the ongoing task matched the type of processing. Figure 6.11 presents these results. Thus, from these studies it is clear that a match in processing between tasks (study and test, ongoing- and prospective-memory tasks) is an important factor in memory retrieval, regardless of the type of memory test one is performing.

Of the encoding specificity effects discussed in this chapter, you can best use to your advantage transfer-appropriate processing in improving your study habits and memory for information. One thing you might consider is to conduct your retrieval practice (see the Retrieval Effects section earlier) with the type of test you will take in mind. If your test is multiple choice, then multiple-choice retrieval practice (i.e., recognizing the correct answers among incorrect choices) will be the best study activity. However, if your test will involve short answers, then retrieval practice that involves recall of the information from cues will be the best study activity. In other words, match the type of processing you use in your study habits with the type of processing you will need to retrieve the information in an exam. And if your exam involves more than one type of problem (e.g.,

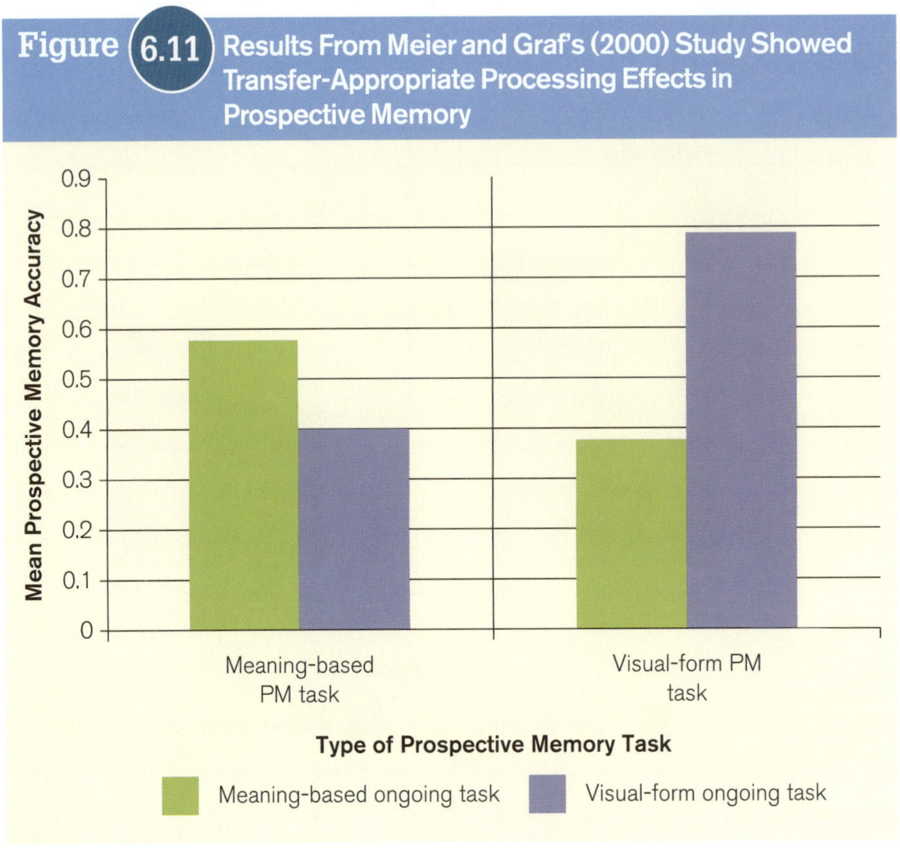

Stop and Think

6.11. Explain the encoding specificity principle. Describe some ways you can use this principle to improve your memory during test taking.

6.12. Godden and Baddeley (1975) found that when people both studied and were tested above water, they remembered more than when they studied above water and were tested underwater. Explain why these results were not due simply to poorer memory when tested underwater.

6.13. Explain why it might be difficult for many students to use the mood-dependent memory effect to improve exam performance.

6.14. Imagine that you have an exam on the material covered in this chapter. Describe some ways that you would prepare for the exam using the concepts covered in this chapter.

multiple choice and short answers), then you may want to do both types of study activities to aid your test performance.

Summary of Encoding-Retrieval Interactions

As you saw in this section of the chapter, both study (i.e., encoding) and test (i.e., retrieval) activities are important to consider when attempting to improve retrieval from long-term memory. Matching the circumstances between study and test, whether this be the environment, your mood, or the processing you do, will increase memory performance. The reason this is important for memory is that you are increasing the overlap in the study and retrieval cues that can help you retrieve information from memory. Even in free-recall memory tests where you are simply asked to recall the studied information without any cues given to guide you, you can provide your own cues by reinstating the context present at study (e.g., things in the environment, the thoughts you had at study during processing). Table 6.1 summarizes the memory retrieval aids we have discussed in this chapter to help you consider which factors that influence long-term memory you might use to help improve your own memory performance. We end this chapter with a further discussion of the way mnemonics can help individuals improve memory performance when they train their minds to use such techniques (see the introduction to this chapter).

Improving Memory

Mnemonics

Image Mnemonic Activity

The suggestions in Table 6.1 may help you perform better on your course exams. However, they are not likely to give you the kind of memory performance described at the beginning of the chapter for the memory champions (e.g., memorizing the order of a deck of cards with just a couple minutes of study). This sort of memory ability requires training and practice using techniques known as mnemonics. **Mnemonics** are memory techniques that have been used by humans for thousands of years to remember information. They rely on the mechanisms of long-term memory to store information in a way that makes it more memorable. For example, read the following sentences, close your eyes briefly and imagine the scenes as you read, count backward by threes from 100, and then try to recall the sentences:

Memory Techniques

The cat walked down the street.

The mailbox was by the curb.

The giraffe ate the leaves in the tree.

The hammer sat on the table.

He wrote on the paper.

The child laughed at the clown.

How many of the sentences could you remember? Let's try it again. Follow the same procedure with the following sentences:

The cat rode a bicycle down the street.

The mailbox danced by the curb.

The giraffe climbed the tree.

Mnemonicizer Exercise

Table 6.1 Summary of Techniques for Improving Retrieval From Long-Term Memory

- Sleeping between the study and test of information you want to remember will help you retrieve that information from long-term memory.
- Encoding information according to its meaning aids long-term memory.
- Spaced repetitions result in better memory than massed repetitions.
- The first information encoded will show the best memory. The last information encoded will show a memory advantage primarily if the delay between encoding and retrieval is very short.
- Reviewing information by means of an intervening test aids later retrieval.
- Matching the circumstances (e.g., environment, mood, processing) of encoding and retrieval aids memory.

Mnemonics: memory techniques that aid memory performance

Memory Improvement Games

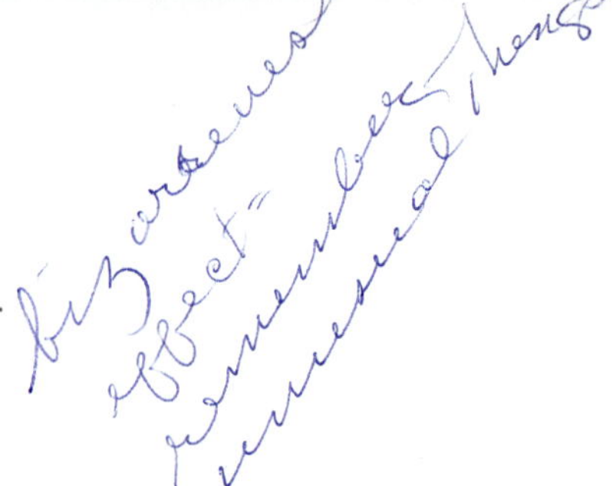

The hammer sang a song to the table.

He wrote on the cow.

The child laughed at the purple sky.

How many of these sentences could you remember? Most people remember the second set better because they invoke strange images that you are more likely to remember. The human mind notices unusual things, and some types of mnemonics use this phenomenon to help you remember. This is known as the bizarreness effect (e.g., McDaniel, Einstein, DeLosh, May, & Brady, 1995) (see Chapter 8 for more discussion of this effect and the role of imagery in memory).

Method of Loci Activity

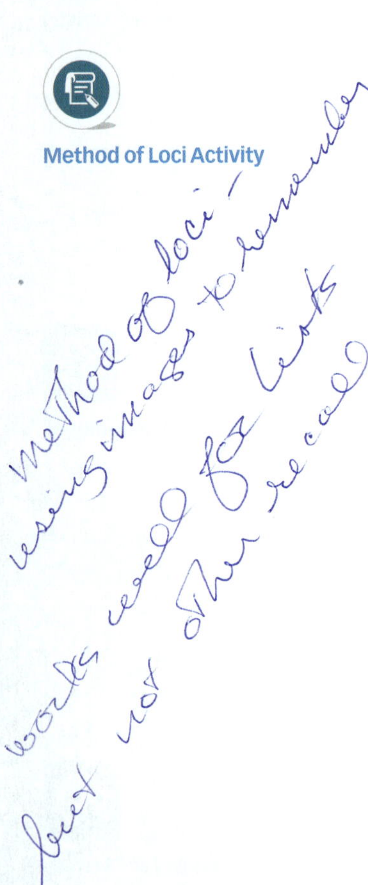

The method of loci is a mnemonic technique often used by the memory champions described by Foer (2011) in his book and involves using images to remember items. One can use this technique by creating images in well-known locations involving items one needs to remember. For example, suppose you wanted to remember the following list of grocery items needed at the store: peanut butter, blueberries, cookies, cheese, bread, sliced turkey, mayonnaise, milk, and apples. To help you remember these words, imagine the place you grew up in that you are most familiar with (e.g., house, apartment). Picture yourself walking up to the front door and think about what it looks like there. Picture yourself holding a jar of peanut butter and smearing it all over the door. Then you go in the door. Go to the first room you encounter. Imagine you are sitting down in this room and having a conversation with a blueberry. Next go to the bathroom. In the bathroom, picture the sink filled to the top with your favorite cookies. Continue moving through the place you are picturing, creating odd images with the objects on the list. Then take a break for ten to fifteen minutes and do not think about the objects in that time. When you come back, try to walk through the place you imagined and recall the objects as you go. You will likely find that you can recall each object quite easily and may remember these objects for some time (try the recall again tomorrow by walking back through the place you imagined again).

Memory champions such as those described by Foer (and Foer himself) create images in their minds of the objects in locations within what Foer calls a "memory palace," which can be any location with set points that can be navigated in one's mind. A familiar route one drives can serve as a "memory palace" as well as one's own home. Foer describes developing and practicing this technique each day for about a year. After that time he was able to use this technique to win the U.S. Memory Championship in 2006.

One thing you might notice about this technique is that it works well for remembering lists of items, but it is not going to make your memory better for every type of information you try to remember. That is one of the drawbacks to using mnemonic techniques. They work well for lists of items but not as well for general knowledge and specific episodes one wishes to remember.

Superior Autobiographical Memory

Until very recently, despite studies looking for such evidence, there was no scientific evidence of what people think of as photographic memory—the type of memory where people claim they can just "picture in their minds" specific episodes or information. Researchers have yet to find clear scientific evidence for this form of memory. However, some recent studies suggest that for a very few individuals, a type of superior autobiographical memory may exist. Autobiographical memories are memories of your day-to-day life (e.g., what you had for breakfast this morning, the day you broke up with your last boyfriend or girlfriend). (Chapter 5 describes this type of

Superior Autobiographical Memory

memory in more detail.) Parker, Cahill, and McGaugh (2006) describe a case study (see Chapter 1 to review the different methods of study used in cognitive psychology) of a woman identified as AJ who claimed to be able to report what occurred on any date past 1980 (during her lifetime). The researchers tested AJ in the lab and found that she did in fact have superior autobiographical memory. She was able to report with near perfect accuracy events from her life and historical events when given a date chosen by the researchers. The researchers verified her personal events from diaries she kept spanning twenty-four years of her life. Because AJ did not know which dates she would be tested on, it is unlikely that she used the mnemonic techniques described in this chapter. In fact, her performance for memorization of lists was below normal levels when tested by the researchers. Thus, her superior autobiographical memory appears to be an untrained ability with an unknown cause.

These researchers have identified ten additional individuals with superior autobiographical memory (LePort et al., 2012). The researchers tested these individuals and found similar memory abilities to those of AJ. All eleven individuals then had an MRI taken of their brains to allow the researchers to examine the size and shape of different brain structures. The results showed that these individuals differed from normal control subjects in the size and shape of their temporal lobe, which is known to be involved in autobiographical memory, and the caudate nucleus, which is known to be involved in skills and habits. The researchers also suggested that the subjects showed some tendencies toward obsessive memory and other habits (e.g., they habitually recall past events in their lives). Thus, these brain structure differences might be responsible for the superior autobiographical memory shown by these subjects, or they could be a result of the abilities these individuals possess. Further research is needed to better understand these abilities and why they occur.

Stop and Think

6.15. What are mnemonics? In what way are they useful in improving memory performance?

6.16. Describe how you might use the method of loci to remember a list of items.

6.17. What is superior autobiographical memory?

6.18. Based on what you learned in this chapter, what techniques do you think will be most useful to you in improving your memory abilities?

THINKING ABOUT RESEARCH

As you read the following summary of a research study in psychology, think about the following questions:

1. Can you connect the researchers' hypothesis in this study to any of the encoding effects discussed in this chapter? In what way(s) are they connected?
2. Can you think of an alternative explanation for the results of the study beyond the explanation offered by the researchers? What type of study might allow the alternative explanation to be ruled out?
3. What type of research design are the researchers using in this study? (Hint: Review the Research Methodologies section in Chapter 1 for help answering questions 3 and 4.)
4. What is the independent variable in this study? What is the dependent variable in this study?
5. What do the results of this study suggest about the purpose of human memory?

(Continued)

(Continued)

Figure 6.12 Mean Recall Results From Nairne et al.'s (2013) Study 2

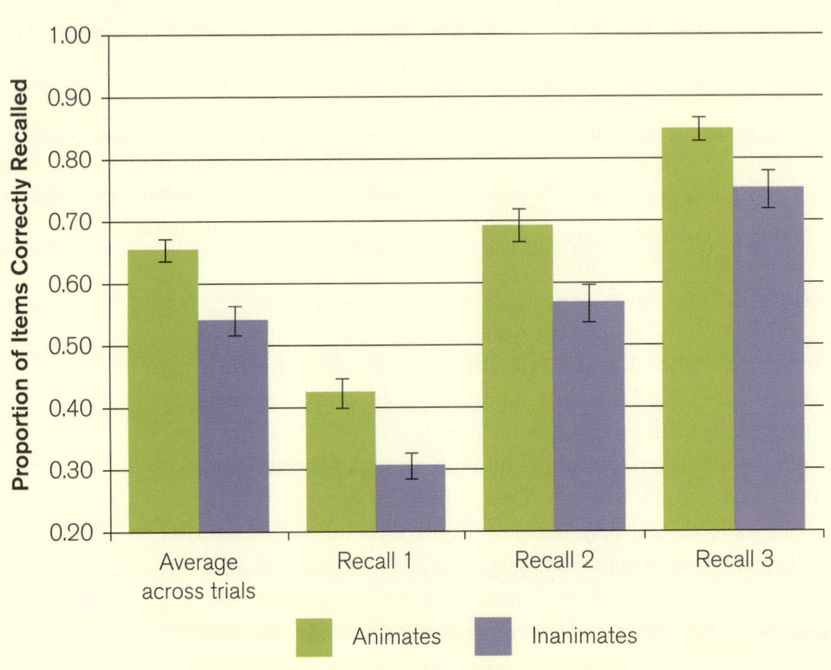

SOURCE: Figure 2, Nairne, J. S., Van Arsdall, J. E., Pandeirada, J. N. S., Cogdill, M., & LeBreton, J. M. (2013). Adaptive memory: The mnemonic value of animacy. *Psychological Science, 24,* 2099–2105.

Study Reference

Nairne, J. S., Van Arsdall, J. E., Pandeirada, J. N. S., Cogdill, M. & LeBreton, J. M. (2013). Adaptive memory: The mnemonic value of animacy. *Psychological Science, 24,* 2099–2105.

Note: Study 2 from this article is described here.

Purpose of the study: The authors of this study argued that animacy (whether or not something is an animate object) is an important factor in long-term memory retrieval. They suggest that this idea is consistent with an adaptive and evolutionary view of memory, as predators of early humans and potential mates are animate objects that would be important to encode and remember. They tested this idea in a study comparing memory for animate (e.g., wolf) and inanimate (e.g., kite) objects, where the groups of items were matched on many other factors (e.g., familiarity of the words, ease of imaging a picture of the items). They hypothesized that the animate objects would be remembered better than the inanimate objects.

Method of the study: Subjects were 54 college students. They were asked to study 24 words in a random order. Half of the words were names of animate objects and half were names of inanimate objects. The words were shown for 5 seconds each, and subjects were asked to try to remember them. After the study list, subjects were asked to complete a digit distractor task for 1 minute. They were then asked to recall the words from the study list in any order. Subjects then repeated the entire procedure (study list, distractor, and recall) two more times to examine effects of repeated exposure and testing of the words.

Results of the study: The results of the study showed that animate objects were recalled at a higher rate than inanimate objects for all three recall tests. Figure 6.12 shows the mean recall results overall and for each of the three recall tests.

Conclusions of the study: The results supported the researchers' hypothesis that animate objects are better remembered than inanimate objects. These results are consistent with an evolutionary perspective of memory development.

CHAPTER REVIEW

Summary

- **Why does forgetting occur and what can you do to prevent it?**

  Forgetting likely occurs due to interference from other information during retrieval and lack of consolidation of memories as they are stored.

- **Which methods of encoding information are effective in increasing retrieval from long-term memory?**

  Encoding information deeply (based on meaning), spaced over time, and with important information first will aid retrieval from long-term memory.

- **Which methods of retrieving information are effective in increasing memory performance?**

  Retrieval practice (i.e., practicing retrieval of information you wish to remember over the long term) will aid later retrieval from long-term memory.

- **In what ways do encoding and retrieval interact to affect long-term memory?**

  A match in circumstances (e.g., mood, environment, physiology, processing) between study and test will result in more cue overlap from study to test, aiding long-term memory retrieval.

- **What are some simple methods you can use to increase retrieval from long-term memory?**

  Table 6.1 summarizes the techniques described in the preceding sections.

- **How effective are mnemonics in increasing long-term memory retrieval?**

  If one trains in the use of mnemonics, these techniques can significantly improve memory for lists of information. However, they will not necessarily improve memory for all types of information.

Chapter Quiz

1. Enter the letter of each effect name with the type of effect it is below.
   (a) encoding effect
   (b) retrieval effect
   (c) encoding-retrieval interaction effect

   ___ level-of-processing effect
   ___ mood-dependent memory effect
   ___ encoding specificity principle
   ___ serial position curve
   ___ testing effect
   ___ transfer-appropriate processing
   ___ spaced repetition effect

2. Which of the following effects shows that long-term memory encoding is based on the meaning of information?
   (a) transfer-appropriate processing
   (b) mood-dependent memory effect
   (c) testing effect
   (d) level-of-processing effect

3. Which of the following effects shows that long-term memories can be strengthened by retrieving them?
   (a) transfer-appropriate processing
   (b) mood-dependent memory effect
   (c) testing effect
   (d) level-of-processing effect

4. Which of the following effects shows that long-term memory retrieval is based on the match in processing type from study to test?
   (a) transfer-appropriate processing
   (b) mood-dependent memory effect
   (c) testing effect
   (d) level-of-processing effect

5. Which of the following effects shows that long-term memory retrieval is based on the match in mental state (e.g., happy, sad, anxious) from study to test?
   (a) transfer-appropriate processing
   (b) mood-dependent memory effect
   (c) testing effect
   (d) level-of-processing effect

6. Consolidation that occurs slowly over time is called ____________ consolidation.
   (a) synaptic
   (b) systems
   (c) neuron
   (d) cortex
7. Which of the following processes is a likely cause of normal forgetting (choose all that apply)?
   (a) interference
   (b) decay over time
   (c) death of neuron cells
   (d) lack of consolidation
8. Is there scientific support for "photographic memory"? Explain your answer.
9. Would you like to have superior autobiographical memory? Why or why not?
10. Describe three study techniques that would improve your test performance.

 Key Terms

Consolidation 129
Deep processing 131
Elaborative encoding 131
Encoding specificity principle 137
Level-of-processing effect 131
Mnemonics 143
Primacy effect 133
Recency effect 133
Serial position curve 134
Shallow processing 131
Spacing effect 132
Testing effect 135
Transfer-appropriate processing 140

 Stop and Think Answers

6.1. Why does forgetting occur?

Forgetting likely occurs due to interference from other information stored in long-term memory and from lack of consolidation, where memories are strengthened as they are stored in neuron connections and in different areas of the brain.

6.2. How do systems consolidation and synaptic consolidation differ?

Systems consolidation is a slow process (days, weeks, months) where the storage of the pieces of memories shifts from the hippocampus to the cortical areas of the brain. Synaptic consolidation is a faster process (hours, days) that occurs in the connections (i.e., synapses) between the neuron cells in the brain.

6.3. What is one way you can increase your retrieval from long-term memory as you study for an upcoming exam?

Sleeping between study and test will aid consolidation and strengthen long-term memories.

6.4. Describe three methods of encoding that can increase retrieval from long-term memory.

Encoding based on meaning (level of processing), spaced over time (spaced repetition), and with important information first (serial position curve) will increase retrieval from long-term memory.

6.5. What is a serial position curve?

The resulting curve when memory performance is graphed according to an item's position in an encoded list: The first items and the last items tend to show higher performance.

6.6. Describe two ways of studying information that would qualify as deep encoding.

Answers will vary, but anything that focuses on the meaning of the information qualifies.

6.7. Based on what you have learned in this section, in what ways can your study techniques for your courses be improved?

Answers will vary depending on current study techniques; see Table 6.1 for a summary.

6.8. What is retrieval practice? What effect does it have on long-term memory?

Retrieval practice is the activity of retrieving information one wishes to remember over the long term. It will increase later memory performance for the practiced information (compared with simply rereading the information).

6.9. Which study-test delays show a memory advantage due to retrieval practice?

Longer study-test delays show the testing effect (better memory for information that received retrieval practice). Short delays (e.g., five minutes) have not shown a benefit of retrieval practice.

6.10. What types of retrieval practice are the most effective? Which of the encoding effects described in the Encoding Effects section do you think may be involved in the more effective retrieval practice techniques?

Active, explanatory, questioning practice activities and spaced retrieval practice will result in the most benefit to long-term memory retrieval. These techniques connect with the level of processing (deep encoding) and spaced repetition effects.

6.11. Explain the encoding specificity principle. Describe some ways you can use this principle to improve your memory during test taking.

The principle states that a match in circumstances from study to test will improve memory performance. Answers will vary for specific techniques.

6.12. Godden and Baddeley (1975) found that when people both studied and were tested above water, they remembered more than when they studied above water and were tested underwater. Explain why these results were not due simply to poorer memory when tested underwater.

Because they also included a group that studied and was tested underwater that produced similar memory results to the group that studied and was tested above water, they can rule out this alternative explanation of their results.

6.13. Explain why it might be difficult for many students to use the mood-dependent memory effect to improve exam performance.

This effect might be difficult to implement because it relies on a match in mood from study to test. Many students are calm when they study but anxious when tested, so it can be difficult to match mood from study to test.

6.14. Imagine that you have an exam on the material covered in this chapter. Describe some ways that you would prepare for the exam using the concepts covered in this chapter.

Answers will vary.

6.15. What are mnemonics? In what way are they useful in improving memory performance?

Mnemonics are techniques for improving memory for a set of items. They rely on well-known or unusual images to remember the information.

6.16. Describe how you might use the method of loci to remember a list of items.

Answers will vary, but the method works by forming images in a well-known place with the items one wishes to remember.

6.17. What is superior autobiographical memory?

A seemingly rare ability found in a few individuals with extremely strong memories of episodes in their lives. These individuals are able to report what occurred in their lives when questioned with a random date in their lives.

6.18. Based on what you learned in this chapter, what techniques do you think will be most useful to you in improving your memory abilities?

Answers will vary depending on current study techniques; see Table 6.1 for a summary.

Student Study Site

Sharpen your skills with SAGE edge at **edge.sagepub.com/mcbridecp**

SAGE edge for students provides a personalized approach to help you accomplish your coursework goals in an easy-to-use learning environment.

Go to edge.sagepub.com/mcbridecp for additional exercises and web resources. Select Chapter 6, Long-Term Memory, for chapter-specific resources. All of the links listed in the margins of this chapter are accessible via this site.

(AP Photo)/Takaaki Iwabu

Memory Errors

Questions to Consider

- Does memory work like a video camera, fully recoding each experience? Why or why not?
- In what ways does memory fail in normal individuals?
- What factors contribute to memory inaccuracies?
- How have researchers studied memory errors?
- How can different types of brain damage or deterioration affect memory accuracy?

Introduction: The Inaccuracy of Memory

On July 28, 1984, as Jennifer Thompson slept in her apartment, a man came into her room. The man raped her, but then Jennifer escaped. During the attack Jennifer thought to herself that in case she survived, she needed to remember all the details of her attacker so that she could help catch and convict him. The police had Jennifer help a sketch artist draw a picture of her attacker. Then the police presented her with a photo lineup where pictures of several men were presented to her as possible suspects. Jennifer identified the photo of Ronald Cotton in the array shown to her as her attacker. Ronald was then brought in for a live lineup. Jennifer again identified him as her attacker. Based primarily on Jennifer's identification of him, Ronald was convicted of the crime and sent to prison. Jennifer felt confident that she had helped put the right person in prison for her attack.

Ronald Cotton was actually innocent of the crime. While in prison, he learned that another inmate had confessed to raping Jennifer Thompson as well as other women. He attempted to have his verdict overturned. Eventually, DNA evidence from the crime was analyzed and it was clear that the inmate who confessed in prison was the man who attacked Jennifer. Ronald was exonerated and set free after eleven years in prison. When Jennifer saw the man who actually attacked her in the courtroom, she had no recognition of him at all, but Jennifer was consumed with guilt over sending the wrong person to prison. Jennifer's case is only one of many where the wrong person was convicted based on eyewitness testimony. The Innocence Project reports that about 75 percent of cases that have been overturned with DNA evidence were for convictions based on eyewitness testimony.

How can our memories be so wrong? In a case where an accurate memory is so important and the person makes a concerted effort to encode the details of the event, the memory of the person who attacked her is still horribly wrong and has devastating consequences. This can occur even in cases where we are intentionally trying to remember something important, as in Jennifer's case. One reason is that our memory does not provide a full and complete recording of our experiences, even in situations where an accurate memory is so important. It probably did not evolve for this purpose (see Nairne & Pandeirada, 2008). Instead, it likely developed to aid us in planning our future, making decisions, and having successful social interactions. Thus, it can be influenced by events that occur after an experience has been stored in our memory. For example, Jennifer's memory of the person who attacked her was likely influenced by the police procedures (e.g., the lineups and the way they were conducted) and the subsequent conviction of a suspect. In addition, Ronald Cotton looked similar enough to the actual assailant so his description seemed to match the general sketch drawn up by the sketch artist before Ronald was arrested. This likely also gave Jennifer confidence in her identification of him in the lineup. Based on their experiences with the serious consequences that can result from such memory errors, Jennifer Thompson and Ronald Cotton, shown together in the photo that opens this chapter, now work together to advocate for changes in the way police conduct photo lineups. Nevertheless, having a memory that works by retrieving information through similarities and connections with our knowledge also has benefits in retrieving accurate memories. In this chapter, we explore the ways in which our memories can be inaccurate, both in normal individuals and in those who have had their memories damaged in some way, and why memory seems to be organized in this way.

The Seven "Sins" of Memory

When you think of people with poor memory abilities, you may think of older individuals who may have some memory deterioration or individuals who have suffered some form of brain damage. But as the opening story shows, even those with normal memory abilities can suffer from drastic memory errors. In his book *The Seven Sins of Memory*, Daniel Schacter (2002) described seven common memory failures that occur in individuals with normal memory abilities (see Figure 7.1). He describes these "sins" of memory as by-products of the way our memories function and typical of everyone to varying degrees. In fact, research on memory errors reviewed in this chapter shows that memory errors, such as the false memory of Ronald Cotton attacking her that Jennifer Thompson experienced, reveal the adaptive mechanisms by which memory operates and how we might design situations like eyewitness questioning to minimize such errors. These mechanisms also help our memories to be more accurate as they aid in retrieval of accurate memories. Later in this chapter, we also consider more atypical failures of memory in individuals with amnesia and types of dementia.

Comstock/Stockbyte/Thinkstock

Photo 7.1 Lineup procedures are important in preserving eyewitness' memory accuracy.

Figure 7.1 The Seven "Sins" of Memory Described by Daniel Schacter (2002)

Transience
Persistence
Absentmindedness
Bias
Blocking
Suggestibility
Source Misattribution

Photo from BananaStock/BananaStock/Thinkstock

Error #1 Transience

The Malleability of Memory

The first memory "sin" is transience. *Transience* is a term for normal forgetting of information over time. In Chapter 6, we described some possible causes of normal forgetting and the form this forgetting takes. Most information is forgotten very quickly after it is encoded, but over time less and less information is forgotten. In other words, the rate of forgetting of information is very high right after encoding, but the rate decreases as the time since encoding increases, such that forgetting slows down (see Figure 6.1). As described in Chapters 5 and 6, most memory researchers have rejected the idea of passive decay over time as the cause of forgetting. Instead, active processes of interference (from older or more recently encoded information) and consolidation (the strengthening of memories through neural cell processes) seem to most heavily influence forgetting. With more interference and less consolidation, more forgetting occurs. Results showing better memory when sleep occurs between encoding and retrieval support both of these descriptions of forgetting: Very little interference occurs while one is sleeping, and consolidation seems to work more effectively (perhaps because of the lack of interference) during sleep. Chapter 6 also describes some encoding methods that seem to result in better memory (i.e., less forgetting of information) such as processing the meaning of information and using imagery mnemonics.

Error #2 Absentmindedness

A lack of attention during encoding or retrieval results in poor memory (see Chapter 4 for further discussion of attention and its effects on cognition). Schacter (2002) terms this phenomenon absentmindedness. A good example of this memory failure is not remembering where you have placed something you need to find, such as your car keys. If you do not pay attention to their location when you put them down, there is a good chance you will not remember where they are (unless you always put them in the same place each time). Not remembering your intentions to perform tasks also falls under the memory failure of absentmindedness. Have you ever intended to go get something from another room in your house, but by the time you get to that room you have forgotten what you went there for because your attention has already wandered off to other thoughts? Remembering to complete a future task (e.g., taking medicine at a certain time, taking cookies out of the oven before they burn, calling your mom before you go to bed) is known as prospective memory (see Chapter 5 for more discussion of prospective memory). Failures of prospective memory are normal (Have you ever completed a homework assignment on time and then forgotten to turn it in?) and are described by Schacter as an absentmindedness "sin" of memory that we all fall prey to from time to time.

Photo 7.2 Not remembering where you left your keys illustrates the memory "sin" of absentmindedness.

Error #3 Blocking

Schacter (2002) describes blocking as an experience of knowing that you know information but being unable to retrieve it. This is also sometimes called a "tip of the tongue" experience.

(Chapter 9 also provides a description of this phenomenon with some other explanations of tip-of-the-tongue phenomena.) Most people have had this experience when they know the name of something (e.g., an actor, the name of a book or movie, a specific word they want to use in their writing) and may be able to remember what letter it starts with or what it sounds like but cannot retrieve the full name or word. This experience can be particularly anxiety provoking when you are blocking on someone's name that you know you know and are in a situation where you need to introduce that person to someone else. This may have even happened to you during an exam: You know that you know the answer to the question, but you just cannot pull it out of your memory. I recently had this experience in trying to remember the name of the fifth Backyardigan character with my son (I forgot Austin). Another example I frequently encounter is that I can remember all but one of the movies nominated each year for an Academy Award. I can typically list all but one but seem to have trouble coming up with the last item in the list. Blocking seems to occur more frequently with proper names and unusual words because the terms are somewhat arbitrary in their assignment: There is no meaning connection to help us associate the name Heather with the person we just met to help us remember her name in the future.

Déjà Vu

Error #4 Source Misattribution

When we remember something as from a different source than the one it was actually learned from, we suffer from source misattribution. For example, there are likely times when you have a thought or idea about something that you think is an original thought you generated, but in reality you read or heard about the idea somewhere else first. This can also happen when you think one person told someone something (e.g., you think your biology professor said there might be a pop quiz in class next week), but later you realize it was someone else who said it (e.g., it was actually your psychology professor who said there might be a pop quiz next week). In this case, you thought the source of this memory was an actual experience of talking to someone, but the reality is that the memory's source is just your own thought. Source misattribution may have played a role in Jennifer Thompson's case. When she identified Ronald Cotton in the police lineup of live suspects, she may have been remembering him from the photo lineup she had already completed instead of from the attack she experienced. Other eyewitness cases have been found to be incorrect due to the "sin" of source misattribution. In these cases, eyewitnesses have erroneously identified someone as having committed the crime that they encountered in another (more innocent) situation.

Misinformation Effect

Error #5 Suggestibility

Suggestibility likely also played a role in Ronald Cotton's case. Jennifer reported that the police confirmed her choice of Cotton as the suspect when she picked him out of the lineup, giving her more confidence that Cotton was the man who attacked her, which likely altered her memory of the attack to fit him as the attacker. As we describe later in this chapter, others' suggestions and statements can alter our memories for events in ways we do not even realize. This can be done both in altering actual memories and creating false memories for events we have never experienced. Have you ever had a clear memory of an event only to later find out that it was your brother, sister, or friend who actually experienced the event? Hearing about and imagining an event multiple times can create a memory for the event that seems real to us as something we experienced. President George W. Bush reported seeing video of the first plane hitting the World Trade Center in the U.S. terrorist attacks of September 11, 2001. However, no video of the first plane was ever found or shown in the media. Thus, it is likely that after hearing reports of the planes hitting the towers of the Trade Center and seeing the video repeatedly of the second plane hitting the building, he unknowingly created a false memory of the first plane that was suggested from these later experiences.

Error #6 Bias

Bias is a similar memory failure to suggestibility. Bias occurs when our current experiences or knowledge alter our memory of a past experience. For example, after going through an unpleasant breakup with a romantic partner, you may remember a happy event you experienced with that partner as more negative than it actually was. This can easily occur when our impressions of people change. Have you ever learned something unpleasant about a friend and then "remembered" that you found that person odd or unlikeable when you first met them? This might have occurred through bias, where your memory of meeting that person has been biased by your later discovery of that person's true personality. Some women later remember the pain of childbirth as less painful than when they were experiencing it because they currently are experiencing happy times with their child. In other words, our current experiences and knowledge affect or bias the way we remember past experiences.

Error #7 Persistence

Persistence is a memory "sin" that can be particularly problematic for us. Do you sometimes hear a song and then later that day hear that song in your mind over and over? This is persistence: experiencing unwanted memories over and over. This particular situation can be annoying but can become more serious and debilitating if the unwanted memory is of a traumatic event. These types of memories are sometimes experienced by soldiers who were in combat and victims of violent crimes and can interfere with an individual's daily life (see Photo 7.3). The re-experiencing of these memories can cause extreme anxiety and sleeplessness that becomes debilitating. In extreme cases, these memories are a primary symptom of post-traumatic stress disorder (PTSD) and can require psychological treatment to decrease them.

BPTU/Shutterstock

Photo 7.3 Experiencing unwanted memories repeatedly (such as memories of combat) illustrates the persistence "sin" of memory.

Summary

Each of the seven "sins" Schacter (2002) described is a by-product of memory failure or error that results from the normal mechanisms under which memory operates in our daily lives. In many cases, memory functioning seems so effortless to us that we do not notice these errors at all. However, when these errors or failures arise (e.g., not remembering an important concept during an exam), we realize the limitations of our memory abilities. While these memory failures can be irritating to us and in some cases have devastating results (as in Ronald Cotton's case and in cases of PTSD), they are actually adaptive to us in our memory functioning. Having the ability to alter or block our memories (even in cases where we do not intentionally alter or block them) keeps us from being overwhelmed by memories we do not need and allows us to quickly retrieve the memories we need through their reconstruction. In fact, the reconstructive nature of memory is an important property of memory functioning that has implications for how we retrieve our memories (e.g., how best to question eyewitnesses) and when we can rely on them for accuracy.

Stop and Think

7.1. Which memory "sin" is the simple forgetting of information from memory?

7.2. Which memory "sins" involve changing an existing memory?

7.3. Can you think of an experience you have had that illustrates the "sin" of blocking? Of source misattribution?

The Reconstructive Nature of Memory

Memory researchers have long known that memory is reconstructive. We do not record and store all aspects of our experiences together. Instead, we encode and store the pieces of an experience (e.g., sights, sounds, scents) and then attempt to put the correct pieces back together when we retrieve our memory of the experience. At times, some of those pieces may be missing or replaced with incorrect pieces of other experiences or from our imaginations. This process occurs automatically, without our awareness, making us feel as if the memories we retrieve are accurate. The study of such errors has revealed the way this process works and what factors can influence this process. In this section, we discuss some of the important studies that have revealed the reconstructive nature of memory and how the reconstruction takes place.

Fake Memory

Bartlett's Studies

War of the Ghosts

Sir Frederick C. Bartlett (1932) conducted studies on subjects' abilities to reproduce simple stories, passages, and figures. Bartlett was interested in the accuracy of reproduction of the text or figures over time and the types of errors subjects made. After asking subjects to study the text or figures, Bartlett asked subjects to reproduce them after increasing intervals of time, beginning with a delay of about fifteen minutes. One of the main texts he used was a Native American folk story that involved a fishing trip for two young men and a battle up the river. As one would expect, he found that subjects could reproduce only some of the text word for word, but they seemed to have remembered many of the main points of the story for long periods of time. However, when subjects made errors in the story, they tended to be consistent with the subjects' cultural biases (the subjects were students in the United Kingdom). For example, "canoes" in the story became "boats" in the reproductions, and "paddling" became "rowing." These errors showed that the subjects relied on their own experiences and knowledge to fill in the details based on their general memory of the events, instead of remembering the details of these events. Bartlett's studies were some of the first to show how memories of experiences are remembered based on the general meaning of the events they want to remember with details filled in (sometimes incorrectly) from subjects' general knowledge.

Let us consider another classic study showing the importance of one's perspective in reducing memory errors. Bransford and Johnson (1972) gave subjects the following passage to read and remember. Read through it and then see how much of it you can recall by covering it up and writing down what you remember:

Identify the Task Activity

> The procedure is actually quite simple. First you arrange things into different groups depending on their makeup. Of course, one pile may be sufficient depending on how much there is to do. If you have to go somewhere else due to lack of facilities that is the next step, otherwise you are pretty well set. It is important not to overdo any particular endeavor. That is, it is better to do too few things at once than too many. In the short run this may not seem important, but complications from doing too many can easily arise. A mistake can be expensive as well. The manipulation of the appropriate mechanisms should be self-explanatory, and we need not dwell on it here. At first the whole procedure will seem complicated. Soon however, it will become just another facet of life. It is difficult to foresee any end to the necessity for this task in the immediate future, but one never can tell. (p. 722)

How well did you remember the passage? Most people cannot remember much of the passage. Bransford and Johnson's subjects remembered about 15 percent to 23 percent (across three experiments) of the ideas in the passage when no topic was given to them. Other subjects were told ahead of time that the passage was about doing laundry, and these subjects remembered from 32 percent to 40 percent of the ideas (in three experiments), significantly improving recall scores. Simply knowing the topic ahead of time allowed the subjects to apply their own knowledge and experience to the passage while they read it and increased their ability to recall the passage accurately. When the topic was given to the subjects after reading the passage (as you were), no improvement in recall was seen. Thus, the effects of subjects' prior knowledge seemed to occur while the passage was being read the first time in interpreting the different parts of it. The subjects' knowledge that the passage was about doing laundry provided them with a schema for the information they were reading.

Schemata and Scripts

A **schema** is a general knowledge structure for an event or situation. For example, after visiting some of your professors' offices, you may have a schema for what a professor's office looks like: books on shelves, a desk, a computer, chairs, a telephone. If you were to visit one of your professor's offices and then try to recall the objects in that office a couple of days later, you might recall objects that fit your schema of a professor's office but were not actually in your professor's office. It seems we rely on our schemata to reconstruct memories of events and experiences that have familiar elements. In fact, Brewer and Treyens (1981) showed that our memory relies on our schemata in an experiment with a similar situation to the professor office visit just described. The subjects in their experiment were asked to wait in the experimenter's office while the experimenter checked that the last subject had finished. After a short time, the subject was taken into another room and asked to describe the office he or she waited in. Subjects could accurately recall many of the objects from the office they waited in, and their schema for a university office likely contributed to that accurate recall, but they also falsely recalled objects that were not in the office. Many of the objects falsely recalled were consistent with a schema of a university office (e.g., books, a filing cabinet). Thus, the office schema may have helped subjects recall objects that were actually there, but it also resulted in recall of objects consistent with the schema that were not present in the office they waited in.

Like schemata, scripts provide a general structure for a familiar event, but they involve an ordered set of actions that one holds in memory for that event. For example, you likely have a script for going out to eat at a restaurant. Think about the sequence of actions that takes place in this scenario. When you enter the restaurant, you approach a desk or podium to be greeted by the host or hostess, where he or she checks your reservation or

Schema: the general knowledge structure for an event or situation

sees if a table is available for you. The host or hostess then takes you to your table with menus if there is no wait for your table. Someone then comes to take drink orders while you read the menu. You can imagine the rest of the scenario and perhaps additional actions that might occur (e.g., a pager given to you if there is a wait for your table, going to the bar for a drink to wait for your table). You likely have additional scripts for other familiar situations. Do you have a script for doing laundry? If so, see how well your script matches the one presented in Figure 7.2. Consider why yours might deviate from the one in the figure. What differences might exist between your laundry experiences and those

Stop and Think

7.4. What is meant by the "reconstructive nature of memory"?

7.5. In what way did Bartlett's studies show that memory is reconstructive?

7.6. How do schemata and scripts aid in reconstructing memories?

7.7. Consider a script or schema you have that many others do not (e.g., how a certain sport is played, how things work at your job). In what ways do you think this script or schema influences your memories or specific experiences you have had in those situations?

Figure 7.2 Script for Doing Laundry

Step 1: Sort dirty clothes according to color (e.g., lights, darks)

Step 2: Bring clothes to washing machine in laundry basket

Step 3: Put clothes in washing machine

Step 4: Select water temperature and other settings

Step 5: Put detergent in machine and start machine

Step 6: When cycle is finished, move clothes to dryer and start dryer

Step 7: When dryer signals clothes are dry, remove clothes and fold them

Photo from © iStockphoto.com/stphillips

of the authors of this text that can account for the differences in the scripts? Also consider how well your script matches the earlier passage from the Bransford and Johnson (1972) study. Do the sentences make more sense in the context of your laundry script? Our own experiences alter the scripts and schemata we develop (as seen in the Bartlett studies), and the context in which we encounter information (e.g., with or without the topic information as in the Bransford and Johnson study) will alter how we encode the information, which then affects whether we can retrieve the information later.

Memory Errors in the Laboratory

As seen in the Bartlett studies, the study of memory errors can teach us much about the way memory typically works. Thus, memory researchers have conducted studies on how memory errors are created and ways to reduce the errors in situations where accurate memory is important (e.g., eyewitness memory). Some clever procedures have been devised for creating memory errors in order to examine the factors that increase or decrease them and better understand why they occur. We begin our discussion of these studies with a popular method of creating false memories (in this case, having a memory for something that did not happen) based on general schemata.

False Memory Activity

The DRM Procedure

In 1995, Roediger and McDermott published a study on false memories with a new methodology based on a much older study by Deese (1950). From the initials of these three authors, the method has become known as the **DRM procedure** and has been used in numerous studies in the past two decades to study the creation of false memories. An example of this method is presented in Figure 7.3. Look at each word in the list in the figure, going down the columns, for a few seconds each. Then cover the words up or turn the page and count backward from 167 for thirty seconds. At the end of thirty seconds, try to write down all the words in the list without looking back at the list. When you are finished recalling the words, check your responses.

Word-Lists Demonstration

Did you include any words not on the list? In particular, did you recall *sleep*, *chair*, *king*, or *cold*? If so, then your memory is like most people's in that you created false memories for these items. Now, let's consider why that might have happened. Look back at the list of words. Do you notice something about the words? In fact, the words all relate to one of four "themes" that correspond to *sleep*, *chair*, *king*, or *cold*. For example, the words in the "bed, rest, awake, tired" list all relate to the theme (or schema) of sleep. Seeing the words for the sleep schema (the first fifteen words in Figure 7.3) likely activated that schema (and the others just listed) for you during your study of the words. Then when you tried to recall the words in the list, your memory relied on the schema (perhaps even unconsciously) to try to recall the words, inserting errors based on the theme words.

In their study, Roediger and McDermott (1995) had subjects study lists as you did in this example. The theme words were not presented in the lists. They then tested the subjects' memory for the lists using both recall (i.e., write down all the words you remember in the list) and recognition (i.e., decide if each word shown was in the list and indicate your confidence in your response) tests. False memories for the theme words were high in both types of tests. Figure 7.4 illustrates their results for these tests. Recall and recognition rates for theme items not presented in the lists were high. Notice that the recall data show the serial position curve, with higher recall for items at the beginning (primacy effect) and the end (recency effect) of the list (see Chapter 6 for further discussion of the serial position curve). The number of false memories for

DRM procedure (Deese-Roediger-McDermott procedure): research methodology that experimentally creates false memories for theme items that are not presented as part of a list of related items

Figure 7.3 An Example of Study Lists From the DRM Procedure

Study each word down the columns for a few seconds each, count backwards for 30 seconds, and then try to recall the words. See the text for further description.

bed	desk	subjects
rest	recliner	monarch
awake	sofa	royal
tired	wood	leader
dream	cushion	reign
wake	swivel	hot
snooze	stool	snow
blanket	sitting	warm
doze	rocking	winter
slumber	bench	ice
snore	queen	wet
nap	England	frigid
peace	crown	chilly
yawn	prince	heat
drowsy	George	weather
table	dictator	freeze
sit	palace	air
legs	throne	shiver
seat	chess	Arctic
couch	rule	frost

False Memory Experiment

theme words was similar to the recall rates of list items in the middle of the list where no primacy and recency effects occur. This makes sense because the theme words not in the lists cannot benefit from list position effects. The graph in Panel B of Figure 7.4 shows the response rates for items that subjects were sure were "old" (studied) and sure were "new" (not studied). Subjects were sure the theme items were "old" almost 60 percent of the time.

Numerous studies have employed the DRM procedure to study false memories for the theme items. These studies have found that false memories for the theme items show remarkable similarities to accurate memories for the list items that subjects have studied. For example, subjects will identify a source for the theme items (e.g., read in a male or female voice) as they do for list items (Payne, Elie, Blackwell, & Neuschatz, 1996). Subjects will also report remembering the presentation of the theme items in the study list with high confidence (Roediger & McDermott, 1995). One study also found that a study-test delay affects list and false memories similarly when delays are relatively short

Tricks of Memory

Figure 7.4 Results From Roediger and McDermott's (1995) Experiment 1

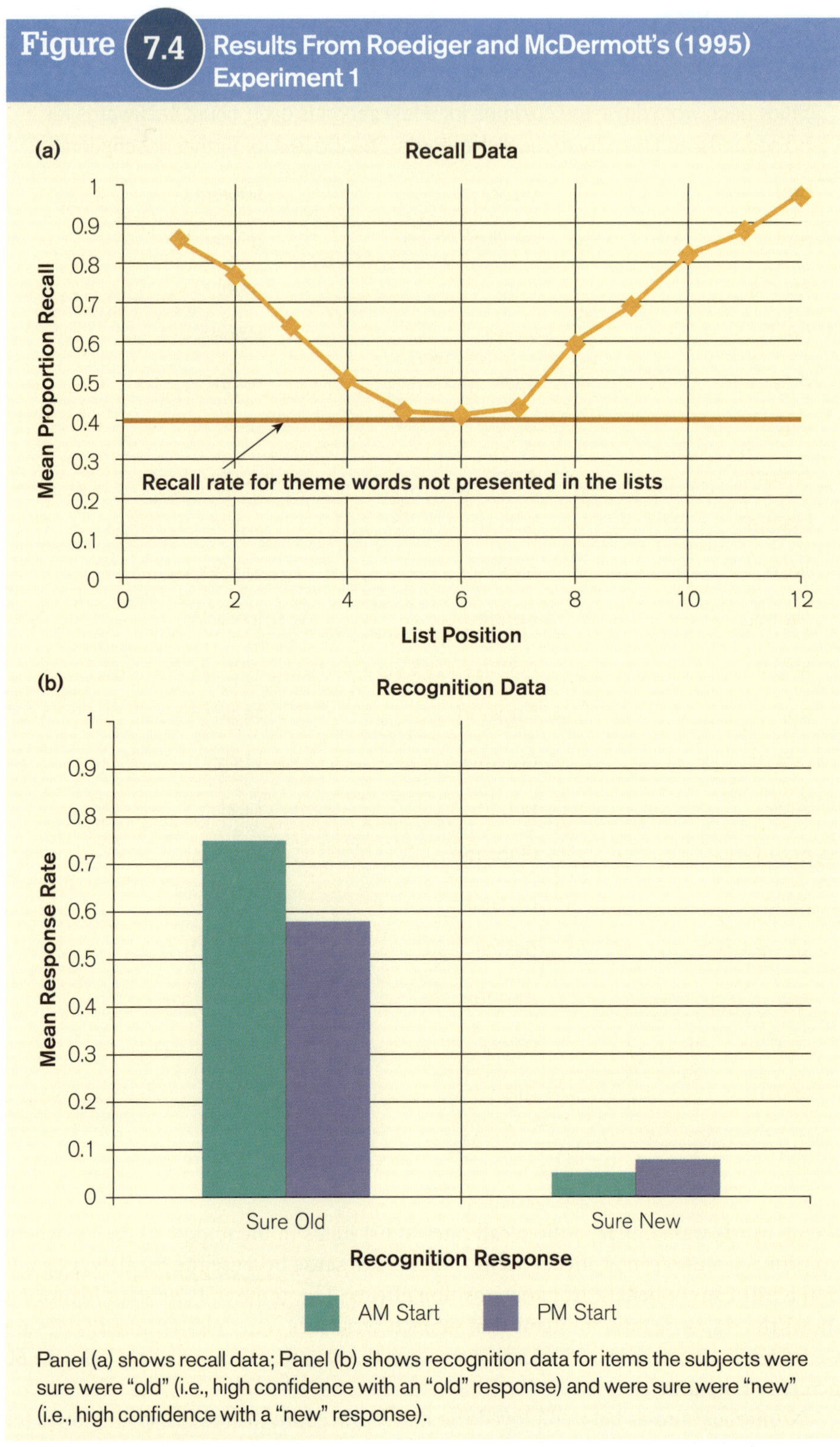

Panel (a) shows recall data; Panel (b) shows recognition data for items the subjects were sure were "old" (i.e., high confidence with an "old" response) and were sure were "new" (i.e., high confidence with a "new" response).

SOURCE: Adapted from Figure 1, Roediger, H. L., III, & McDermott, K. B. (1995). Creating false memories: Remembering words not presented in lists. *Journal of Experimental Psychology: Learning, Memory, and Cognition, 21*, 803–814.

(Colbert & McBride, 2007). Studies have even shown that electrophysical brain activity is similar for true recognition of list items and false recognition of theme items (Düzel, Yonelinas, Mangun, Heinz, & Tulving, 1997; see Chapter 2 for the details of this study).

Why does the presentation of themed lists in the DRM procedure produce such strong false memories for the nonpresented theme words? Researchers (e.g., Gallo, 2010; Roediger & McDermott, 1995) have suggested that two important memory processes are at play in the creation of false memories in the DRM procedure. The first process is activation of related items in memory. In Chapters 5 and 6, we discussed the idea that long-term memory organizes concepts by associations between the concepts (see Figure 5.2). When concepts (e.g., words) are presented, those concepts become activated in the network organization in long-term memory. When a concept or schema becomes activated, that activation then spreads to other related concepts in the network. (See Chapter 10 for further discussion of spreading activation in concepts.) Thus, when words like *dream*, *night*, *bed*, and *blanket* are presented, these concepts or schemata are activated in memory along with the related concept of sleep, even though *sleep* is not presented in the list. This spread of activation then causes *sleep* to seem similar to the actual list items in memory. When one attempts to remember the list items, the second process of source monitoring further works against accurate identification of list items. When we attempt to recall or recognize items, we consider whether a generated (in recall) or presented (in recognition) item was actually studied in the list. In other words, we try to determine the source (previously studied versus encountered somewhere else) of the item to decide if it was studied or not. When we source monitor for the theme items that were not presented, source misattribution (one of the "sins" of memory) can occur, allowing us to believe the item was studied along with the related list items. After all, it was activated in memory like the list items so it seems to us like a list item when we attempt to retrieve the list items. Additional activation of the theme items can also occur at test when the related list items are encountered (e.g., Coane & McBride, 2006), further confusing the two types of items in memory. Thus, both activation and source monitoring work together to produce false memories in the DRM procedure. Therefore, this theory is called the activation-monitoring theory of false memory creation.

Flash-Bulb Memories

A related theory of false memories, called fuzzy trace theory, suggests that when the themed lists are presented for study in the DRM procedure, a gist for the list is created and stored in memory. The gist matches the theme items closely because the lists were created to correspond to that theme item. When items are retrieved in a later memory test, the gist for the list is easily available (like the main ideas of the story in the Bartlett studies), whereas the details of the specific items have been lost (like the details of the story in the Bartlett studies). Thus, the theme items are falsely remembered as the gist for the list. This description of false memory creation is known as fuzzy trace theory (e.g., Brainerd & Reyna, 1998). Both the activation-monitoring and fuzzy trace theories have been supported by research studies and show some similarities in the way they describe false memories. In fact, they have been difficult to separate in tests of their predictions (Gallo, 2010).

In summary, the DRM procedure was an important step in helping us better understand memory errors because it allows researchers to easily and harmlessly create false memories in the laboratory so the factors that influence their creation can be studied. However, one drawback to this methodology is how different it may be from real-world creation of false memories. Some of the processes are likely to be similar in the DRM procedure and real-world false memories like the Ronald Cotton case (e.g., source misattribution), but critics of this method argue that studying a list of related words under controlled conditions is not similar enough to real-world situations such as experiencing or witnessing a crime. Other methods that better model real-world

Stop and Think

7.8. How does the DRM procedure create false memories?

7.9. In what way are the false memories created by the DRM procedure "reconstructive"?

7.10. In what ways are the false memories created by the DRM procedure similar to accurate memories?

7.11. Consider a situation where it might be easy to make a source misattribution error in your life. Can you think of anything you can do to help you prevent this error?

situations are needed to address this criticism. We next turn our discussion of false memories in the laboratory to these more realistic methods of study.

Eyewitness Memory Studies

Eyewitness Test

The Fiction of Memory

One of the most important real-world applications of knowledge about memory errors is in judging the accuracy of eyewitness memory. Numerous criminal investigations and legal cases rely on statements from eyewitnesses. The accuracy of their memory can strongly influence whether the correct person is arrested for a crime and whether that person is convicted of that crime. To better understand how accurate eyewitness memory really is, memory researchers have conducted studies that examined the effects of various factors on eyewitness memory. One factor that has emerged as important in altering the accuracy of an eyewitness' memory is what the witness is exposed to after he or she witnesses the event, termed postevent information (Loftus, 2005). When the postevent information is incorrect or misleading, it can result in memory errors from the witness.

In a classic study examining the effects of postevent information that might be given in questions asked of eyewitnesses by investigators, Elizabeth Loftus and John Palmer (1974) asked subjects to watch videos of car accidents. After viewing the films, subjects were asked to recall what happened and then asked some questions about what they had seen. One key question asked subjects "How fast were the cars going when they _____ each other?" with the blank filled in with a specific verb that suggested a particular description of the crash. The researchers used the verbs *smashed*, *collided*, *bumped*, *hit*, and *contacted* for different groups of subjects. They found that the speed estimate subjects gave depended on the verb they were given in the question, with higher estimates of speed given for more violent verbs (e.g., *smashed*). Figure 7.5 illustrates the method and results of this study. In a second experiment, subjects viewed a car accident video and then received the speed estimate question with either *smashed* or *hit* as the verb. Again, higher speed estimates were given for *smashed* than for *hit*. A week later, the subjects returned and were asked again about the car accident in the video. This time they were asked if they saw any broken glass in the video, another suggestive question about the nature of the crash. A larger percentage of people said they saw glass if they had been asked the speed question with the verb *smashed* (32 percent) than if they had been asked with the verb *hit* (14 percent). No broken glass appeared in the video; these reports were false memories about the accident influenced by the type of question subjects were asked about the video they saw. Such results are known as the **misinformation effect** because subjects are mislead by suggestive information given (in statements or questions) after they have witnessed an event. This information changes their memory of the event to create memory errors. The misinformation effect provides another example of the memory "sin" of suggestibility.

Witnesses are also vulnerable to the misinformation effect when exposed to incorrect postevent information about an event, such as when they hear other witnesses' inaccurate accounts of the event. For example, Stark, Okado, and Loftus (2010) simulated witnessing a crime by having subjects view photos of a man stealing a woman's wallet. The next day the subjects heard a description of the crime that contained inaccurate information (e.g., the description suggested that the man put the wallet in his pants pocket when the photos showed him putting it in his jacket pocket). They then answered a series of questions about the event depicted in the photos. When subjects heard inaccurate information about the crime in the postevent description of the crime, they were more likely to answer questions about those details incorrectly. Thus, subjects had more false memories for details of the crime when they were exposed to inaccurate information after the crime, as might occur if they heard others' inaccurate descriptions of the crime. Studies also suggest that memory errors due to misinformation are long lasting

Misinformation effect: a memory result where subjects have false memories for an event based on suggestive information provided by others

Figure 7.5 Results From the Loftus and Palmer (1974) Study Showing the Misinformation Effect in Which Subjects Were Shown Videos of Car Accidents

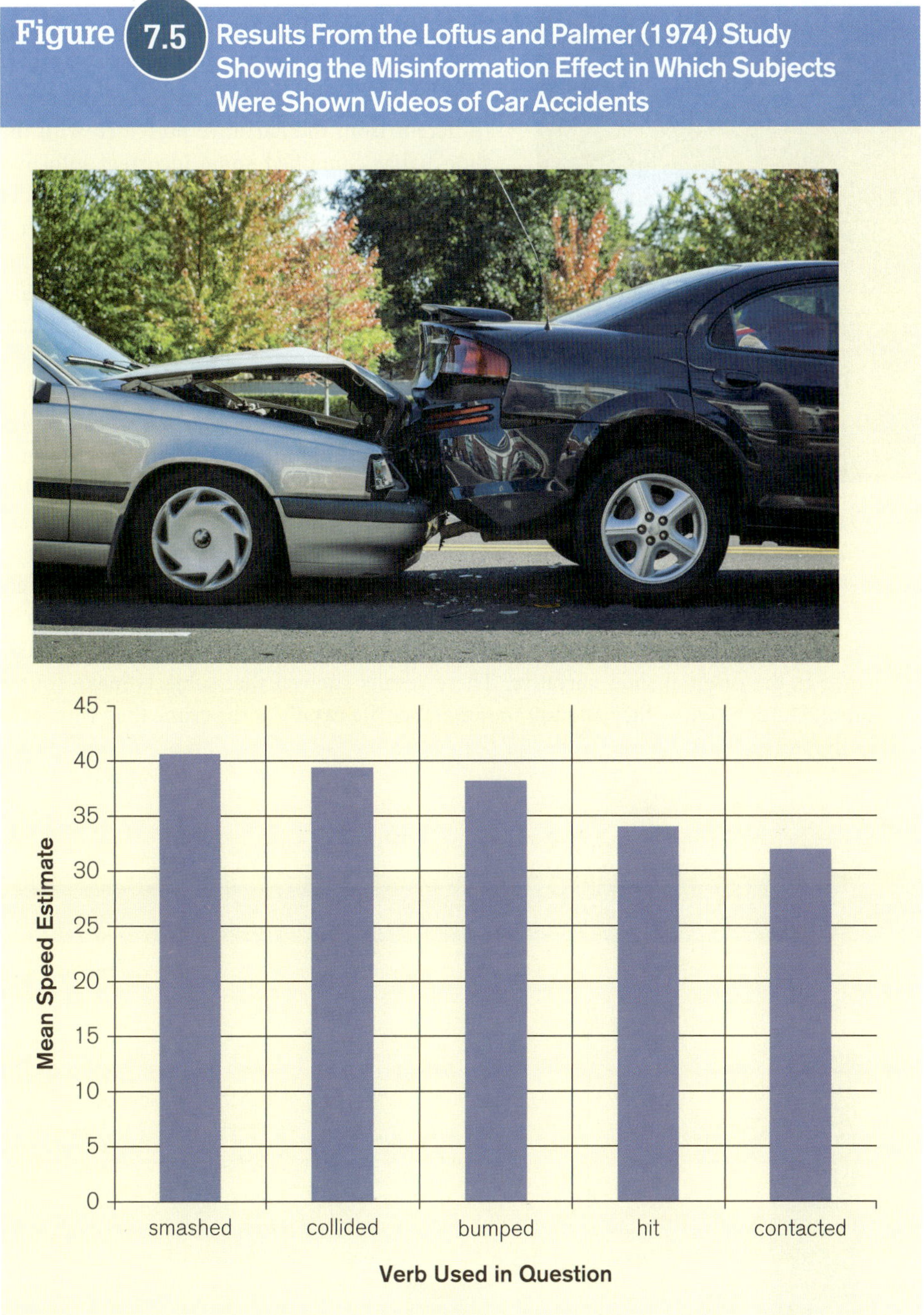

Photo from © Can Stock Photo Inc./rjcphoto

(e.g., more than a year; Zu et al., 2002) such that they can affect eyewitnesses for the length of a criminal case.

Some of the same processes that create false memories in the DRM procedure are suggested as mechanisms of memory errors in eyewitnesses. For example, hearing incorrect information about an event one experiences can "activate" those details about the event, with a source misattribution later causing one to think they are part of his or her memory of the event instead of from another source (e.g., another witness). Stephen Lindsay's (1990) study showed that such source misattributions occur for postevent misinformation. In this study, subjects viewed slides of a crime where a man steals items

Photo 7.4 In Lindsay's (1990) study, slides of a crime were shown with a narrative in a female voice. A postevent description of the crime was then presented in the same female voice or in a male voice.

from an office (see Photo 7.4). The slides were shown along with a verbal narrative of the events in the slides presented in a female voice. Subjects then heard a postevent description of the crime (different from the narrative presented with the slides) that contained some incorrect information about the slides, as was done in the Stark et al. (2010) study. However, half of the subjects heard the postevent description in the same female voice as the original slide narrative, making it difficult for the subjects to discriminate between the two descriptions. The other subjects heard the postevent description in a male voice, allowing them to distinguish the two descriptions better in their memories of the descriptions. Subjects then answered questions about the crime depicted in the slides. The results are shown in Figure 7.6. Subjects who heard the male voice in the postevent description were less likely to be influenced by the incorrect information in the description than subjects who heard the postevent description in the same female voice as the original slide narrative. These results showed that subjects make source misattributions when they attempt to remember the details of the crime they witnessed in the slides.

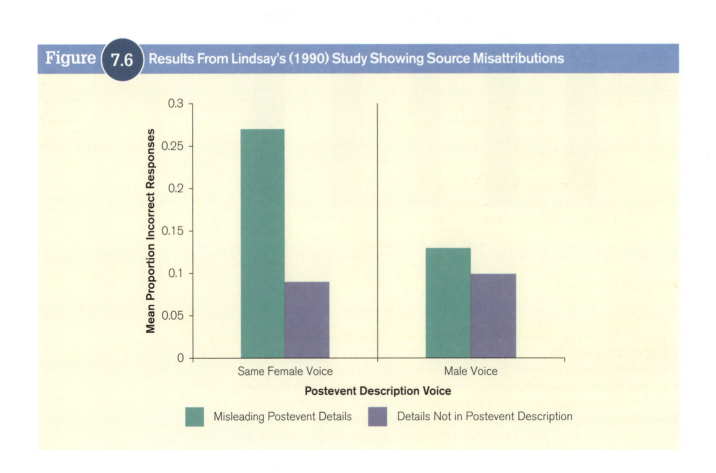

Figure 7.6 Results From Lindsay's (1990) Study Showing Source Misattributions

Applications of Eyewitness Memory Research

Given what we now know about eyewitness memory and the factors that influence its accuracy, what can we do to make eyewitness memory errors less likely? One thing we can do is change the way eyewitnesses are questioned, and police units around the world are making these changes to reduce the chance that inaccurate eyewitness testimony contributes to wrongful convictions. The changes focus on preventing suggestibility or leading information from the administrators of suspect lineups. The research conducted by cognitive psychologists showing misinformation effects from different types of postevent information has directly led to these specific reforms in police procedure (Wells et al., 1998).

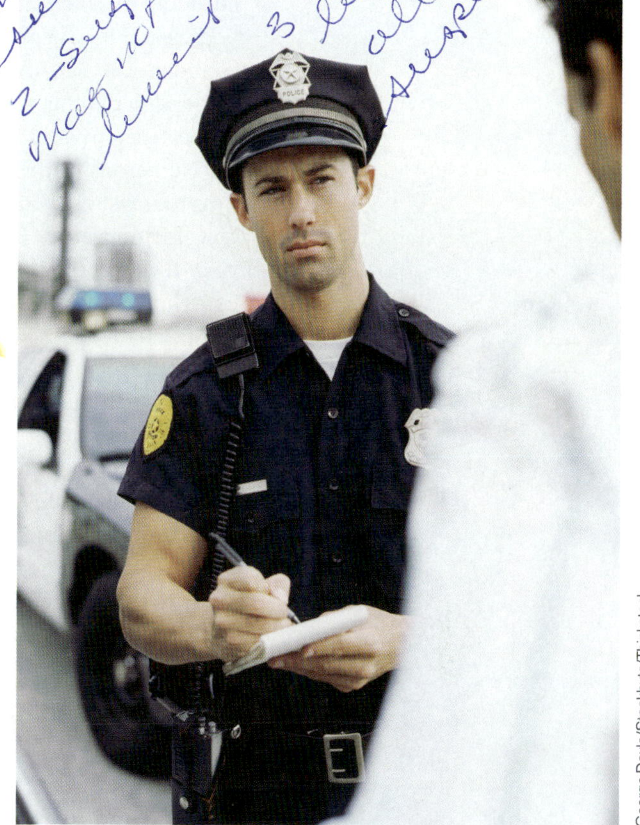
George Doyle/Stockbyte/Thinkstock

Photo 7.5 Police departments are changing the way they question witnesses to reduce suggestibility errors in suspect identification.

For example, many police departments in the United States now require a double-blind suspect lineup, where the person who administers the lineup to the witness does not know which person is the suspect to avoid the possibility of biasing the witness to choose the suspect or confirming his or her choice in the lineup as the suspect. This type of confirmation bias occurred in the lineup in the Jennifer Thompson case described at the beginning of the chapter (where a double-blind lineup was not used) and may have contributed to the wrongful conviction of Ronald Cotton. Research has shown that this confirming feedback can increase a witness' confidence in his or her choice, even if that choice is incorrect (e.g., Wells & Bradfield, 1998). In addition, a warning is often given to witnesses that the suspect may not be present in the lineup. This reduces the chance that the witness will assume the person who committed the crime is in the lineup and will choose someone in the lineup even if he or she is not sure the person in the lineup is the correct person. This instruction gives someone the option of saying that the person he or she remembers is not present in the lineup. Suggestibility is also reduced when lineups are created with similar-looking individuals to avoid the suspect standing out as the only person who looks like who the witness remembers. Higher suggestibility may have also occurred in Jennifer Thompson's case because Ronald Cotton looked like the actual perpetrator. Finally, research (e.g., Steblay, Dysart, Fulero, & Lindsay, 2001) has shown that showing possible suspects to the witness one at a time, instead of all at once, decreases false identifications in lineups. Such sequential lineup procedures are replacing the traditional simultaneous lineup procedures in many police departments. Thus, results from research in eyewitness memory are helping to reduce the problem of suspect misidentification.

Eyewitness Testimony

Research is also helping police departments find ways to question witnesses that prevent memory errors through postevent misinformation. The development of the cognitive interview (e.g., Geiselman, Fisher, MacKinnon, & Holland, 1986) has helped police question witnesses in a way that limits suggestibility and misleading information. The interview relies on four techniques designed to enhance retrieval of the details of an event (Memon, Meissner, & Fraser, 2010). The techniques come from basic principles of memory processing (some of which are discussed in Chapter 6 of this text). In the cognitive interview, the witness is asked to conduct a detailed retrieval of the event he or she experienced such that (1) the original context is reinstated in the witness' minds (e.g., encoding specificity; see Chapter 6), (2) the witness reports everything he or she remembers even if it is incomplete to allow for retrieval of information a witness may have less confidence in, (3) the witness takes different perspectives of the event in his or her retrieval (e.g., other witnesses'), and (4) the witness retrieves events in different temporal orders (e.g., forward in time, backward in time).

Numerous studies have found that the cognitive interview increases accurate witness retrieval of event details compared with typical police questioning procedures. In fact, Memon et al. (2010) conducted a statistical review (called a meta-analysis) of sixty-five experiments involving the cognitive interview and showed that across these experiments, the cognitive interview increases retrieval of correct details of events with only a small increase in the number of incorrect details retrieved. Further, the Memon et al. study showed that the increase in correct details was highest for older adults, meaning that the cognitive interview may be particularly useful for older eyewitnesses, who are typically more influenced by misleading information (e.g., Cohen & Faulkner, 1989) and prone to source monitoring errors (e.g., Hashtroudi, Johnson, & Chrosniak, 1990). Based on the research showing positive effects of the cognitive interview, in 1999 the National Institute of Justice distributed training manuals for the cognitive interview to all U.S. police departments. Campo, Gregory, and Fisher (2012) conducted a field study to determine if South Florida police officers were using the technique described in these training manuals in their questioning of witnesses. Unfortunately, they found that the interviews sampled did not successfully use the cognitive interview techniques. Thus, there is room for improvement in translating the results of psychological science to real-world situations in this area.

Summary and Conclusions

Laboratory research in memory errors is providing us with a better understanding of how memory errors occur and ways they can be reduced in real-world situations. From the results of these studies, it is clear that memory errors result from normal underlying memory processes (e.g., familiarity of recently encoded information due to activation, source misattributions) and are therefore by-products of efficient memory mechanisms that do not "record" events in their entirety. Instead, our memories are reconstructive, relying on our schemata of events, prior knowledge, and our biases to put the pieces of a past event back together into a coherent whole. Understanding these processes has helped researchers better understand the limits of eyewitness memory accuracy and how we can avoid some of the errors in suspect identification and detail retrieval that can occur when witnesses are questioned or asked to view a suspect lineup. The results of these studies have aided in the development and implementation of improved police procedures to increase the accuracy of eyewitness memory.

Stop and Think

7.12. In what ways has research in eyewitness memory modeled real-world eyewitness situations?

7.13. Based on the results from research in eyewitness memory, what factors seem to increase memory errors in a witness?

7.14. What recommendations for questioning witnesses and conducting suspect lineups have come from the research in this area?

7.15. Consider an event you witnessed where it was later important for you to remember the details of the event (e.g., witnessing an accident or crime, experiencing an accident or crime). What factors occurred during or after the event that may have decreased your memory accuracy for the details of the event?

Although many of the errors presented in this chapter seem to have negative consequences, there may be a positive side to the creation of some kinds of errors. In a number of studies, Loftus and colleagues (e.g., Thomas & Loftus, 2002) have shown that imagining an event can create a false memory for that event. However, if one imagines a negative event related to something he or she wishes to avoid, the false memory can work to aid in avoiding that item or situation in the future. As an example of a positive application of false memory through imagining events, Clifasefi, Bernstein, Mantonakis, and Loftus (2013) reported that subjects who had false memories created by suggestions from researchers of an earlier event when they got sick drinking vodka showed a decreased preference for drinking vodka in the future. Thus, false memories might provide a useful way to avoid negative stimuli (like drinking too much alcohol) for individuals who wish to do so.

Memory Illusions

False Memories in Mice

Clinical Memory Failures—Amnesia

Up to this point in the chapter, we have been discussing typical memory failures in a normally functioning memory system. We now turn our discussion to nontypical memory failures in clinical cases. Such failures take two forms: (1) a fairly immediate and discrete memory failure, such as in amnesic cases where a brain lesion has occurred due to an accident or disease or (2) a progressive deterioration of memory that becomes worse over time.

Types of Amnesia

Chapter 5 began with the story of Clive Wearing, who suffers from extreme **amnesia**. After suffering from a form of encephalitis, he was no longer able to remember events that he experienced and had forgotten many of the events of his past. Such cases are atypical, but they can occur when one suffers damage in particular brain areas due to a disease or accident. In Chapter 2, we presented another well-known case of amnesia in a

Amnesia: a memory deficit due to a brain lesion or deterioration

Figure 7.7 Cases Like H. M.'s Have Shown That the Hippocampus Is an Important Brain Area for Explicitly Retrieving Memories

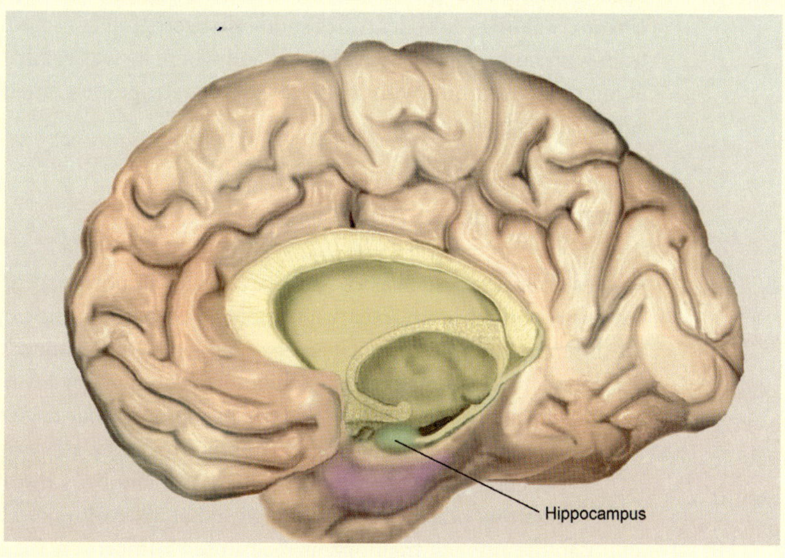

SOURCE: Adapted with permission from D. L. Schacter and A. D. Wagner, "Remembrance of Things Past," *Science, 285*, pp. 1503–1504. Illustration: K. Sutliff. © 1999 American Association for the Advancement of Science. Reprinted with permission from AAAS.

Figure 7.8 Retrograde and Anterograde Amnesia

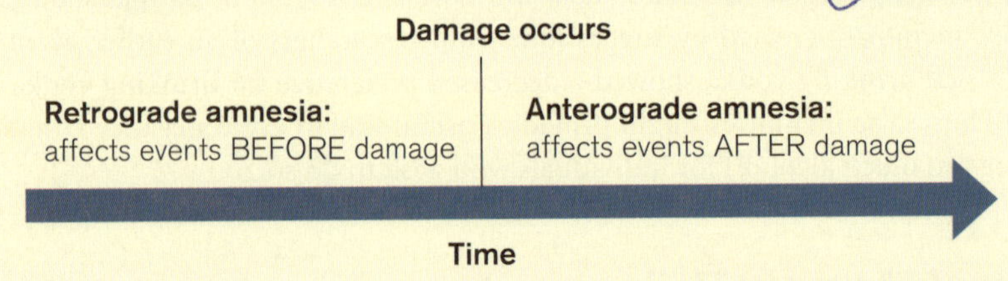

Damage occurs

Retrograde amnesia: affects events BEFORE damage

Anterograde amnesia: affects events AFTER damage

Time

Retrograde amnesia involves difficulty in retrieving memories for events before the injury. Anterograde amnesia involves difficulty in retrieving memories for events after the injury.

man known as H. M., whose name was revealed as Henry Molaison after his death in 2008. H. M. suffered from epilepsy as a child that was severe enough to disrupt his daily life. When he was eighteen, surgery was performed in an attempt to reduce the frequency and severity of his seizures. Unfortunately, the surgery had an even more debilitating side effect: H. M. lost his ability to explicitly retrieve events that occurred after his surgery. During the surgery, the area known as the **hippocampus** (see Figure 7.7) in the medial temporal lobe was damaged in H. M.'s brain, which caused his **anterograde amnesia** (see Figure 7.8). In other words, H. M. could remember who he was, his family, and his life up until the surgery but could not remember people he met or events he experienced after the surgery.

Amnesic Patients

The other type of amnesia is **retrograde amnesia** (see Figure 7.8), which involves loss of memory for events that occurred before the brain damage. This might be the form of amnesia you first thought about when reading the title of the section, as it is the one commonly portrayed in movies and TV shows. This type of amnesia is most common after a head injury (e.g., due to swelling of brain tissue) but is typically short-lived (i.e., many of the memories are eventually recovered) and limited to the events that occurred shortly before the damage. However, extreme cases of retrograde amnesia have been documented. For example, Doug Bruce, depicted in the documentary film *Unknown White Male*, describes suddenly becoming conscious one day on a New York train with no memory of who he was and where he was headed. Doctors who examined Doug diagnosed him with a severe case of retrograde amnesia. However, this type of amnesia is extremely rare.

Case Study of H.M.

Amnesia and Implicit Memory

Studies of amnesics such as H. M. have revealed important distinctions between types of memories and the brain areas responsible for these memories. In Chapter 5, we described the difference between implicit and explicit forms of memory. Much of our discussion in Chapters 5 to 7 has focused on explicit forms of memory involving intentional retrieval of a previous episode. This is the type of memory that is generally a problem for the types of amnesias described earlier. Implicit memory, however, involves unintentional retrieval of memory. In some cases, implicit memory is involved in a task without us being aware that our memory is being used at all. Amnesics like H. M. have shown the ability to use implicit memory, as measured by improvement on skills tasks performed over a series of days or weeks that they have no memory of having performed in the past.

Hippocampus: the area of the brain important for memory encoding and retrieval

Anterograde amnesia: a memory deficit for information or experiences encountered after a brain lesion

Retrograde amnesia: a memory deficit for information learned or experiences encountered before a brain lesion

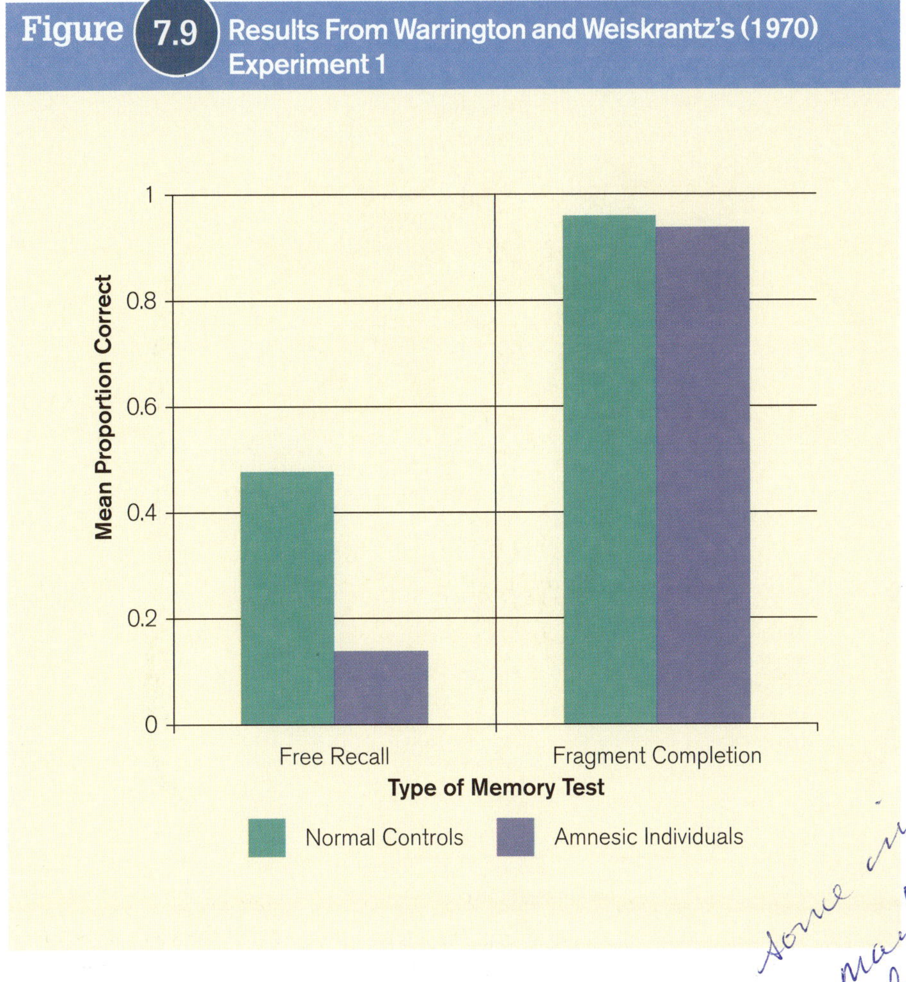

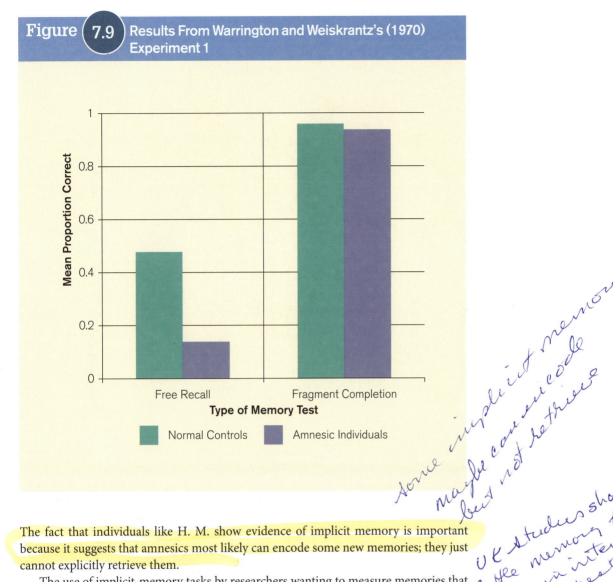

Figure 7.9 Results From Warrington and Weiskrantz's (1970) Experiment 1

The fact that individuals like H. M. show evidence of implicit memory is important because it suggests that amnesics most likely can encode some new memories; they just cannot explicitly retrieve them.

The use of implicit-memory tasks by researchers wanting to measure memories that are not intentionally retrieved increased significantly in the 1970s and 1980s. This increase was due in part to findings from two researchers in the United Kingdom showing that amnesics who have little to no memory for studied items in intentional-retrieval tests (e.g., recall, recognition) exhibit normal memory performance on implicit-memory tasks, like identifying word fragments (Warrington & Weiskrantz, 1968, 1970, 1974). Figure 7.9 illustrates the results from one of these studies comparing amnesics with normal control subjects. The amnesic subjects showed lower performance on the free-recall test than the normal control subjects (the small amount of memory they showed on this test is likely due to guessing guided by implicit memory) but showed similar performance to normal control subjects on the fragment completion test. In other words, when they were intentionally retrieving studied items, the amnesic subjects performed poorly, but when they were simply asked to complete a related task without any reference to the studied items, the amnesic subjects showed performance indicating typical implicit memory. These results suggest that amnesics such as H. M. have not lost the ability to make new memories as was once believed. Instead, it seems that amnesics may have lost the ability to intentionally retrieve memories. Thus, amnesics seem to have deficits in explicit memory but do not typically show deficits in implicit memory.

Who Was H.M.?

Figure 7.10 Neural Plaques and Tangles in Alzheimer's Patients

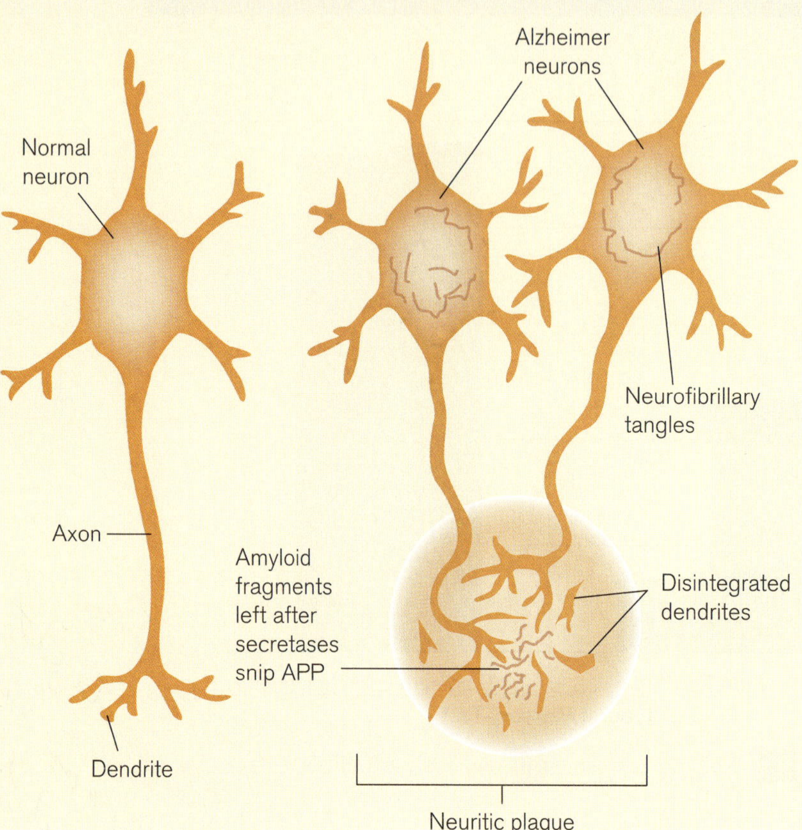

Neuronal plaques and tangles present in Alzheimer's disease patients cause disruption of brain functioning resulting in progressively more severe dementia.

Amnesia in Alzheimer's disease

Neuropharmacology and Alzheimer's Disease

Plaques: bundles of protein that develop in the synapse, characteristic of Alzheimer's disease

Tangles: protein fibers that develop in a neuron's nucleus characteristic of Alzheimer's disease

Unlike the cases of amnesia just described that occurred somewhat suddenly after an injury, memory abilities can also deteriorate over time. One of the more common causes of progressive amnesia is Alzheimer's disease. It is believed that Alzheimer's disease occurs when neuron (i.e., brain cell) function is disrupted by plaques and tangles. **Plaques** are bundles of protein (generally beta amyloid protein) that develop in the space between neurons known as the synapse (see Chapter 2 for further discussion of neurons and their functions), disrupting communication between neurons. As the plaques spread throughout the brain, neuron communication deteriorates causing more severe dementia. **Tangles** are protein fibers (tau amyloid protein) that develop in a neuron's nucleus, decreasing its ability to function properly. As more tangles spread throughout the neurons in the brain, less cognitive functioning occurs, resulting in dementia. See Figure 7.10 for a depiction of plaques and tangles in neurons. Neuron functioning is disrupted by both plaques and tangles in Alzheimer's patients. Over time, massive cell loss drastically reduces brain mass (see Photo 7.6). Neuron function disruption seems to begin in the hippocampus in the early stages of

Alzheimer's disease (Gosche, Mortimer, Smith, Markesbery, & Snowdon, 2002). Because the hippocampus is important in explicit memory retrieval (as already described), this is likely the cause of memory problems that signal the beginning of the disease symptoms.

The incidence of Alzheimer's disease is expected to rise with an increased aging population. Thus, prevention of the disease is a key research area in neuroscience. Current research suggests that both physical and cognitive activity can help reduce the incidence of the disease. For example, Erickson et al. (2011) showed that aerobic exercise increased the size of the hippocampus, which led to memory improvements in elderly subjects. Belleville et al. (2011) also showed that in individuals with mild cognitive impairment (often a precursor to Alzheimer's disease), memory training with a cognitive task increased brain activity in areas related to memory on a later task. Better understanding of the link between brain function and these activities will aid efforts to reduce Alzheimer's disease in the elderly.

Healthy Brain

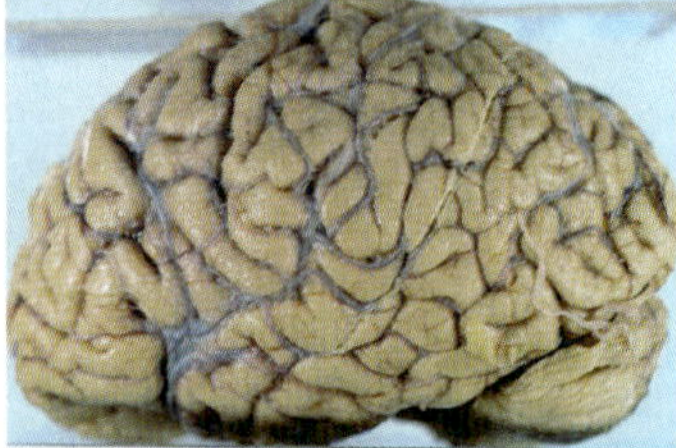

Brain with Alzheimer's

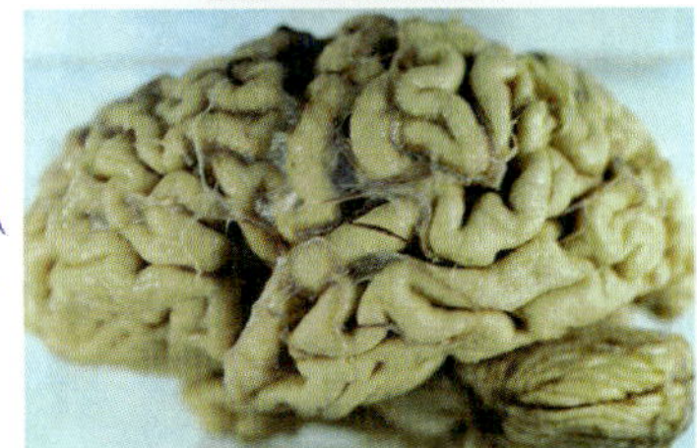

Science Source

Photo 7.6 Comparison of Alzheimer's disease–damaged and normal brain.

Amnesia in Childhood

Amnesia (**childhood** or **infantile amnesia**) has also been used to describe the phenomenon of a lack of memory of one's life before the age of five (the age range can vary by individual). However, amnesia in this case does not mean a complete absence of memories for this time period. Many people can remember a few episodes from before this age, especially if they have strong emotional content, but far fewer memories exist for this age range than for later in one's life (Richmond & Nelson, 2007). Can you remember any episodes from your life from age two or three? My family moved to California when I was almost five; thus, I have many memories of growing up in Southern California but very few memories of living near Philadelphia where we lived before we moved. One suggestion for the cause of this lack of early childhood memories is that the areas of the brain (e.g., the hippocampus and the surrounding medial temporal lobe) responsible for very long-term storage of memories are not yet fully developed. The lack of a fully developed knowledge structure may also contribute to this phenomenon because, as we have discussed, connections to current knowledge are important for memory encoding. However, this does not mean that children of this age do not store information in long-term memory. My son can recite most of the dialogue from the Pixar *Cars* movies and remember going on the Buzz ride at Disney World, showing that he is storing information in long-term memory. However, as he gets older, he will not likely retain memories of our trip to Disney World, as those memories tend not to be stored over a longer time range. In addition, childhood amnesia seems to be specific to episodic memories. Semantic and implicit memories do not seem to show the same types of deficits in young children.

Stop and Think

7.16. Describe the two types of amnesia based on the types of events that are forgotten.

7.17. Describe the two ways that amnesia can develop in individuals.

7.18. Are anterograde amnesics able to encode new memories? How do you know?

7.19. What is the proposed cause of amnesia in Alzheimer's patients?

7.20. Imagine someone who is becoming elderly in your family has come to you for advice based on your knowledge of cognitive psychology on how to keep his or her memory abilities strong as he or she ages. What advice would you give this person?

Childhood Amnesia

Childhood amnesia (infantile amnesia): a phenomenon where many episodic memories of early childhood are inaccessible in later life

THINKING ABOUT RESEARCH

As you read the following summary of a research study in psychology, think about the following questions:

1. Describe the memory errors the subjects in this study made. What is the likely cause of the errors?
2. In what way(s) is the method of this study similar to the DRM procedure described in this chapter?
3. What type of research design are the researchers using in this study? (Hint: Review the Research Methodologies section of Chapter 1 for help in answering questions 3 and 4.)

Figure 7.11 Results From the Castel et al. (2007) Study Showing Benefits and Detriments of Expertise on Memory

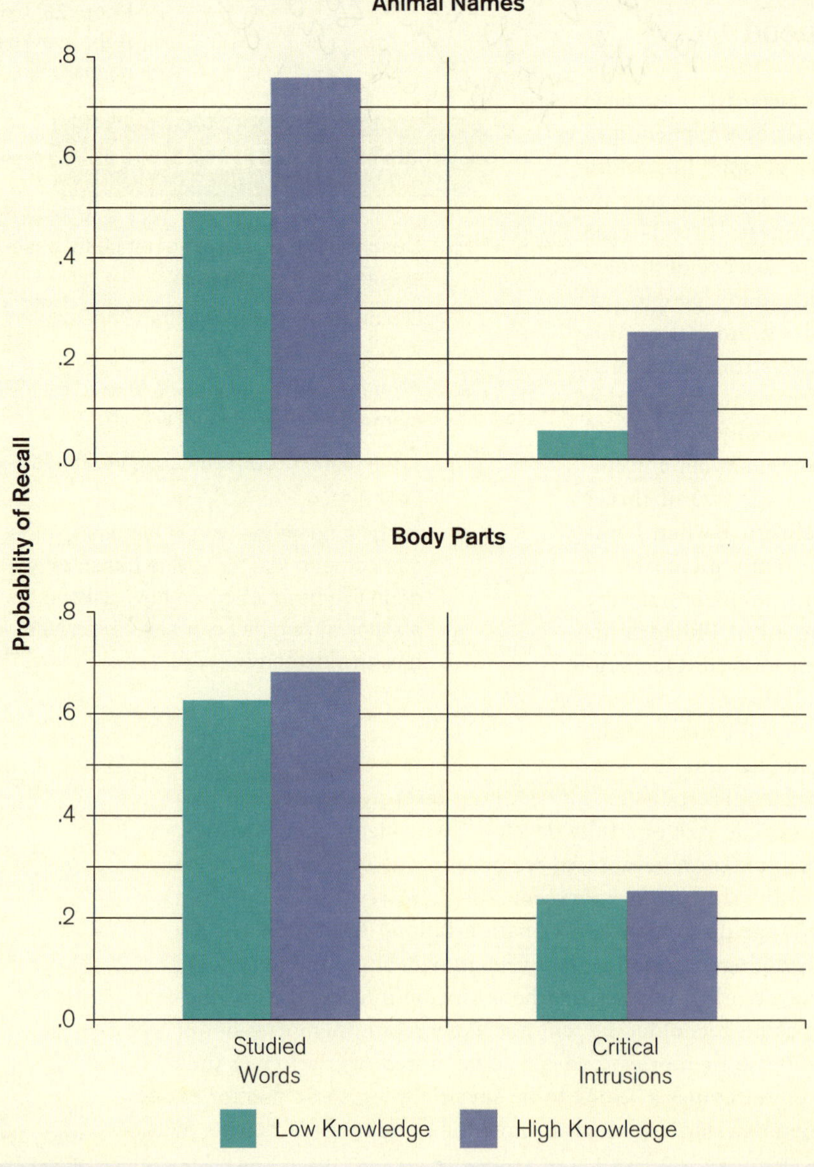

SOURCE: Figure 1, Castel, A. D., McCabe, D. P., Roediger, H. L., III, & Heitman, J. L. (2007). The dark side of expertise: Domain-specific memory errors. *Psychological Science, 18*, 3–5.

4. What is the independent variable in this study? What is the dependent variable in this study?
5. What do the results of this study suggest about the purpose of human memory?

Study Reference

Castel, A. D., McCabe, D. P., Roediger, H. L. III, & Heitman, J. L. (2007). The dark side of expertise: Domain-specific memory errors. *Psychological Science, 18*, 3–5.

Purpose of the study: The researchers were interested in the effects of memory for expertise-related information. Subjects who were experts in American football and nonexpert subjects were tested for their memory of animal names, where each animal name was also the name of an American football team. They hypothesized that American football experts would remember more of the animal words than nonexperts but that they would also have more false memories for animal team name words that were not presented.

Method of the study: Subjects were 40 college students. They were asked to study two lists of 11 words in a random order. One of the study lists contained 11 animal names that were also names of American football teams (e.g., falcons, broncos, colts, jaguars). The other study list contained 11 body part names (e.g., toes, arm, stomach, neck) and was used as a control comparison list. Three items of each type (animal/team words and body parts) were not presented in the lists. These items served as possible false-memory items in the memory test. The words were shown for 1 second each. After both lists had been presented, subjects were asked to complete a filler task for 10 minutes. They were then asked to recall the words from each study list for 4 minutes. After the memory test, subjects completed a questionnaire to assess American football knowledge. Scores on this questionnaire were used to divide the subjects into expert and nonexpert groups of equal size.

Results of the study: For the animal/team words, expert subjects recalled more words than the nonexperts but also falsely recalled more words than the nonexperts. No differences were found between the expert and nonexpert groups for the body part words. Figure 7.11 shows the mean recall results for each word type and group of subjects.

Conclusions of the study: The results supported the researchers' hypothesis that expertise affects both accurate and false memory for information in the area of expertise. These results illustrate both beneficial and detrimental effects of expertise on memory.

CHAPTER REVIEW

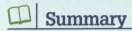

Summary

- **Does memory work like a video camera, fully recoding each experience? Why not?**

  Research has shown that memory is reconstructive, putting the pieces of our memories back together when we retrieve them. The memory errors seen in individuals support this idea, rather than a "video camera" mechanism of memory.

- **In what ways does memory fail in normal individuals?**

  Schacter (2002) described seven "sins" of memory as normal memory failures: transience (normal loss of information over time), absentmindedness (forgetting due to lack of attention), blocking (forgetting due to interference from other information), source misattribution (memory errors due to misattribution of the source of information), suggestibility (memory errors due to suggestions from outside sources), bias (memory errors due to our own experiences after the information was originally encoded), and persistence (unwanted memories of information that persist).

- **What factors contribute to memory inaccuracies?**

  In general, normal memory processes can contribute to memory errors. For example, use of schemata, scripts, and our previous knowledge of events and concepts to reconstruct memories can result in errors. In cases of eyewitness memory, exposure to misleading information or inaccurate suggestions can result in memory errors.

- **How have researchers studied memory errors?**

  The DRM procedure has been used to study how memory errors occur and what influences their creation. In this procedure, themed lists are presented and subjects typically show false memories for the themes that are not presented. Researchers have also studied memory for events by presenting subjects with a video or slides of an event, questioning them about the event or exposing them to other accounts of the event, and then testing their memory for the event they saw. These studies have helped us understand the factors that influence witness memory accuracy.

- **How can different types of brain damage or deterioration affect memory accuracy?**

  Amnesia can occur due to brain injury or disease. It can happen suddenly, caused by an accident or illness, or progressively, as in Alzheimer's disease. Both retrograde amnesia (loss of memory for events before the injury) or anterograde amnesia (loss of memory for events after the injury) can occur.

Chapter Quiz

1. Which memory "sin" is primarily due to a lack of attention at encoding or retrieval?
   (a) absentmindedness
   (b) persistence
   (c) suggestibility
   (d) blocking
2. Which memory "sin" results in unwanted memories?
   (a) source misattribution
   (b) persistence
   (c) suggestibility
   (d) bias
3. Which memory "sin" is synonymous with normal forgetting over time?
   (a) bias
   (b) persistence
   (c) suggestibility
   (d) transience
4. Which type of amnesia results in an inability to explicitly retrieve memories from after the brain damage has occurred?
   (a) semantic amnesia
   (b) anterograde amnesia
   (c) cortical amnesia
   (d) retrograde amnesia
5. Loftus's studies of eyewitness memory showed that ______________ can alter the memory for an event.
   (a) a person's schema
   (b) postevent information or suggestions
   (c) thematic activation
   (d) lack of confidence
6. A script is
   (a) the general meaning or gist of the information.
   (b) a cause of amnesia.
   (c) a stored set of actions typical of an event.
   (d) a network of stored concepts.
7. I have a memory that I took my medicine this morning, but in reality, I only thought about taking my medicine. This type of memory error represents the ________ "sin" of memory.
   (a) suggestibility
   (b) bias
   (c) transience
   (d) source misattribution
8. I arranged to call my friend at 3:00 p.m. when she had a break in her schedule. However, during the day, I was busy with many tasks and forgot to call at the scheduled time. This type of memory error represents the ________ "sin" of memory.
   (a) source misattribution
   (b) blocking
   (c) transience
   (d) absentmindedness
9. Explain why memory is described as reconstructive.
10. How do we know that amnesics like H. M. can store new memories?
11. Describe the two types of neuron function disruptions that occur in Alzheimer's disease.

12. How has research in eyewitness memory changed police procedures in some departments?

13. Describe a situation where you (or someone you imagine) experienced the memory "sin" of bias.

Key Terms

Amnesia 169
Anterograde amnesia 170
Childhood (infantile) amnesia 173
DRM procedure (Deese-Roediger-McDermott procedure) 160
Hippocampus 170
Misinformation effect 164
Plaques 172
Retrograde amnesia 170
Schema 158
Tangles 172

Stop and Think Answers

7.1. Which memory "sin" is the simple forgetting of information from memory?

Transience

7.2. Which memory "sins" involve changing an existing memory?

Source misattribution, bias, and suggestibility all involve changing an existing memory.

7.3. Can you think of an experience you have had that illustrates the "sin" of blocking? Of source misattribution?

Answers will vary, but blocking involves lack of retrieval of information you know due to competing information you are retrieving at the same time. Source misattribution involves incorrectly attributing the source of information, such as thinking you said something when someone else did.

7.4. What is meant by the "reconstructive nature of memory"?

Memory is not a recording process. Instead, pieces of experiences are stored and then put back together in the retrieval process. Missing pieces can be filled in based on our general knowledge, biases, or postevent suggestions, creating memory errors.

7.5. In what way did Bartlett's studies show that memory is reconstructive?

Subjects in these studies recalled the details of a story based on their own schemata for the events in the story. Their existing knowledge for these events changed their memories of the story as they attempted to retrieve it, showing that the story was reconstructed with pieces filled in from preexisting schemata.

7.6. How do schemata and scripts aid in reconstructing memories?

They help us fit information into our existing knowledge structure at encoding and fill in pieces of the memory for an event based on this existing knowledge structure at retrieval.

7.7. Consider a script or schema you have that many others do not (e.g., how a certain sport is played, how things work at your job). In what ways do you think this script or schema influences your memories or specific experiences you have had in those situations?

Answers will vary.

7.8. How does the DRM procedure create false memories?

Themed lists are presented without the theme items, and then false memories for the presentation of the theme items are created based on activation of the theme from the list items and source misattribution for the source of the activation at retrieval.

7.9. In what way are the false memories created by the DRM procedure "reconstructive"?

In retrieving the list items, one "reconstructs" the lists based on their meaning and the theme items are erroneously retrieved due to this reconstruction.

7.10. In what ways are the false memories created by the DRM procedure similar to accurate memories?

Subjects report confidence and recollective experiences (i.e., they claim to "remember" seeing or hearing the theme items in the list) for the theme items just as they do for list items. General memory process (e.g., forgetting and brain function) also seem to be similar for false and accurate memories in the DRM procedure.

7.11. Consider a situation where it might be easy to make a source misattribution error in your life. Can you

think of anything you can do to help you prevent this error?

Answers will vary, but being aware of the possibility of errors and paying attention to the source of information can help reduce the errors.

7.12. In what ways has research in eyewitness memory modeled real-world witness situations?

This research has used a method where subjects are exposed to an event and then questioned about their memory for the event, just as eyewitnesses are in real-world situations. Postevent information is also sometimes used as it is in real-world situations.

7.13. Based on the results from research in eyewitness memory, what factors seem to increase memory errors in a witness?

Suggestive questioning and exposure to inaccurate or misleading information can lead to memory errors in these situations.

7.14. What recommendations for questioning witnesses and conducting suspect lineups have come from the research in this area?

Using neutral questioning (such as in the cognitive interview technique), presenting lineups with the possibility that no suspect is present, avoiding confirmations of lineup responses, and avoiding pop-out lineups where the suspect is the only one who looks like the perpetrator description are all recommendations that have come from research in this area.

7.15. Consider an event you witnessed where it was later important for you to remember the details of the event (e.g., witnessing an accident or crime, experiencing an accident or crime). What factors occurred during or after the event that may have decreased your memory accuracy for the details of the event?

Answers will vary, but bias and postevent information can be factors in this situation.

7.16. Describe the two types of amnesia based on the types of events that are forgotten.

In anterograde amnesia, memories formed after the brain damage occurred cannot be retrieved. In retrograde amnesia, memories formed before the brain damage occurred cannot be retrieved.

7.17. Describe the two ways that amnesia can develop in individuals.

Amnesia can occur suddenly, such as from an accident or illness, or progressively, such as in Alzheimer's disease.

7.18. Are anterograde amnesics able to encode new memories? How do you know?

Anterograde amnesics can form new memories that can be retrieved implicitly. This has been shown with research using implicit-memory tasks, where retrieval is not explicit (i.e., intentional).

7.19. What is the proposed cause of amnesia in Alzheimer's patients?

The proposed cause of Alzheimer's disease is the formation of plaques and tangles in the brain that disrupt neuron function and communication.

7.20. Imagine someone who is becoming elderly in your family has come to you for advice based on your knowledge of cognitive psychology on how to keep his or her memory abilities strong as he or she ages. What advice would you give this person?

Answers will vary, but research has shown that engaging in aerobic exercise and cognitive tasks can prevent the type of dementia seen in Alzheimer's patients.

Student Study Site

SAGE edge™

Sharpen your skills with SAGE edge at **edge.sagepub.com/mcbridecp**

SAGE edge for students provides a personalized approach to help you accomplish your coursework goals in an easy-to-use learning environment.

Go to edge.sagepub.com/mcbridecp for additional exercises and web resources. Select Chapter 7, Memory Errors, for chapter-specific resources. All of the links listed in the margins of this chapter are accessible via this site.

CALIFORNIA
1

Imagery

Questions to Consider

- What is an image? How do images contribute to cognitive tasks?
- How are visual images represented and manipulated in our minds?
- How do pictures aid memory?
- What effect does bizarre imagery have on memory?
- How is imagery used in mnemonics?
- How do visual images help us navigate in our environments?
- How do nonvisual images aid in cognition?

Introduction: Visual Imagery in Everyday Life

When I am having a bad day, I sometimes close my eyes and imagine I am driving my Jeep up Pacific Coast Highway. The sun is shining, the wind is whipping the loose strands of my hair around, and I can smell the saltiness of the air. I drive past the length of Newport Beach and keep right on going until I hit the Huntington Beach Pier. There I park and watch the waves crash, full of surfers near the pier. I have a clear visual image of this scene in my head even as I type it out on the page.

I can easily create this visual image because it is a scene I have encountered many times. Driving up Pacific Coast Highway in the places described here was something I did often when I had a bad day while I was in graduate school in Southern California. Living now in Central Illinois, I cannot experience that drive when I have a bad day so instead I imagine it in my head and it is almost as if I am there. I feel calmer and more centered, as I used to when I actually took that drive. But even if I had never been on Pacific Coast Highway before, I could still create an image in my head of what it might be like from pictures I have seen or descriptions I have heard before. In reading my description, you may have created a visual image of yourself in the driving scene, even if you have never been to the California coast.

Our ability to imagine a visual scene plays a part in many cognitive tasks we perform. I access my memory of driving on Pacific Coast Highway when I want to relax. As we discussed in Chapter 6, visual images can be useful mnemonics to help us remember information that is not inherently visual. We can also use visual images to help us predict the future in "seeing" how objects and scenes can change over time as we navigate through complex environments. We focus on imagery in this chapter and how it relates to many of the cognitive processes (e.g., memory, perception, problem solving) covered in other chapters of this text.

Mental Images and Cognition

Alan Baddeley: Visual Imagery

Imagery has been known as a useful cognitive tool since ancient times. It was used as a mnemonic device by Roman orators and is used today by people who develop their memorization abilities for competition (Foer, 2011). In fact, mental images are important not just in memory but in many of the cognitive processes discussed in this text. We collect images of the world around us as we navigate and interpret information using our perceptual processes. We create images of situations as we attempt to solve problems we encounter in our daily lives. As we communicate with others, we often create images of situations we want to relate through language or of situations others are describing to us.

Mental Imagery Research at Lund University

Consider some situations where imagery is useful in your everyday tasks. When you meet a friend in a busy place, you might use a mental image you have of your friend's face or his or her other features to scan the environment for someone who looks like your friend. You probably also use mental imagery to retrieve facts and knowledge (i.e., semantic memories), such as the location of various mid-Atlantic states in the United States or whose photo is on the U.S. five dollar bill. You probably also convey information to other people about your experiences using mental images of those events, such as who was at a party you were at last weekend or who was the star of a movie you recently saw. In my recent attempts to learn Japanese hiragana language symbols, I have used mental images of objects I am familiar with to memorize the phonemes that correspond to the symbols (e.g., ま creates an image for me of a mother holding a child and equates to the phoneme *ma*).

Thus far, we have considered examples of images that are primarily visual, but images are mental re-creations of sensory information from the outside world and can be visual, auditory (i.e., sounds), olfactory (i.e., smells), or tactile (i.e., touches). When we re-create in our minds (i.e., an episodic memory) a scene we have experienced, we can access the visual pieces of the scene (e.g., trees and stretches of grass in a park where we had a picnic), the smells that accompanied the scene (e.g., fresh-cut grass in a park), sounds that were present (e.g., laughter of children in the nearby playground), and the tactile sensations we experienced (e.g., the coolness of a breeze on our arms). From these examples, it may be clear that imagery and episodic memory (i.e., memories of our experiences) are closely connected. But imagery can be created without having a memory of the experience, as mentioned in the introduction to the chapter. You can create an image in your mind of what it might be like to stand on the moon with lowered gravity, hearing the sound of your breath in the space suit you would be wearing and seeing Earth from such a distance. You can create these images even though you have no memory of having been on the moon by using the knowledge you have about the moon and your reasoning abilities to make a good guess about what that experience might be like.

Decoding Visual Imagery During Sleep

The Debate on Propositional and Spatial Representations

Given the importance of imagery for our cognitive abilities, researchers have investigated how images are created and held in our mind. Experiments in the 1970s spawned two primary ideas about how images are held and manipulated in our minds, each of which relies on the representationalist approach to cognition described in Chapter 1. One idea is that mental images are represented spatially, in the same way that objects or scenes are perceived when looking at them. Stephen Kosslyn (e.g., Kosslyn, Ganis, & Thompson, 2006) has been one of the strongest proponents of this view and conducted many experiments to test this idea. He reasoned that subjects asked to do a "mental travel" task, where they have to access different locations of an object or scene, should show longer response times in the task for larger distances across locations if, in fact, they are accessing a **spatial representation** of the image to complete the task. This type of task is known as mental scanning.

Stephen Kosslyn: The Imagery Debate

In one study using a mental scanning task, Kosslyn (1973) asked subjects to consider drawings of objects (e.g., a plane, a lighthouse) like those shown in Figure 8.1. He asked them to then create an image of the object they had seen and focus on a part of the object (e.g., the plane's propeller). The subjects were asked to verify if a description of the object was accurate for another part of the object they were not yet focused on (e.g., Does the plane have a tail fin?). Time to verify the description was recorded on each trial. Results from this study showed that the farther away on the object the verification task was (e.g., the plane's tail) from the starting point in the image (e.g., the plane's propeller), the longer it took subjects to complete the task. From these results, Kosslyn argued that mental images exist as spatial representations in the mind that we can access to complete a task.

Kosslyn further supported his argument with additional experiments. For example, in one study (Kosslyn, Ball, & Reiser, 1978), subjects were asked to study the locations of objects on the map of a fictional island (see Figure 8.2 for an example). They were then asked to imagine the map of the island and go to a specific location on the island. Finally, they were asked to mentally move from that location to another location on the island. You may imagine this task more easily with something familiar to you. Imagine you are standing at your front door. From there, go to your bedroom. This is the task Kosslyn

Spatial representation: the idea that visual information is represented in analog form in the mind

Figure 8.1 Simple Objects Like Those Imagined by Subjects in Kosslyn's (1973) Experiment

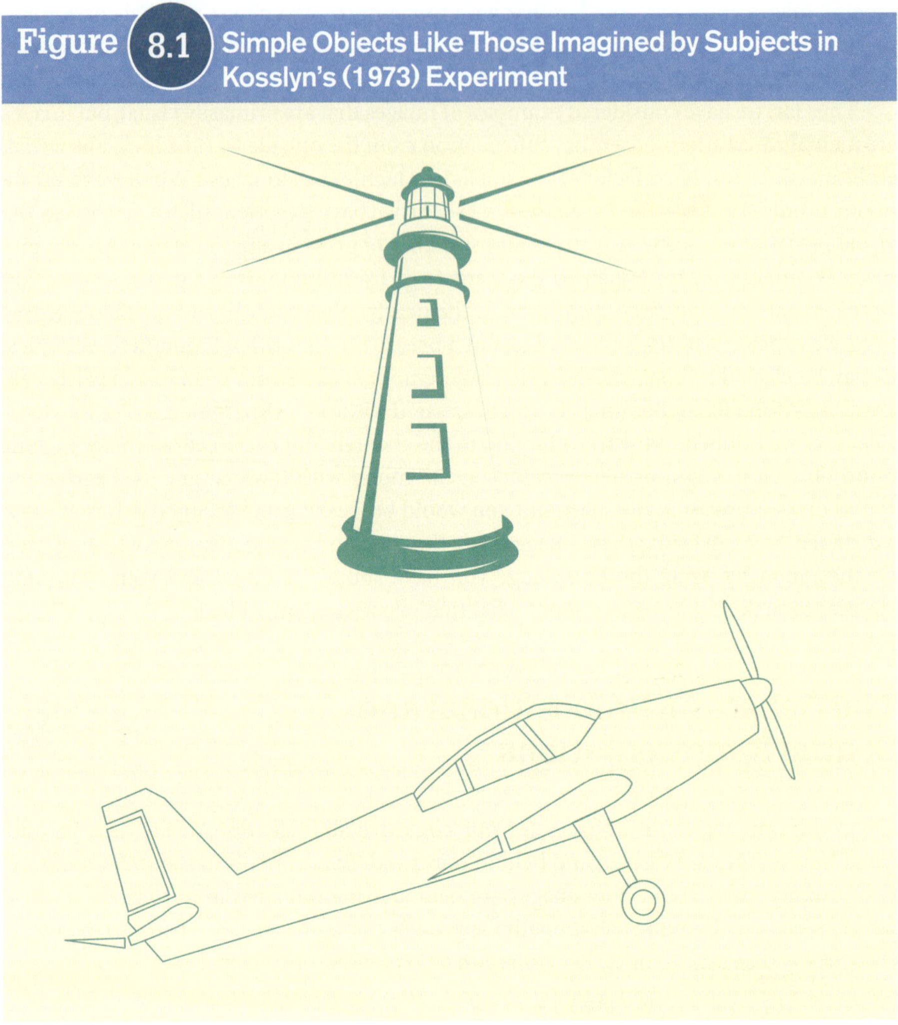

et al.'s subjects were given, but they were asked to mentally "move" around on the island they had studied (seen in Figure 8.2). The time it took them to "mentally travel" between locations depended on the actual distance between the locations on the map, suggesting that subjects were moving around on a spatial representation of the map in their minds. Similar results were also reported by Pinker and Kosslyn (1978) for three-dimensional scenes and by Shepard and Metzler (1971) for the rotation of three-dimensional objects (see Figure 5.11).

Despite the evidence for spatial representations of mental images provided by Kosslyn and colleagues, another researcher suggested a different idea about how mental images are represented in the mind. Pylyshyn (1973) argued that mental images actually represent **propositional representation**, rather than spatial. An example of a proposition is the way you might think of a sentence. Because you know how sentences are structured, you can assign each word to a part of the structure. For example, for the sentence "The boy flew his kite," you know that *The boy* is the subject of the sentence, *flew* is the verb, and *his kite* is the object of the verb (see Figure 9.2 for another example of a propositional representation of a scene). Knowing the purpose of each of these parts allows you to interpret the sentence and understand the ideas presented in it. Contrast this with the spatial representation of this sentence seen in Photo 8.1. Both the propositional and spatial representations have the same meaning and represent the same ideas; they just represent those ideas in different ways. The propositional-representation view

fMRI in Mental Imagery Research

Propositional representation: the idea that visual information is represented nonspatially in the mind is consistent with ideas about the way language is represented in the mind (see Chapter 9 for more discussion).

Figure 8.2 Fictional Map Used in the Kosslyn, Ball, and Reiser (1978) Study

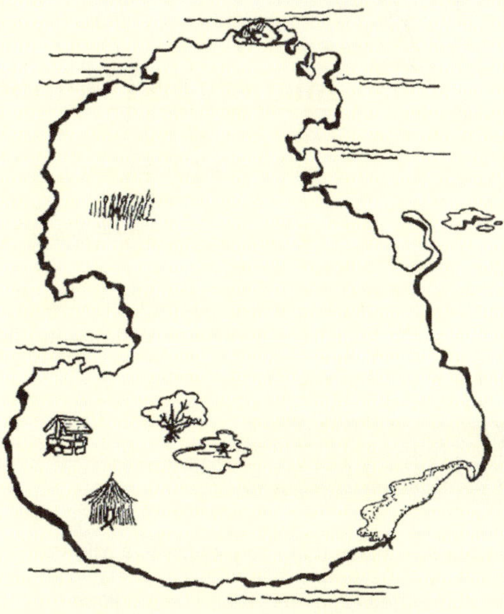

In a study by Kosslyn, Ball, and Reiser (1978, Experiments 2 and 3), subjects were asked to "mentally travel" across a map of a fictional island to different locations. Time to travel was longer for locations that were farther apart (e.g., longer from hut to grassy area than from hut to well).

SOURCE: Figure 2, Kosslyn, S. M., Ball, T. M., & Reiser, B. J. (1978). Visual images preserve metric spatial information: Evidence from studies of image scanning. *Journal of Experimental Psychology: Human Perception and Performance, 4,* 47–60.

Pylyshyn (1973) argued that mental images that seem spatial might actually be propositions of the objects. He suggested that the phenomenological experience of accessing a spatial mental image did not necessarily mean that this was the mode in which our mind had represented the image. You might think of this like the heat you feel from a light bulb while reading—the heat you feel contributes nothing to the reading process (Kosslyn et al., 2006). It is a just a by-product of using a lamp to read by. In this way, the sensory images we experience may be like the heat—we experience them, but they are not part of the process of representing images in our minds. It is possible that the actual representation (a propositional representation) is beyond our conscious experience. Pylyshyn (1981) argued that the task of imagining something happening (like the "mental travel" tasks Kosslyn and colleagues used in their studies) has a temporal sense that the subjects understand and that they mimic this idea of the unfolding of time in the task. He claimed this was why the response times were longer for larger distances, not the idea that images are actually represented spatially within one's mind.

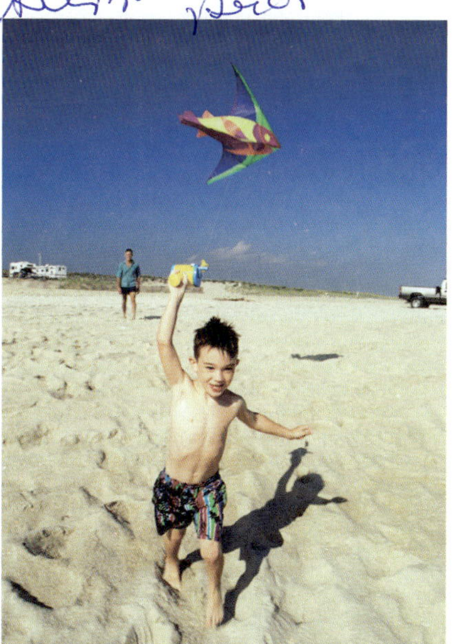

Photo 8.1 Spatial representation of the sentence "The boy flew his kite."

Pylyshyn's argument for propositional representations is compelling, but spatial representation has been the majority view and is supported by more data (e.g., Kosslyn's studies already described) than the propositional view. To counter Pylyshyn's suggestion that spatial representation does not occur for mental images, Kosslyn and his colleagues conducted further studies that examined brain activity during mental imaging. For example, Kosslyn et al. (1993) showed that visual mental imagery tasks activate visual cortex areas in the brain, suggesting that mental imagery activates brain regions that are also activated in perception. Kosslyn, Thompson, Kim, and Alpert (1995) further showed that the size of an object one is imagining is related to the location of brain activation in primary visual cortex areas due to the spatial organization of the visual cortex (see Chapters 2 and 3 for more discussion of the organization of the visual cortex). Slotnick, Thompson, and Kosslyn (2012) more recently reported that brain areas involved in visual memory tasks are also involved in visual mental imagery tasks. These results suggest that the memory accessed in the imagery task is perceptual. Thus, recent neuroimaging studies provide additional support for

Stephen Kosslyn: Mental Imagery and Perception

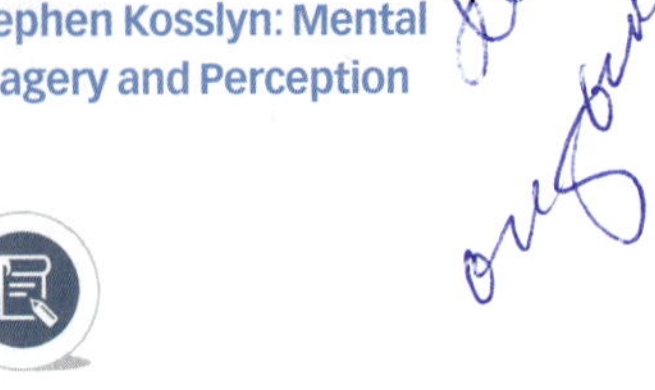

Imagery and Memory Activity

the spatial-representation view of imagery. However, Pylyshyn (2002, 2003) has continued to argue for propositional representation of images, claiming that neuroimaging data do not necessarily illustrate the representational processes that occur for images. Therefore, the debate over how images are represented in the mind is ongoing.

Imagery and Memory

Consider the following words. Read each one to yourself:

house, dream, justice, kite, giraffe, cute, first, whale, trust, paper, hope, clock

Now cover them up, count backward by threes from forty-five, and try to write down all the items you read. It is unlikely that you remembered all of the words, but consider which type of word you remembered the best. *House*, *kite*, *giraffe*, *whale*, *paper*, and *clock* are all concrete objects, whereas *dream*, *justice*, *cute*, *first*, *trust*, and *hope* are more abstract concepts and less easily imagined. Most people remember more of the concrete objects, a result known as the concreteness effect.

> **Stop and Think**
>
> 8.1. Describe two cognitive tasks that imagery plays a role in.
>
> 8.2. Explain the difference between spatial and propositional representations of images.
>
> 8.3. Imagine you are standing outside the building you are in now. In your mind, go to the library on your campus. Now imagine you are once again outside the building you are in now. In your mind, go to the student center on your campus. According to research results reported in this chapter, which "mental travel" task should take longer? Why?
>
> 8.4. The sentence "The cow behind the fence chewed on the green grass" is an example of which type of image representation?

From our discussion of imagery so far in this chapter, you might have noticed the strong connection between imagery and some types of memories. For example, images seem to play a role in many episodic memories we recall from events we have experienced in our lives. In fact, many studies have shown that images can aid memory compared with other forms of information (e.g., words): Pictures are better remembered than words, words that are more easily imaged (i.e., concrete objects) are better remembered, and sentences that create bizarre images are better remembered than sentences that invoke more common images. Finally, as described in Chapter 6, images play a role in mnemonics (i.e., memory aids for encoding lists of information). We now consider each of these imagery effects on memory.

The Picture Superiority Effect

About fifty years of research in memory has shown one fairly consistent result: Pictures are better remembered than words. This effect, known as the **picture superiority effect**, was most frequently seen in studies conducted by Alan Paivio (1991). For example, in one such study (Paivio & Csapo, 1973), subjects studied pictures or word labels for the pictures and then recalled the items they had studied. In a number of different study conditions, pictures were better recalled than words in the memory test. This result has been replicated many times in the decades since Paivio began his research in this area.

Picture superiority effect: a result showing that memory for pictures is superior to memory for words of the same concepts

To explain the picture superiority effect, Paivio (1975, 1986, 1991, 1995) has suggested that pictures produce automatic encoding in two modalities when they are studied, whereas words only produce encoding in one modality, an idea known as dual-coding theory. According to dual-coding theory, words produce only a verbal code (the word itself) when studied, but pictures produce both an image code (the picture itself) and a verbal code (the label for the picture). If you consider the two ways that mental images might be represented in the mind described earlier (i.e., spatial and propositional representations), this would be like having both types of representations stored for each picture item but only the propositional representation stored for each word item. Paivio proposed that both the image code and the verbal code for pictures are automatically encoded into memory when they are studied. This results in two separate and distinct cues (the image code and the verbal code) accessed at retrieval. This provides a better opportunity for one to retrieve a studied picture compared with a studied word that can be retrieved through the verbal code but not an image code.

You may notice that dual-coding theory relies on an important assumption: that pictures will be automatically labeled at study, but words will not be imagined as frequently as pictures are labeled. Snodgrass and McClure (1975) supported this assumption in their research. They instructed subjects to study words and pictures under two conditions: either to memorize the label of the item or to imagine the item. They showed that memory for pictures was similar under these two conditions but that memory for words improved when they were asked to imagine the item. These results are shown in Figure 8.3 and suggest that labeling occurs naturally for pictures (no extra instruction is needed) but that words are not always automatically imagined—an instruction to imagine them is needed to increase their memory to a level similar to that for pictures.

The Concreteness Effect

The effect illustrated in the demonstration at the beginning of this section, where more concrete objects are remembered than abstract ones, is known as the **concreteness**

Concreteness effect: a result showing that memory for concrete concepts is superior to memory for abstract concepts

Figure 8.3 Results From Snodgrass and McClure's (1975) Study Showing Improved Memory for Words When Items Are Imagined

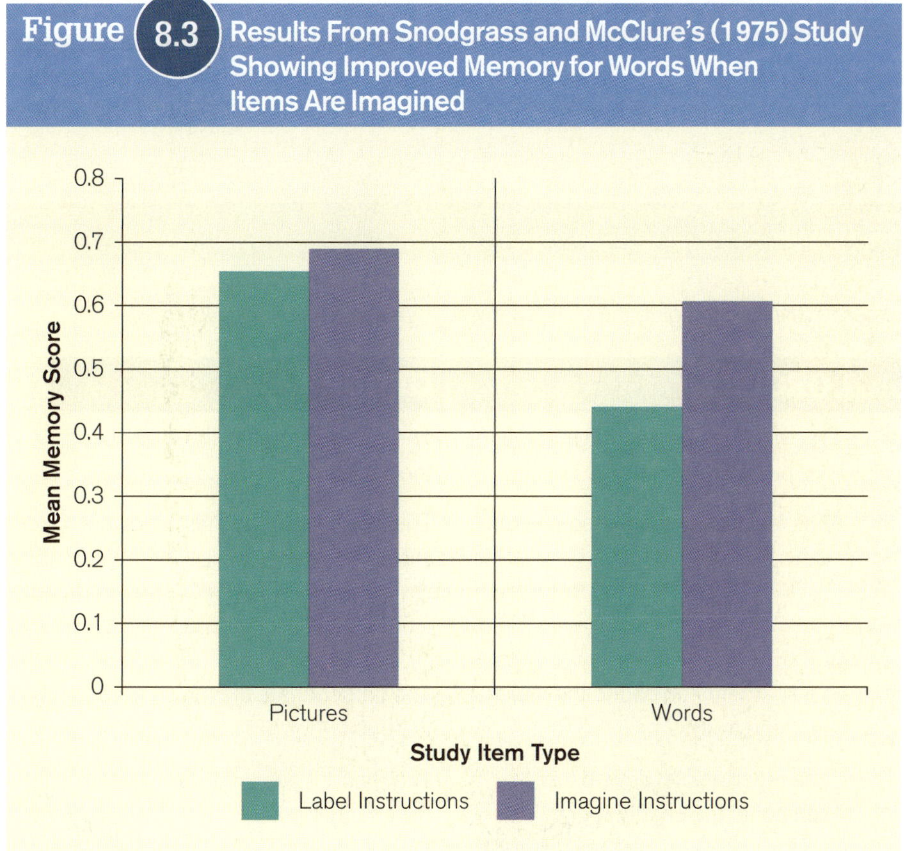

effect. Paivio and colleagues (e.g., Paivio & Csapo, 1973; Paivio & Madigan, 1968) also showed this effect in their studies with higher recall for concrete item labels (e.g., *apple*, *hotel*, *pencil*) than more abstract item labels (e.g., *crime*, *death*, *gravity*). Dual-coding theory was also suggested as the explanation for this effect. Although words are not automatically imagined in every case, it is likely that some word items may be imagined during encoding or retrieval, with more concrete objects imagined than abstract items (which are more difficult to imagine). Thus, this effect is also consistent with the dual-coding idea that relies on image coding of some items.

The Bizarreness Effect

Memorizing Through Storytelling

As described in Chapter 6 (also see the Image Mnemonic Activity on this effect in Chapter 6), the **bizarreness effect** is shown when any information that evokes an unusual image is better remembered than information that evokes more typical images. For example, McDaniel and Einstein (1986) found that sentences like "The dog rode the bicycle down the street" were better remembered than sentences like "The dog chased the bicycle down the street." The first sentence creates an unusual image, whereas the second sentence creates a more common image. An interesting part of their results was that subjects showed the bizarre sentence memory advantage when sentence type was manipulated within subjects (i.e., subjects received both bizarre and common sentences) but not when sentence type was manipulated between subjects (i.e., subjects received only bizarre or common sentences). From this finding, McDaniel and Einstein suggested that the bizarreness effect is caused by the distinctiveness of the bizarre image as compared with the common image. The bizarre sentences seem to stand out when one tries to remember sentences of both types. However, when only one type of sentence is studied, bizarre sentences are less distinct because they are all of the same type. Thus, the bizarre nature of the image only aids memory when it stands out against other studied information.

Bizarreness Effect Activity

Bizarreness effect: result showing that memory for unusual images is superior to memory for typical images

Consider the sentences in Table 8.1. Choose one of the columns of sentences to read, and as you read them, try to form a mental image of the scene depicted in the sentence. Then cover up the sentences and try to recall each one. Check your answers when you're

Table 8.1 Bizarreness Effect Activity

Choose one of the groups of sentences to read and imagine the scene depicted by each sentence as you read.

GROUP 1	GROUP 2	GROUP 3
The plumber lifted the mop out of the bucket.	The plumber juggled the mop out of the bucket.	The plumber juggled the mop out of the bucket.
The teacher sorted the homework in his file.	The teacher sorted the homework in his file.	The teacher burned the homework in his file.
The maid spilled ammonia on the table.	The maid licked ammonia on the table.	The maid licked ammonia on the table.
The gardener unloaded the mulch from the truck.	The gardener unloaded the mulch from the truck.	The gardener ate the mulch from the truck.
The reporter interviewed the senator at the charity event.	The reporter interviewed the senator at the charity event.	The reporter painted the senator at the charity event.

done. How well you remembered them likely depended on the group you chose to read. In Group 1, all of the sentences evoke common images. In Group 2, some of the sentences evoke bizarre images and some evoke common images. In Group 3, all of the sentences evoke bizarre images. According to McDaniel and Einstein's (1986) research, the bizarreness effect should be strongest for Group 2 where the sentence types are mixed (i.e., manipulated within subjects), as compared to when different sets of subjects are assigned to read either Group 1 or Group 3 sentences of only one type (i.e., manipulated between subjects). This example illustrates how distinctiveness can influence memory: The bizarre sentences in Group 2 stand out against the rest and are better remembered.

Distinctiveness has also been proposed to explain the picture superiority effect described earlier in this chapter (e.g., Mintzer & Snodgrass, 1999). Although the picture superiority effect can be produced with between-subjects manipulations of item type (i.e., when different groups of subjects study words and pictures), pictures seem to be more distinctive from one another than words are, which allows the individual pictures to stand out against the other items.

Imagery and Mnemonics

Method of Loci Exercise

In Chapter 6, we described some techniques for improving memory for lists of items called mnemonics. As you may recall, some of the best mnemonics rely on images of the objects one wishes to remember placed in familiar locations along a known route (e.g., your drive or walk home). This technique is known as the **method of loci**, and, as described by Foer (2011), the more bizarre the images created when using the technique, the better they are remembered. In other words, the bizarreness effect can help one remember lists of items when applied as a mnemonic.

Method of loci: a memory aid where images of to-be-remembered information are created with locations along a familiar route or place

Another technique, known as the **pegword mnemonic** technique, also involves the connection of different words with images. In the pegword mnemonic, specific words that rhyme with numbers are used as place holders in an ordered list (e.g., one–bun, two–shoe, three–tree). These pegwords are then associated with items you wish to remember in order. For example, suppose you needed to memorize a speech on the lobes of the brain. If the first topic in your speech is the frontal lobe, you might imagine a

Pegword mnemonic: a memory aid where ordinal words (e.g., one, two) are rhymed with pegwords (e.g., bun, shoe) to create images of pegwords and to-be-remembered items interacting

Siri Stafford/Photodisc/Thinkstock

Hemera Technologies/PhotoObjects.net/Thinkstock

Photo 8.2 The pegword mnemonic technique involves the connection of placeholder words (e.g., one–bun, two–shoe, three–tree) with items one wishes to remember.

hamburger bun sitting at your front door (see Photo 8.2) to connect the *bun* (meaning one) with the "frontal" topic in your speech. If the next topic in your speech is the occipital lobe that involves processing of visual information, you might imagine a shoe with eyes to connect the pegword *shoe* (for two) with the visual processing task of the occipital lobe. In this way, images are used to connect the pegwords that indicate order of the list with the items you wish to remember. Use of mnemonics will not improve your general memory abilities, but it can help you remember lists of information for exams, remember sections of a speech you need to give, or help you remember names of people you meet. The creation of images, especially bizarre images, can help you more easily remember this information.

Metacognition of Visual Imagery

The Dark Side of Imagery

Although many of the effects of imagery on memory are positive, imagery can also hurt memory in some cases. In Chapter 7, we discussed the types of memory errors that can occur, along with the conditions that contribute to those false memories. One thing that contributes to false memories that we have not yet discussed is imagery. Several studies have now shown that when one is asked to imagine an event that never occurred, this can sometimes create a false memory for the event as if it actually happened.

Elizabeth Loftus and others have shown the effects of imagining events on memory for the events in numerous studies. For example, Loftus (1993) has shown that subjects who are asked to "remember" the time they were lost in the mall when they were a child are able to recall details of the event, even though every subject in these studies was never actually lost in a mall as a child (as verified by their family members). Thomas and Loftus (2002) showed that just imagining an event a few times can create false memories for having experienced the event. In this study, subjects were asked to perform or imagine either common tasks (e.g., roll a pair of dice, flip a coin) or bizarre tasks (e.g., sit on a pair of dice). After imagining the tasks they did not perform a few times, many of the subjects reported having performed both the common and the bizarre tasks. Thus, imagining events that never happened can have the unintended effect of creating a false memory for those events. These studies show that although in most cases imagery can aid memory retrieval, it can also create memory errors that could be damaging if one is asked to imagine a negative event, such as a crime.

Stop and Think

8.5. Describe each of the following effects: the picture superiority effect, the concreteness effect, and the bizarreness effect.

8.6. In what way can each of the effects listed in Stop and Think 8.5 aid in the use of mnemonics to improve memory for information?

8.7. Describe how you might use the pegword mnemonic technique to remember a grocery list of items you need to buy.

8.8. Mnemonics can aid memory for specific lists of information, but they do not improve general memory abilities for all information. Why do you think mnemonics have this limited effect on memory?

Imagery in Problem Solving and Wayfinding

Pick a Card Activity

Imagery is useful in remembering information, but it can also be useful in other cognitive tasks such as problem solving and navigating in the environment. Consider the following problem: You have a deck of fifty-two playing cards. You choose a card at random from the deck. What is the probability that the card is a spade (see Photo 8.3)? While considering this problem, did you imagine the deck and the different suits of c that are in a deck? If so, then you used imagery to help solve the problem. Imagery is not necessary to solve this problem, but it can be helpful if you are not very familiar with playing cards. (The answer is 25 percent, because there are four suits in the deck, giving you a one-in-four chance of choosing a spade.)

Stockbyte/Stockbyte/Thinkstock

Photo 8.3 Imagery can aid in problem solving, such as determining the probability of choosing a spade at random from a deck of cards.

Imagery in Problem Solving

In fact, recent research has shown that reasoning abilities can be aided by mental imagery. Consider another problem involving the gears seen in Photo 8.4. If the gear on the right is turned clockwise, which direction will the gear on the left turn? Research suggests that creating a mental image of this gear system and moving the image in your mind can help you solve the problem. Hegarty (2004) reviewed research studies showing that when subjects attempt to solve problems like the gear system problem shown in Photo 8.4 or a pulley system problem, the reaction time in solving the problem depended on the amount of movement required by the system in the problem. Further, asking subjects to mentally imagine the problem did not change their reaction times, suggesting that mental imaging is something they will do on their own to solve the problem.

Hegarty (1992) also showed that in solving complex problems, the mental simulation is done in parts to arrive at the final solution. Try to solve the problem in Figure 8.4. Which direction will the top left wheel move? In order to solve this problem, you might think through each part of the system's movement (e.g., pulling the rope on the right will make the top right wheel move clockwise, which will then move the bottom wheel counterclockwise, which then moves the top left wheel counterclockwise). Hegarty gave subjects pulley systems like the one shown in Figure 8.4. She then gave them statements to verify (e.g., True or false? If the block on the bottom is pulled, the bottom wheel will turn clockwise) and recorded the reaction time to verify the statements. The reaction time results are shown in Figure 8.5. As can be seen in the graph, subjects took longer to verify statements that involved more parts of the pulley system. This result suggests that subjects are not moving all the parts of the mental image of the system simultaneously. Adding more parts to the problem adds more time for subjects to imagine a solution.

Pulley System Problem Activity

Moulton and Kosslyn (2009) argued that imagery serves a primary role in prospective cognition—our ability to make predictions about how things will occur in the future. They suggest that imagery allows knowledge to be generated about specific events, which then allows for predictions to be made about those events. In other words, imagery allows for the prediction of various solutions to problems from the knowledge gained in the mental simulation of the problem. However, visual imagery is not the only strategy used in problem solving. Rule-based strategies are also used in many problems. For example, in the gear system problem in Photo 8.4, you might know a general rule about gears—that they move in opposite directions where they are connected. This rule could be used to answer the question posed in Photo 8.4 without creating a mental image of the system and moving it in your mind. Using a mental imagery strategy is an example of a spatial representation of the problem. Using a rule-based strategy would involve a propositional

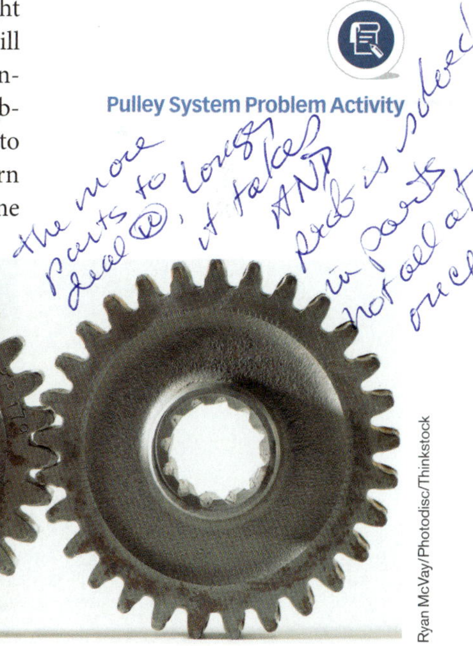

Ryan McVay/Photodisc/Thinkstock

Photo 8.4 Research shows that mental imagery can aid in the solution of problems, such as with this gear system. If the gear on the right is turned clockwise, which direction will the gear on the left turn?

Figure 8.4 Pulley System Problem Similar to Those Used in Hegarty (1992)

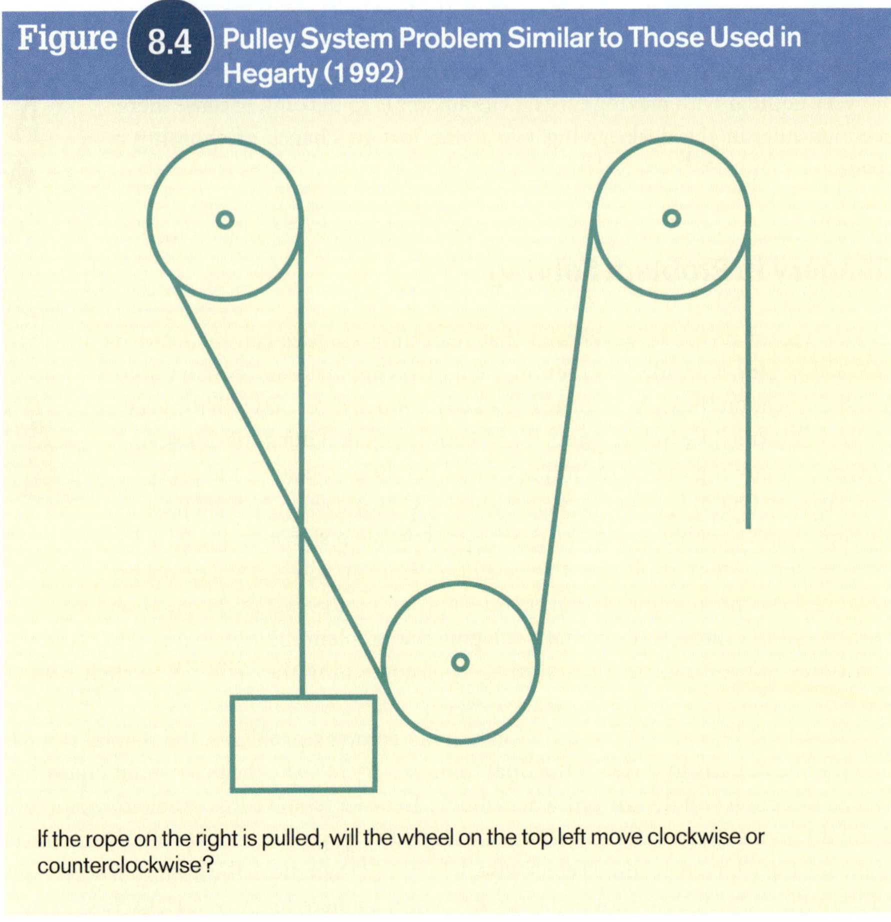

If the rope on the right is pulled, will the wheel on the top left move clockwise or counterclockwise?

Figure 8.5 Results From Hegarty's (1992) Experiment 1 for Pulley System Statements That Involved Movement (collapsed across the two pulley systems used)

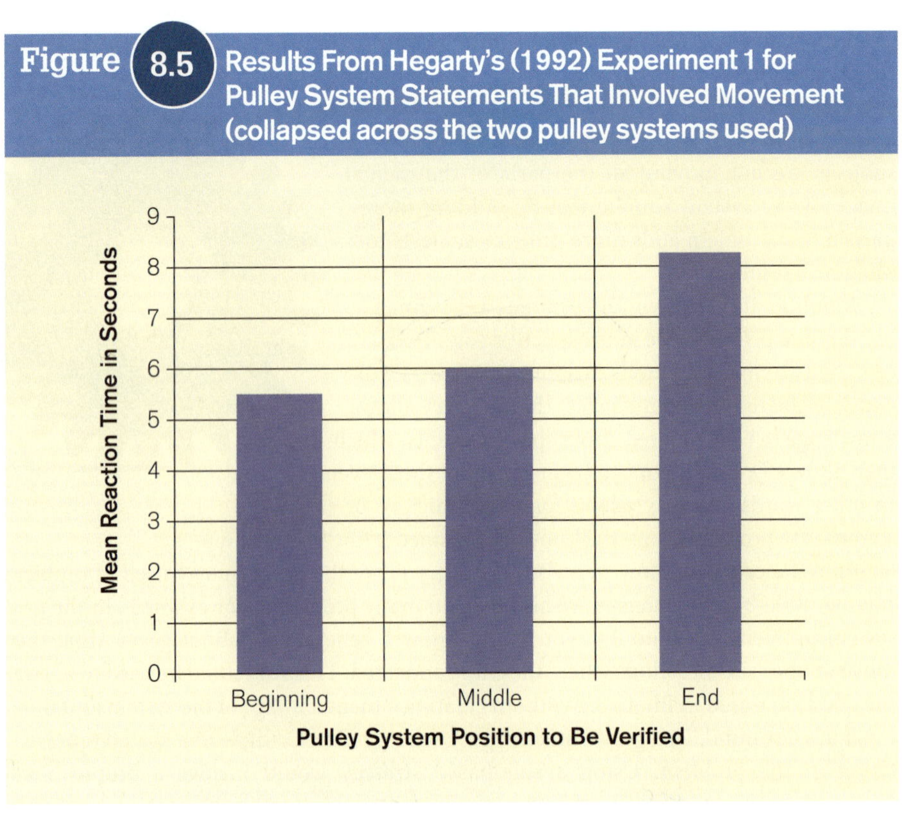

representation of the problem. Thus, imagery seems to play a role in problem solving, regardless of the type of representation (spatial or propositional) from which the imagery is formed.

Imagery in Wayfinding

Imagery seems to be helpful as well in another type of problem-solving task: navigating our environment. Foley and Cohen (1984) argued that in making judgments about a large-scale environment (e.g., a large building) subjects who made accurate judgments constructed a "working map" of the environment. They found that two types of imagery contributed to the "working map" representation subjects created: scenographic and abstract imagery. **Scenographic imagery** is what one would see walking through the environment. **Abstract imagery** is a maplike image overview of the environment (see Figure 8.6 for examples). Their study showed that both types of imagery contributed to subjects' knowledge of the environments they were asked to judge.

Examples of Abstract Imagery

Some studies have shown that, although both types of imagery contribute to wayfinding, abstract imagery is more helpful in navigating an environment (e.g., Abu-Obeid, 1998; Foley & Cohen, 1984). However, in a study comparing a route perspective (directions are given in terms of what the person following them will see on the route, allowing for scenographic images) and a survey perspective (directions are given as if following a map overview of the route, allowing for abstract images), Padgitt and Hund (2012) found that the route perspective resulted in better wayfinding performance in a university building. Thus, the effectiveness of the two types of imagery may depend on the complexity of the environment, the means of following the instructions (i.e., step by step or from memory), individual differences in sense of direction, or other factors.

Stop and Think

8.9. Describe how imagery can aid in problem solving and navigating an environment.

8.10. In what way are the results of Hegarty's studies involving pulley problems similar to the results of Kosslyn et al.'s studies in navigating a fictional island from a studied map?

8.11. Describe the difference between scenographic imagery and abstract imagery in navigating an environment. Which of these seems to be more helpful in successful navigation?

Neuroscience of Wayfinding

From the research reviewed here, it is clear that imagery is related to several important cognitive tasks necessary for daily activities. Memory, problem-solving, and navigation abilities all include some role for imagery in tasks relying on these abilities, with imagery as a key component in superior performance on these tasks. However, most of the imagery helpful in these cognitive tasks is visual. In the next section, we consider how nonvisual imagery can aid in motor tasks such as sports performance.

Nonvisual Imagery

Paivio's dual-coding theory, described earlier in this chapter, suggests that imagery has two inherent codes, a verbal code (as in the word label for pictures) and a nonverbal code (as in the visual image of a picture). The nonverbal code can include visual information or information from other modalities, such as auditory, olfactory, or tactile information. Some researchers have investigated these nonvisual codes as they pertain to motor tasks, such as grasping an object, hitting a baseball, or running. In some cases, these nonvisual codes can be easily translated into a verbal code (Klatzky, McCloskey, Doherty, Pellegrino, & Smith, 1987), but in other cases, verbal translation is more difficult (e.g., explaining verbally what is involved in running). But kinesthetic imagery, regardless of the verbal

Scenographic imagery: the image of an environment based on landmarks encountered in that environment along a navigated route

Abstract imagery: an image of an environment based on an overview of the environment

Figure 8.6 Examples of Scenographic Images (Panel A) and an Abstract Image (Panel B) of a University Building

Panel A

View facing the men's room after getting off the elevator

View of the doors at the entrance to the plaza

View of the junction between the two parts of the basement level in front of Room 20J

View at end of hallway in front of Room 17 containing the PRC and computer lab

Panel B – Abstract image of the basement level of DeGarmo Hall at Illinois State University

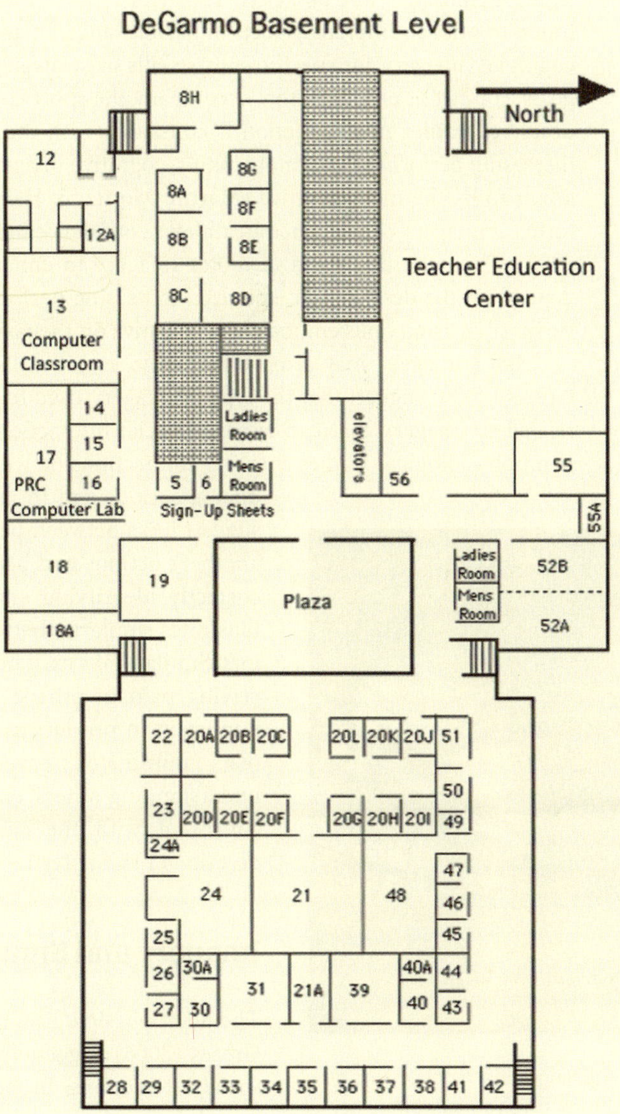

DeGarmo Basement Level

access to the imagery, has been shown to influence the way we perform motor tasks. Such imagery has been called internal imagery (Jeannerod, 1995), as it is experienced from within as if one were performing the action with one's body (i.e., "muscular imaging"; Epstein, 1980).

Affordance Perception

In some early work in this area, Klatzky et al. (1987) showed that subjects could report the correct hand shape for grasping different objects (see Photo 8.5) without actually grasping those objects, suggesting that the subjects had access to a motor image for the task. In this case, the image was also available verbally, as subjects could make a verbal report. In another study by Klatzky, Pellegrino, McCloskey, and Doherty (1989), these researchers showed that when asked to judge whether an action could be performed (e.g., crumple a newspaper versus climb a grape), subjects more quickly identified performable actions when they were preceded by an appropriate hand configuration for the action. This suggests that subjects benefitted in judging the actions from the motor imagery provided by the hand configuration cues.

Visualization for a Gymnast

Thomas Northcut/Stockbyte/Thinkstock

Photo 8.5 Subjects in Klatzky et al.'s (1987) experiments could identify the correct hand configuration for grasping specific objects.

In other studies, researchers have considered the benefit of **motor imagery** to sports performance (see Photo 8.6). A long line of studies has shown that motor imagery, in the form of muscular rehearsal within one's mind, can benefit performance in sports such as skiing, gymnastics, and basketball (Epstein, 1980). Different types of imagery have been found to impact different aspects of performance. Imagery has been classified as either cognitive (imagery for specific sports skills or strategies) or motivational (imagery for goals, coping, or emotions that accompany the sport competition). The motor imagery described earlier in this section is consistent with the cognitive type of imagery. For increasing performance of motor skills, cognitive imagery that focuses on specific skills seems to be the most effective (Martin, Moritz, & Hall, 1999). However, motivational forms of imagery can enhance an athlete's confidence in his or her abilities (Martin et al., 1999). Thus, the best form of motor imagery in enhancing sports performance may depend on the desired outcome (e.g., increasing performance of a specific motor skill versus increasing one's emotional perspective on the task).

Motor imagery may also be related to social skills and interactions. Decety and Grèzes (2006) suggest that the type of imagery used to enhance motor performance is related to imagery that can enhance social interactions. They review evidence from neurophysiological studies showing connections between brain areas involved in producing actions and in imagining actions. They further suggest links between perceiving one's own actions and another's actions and between imagining emotions and correctly identifying another's emotional state, which illustrates similarity between imagery and social behaviors. Similar links exist between imagining pain and perceiving pain in others. Thus, motor imagery may be important in producing active interactions with others (e.g., coordinated movements and synchrony) and in understanding others' emotional states. These ideas are consistent with the embodied cognition perspective described in Chapter 1.

© iStockphoto.com/GoodLifeStudio

Photo 8.6 Research suggests that imagining yourself performing a free throw shot using motor imagery can improve your performance.

Stop and Think

8.12. Explain what is meant by motor imagery. Describe an example from your life for this concept.

8.13. What is the difference between cognitive imagery and motivational imagery? Which one seems to enhance performance more in a specific sports skill (e.g., making a free throw)?

8.14. Describe what is meant by Barsalou's concept of "grounded cognition." How does this approach to cognition differ from the representationalist approach with which the chapter started?

Imagery and Simulation

The neurophysiological results described by Decety and Grèzes (2006) suggest that imagery may play a role in social interactions. In fact, imagery may precede many social interactions as we consider what we might say to someone in certain situations before we encounter them, what emotions specific social situations might elicit in us before we experience them, or what movements we must make to navigate a social environment without tripping and embarrassing ourselves. In other words, social interaction often requires simulation of these actions and emotions in order to determine the best way to handle a social situation. Thus, imagery may be part of the broader process of simulation that we do every day as we interact with our environment.

This idea was suggested by Barsalou (2008) in describing the role of cognitive processes in our goals for perception and action in our environment. He calls this perspective "grounded cognition," as it involves considering cognition as a means for achieving goals that may be bodily, social, or simulative. Barsalou presents evidence to support the argument that simulation is the way in which information is represented in the mind. He argues that imagery plays a primary role in such simulation, suggesting that the imagery we have described in this chapter is not a compartmentalized cognitive process on its own. Instead, it is an important process in grounded cognition, where cognition involves simulation and the interaction of the body and the environment. Thus, cognition is a broad interactive process rather than the accumulation of different operations from independent processes of perception, memory, and language. This way of viewing cognition is becoming more popular as research areas of cognition have interacted and overlapped more in the past few decades.

Mental Rehearsal

Motor imagery: a mental representation of motor movements

THINKING ABOUT RESEARCH

As you read the following summary of a research study in psychology, think about the following questions:

1. In what ways is this study similar to studies examining the role of visual imagery in cognitive tasks presented in this chapter?
2. What was the manipulated variable in this experiment? (Hint: Review the Research Methodologies section in Chapter 1 for help in answering this question.)
3. What was the purpose of the control condition? In what way would the researchers' conclusion have been limited if the control condition had not been included?
4. If the researchers had chosen to look at brain activity during the moral judgment task instead of looking at inhibition due to the type of interference task, what results would you expect for this study?

Study Reference

Amit, E., & Greene, J. D. (2012). You see, the ends don't justify the means: Visual imagery and moral judgment. *Psychological Science, 23*, 861–868.

Note: Experiment 2 of this study is presented.

Purpose of the study: The study was conducted to investigate the role of visual imagery in moral judgments. The researchers considered two possible contributions to moral judgments: favoring the rights of an individual (e.g., it is wrong to harm a single individual, even if doing so would save others) and favoring the greater good (i.e., it is better to harm a single individual than many). The authors predicted that, due to its connection to emotional content, visual imagery contributes to judgments favoring the individual (a more emotional choice), whereas verbal processing contributes to favoring the greater good (a more logical, less emotional choice). They tested this hypothesis by adding interference to a moral judgment task that would inhibit either visual or verbal processing in the judgments.

Method of the study: Subjects were given a number of moral dilemma scenarios that produced a conflict where killing a single person would save several other people. Subjects rated the acceptability of killing the single person (resulting in saving several others) on a 1 (completely unacceptable) to 7 (completely acceptable) scale. During the moral judgment task, they also performed a visual or verbal task to manipulate the type of processing (visual imagery or verbal processing) required in the second task. The visual task involved judging whether a specific shape had been presented 2 shapes earlier within a series of 10 shapes shown to the subject. Thus, subjects had to access visual images of the presented shapes to make their response. The verbal task was the same, but the names of the shapes (e.g., circle, square) were presented instead of the actual shapes. By requiring the subjects to complete two tasks at once, the researchers created a situation where the secondary task could interfere with the

(Continued)

(Continued)

judgments about acceptability of the choice to kill one person (and save several others) in the moral judgment task. Thus, in the visual task condition, subjects were inhibited in their visual imagery abilities in the moral judgment task. In the verbal task condition, they were inhibited in their verbal processing in the moral judgment task. Finally, some scenarios were presented without a second task to create a control condition.

Results of the study: The visual task condition resulted in higher mean acceptability rating (subjects were more likely to allow the single individual to be killed) than in the verbal processing condition or the control condition. This result indicates that visual imagery inhibited by the visual interference task is important in making judgments that would favor saving the individual in the moral scenarios presented. Because subjects were less able to create visual images in the moral judgment task (due to the interfering visual task), they favored killing the individual more than in the verbal or control task conditions.

Conclusions of the study: In this experiment, the researchers' hypothesis was partially supported by the result that a visual interference task inhibited favoring the individual. However, a verbal interference task did not influence moral judgments as compared with the control condition. But from the results the researchers did obtain, they concluded that visual imagery contributes to the favoring of individuals in moral judgments.

CHAPTER REVIEW

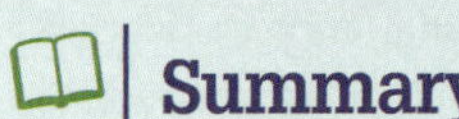

Summary

- **What is an image? How do images contribute to cognitive tasks?**

  An image is a representation of something (e.g., an object, a scene, a movement, a sound) in your mind. Images contribute to many cognitive tasks including memory, perception, problem solving, and environment navigation by aiding in the processes that accompany these tasks.

- **How are visual images represented and manipulated in our minds?**

  There are two ideas about how images are represented in our minds: spatial and propositional. Spatial images represent things in their original form, whereas propositional images represent the meaning and associations of the thing being represented. It is still debated as to whether images are represented spatially or propositionally.

- **How do pictures aid memory?**

  The picture superiority effect has shown that pictures are generally better remembered than words. One idea about why this is the case is dual coding of pictures where both the visual and verbal information is stored for pictures but only verbal information is stored for words. More stored codes generally produce better retrieval. Pictures may also be more distinctive than words and thus more easily retrieved.

- **What effect does bizarre imagery have on memory?**

  Bizarre imagery aids memory. It has been proposed that bizarre images are more distinctive and thus more easily retrieved.

- **How is imagery used in mnemonics?**

  Imagery is useful in mnemonic techniques in associating something meaningful to information we wish to remember. Bizarre images can aid in making that information more distinctive in memory.

- **How do visual images help us navigate in our environments?**

  Visual images can aid navigation in providing landmarks to follow (e.g., retrieving these images from memory) or in providing an overview image of an environment to follow in navigating that environment.

- **How do nonvisual images aid in cognition?**

  Nonvisual images aid cognition as well. For example, motor images can enhance sports performance through the mental practice of muscle movements.

Chapter Quiz

1. The sentence "Twelve blackbirds flew through the cloudless blue sky and landed at the top of a large oak tree" is an example of what type of imagery?
   (a) spatial imagery
   (b) propositional imagery
   (c) motor imagery
   (d) all of the above
2. A video showing twelve blackbirds flying and landing on the top of a large tree is an example of what type of imagery?
   (a) spatial imagery
   (b) propositional imagery
   (c) motor imagery
   (d) all of the above
3. Imagining yourself jumping over a small fence is an example of what type of imagery?
   (a) spatial imagery
   (b) propositional imagery
   (c) motor imagery
   (d) all of the above
4. The description of images as spatial proposed by Kosslyn and others illustrates the ___________ perspective of cognition.
   (a) embodied cognition
   (b) representational
   (c) biological
5. The description of images as important in simulations that help aid the fulfillment of perceptual goals illustrates the ___________ perspective of cognition.
   (a) embodied cognition
   (b) representational
   (c) biological
6. Remembering words like *book*, *tree*, and *butterfly* better than words like *justice*, *meaning*, and *life* illustrates the ______________ effect.
   (a) bizarreness
   (b) picture superiority
   (c) concreteness
7. Explain the difference between spatial and propositional representations.
8. How have studies of brain activity helped support the spatial representation view of imagery?
9. Provide some examples of the bizarreness effect from your life.
10. When finding a place you have never been, do you rely more on scenographic or abstract images? Provide some examples that illustrate this.
11. Explain how motor imagery is different from other forms of imagery discussed in this chapter. Provide an example of motor imagery from your life.

Key Terms

Abstract imagery 193
Bizarreness effect 188
Concreteness effect 187
Method of loci 189
Motor imagery 196
Pegword mnemonic 189
Picture superiority effect 186
Propositional representation 184
Scenographic imagery 193
Spatial representation 183

Stop and Think Answers

8.1. Describe two cognitive tasks that imagery plays a role in.

Answers will vary, but many cognitive tasks in the areas of memory, problem solving, perception, and language seem to rely partly on imagery of some form.

8.2. Explain the difference between spatial and propositional representations of images.

Spatial representations are essentially representations of an object or scene as it appears in reality. You can "map" each portion of the actual object or scene onto the image. Propositional representations do not retain the physical properties of the object or scene in the image as they appear in reality. Instead, these properties are recoded into a form with the same meaning but not the same analogical content.

8.3. Imagine you are standing outside the building you are in now. In your mind, go to the library on your campus. Now imagine you are once again outside the building you are in now. In your mind, go to the student center on your campus. According to research results reported in this chapter, which "mental travel" task should take longer? Why?

Whichever route is longer should take longer to travel in your mind because most studies have shown that individuals take longer to complete mental travel tasks when the travel is farther in reality.

8.4. The sentence "The cow behind the fence chewed on the green grass" is an example of which type of image representation?

This is a propositional representation. It retains the meaning of an image but not the physical properties of the image. A picture of a cow behind a fence eating green grass would be a spatial image of this scene.

8.5. Describe each of the following effects: the picture superiority effect, the concreteness effect, and the bizarreness effect.

The picture superiority effect is a common result showing higher memory for studied pictures than studied words. The concreteness effect is shown by higher memory for concrete objects than for abstract concepts. The bizarreness effect is the finding that information containing unusual images (e.g., the blue cow danced in the field) is better remembered than information containing common images (e.g., the brown cow ate in the field).

8.6. In what way can each of the effects listed in Stop and Think 8.5 aid in the use of mnemonics to improve memory for information?

Distinctiveness seems to be important in each of these effects. Items better remembered tend to be more distinct from other items. Dual coding (e.g., verbal and pictorial image codes) may also play a role in these effects.

8.7. Describe how you might use the pegword mnemonic technique to remember a grocery list of items you need to buy.

Answers will vary, but the key is to create an image of each item interacting with the images created in the rhymes (e.g., for "one is a bun" imagine a box of cereal sandwiched within a hamburger bun).

8.8. Mnemonics can aid memory for specific lists of information, but they do not improve general memory abilities for all information. Why do you think mnemonics have this limited effect on memory?

Mnemonics rely on images. Thus, the specific images created are tied to specific material to be remembered. These images aid memory for this specific material but will not help you remember other information that is not part of the image.

8.9. Describe how imagery can aid in problem solving and navigating an environment.

Studies have shown that imagining a place (e.g., with an overview map or landmarks in that place) can aid in navigation.

8.10. In what way are the results of Hegarty's studies involving pulley problems similar to the results of Kosslyn et al.'s studies in navigating a fictional island from a studied map?

The Hegarty studies suggest that individuals are solving problems through the manipulation of a spatial image. It takes longer to respond when the image must be manipulated more. This is similar to the Kosslyn et al. studies where subjects took longer to mentally travel from one location to another on a map.

8.11. Describe the difference between scenographic imagery and abstract imagery in navigating an environment. Which of these seems to be more helpful in successful navigation?

Scenographic imagery involves landmarks along a route. Abstract imagery involves an overhead view (like a map) of a place. Some studies have shown that scenographic information is more helpful; however, the influence of these two types of imagery may also depend on the factors surrounding the task (e.g., complexity of the environment).

8.12. Explain what is meant by motor imagery. Describe an example from your life for this concept.

Motor imagery is a nonvisual form of imagery that involves mental practice of motor movements. Examples will vary but should involve some kind of motor movement you can imagine yourself performing.

8.13. What is the difference between cognitive imagery and motivational imagery? Which one seems to

enhance performance more in a specific sports skill (e.g., making a free throw)?

Cognitive imagery involves imagery for specific sports skills or strategies (e.g., a movement involved in performing some type of sports skill). Motivational imagery involves imagery for goals, coping, or emotions that accompany sports competition. Current research suggests that cognitive imagery is more helpful in improving specific sports skills.

8.14. Describe what is meant by Barsalou's concept of "grounded cognition." How does this approach to cognition differ from the representationalist approach with which the chapter started?

Barsalou's concept of grounded cognition posits that cognition aids us in tasks, like navigating our environment and achieving specific perceptual goals. He discusses the importance of imagery and simulation in such cognition. This view illustrates the embodied-cognition perspective, whereas Kosslyn's spatial-imagery argument illustrates the representationalist view of the study of cognition.

Student Study Site

Sharpen your skills with SAGE edge at **edge.sagepub.com/mcbridecp**

SAGE edge for students provides a personalized approach to help you accomplish your coursework goals in an easy-to-use learning environment.

Go to edge.sagepub.com/mcbridecp for additional exercises and web resources. Select Chapter 8, Imagery, for chapter-specific resources. All of the links listed in the margins of this chapter are accessible via this site.

© AF archive/Alamy

Language

Questions to Consider

- What is language?
- How do we get from a string of sounds or marks on a page to something meaningful?
- How do we go from thoughts to spoken language?
- How do we acquire language?
- How does human language differ from animal communication?

Introduction: A Simple Conversation

Consider the following scene in a local coffee shop. Bill is sitting at a corner table and is approached by another young man.

TED: *"Hey Bill."*

BILL: *(looks up) "Ted! What's up?"*

TED: *(sits in the chair across from Bill) "Last week I was talking to Rufus and Elizabeth after the circus. Man, the stuff he knows is dangerous."*

BILL: *"Dangerous? I think he just needs a day of rest and a box of tissues and he'll be alright."*

TED: *(initially looks confused) "Um . . . no, not a stuffy nose, THE STUFF HE KNOWS. You know, all the knowledge about what happens in the future."*

BILL: *(laughs) "I got it dude. What was he talking about this time?"*

TED: *"Well, he was reading a newspaper and I was reading over his shoulder. The paper must have been from some time in the far future."*

BILL: *"Why do you say that Ted?"*

TED: *"Well, the headlines were really bizarre, but Rufus didn't even bat an eye. He acted like everything was perfectly normal. Man, things in the future must be really weird."*

BILL: *"Give me an example of the headlines."*

TED: *"Well, it was last week, but I remember one of them. It was 'Enraged cow injures farmer with ax.' Can you imagine it? In the future, cows carrying axes!"*

BILL: *(laughs again) "Ted, I think that you misinterpreted that headline. I think that the farmer was probably the one with the ax."*

TED: *"Man, Bill, I'm glad I ran into you. I've got to go call my uncle and tell him not to worry about his cow Betsy. Party on, dude."*

Ted then gets up and leaves the coffee shop, while Bill laughs quietly to himself.

Most of the time communication using language feels relatively effortless and easy. However, as the opening story exemplifies, sometimes we stumble and communication fails. Bill misinterprets some of what Ted says because two things sound similar. Ted misinterprets the newspaper headlines because there are two possible meanings depending on how we build the underlying grammar of the headline. The failures (and successes) of our language use reveal that the apparent ease belies an incredibly complex system of information and processes. This chapter provides an introduction into psycholinguistics, a subfield of cognitive psychology that examines how we use language. As the term suggests, this area is heavily influenced by concepts from the fields of linguistics (which examines the structure of human language) and psychology (primarily cognitive psychology). In some respects, our discussion of the processing of language mirrors our discussions of memory. In the chapters on memory (see Chapters 5, 6, and 7) we discuss the processes of encoding (getting information into memory), storage (holding and organizing memories), and retrieval (getting information out of memory). For language, we focus on similar processes: comprehension (understanding language coming in), the mental lexicon (our storage of language information), and production (mapping thoughts onto language and articulating them). In this chapter, we start with a discussion of what language is and how it is structured. We briefly review research and theory about how we use and acquire language. We close with a brief discussion of how human language use differs from other methods of communication used by both humans and animals.

What Is Language?

Crash Course: Language

Philosophers and linguists have offered a number of answers to the question, What is language? It is a hard question to answer. Most definitions agree that language is used for multiple functions, the primary of which is to exchange information between individuals. In the opening story Bill and Ted are talking with one another with the goal of passing along information between the two. Bill wants to know how Ted is doing, and Ted wants to relate his experience with Rufus. The same basic purpose is true of the textbook you are reading. Our goal, as authors, is to convey concepts about cognitive psychology. The medium through which we are trying to accomplish this is the words and sentences you are currently reading.

Structure of Language

Most theories of language assume it consists of different kinds of linguistic domains: form (phonology and orthography), meaning (semantics), grammar (syntax), and use (pragmatics). Psycholinguistic theories have borrowed many of the concepts from these domains, proposing that language processing involves different levels of language elements. Consider our story. It is made up of several elements: sounds (or letters), words, phrases, and sentences. These elements are related to each other hierarchically. That is, words are made up of sounds, phrases are made up of words, sentences are made up of phrases, and our story dialogue is made up of sentences. The traditional psycholinguistic theoretical approach has been to assume that each of these levels of language consists of representations and rules (consistent with the representational approach to cognition discussed in Chapter 1). This approach allows for the productive nature of language. We are able to produce and understand a potentially infinite set of sentences, including those we have never heard before. The following subsections illustrate this approach for different levels of linguistic information.

Language Form: Phonology and Orthography

Consider the sounds that make up the first spoken line of our story "Hey Bill." There are five distinct sound units, two vowels and three consonants: /h/, /eI/, /b/, /I/, and /l/. These sound elements are called **phonemes**. Different languages are made up of

Phonemes: distinct sound units that comprise a language

different sets of phonemes (e.g., American English has roughly forty phonemes, Native Hawaiian has as few as thirteen, while some African languages may have more than one hundred). In addition to the individual phonemes, languages have rules that specify how to put the phonemes together (e.g., rules for syllables). For example, in English we can put the /p/ and /t/ phonemes together in some contexts (e.g., *captain*) but not in others (e.g., English does not have a word that begins with both together as in the nonword *ptain*).

Notice that there is not a one-to-one correspondence between the sounds (phonology) and the letters that make up a language (orthography). Consider Bill's mishearing of Ted's "the stuff he knows" as "the stuffy nose." Had Bill read Ted's comment instead of hearing it, he would not have made the mistake. As speakers learning English as a second language will tell you, the spelling-to-sound rules are not simple. For example, consider the letter *c*; sometimes it is pronounced with the /s/ phoneme and sometimes the /k/ phoneme (*circus* has both). The differences between the two kinds of stimuli (e.g., letters are made up of visual lines and curves that we see; sounds are made up of vibrations in the air that we hear) illustrates the flexibility of our comprehension processes to handle two sets of representations to achieve the same basic communicative goals. We discuss this in greater detail later in this chapter.

Morphology: Language Interface of Form, Syntax, and Semantics

Above these form levels in the hierarchy is morphology. Morphological units (**morphemes**) are the smallest representations that convey meaning and grammatical properties. Consider Ted's utterance about the headline: "'Enraged cow injures farmer with ax.' Can you imagine it? In the future, cows carrying axes!" In some cases, what we think of as "words" are single morphemes (e.g., *cow* and *imagine*), but in many cases "words" are made up of multiple morphemes (e.g., *cows* is made up of *cow* and the plural morpheme *-s*). Additionally, not all morphemes have the same properties, so they interact with the rules of morphology differently. For example, free morphemes can stand alone (e.g., *cow*), while bound morphemes must be attached to other morphemes (e.g., the plural *-s*). Sometimes morphemes are used to add grammatical features (e.g., the past tense inflectional morpheme *-ed* may be added to indicate that the event occurred in the past); in other cases added morphemes result in a change of the meaning or syntactic class (e.g., noun or verb) of a word (e.g., in *farmer* the *-er* changes the meaning of *farm* from "a place to grow food" to "a person who grows food").

Our story also illustrates how the phonological and morphological levels may interact in interesting ways. Consider what happens when we add the plural morpheme to the following words: *ax* and *cow*. Listen to how you pronounce the plural morpheme in the two cases. For *cows* we use the /z/ phoneme, for *axes* we use the /Iz/ (there is a third too: with *bikes* we use /s/). The rules change how the plural morpheme is phonologically realized depending on the phonological environment. Thus, the morphological level is the point at which form, syntax, and semantic information interact.

Syntax (Grammar)

The next level of representation in the hierarchy is typically **syntax**. At the most basic, this is the level of representations and rules that specifies the ordering of words. Consider two sentences with exactly the same words but two very different meanings: "Man bites dog" and "Dog bites man." It is easy to see that the word order is important for the overall meaning. Consider too what happens if we reorder the words as "Bites man dog." This ordering makes very little sense, and we easily recognize it as an illegitimate sentence. Syntactic structure is the abstract representation that specifies how the words are related, not by meaning but rather the grammatical properties (e.g., nouns and verbs) of the words. The elements and rules of syntax are similar to the grammar you may have

Morphemes: the smallest units of a language that contain meaning

Syntax: the rules structure of a language

learned back in your early language arts classes of your youth. Consider the following basic phrase structure rules for English:

1. A sentence (S) is made up of a noun phrase and a verb phrase [S: NP + VP]
2. A noun phrase (NP) is made up of a noun (N) that may be modified by an article, an adjective, and a prepositional phrase [NP: (art) (adj) N (PP)]
3. A prepositional phrase (PP) is made up of a preposition followed by a noun phrase [PP: Prep + NP]

So the reason "Bites man dog" does not make sense is that it does not follow the rules of English. (English does not allow a sentence that starts with a verb followed by two nouns.)

This underlying syntactic structure is not simply the linear ordering of the words (surface structure). In fact, it is not uncommon to have multiple underlying structures corresponding to the same surface structure. Consider the headline that caused Ted some confusion: "Enraged cow injures farmer with ax." The two interpretations (the cow has the ax or the farmer has the ax) correspond to two different syntactic structures. Figure 9.1 shows a "tree structure" that shows how the different syntactic chunks (constituents) may be arranged. In Figure 9.1a, the prepositional phrase "with ax" is part of the verb phrase, modifying the verb *injures*. Figure 9.1b shows a syntactic structure in which "with ax" is part of the object noun phrase, modifying the noun *farmer*. So the overall meaning depends not only on the meanings of the individual words but also on the abstract syntactic structure represented in the figures by the tree structures above the sentences.

Figure 9.1 Different Syntactic Structures of a Newspaper Headline

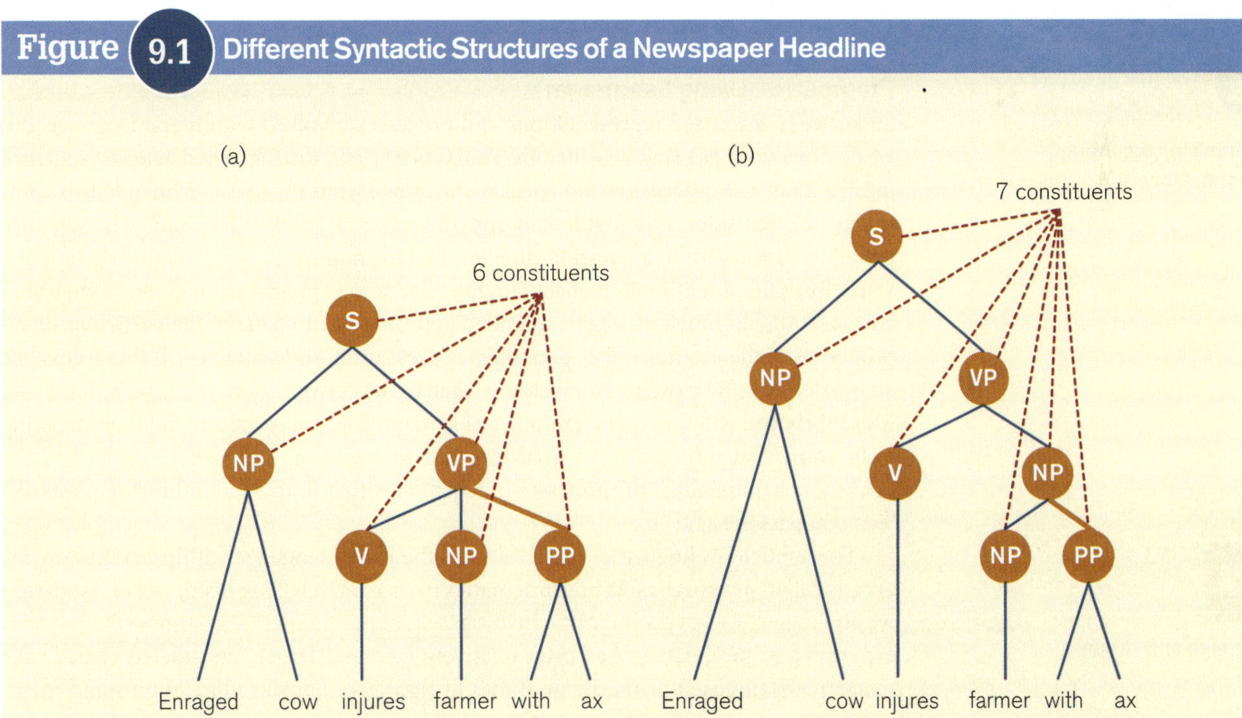

Two sentences with identical surface structures can have two different interpretations depending on the underlying abstract syntactic structure. In (a) there are six constituent nodes, and the prepositional phrase (PP) modifies the verb phrase (VP), resulting in an interpretation of "the cow injures with the ax." In (b) there are seven constituent nodes, and the prepositional phrase is attached to the noun phrase (NP), modifying *farmer* and resulting in an interpretation of "the farmer with the ax."

Semantics (Meaning)

Levels of representation above syntax are related to meaning—**semantics**. Most psycholinguistic theories make a distinction between linguistic elements like words and the mental concepts with which they are related (see Chapter 10 for a more detailed discussion of concepts). Shakespeare's "a rose by any other name would smell as sweet" illustrates this distinction. The flower name *rose* is a word, with phonological (made up of phonemes /r/ /oa/ /z/) and syntactic properties (noun), while the concept corresponding to a rose might include features like these: scented flower from genus Rosa, comes in many colors and varieties, stems often have thorns. However, there are theoretical debates over how the linguistic and conceptual systems are related. Some theories don't include separate semantic and conceptual representations. In these views, the semantic representations are the conceptual representations corresponding to words and sentences (e.g., Jackendoff, 1994, 2010). Other theories include semantic representations within the language processing systems separate from the conceptual system (e.g., Pavlenko, 1999). In these theories the semantic representations serve to map verbal labels to their corresponding concepts. For example, consider the case of a Spanish-English bilingual speaker (Francis, 2005). The speaker may have a single concept for ROSE, while having two separate semantic representations, one for English (*rose*) and one for Spanish (*rosa*). These semantic representations may include information about what kinds of roles the words may play or require in a sentence (e.g., who does what to whom). This information is particularly important for verbs. For example, the verb *give* requires an agent to give a theme to a recipient (e.g., "Mary gives the apple to John" sounds good, but "Mary gives the apple" sounds incomplete).

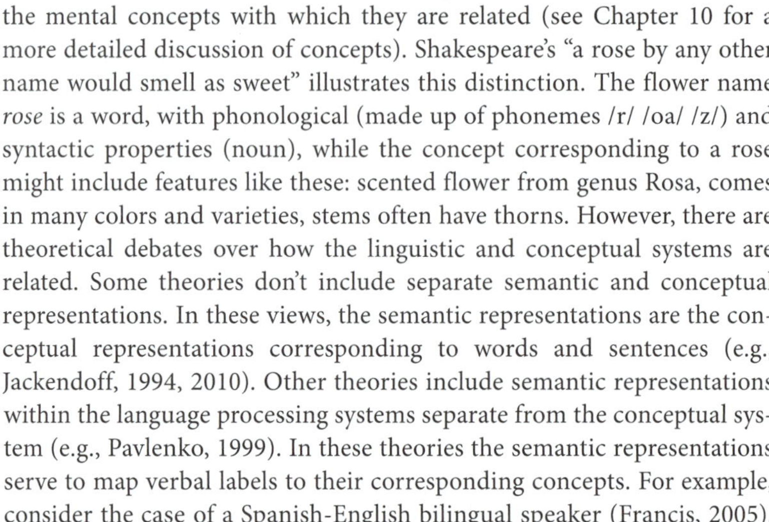

Photo 9.1 Changing the name of the rose doesn't change the concept of what a rose is.

Listening for Nonliteral Meaning Activity

Pragmatics (Using Language)

So far we've discussed representations and processes involved with literal language, but we do not always use language literally. Paul Grice (1989) distinguished between sentence meaning (as just described) and speaker meaning (what the speaker intended to communicate). Consider Bill's first line in our conversation, "Ted! What's up?" The sentence meaning appears to be a question directed to Ted inquiring about what things are elevated, but Bill's intention is probably to greet Ted and express a willingness to engage in conversation. So much of what is intended appears to be outside of the particular literal properties of the utterance (i.e., phonological, semantic, and syntactic). If this seems like an isolated case, take twenty minutes and listen to the conversations going on around you. Most likely you will find many examples of situations where people intend their meaning to be somewhat different from what they literally say (e.g., idioms like "he kicked the bucket," metaphors like "my professor butchered my first draft," and indirect requests like "can you pass the salt?").

Language and Thought

The subfield of linguistics that examines the use of language within particular contexts is called **pragmatics**. While pragmatics has a relatively long history of investigation within linguistics, psycholinguistic investigation of pragmatics (sometimes referred to as experimental pragmatics) has been relatively rare and largely considered outside the mainstream (focused primarily on issues of figurative language like idioms and metaphors). However, within the past decade, research examining these issues is on the rise (Noveck & Reboul, 2008).

Semantics: meaning contained within language

Pragmatics: the examination of how language is used in particular contexts

Language is more than a simple string of letters or sounds. Instead, this set of finite elements (letters and sounds) is combined in systematic ways to convey a potentially infinite set of meanings. In other words, language is a complex hierarchical system of abstract representations and rules for combination. As you might expect with such a complex system, the mental processes we use to process language are complex as well. The next section provides an overview of how we comprehend and produce language.

Stop and Think

9.1. Identify the phonemes in the sentence "Ted quietly chatted with Bill."

9.2. Identify the morphemes in the sentence "Ted quietly chatted with Bill at the coffee shop."

9.3. What are two different interpretations of the sentence "Groucho shot an elephant in his pajamas"? How are the interpretations linked to syntax?

How Do We Process Language?

In 1861 Paul Broca examined a patient, Tan (the only word that he could speak freely), who had been unable to speak for twenty-one years. Tan seemed to retain his ability to understand language, but his ability to produce language was severely impaired. After his death, Broca performed an autopsy and discovered that Tan had suffered brain damage in the left inferior frontal region of his cortex (see Figure 9.2). This was the first documented case of expressive aphasia (also known as **Broca's aphasia**). Patients with damage to this region of the brain have speech typically characterized as slow, effortful, and halting, lacking in most grammatical words (e.g., articles, prepositions).

Wellcome Library

Photo 9.2 Paul Broca

Broca's aphasia: a deficit in language production

Wernicke's aphasia: a deficit in language comprehension

Fifteen years later Karl Wernicke (1874) described a patient who apparently had the opposite problem. His patient had suffered damage to the posterior part of his temporal lobe and was described as having relatively fluent, syntactically intact production but impaired comprehension. Patients with damage to this area who exhibit similar deficits are diagnosed as having **Wernicke's aphasia**. This early dissociation between language production and language comprehension processes shaped how later psycholinguists developed their lines of research and theories about how we use language. In particular, until relatively recently, most research has focused on either production or comprehension processes.

During the early half of the twentieth century psychological theory and research was dominated by behaviorism. Within this tradition, language processing was described with the same principles of behavior used to describe nonverbal behaviors. These views are best exemplified in B. F. Skinner's (1957) book *Verbal Behavior*. The

Figure 9.2 Tan's (real name Louis Leborgne) Brain *(left)* and MRI of Tan's Brain *(right)*

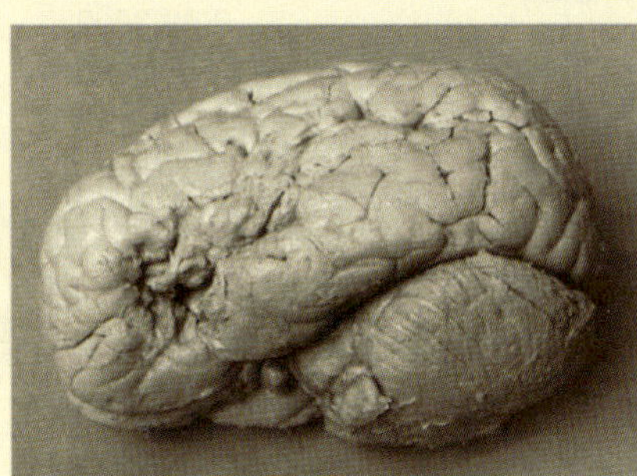

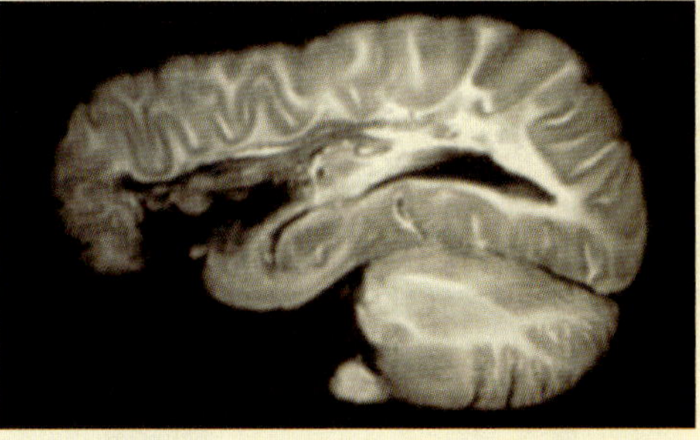

SOURCE: Figure 2 and Figure 3, Dronkers, N., Plaisant, O., Iba-Zizen, M., & Cabanis, E. (n.d.). Paul Broca's Historic Cases: High Resolution MR Imaging of the Brains of Leborgne and Lelong. *Brain,* 1432–1441.

field of modern psycholinguistics is typically traced to the 1950s (see Levelt, 2012, for an excellent review of pre-Chomskyan psycholinguistic research). This early formative decade saw several interdisciplinary seminars and conferences that brought psychologists and linguists together as well as several key publications (e.g., George Miller's textbook *Language and Communication*, 1951; Karl Lashley's article, "The Problem of Serial Order in Behavior," 1951). In 1959 Noam Chomsky published a review of B. F. Skinner's book (also see Chapter 1), arguing that language acquisition and processing cannot be adequately explained by behaviorist principles alone. This review and Chomsky's book *Syntactic Structures* (1957) laid the groundwork that would radically change both the fields of linguistics and psychology. Research in the 1960s was largely focused on looking for evidence of the psychological reality of Chomsky's proposed generative and transformational grammar. From the early 1970s to today, the field has become increasingly more interdisciplinary. Linguistic theory no longer plays the dominant role. Instead, the field has embraced theories and traditions in a wide variety of areas, including cognitive psychology, linguistics, artificial intelligence, philosophy, and neuroscience.

The following sections briefly describe research in language comprehension and production separately and then describe approaches that examine production and comprehension processes working together.

Language Comprehension

Listening for Ambiguity Activity

Someone understanding language (whom we will call the "comprehender") is largely at the mercy of the language producer. The comprehender's job is to try to reconstruct the intended meaning of the speaker (or writer). Normally this process feels very easy, but when you consider the potential for ambiguity, at nearly every level of representation, it is amazing that we ever understand anything at all. Consider what you have to do to understand the sentence "The cat chased the rat." You must identify the sounds (or letters) that make up the words, retrieve their meanings, build the appropriate syntactic structure, and then combine that information into an overall interpretation of the sentence (see Figure 9.3). In the following subsections we briefly review these major subareas of research in language comprehension.

Figure 9.3 An Overview of Language Comprehension

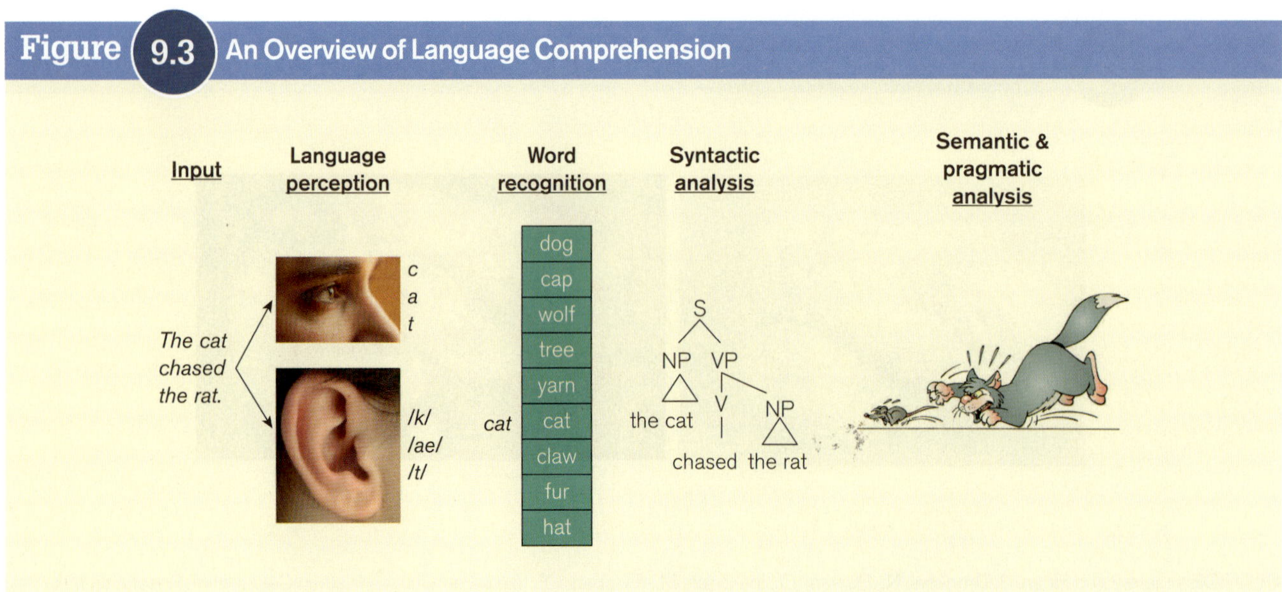

Photo of eye: Hemera Technologies/AbleStock.com/Thinkstock; *photo of ear:* © iStockphoto.com/bobbieo; *cat chasing rat:* © iStockphoto.com/FerasNouf

Language Perception

Most of the language that we try to understand is either spoken or written (leaving aside things like sign language or reading braille). Whether we are reading or listening to the sentence we usually come to the same interpretation, so it might be easy to assume that comprehension processes for spoken and written language are the same. However, there are some big differences between the two systems, at least at the initial stages. Consider the problem that Bill and Ted had with the sentence "The stuff he knows is dangerous." When the sentence is written it isn't ambiguous. However, in the story the sentence is spoken, which resulted in Bill's misinterpretation of the sentence as "The stuffy nose is dangerous." In many ways written language is much clearer than spoken language. Written language is perceived by the visual system. It is typically persistent (outside of TV news crawls, the words stay visible on the page), letters are typically distinct from one another, there are spaces between words, and some words that sound identical are spelled differently. In contrast, spoken language comes in via the ears. It is transient (it unfolds over time and then fades away), and the phonemes and words don't typically have gaps between them. In fact, the sounds often overlap to some degree, called **coarticulation**. Figure 9.4 shows the sound spectrograms for "The stuff he knows is dangerous" and "The stuffy nose is annoying." Notice that the words all seem to blend together such that it is difficult to see where one word ends and the next begins. Despite this, we are able to recognize language spoken by different people with different voices speaking at different levels (e.g., whispering, talking, or yelling) and different rates. These variables result in different acoustic properties of the language (in the case of written language, consider different handwritings and fonts). It turns out that it is very difficult to identify particular core common features that correspond to particular phonemes. This is referred to as the **invariance problem**. So, given the complexity and variability of the language input, how do we identify the phonemes in the signal?

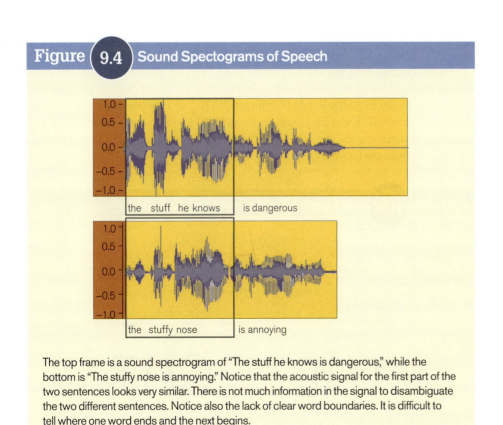

Figure 9.4 Sound Spectograms of Speech

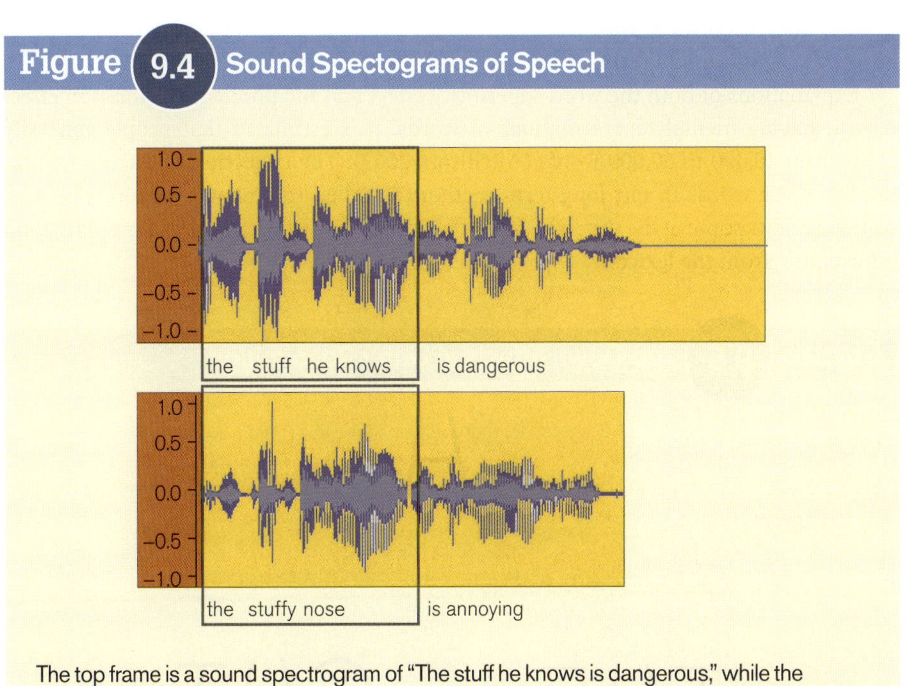

The top frame is a sound spectrogram of "The stuff he knows is dangerous," while the bottom is "The stuffy nose is annoying." Notice that the acoustic signal for the first part of the two sentences looks very similar. There is not much information in the signal to disambiguate the two different sentences. Notice also the lack of clear word boundaries. It is difficult to tell where one word ends and the next begins.

SOURCE: Copyright © 2014 members of the Audacity development team.

Coarticulation: an issue in language comprehension due to the overlapping of sounds in spoken language

Invariance problem: an issue in language comprehension due to variation in how phonemes are produced

Research suggests that we treat language-related stimuli differently from other stimuli. While most sounds are perceived along a continuum, speech is perceived as discrete categories (Liberman, Harris, Eimas, Lisker, & Bastian, 1961; Liberman, Harris, Hoffman, & Griffith, 1957). This process is called **categorical perception**. Eimas and colleagues (Eimas, Siqueland, Jusczyk, & Vigorito, 1971) demonstrated that infants (one- and four-month-olds) can distinguish between different phonemes. In fact, it is generally believed that infants can distinguish between most phonological units of the world's languages. Interestingly, as they experience language, they typically lose their ability to make distinctions between phonological contrasts not found in their native language contexts. For example, English makes a distinction between /r/ and /l/ phonemes, but Japanese does not. In Japanese, the /r/ and /l/ sounds are considered part of the same category of speech. Young Japanese infants can make the distinction; however, as they get older and experience Japanese in their environments, they lose that ability (e.g., Iverson et al., 2003; Kuhl et al., 2006).

Using Top-Down Information Activity

Another processing feature of language perception is top-down contextual information. In other words, we use information we already know about words to help us interpret incoming language. Consider the "letter" in the top part of Figure 9.5. Is it an *A* or an *H*? Now consider it in the bottom half of the figure. Most people interpret it as an *H* when in *THE* and as an *A* when in *CAT*. Letters are easier to identify if they are embedded within words compared to nonword contexts or in isolation. This is called the word superiority effect (see Figure 9.6; Reicher, 1969). Contextual information can even be used to fill in missing information. Richard Warren (1970) presented listeners with the sentence "The state governors met with their respective legislatures convening in the capital city," but he removed the first /s/ in *legislatures* and replaced it with a cough. The listener's task was to report where the cough had occurred and whether he or she noticed anything else about the sentence. Not only were his participants unable to correctly identify the location of the cough, none of them noticed that the /s/ was missing. Instead, they used their knowledge of the word to "fill in" the missing input. This is known as the **phoneme restoration effect**.

Word Superiority Experiment

Explanations of both the word superiority effect and the phoneme restoration effect rely on having mental representations of words. It is estimated that people generally know from 40,000 to 60,000 words (Aitchison, 2003). The collection of the representations of these words in our long-term memory is called the mental lexicon. The next section reviews some of the processes and effects involved with recognizing and retrieving information from the lexicon.

Figure 9.5 Top-Down Effects in Letter Recognition

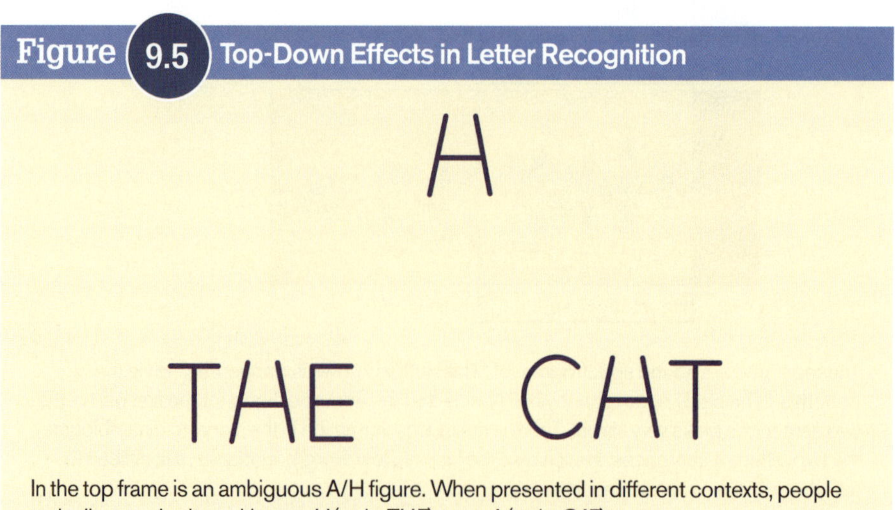

In the top frame is an ambiguous A/H figure. When presented in different contexts, people typically perceive it as either an *H* (as in *THE*) or an *A* (as in *CAT*).

Categorical perception: an issue in language comprehension due to the categorization of phonemes

Phoneme restoration effect: the use of top-down processing to comprehend fragmented language

Figure 9.6 The Word Superiority Effect

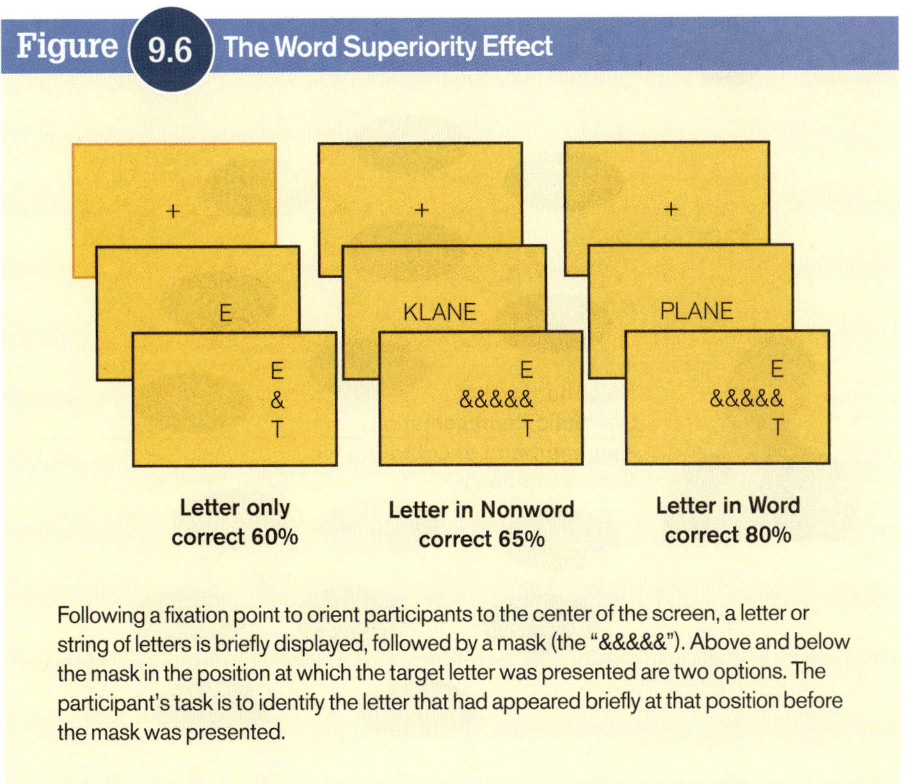

Following a fixation point to orient participants to the center of the screen, a letter or string of letters is briefly displayed, followed by a mask (the "&&&&&"). Above and below the mask in the position at which the target letter was presented are two options. The participant's task is to identify the letter that had appeared briefly at that position before the mask was presented.

Stop and Think

9.4. What are the major differences between spoken and written language?

9.5. How are speech sounds processed differently from other kinds of sounds?

9.6. What processing features may be used to help understand degraded stimuli (e.g., reading a faded photocopy or understanding somebody speaking with a stuffy nose)?

Lexical Recognition and Access

Imagine that you are reading something in a language that you don't know, but you have access to a translation dictionary with 50,000 words in it. Looking up each word would make reading the sentence take a long time. Now consider how long it took you to read this sentence in a language that you know, using your own mental dictionary. You were much faster. Research has shown that it takes as little as 200 milliseconds to recognize a word (in the case of spoken language, this may be even before the end of the word is heard). Recognition of the word is only part of the issue; following recognition we access the word (Balota, 1990; Balota & Chumbley, 1984). If we consider a dictionary as our metaphor for the lexicon, recognition would be when we find the word. Access would correspond to reading the entry for the word, which would typically include how it is pronounced, what part of speech it is, and what its meanings are. The speed (and accuracy) with which we can accomplish this feat is a function of how we organize our lexicons and the extent to which we can use contextual information.

A typical dictionary is arranged in alphabetical order; however, research suggests that our mental lexicon is organized along many other dimensions (see Figure 9.7). Researchers have identified a wide variety of variables that impact word recognition. Perhaps the most powerful variable is how often a word is used—its lexical frequency. The more frequently a word is used, the faster that word is recognized (e.g., Monsell, 1991). "Neighboring" words (those that have similar spellings) also affect recognition.

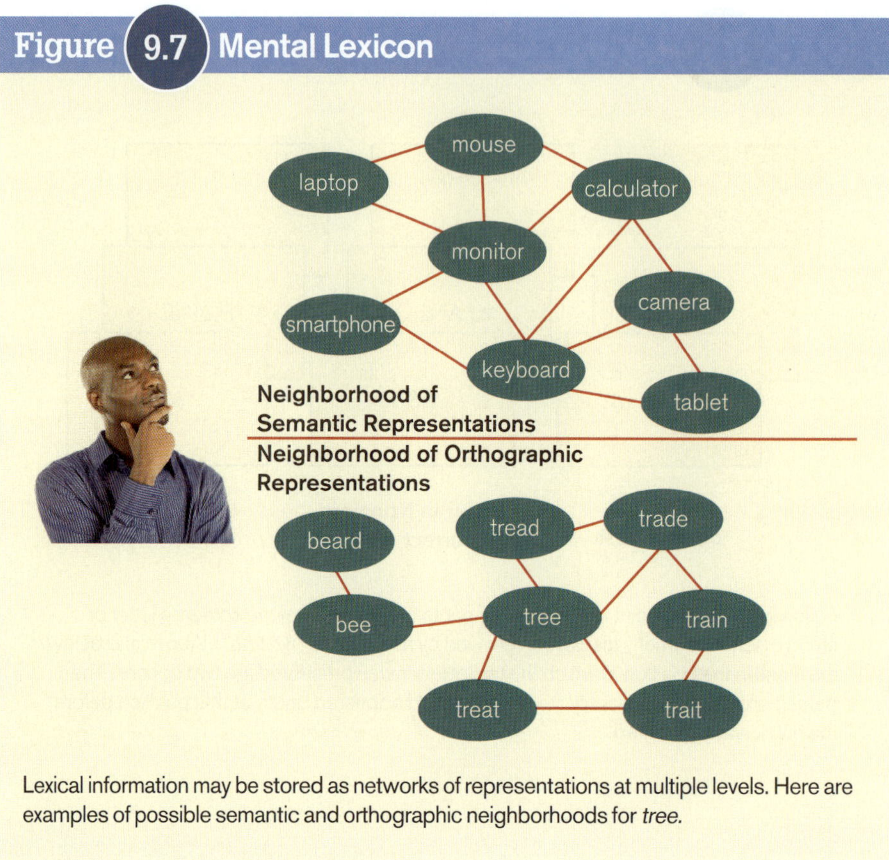

Lexical information may be stored as networks of representations at multiple levels. Here are examples of possible semantic and orthographic neighborhoods for *tree.*

Photo: BananaStock/BananaStock/Thinkstock

Generally, words with large neighborhoods (the set of words that differ by changing one letter) have more competition and take longer to recognize. Morphologically complex words take longer than morphologically simple words (*hunter* made up of *hunt* and *-er* takes longer to recognize than *daughter*, which is a single morpheme).

Lexical Ambiguity

Properties of the word alone are not the only factors that affect word recognition; the context in which they occur also matters. Words may be "primed" by other words (see Figure 9.8). Meyer and Schvaneveldt (1971) presented participants with a list of strings of letters and asked them to respond with a yes or no as to whether they were real words (a lexical decision task). They demonstrated that people recognize a word (e.g., *doctor*) faster if it is preceded by a semantically related word (e.g., *nurse*) compared to an unrelated word (e.g., *shoes*). Similar results have been found for phonological and orthographic (spelling) primes.

Lexical Decision Experiment

Context also impacts access to a word's meaning. David Swinney (1979) used a cross-modal priming task in which participants listened to a sentence while watching a display. At some point during the sentence, a string of letters appeared on the display and the participants performed the lexical decision task. Consider the following critical passage: "Rumor had it that, for years, the government building has been plagued with problems. The man was not surprised when he found several spiders, roaches, and other bugs in the corner of his room." Shortly after hearing the word *bugs* participants saw either *ant* (related to the insect meaning of *bug*, consistent with the context), *spy* (related to the listening-device meaning of *bug*, inconsistent with the context), or *sew* (unrelated to any meanings of *bug*). If the word appeared right after the word *bugs*, then both *ant* and *spy* were recognized faster than *sew*. However, if the word appeared 200 milliseconds after *bugs*, only *ant* was primed (*spy* and *sew* were the same). This shows that initially

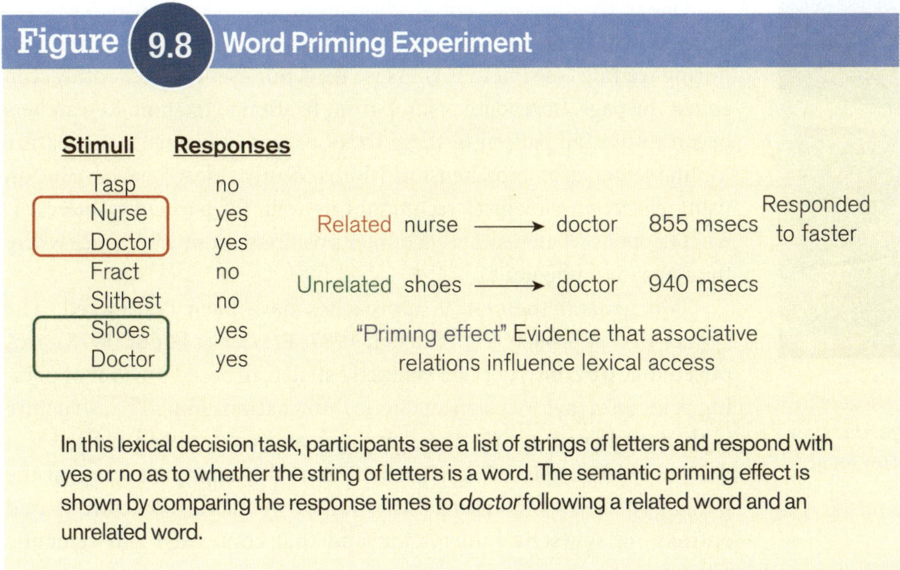

In this lexical decision task, participants see a list of strings of letters and respond with yes or no as to whether the string of letters is a word. The semantic priming effect is shown by comparing the response times to *doctor* following a related word and an unrelated word.

both meanings were accessed, but shortly afterward, only the contextually appropriate meaning remained. Further research (e.g., Rayner & Duffy, 1986; Simpson & Burgess, 1985) has found that the relative frequency of the word's meanings turns out to be an important variable.

> **Stop and Think**
>
> 9.7. What factors impact how quickly a word is recognized?
>
> 9.8. What factors are important in accessing the appropriate meaning of a word?

As we have seen, a number of variables impact how quickly we recognize a word and access its meaning. One of these important factors is the sentence context in which words appear. This shouldn't be surprising since most words aren't understood in isolation but rather as they appear in sentences. The next section describes some of the theory and research examining how we process sentences.

Interpreting Sentences: Syntactic Analysis

Interpreting Syntax Activity

As discussed earlier, recognizing and accessing words is not the end of comprehension. Building the syntactic structure (called **syntactic parsing**) impacts how a sentence is understood. Consider our headline "Enraged cow injures farmer with ax." As we hear or read this sentence, how do we decide which structure (see Figure 9.1 again) we build? Early approaches suggested that we primarily use syntactic information to make this decision.

Chomsky (1957, 1965) made a distinction between **deep structure** (derived from phrase structure rules like those discussed earlier) and **surface structure** (the linear order that actually gets produced). Transformations of the deep structure (e.g., adding, deleting, and moving syntactic constituents) result in the final surface structure. These processes were proposed to explain things like why the active sentence "the dog bit the man" and the passive sentence "the man was bitten by the dog" can mean the same thing. They both come from the same underlying deep structure, but the passive version has undergone a transformation to make it passive (the passive transformation rule would be something like this: move the second NP *the man* to the front, add *was* before the verb, add *-en* to the verb, and add *by* before the first NP *the dog*). While details of Chomsky's theory have changed, it set the stage for much of the research on how we syntactically analyze a sentence.

Syntactic parsing: building the syntactic structure of a sentence

Deep structure: the meaning of a sentence

Surface structure: the order of words presented in a sentence

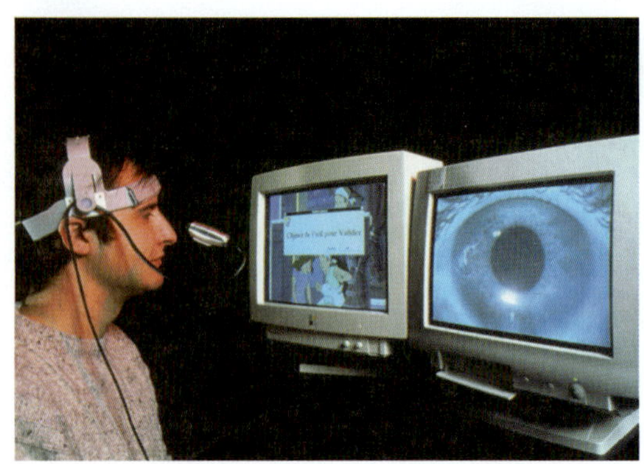

Pascal Goetgheluck/Science Source

Photo 9.3 Early eye-tracking methods used lasers to track the movements and fixations of the eye. Using new technologies, more recent methods allow for a much greater freedom of head motion.

One of the most influential advances in this area of research was the development of technology and procedures to measure eye movements during reading (see Photo 9.3). As we read, our eyes don't smoothly scan across the page. Instead, they jump from fixation to fixation. Researchers began to use the pattern of these fixations and movements to measure "online sentence" comprehension. More recently, researchers have begun using electrophysiological techniques as well. Of particular interest is what happens when readers encounter positions within a sentence where the syntax is ambiguous.

Two general theoretical approaches have been considered. The syntax-first approach (e.g., Frazier, 1987; Frazier & Fodor, 1978) proposed that we construct one syntactic structure based on a set of parsing principles that focus on syntactic information alone. That structure is then evaluated against the semantics and context and revised if it does not make sense. A key prediction of this approach was that the parsing processes computes the initial syntactic structure based entirely on syntactic information and that contextual and semantic information is only used afterward.

Eye Tracking Experiment

One of the syntactic principles proposed was that simpler structures are preferred over complex ones. Consider Figure 9.1 again. The syntactic structure on the left (9.1a) is considered the simpler structure because it has fewer branching points or nodes (six constituents), while the one on the right (9.1b) is more complex because it has more nodes (seven constituents). To test the predictions of this syntax-first approach, Rayner, Carlson, and Frazier (1983) had people read sentences similar to our ambiguous headline. Consider the following pair of sentences.

a. The spy saw the cop with the binoculars, but the cop didn't see him.

b. The spy saw the cop with the revolver, but the cop didn't see him.

The syntax-first approach predicted that when participants read these sentences, in both (a) and (b) the initial syntactic structure built should be the simpler one in which the prepositional phrase ("with the binoculars/revolver") modifies the verb phrase ("the spy saw with the binoculars/revolver"). In the case of sentence version (a), this interpretation makes sense (the spy saw with the binoculars). However, this structure does not make sense in version (b) (the spy saw with the revolver), which should result in a slowing down of reading when getting to the "but the cop didn't see him" part of the sentence. Rayner et al.'s results were consistent with this prediction (see Figure 9.9).

Central to the syntax-first approach is the idea that the initial structure is based on syntactic properties alone. However, a number of research findings led to the development of an alternative interactive approach that suggests that other variables may influence the initial parse (e.g., Altmann, 1998; Gibson & Pearlmutter, 1998). For example, Taraban and McClelland (1988) presented readers sentences with the same syntactic ambiguity that Rayner et al. investigated but with stronger semantic information biasing the more complex interpretation.

c. The police arrested the mastermind behind the hideout, but they forgot to read him his rights. (simpler structure)

d. The police arrested the mastermind behind the crimes, but they forgot to read him his rights. (more complex structure)

Using these sentences, they found the opposite pattern of results. Even though sentence (d) has a more complex syntactic structure, reading times were faster in (d) than in (c). Results like these demonstrate strong support for the interactive approach to syntactic analysis.

Figure 9.9 Rayner et al.'s (1983) Reading Time Results

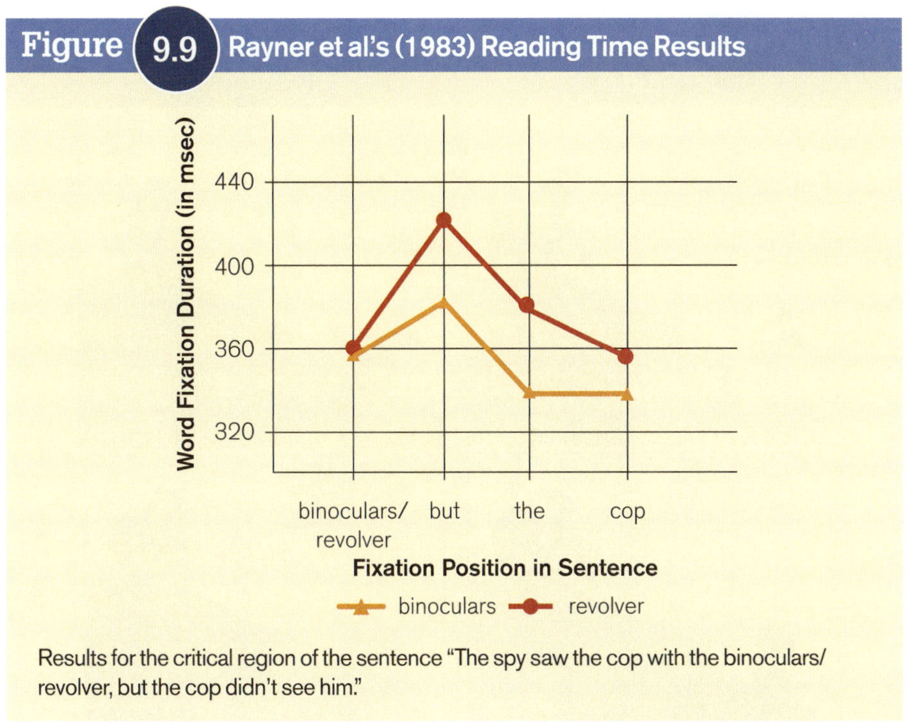

Results for the critical region of the sentence "The spy saw the cop with the binoculars/ revolver, but the cop didn't see him."

The review of research in this section demonstrates that understanding the meaning of a sentence involves more than just knowing the meanings of the words. The underlying syntactic structure plays an important role as well. Similarly, meaning may not end with the meaning of isolated sentences. Most of the time we are not trying to comprehend sentences in isolation but are trying to understand a series of related sentences, paragraphs, and entire stories. The next section describes some of the processes we use to build structures within texts.

Stop and Think

9.9. What is the difference between deep and surface structure? What are syntactic transformations?

9.10. How do the syntax-first and interactive approaches differ with respect to resolving syntactic ambiguity?

Beyond the Sentence: Texts and Discourse

Consider our opening story again. Understanding the entire passage involves building structures larger than individual sentences. At one point Ted says, "Man, the stuff he knows is dangerous." Who does *he* refer to? Within that sentence there is not a good candidate. However, if you look back a sentence, you will see that there are two people mentioned. In this case *he* refers to Rufus and not Elizabeth because of the male pronoun used. But suppose that the preceding sentence contained "Rufus and Bach" instead. How do we decide which person *he* refers to in that case?

Reading in the Brain

Arnold, Eisenband, Brown-Schmidt, and Trueswell (2000) used an eye-tracking procedure to investigate the kinds of cues used to figure out the correct pronoun antecedents. They had people listen to sentences like "Donald is bringing some mail to Mickey [or Minnie] while a violent storm is beginning. He's [or She's] carrying an umbrella, and it looks like they're both going to need it." Simultaneously, they were looking at pictures like those in Figure 9.10 (in all of the pictures the correct antecedent is the character with the umbrella). They examined two cues: gender (if both characters are the same or different gender) and accessibility (typically things mentioned first are more accessible than things mentioned second). They monitored what people looked at in the pictures as they heard the sentences. Their results showed that people use both gender and accessibility information to quickly determine the correct antecedent for the pronouns.

Figure 9.10 The Four Conditions Used in the Arnold et al. (2000) Study

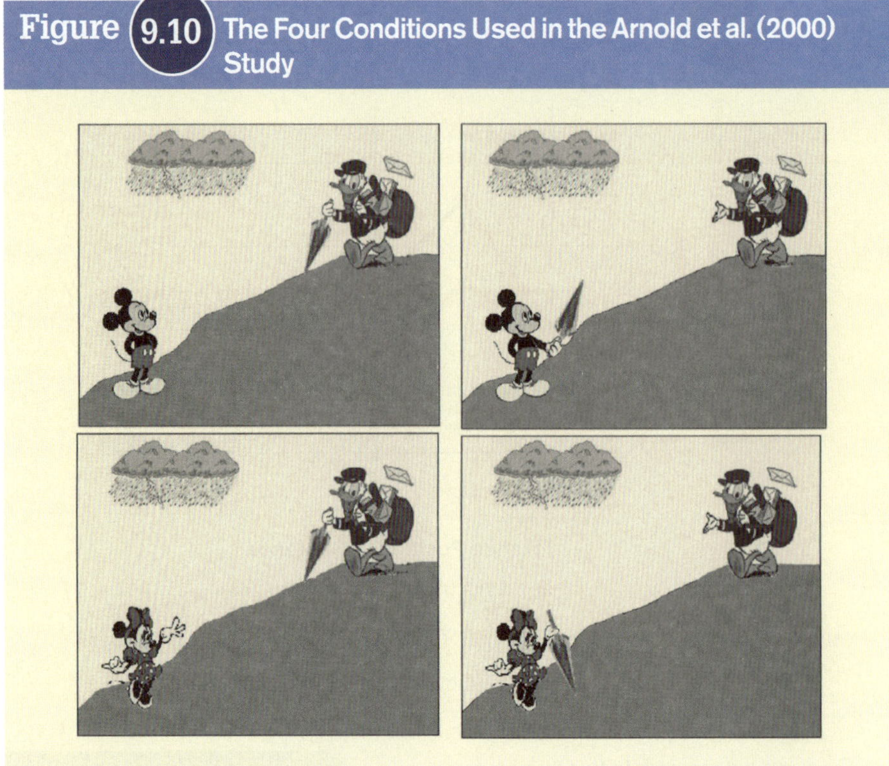

SOURCE: Figure 1, Arnold, J. E., Eisenband, J. G., Brown-Schmidt, S., & Trueswell, J. C. (2000). The rapid use of gender information: Evidence of the time course of pronoun resolution from eye tracking. *Cognition, 76,* B13–B26.

Using a pronoun to refer back to something in another sentence (called **anaphoric inference**) is one way in which we use inferences to bind sentences together into cohesive texts (things make sense from one sentence to the next) and coherent structure in discourse (the whole text makes sense with what we know about the world). Inferences are interpretations of the story that go beyond what is actually stated. They help tie the story together, forming a cohesive whole, rather than a list of disconnected sentences. There are many types of inferences. Consider the following:

> Dick and Harry got the picnic basket out of the trunk. The beer was warm. Dick accidentally shot his hunting partner later that afternoon.

We may make the following inferences: the beer was warm because it was in the trunk; the trunk was hot because it was a hot day; Dick and Harry drank the beer; Dick had a gun; and Dick and Harry went hunting together. Not all types of inferences are automatically generated as we comprehend the text, and others may only be made when we later recall the story (McKoon & Ratcliff, 1992; Singer, 1994). Furthermore, a comprehender's goal (e.g., why somebody is reading a particular text) has also been demonstrated to have an impact on what inferences are made (VanDenBroek, Lorch, Linderholm, & Gustafson, 2001). For example, if you read a book to study for an exam, you may emphasize drawing inferences that draw connections within the text. In contrast, when reading for pleasure, you may instead emphasize drawing connections with your own experiences or background knowledge.

The end product of comprehension is a mental representation of what the entire discourse is about. This representation is typically called a mental or situational model (Zwaan & Radvansky, 1998; Johnson-Laird, 1983). Think back to our opening story. What is your interpretation? Is it an image of two guys sitting in a coffee shop, sipping their drinks, discussing events that one of them had experienced earlier? One way to

Anaphoric inference: using a pronoun to refer to something in a previous sentence

think of a situational model is as a mental simulation of the events evoked by the language that you understood. This is somewhat different from the scripts and schemata discussed in Chapters 7 and 10. Those are mental representations of stereotypical events. The situational model is a mental representation of the current interpretation, which may be influenced by inferences drawn from a schema. For example, our story does not describe the coffee shop where Bill and Ted are talking, but your situational model may contain inferences drawn from what you expect at a typical coffee shop (e.g., Bill and Ted are sitting at a small table with two chairs, Ted has a cup of coffee in front of him).

Visual Representations During Language Processing

Support for this approach comes from findings suggesting that language comprehension is tightly connected to the perceptual representations of the situations described. Zwaan, Stanfield, and Yaxley (2002) had comprehenders read a sentence that implied something about the shape of objects (e.g., "The egg was in the carton" or "The egg fried in the pan") and then presented a picture of an object to be named (see Figure 9.11). They found that naming times were slower if the implied shape in the sentence mismatched the pictured shape than if they matched. Glenberg and Kaschak (2002) found evidence that the situational model may include action components. They presented comprehenders with sentences that implied action in a particular direction (e.g., "close the drawer" implies action away from you, while "open the drawer" implies action toward you). Their comprehenders had to decide whether the sentences made sense and indicate their decision either by pressing a button close to them or away from them. Sentences that implied action in a direction consistent with the response direction (e.g., if "yes it makes sense" was a button close to the body and the sentence was "open the drawer") were verified faster than those that were inconsistent.

Recent neurophysiological results also support this approach. For example, using fMRI data (a brain imaging technique; see Chapter 2 for more details), Hauk, Johnsrude, and Pulvermüller (2004) found overlapping brain area activation (see Figure 9.12) when people read action words (e.g., *lick*, *pick*, and *kick*) and when they performed related actions (instructed to move their tongue, finger, and foot).

Figure 9.11 Examples of the Kinds of Stimuli Used in the Zwaan et al. (2002) Study

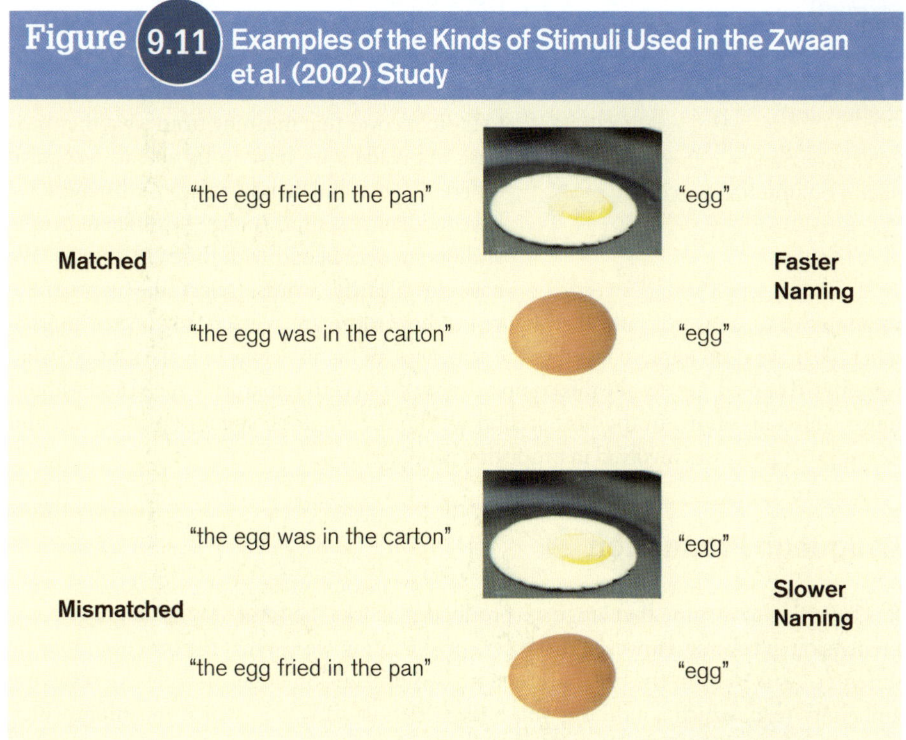

Photos: *fried egg:* George Doyle/Stockbyte/Thinkstock; *unbroken egg:* Stockbyte/Thinkstock

Figure 9.12 fMRI Images From the Hauk et al. Study

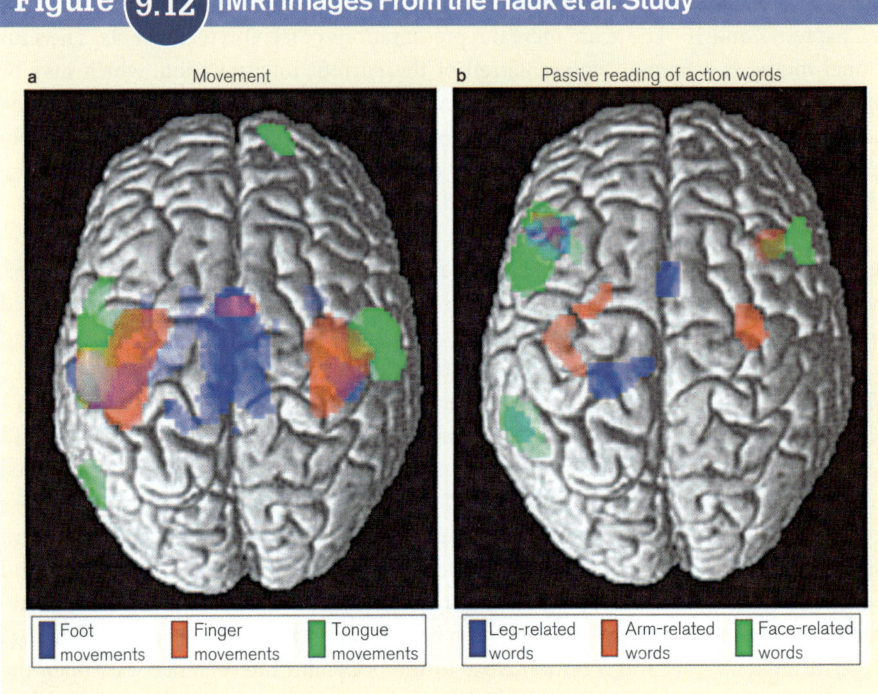

The frame on the left shows brain activation for three different movements. The frame on the right shows brain activation reading action-related words.

SOURCE: Hauk, O., Johnsrude, I., & Pulvermüller, F. (2004). Somatotopic representation of action words in human motor and pre-motor cortex. *Neuron, 41*, 301–307.

Stop and Think

9.11. What processes are used to combine separate sentences into a cohesive and coherent structure?

9.12. What is a situational model? What evidence is there that we generate these models during comprehension?

As the preceding section suggests, understanding language involves a complex set of procedures. In many ways we are at the mercy of the speakers and authors. They know what thoughts they are trying to convey, and our job, as comprehenders, is to try to recover that meaning from what they produce. As readers we have to be able to recognize different fonts and handwriting. As listeners we have to identify sounds spoken by different people at different speeds and with different accents. We have to identify words, select the appropriate meanings of those words, and then figure out how those are syntactically related to each other. Then we need to piece together the sentences, filling in details to make sense of what we've heard or read. Yet despite this complexity, we do so with remarkable speed and without much conscious effort. In the next section we flip the language system upside down and examine the processes involved in producing language.

Language Production

It is tempting to assume that language production works the same way as language comprehension in reverse. However, on closer consideration we see that the processes may be different. As we saw in the previous section, comprehension largely is a case of resolving ambiguity (e.g., which sound did you hear, which word was it, which meaning, which syntactic structure). In contrast, when producing language, you are typically in control of the situation. You know what ideas to convey and who your audience is; you can select which words to use, the order to put them in, and the rate at which to speak. There is much less ambiguity to resolve during production. However, there is an interesting paradox. Even though we are in total control, when we make mistakes producing language, it is typically at the expense of meaning, while maintaining the correct form. In other words, even though the purpose of producing an utterance is to convey meaning, the mistakes we make often show disruptions in meaning but appear to obey the rules corresponding to other levels of representation (e.g., syntax and phonology). The following section describes some of the ways in which language production processes have been examined.

Abstraction in Speech Production

Making Mistakes: Speech Errors

The processes of language production begin with mapping our thoughts (or message) onto linguistic representations. This presents a challenge to doing research because manipulating thought in carefully controlled experimental designs can be difficult (Bock, 1996). However, while the input to language production is difficult to manipulate, the output of the process, produced language, provides a rich set of data for analysis. Sit down and listen to a conversation going on nearby. Generally you will find that our productions are remarkably fluent and accurate. However, they do contain false starts, hesitations, "ums" and "uhs," and from time to time mistakes (Erard, 2007). While speech errors are often referred to as "slips of the tongue," analyses of the pattern of errors suggest that most of them result from higher-level processes rather than the motor control of the tongue. Collections of speech errors have provided the foundation of most theories of language production (e.g., Dell, 1986; Fromkin, 1971; Garrett, 1975).

Listening to Speech Activity

Table 9.1 gives a sampling of the wide variety of speech errors that have been collected and analyzed. Errors appear to involve all of the linguistic units we have discussed in this chapter. Researchers have noted several regularities in the errors we make. For example, errors resulting from the interaction between two representations appear to be constrained to interacting elements of the same type. In other words, most word errors involve words from the same syntactic category. In sound errors, most vowels interact with other vowels and consonants with other consonants. Regularities like these suggest that words, syntax, and sounds are likely to be processed separately during production. Analyses have also revealed that sound errors typically involve elements relatively close together, while word errors may involve words farther apart, again suggesting that lexical and phonological processing may occur separately. Another regularity is that sound errors result in actual words more often than expected by chance. Furthermore, when these sound errors result in nonwords, the nonwords typically conform to the phonological rules of the speaker's language. These regularities suggest that the interaction between lexical and phonological processes may be complex.

What Speech Errors Reveal

These kinds of regularities led Merrill Garrett and others to propose that language production proceeds through a series of processes: conceptualization, formulation, and articulation (e.g., Garrett, 1975, 1988; Levelt, 1989). Conceptualization is the level of thought, where we piece together the nonverbal situational model (the "message") we want to talk about (see Figure 9.13). Formulation is the grammatical processing stage during which the message is mapped onto linguistic units. Garrett proposed that this happens in two stages. First is the functional stage of processing where we select semantically appropriate lexical items and assign them to functional roles (e.g., subject, verb, object). Following this is the positional stage, during which a syntactic structure corresponding to the functional roles is built and lexical items are inserted into the syntactic structure. Following the positional stage, the form information (e.g., sounds, spellings) of the words is specified, and finally we articulate (say or write) the utterance. The theory predicts a separation of semantic, syntactic, and phonological processes during production. The separation of the meaning from the syntax and form explains the production paradox. Since meaning processing is completed earliest, errors resulting late in the production process may disrupt meaning while conforming to syntactic and form constraints.

Table 9.1 Types of Speech Errors

TYPE	EXAMPLES: INTENDED → PRODUCED ERROR	UNIT INVOLVED
SOUND ERRORS		
Exchange	York library → "lork yibary"	Phoneme
Anticipation	Reading list → "leading list"	Phoneme
Perseveration	Beef noodle → "beef needle"	Phoneme
Addition	Blue bug → "blue blug"	Phoneme
Shift	Black boxes → "back bloxes"	Phoneme
Deletion	Same state → "same sate"	Phoneme
MORPHEME ERRORS		
Exchange	Thinly sliced → "slicely thinned"	Stem
Anticipation	My car towed → "my tow towed"	Stem
Perseveration	Explain … rule insertion → "rule exsertion"	Prefix
Addition	Some weeks → "somes weeks"	Inflectional suffix
Shift	Gets it → get its	Inflectional suffix
WORD ERRORS		
Exchange	Writing a letter to my mother → "writing a mother to my letter"	Noun
Anticipation	Sun is in the sky → "sky is in the sky"	Noun
Perseveration	Class will be about discussing the test → "discussing the class"	Noun
Addition	These flowers are purple → "these purple flowers are purple"	Adjective
Shift	Something to tell you all → "something all to tell you"	Quantifier

SOURCE: Dell, G. S. (1986). A spreading-activation theory of retrieval in sentence production. *Psychological Review, 93*, 283–321.

Separation of Semantics, Syntax, and Form

As in language comprehension research, much of the research in language production has focused on the nature of the relationship among semantic, syntactic, and form processing. You may already have had an experience supporting the idea that semantics and form processing are separated during language production. Think about a time during which you found yourself having trouble remembering the name of a famous movie star or the word for some obscure object. Often when in this state you may know that you

Figure 9.13 An Overview of Language Production

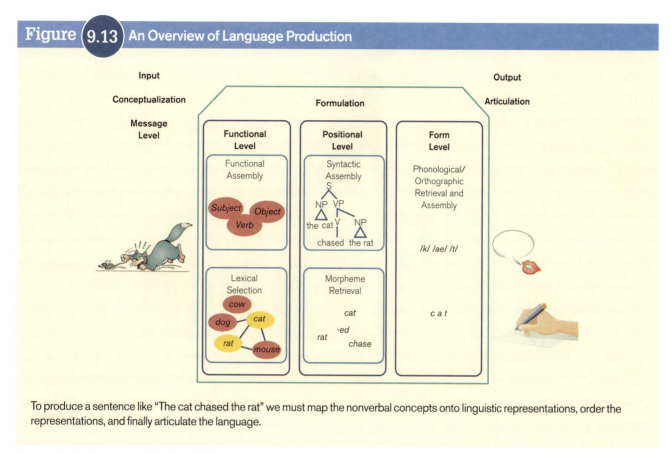

To produce a sentence like "The cat chased the rat" we must map the nonverbal concepts onto linguistic representations, order the representations, and finally articulate the language.

Photos: *Cat chasing rat:* Feras Nouf/Istock/Thinkstock; *photo of mouth:* © iStockphoto.com/proyeksie; *photo of hand writing:* © iStockphoto.com/acrylik

know the word, and remember some details of the word, but you just cannot retrieve it at that moment. This feeling is called the tip-of-the-tongue state (James, 1890). It is thought to reflect a state in which you have accessed the semantic and syntactic representations of a word but not the phonological form of the word. Vigliocco, Antonini, and Garrett (1997) demonstrated that when Italian speakers were in this state, they had access to semantic and syntactic features of words (Italian specifies the grammatical genders masculine and feminine for nouns) but not the letters and phonemes of the words.

Schriefers, Meyer, and Levelt (1990) provided an experimental demonstration of the separation of semantic and phonological processing during production. They presented speakers with object pictures to be named, while simultaneously ignoring a word they heard over headphones. They manipulated two variables: the relationship between the pictures and the words (if the picture was a dog, then the interfering words could have been *dot*, phonologically related; *cat*, semantically related; or *ship*, unrelated) and when the interfering word appeared relative to the picture (150 milliseconds before the picture, at the same time as the picture, or 150 milliseconds after the picture). The results of their experiment are presented in Figure 9.14. When the distractor word was presented early, there were clear effects of hearing a semantically related word but not a phonologically related word (relative to the unrelated control word condition). The pattern is different when the distractor was presented later: no effect of a semantically related word but an effect of a phonologically related word. However, further research has suggested that this division may not be so distinct (e.g., Cutting & Ferreira, 1999; Damian & Martin, 1999; Peterson & Savoy, 1998).

Tip-of-the-Tongue Phenomenon

Figure 9.14 Results of Schriefers et al.'s (1990) Study

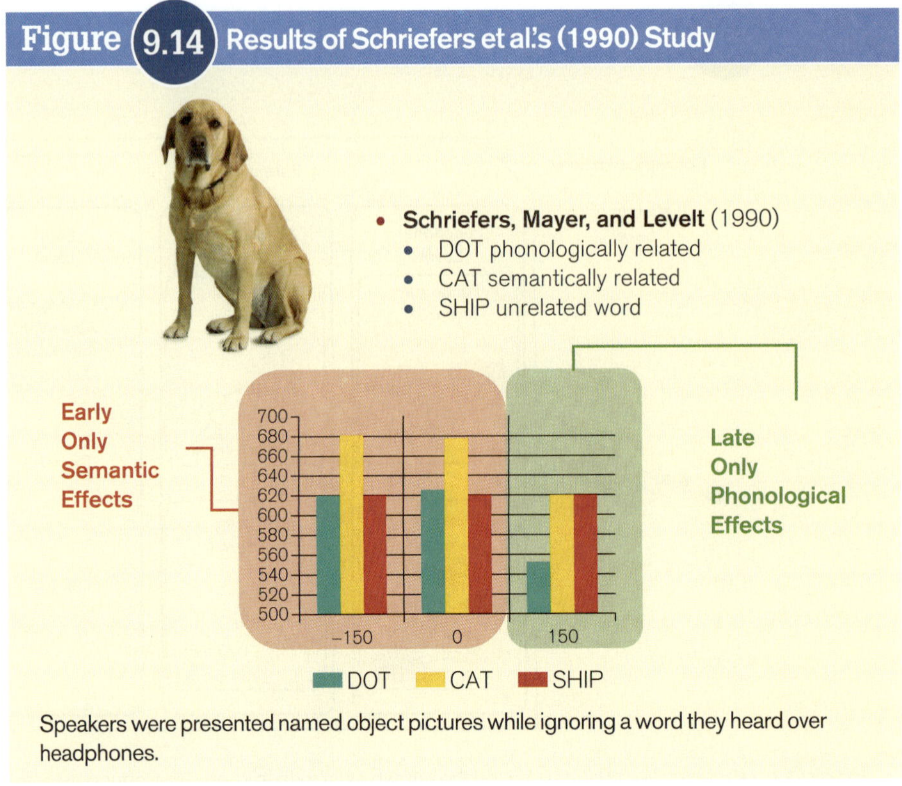

Speakers were presented named object pictures while ignoring a word they heard over headphones.

Dog photo: Photodisc/Thinkstock

Experiments examining agreement processes (e.g., subject-verb agreement, pronoun gender agreement) have been used to explore the separation of semantic and syntactic levels of processing in production. Consider the following sentence.

a. The knife is on the table.

At first it may seem straightforward. The subject of the sentence is singular (referring to a knife), so you need to use the singular verb form *is*. But now consider the sentence in (b).

b. The scissors are on the table.

In this sentence the subject refers to a single pair of scissors, but the correctly agreeing verb form is *are*. The word *scissors* demonstrates that the property of the plural form has both a semantic and syntactic component to it. To examine how these semantic and syntactic components are used in production, Kathryn Bock and colleagues (e.g., Bock & Eberhard, 1993; Bock & Miller, 1991; Humphrey & Bock, 2005) used a sentence completion task in which speakers were presented with the beginning of a sentence up to but not including the verb.

c. The cutting board under the knives . . .

d. The cutting board under the scissors . . .

The speaker's task was to repeat and complete the sentence fragment. When presented with sentences like those presented in (c) and (d), speakers made errors and completed the sentences using a plural verb (e.g., "The cutting board under the knives are getting old"). The results suggest that notional and grammatical number agreement processes operate differently at separate stages during production.

Research examining production and comprehension of language suggests that many of the same levels of representation may be involved in both behaviors. However, because comprehenders and producers start with different inputs (spoken or written language versus thought), the processes involved may operate differently. Most research has focused on either comprehension or production as independent processes. Recently, some researchers have begun examining how production and comprehension processes are directly related to each other.

Stop and Think

9.13. What is the paradox of production?

9.14. What evidence has been used to suggest that semantic and phonological processing are separated during language production?

Dialogue: Production and Comprehension Together

Up until this point our discussion has focused on either language comprehension or production in isolation. However, if we look back to our opening story, it is a dialogue between Bill and Ted. This is the typical situation in which language is used, with multiple individuals taking turns as comprehenders and producers. Herb Clark (1996) characterized using language as a joint action akin to dancing. Like dancing, language users need to coordinate their linguistic actions, often rapidly switching between roles as a speaker and a listener, to successfully communicate ideas. So how are comprehension and production processes related to one another?

Photo 9.4 Language is a coordinated joint activity like dancing.

As noted in the previous section, our utterances are generally fluent and accurate. One proposal to account for this is that we use our comprehension system to monitor our ongoing productions, not only after we have said them but also before their actual articulation. Levelt (1983) called this approach the perceptual loop. The theory is that even before we articulate our planned utterances, we run our "inner speech plan" through our comprehension system to look for errors so that we can make corrections before articulation. Zenzi Griffin (2004) reported findings consistent with this proposal. She monitored speakers' eye movements while they described pictures. She found that speakers gazed at named objects longer when they named them incorrectly and then corrected the error. However, recent evidence suggests that comprehension alone may not be sufficient for monitoring errors (e.g., Huettig & Hartsuiker, 2010; Nozari, Dell, & Schwartz, 2011; Vigliocco & Harsuiker, 2002). Even our disfluencies (e.g., "ums" and "uhs") may be meaningful. Fox Tree (2001) has suggested that the "ums" and "uhs" we produce may be used to signal comprehenders of upcoming production difficulties. Research findings like these provide strong support for the notion that we may use our production and comprehension processes together during language use.

Garrod and Pickering (2004) proposed a framework to describe how production and comprehension processes interact during dialogue. Their theory, called the alignment theory, proposes that the goal of conversation is the alignment of the representations of the speaker and listener. That is, successful communication involves aligning the phonological, syntactic, semantic, and situational models in both participants for successful communication. They proposed that the mechanism through which alignment occurs is priming, like that discussed earlier in the chapter. As people converse, they often repeat sounds, words, syntax, and meanings. Over the course of the dialogue, via priming, the sets of representations activated in the people become more and more coordinated.

Mounting evidence demonstrates that participants in dialogues coordinate semantic, syntactic, and lexical representations. Garrod and Anderson (1987) had pairs of people verbally talk each other through a maze. They found that their participants tended to use the same terms and phrases to refer to where they were in the maze. Branigan, Pickering, and Cleland (1999) demonstrated that people tend to repeat the syntactic structures they use.

Richardson and Dale (2005) provided particularly striking evidence of the coordination between speakers and comprehenders. They monitored the eye movements of speakers describing their favorite scene from the television show *Friends* while presented with an array of the characters from the show. They also measured the eye movements of a separate group of participants, who viewed the same character array while they listened to recorded descriptions provided by the first group. Results showed a large overlap in the gazes of the two groups. In other words, the listeners typically looked at the same characters at the same time as those who produced the language.

> **Stop and Think**
>
> 9.15. How might we use our comprehension processes to aid our productions?
>
> 9.16. What is some of the evidence that speakers and listeners align their linguistic representations during dialogue?

In most situations in which we use language, we act as both a producer and a comprehender. Given that we have the capacity to do both highly related activities, it may not be surprising that the processes are interrelated. Consider that point in our lives when we do not have the capacity to be full-fledged participants in dialogues, when we are infants learning language. How do we acquire our language representations in the first place? The next section provides a brief discussion of research examining how we acquire language.

Acquiring Language

The Wild Boy of Aveyron

After reading the previous sections of this chapter describing how complex language and the mental processes that underlie its use are, you may be amazed at how quickly and effortlessly we use language. What is perhaps even more amazing is how we acquire language in the first place. If you've ever tried to learn a second language as a teenager or an adult, think about how long and hard the process was. Compare that with infants and children learning their first language (shown in Photo 9.5). How do they do it and make it seem so easy? We begin this section with a brief description of typical language development and follow with a summary of theoretical and empirical approaches to the investigation of this behavior.

Typical Language Development

There is great uniformity in the pattern of language development across languages and cultures. Newborns enter the world without being able to use language, but evidence suggests they have some experience and knowledge very early on, perhaps even before birth. DeCasper, Lecanuet, Busnel, Granier-Deferre, and Maugeais (1994) had mothers read stories to their fetuses during pregnancy. At the thirty-eighth week a new or old story was read while the fetuses' heart rates were measured. Heart rates slowed in response to the old stories, demonstrating that even in the womb, fetuses could distinguish between the two stories. Mahler et al. (1988) demonstrated that four-day-old infants could distinguish between spoken French and Russian. As already mentioned earlier in the chapter, one-month-old infants can distinguish between most of the phonological contrasts of all the languages of the world. By their sixth month, infants typically can recognize their own names and respond to "no." From six to twelve months they can recognize names of familiar objects, foods, and body parts (Bergelson & Swingley, 2012). From age one to two years, children can point to objects and pictures when named and understand some requests or questions (e.g., "Push the truck" or "Where's the horsey?"). At this age children often exhibit overextension, applying the words they know to more things than adults do (e.g., *doggie* may be used to refer to all four-legged animals) and underextension (e.g., using *car* to refer to a particular car rather than all cars). It is estimated that children typically understand nearly three times more words than they produce at this stage. Vocabulary growth continues rapidly, and by the third year the vocabulary gap between production and comprehension narrows. Also by the third year they can answer who, what, and where questions.

Photo 9.5 Children at these ages begin learning to use language.

How Babies' Brains Practice Speech

Language production typically lags behind language comprehension, in areas other than vocabulary as well. Early vocal behavior consists of nonlinguistic vegetative sounds (e.g., crying, burps, sucking noises), but as early as six weeks, infants begin cooing vowel sounds. By four to five months they begin babbling and producing clear consonant vowel clusters (e.g., *ba*, *gi*), followed by reduplicated babbling (e.g., *baba*, *gigi*). By ten months infants begin to show more complex babbling, combining sounds into incomprehensible wordlike utterances (e.g., *dab gogotah*), and by twelve months their utterances may be showing evidence of the phonological rules of their environmental language. At this point they may begin to use their first words, often pointing at things to which they refer. These words are usually unique to the child, rather than fully formed adult forms (e.g., *baba* for *bottle*). By their second birthday they may use two hundred to three hundred words (typically focused on the "here and now," like important people and objects that can be moved or manipulated), and by their third birthday they can use one thousand words. Nouns typically appear before verbs. Children's utterances initially consist of single words, but in their second year they start to combine words to produce longer "telegraphic" speech, leaving out grammatical words (e.g., articles like *the* and *a* and prepositions like *by* and *for*). By their third year their utterances continue to get longer and more complex. They typically use full sentences and can form questions, make negative statements, and use grammatical morphemes.

Infants don't learn language in isolation; instead they are typically actively engaged in highly interactive and social contexts. Parents talk to and play with their children (Hart & Risley, 1995, estimated that parents direct three hundred to four hundred utterances an hour to their children). Speech directed at infants (called child-directed speech) typically differs from that between adults. It typically has fewer words, less complex syntax, more repetition, and exaggerated prosodic structure (higher pitched, slower, longer pauses, and distinctive contours). These speech simplifications provide infants important cues that assist in their language learning (Dominey & Dodane, 2004). Eye contact and smiling provide strong social cues. Snow (1977) has argued that as early as one month infants learn some basic turn-taking rules of conversation through the playful "dialogues" with their caregivers (e.g., "Ooh, was that a burp? Are you burping at me?" The parent then pauses and waits until the infant makes another vocalization. "You were! You were burping at me."). Parent-infant interactions provide a rich environment, full of linguistic information to help the child learn language.

As children get older, their language use gets more sophisticated. They continue their vocabulary explosion (e.g., by the age of six they may have a vocabulary of 14,000 words), their utterances get longer, and their syntax grows in complexity. Additionally, they may begin to learn a new medium of language use: reading. Overall, the speed and apparently effortless nature of our ability to use language is amazing. The next sections review some of the theoretical approaches taken to explain how we are able to do it.

Nature or Nurture: Mechanisms for Learning Words and Syntax

Theories of Language Development

How we acquire language is a matter of ongoing debate. Some approaches place the theoretical emphasis on experience (nurture) while others focus on biological predisposition (nature). The behaviorist approach, as advanced by B. F. Skinner (1957), theorized that language learning could be explained through principles of reinforced imitation. Chomsky (1959) argued against this explanation because it could not account for the infinite productivity of language; children can comprehend and produce utterances they have never heard before. Chomsky instead proposed that we come innately prewired with knowledge about language and that language acquisition is a maturational process, like learning to walk. Children learn language in a predetermined way when in an appropriate language context. These two approaches exemplify two extremes of the nature versus nurture debate. Somewhere between these two extremes are the interactionist approaches (e.g., Golinkoff, Mervis, & Hirsh-Pasek, 1994; Markman, 1989), which propose that language learning is the result of the interaction between experience and biological predispositions for language and cognition.

Language and the Mind

For example, Golinkoff, Hirsh-Pasek, and colleagues proposed the emergent coalition model (Hirsh-Pasek, Golinkoff, & Hollich, 2000). The model hypothesizes that early word learning begins associatively but transitions to social and cognitive constraint-driven processes. They argue that infants are born with biases to attend to and integrate attentional (e.g., perceptual salience, temporal contiguity), social (e.g., eye gaze, social context), and linguistic (e.g., grammar, intonation) cues when learning words. Over time, the relative importance of these cues may change. In a series of studies (Hollich et al., 2000; Pruden, Hirsh-Pasek, Golinkoff, & Hennon, 2006), they presented two objects to infants (ten, twelve, and twenty-four months old) with a person situated between the objects. During the learning phase of the experiment, the researchers manipulated the perceptual salience of the objects: one object was very interesting (e.g., brightly colored, moving parts) while the other was less interesting (e.g., dull color, stationary). They also manipulated the social cues by having the person naming the object (e.g., "Look a modi!") stare at one of the objects (see Figure 9.15). This allowed the researchers to see how the attentional and social cues interact during learning. Following the learning phase, they tested whether the infant had learned the name. This was done in three ways: (1) they presented the two objects and asked the child to look at the object with the label (e.g., "Can you find the modi?"), (2) they presented a "new label" to see if the infant would look away, and (3) they mentioned the original label to see if the infant's gaze returned to the object. The results showed that ten-month-old infants used only the perceptual salience to connect the name to the object, twelve-month-old infants learned the name only when the perceptual and social cues aligned, and twenty-four-month-olds

Figure 9.15 An Example of the Learning Phase Used in Hollich et al. (2000)

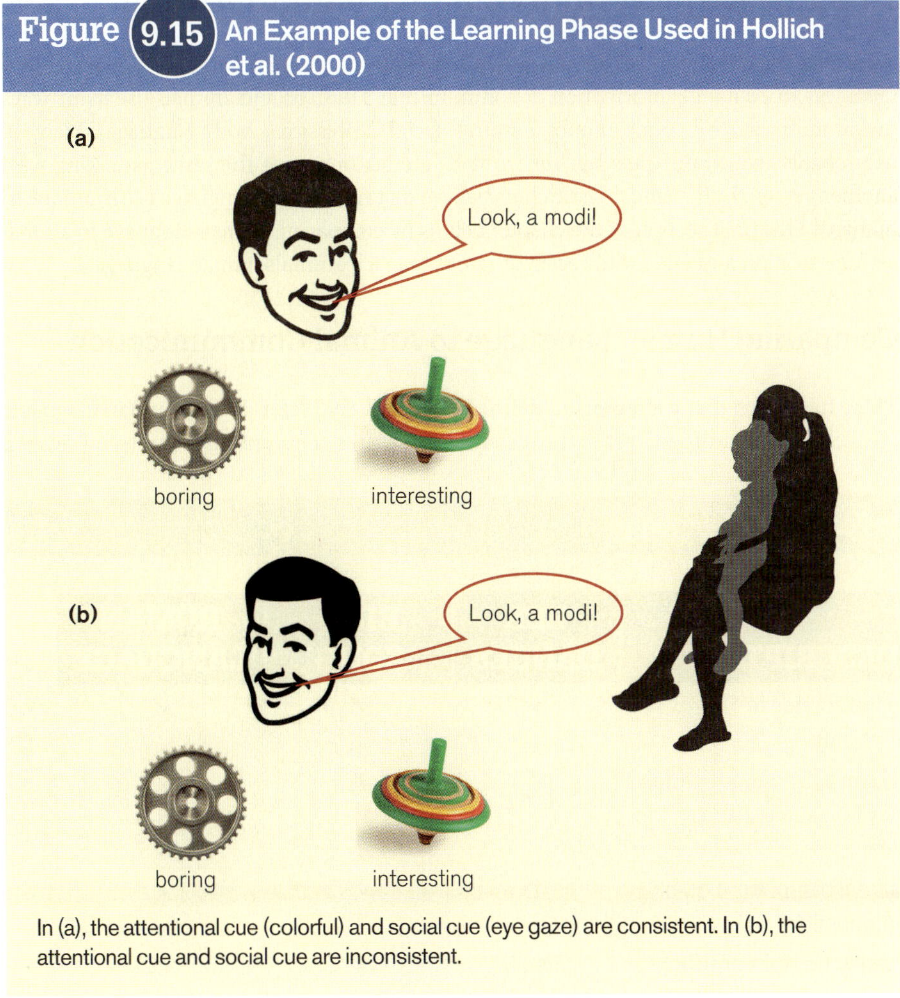

In (a), the attentional cue (colorful) and social cue (eye gaze) are consistent. In (b), the attentional cue and social cue are inconsistent.

learned the names using only the social cues. Brandone, Pence, Golinkoff, and Hirsh-Pasek (2007) used a similar methodology to examine verb learning. They found that two-year-olds were able to learn new verbs when perceptual cues (whether an action produced a result like a sound or a light) and speaker cues (both linguistic and social cues) matched but not when they mismatched.

Results like these suggest that children have cognitive biases that interact with a rich linguistic and social environment in which they learn language. What does this suggest about the uniqueness of language for humans? Can animals use language? The final section of this chapter examines this question.

Stop and Think

9.17. What are the major linguistic milestones of a six-month-old infant? A twelve-month-old infant? A two-year-old child?

9.18. Why do Chomsky and others propose that much of language acquisition is driven by innate knowledge of language?

9.19. How does the emergent coalition model describe the process of word learning in infants?

Human Language and Animal Communication

We started the chapter by asking the question "What is language?" Part of the answer is that it is a way to exchange information or communicate. Humans and animals use many ways to communicate (e.g., pheromones, gestures, facial expressions, body language). Many of us probably talk to our pets but realize that interaction is not the same as talking with another person. In fact, most researchers believe that full-fledged language use is unique to humans. This final section of the chapter begins by comparing human language to animal communication and ends with recent attempts to teach animals human language.

Comparing Human Language to Animal Communication

There have been many attempts to define the unique characteristics of human language. Hockett (1960) outlined a set of thirteen design features of communication (see Table 9.2

Table 9.2 Hockett's Design Features of Language

FEATURE	DESCRIPTION	BEE DANCES	BIRD SONG	HUMAN LANGUAGE
Vocal-auditory channel	Using the sounds to communicate	×	✓	✓
Broadcast transmission and directional reception	Sounds are broadcast widely but may be used to localize the speaker	✓	✓	✓
Rapid fading	The signal disappears quickly after production	?	✓	✓
Interchangeability	Users may be both producers and comprehenders	limited	×	✓
Total feedback	Speakers have access to their own productions	?	✓	✓
Specialization	The speech organ has been adapted for the task			✓
Semanticity	The signals have meaning	✓	✓	✓
Arbitrariness	No direct connection between the sound and the meaning	×	in part	✓
Discreteness	The signal is made of separate units	×	✓ if semantic	✓
Displacement	Can communicate about things removed from time and space	✓	?	✓
Productivity	Can use unique combinations that have not occurred before	✓	?	✓
Traditional transmission	Can be taught and learned	×	?	✓
Duality of patterning	Combinations of meaningless parts result in meaningful units	×	?	✓

SOURCE: Demers, R. A. (1988). Linguistics and animal communication. In F. J. Newmeyer (Ed.), *Linguistics: The Cambridge Survey* (pp. 314–335). New York: Cambridge University Press.

for a complete list). He proposed that although different systems of animal communication may include some of these features, only human language includes all of them. These features include aspects of language related to issues we have discussed earlier in the chapter: productivity, semanticity, arbitrariness, duality of patterning, and traditional transmission. Hauser, Chomsky, and Fitch (2002) have proposed that the minimum distinguishing characteristic of human language is recursive syntax. Recursion occurs when a rule calls for a version of itself. For example, consider the phrase structure rules we discussed earlier. A noun phrase includes a noun that may be modified by an article, adjective, or prepositional phrase. A prepositional phrase is made up of a preposition and a noun phrase. Recursion results because the noun phrase can contain a prepositional phrase, which can in turn contain a noun phrase. So how do systems of animal communication stack up?

As every dog owner knows, dogs bark, but are they "saying" anything? Most researchers agree that the functions of barking are primarily for warning, territory marking, defense, and protest. Pongrácz, Molnár, and Miklósi (2006) found that people are able to use acoustic properties of dog barks to categorize them as aggressive or happy and playful. While this evidence suggests that barking may serve a communicative role, it falls far short of the complexities exhibited by language. Perhaps surprisingly, bees exhibit a system that shares more features with humans. Honeybees dance to communicate the location of nectar sources (von Frisch, 1967). The angle of the dance indicates the direction, and the rate of looping indicates the distance. The bee system of communication exhibits some features (e.g., displacement, semanticity, and productivity) but not others (e.g., discreteness, arbitrariness, and duality of patterning). Perhaps the system of animal communication that comes closest to human language is that of songbirds. Many birds use calls to signal particular behaviors (e.g., warning alarm, coming in for a landing); others also use songs. Songs, typically limited to males, are used to attract females and repel other males of the same species. The songs are structurally complex, made up of individual notes combined into ordered subparts. However, whereas a hallmark of human language is how word order and syntax are associated with meaning, variations in birdsongs have not been demonstrated to reflect differences in meaning. Gentner, Fenn, Margoliash, and Nusbaum (2006) have demonstrated that European starlings could be trained to distinguish between song sequences containing recursive and nonrecursive structures. However, the ability to distinguish recursion does not demonstrate that starlings can use recursion in their songs (Corballis, 2010).

Courtesy of The Alex Foundation

Photo 9.6 Alex, an African grey parrot trained by Irene Pepperberg.

There is little convincing evidence that the communication systems of animals meet the currently accepted definitions of human language, offering strong support for the notion that language use is unique to human beings. Does this mean that animals can't learn to use language? We address this next.

Irene Pepperberg

Attempts to Teach Animals Human Language

The human vocal system has evolved to allow for speech (Liberman, 1984). No other animals' vocal systems are adapted for this capability. Parrots can be taught to mimic human-sounding speech, but mimicking speech isn't the same as using language. Irene Pepperberg (2009) attempted to teach Alex (see Photo 9.6), an African grey parrot, language. With thirteen years of language instruction, Alex was able to demonstrate some remarkable abilities. Alex had a vocabulary of nearly eighty words, could distinguish

Alex the Parrot

Photo 9.7 Chimpanzees have been taught American Sign Language.

between things of different colors and composition, and demonstrated the ability to make some unique combinations of words. Chaser, a border collie, was trained to recognize and distinguish the proper names of more than one thousand objects (Pilley & Reid, 2011). Her trainers have argued that she has an awareness that maps words onto referent objects. Sofia, a mixed-breed dog, (Ramos & Ades, 2012) can reportedly respond to requests resulting from unique combinations of action and object terms. But perhaps the most famous and intensive attempts to teach language to animals have involved chimpanzees.

Washoe, a female chimpanzee, was brought up as a human child and taught to use American Sign Language (Gardner & Gardner, 1969). From morning to night, all communication between Washoe and her caregivers was with sign language (sign language was also used between caregivers when in Washoe's presence). Using daily records of Washoe's signing, the experimenters estimated that she could use from 150 to 200 signs, from many different syntactic classes. Caregivers argued that she demonstrated behaviors similar to those of human children learning language, including overgeneralization of words, and could create new signs generatively (e.g., combined signs for "water" and "bird" to refer to a duck). Fouts, Fouts, and Van Canfort (1989) reported that Washoe's adopted son Loulis (she cared for a ten-month-old chimpanzee following the death of her own newborn) learned to use sign language from other signing chimpanzees. Another chimpanzee, Sarah, was taught an artificial language consisting of plastic symbols of different shapes, sizes, and textures (Premack & Premack, 1972; Premack, 1988). Sarah had a "reading" and "writing" vocabulary of nearly 130 words. Researchers claim she was able to understand the words in the absence of their referents, suggesting that she was able to demonstrate key characteristics of language (e.g., semanticity, arbitrariness, and displacement). Sarah could also follow simple written instructions like "insert banana pail" as well as more complex ones like "insert apple pail banana dish" (meaning put the apple into the pail and the banana onto the dish).

Stop and Think

9.20. What are the characteristic features of human language?

9.21. How do the dances of bees compare to human language?

9.22. How does the performance of chimpanzees taught to use language compare to human children learning language?

Whales and Language

While the feats of these animals are impressive, the debate over whether language is a uniquely human behavior still continues. Many researchers argue that animal behaviors like those described fall short of most characterizations of full-fledged language use in both human adults and children (e.g., Terrace, Pettito, Sanders, & Bever, 1979). Other researchers argue these behaviors demonstrate that animals have the capacity for a simple, symbolically based language system (e.g., Savage-Rumbaugh et al., 1993).

THINKING ABOUT RESEARCH

As you read the following summary of a research study in psychology, think about the following questions:

1. What aspects of language are being examined in this study?
2. What is the independent variable in this study?
3. What is the dependent variable in this study?
4. What alternative explanations can you come up with to explain the results of this study?

Study Reference

Emberson, L. L., Lupyan, G., Goldstein, M. H., & Spivey, M. J. (2010). Overheard cell-phone conversations: When less speech is more distracting. *Psychological Science, 21*, 1383–1388.

Note: Experiment 1 of this study is described.

Purpose of the study: The authors wanted to determine whether hearing one side of a cell phone conversation is more distracting than listening to the entire conversation. It was hypothesized that hearing only one-half of a conversation puts the listener into a less predictable state, which would in turn impair his or her ability to pay attention and perform a concurrent task.

Method of the study: Participants were instructed to complete two tasks: track a moving dot with a computer mouse and respond to letters on a computer screen (choice reaction time task, respond only if one of four letters popped up). While doing that task, they sometimes heard speech played over speakers. There were two kinds of speech: dialogues (both sides of a conversation) and "halfalogues" (one side of a conversation).

Results of the study: Performance on both tasks was worse for halfalogues than dialogues. These results are presented in Figure 9.16.

Conclusions of the study: The authors concluded that because conversations are coordinated behaviors, speech in a halfalogue is less predictable than a complete dialogue. They argued that the decreased predictability of the halfalogue automatically pulled away attentional resources, which resulted in fewer resources and thus poorer performance on the two tasks.

Figure 9.16 Results of Emberson et al.'s (2010) Experiment 1

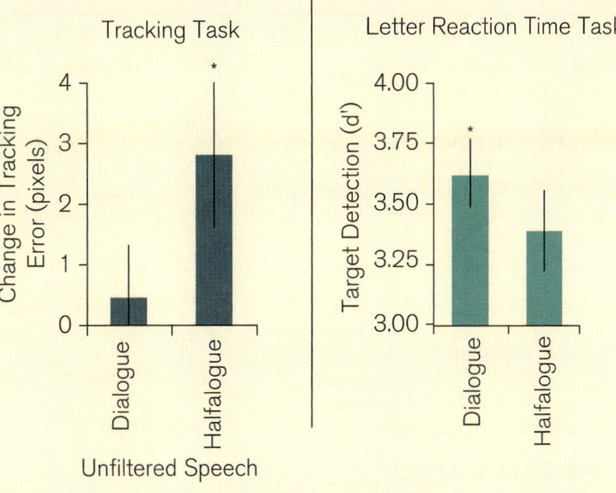

SOURCE: From Emberson, L. L., Lupyan, G., Goldstein, M. H., & Spivey, M. J. (2010). Overheard cell-phone conversations: When less speech is more distracting. *Psychological Science, 21,* 1383–1388.

CHAPTER REVIEW

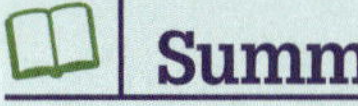

Summary

- **What is language?**

Language is a system constructed from multiple levels of representations to convey meaning. Each level of representation uses rules to combine elements together to form other representations. These levels of representations include form (spelling and sounds), grammar (syntax), and meaning (morphemes and semantics).

- **How do we get from a string of sounds or marks on a page to something meaningful?**

  The major problem in language comprehension is to resolve potential ambiguities to recover the intended meaning of the producer. This process is accomplished through a series of processing stages using information in the signal as well as contextual information about the words, grammar, and world knowledge.

- **How do we go from thoughts to spoken language?**

  Language production involves levels of representations similar to those in comprehension; however, the system has evolved not to resolve ambiguity but rather to get the form of the output correct. In dialogue, perhaps the most typical way in which we use language, both language production and comprehension process are involved. Alignment theory proposes that successful communication arises when the participants' linguistic and situation model representations are aligned. Alignment is achieved largely through automatic priming mechanisms.

- **How do we acquire language?**

  Infants and children learn language rapidly and without explicit instruction. Production abilities tend to lag behind comprehension initially, but the gap is typically closed by the second year. Patterns of acquisition appear to be relatively stable across different individuals and cultures, suggesting to some that humans have an innate ability to learn language. Others believe the acquisition of language results from interactions between cognitive biases and language experience.

- **How does human language differ from animal communication?**

  Animals use systems of communication that share some of the features of human language but not all. Attempts to teach animals to use systems of human language have had limited success.

Chapter Quiz

1. Enter the letter for the correct definition next to the terms below.
   (a) the smallest unit of language that has meaning
   (b) perceiving a continuous stimulus as discrete categories
   (c) a representation of what a text is about
   (d) chunks of syntactic representations
   (e) the sound representations that make up human languages
   (f) building the grammatical structure of a sentence
   (g) the characteristic that words have meaning
   (h) the collection of word representations in our long-term memory
   ___ Constituent
   ___ Categorical perception
   ___ Mental lexicon
   ___ Morpheme
   ___ Phoneme
   ___ Semanticity
   ___ Situational model
   ___ Syntactic parsing
2. What does it mean that language is hierarchically structured?
3. What are the phoneme restoration and word superiority effects? What process do they illustrate?
4. What is the syntax-first approach to parsing?
5. What is an inference? How is it used to help with language comprehension?
6. What is the "paradox" in language production?
7. What design feature of language corresponds to the use of unique combinations of representations to produce an infinite number of utterances?
   (a) duality of patterning
   (b) semanticity
   (c) productivity
   (d) innateness
8. Washoe was
   (a) an African grey parrot.
   (b) a child raised in a language-free environment.
   (c) a chimpanzee taught to use human language.
   (d) a speech error demonstrating categorical perception.
9. In the sentence "Connor teased Daphne" the *-ed* is a
   (a) phoneme.
   (b) bound morpheme.
   (c) free morpheme.
   (d) syntactic constituent.

10. Evidence suggests retrieval of words from the mental lexicon is affected by
    (a) lexical frequency.
    (b) orthographic neighborhoods.
    (c) morphological complexity.
    (d) all of the above

Key Terms

Anaphoric inference 218
Broca's aphasia 209
Categorical perception 212
Coarticulation 211
Deep structure 215
Invariance problem 211
Morphemes 206
Phoneme restoration effect 212
Phonemes 205
Pragmatics 208
Semantics 208
Surface structure 215
Syntactic parsing 215
Syntax 206
Wernicke's aphasia 209

Stop and Think Answers

9.1. Identify the phonemes in the sentence "Ted quietly chatted with Bill."

/t/ /e/ /d/ /k/ /w/ /ai/ /e/ /t/ /l/ /i/ /ch/ /æ/ /t/ /I/ /d/ /w/ /I/ /th/ /b/ /I/ /l/

9.2. Identify the morphemes in the sentence "Ted quietly chatted with Bill at the coffee shop."

Ted quiet –ly chat –ed with Bill at the coffee shop

9.3. What are two different interpretations of the sentence "Groucho shot an elephant in his pajamas"? How are the different interpretations linked to syntax?

In one case, Groucho is wearing his own pajamas. In the other interpretation, the elephant is wearing Groucho's pajamas. The difference syntactically has to do with what the prepositional phrase "in his pajamas" modifies (either "shot in his pajamas" or "elephant in his pajamas").

9.4. What are the major differences between spoken and written language?

Written language is typically persistent, with clear delineations between letters and words, and is processed by the visual system. Spoken language is transient (it fades rapidly over time), without clear boundaries between phonemes and words, and is processed by the auditory system.

9.5. How are speech sounds processed differently from other kinds of sounds?

Most sounds are perceived as continuous. However, speech sounds are perceived as discrete categories.

9.6. What processing features may be used to help understand degraded stimuli (e.g., reading a faded photocopy or understanding somebody speaking with a stuffy nose)?

In addition to using information from the signal itself, contextual information about words and meaning are used to resolve potential ambiguities.

9.7. What factors impact how quickly a word is recognized?

Lexical frequency, morphological complexity, orthographic and phonological neighborhood size, and semantic priming.

9.8. What factors are important in accessing the appropriate meaning of a word?

The context in which a word is used and the frequency of alternative meanings.

9.9. What is the difference between deep and surface structure? What are syntactic transformations?

Deep structure is the syntactic structure formed from meaning through the use of phrase structure rules. Surface structure is the final linear ordering of words in a sentence that result after transformations of the deep structure.

9.10. How do the syntax-first and interactive approaches differ with respect to resolving syntactic ambiguity?

The syntax-first approach uses only syntactic information to build the initial syntactic structure of a sentence. Semantic and contextual information is used afterward to build a new structure if necessary. Interactive approaches use other sources of information (in addition to syntactic information) to build the initial structure.

9.11. What processes are used to combine separate sentences into a cohesive and coherent structure?

Inferences are used to connect sentences together and integrate world knowledge into the ongoing understanding of the text.

9.12. What is a situational model? What evidence is there that we generate them during comprehension?

A situational model is a dynamic representation (a simulation) of the interpretation of the text. Research suggests that the situational model may be perceptual (e.g., orientation information) and action (e.g., direction of movement) aspects inferred by the text.

9.13. What is the paradox of production?

If the producer knows the meaning of what he or she wants to say and is in control of the situation, then why do most speech errors appear to obey syntactic and form regularities at the expense of disruptions in meaning? The answer appears to be that meaning is processed separately and earlier than syntactic and form information.

9.14. What evidence has been used to suggest that semantic and phonological processing are separated during language production?

The tip-of-the-tongue state is an example in which the semantic but not form information has been accessed. Experiments using the picture-word interference task show an early stage of primarily semantic processing followed by a later stage of phonological processing.

9.15. How might we use our comprehension processes to aid our productions?

Evidence suggests that we may use comprehension to monitor what we plan to say, allowing us to detect and repair faulty utterances.

9.16. What is some of the evidence that speakers and listeners align their linguistic representations during dialogue?

The repeated use of words and syntax between participants engaged in dialogue suggests the alignment of our linguistic representations. This is also supported by the coordination of gaze durations between speakers and listeners watching the same visual array of photos during the description of a television show.

9.17. What are the major linguistic milestones of a six-month-old infant? A twelve-month-old infant? A two-year-old child?

From six to twelve months infants can recognize names of familiar objects, foods, and body parts. Six-month-olds typically produce reduplicated babbling, while twelve-month-olds begin to produce their first words. From age one to two years, children can point to objects and pictures when named and understand some requests or questions. By their second birthday, they typically produce two hundred to three hundred words and are beginning to combine the words into short "telegraphic" utterances.

9.18. Why do Chomsky and others propose that much of language acquisition is driven by innate knowledge of language?

Language acquisition appears to follow the same basic pattern across different languages and cultures. This suggests that it may be a maturational rather than learned process (like walking). Additionally, language is productive, meaning that we can understand and produce sentences we have never experienced before, suggesting that reinforcement of past experiences is not sufficient for language learning.

9.19. How does the emergent coalition model describe the process of word learning in infants?

The model proposes that infants initially attend primarily to perceptual and attentional cues early. However, as they get older they use other linguistic and social cues (either in combination or alone). This reflects a developmental shift in the use of relevant cues.

9.20. What are the characteristic features of human language?

Table 9.2 lists the thirteen characteristics of human language proposed by Hockett. More recently Chomsky and others have proposed that the presence of recursion in syntax is the hallmark of human language.

9.21. How do the dances of bees compare to human language?

The bee system of communication exhibits some features (e.g., displacement, semanticity, and productivity) but not others (e.g., discreteness, arbitrariness, and duality of patterning).

9.22. How does the performance of chimpanzees taught to use language compare to human children learning language?

Attempts to teach animals to use systems of human language have had limited success. While animals may learn some words (many fewer than do human children), animals fail to learn to use all but the most simple syntax.

Student Study Site

Sharpen your skills with SAGE edge at **edge.sagepub.com/mcbridecp**

SAGE edge for students provides a personalized approach to help you accomplish your coursework goals in an easy-to-use learning environment.

Go to edge.sagepub.com/mcbridecp for additional exercises and web resources. Select Chapter 9, Language, for chapter-specific resources. All of the links listed in the margins of this chapter are accessible via this site.

CBS Photo Archive/Contributor/Getty Images

Concepts and Knowledge

Questions to Consider

- What is a concept?
- How are concepts mentally represented?
- How are concepts and knowledge organized?
- What do we use concepts for?

Introduction: Game Night

Game night is always a big hit at our house. Sometimes we play a variation of the old $10,000 Pyramid *TV game show. In our version of the game, one person names exemplars and the rest of the players have to figure out what category the exemplars are from (e.g., Charlie says, "bird, airplane, baseball, bat." Isabel calls out, "things that fly"). Points are awarded for the number of exemplars and for guessing the correct category. Sometimes the categories are fairly straightforward (e.g., robin, sparrow, hawk, cardinal, penguin, ostrich: "birds"), but other times they are more difficult (e.g., wallet, photo album, laptop computer, cell phone, jewelry, vintage vinyl record collection, guitar: "things you would take from your burning house"). Other popular hits on game night include Bridge (the classic card game), Beyond Balderdash, Ticket to Ride, Munchkin, and Apples to Apples. When I announce, "Kids, let's do a game night tonight. Go pick out a game," the kids run off to the playroom and return (after some heated discussion sometimes) with the night's game. How do they know what to count as a game? Part of the answer lies in the fact that they've had a lot of experience with games (my son even watches an Internet show that showcases a different "tabletop game" each episode). Based on these experiences they are able to recognize and select things that fit their mental concept of "game."*

This chapter is about the pieces of our mental world: concepts and knowledge. The material is closely related to discussions of semantic memory in Chapter 5 and of language meaning in Chapter 9. In his book The Big Book of Concepts, *Gregory Murphy (2002, p. 1) opens with "Concepts are the glue that holds our mental world together." Concepts are our mental representations of categories of things in the world. Being able to recognize and group things into mental categories is an extremely important cognitive ability. It allows us to identify what something is, what the properties of that thing are, and how we can behave with the thing (e.g., Should we eat it? Will it hurt us? What can we use it for?). For example, imagine that you were handed the object in Photo 10.1. You may not know what to do with it. However if somebody told you it was a fruit (it is a pitaya or dragon fruit), then you would probably assume that it is something you can eat, that it probably has seeds, and that it may be sweet. You would base these assumptions on what you know about the concept of fruit. Furthermore, if somebody were to show you another one, you would be able to recognize it as a fruit, with the properties of fruit, without needing to be told these things again. Indeed, without our ability to categorize like this, we would have to identify and learn the properties of things anew each and every time we encountered an object.*

We begin this chapter with the classical view of concepts as definitions and then review the theoretical and empirical problems with this view. Then we describe three alternative views. Following this, we describe how concepts are used for categorization, organized into larger structures of knowledge, combined together, and used to make inductive inferences.

Photo 10.1 A dragon fruit.

What Are Concepts?

The Classical Approach: Concepts as Definitions

If somebody were to ask you, "What is a square?" you may come up with something like "a closed four-sided figure, composed of four straight lines of equal length, joined at ninety-degree angles." This definition of square works quite well. The set of features are necessary (identifying the features something must have to be a square) and sufficient (if something has all of these features, then it must be a square) for identifying members of the category. The advantage of this approach is that using a definition is a relatively easy way to identify whether an object is or is not a member of the category. All one needs to do is to match the features of the object with the features listed in the definition. This view of concepts as definitions with lists of necessary and sufficient properties can be traced back to early Greek philosophers (e.g., Plato and Aristotle) and was generally assumed until the mid-twentieth century. However, in the last century philosophers and psychologists began identifying problems with this view.

Photo 10.2 Ludwig Wittgenstein

Theoretical Problems With Definitions as Concepts

Crash Course: Cognition

Let's change our example. Suppose that somebody asked you, "What is a game?" As with our square example, you would probably try to think up a definition of what a game is. However in contrast with the square example, you would probably find it difficult to come up with a single definition that adequately captures everything you categorize as a game. Philosopher Ludwig Wittgenstein (1953), shown in Photo 10.2, used the concept of "game" as part of a theoretical argument against the definition approach to concepts. He argued that it may not be possible to identify a list of necessary and sufficient features for many categories, in particular "real-world" categories. Consider what is common to board games. Now extend that to card games, ball games, and to the Olympic Games. What features are common to them all? Here are some possible features of games: have competition (winners and losers), have an aspect of luck and/or skill, provide fun or amusement. But consider a child throwing a ball against the garage and catching it. Is she playing a game? If the answer is yes, then who are the winners and losers? Wittgenstein (1953) argued that the category members shared a family resemblance. That is, it is usually easy to see that children look like their parents, although it may be difficult to pinpoint the precise set of features they share (see Photo 10.3). Family resemblance points not to a single set of defining features but rather to members of categories connected by overlapping sets of features. In this approach, concepts are not defined by necessary and sufficient features but rather connected by a series of overlapping similarities across features. Consider another of Wittgenstein's examples: the concept of "chair." Look at the objects presented in Photo 10.4. Most people would agree that they are all examples of their concept of chair. However, while it may be easy to agree about how best to categorize these objects, it is not as easy to agree on a common definition of what a chair is. Give it a try. Write down what you believe are the necessary and sufficient features of a chair. Compare your definition with those of other students in your class. Chances are you won't find the

Photo 10.3 A mother and her two daughters. Notice the family resemblance between the three.

What Is a Chair? Activity

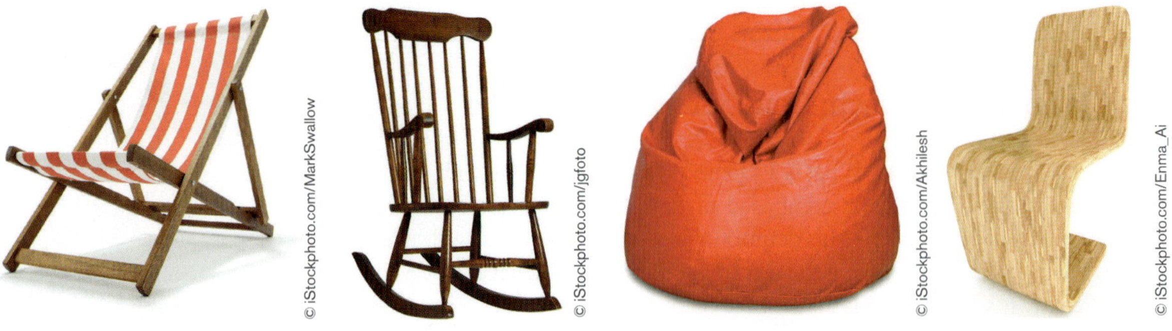

Photo 10.4 Examples of the concept "chair."

same level of agreement about the features as you did with the categorization of the pictures. Wittgenstein's theoretical arguments are generally viewed as strong evidence against the classical definition approach of concepts.

Empirical Problems With Definitions as Concepts

In addition to Wittgenstein's theoretical arguments, many empirical findings suggest that the classical view of concepts as definitions is incorrect. One characteristic of the definition approach is that it determines whether something is part of a category, but once something is determined to be a category member it does not make distinctions between category members. However, McCloskey and Glucksberg (1978) demonstrated that category boundaries are not always so clear-cut. They presented their participants with pairs of words. The second word was a category name. The participants' task was to quickly judge whether the first word was a member of that category (e.g., dog-mammal, participants should indicate yes). Their results indicated that for some items, this task was easy: Items were either clear members (e.g., chair-furniture, yes) or clear nonmembers (cucumber-furniture, no). However, some items were much more difficult (e.g., bookcase-furniture; curtains-furniture). For these items, there was disagreement across participants (with some responding yes and others no) as well as within participants across different testing sessions (for some items they changed their minds 22 percent of the time). The data suggest that we do not treat all members of a category equally. Instead we behave as if some members of a category are "better" than others. For example, take a minute and write down all of the birds you can think of. Chances are that birds like "robin," "blue jay," and "sparrow" are category members you wrote down early in your list. But consider birds like "ostrich" and "penguin." Where did these birds fall on your list (if they made it at all)? These members are usually considered much less "typical" than birds like "robin" and "sparrow."

Birds Activity

Rosch and Mervis (1975) presented participants with twenty members of six categories (see Table 10.1 for three examples) and asked participants to rate the typicality of each member. A separate group of participants was asked to list attributes of each of the members. Some attributes were listed more frequently than others. Exemplars that had more of these frequent attributes were considered more typical members of the category. Rosch and Mervis interpreted these findings as support for Wittgenstein's family resemblance view. They argued that concepts are overlapping networks of attributes. Typicality of members within a category depends on how they compare to an abstract combination of the most frequent attributes. So, typical category members have many frequent attributes (i.e., features common to many category members) and very few attributes that are frequent in other categories. This theory is discussed in greater detail later in the chapter.

Typicality effect: a result where more common members of a category show a processing advantage

The **typicality effect** is among the most common empirical findings in cognitive psychology and has been found using a wide range of methodologies beyond rating

Table 10.1 Categories and Exemplars Used in Rosch and Mervis (1975)

Exemplars are listed from most typical to least typical. The bottom rows list the number of features common to the five most and least prototypical exemplars

		CATEGORY		
		FURNITURE	**WEAPON**	**CLOTHING**
Most typical		Chair	Gun	Pants
		Sofa	Knife	Shirt
		Table	Sword	Dress
		Dresser	Bomb	Skirt
		Desk	Hand grenade	Jacket
		Bed	Spear	Coat
		Bookcase	Cannon	Sweater
		Footstool	Bow and arrow	Underpants
		Lamp	Club	Socks
		Piano	Tank	Pajamas
		Cushion	Teargas	Bathing suit
		Mirror	Whip	Shoes
		Rug	Icepick	Vest
		Radio	Fists	Tie
		Stove	Rocket	Mittens
		Clock	Poison	Hat
		Picture	Scissors	Apron
		Closet	Words	Purse
		Vase	Foot	Wristwatch
Least typical		Telephone	Screwdriver	Necklace
Number of features in common	5 most typical exemplars	13	9	21
	5 least typical exemplars	2	0	0

tasks. For example, Rips, Shoben, and Smith (1973) used a speeded category verification task in which they presented participants with sentences like "A robin is a bird" or "An elephant is a bird." Participants had to respond with "True" or "False" as quickly as they could. They found that responses were much faster for typical members of a category (e.g., "A robin is a bird") than for atypical members (e.g., "A chicken is a bird"). As in our demonstration earlier, Mervis, Catlin, and Rosch (1976) showed that typical items are produced first when prompted to produce category members. Typical items are usually learned first (e.g., Meints, Plunkett, & Harris, 1999) too. When mentioning two category members together, the more typical member is usually mentioned first (e.g., "robins and penguins" rather than "penguins and robins"; Kelly, Bock, & Keil, 1986). Garrod and Sanford (1977) demonstrated that reading time of an anaphor is faster ("the vehicle" in "the vehicle narrowly missed the pedestrian") if the antecedent it refers to is a typical category member (e.g., "the car" versus "the bus" in "the bus/car came roaring around the corner").

Stop and Think

10.1. What are necessary and sufficient properties of a concept?

10.2. What are the major theoretical and empirical arguments against concepts as definitions?

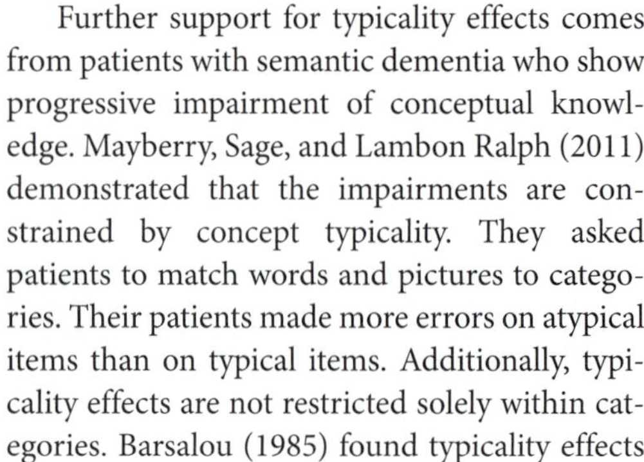

Further support for typicality effects comes from patients with semantic dementia who show progressive impairment of conceptual knowledge. Mayberry, Sage, and Lambon Ralph (2011) demonstrated that the impairments are constrained by concept typicality. They asked patients to match words and pictures to categories. Their patients made more errors on atypical items than on typical items. Additionally, typicality effects are not restricted solely within categories. Barsalou (1985) found typicality effects for exemplars outside of categories. For example, a chair is considered a better nonmember of the category "bird" than a butterfly is, further demonstrating that category membership is not an all-or-none process.

A World Without Words

While the definition approach may hold some intuitive appeal and work for some artificial categories (e.g., "square"), it has generally fallen out of favor as a processing model. Its main failings include the absence of clear necessary and sufficient features, no clear categorical boundaries, and typicality effects for category and noncategory members. The section that follows briefly discusses alternative theoretical approaches proposed to explain how we mentally represent concepts.

Alternative Approaches to Concepts

Many theoretical approaches to concepts have been proposed to replace the classical definitional approach. This section briefly reviews several of these approaches. Keep in mind that within each of these approaches are many individual theories, each with their own specific details (much like the categories they have been constructed to explain).

Prototype Approach

The **prototype approach** grew primarily from the theoretical and empirical work initially developed by Eleanor Rosch (Rosch & Mervis, 1975) (sometimes this approach is referred to as the family resemblance or probabilistic approach). This approach views concepts as abstract representations (prototypes) that summarize the common and distinctive attributes of the members of the category that comprise the concept (e.g., Hampton, 1979; Smith, Rips, & Shoben, 1974). The prototype of a category is essentially a weighted average of the important features of its members. Important features are those shared by most of the members (common) and not by members of other categories (distinctive). Category membership is determined by virtue of the similarity of the object's attributes to the prototype's attributes.

Think back to our opening story about all of the things my family considers games. Bridge involves two pairs of people competing against each other at cards to reach at least 100 points first. It consists of multiple rounds of hands, with each hand consisting of a bidding stage and a playing stage. Beyond Balderdash consists of a group of people making up potential definitions of an obscure word, the basic plot corresponding to an obscure movie title, or things that happened on a particular date. These made-up things are read aloud, along with the actual answer, and players vote for the one they believe is the actual answer. Points are awarded for getting the correct response or having other players vote for the response you wrote. Ticket to Ride involves building railroads along different routes across a board with a map on it. Longer routes are awarded more points. Players randomly select cards with target routes (e.g., Los Angeles to Miami) that the player is awarded extra points for achieving. At the end of the game, the player with the most points wins. Table 10.2 presents feature lists for five potential members of the concept of "game." Looking over these examples, one might abstract a prototype for games

Prototype approach: the idea that concepts are represented based on a typical (common) instance of that concept

as things that have a system of rules and use cards where players compete for points and the highest point getter is the winner. Now let's suppose we encounter Yahtzee for the first time. Would it fit into our concept of "game"? According to the prototype approach, we would compare the features of Yahtzee to our prototype features. While Yahtzee doesn't include the use of cards, it does share the other features with our prototype. Now consider playing catch (throwing a baseball between two individuals). Would we consider that a game? Maybe not, since there does not seem to be much overlap of features. Suppose that we had two pairs of people tossing the ball, with each team counting the number of successful catches and declaring the team with the highest count the winners. Now the scenario overlaps more with the features of our prototype, and our judgment of it may change to include it as part of the concept.

However, not all researchers accept the idea of a single abstract representation that spans an entire concept. Instead, they propose an approach grounded in the belief that categorization of new objects is based on specific memories of past examples, rather than something like a single prototype.

Table 10.2 Sample Feature Lists of the Concept "Game"

BRIDGE	BEYOND BALDERDASH	TICKET-TO-RIDE	YAHTZEE	PLAYING CATCH
Played for enjoyment	Played for enjoyment	Played for enjoyment	Played for enjoyment	Played for enjoyment
Pairs of players compete	Players compete for points	Players compete for points	Players compete for points	Uses a ball
Uses playing cards	Uses cards with targets to be elaborated upon	Uses a board with a map	Uses dice	Players take turns throwing and catching the ball
Play ends when a specified point total is reached	Players keep track of points by moving game pieces on a board	Uses cards with designated routes	Points are awarded for rolling specified dice outcomes	
Has two phases: bidding and playing	Play ends when a specified point total is reached	Players get points for creating train routes	Players take turns rolling the dice	
Points are awarded for number of tricks taken during the play, as a function of the bid	Players vote for correct answer	Players get extra points for completing routes designated on cards	Each turn consists of up to three rolls of the dice	
	Points awarded for correct answer	Player with the most points wins		
	Points awarded for other players voting for your answer	Players keep track of points by moving game pieces on a board		

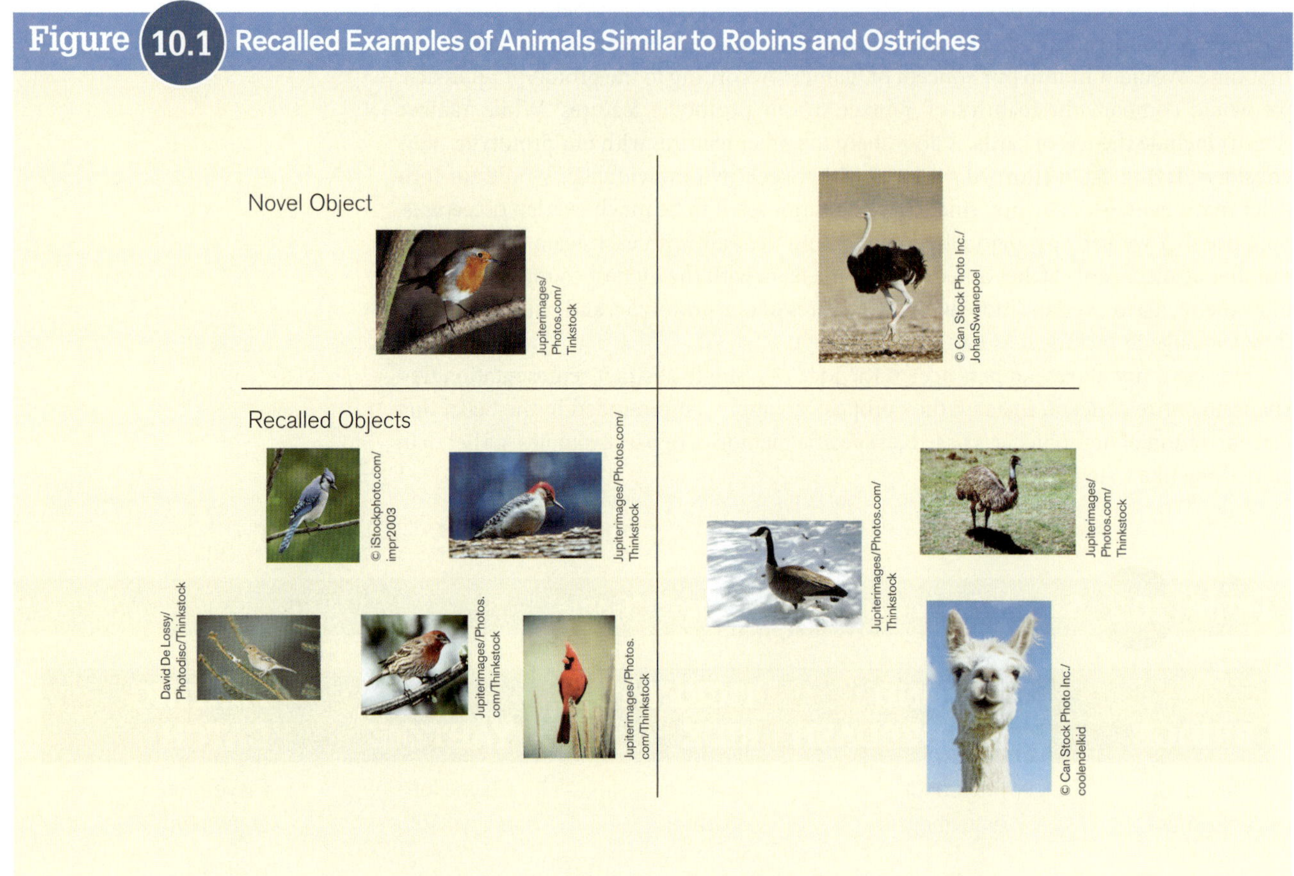

Figure 10.1 Recalled Examples of Animals Similar to Robins and Ostriches

Exemplar Approach

The **exemplar approach** (e.g., Medin & Schaffer, 1978) proposes that concepts consist of separate representations of experienced examples of the category. In other words, categorization of an object is accomplished by comparing it to all of your memories of similar things. Staying with our games example, suppose you open up a present and it is a colorful box containing some dice, a deck of cards, some plastic tokens, a board, and a set of rules. These contents may bring to mind specific experiences you have had that involve objects with similar features (e.g., Monopoly, Candy Land, Risk) so that you compare the memory of these objects with the new one in front of you and determine that it is a board game. The major difference between this approach and the prototype approach is that comparisons are being made to memories of actual experiences rather than an abstraction of those experiences.

So how does this approach explain the typicality results? Recall that the most typical items of a concept are those that are similar to many other members of the concept. So on average, the more typical of a concept an object is, the more similar it will be to recalled members of that concept. The less typical of the concept an object is, the fewer members of that concept that will be recalled. Additionally, the object may have many features similar to members of other concepts, resulting in the retrieval of memories of noncategory objects. For example, suppose you see a robin for the first time. It may bring to mind memories of many birds (e.g., sparrows, cardinals, woodpeckers, and blue jays). The high similarity of features between robins and these remembered birds results in "robin" being interpreted as a typical member of the concept "bird " (see Figure 10.1). However, suppose you saw an ostrich. Ostriches don't share many features with most common birds. They aren't small and don't fly or hang out in trees. Instead they are big,

Exemplar approach: the idea that concepts are represented based on exemplars of the category that one has experienced previously

Figure 10.2 Examples of Stimuli Like Those Used in the Allen and Brooks (1991) Study

	BODY SHAPE (0-CURVES, 1-ANGULAR)	LEG LENGTH (0-SHORT, 1-LONG)	SHADING (0-BLANK, 1-SPOTTED)	CATEGORY RULE BUILDER HAS AT LEAST TWO: ANGULAR BODY, LONG LEGS, SPOTS
	0	1	1	Builder
	1	1	0	Builder
	0	0	1	Digger
	1	1	1	Builder
	1	0	0	Digger
	1	1	1	Builder
	0	0	0	Digger

with a long neck and long legs, and have feathers that look like fur. If you have encountered an emu before, an ostrich will probably come to mind, but not many other birds are likely to (maybe swans and geese). You might even think of other large animals like alpacas. As a result of these recalled memories, ostriches are considered much less birdlike than the robin.

A lot of research has attempted to distinguish between the exemplar and prototype approaches. Much of this work has used experimental paradigms in which participants are taught new artificial concepts and then tested with novel examples. The advantage of using artificial concepts is that researchers can tightly control the features involved and can examine how the concepts are initially acquired. For example, Allen and Brooks (1991) presented participants with cartoon animals having different environmental background contexts (e.g., desert or forest scene). They systematically manipulated features of the cartoon characters. Participants had to learn a rule to categorize the cartoon characters into either "diggers" (who dig holes to live in) or "builders" (who build homes from materials in their environment). Half of the participants were explicitly told the rule; the others were not told the rule. Of the five features manipulated, three were relevant to the categorization (i.e., leg length, angularity of body type, spotted or not) and two were not (i.e., number of feet and length of neck). Figure 10.2

Thinking Intuitively

Figure 10.3 Examples of "Good" and "Bad" Matches Used in the Allen and Brooks (1991) Study

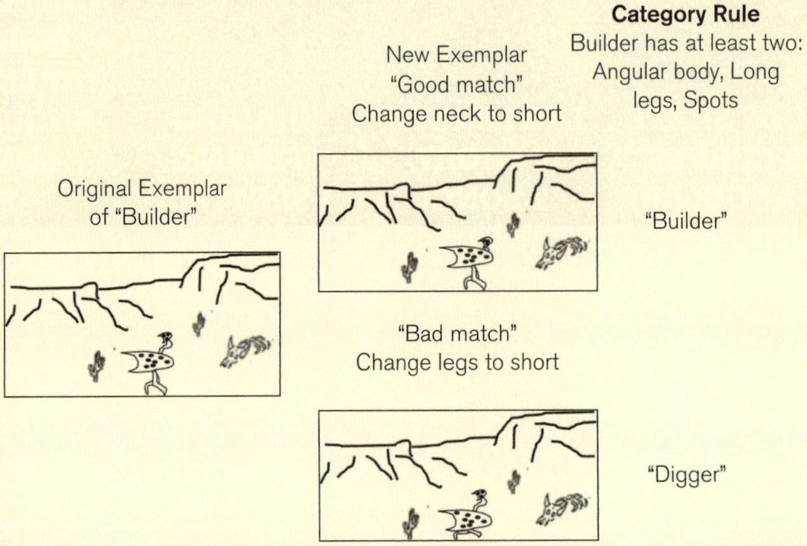

Category Rule
Builder has at least two:
Angular body, Long legs, Spots

New Exemplar
"Good match"
Change neck to short

Original Exemplar of "Builder"

"Builder"

"Bad match"
Change legs to short

"Digger"

In both the good and bad match cases the new exemplars differed from the original by one feature. In the good match example, the neck length was changed, but because the character still has long legs and spots it remains a builder. In the bad match example, the legs were shortened, resulting in the character belonging to the digger category. Participants were better at categorizing the good matches than the bad matches.

presents some examples of these artificial stimuli. Participants were trained to learn the categorization rule using eight exemplars. Following the learning phase, participants were then tested with new examples. The researchers could vary the similarity of the new test items to the exemplars used in the learning phase by manipulating the nonrelevant features (number of feet and length of neck as well as the environmental context). The researchers could create new items that were either "good" or "bad" matches. Bad matches were created by keeping irrelevant features constant (same background, number of feet, and neck length) but changing one of the critical features resulting in the item being a member of the other category (see Figure 10.3). Good matches were created by changing a feature that did not change the category. Participants were slower and made more errors categorizing "bad matches" than "good matches" (see Figure 10.4). This finding suggests that participants were relying on the similarities to the specific learned exemplars rather than relying on an abstraction like a prototype.

Mack, Preston, and Love (2013) compared computational models of the exemplar and prototype approaches with fMRI scans of people's brains as they performed a categorization task. Prior to scanning, participants were taught to categorize novel objects into two categories. Following this, they then categorized old and new objects while in the fMRI scanner. Both the exemplar and prototype models accounted well for the behavioral data. The researchers then used the two models to compute the representational match between the test objects and the different representations (exemplars versus prototypes). They then compared these representational matches with the brain response data. Their results indicated that the exemplar model provided a better prediction than the prototype model for most of their participants.

Figure 10.4 Results of the Allen and Brooks (1991) Study

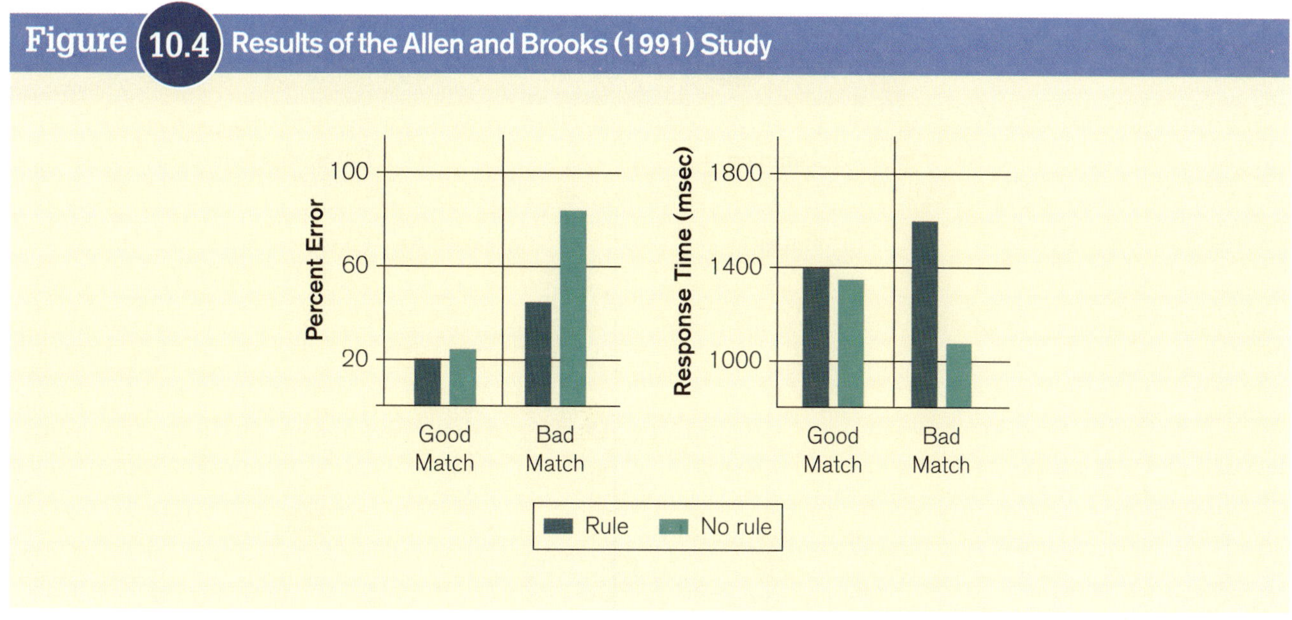

While most of the results from experiments using artificial concepts favor the exemplar approach over the prototype approach (see Murphy, 2002, for a review), it is important to recognize a potential limitation of such research. The conceptual structures used in these artificial concepts are very simple relative to naturally occurring concepts. So for naturalistic concepts like games or birds, we can develop much richer prototypes and have more exemplars with which to make comparisons. Indeed, evidence suggests that we may use both approaches, depending on context. Malt (1989) used pictures of real animals in a priming task that allowed her to investigate whether exemplars or prototypes were activated during a categorization task. Across a series of experiments, her results suggested that we may use both exemplar and prototype representations to make categorical decisions.

In many respects, the prototype and exemplar approaches are similar. In both, concept learning and categorization involve identifying features and making comparisons to either an abstract prototype or other recalled exemplars. However, both approaches place a heavy emphasis on observable features and also largely ignore the role of prior knowledge in learning and using concepts.

Concepts Based on World Knowledge Approach

Barsalou (1985) examined the typicality of taxonomic concepts like those used in Rosch and Mervis's (1975) study along with a set of goal-derived concepts (e.g., birthday presents, foods not to eat on a diet, things to take from your house if it is on fire). Goal-derived concepts are categories of things grouped together, not because of shared observable features but rather how well their members satisfy a particular purpose. Barsalou measured three variables: central tendency (essentially a measure of family resemblance), frequency of instantiation (how often an item was considered a member of a category), and how well an item satisfied the goal (which Barsalou called the "ideal"). His results indicated that all three variables were important to determining an item's typicality. Because the exemplar and prototype approaches depend on observable features, the finding of an abstract feature like goal directedness (the ideal) is problematic for these approaches. Results like these have led some theorists to develop an approach in which conceptual structures are part of a larger system of general knowledge.

Figure 10.5 Examples of Stimuli Used in the Lin and Murphy (1997) Study

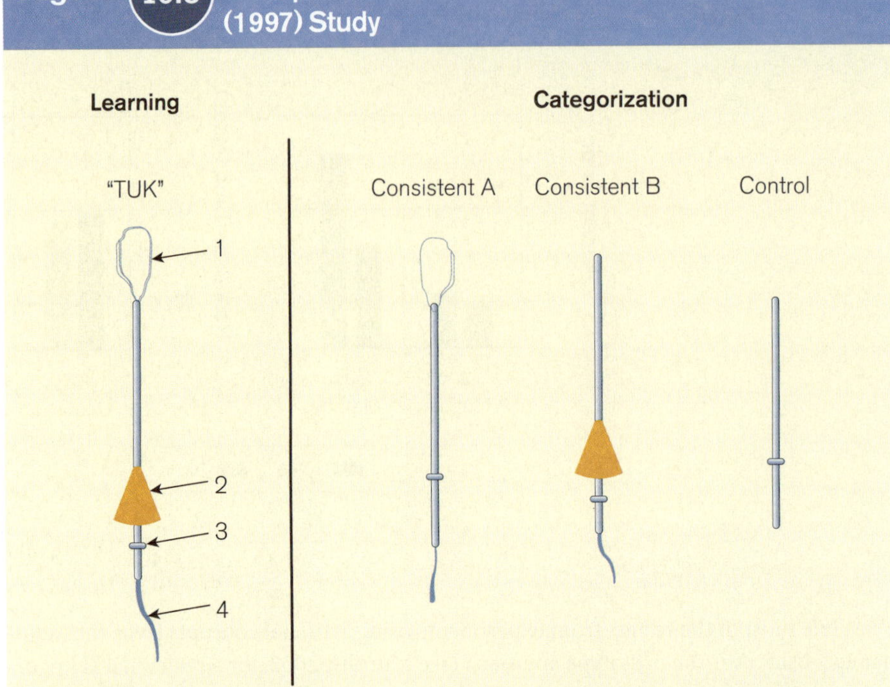

Participants were shown examples of this novel tool (a tuk) and provided one of two stories that explained the function of the tool's parts. Story A relayed that the tuk was a hunting tool consisting of a loop (Part 1) that could be hooked around the prey's neck, a guard to protect the hunter's hand (Part 2), a handle (Part 3), and a drawstring to pull the loop tight (Part 4). Story B explained that the tuk was used to spray pesticides; it consisted of a loop to hang the tuk for storage (Part1), a bottle to hold the pesticide (Part 2), a control screw (Part 3) that could be opened or closed, and a hose through which the pesticide could flow (Part 4).

In Chapters 7 and 9 we introduced the concepts of schemata and scripts as representations of knowledge. Cohen and Murphy (1984) argued that prototypes are better represented as schemata than as unstructured lists. For example, rather than representing a bird as an unstructured list of weighted features, a schema for "bird" would be a structured set of dimensions (often called slots) that can be specified with particular values. Our schema for birds may include dimensions for physical characteristics like "outer skin: feathers"; "number of legs: two"; "mouth type: beak"; "movement: flies, walks, swims." Furthermore, the dimensions may be connected such that they may restrict the values they can take. For example, number of legs and movement might be connected such that if the object has no legs, then movement can't take "walks" as a value. This approach represents a move toward richer conceptual representations incorporating broader pieces of general knowledge.

Murphy and Medin (1985) argued that similarity-based theories of concepts fall short of adequately describing why concepts are coherent or meaningful because they don't take into account our theories of how the world works. Consider our concept of "bird" again. The properties "has wings," "is covered in feathers," "lives in nests," and "can fly" are related to each other. Lists of features may capture the fact that these features often co-occur, but the theory approach goes beyond simple correlation. Our knowledge about the world provides a reason that explains the co-occurrence of these features: lightweight feathers and wings allow birds to fly, which in turn allows them to nest in trees high above many predators. The causal relationships between these

Figure 10.6 Results From the Lin and Murphy (1997) Study

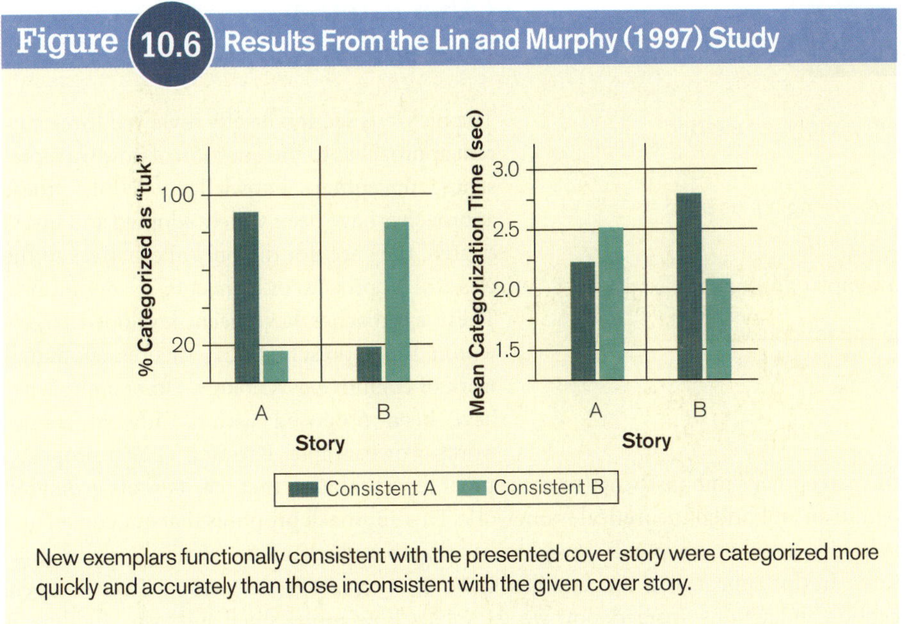

New exemplars functionally consistent with the presented cover story were categorized more quickly and accurately than those inconsistent with the given cover story.

features are part of our general world knowledge, and their use as part of the conceptual process can explain how and why the features in our conceptual representations stick together. Similarly, knowledge may also play a role in explaining why an ostrich, which does not have the highly salient bird feature "can fly," is still considered a member of the category if we consider that the reason it can't fly is that it is too heavy for its wings to carry it aloft. The theories approach may also explain why some features are listed while others are not. For example, even though birds and airplanes are both often brightly colored, we would probably only list it as a feature for birds because it is not a particularly salient or important property of airplanes. In contrast, a feature like "has wings" is salient for both concepts and will likely be listed for both birds and airplanes.

Lin and Murphy (1997) examined the influence of knowledge within a categorization task. They had two groups of participants learn about an artificial tool (a "tuk"), like that shown in Figure 10.5, and read a story about how the tool was used. The main experimental manipulation was in the functional importance of some of the features in the two stories. In Story A, Part 1 is critical to the functioning of the tool (used to capture the prey) but not in Story B (used to hang the tool for storage). The opposite is the case for Part 2 (it stores the pesticide for Story B; in Story A it protects the hunter's hand). In the learning phase of the study, participants were shown exemplars of each category along with either Story A or Story B and asked to memorize what the category was about. During the categorization phase, participants were given single exemplars (see the right side of Figure 10.5) and asked to answer quickly as to whether the item was a tuk (they also asked participants to rate how typical they thought the items were of the category). Some of the exemplars lacked the critical functional feature, making them inconsistent with the story the participants had heard during the learning phase. Across a series of experiments, with participants who were given Story A during learning, exemplars consistent with Story A were categorized as a "tuk" more often, rated as more typical, and categorized faster than those inconsistent with Story A (see Figure 10.6). These results clearly demonstrate the importance of general background causal knowledge for our conceptual system (Carey, 1985; Keil, 1989; Rips, 1989).

Stop and Think

10.3. What is a prototype? How are prototypes used to represent concepts?

10.4. What is an exemplar? How are exemplars used to represent concepts?

10.5. How are the prototype and exemplar approaches similar?

10.6. How might world knowledge impact conceptual representations?

Other Alternative Approaches to Concepts

The previous section briefly reviewed three current approaches to the question of how we represent conceptual knowledge. While these approaches have been widely adopted and investigated, they are not the only alternatives to the classical approach of concepts as definitions. These approaches have been developed largely within the representational theoretical framework of cognitive psychology. Other approaches have been proposed within different frameworks. For example, Barsalou (1999) proposed the perceptual symbols theory of conceptual representation that has its roots grounded within an embodied theoretical framework. This approach proposes that our conceptual system is largely perceptually based rather than based in amodal symbolic representations. In this approach, a concept like "apple" isn't represented separately from our perception and actions. Instead, how we see apples, how apples smell and taste, and how it sounds and feels when we bite into an apple are all directly part of our represented concept of apple. A number of models of the conceptual system have also been proposed within connectionist frameworks (e.g., Cree, McRae, & McNorgan, 1999; Rogers & McClelland, 2004; Smith & Minda, 2000) inspired by neural networks. Network models like these highlight a feature of concepts that we have not yet discussed in this chapter: Individual concepts are typically organized as part of larger knowledge structures. The next section reviews approaches proposed about how concepts are organized.

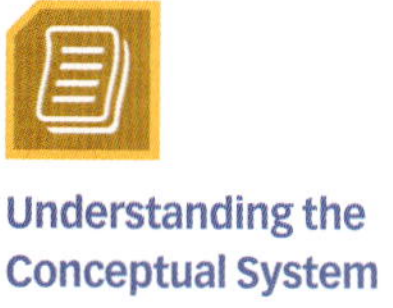

Understanding the Conceptual System

Organizing Our Concepts

Conceptual Hierarchies

To this point we have dealt primarily with examples in which we are trying to decide whether something is a member of a particular isolated concept. However, our conceptual world rarely breaks down into such a circumscribed situation. Consider the activity being played in Photo 10.5. We can describe the picture as people playing a game, or a card game, or poker, or perhaps even a particular type of poker (e.g., 5 card draw or Texas hold 'em). The point is that single objects or events are typically members of many different larger or smaller categories. Empirical studies have demonstrated that concepts are typically structured hierarchically. Based on work examining a broad range of cultures, Berlin (1992) argued that this is a universal feature of all natural world categories. Figure 10.7 shows a simplified conceptual hierarchy for games. Categories higher in the figure are referred to as superordinate to lower levels, while categories lower are referred to as subordinate to higher levels. The links between concepts represent "is a" relations, in the sense that "poker" is a member of "card games." One of the features of this organization is that subordinate categories may inherit the properties of their superordinate categories. For example, if you learn something new about the category "card games," you may be able to generalize this new knowledge to all of the subcategories of card games. This feature allows us to know a lot about something that we may never have actually encountered once we learn what category it belongs to. Furthermore, these relationships are assumed to be transitive. That is, if poker is a kind of card game, and Texas hold 'em is a kind of poker, then Texas hold 'em is a kind of card game with all of the properties of a card game.

Basic-Level Concepts

Consider the pictures in Photo 10.6. What would you call each thing? Most people will answer this question with "dog," "flower," and "car." However, other reasonable answers could include "border collie," "daisy," and "Ford Thunderbird," or "animal," "plant," and "vehicle." Another widely found finding is that one level is typically privileged over other levels. These privileged levels are typically referred to as **basic-level concepts**. Roger Brown (1958) observed that parents typically prefer to use these middle levels of the hierarchy of concepts when speaking to their children. Research has established a wide variety of basic-level effects: children learn basic categories and their names before other levels (e.g., Anglin, 1977), basic categories typically share common shapes and movements (e.g., Rosch, Mervis, Gray, Johnson, & Boyes-Braem, 1976), they allow for faster categorization of pictures (e.g., Tanaka & Taylor, 1991), and they are used more frequently in free naming (e.g., Cruse, 1977).

Rosch and her colleagues (e.g., Rosch, 1978; Rosch et al., 1976) argued that basic-level objects are those at which the category members share the highest number of features. This suggests that basic-level concepts are more informative than other levels (e.g., Markman & Wisniewski, 1997; Murphy & Brownell, 1985). Basic levels provide a lot of information about the categories and are also distinct from other concepts at a similar level in the hierarchy (Murphy & Lassaline, 1997). For example, consider the basic categories of cats and dogs. Knowing that something is a cat is very informative; you can infer many

Brand X Pictures/Stockbyte/Thinkstock

Photo 10.5 People enjoying a game of poker.

Figure 10.7 Simplified Hierarchy of "Games" Concept

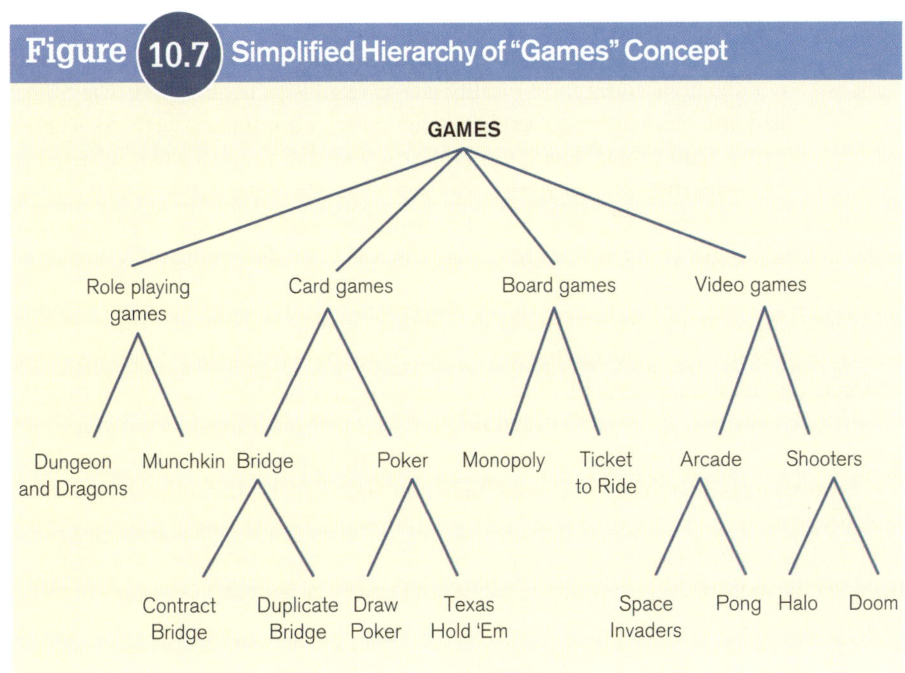

Basic Concepts Activity

Learning Concepts Through Illustration

Basic-level concept: level of concept hierarchy where common objects (e.g., dog) reside

Photo 10.6 Basic concepts activity.

properties about it (e.g., it meows, chases mice, has whiskers, purrs). You also know that dogs and cats are distinct concepts (e.g., dogs bark, chase cats, have a wet nose). **Superordinate concepts** (e.g., mammals and reptiles) tend to be distinctive but not as informative. **Subordinate concepts** (e.g., spaniels and border collies) tend to be informative but not as distinctive.

Superordinate concept: the level of concept hierarchy where general categories of the basic-level concepts (e.g., mammal) reside

Subordinate concept: the level of concept hierarchy where specific exemplars of a basic-level concept (e.g., husky) reside

Cognitive economy: the idea that concept information is stored at the most efficient level of the hierarchy

Organizational Approaches

Stored-Network Approaches

How these hierarchies and basic levels are mentally represented is a matter of theoretical and empirical debate. One theoretical approach is that these hierarchies are stored in memory as networks of relationships. For example, consider the model of semantic memory (see Figure 10.8). This model, proposed by Collins and Quillian (1969), is a network of related concepts and their associated features. Links in the model correspond to different kinds of relationships. "Is a" links represent the hierarchical structure, while the "has," "is," and "can" links represent the properties associated with the concepts. Collins and Quillian proposed that when an object is categorized, "activation" (think of it as a kind of mental flow of information) spreads from that object's corresponding concept node to other associated nodes. For example, to verify the statement "A canary is a bird," activation would spread from the concepts "canary" and "bird." If the spreading activations intersected, then the answer would be "yes." A major advantage of this organization is one of **cognitive economy**. For example, features shared by all animals can be stored at the animal level and need not be stored at any of the subordinate levels (e.g., bird, fish, robin, or trout). In addition to efficient mental storage, this organization also allows for property inheritance and generalization of new objects. For example, upon learning that a horse is an animal, the concept "horse" would inherit the features associated with the concept "animal." The model predicted distance effects: The more "is a" links that need to be traversed, the longer the verification times. Early research using a speeded property verification task (e.g., reply "true" or "false" as quickly as you can to the following statements: "A canary is red," "A rose has roots") supported the model's predictions.

However, further research yielded problems for the model. It was not able to account for typicality effects (e.g., Rips et al., 1973). The model had no mechanism to explain why some subordinates were considered better than others. Hampton (1982) found that the transitive inheritance of properties is sometimes violated. For example, while people agree with the two statements "A lamp is a kind of furniture" and "A car headlight is a kind of lamp," they don't verify the transitive combination "A car headlight is a kind of furniture."

Consistent with the normal scientific process, a wide variety of other network models have been developed and tested in response to these (and other) limitations. For example, Collins and Loftus's (1975) revised semantic network model proposed changes to how activation was spread and the addition of variable weighting on the connections between concepts (e.g., to capture typicality effects, the link between "robin" and "bird" would be stronger than the link between "penguin" and "bird"). Many other models have been proposed (e.g., Anderson, 1976; Anderson & Bower, 1973; McClelland & Rumelhart, 1981; Nelson, Kitto, Galea, McEvoy, & Bruza, 2013). In fact, the stored-network approach is among the most widely adopted and persistent theoretical approaches within cognitive psychology.

Semantic Networks and Spreading Activation

Figure 10.8 Simplified Version of Collins and Quillian's (1969) Taxonomic Hierarchy Model

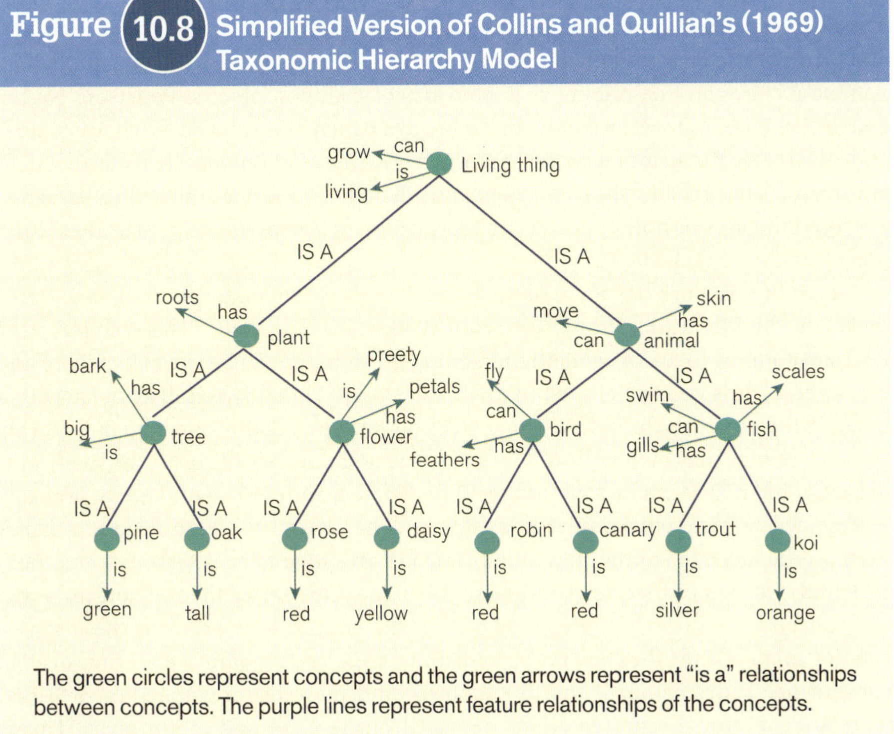

The green circles represent concepts and the green arrows represent "is a" relationships between concepts. The purple lines represent feature relationships of the concepts.

Feature Comparisons Approaches

An alternative to the stored network view is that hierarchical relationships are computed using reasoning processes rather than being directly stored in a semantic network. In this approach, deciding how concepts are related involves comparing features of the two concepts. In other words, if you were encountering a tapir for the first time, and trying to decide whether it is an animal (see Photo 10.7) you would compare the features stored with the concept "animal" to the features of the tapir (a roughly pig-shaped herbaceous mammal found in regions of the Southern Hemisphere). Given that tapirs share features with animals (e.g., can move and have skin, eyes, ears, and mouth), you would make the inference that they are considered animals. Typicality effects would reflect the degree of overlapping similarity of features.

Recently, several other feature-based models have been proposed using a variety of frameworks. While the details of these accounts are complex and beyond the scope of our current review, they are similar in that none of the models includes explicit representation of hierarchical conceptual structure (and in some cases no direct representations of concepts). However, even without these relationships explicitly represented, the models can simulate the effects demonstrated in the research (e.g., Hampton, 1997; Murphy, Hampton, & Milovanovic, 2012).

Vladimir1965/istock/Thinkstock

Photo 10.7 A tapir.

Neuroscience-Inspired Approaches

Patients with semantic dementia suffer from the progressive impairment of their conceptual knowledge. Elizabeth

Warrington (1975) described three patients who had impairments in their conceptual knowledge reflected in deteriorated vocabulary (both production and comprehension) and their knowledge about the properties of objects. These patients often had difficulty naming pictures and describing characteristics of common objects. Patterson, Nestor, and Rogers (2007) showed a picture of a zebra to a patient who replied that it was a horse and asked what the stripes were for. Neuroscientists have examined the pattern of deficits that patients exhibit (those with semantic dementia as well as other disorders) and proposed theories of how concepts are represented in our brains (e.g., Barsalou, 2010; Mahon & Caramazza, 2009).

Much of this work has focused on "where" in the brain concepts are located. In a review of the literature, Thompson-Schill (2003, p. 288) wrote, "The search for the neuroanatomical locus of semantic memory has simultaneously led us nowhere and everywhere." It is widely believed that our conceptual knowledge is distributed across multiple regions of the brain, involving areas for both perception and action. Knowing about an orange may involve how it looks (round and orange), the taste, the smell, how to peel it, and how it can be split into sections. These features of an orange are probably represented in different brain regions. One of the central theoretical questions has been on the mechanism that ties all of these features together. Patterson et al. (2007) reviewed two sets of theories addressing this issue. One set of theories suggests that our concepts are directly represented within the connections between these sensorimotor areas. Other theories propose distinct areas of the brain (sometimes called convergence zones or hubs) that function to bind these features together such that there are conceptual representations distinct from sensory and motor areas. This is similar to the ideas described in Chapter 5 about how episodic memories are encoded and stored, where the relevant features (e.g., sensory features) are stored in the appropriate areas of the cortex (cortical areas specialized for that sense) and features bind during encoding.

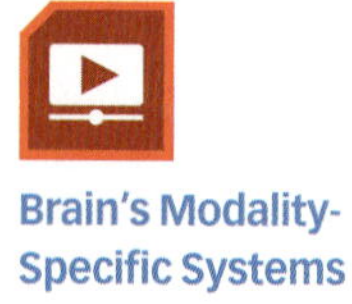

Brain's Modality-Specific Systems

Figure 10.9 represents these two views. The top half of the figure represents the approaches in which concepts are represented in the network of connections. The green lines represent the connections between the different cortical systems. The left side of the figure shows the widely distributed brain regions involved in representing objects. These areas correspond to regions responsible for the processing of sensory, motor, and linguistic information. The right side of the figure shows schematic models of the proposed conceptual systems. The bottom half of the figure represents the approaches in which the conceptual system includes an area of convergence (shown in pink in the bottom left part of the figure) where information from different cortical regions is bound together. Connections between the cortical regions and the convergence zone are depicted by the red lines.

Stop and Think

10.7. What are superordinate, basic, and subordinate levels of concepts?

10.8. What empirical evidence suggests that basic-level concepts are processed differently from other levels of concepts?

10.9. How do network models represent the hierarchical structure of concepts?

Summary of Conceptual Organization

Concepts are not isolated representations floating around in unstructured semantic memory spaces. Rather, concepts appear to operate in relatively stable and predictable organizational structures. While the structure of these systems is clearly related to each individual's concepts and experience, there is remarkable similarity between individuals across languages and cultures. We group things together into similar

Figure 10.9 Two Theoretical Approaches Described in Patterson et al. (2007)

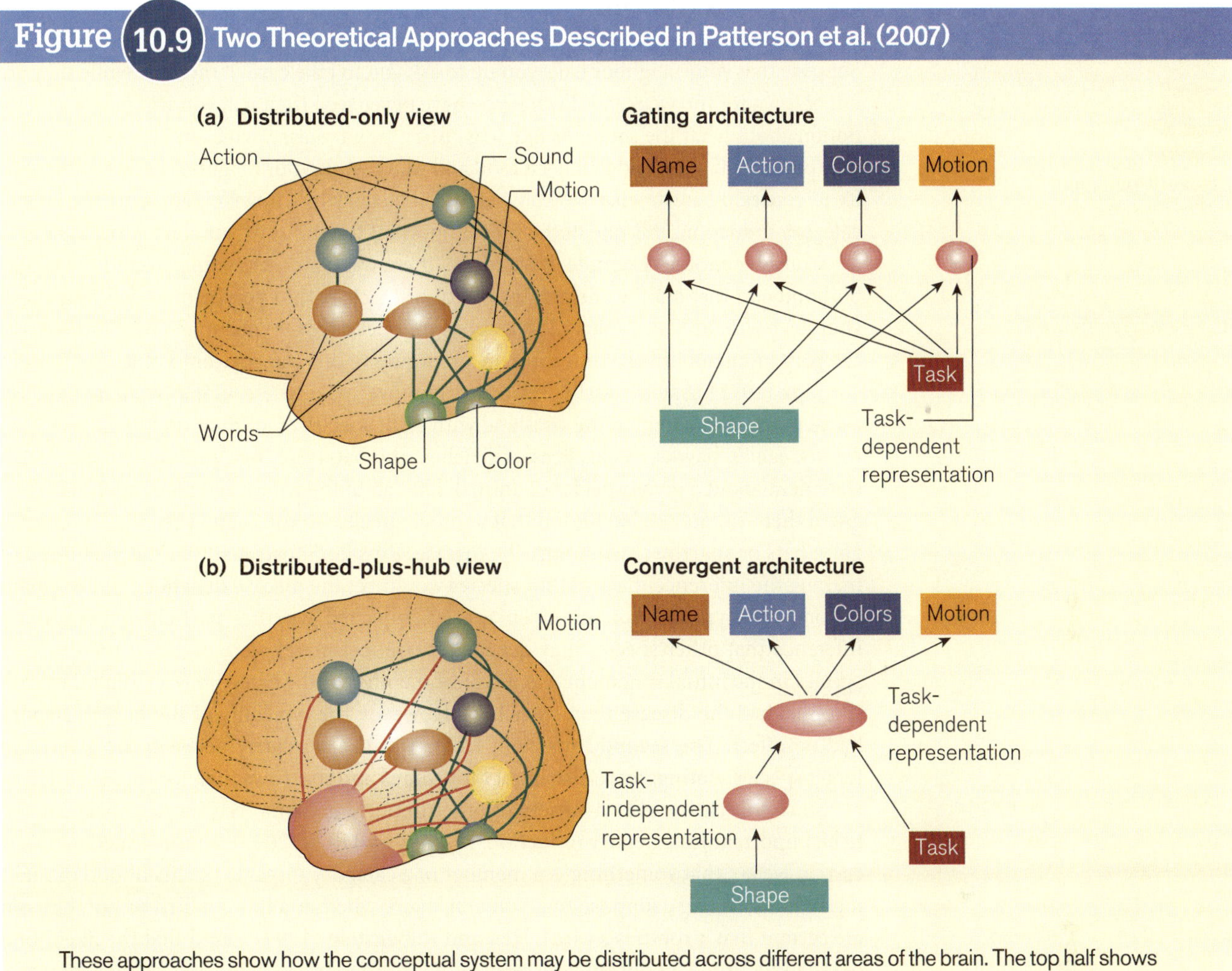

These approaches show how the conceptual system may be distributed across different areas of the brain. The top half shows the concepts as a network of connections. The bottom half shows the concepts as a separate bound convergence zone.

SOURCE: Patterson, K., Nestor, P. J., & Rogers, T. T. (2007). Where do you know what you know? The representation of semantic knowledge in the human brain. Nature Reviews: Neuroscience, 8, 976–987.

categories and typically treat particular kinds of categories as basic for many tasks. How and why we represent these regularities is a matter of ongoing empirical and theoretical debate.

Using Concepts: Beyond Categorization

Up until this point we have focused our review on research investigating how we use concepts to categorize the world around us. However, we use categories for other purposes as well. We use concepts to make predictions about the properties of new objects and categories. This process is called category induction. Our use of stereotypes to make predictions about people is based on social concepts. We can also combine concepts productively, which may result in the combination of new concepts. There are also individual differences in what we know and have experience with. So one might ask how the conceptual systems for experts may differ from those of novices. Explorations of how we use concepts beyond categorization processes have implications for theories of how they are represented in our cognitive systems. The final section of this chapter briefly reviews the research on some of these other conceptual processes.

Category Induction

Category Induction

Suppose that your neighbor calls you up to ask you to take care of their cat while they are out of town for the weekend. Even if you have never seen their cat, you will have a general notion about what the cat looks like (e.g., furry, pointed ears, whiskers) and know that it may purr if you pet it and will need food and water while your neighbor is away. This ability to generalize from what we know about a category to a novel object is an example of category induction. It is one of the most important functions of our conceptual system.

Consider another example. If I told you there was a sickness going around the neighborhood and that another neighbor's parrot was sick, would you be more worried about your pet parrot or your canary? What about your pet dog? Or your son? These instances of category induction involve inferring the properties of one category onto other categories.

Rips (1975) systematically examined how we make these kinds of inferences. He asked participants to imagine an island with eight species of animals on it (i.e., sparrows, robins, eagles, hawks, ducks, geese, ostriches, and bats). He then presented them with a statement about a given species of animal, like "all of the robins have a disease." He then asked them to rate the likelihood that another species on the island (i.e., the target category: bats or sparrows) would get the disease. Rips demonstrated that the likelihood of making the inference that another species would get the disease depended on two main factors. The typicality of the given species impacted whether participants made the inference that other species may get the disease. Estimates were higher if the diseased species in the initial statement was a typical member of the category (e.g., higher ratings if robins had the disease than ostriches). However, the typicality of the target category had no effect. The second important factor was the similarity between the given and target species. Ratings were also higher for robins and sparrows than for robins and bats.

Since this early study, a variety of other important characteristics have been shown to be important for category induction. Murphy and Ross (2005) demonstrated that how certain we are that something is a member of a category impacts the likelihood of making inductions (e.g., suppose that you aren't sure whether a bat is a bird or not, but you are certain that a robin is a bird). Heit and Rubenstein (1994) found that the likelihood of the induction depends on how relevant it is to the kind of categories being compared. For example, you are more likely to make an inference about an anatomical property (e.g., the heart rate) than a behavioral property (e.g., migration patterns) between two species that are both mammals (e.g., a bear and a whale). However, if the two categories are instead related by virtue of their environment (a tuna and a whale both live in the sea), then you are more likely to make the induction about a behavioral property (e.g., migration patterns). In other words, our world knowledge about how properties are related to their categories has an impact on the inferences we make between categories. Similarly, Lassaline (1996) showed that the sharing of causal relationships of features between categories impacts inductions. For example, suppose that you were told that

1. A tenrec has a weak immune system, pale skin, and an acute sense of smell.
2. A spinosa has a weak immune system and pale skin.

Then you were asked about the likelihood that a spinosa has an acute sense of smell. The likelihood of making the induction increased if participants were also given a causal relationship between some of the features of the animals (e.g., for both animals a weak immune system causes their pale skins).

Stereotypes

We also make inductive inferences in our day-to-day social lives. Imagine that you are attending a local neighborhood mixer and are introduced to Steve. Steve seems friendly and outgoing, is dressed head to toe in black, and has spiked bleached-blond hair. He splits time discussing the different qualities of Fender and Gibson guitars and the novel he recently finished. If somebody were to ask you whether you thought Steve was a professional musician or a psychology professor, chances are pretty high you would answer that he is a musician. We often make decisions like these based on a person's appearance, actions, and the context to classify the person into social categories. These processes appear very similar to those used when we examined the object in Photo 10.1. Once we recognize it as a type of fruit, we infer many properties, such as that it is edible and it may be sweet and have seeds.

Implicit Association Test

Much of what we read or hear about on the news is about the negative consequences of using stereotypes, particularly with respect to targets of social stereotyping behaviors. Why do we use stereotypes when we make judgments and decisions about people? Social psychologists have adopted many of the conceptual theories discussed here when developing theories of how and why we use stereotypes. One common view is that using stereotypes is a fundamental and cognitively efficient way to interact in social contexts (Macrae, Milne, & Bodenhausen, 1994). It has been proposed that stereotypes are involved as part of a two-stage process (e.g., Banaji & Greenwald, 1994, Devine, 1989). The first stage is an automatic activation of stereotypic knowledge within some kind of stored representation of knowledge. In other words, when we encounter other people, we quickly sort them into social categories based on their readily available features. In the encounter with Steve, we may initially categorize him as a musician based on his appearance and his interest in guitars. This initial stage may later be followed by a second, more controlled deliberate stage of processing (see Chapters 4 and 12 for more discussion of automatic and controlled processing). As we learn more about Steve (e.g., that he works at the local university and does research examining scientific reasoning), we are able to overcome the initial stereotyping processes and correctly categorize him as being a psychology professor (Macrae, Bodenhausen, & Milne, 1995).

A common assumption in these theories is that the stereotypic knowledge is learned and represented in the same way as the conceptual systems we have been discussing in this chapter. In their review, James Hilton and William von Hippel (1996, p. 240) define stereotypes as "beliefs about characteristics, attributes, and behaviors of members of certain groups. More than just beliefs about groups, they are also theories of how and why certain attributes go together." Brewer, Dull, and Lui (1981) demonstrated that stereotypes of the elderly may be represented hierarchically (e.g., subordinates: grandmother, elder statesman, senior citizen) and that within this hierarchy most stereotypical behaviors appear to operate at a basic level, rather than at more general superordinate or subordinate levels. Findings like these support the notion that stereotype conceptual representations may operate in much the same way as our more general conceptual system.

Expertise

Look back at Figure 10.1 and name as many of the birds as you can. If you are like me, you may not feel like you know a lot about birds. However, you may know somebody who knows a lot about birds (e.g., the person reads about birds, often goes on bird-watching vacations). How might being an expert about a particular domain impact our concepts and organization of concepts within that area of expertise?

Expertise Effects Demonstration

Murphy and Wright (1984) compared feature lists generated for psychological disturbances (e.g., childhood emotional disorders) by groups, with levels of experience ranging from expert (e.g., practicing clinical psychologists) to novice (e.g., undergraduates). Their results indicated that experts have richer conceptual representations and higher levels of agreement in their feature lists for categories. Tanaka and Taylor (1991) examined the hierarchical conceptual structures for samples of bird and dog experts. They found that within their areas of expertise (e.g., the dog conceptual space for the dog experts), experts' basic levels of categorization shifted to a lower level of the hierarchy (e.g., to a level that nonexperts typically considered subordinate). However, when those same experts were tested in a domain outside of their area (e.g., the bird conceptual space for dog experts), they considered the usual level of the hierarchy to be the basic level. Medin, Lynch, Coley, and Atran (1997) examined categorization and inductive reasoning in three types of tree experts (landscapers, taxonomists, and parks maintenance workers). They found that the different group experts structured their conceptual systems differently. Landscapers tended to structure their categories along goal-derived purposes (e.g., how the trees are used), while taxonomists and maintenance workers structured their categories along scientific and folk-defined taxonomies, respectively. However, across types of experts, inductive reasoning suggested that the genus-level categories were treated as the basic level of their hierarchies.

Conceptual Combination

Think about an apple. What features would you list that make up the prototypical apple? Are the colors white or brown on your list? Probably not. Now consider the term "peeled apple." Chances are that if you were to list the features of the combined concept it would include the feature of white (and maybe brown if you think about what happens to a peeled apple when exposed to the air for a few minutes). We opened this chapter with "Game night is always a big hit at our house." If we consider word meanings as labels that represent concepts (see Chapter 9 for more discussion of word meaning and concepts), then we can think of a sentence as representing a large complex concept made up of the combination of smaller concepts. How do we combine individual concepts into larger, more complex concepts?

Stop and Think

10.10. What is category induction? What factors have been shown to impact the processes of category induction?

10.11. How are stereotypes related to concepts?

10.12. How does expertise impact conceptual organization?

Most of the work on conceptual combination has focused on relatively small combinations (e.g., *peeled apple, game night*). Research suggests that the process is not simply the intersection of the two categories (e.g., the concept "game night" is not the things that are both in the categories of "game" and "night"). Smith and Osherson (1984) presented participants with pictures like those in Photo 10.8. They found that a picture of a red apple was judged to be more typical of the combined concept "red apple" than it was of either simple concept "apple" or "red things." Interestingly, for atypical things like a picture of a brown apple, the effect is even larger. In this case the picture was rated as somewhat typical of "brown things," not typical of "apples," and very typical of "brown apples."

Jupiterimages/Creatas/Thinkstock

Hemera Technologies/PhotoObjects.net/Thinkstock

Photo 10.8 A red apple and a brown apple.

Standard prototype and exemplar models did not have mechanisms that could easily account for effects like these. Smith, Osherson, Rips, and Keane (1988) proposed a model in which concepts are represented as prototype schemata with dimensions and values (see our earlier discussion of Cohen & Murphy, 1984). While the Smith et al. (1988) model captured the early data well, further research has revealed limitations of the model. For example, sometimes it is difficult to predict which dimensions of the combined categories modify each other. For example, compare the changes to "apple" and "farmer" when modified in "organic apple" and "organic farmer."

The Future of Research and Theory of Concepts

The review in this chapter reflects many of the central findings in the psychological investigation of concepts and knowledge. The theories presented represent the dominant approaches developed to explain the research. At this point you may be asking yourself, "Which approach is the correct one?" Unfortunately, there isn't a simple answer to this seemingly easy question. None of the theoretical approaches can account for all of the data. In fact, the research reviewed in this chapter focused largely on relatively simple concepts of concrete objects. Researchers have also identified and explored other interesting aspects of concepts. Given what you now know about concepts, think about some of the following questions: How do children acquire concepts?, Are there differences between natural and artificial categories?, How are abstract concepts like "love" and "justice" and verb concepts like "run" represented?, and Where and how are concepts represented in the brain? Rather than abandon the approaches, researchers continue to develop and test new, more complex approaches.

THINKING ABOUT RESEARCH

As you read the following summary of a research study in psychology, think about the following questions:

1. What aspects of concepts are examined in this study?
2. What are the independent variables in this study?
3. What are the dependent variables in this study?
4. What alternative explanations can you come up with to explain the results of this study?

Study Reference

Sloutsky, V. M., Kloos, H., & Fisher, A. V. (2007). When looks are everything: Appearance similarity versus kind information in early induction. *Psychological Science, 18,* 179–185.

Purpose of the study: The authors examined the categorization and inductive processing of 4- and 5-year-olds. Of particular interest was whether young children base their categorical inductions on category membership or physical similarity. This summary describes only the first experiment of the research article.

Method of the study: The researchers presented children with pictures of artificial buglike animals ("ziblets" and "flurps," see Figure 10.10). The animals were created by combining six attributes: body, tail, antennae, wings, buttons, and fingers. The two categories of animals were defined by the relationship between the number of buttons and fingers: one category had more fingers than buttons, the other fewer fingers than buttons. The children were told a story about getting a new pet from the store. The store had nice, friendly ziblets and wild, dangerous flurps. The children were told the rules about how to tell ziblets from flurps (by counting their fingers and buttons), along with examples of each type. During a learning phase, the children were presented with novel bugs and asked to categorize them as either ziblets or flurps and were provided feedback as to whether they were correct (along with a reminder of the distinguishing rules). This was then followed by categorization trials (like the learning trials but without feedback). Then the children were given an induction task, consisting of three animals. For one animal, they were told that it had a hidden property (e.g., it has thick blood), and they were then asked to select from the other two which one had the same hidden property. The researchers were able to construct stimuli so that they could directly compare category membership against similarity of appearance. An additional final categorization task was performed to ensure that the children had not forgotten the categorization rule.

Results of the study: The results are presented in Figure 10.11. The children demonstrated clear use of category membership in the categorization task. In contrast, on the induction task, the children rarely used category membership when making their selections. Instead, the evidence suggests they used physical similarity to the

(Continued)

(Continued)

Figure 10.10 Stimuli From the Sloutsky et al. (2007) Study

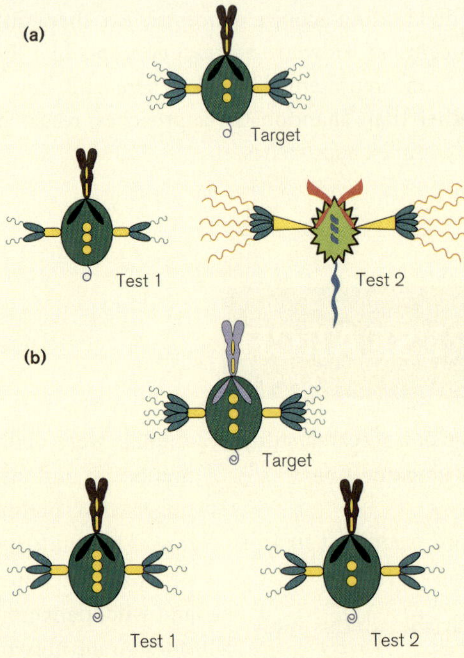

SOURCE: Figure 2, Sloutsky, V. M., Kloos, H., & Fisher, A. V. (2007). When looks are everything: Appearance similarity versus kind information in early induction. *Psychological Science, 18*, 179–185.

Figure 10.11 Results From the Sloutsky et al. (2007) Study

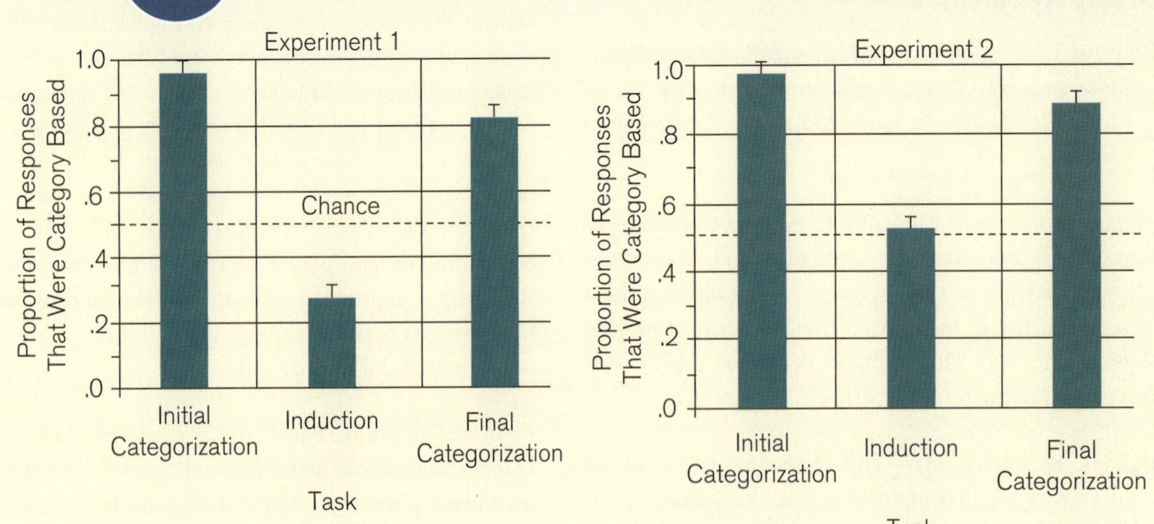

The bars indicate the proportion of the responses that were categorically based.

SOURCE: Figure 3, Sloutsky, V. M., Kloos, H., & Fisher, A. V. (2007). When looks are everything: Appearance similarity versus kind information in early induction. *Psychological Science, 18*, 179–185.

item with the given hidden trait to make their inductive selection.

Conclusions of the study: The authors concluded that young children (4- and 5-year-olds) able to make categorization judgments with new categories do not use category membership to make inductive inferences.

CHAPTER REVIEW

Summary

- **What is a concept?**

  A concept is a mental representation of a category of things in the world. The conceptual representation is a mental organization of the knowledge we have about categories of things stored in our long-term memories.

- **How are concepts mentally represented?**

  The chapter reviewed three main approaches. The classical approach of categories as definitions has generally been refuted on both theoretical and empirical grounds. The prototype approach is that concepts are represented as an abstract average of representative features of the items in a category. The exemplar approach is that concepts are based on similarities to retrieved memories of previously encountered category members. The knowledge-based approach suggests that conceptual representations must also include theories about how different features are related.

- **How are concepts and knowledge organized?**

  Concepts appear to be organized hierarchically, with general superordinate groupings and more specific subordinate groupings. There is theoretical debate as to whether these hierarchical relationships are directly represented in long-term memory or computed through feature comparisons. Additionally, certain levels of the hierarchy are treated as basic-level concepts, showing preferred processing.

- **What do we use concepts for?**

  Concepts may underlie most of our cognitive processes. We use them to categorize things, allowing what we already know about a concept to apply to new instances. Similarly, we can use concepts to make inferences about other similar concepts. We can also combine categories to productively create new and potentially more complex concepts.

Chapter Quiz

1. The classical approach to concepts is that they are mental representations of
   a) the averaged features of all members of a category.
   b) the collection of all retrieved memories of encounters with members of a category.
   c) a definition consisting of necessary and sufficient features of all members of a category.
   d) how and why features of category members are related to one another.
2. Rips et al. (1973) demonstrated that people verify "a robin is a bird" faster than "a chicken is a bird." This is an example of
   a) an exemplar effect.
   b) a typicality effect.
   c) a basic-level effect.
   d) category induction.
3. Consider the concept of an apple. Match the concept label with its label within a conceptual hierarchy.
   a) Basic level
   b) Superordinate level
   c) Subordinate level

   ___ Golden delicious
   ___ Fruit
   ___ Apple

4. A schema representation for the concept "bird" consists of
   a) an unordered list of common features.
   b) a list of common features ordered in terms of their typicality.
   c) a structured set of dimensions with particular values for the dimensions.
   d) all of the recalled memories of past experiences with birds.
5. Imagine you read in the paper that a particular model of automobile had recently been recalled because of electrical issues. Based on the research on category induction, which of the following inferences would you most likely make?
   (a) That your car might develop electrical issues
   (b) That your house might develop electrical issues
   (c) That your truck might develop electrical issues
   (d) That your car might develop mechanical issues
6. Summarize the methods and conclusions from the Allen and Brooks (1991) study.
7. Summarize the methods and conclusions from the Lin and Murphy (1997) study.
8. Compare and contrast the exemplar and prototype views of concepts.
9. Why is the lack of transitive inheritance properties (Hampton, 1982) a problem for the Collins and Quillian (1969) model?
10. How does expertise in an area impact our conceptual representations?
11. How are stereotypes similar to other concept representations?

Key Terms

Basic-level concept 253
Cognitive economy 254
Exemplar approach 246
Prototype approach 244
Subordinate concept 254
Superordinate concept 254
Typicality effect 242

Stop and Think Answers

10.1. What are necessary and sufficient properties of a concept?

Necessary and sufficient properties are those that define whether something is or is not a member of a category.

10.2. What are the major theoretical and empirical arguments against concepts as definitions?

Necessary and sufficient property definitions are generally difficult to derive for naturally occurring categories. Additionally, category membership does not appear to be all or none. Instead, some members of a category differ in how typical they are of the concept.

10.3. What is a prototype? How are prototypes used to represent concepts?

A prototype is an abstract average of representative features of the items in a category. Category membership is determined by comparing the features of an object with the features of the prototype representation.

10.4. What is an exemplar? How are exemplars used to represent concepts?

Exemplars are retrieved memories of previously encountered things. Category membership is determined by comparing the features of an object with the features of recalled exemplars of different categories.

10.5. How are the prototype and exemplar approaches similar?

Both the prototype and exemplar approaches rely on similarity comparisons of features between the current object and representations retrieved from memory.

10.6. How might world knowledge impact conceptual representations?

Theories about how features are related to one another have been shown to have an impact on how items are categorized and what kinds of categorical inferences are made.

10.7. What are superordinate, basic, and subordinate levels of concepts?

Evidence suggests that concepts are organized hierarchically, with general superordinate groupings and more specific subordinate groupings. Basic-level concepts are particular levels of the hierarchy shown to be processed preferentially. Members of basic-level concepts show high levels of similarity within their category and distinctiveness from things belonging to other concepts.

10.8. What empirical evidence suggests that basic-level concepts are processed differently from other levels of concepts?

There are many demonstrations of basic-level preferences. These include how children tend to learn basic-level category names early and how basic-level names allow for faster categorization and naming of pictures and show higher levels of category induction.

10.9. How do network models represent the hierarchical structure of concepts?

A common assumption in many theories of conceptual structure is that hierarchical relationships are directly stored as part of the concepts. For example, the concepts "robin" and "bird" would share an "is a" link. Alternatively, some approaches suggest that hierarchical relationships may be computed through feature comparisons. In other words, we can decide that a robin is a bird by virtue of the feature overlap between the concepts "bird" and "robin."

10.10. What is category induction? What factors have been shown to impact the processes of category induction?

Our ability to generalize from what we know about a category to a novel object is an example of category induction. The typicality of category members and the feature similarity between the two concepts involved in the induction have been shown to impact the likelihood of making the induction.

10.11. How are stereotypes related to concepts?

Stereotypes have been characterized as conceptual representations of social categories. Like general concepts, stereotypes have been demonstrated to have hierarchical structure and basic levels.

10.12. How does expertise impact conceptual organization?

Experts have more experience and knowledge within particular domains. Evidence suggests that within their domains of expertise, experts may develop different hierarchical structures related to their experience and knowledge, as well as treat lower levels as their preferred basic level of representations.

Student Study Site

Sharpen your skills with SAGE edge at **edge.sagepub.com/mcbridecp**

SAGE edge for students provides a personalized approach to help you accomplish your coursework goals in an easy-to-use learning environment.

Go to edge.sagepub.com/mcbridecp for additional exercises and web resources. Select Chapter 10, Concepts and Knowledge, for chapter-specific resources. All of the links listed in the margins of this chapter are accessible via this site.

Philip Lee Harvey/The Image Bank/Getty Images

Problem Solving

Questions to Consider

- How often and what kind of problems do you solve every day?
- How do you solve problems: through trial and error, through conscious deliberation, or do solutions just suddenly occur to you?
- Why are some problems more difficult to solve than others?
- What gets in your way when trying to solve problems?
- How do expert problem solvers differ from novices?

Introduction: Problem Solving in Daily Life

Consider what might be a typical morning. Your alarm goes off and you stumble out of bed faced with a decision about what to wear that day. You've got a job interview in the afternoon, but you also want to hit the gym in the morning. You decide to dress in your sweats now, carry your nice clothes, and shower at the gym. You've got time for a quick breakfast, but you realize that you are out of milk. You are going to need to figure out a way to go to the store to buy some, but with your interview followed by your evening section of your psychology seminar course, you aren't sure when you'll have the time. But for now you are hungry, so you sit down to a cup of coffee and the Sudoku puzzle in the morning paper. You notice that there is a new kind of puzzle, KenKen. It looks similar to Sudoku, but as you try to solve it, you find that it is much harder for you to solve than the Sudoku you do every morning. After trying to finish your puzzles you head upstairs to pack your interview clothes, and a solution suddenly hits you. Instead of packing the clothes into your gym bag, you grab a small cooler and pack them into that. You realized that you should have time to grab some milk from the corner store before your interview, and it should keep cold in the cooler during both the interview and your seminar class. Happy with this solution, you head to the gym (and on the way begin to wonder what you will do with the cooler during your interview).

Types of Problems and Strategies

This opening story illustrates how our days are full of problems we try to find solutions for. The problems we face vary in size and scope: Some are little (e.g., solving the puzzle in the newspaper, figuring out what to wear), while others are larger (e.g., how to get a good job). Many people consider our problem-solving abilities to be the prototype of "higher thought," a centerpiece of our cognitive processes. Typically, the problem-solving process has been described as a cycle of stages (e.g., Bransford & Stein, 1993; Dewey, 1910; Polya, 1954; Pretz, Naples, & Sternberg, 2003; Wallas, 1926). These stages typically include processes like the following:

- *Recognize and identify the problem*
- *Define and mentally represent the problem*
- *Develop a solution strategy*
- *Allocate mental resources for solving the problem*
- *Monitor progress toward the goal and evaluate the solution*

This cycle is not intended to imply serial stages of processing. Instead, it is intended to describe the kinds of cognitive processes involved in solving problems. This chapter focuses on research and theory on the first four stages of the cycle.

Recognizing and Identifying a Problem

Researchers studying problem solving typically describe a problem as a situation in which there is a difference between a current state and a desired goal state. Problem solving is the process of developing a solution (or set of solutions) designed to change the state of affairs

Figure 11.1 A Sudoku Puzzle

	8				2			
			7	3	9		2	
9		7				3		5
	4	2	1	9		6		
1		5				9		4
		9		8	4	5	1	
2		6				7		8
	9		8	7	1			
			5				3	

Try to fill in the empty cells with numbers from 1 to 9. Each three-by-three box, each row, and each column may not have any repeated numbers (each may only have the numbers 1 to 9 in them).

from the current state to the goal state. Consider three parts of our opening story that may be considered problems. Getting dressed in the morning involves the need to move from the state of undress (the current state) to getting dressed for the day (the goal state). On normal days you may not consider this a problem since you probably have a ready solution available. However, in our story special circumstances require a different solution, one in which you can dress appropriately for both a job interview and a workout at the gym. Rather than using your usual dressing solution, you have to come up with an alternative plan. Solving the puzzle in the morning paper is also an example of a problem. Consider the Sudoku puzzle in Figure 11.1 (the solution is found in Figure 11.16 at the end of the chapter). A Sudoku puzzle is typically a nine-by-nine grid with some of the cells blank and the others containing numbers. Your task is to complete the grid by filling in the empty cells with numbers, with the constraint that each row, column, and three-by-three cell doesn't have any repeated numbers. Sudoku puzzles are set up so that there is only one correct solution. These features make the Sudoku a **well-defined problem**. This doesn't mean that it is necessarily an easy problem to solve but rather that the goals and constraints are known, and by applying particular procedures a correct solution can be found. In contrast, the problems of getting a job, getting dressed for the day, or even arranging your day so that you can get milk, work out, and go to class and a job interview don't typically have a single correct solution. Problems like these are considered **ill-defined problems**. Ill-defined problems lack clear paths between the current and goal states. As a result, ill-defined problems are often much more difficult to mentally represent, identify solution strategies for, and solve. Goel (2010) argues that performance patterns of brain-damaged patients (particularly those with frontal lobe lesions) suggest that there are neuropsychological differences between well- and ill-defined problems.

Well-defined problem: a problem that has a clearly defined goal state and constraints

Ill-defined problem: a problem that lacks a clearly defined goal state and constraints

Stop and Think

11.1. Make a list of some of the problems you have already faced today.

11.2. For each problem in Stop and Think 11.1, identify the initial and goal states and how you went about solving the problem.

11.3. Which of the problems in Stop and Think 11.1 would you classify as well-defined and which as ill-defined? What characteristics of the problems led you to classify them in that way?

Defining and Representing Problems

Defining and representing a problem is the process of stating the scope and goal of the problem and organizing the knowledge needed for addressing the problem. This knowledge includes mentally representing the current and goal states, the rules or constraints, and the allowable operations available to solve the problem.

Moving Pennies Activity

For example, consider the pennies in Figure 11.2. The problem is to move two pennies so that all of the pennies are touching three and only three other pennies. Give the problem a try. Can you find the solution? The solution, given in Figure 11.3, is the same for initial states (a) and (b). People typically find the problem difficult to solve because they represent the problem in two dimensions, as if sliding the pennies on a table. As a result, they don't consider lifting the pennies and stacking them. In other words, they don't consider moving the pennies in the third dimension an allowable operation. Initial state (b) is usually found to be more difficult than (a) because in (a) there are no places where they can slide a penny so that it touches three other pennies. As a result, people are quicker to change their representation of the problem in (a) to allow for stacking of the coins. In contrast, people who start with (b) typically maintain their two-dimensional representation of the problem longer because there are some places where they can move the pennies that touch three others, suggesting that they are getting closer to the final goal state.

Dominos and a Chessboard Activity

Consider another problem illustrated in Figure 11.4. The task is to determine whether you can cover an eight-by-eight checkerboard with dominos. Each domino can cover two checker squares. The catch is that the checkerboard has been distorted by the removal of the two diagonal corner squares. Give it a try. Can you cover the entire board with dominos (the dominos can't hang off of the edges or be altered in any way)? If you aren't certain of your answer, consider the same problem but with Figure 11.5 instead. Most people find the problem much easier to solve when they alter their representation of the problem this way. Here you can easily see that both of the removed squares are white and that each domino will cover one red square and one white square. However, if two white squares are removed, then there are thirty-two red squares and thirty white squares and no way to cover the entire board with the dominos.

Figure 11.2 Pennies Problem: Is There a Way to Move Two Pennies Such That All of the Pennies Touch Three and Only Three Other Pennies?

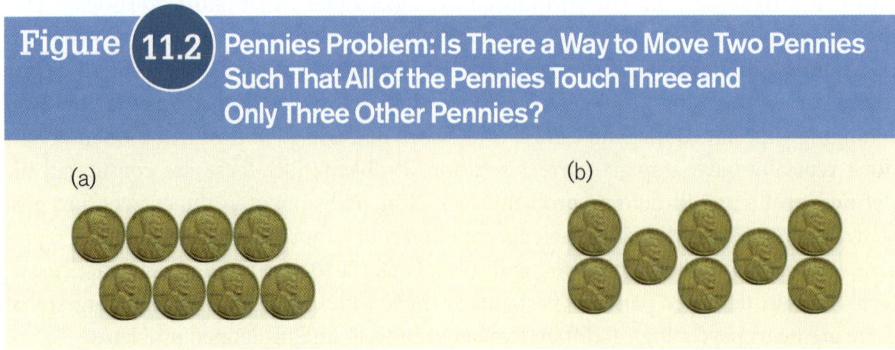

Photo of penny: Photos.com/Photos.com/Thinkstock

Figure 11.3 Solution to the Pennies Problem

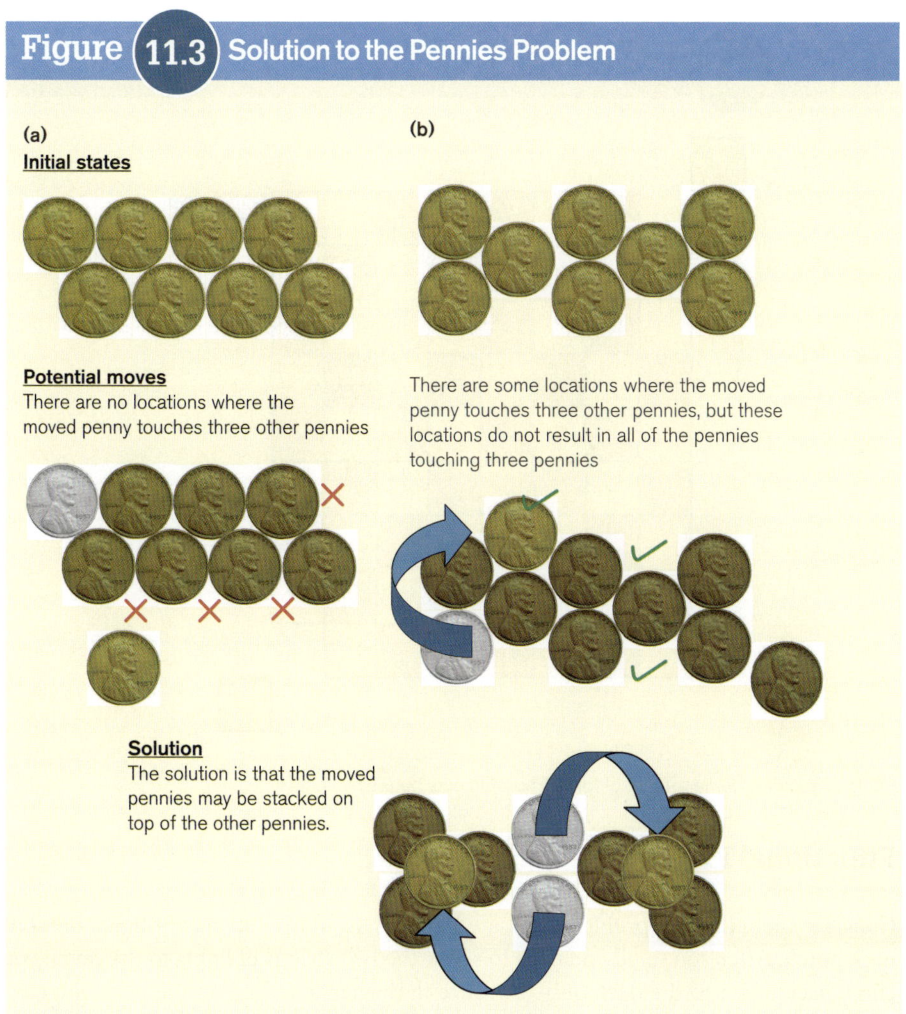

(a)
Initial states
(b)
Potential moves
There are no locations where the moved penny touches three other pennies
There are some locations where the moved penny touches three other pennies, but these locations do not result in all of the pennies touching three pennies
Solution
The solution is that the moved pennies may be stacked on top of the other pennies.

Photo of penny: Photos.com/Photos.com/Thinkstock

Figure 11.4 Domino and Distorted-Checkerboard Problem

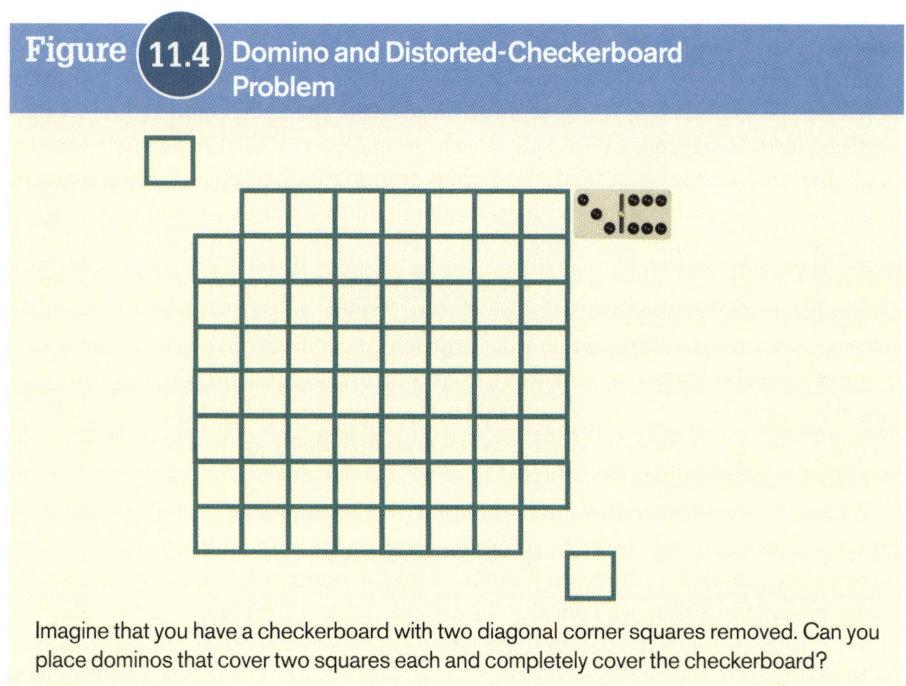

Imagine that you have a checkerboard with two diagonal corner squares removed. Can you place dominos that cover two squares each and completely cover the checkerboard?

Photo of domino: Hemera Technologies/PhotoObjects.net/Thinkstock

Figure 11.5 Variation of the Distorted-Checkerboard Problem

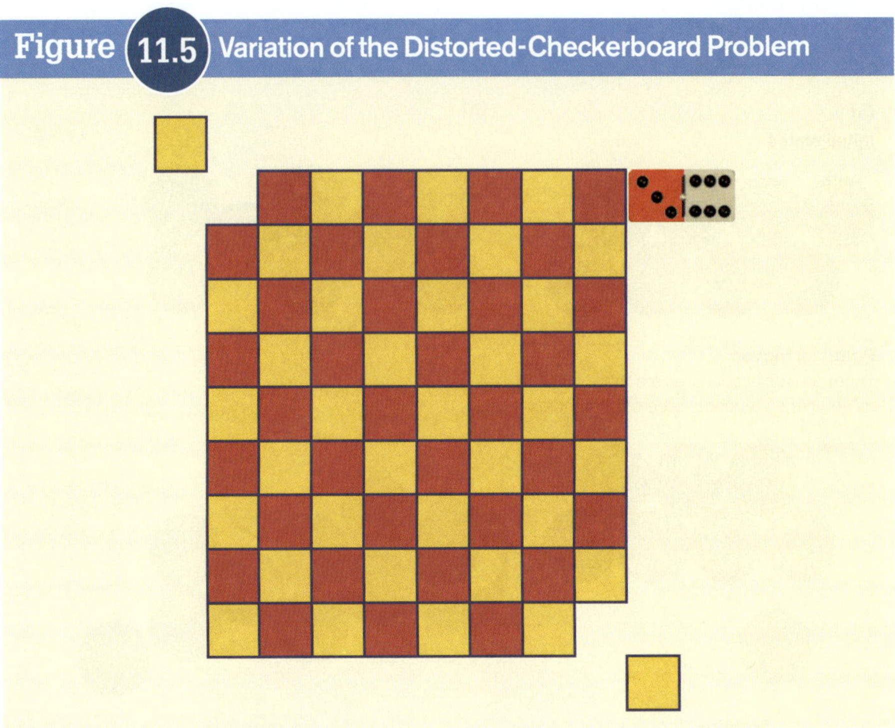

Photo of domino: Hemera Technologies/PhotoObjects.net/Thinkstock

Functional Fixedness

Two Strings Problem Activity

Consider the following problem. You are hanging decorative strings of lights on your back porch. After you finally manage to screw the two strings of lights to the eaves, you climb back down to the deck only to realize that when standing on the deck you can't reach both sets of dangling lights. To make them work you need to plug them into each other. You don't want to climb back up with your screwdriver and take one down. Is there a way to grasp both ends of the lights without going back up the ladder? Many people are stumped by this problem. Here is a hint: The screwdriver is the key to the solution. When most people think of a screwdriver, they think about the function of turning screws. However, for this problem, the screwdriver can be used for a different function. The solution is to tie the screwdriver to one of the strings of lights and swing it back and forth (see Figure 11.6).

Overcoming Functional Fixedness

Functional fixedness is focusing on how things are usually used, while ignoring other potential uses. Gestalt psychologists identified this bias as a common barrier to our ability to solve problems (Maier, 1931). When faced with a problem, we retrieve information about the objects in it (e.g., string lights, ladder, screwdriver) and search for similar problems involving similar objects. When we start developing potential solutions, they are based in part on what functions the objects can perform. In the case of the screwdriver, based on how we've used it before, the functions that we consider probably involve turning screws, not using it as a weight for a pendulum. As a result, the representation of the problem space may not even include using the screwdriver in this way as a potential solution.

Functional fixedness: focusing on how things are typically used and ignoring other potential uses in solving a problem

These three problems demonstrate that the way we represent problems can have a powerful impact on our ability to solve problems. In the pennies problem, if we don't represent the problem in three dimensions, then the solution (stacking the coins) isn't going to be a possibility we consider. In the checkerboard example, representing the problem without colors doesn't preclude finding the correct solution, but it also doesn't highlight the importance of considering neighboring squares as an important feature of

Figure 11.6 The Two String Problem

the problem. The addition of colors to both the board and the dominos spotlights this characteristic, often making it much easier to find the correct solution. In other words, how we mentally represent a problem can both help or hinder finding the solution. The next section describes how we find solutions to problems.

Stop and Think

11.4. Consider the following problem. You have a jug of apple juice and a container of water. After putting both the apple juice and the water into a large pitcher, the apple juice and water remain separate. How does this happen?

11.5. As you consider potential solutions to the problem in Stop and Think 11.4, think about how you mentally represent it. What assumptions about the problem does your mental representation lead you to make?

11.6. A solution to the problem in Stop and Think 11.4 is that the water is frozen in the form of ice cubes. Do you think that you would have thought of the solution if the problem had stated "a tray of water" instead of a "container"?

Developing Solutions to Problems: Approaches and Strategies

Consider again the Sudoku problem in Figure 11.1. Go ahead and try to solve the puzzle, but while you do talk out loud about how you are trying to find the solution. What sorts of things did you find yourself saying? This method of thinking aloud is a commonly used methodology in research on problem solving. Unlike many of the cognitive processes discussed in this book, many of the processes underlying problem solving may be accessible to internal introspection. By having people think aloud while solving problems, researchers may gain insights into how people represent the problem, what information they are attending to, and what strategies they attempt to use. However, one needs to be cautious and keep in mind that some of the processes may not be consciously accessible, and furthermore, people may not report all of what is consciously available (e.g., they may not report strategies they began to consider but then rejected). Consider your own verbal reports of how you tried to solve the Sudoku puzzle. Do you feel that you were able to describe everything that went through your mind as you solved the puzzle? The next sections describe some of the strategies researchers propose we use to solve problems.

Sudoku Activity

Jays and Youngsters Solve Aesop Problem

Associationist Approach: Trial-and-Error Strategy

Early theories of problem solving focused primarily on trial and error. The idea was that when faced with a problem we try out a solution and see if it works. If it doesn't work, then we try another. This process is repeated until the problem is solved. Over time, as we accumulate associations between problems and successful solutions, we use these associations when encountering new problems. If the new problems are similar to old ones, then we will try to apply the solutions we used for the old ones (e.g. Thorndike, 1911). This approach to problem solving is known as the associationist approach.

Stop and Think

11.7. Think about some of the problems you encounter in your own life. What are some situations where you try to solve them through trial and error? Are there ways in which these different situations are similar?

11.8. Are there other problems that you'd never consider trying to use trial and error to solve? Why would trial and error not work well in these situations?

Generally trial-and-error approaches work well when there are relatively few possible solutions. For example, if your problem is trying out what clothes to wear to your job interview and you only have three suits, then you can try each suit on and it won't take very long. However, if you also have three dress shirts and two pairs of nice shoes, then the number of possible combinations quickly grows. Trying each suit with each shirt and each pair of shoes results in eighteen possible combinations (three suits X three shirts X two pairs of shoes).

Now think back to the Sudoku problem. If you have not done many Sudoku problems already, you may go about trying to find the solution using the method of trial and error, filling in all of the empty spaces with numbers and then seeing if your solution fit the puzzle constraints. However, chances are that you would get frustrated with using this strategy for this problem. While it is true that using this method, trying every number in every empty square, will ultimately result in the correct solution to the puzzle, it will likely take a very long time (with forty-five empty slots, and nine possible numbers in each one, there are over a trillion possibilities to check). So while trial and error might work for relatively simple problems, usually other strategies are necessary.

Gestalt Approaches

Insight Learning in a Chimp

Psychologists in the Gestalt tradition of the 1900s argued against purely associationist theories of problem solving (e.g., Duncker, 1945, Köhler, 1959). They argued that associationist theories predicted that problem solving was generally a gradual process and that many nonsensical errors should occur when people try to solve problems. However, when researchers began using think-aloud protocols, it became apparent that problem solvers appeared to use systematic strategies, rather than trial and error. The Gestalt approach is that a problem solver goes beyond past associations, and solutions arise out of new productive processes. These productive processes include creating mental representations of information structured to achieve particular goals (for a similar perspective, see the Gestalt approach to perception in Chapter 3). Often the solution is the result of a sudden breaking away from past associations, resulting in a reorganization of the mental representation of the problem. Other times problems are solved by recognizing that a past problem, even one that differs in surface features, shares an underlying structure and solution with the current problem (e.g., Wertheimer, 1945).

Insight

Using the think-aloud method, Gestalt psychologists noticed that people often get the feeling that the solution to a problem suddenly occurs to them, a kind of "aha" experience, rather than gradually developing over multiple attempted solutions. In our opening story the solution to the problem, to carry the clothing in a cooler, suddenly came upon the person. Think back to when you tried to solve the earlier pennies and checkerboard problems. If you were able to come up with the solution, did you experience it as an "aha" moment, or was it the result of a more gradual solution process?

John Kounios: The Neuroscience Behind Epiphanies

Not all problems are solved using **insight**. Insight problems are typically those in which solvers cannot initially find a solution and have often stopped consciously thinking about the problem, when suddenly the correct solution emerges into consciousness (e.g., Duncker, 1945, Maier, 1931, Metcalfe & Wiebe, 1987). Gestalt psychologists theorized that we unconsciously continued to process the problem, searching for solutions during the incubation period following initial attempts to solve the problem. Much of their research attempted to describe which conditions promoted insightful solutions. They argued that insightful solutions often result when particular barriers to problem solutions are overcome. Some of the barriers they identified are discussed later in this chapter. For example, in our pennies example, the solution required changing from representing the problem as one in a two-dimensional space (so only sliding the coins was allowed) to one in a three-dimensional space (allowing for the coins to be stacked). In this case, insight happened when you suddenly realized that you could restructure how you represent it and the solution to the problem became apparent.

Creativity Test: Insight Problems

While the work of the Gestalt psychologists described the conditions under which insightful problem solving may occur, what exactly insight is has been a controversial research question (e.g., Weisberg, 1988; Weisberg & Alba, 1981). Researchers have proposed a number of processes that may underlie insight problem solving (e.g., Kaplan & Simon, 1990; Knoblich, Ohlsson, Haider, & Rhenius, 1999). For example, Janet Davidson and colleagues (e.g., Davidson, 1995; Davidson & Sternberg, 1986) proposed three mental processes involved: selective encoding, selective combination, and selective comparison. Selective encoding contributes to restructuring so that information originally viewed as irrelevant becomes viewed as relevant. For example, in our checkerboard example, when you mentally added color to the board and domino, the critical information about the importance of neighboring squares becomes relevant. Selective combination is when a previously nonobvious framework for relevant features becomes identified. The realization that the pennies can be moved in three dimensions, not just two, is an example of selective combination. Selective comparison is when you discover a nonobvious connection between new information and prior knowledge.

Figure 11.7 The Nine-Dot Problem: Connect the Dots With Four Straight Lines

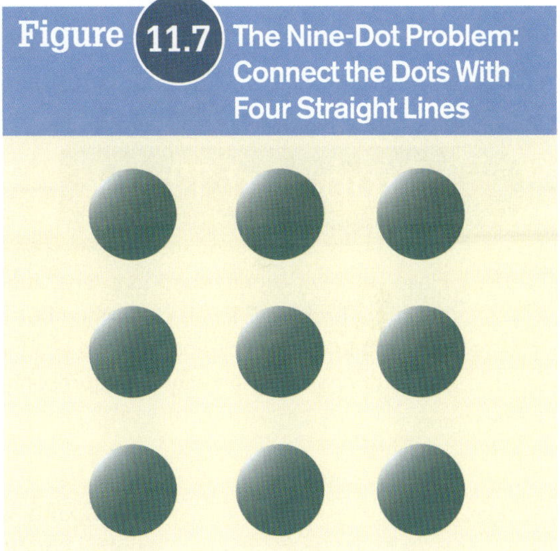

9-Dot Problem Activity

Let's consider another problem. Look at the dots in Figure 11.7. Your task is to connect all of the dots using four straight lines. Go ahead and give it a try. If you are having trouble, think about our solution to the pennies problem where we had to restructure the problem and break outside the boundaries of two dimensions. The key, as in the pennies problem, is to represent the problem without borders (you can find the solution in Figure 11.8). In the pennies problem the borders limited the problem space to two dimensions. In the nine-dot problem, the borders limit the figure to the implied edges of a square made by the arrangement of the dots. If you were able to recognize the similarity between the two solutions (to "think outside the boundaries") to these problems, you were using the process of selective comparison.

Insight: suddenly realizing the solution to a problem

Figure 11.8 The Nine-Dot Solution: The Key Is to Represent the Problem Without Borders

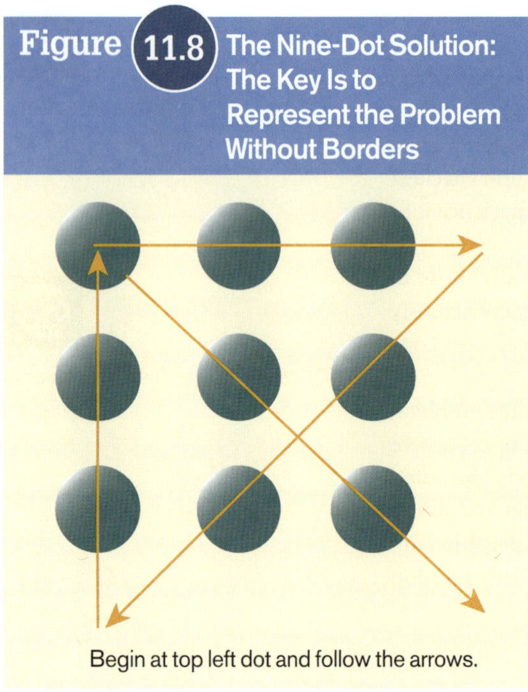

Begin at top left dot and follow the arrows.

The difficulty of the nine-dot problem has been linked to a variety of factors that influence how we mentally represent the problem. Gestalt psychologists argued that perceptual grouping principles (see Chapter 3 for more details) make us think of the nine dots as grouped as a single figure and that the white space around it is background (Maier, 1930). Our attempts to solve the problem are biased such that we limit the lines we draw to stay within the borders of the figure. Disrupting the likelihood of grouping the dots as a single figure can increase the solution rate (Chronicle, Ormerod, & MacGregor, 2001; Kershaw & Ohlsson, 2004). Giving problem solvers the first line or two, reducing the number of possible solutions, increases the solution rate (MacGregor, Ormerod, & Chronicle, 2001). Past experience with problems with similar solutions also can increase solution rates (Kershaw & Ohlsson, 2004; Weisberg & Alba, 1981).

Past experience can be critical for solving problems. If you have encountered a problem before, and were able to solve it, then you can probably solve the current problem using that same solution (in which case you may even think "not a problem"). You have probably done this yourself. When you are working on homework problems assigned at the end of a chapter, do you go back and look at a sample problem that was worked through earlier in the chapter?

Stop and Think

11.9. Have you ever experienced that "aha" feeling when solving a problem? If you can remember what the problem and your solution was, do you think it was the result of changing the way you represented the problem?

Chi and Snyder (2012) examined the role of past experience for solving the nine-dot problem. They used a technique called transcranial direct current stimulation (tDCS) to temporarily inhibit their participants' right anterior temporal lobe (tDCS can also be used to temporarily stimulate as well). tDCS is a noninvasive procedure in which a weak direct current is applied directly to the scalp (see Chapter 2). Chi and Snyder (2012) gave their participants nine minutes to solve the nine-dot problem, three minutes before stimulation, three minutes during stimulation, and three minutes immediately after stimulation. Participants were randomly assigned to either the stimulation condition or a "sham" control condition (in which they did not receive stimulation). They found that 40 percent of the participants who received stimulation were able to solve the problem. In comparison, none of those in the control condition solved it. Chi and Snyder proposed that the stimulation temporarily inhibited their participants' reliance on past experiences, which in this case corresponded to the participants viewing the dot patterns as being bounded by a square. In other words, the stimulation essentially allowed them to think outside of the box and find the solution to the problem.

Mental Set

Cups and Water Problem Activity

Luchins (1942) presented people with the following problem. Imagine that you have three containers of water. You want to end up with 100 cups of water. You start out with three different-sized containers: Container A holds 21 cups, Container B holds 127 cups, and Container C holds 3 cups. How can you measure out 100 cups? The solution is to fill up Container B (127 cups), then remove water from Container B with Container C twice

(127 – 2 × 3 = 121), and then use Container A once to remove water from Container B (121 – 21 = 100). Now you try a few:

Trial 1) Target: 18 cups A: 23, B: 49, C: 4

Trial 2) Target: 21 cups A: 9, B: 42, C: 6

Trial 3) Target: 22 cups A: 18, B: 48, C: 4

Mental Set

Did you notice that all three trials could be solved using the same solution as our original problem (B – 2C – A)? Did you solve all three additional problems in the same way? Go back and look at Trial 3. Did you notice a much more direct solution? You could have just filled A and C and added them together. If you didn't notice this, but instead used the same solution as you did for the others, then you were using a **mental set** bias. Mental set is similar to the functional fixedness bias. We tend to use the same set of solutions for similar problems, even if there are other, simpler solutions available. Both solutions are correct. While the A + C solution may be simpler than the B – 2C – A solution, it is typically more work to come up with that solution given your recent history of using the longer solution. It is faster to recall and use the method you just used than to generate a new possible solution (Bilalic, McLeod, & Gobet, 2008).

Analogical Transfer

In the preceding example of the water containers, all of the puzzles are so similar that you probably thought of them as essentially the same problem. A similar process can happen with problems that, on the surface, may seem like completely different problems. However, under the surface the problems might have a similar structure. This is the strategy of **analogical transfer**, using the same solution for two problems with the same underlying structure.

Try to solve a variation of a problem Karl Duncker gave his participants (Duncker, 1945).

Radiation Problem Activity

> Imagine that you are a surgeon and your patient has an inoperable stomach tumor. However, one possible surgical method you think might work is to use a beam of radiation. A high-intensity beam should destroy the tumor. However, at high intensities, the beam will also destroy the surrounding healthy tissue. How can one cure the patient with these beams and, at the same time, avoid harming the healthy tissue that surrounds the tumor?

Do you have the solution yet? If not, consider the following hints: (1) What if you could adjust the intensity of the beams? and (2) What if you had more than one beam? With these hints people often come up with the solution of using multiple low-intensity beams to converge on and destroy the tumor without harming the surrounding tissue (called the "dispersion solution"). Duncker's radiation problem is a classic example of an insight problem. People usually have great difficulty solving the problem without revising their mental representation of the problem to include the potential of multiple adjustable-intensity beams. But if you had previously solved a problem with a similar solution, would it make it easier to solve the radiation problem? Mary Gick and Keith Holyoak tested this in a series of experiments.

Before giving people the radiation problem, Gick and Holyoak (1980) presented them with a different problem like this one.

> A small country is ruled by a dictator living in a strong fortress situated in the middle of the country, surrounded by villages. Many roads radiate outward from the fortress like spokes on a wheel. A general vows to capture the fortress and free the country.

Mental set: a tendency to use the same set of solutions to solve similar problems

Analogical transfer: using the same solution for two problems with the same underlying structure

> The general knows that if his entire army could attack the fortress at once it could be captured, but the dictator had planted mines on each of the roads. The mines were set so that small bodies of men could pass over them safely; however, any large force would detonate the mines, destroying the villages. A full-scale direct attack on the fortress therefore appeared impossible. The general solved the problem by dividing his army up into small groups and dispatched each group to the head of a different road. When all was ready he gave the signal, and each group charged down a different road. All of the small groups passed safely over the mines, and the army then attacked the fortress in full strength. In this way, the general was able to capture the fortress and overthrow the dictator.

While the surface features of this problem are different from those of the radiation problem, the structure of the underlying problems is similar (see Table 11.1). Gick and Holyoak found that 70 percent of the people who received the army problem and its solution solved the radiation problem using the dispersion solution, compared to only 10 percent of the people who didn't get the army problem. Some participants received slightly different versions of the army problem. In one variation the general finds an unmined road to the fortress, so the solution is to send the entire army down this road to attack. This is analogous to a different solution to the tumor problem, aiming the radiation beam at the tumor in a way to bypass the tissue (e.g., aiming it down the patient's throat). With the unmined-road initial story, only 10 percent of participants arrived at the dispersion solution for the radiation problem, and 70 percent proposed an open-passage solution. Another group of people were presented a version of the story in which the army general is ordered to parade throughout the entire country. If the dictator is not impressed by the parade, the general will be dismissed. This version

Table 11.1 Structural Similarities Between the Radiation and Army Problems

	RADIATION PROBLEM	ATTACKING ARMY PROBLEM
Problem statement	Doctor has radiation beams.	General has an army.
	Patient has a tumor.	Country has a dictator.
	Tumor is surrounded by healthy tissue.	Dictator is living in a fortress sitting at the center of country surrounded by villages.
Desired goal	Destroy the tumor with beams.	Capture the fortress with army.
Problem constraints	High-intensity beams destroy tumor and healthy tissue.	Entire army can capture fortress, but large group detonates mines on road destroying army and villages.
	Low-intensity beams don't destroy tumor or harm healthy tissue.	Small groups of men can safely pass over roads but cannot capture the fortress.
Solution	Use several low-intensity beams from different directions that converge on the tumor and destroy it.	Separate the army into smaller groups of men. Send each group down separate roads and attack the fortress simultaneously.
Goal state	Tumor is destroyed.	Fortress is captured.
	Healthy tissue is unharmed.	Army and surrounding villages are intact.

SOURCE: Adapted from Gick, M. L., & Holyoak, K. J. (1980). Analogical problem solving. *Cognitive Psychology, 12,* 306–355.

of the problem has a similar solution to the radiation problem but has a much less analogous desired goal: producing an impressive parade instead of capturing a fortress. Only 50 percent of the people receiving this story solved the radiation problem with the dispersion solution.

The Gick and Holyoak (1980) experiments demonstrate that past experience with analogous problems can be a powerful strategy for solving problems (sometimes called positive transfer). However, there was one surprising result across their experiments: Unless explicitly told that the two problems might be related, participants rarely recognized and used the analogous relationship between the problems when trying to solve the radiation problem (30 percent solved without the hint, 70 percent solved with the hint). What may underlie their difficulty? To use the analogical transfer strategy one needs to retrieve an appropriately related problem, map the pieces of the new problem onto the structure of the retrieved problem, and then correctly generalize the solution that arises out of the mapping process. These processes rely on recognizing the similarity between the different problems. However, there are two levels of similarity to consider. One is the similar surface features of the context (e.g., medical, military), objects (e.g., tumor, doctor, radiation beam, healthy tissue, dictator, army, general, villages), and actions (e.g., armies attacking, beams destroying tissue) of the problems. The other level is the underlying structure of the problem (dictator = tumor, army = radiation beam; see Table 11.1). As Gick and Holyoak's studies show, the key to using analogous solutions is using problems with similar underlying structures. However, we are often strongly influenced by the similarity of the surface structure of the problems (e.g., Holyoak & Koh, 1987; Novick, 1988; Ross, 1984, 1989; Ross & Kilbane, 1997).

Sometimes the surface structure and the underlying structural relationships are strongly related. In these cases, retrieval, guided by surface similarity, can be beneficial, leading to positive transfer between problems. However, we also have experience with problems that are similar on the surface but require very different solutions. In these situations, using problems that have strong surface similarities but different underlying structures leads individuals to attempt the wrong solutions (as did the participants in Gick and Holyoak's unmined-road story condition). This is referred to as negative transfer. In other words, if you try to use analogical transfer to solve problems, the problems that you retrieve from past experience may reflect the similarity of surface features rather than the critical structural similarities between problems. Furthermore, the strong influence of surface similarity may interfere with searching memory for problems with underlying structural similarity. For example, Gick and Holyoak's participants rarely noticed the relevance of the army problem, even though it was presented immediately before the radiation problem. However, when they were given a hint that the army problem might be useful, encouraging them to recall its details, then they were able to make use of the analogous underlying structure.

Stop and Think

11.10. Consider the following problem. The local baseball team holds tryouts for new pitchers and catchers. They invited sixteen players at each position to try out for the team. On the day of the tryouts, the weather is windy, so the coaches decide to have all of the players try out at the same time. However, two of the catchers have to cancel at the last moment. Can the coaches pair up the remaining players and have them all try out at the same time? Does this problem remind you of any of the problems earlier in the chapter?

11.11. Compare the underlying structure of the baseball player problem in Stop and Think 11.10 and the checkerboard and dominos problem (see Figures 11.4 and 11.5). List the problem statement, desired goal, problem constraints, and solution for each. Would you consider the two problems to be analogous?

Summary

The Gestalt approach to problem solving was focused on the structure of the representation of the problem. Insight solutions arise from a restructuring of the representation.

Mental sets and analogous solutions arise from using past solutions. However, most of the research was primarily descriptive, focused on describing when insight and analogical reasoning occurred. With the development of the computer and the information processing approach to cognition, a new approach to problem solving emerged that focused on the underlying processes involved in solving problems.

Problem Solving as Problem Space Searches

In the early 1960s Allen Newell and Herb Simon developed a computer program for problem solving called the General Problem Solver (GPS for short). By the 1970s their approach radically changed the way cognitive psychologists theorized about human problem solving. Newell and Simon proposed that problem solving typically proceeds by dividing the larger problem into smaller problems, searching for solutions to the smaller problems, and evaluating these solutions to see if they bring you closer to solving the larger problem. Consider an example from Newell and Simon (1972, p. 416):

> I want to take my son to nursery school. What's the difference between what I have and what I want? One of distance. What changes distance? My automobile. My automobile won't work. What is needed to make it work? A new battery. What has new batteries? An auto repair shop. I want the repair shop to put in a new battery; but the shop doesn't know I need one. What is the difficulty? One of communication. What allows communication? A telephone . . . and so on.

Algorithm Demonstration

The overall problem is that the current state (my son is at home) does not match the goal state (my son is at school). Finding the solution to this problem consists of a guided search through a problem space. The problem space consists of a mental representation of the set of intermediate states, subgoals, and operators (the actions that can be performed to change a state). In the example, the problem solver recognizes that a car can be used to drive his son from home to school (so driving the car is an operator here). But in this case the car isn't running. So a subgoal is to change the current state and get the car to run. This subproblem is solved by buying a new battery at the store (so buying a battery is another operator). Newell and Simon proposed that there are different ways to search through the problem state. By using an **algorithm**, you can consider the entire problem space, searching every possible solution. While this guarantees finding the solution (assuming there is one), if the problem space is especially large, we may not have the resources available to search the entire space. In contrast, **heuristic** searches consider only part of the search space. Instead of considering all possible solutions, we instead mentally consider potential chains of subproblems, evaluating how each operator changes the current state.

Heuristics Demonstration

Consider the Tower of Hanoi problem depicted in Figure 11.9. This puzzle involves three different-sized discs that can be moved back and forth on three pegs. The goal of the puzzle is to move the discs from the first peg to the final peg. The rules are that you can only move one disc at a time, only the top disc of a stack may be moved, and discs may only be placed on top of either an empty peg or a larger disc. The operator in this puzzle is moving a disc from one peg to another. The problem space consists of all the possible moves that can be made.

Algorithm: a prescribed problem-solving strategy that always leads to the correct solution in problems with a single correct solution

Heuristic: a problem-solving strategy that does not always lead to the correct solution

Figure 11.10 shows the problem space for the first move. There are two possible moves, to move the red disc to the middle peg or the final peg. After either of these moves there are several possible moves. We could move the red disc again, either to the other empty peg (taking us to the alternative-position option on the first move) or back on top of the green peg (putting us back to the initial state). Neither of these options gets us closer to our final goal state. The other options are to move the green disc to the empty peg (which one is empty depends on which move we made in Step 1). Figure 11.11 shows

Figure 11.9 The Tower of Hanoi

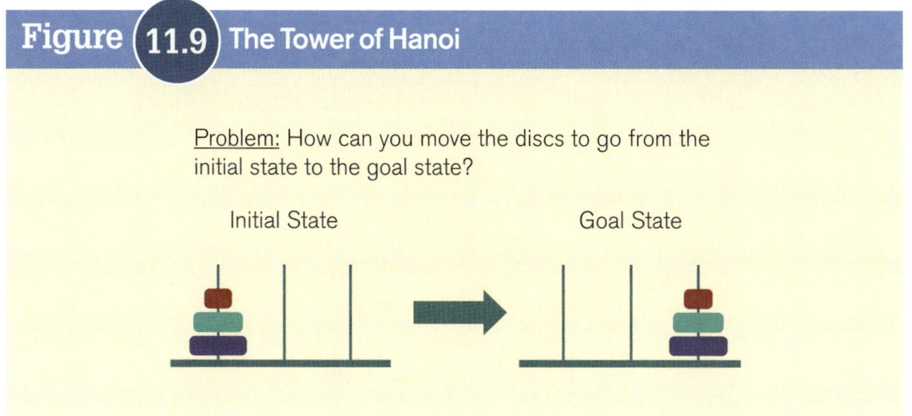

Problem: How can you move the discs to go from the initial state to the goal state?
Initial State
Goal State

Figure 11.10 The Problem Space for the First Move of the Tower of Hanoi Puzzle

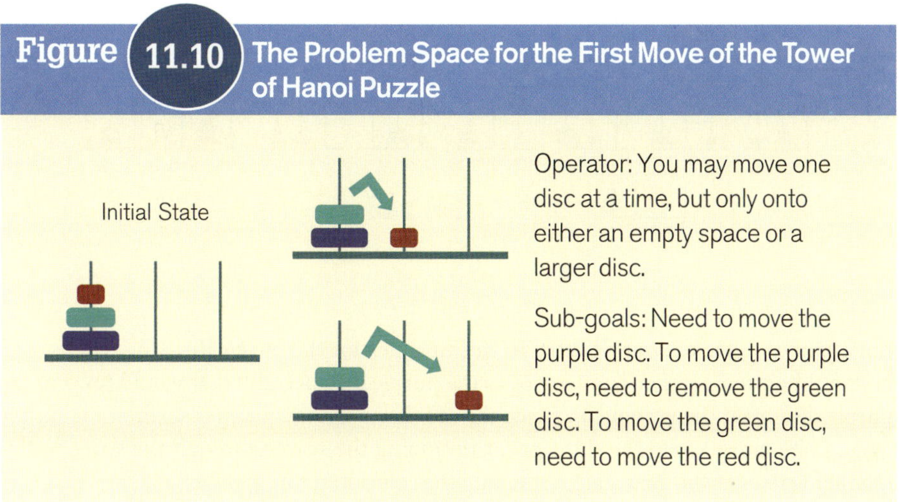

some of the problem space (not all of the possible moves and intermediate states are shown in the figure). While there are many paths that will result in the final solution, the most efficient solution path is indicated by the red arrows.

Initial State
Operator: You may move one disc at a time, but only onto either an empty space or a larger disc.
Sub-goals: Need to move the purple disc. To move the purple disc, need to remove the green disc. To move the green disc, need to move the red disc.

Newell and Simon argued that we solve problems by mentally working our way through the problem space. However, as we can see, even relatively simple problems can result in very large problem spaces. Rather than search every possible path through the space, Newell and Simon proposed that we guide our search through the space using particular heuristic strategies. The following section briefly describes three of the many heuristic search processes that have been proposed.

Means-Ends Strategy

Newell and Simon's GPS computer program used the **means-ends strategy**. The means-ends strategy guides the search through the problem space by repeatedly comparing the current state of the problem to the goal state, identifying the differences and developing subgoals. As each subgoal is achieved, the intermediate state gets closer to the goal state. Newell and Simon's story about driving their son to school is an example of using this strategy. The Tower of Hanoi problem can be broken down in a similar way. All of the discs need to be moved onto the final peg, but only one peg can be moved at a time. To move the purple disc, the green disc needs to be removed. To move the green disc, the red disc needs to be moved. So the first subgoal is to move the red disc. Once the red disc is moved, then the green disc can be moved onto the empty peg. However, now there is

Means-ends strategy: a problem-solving strategy that involves repeated comparisons between the current state and the goal state

Figure 11.11 Some of the Problem Space for the Tower of Hanoi Puzzle

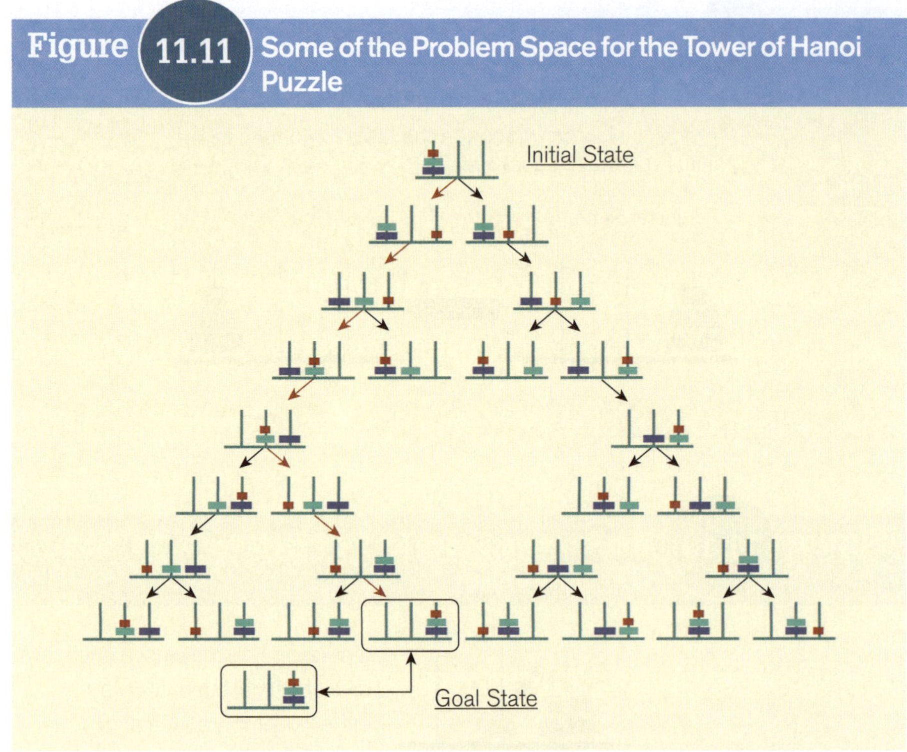

not a spot to move the purple disc. To free up a peg for the purple disc, the red disc can be moved onto the green disc (not onto the purple disc because that would prevent the purple disc from being moved). Once the red disc is on the green disc, then the purple disc can be moved onto the third peg. Continuing the search through the space in this manner arrives at the goal state, providing the solution to the puzzle.

Hill-Climbing Strategy

You may have noticed that the means-ends strategy provided a straightforward solution that worked, if in the initial step the red disc was moved onto the third peg (see the left side of Figure 11.11). However, if the red disc was initially moved onto the middle peg, which satisfies the subgoal of freeing up the green disc, then the search through the problem space will take much longer to reach the final goal state (see the right side of Figure 11.11). So how do we decide which move to make on our first turn? One possibility is to look ahead at the impact of making the two choices. If the problem space is small enough, this may be possible, but even in this small problem, that would require thinking through many possible solution paths. An alternative is to use the heuristic of hill climbing. The **hill-climbing strategy** is to select the operator that results in a change most similar to the goal state. On the first move, the red disc could be moved to either the middle or third peg. Moving it to the third peg is more similar to the goal state than moving it to the middle peg. In this case, this turns out to lead to the shortest path through the problem space.

Hill-climbing strategy: a problem solving strategy that involves continuous steps toward the goal state

Working-backward strategy: a problem-solving strategy that involves beginning with the goal state and working back to the initial state

Working-Backward Strategy

Another strategy is to try searching through the problem space backward, starting from the goal state (**working-backward strategy**). Again, consider the Tower of Hanoi problem. The final state has the purple disc on the final peg. To get it there we need to move the green and red discs to the middle peg, so that the purple disc can be moved to the final peg. If the green and red discs are both in the middle, the green disc needs to be on the bottom, so the green disc needs to be moved onto it when it is empty. So the first move should be to move the red disc to the final peg, so that the green disc can be placed in the middle. Then place the red disc onto the green disc, which frees up the final peg for the purple disc.

Stop and Think

11.12. Think back to how you tried to solve the Sudoku problem in Figure 11.1 How did you decide on your first move? Did you focus on the overall solution to the problem, or did you identify a subgoal to try to solve?

11.13. Think about the problem-solving strategies described in this section. Can you think of some examples from your own life where you used these strategies to solve a problem?

Summary of Approaches and Strategies

There is no single problem-solving mechanism for all problems. This is critical because of the vast variety of problems we are faced with on a day-to-day basis. When faced with a problem, we have many potential strategies available to solve it. If it is a relatively simple problem, then trial and error may yield the solution. If we have solved similar problems before, we may be able to use past solutions. Sometimes using one strategy doesn't work, so we try another one. Regardless of the strategy we use, we use it within our system of cognitive processes. The next section reviews how the processes of perception, attention, memory, language, and knowledge impact how we solve problems.

Allocating Mental Resources for Solving the Problem

Working Memory and Problem Solving

Think back to when you tried to solve the Sudoku puzzle. Chances are that if you tried a trial-and-error strategy of filling in numbers randomly, you got frustrated quickly. The problem space is too large. Rather than thinking about the final goal (getting all of the empty slots filled), most people instead focus on subgoals, trying to complete rows and columns. For example, you can quickly rule out a 2 in the upper-left empty box; it cannot be correct because there is another 2 already in the row (and the column too; see Figure 11.12[a]). You may then try a 3, which seems to be a good solution because it fits the constraints: There are no other 3s in the row, column, or three-by-three box (see Figure 11.12[b]). Using this sort of approach involves your attention system (see Chapter 4 for more discussion of attentional processes). You have to search the rows and columns, looking for other 2s and 3s, while ignoring the other numbers. Using the same constraints you can rule out the numbers 1, 2, 7, 8, and 9, leaving 3, 4, 5, and 6 as possible numbers for that square. Often, when trying to solve a Sudoku, people will write down these possible numbers for that square rather than trying to keep all of these possibilities in mind. This is because holding the possibilities for each square quickly surpasses the limits of our working memory system (see Chapter 5 for a discussion of working memory).

Our ability to solve problems is constrained by our cognitive systems. Consider the effects of our long-term memory processes (Ohlsson, 1992). When we encounter a problem, we retrieve knowledge that we bring to bear on the problem. The information we retrieve determines the way we initially represent the problem. How the problem is presented, what words are used (e.g., Salomon, Magliano, & Radvansky, 2013), and whether it is presented with a diagram (e.g., Larkin & Simon, 1987) impact what knowledge is retrieved. This knowledge includes conceptual information about the features and functions of parts of the problems, as well as past solutions. We use this retrieved information to define the problem space. This information also impacts how we allocate our attention (e.g., Grant & Spivey, 2003; Wiley & Jarosz, 2012), guiding what information to focus on and what information to ignore. Our working-memory capacity places limits on how much information about the

Figure 11.12 Potential Solutions in the Problem Space of the Sudoku Puzzle Given in Figure 11.1

Potential solutions in the problem space of the Sudoku puzzle given in Figure 11.1. The yellow box indicates a possible locations for a potential solution number. The red boxes indicate reasons that rule out that possible solution.

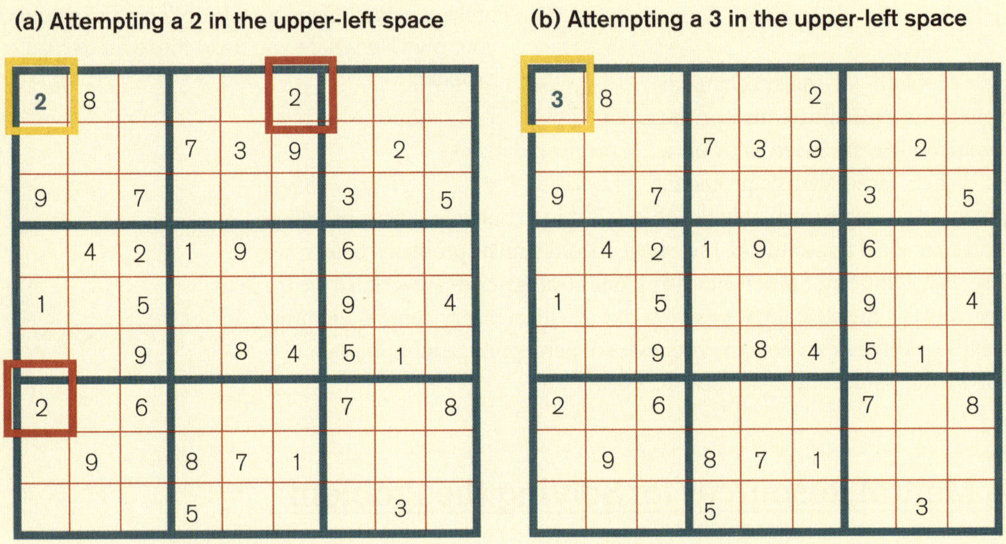

(a) Attempting a 2 in the upper-left space

2	8				2			
			7	3	9		2	
9		7				3		5
	4	2	1	9		6		
1		5				9		4
		9		8	4	5	1	
2		6				7		8
	9		8	7	1			
			5				3	

(b) Attempting a 3 in the upper-left space

3	8				2			
			7	3	9		2	
9		7				3		5
	4	2	1	9		6		
1		5				9		4
		9		8	4	5	1	
2		6				7		8
	9		8	7	1			
			5				3	

problem we can process. These limits constrain how much information about the problem is available and the search through the problem space (Chein & Weisberg, 2014; Thomas, 2013).

Look at the problem in Figure 11.13. Imagine that the problem is made up of matchsticks arranged like a math problem. However, the math problem as stated is wrong and needs to be fixed. How can you fix the problem so that it is true by only moving a single matchstick? The solution to the problem is given below it. Gunther Knoblich and colleagues (1999) have examined how people solve matchstick arithmetic problems like these. When we first encounter a problem like this we retrieve information about math and Roman numerals. Part of our math knowledge includes rules about how we can or cannot manipulate numbers and formulae. Based on our past experience, we construct our initial problem space in a way that is constrained by these rules. Due to working-memory constraints, we probably also initially represent the elements of the problems as meaningful information chunks (see Chapter 5 for more details). For example, rather than representing VII as four matchsticks, we think of it as the number 7. The same is true for the mathematical operators for equals, addition, and subtraction. However, some chunks may be "tighter" than others. For example, the Roman numerals III and VI are compositional, made up of three ones and a five and a one, respectively. In contrast, the numerals V and X cannot be decomposed in the same way. Knoblich et al. (1999) argued that the inclusion of these math rules and chunks is what makes solving these problems difficult. Furthermore, they predicted that the difficulty of the problems should vary as a function of how much the solution depends on the ease with which we can relax our representations of the rules and decompose the chunks.

Figure 11.14 offers a few more of these problems for you to try (some solutions are presented in Figure 11.15). Chances are that you will be able to solve the first problem in (a) fairly quickly. Problems like this one require decomposing a loosely chunked Roman numeral and relaxing a fairly low-level rule of math. Additionally, the solution is similar to the first example you saw. The second problem in (b) was probably harder because it requires decomposing the equals sign, which is more tightly chunked. The third problem in (c) is the hardest, requiring the decomposition of a tightly chunked representation of X. Knoblich et al. (1999) had participants solve problems like these, systematically varying the level of rule and degree of chunking needed for the solution. These two variables correctly predicted how quickly their participants were able to solve the problems.

In a follow-up study, Knoblich, Ohlsson, and Raney (2001) examined the eye movements of participants trying to solve matchstick math problems. Since people tend to stare (fixate) at things they are thinking about, the researchers predicted that their eye movements would reflect how their participants were trying to solve the problems. Eye movements tended to look similar when participants first encountered the problems. They tended to focus on the Roman numerals, rather than the mathematical operators, suggesting that their initial problem spaces were biased to consider only some elements of the problems. Additionally, for the difficult problems, such as (b) and (c), the longer they worked on a problem, the longer their fixations became, suggesting that they had reached an impasse and were considering fewer potential solutions. However, at later stages of problem solving the eye movements of participants who were able to solve the problems changed. These participants shifted their gazes to the critical elements of the problems (e.g., the plus sign or the individual parts of decomposable Roman numerals). The researchers interpreted these patterns of data as consistent with the theory that the initial representation of the problems led to an inability to focus attention on the critical aspects of the problem, leading to an impasse. However, participants who were able to relax the constraints imposed by typical mathematical rules and could decompose the initially chunked representations could rerepresent the problems. The re-represented versions of the problem then allowed them to attend to the critical parts of the problem and find the solution.

Figure 11.13 Matchstick Problem and Solution

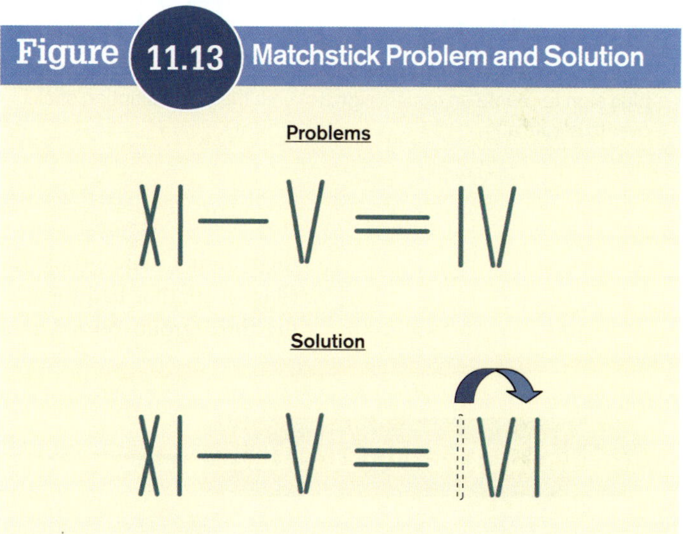

Figure 11.14 Matchstick Problems

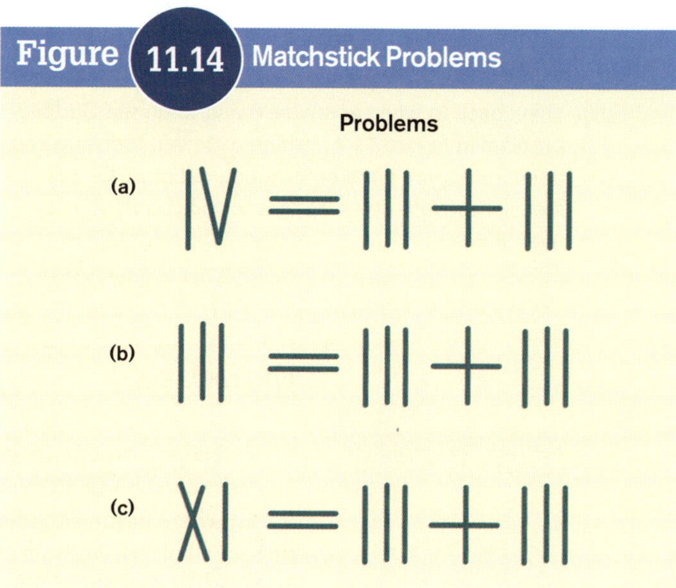

Traditionally, neuropsychologists studying problem solving have focused on measuring the impact of brain damage (via injury or disease), documenting the correlated deficits with localization of brain lesions. With the development of modern neural imaging techniques, this focus has begun to shift away from localization of function toward understanding cognitive mechanisms. However, many traditional problem-solving tasks are difficult to study using neural imaging techniques (Luo & Knoblich, 2007). For example, the nine-dot problem, the water jug problem, and matchstick

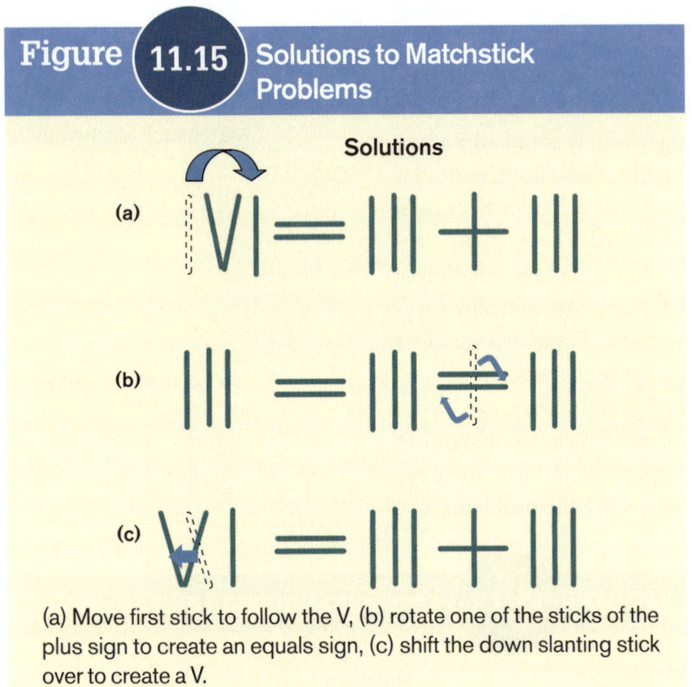

Figure 11.15 Solutions to Matchstick Problems

(a) Move first stick to follow the V, (b) rotate one of the sticks of the plus sign to create an equals sign, (c) shift the down slanting stick over to create a V.

arithmetic problems rely on different pieces of information and vary with difficulty. Also, many imaging techniques require multiple trials, but for many problems once you have an insight and discover the solution, future versions of the problem may no longer be insightful. However, cognitive neuroscientists have begun to develop new problem-solving tasks better suited for investigation with these imaging technologies.

John Kounios and Mark Beeman performed a series of experiments using both EEG and fMRI to examine insight problem solving (e.g., Bowden, Jung-Beeman, Fleck, & Kounios, 2005; Jung-Beeman et al., 2004; Kounios & Beeman, 2009). Generally their studies indicate that insight is the result of a series of brain states that operate at different time scales. In particular, their results implicate an important role of the anterior temporal lobe (ATL) for solving insight problems. Chi and Snyder (2011) further investigated the role of the right ATL by having participants solve matchstick arithmetic problems. They randomly assigned their participants to one of three conditions and used tDCS (described earlier in the chapter) to selectively stimulate different regions of their brains. One group had their right ATL excited and their left ATL inhibited (R+L-), another had their left ATL excited and their right ATL inhibited (R-L+), and the third group served as a control comparison group. They found that the R+L- participants solved more of the insight problems than the other two groups. They suggested that this was probably due to diminishing top-down information, the interruption of mental set, and potentially improved participants' set-switching abilities.

It should be apparent from the research reviewed in this section that solving problems happens within our cognitive architecture. How we identify, represent, solve, and evaluate problems must involve many (if not all) aspects of our cognitive processes. In other words, potentially all of the research and theory discussed in the other chapters of this book impact our ability to solve our day-to-day problems.

Stop and Think

11.14. Imagine that the GPS function on your phone is not working and you are driving to Disney World. What cognitive processes are you likely to rely on as you navigate your trip?

11.15. Think back to when you were trying to do the Sudoku problem in Figure 11.1. Where were you focusing your attention as you were considering options? Do you find it easier to write down options, or do you try to keep them in memory?

Expertise

Given that past experience has such a dramatic impact on how we solve problems, you may ask yourself whether you can become an expert problem solver. The answer is yes, at least within particular domains. If you practice doing Sudoku, you will become a better Sudoku player. The same is true for other domains, like playing chess, doing physics problems, or coaching gymnasts.

Experts Versus Novices

What makes an expert problem solver so much better than a novice? Given the complexity of problem solving already outlined earlier in the chapter, it should come as no surprise that it is a combination of factors.

MythBusters' Adam Savage on Problem Solving

Perception and Attention

As we gain experience with different types of problems, we learn which details of the problems are relevant and which are not (e.g., Haider & Frensch, 1999). For example, Moreno, Reina, Luis, and Sabido (2002) monitored the eye movements of expert and novice gymnastic coaches while they viewed gymnastic routines. They found that the expert coaches had longer fixations on regions critical to the performances and fewer, shorter fixations on nonrelevant areas. Lesgold et al. (1988) compared the ability of radiologists with over ten years of experience to residents in finding tumors in X-rays. While both groups were able to find the main problems, experts were also able to detect a greater number of critical features and subtle cues and the relationships between these.

Memory

Experts also mentally group aspects of the problems differently than novices do. For example, chess experts can remember where virtually all of the pieces of a chessboard are during a game. They can do this because their past experience of thousands of games allows them to chunk the pieces in meaningful ways (e.g., in terms of defensive structures). To further support this idea, Reingold, Charness, Pomplun, and Stampe (2001) measured the eye movements of chess experts and novices. They showed that expert players spent more time looking between pieces than at individual pieces, suggesting that they were focused not on the individual pieces but rather on the overall structures on the board. This difference allows experts to focus on higher-order problem goals, reducing the problem space. However, if experts are presented with a board on which the pieces have been arranged randomly, their memory performance is similar to that of less experienced players (Chase & Simon, 1973; de Groot, 1966).

When experts are reminded of past solutions, as in the case of analogical transfer, they are more likely than novices to focus on the underlying structural features of the problems. To illustrate this, Novick (1988) presented students with a series of math word problems, some of which were structurally similar, others of which were only similar on the surface. She demonstrated that experts (those scoring from 690 to 770 on the math SAT test) showed greater positive transfer between analogous problems relative to novices (those scoring from 500 to 650 on the math SAT). Furthermore, experts showed less negative transfer between nonanalogous problems that shared surface features. This result demonstrates that experts and novices differ in their initial problem representations. Chi, Feltovich, and Glaser (1981) found similar results for physics problems comparing advanced doctoral students (experts) to undergraduate physics majors (novices). They found that the advanced students were able to see past surface features and perceive the underlying structure of the problems.

Better Strategies

Experts also generally spend more time analyzing problems, adding relevant knowledge to their representation and planning their solutions (Chi, 2006). While novices and experts may have the same strategies available to them, experts are better at predicting and using more effective strategies. For example, chess experts and novices both look ahead for approximately the same number of moves (e.g., if I move my pawn, then she moves her bishop, then I move the knight), but the look-ahead of experts is typically focused on more knowledge-based searches focused on higher-order goals (e.g., good

The Expert Mind

defensive structure rather than just reacting to a particular move of an opponent) (Gobet & Simon, 1996).

One of the most persistent findings in the research on expertise is that experts' problem-solving advantages are restricted to problems within their domain of expertise. While chess masters can remember where all of the pieces on a chessboard are, they can only do it if the pieces are arranged in a meaningful game-related way. Furthermore, if you measure chess experts' ability to remember the location of checkers or cards played in a hand of bridge, their chunking capacities will look like those of novices (with comparable experience with checkers or bridge). So one question you might have is, outside of becoming an expert in a particular field, is there a way to improve your general problem-solving abilities?

Becoming a Better Problem Solver

Given what we know about the processes that underlie problem solving, what can we do to become better problem solvers? A search of bookstores and the Internet yields a vast selection of advice. One research-motivated approach is the **IDEAL framework** proposed by John Bransford and Barry Stein (1993). It is based on the same basic problem-solving cycle that has guided the structure of this chapter. *IDEAL* stands for Identify problems and opportunities, Define goals, Explore possible strategies, Anticipate outcomes and act, and Look back and learn. They suggest that effective problem solvers view problems as opportunities and actively seek them out. In other words, they gain practice recognizing and identifying problems. Defining refers to representing the problem and identifying the goals and potential operations. Good problem solvers recognize that how they represent a problem has an impact on how they try to solve it. One effective approach is a willingness to "think outside of the box" and try different ways of representing the problem. Additionally, they recognize the possibility of multiple strategies that can be explored to search the problem space for a way to achieve the goal. Good problem solvers are willing to try to actively evaluate the effects of these strategies. Understanding how and why solutions work is also important because it helps encode the underlying structural components of problems rather than the surface features. Becoming more aware of the cycle of problem solving and employing strategies targeting these stages can lead to better general problem solving.

Figure 11.16 Sudoku Solution From Figure 11.1

3	8	**1**	**6**	**5**	2	**4**	**9**	**7**
6	**5**	**4**	7	3	9	**8**	2	**1**
9	**2**	7	**4**	**1**	**8**	3	**6**	5
8	4	2	1	9	**5**	6	**7**	**3**
1	**3**	5	**2**	**6**	**7**	9	**8**	4
7	**6**	9	**3**	8	4	5	1	**2**
2	**1**	6	**9**	**4**	**3**	7	**5**	8
5	9	**3**	8	7	1	**2**	**4**	**6**
4	**7**	**8**	5	**2**	**6**	**1**	3	**9**

IDEAL framework: a step-by-step description of problem-solving processes

THINKING ABOUT RESEARCH

As you read the following summary of a research study in psychology, think about the following questions:

1. Which of the approaches to the study of cognition do you think these researchers used in their experiments on problem solving: representationalist, embodied, or biological (see Chapter 1 for a review of these approaches)?
2. What are the independent variables in this study?
3. What are the dependent variables in this study?
4. In what way might these results be useful for everyday problem solving?

Study Reference

Grant, E. R., & Spivey, M. J. (2003). Eye movements and problem solving: Guiding attention guides thought. *Psychological Science, 14*(5), 462–466.

Purpose of the study: The researchers examined whether participants' ability to solve Duncker's radiation problem (see the Analogical Transfer section earlier in the chapter) could be improved by manipulating how and where they look at the problem.

Method of the study: In the first experiment, the researchers examined the eye movements of participants looking at the diagram in Figure 11.17, while trying to solve Duncker's radiation problem. They compared the fixation patterns of participants who were able to solve the problem without hints to those who needed hints. The second experiment again examined Duncker's radiation problem. This experiment compared three groups of participants: One group examined the diagram used in Experiment 1; the other two groups examined an animated version of the figure. One version of the animated figure was constructed to highlight the regions of the figure that the results of Experiment 1 identified as a critical feature (i.e., the oval perimeter that represented the skin subtly pulsing). The other version of

Figure 11.17 Diagram Shown to Subjects in the Grant and Spivey (2003) Study

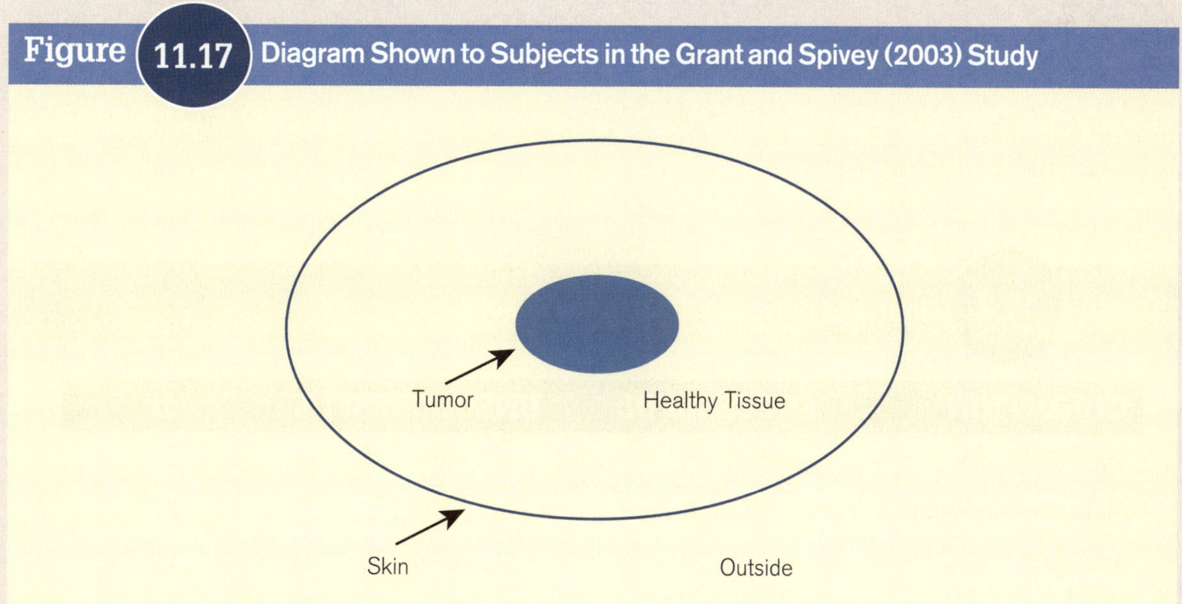

SOURCE: Figure 1, Grant, E. R., & Spivey, M. J. (2003). Eye movements and problem solving: Guiding attention guides thought. *Psychological Science, 14*(5), 462–466.

(Continued)

(Continued)

Figure 11.18 Results From Grant and Spivey's (2003) Experiment 1

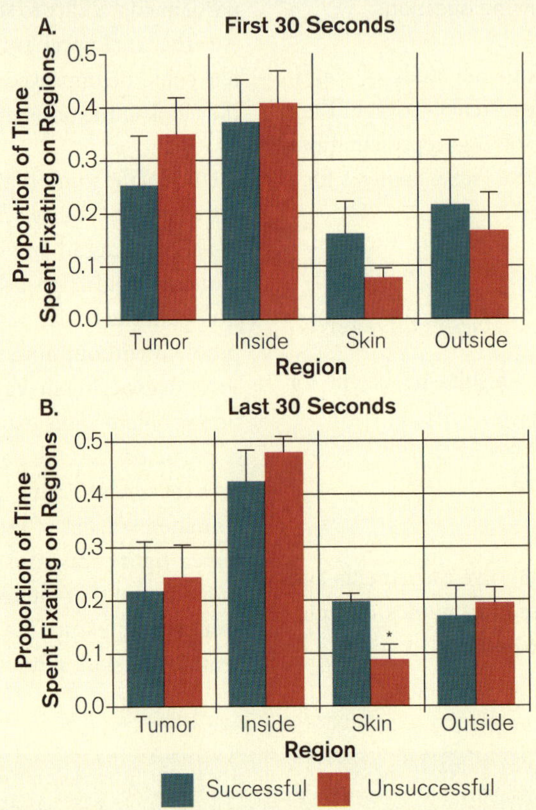

SOURCE: Figure 2, Grant, E. R., & Spivey, M. J. (2003). Eye movements and problem solving: Guiding attention guides thought. *Psychological Science, 14*(5), 462–466.

Table 11.2 Grant and Spivey's (2003) Study Results

CONDITION	SUCCESSFUL	UNSUCCESSFUL	*n*
Static (Experiment 1)	36% (5)	64% (9)	14
Static (Experiment 2)	37% (10)	63% (17)	27
Animated tumor	33% (9)	67% (18)	27
Animated skin	67% (18)	33% (9)	27

SOURCE: Table 1, Grant, E. R., & Spivey, M. J. (2003). Eye movements and problem solving: Guiding attention guides thought. *Psychological Science, 14*(5), 462–466.

the animated figure highlighted a feature (the tumor subtly pulsing) that Experiment 1 results suggested were noncritical.

Results of the study: Eye fixation data from Experiment 1 showed that in the last 30 seconds of problem solving, subjects who looked at the skin in the diagram were more likely to solve the problem than to be unsuccessful. This result shows that the skin is the most relevant feature of the diagram for solving the problem. This difference did not occur in subjects looking at other parts of the diagram during this time (see Figure 11.18). As the results in Table 11.2 illustrate, successful performance in solving the problem across both experiments occurred most often when the diagram was animated to highlight the most critical feature for solving the problem (i.e., the pulsing skin).

Conclusions of the study: From the results of the two experiments, the researchers concluded that problem solving is enhanced when one focuses attention on the visual aspects of a problem relevant for finding a solution.

CHAPTER REVIEW

Summary

- **What kind of problems do you solve every day?**

  Some of the problems we solve every day are well-defined, with clearly stated goals and strategies for achieving those goals. Others are ill-defined, with fuzzier goals and fewer clear pathways to their solutions.

- **How do you solve problems: through trial and error, through conscious deliberation, or do solutions just suddenly occur to you?**

  Trial and error works as a strategy for relatively simple problems, but we typically use other strategies for more complex problems. Often we break the problem down into subproblems, working on solving those to achieve our larger goal. Sometimes we get stuck until we change how we represent the problem and a solution emerges.

- **Why are some problems more difficult to solve than others?**

  Problems with clearly defined goals and constraints are typically easier to solve than those that are less clear. Problems that we have had past experience with are typically easier than those that are new to us. Problems that require us to represent relevant information in a way different from how we usually think of things are also typically difficult.

- **What gets in your way when trying to solve problems?**

  We solve problems within our cognitive systems, and sometimes those systems have limitations that impact our ability to solve problems. We have limits on how much information we can attend to and hold in working memory at one time. To overcome this, we often chunk information together. Sometimes the information is chunked in a way that facilitates finding a solution. However, other times the information is grouped together in a way that interferes with finding a solution. Sometimes the problem has so many potential paths to achieving a goal that we can't consider them all and as a result miss the right one.

- **How do expert problem solvers differ from novices?**

  We all draw upon our past experiences to solve problems. Within their domain of expertise, experts have a much larger array of experiences compared to novices. This experience allows experts to focus their attention on the most relevant aspects of a problem, to focus on the underlying structure of a problem instead of surface features, to represent a problem in the most efficient way, and to retrieve past solutions to similar problems.

Chapter Quiz

1. The problem-solving cycle includes all but the following stages:
   (a) recognize and identify the problem
   (b) define and mentally represent the problem
   (c) monitor progress toward the goal and evaluate the solution
   (d) create alternative kinds of problems
   (e) develop a solution strategy
   (f) allocate mental resources for solving the problem
2. Researchers typically describe a problem as
   (a) the difference between past problems and the current problem.
   (b) the difference between a current state and a desired state.
   (c) the difference between an insight and a representation.
   (d) the similarity between past problems and the current problem.
   (e) the similarity between attention and working memory.
3. The checkerboard and dominos problem illustrates that
   (a) games are a kind of problem-solving task.
   (b) how we represent a problem can have an impact on our ability to find a solution.
   (c) functional fixedness can make finding solutions easier.
   (d) monitoring progress toward the goal is rarely done.
   (e) the trial-and-error strategy is a fast and efficient method for finding a solution.
4. The associationist approach describes most problem solving as involving
   (a) insight.
   (b) analogy.
   (c) chunking.
   (d) trial and error.
   (e) searching through a problem space.
5. Gestalt psychologists proposed that problem solving
   (a) often involved unconscious processing of a problem.
   (b) sometimes involved insight.
   (c) involves thinking aloud.
   (d) is impacted by past experience.
   (e) All of the above answers are correct.
6. Successfully solving a problem using the analogy transfer strategy typically results from
   (a) focusing on the surface features of the problem.
   (b) focusing on the underlying structure of the problem.
   (c) focusing on both the surface features and underlying structure of the problem.
   (d) ignoring both the surface features and underlying structure and instead relying on insight to solve the problem.
7. Newell and Simon proposed that problem solving involves a search through a problem space. What is a problem space?
   (a) the part of memory where we store all of our past experience with problems
   (b) a mental representation of the set of intermediate states, subgoals, and operators
   (c) the combination of the articulatory loop and spatial sketchpad components of working memory
   (d) the mental set of typical functions that objects usually are used for
8. A hill-climbing strategy for problem solving is
   (a) an approach that starts at the top of a set of potential solutions and works down the set.
   (b) an approach in which operators are selected if they result in changing the current state to something that is closer to the goal state.
   (c) an approach in which you work through the problem space in reverse, starting with the goal state and working backward to the initial state.
   (d) an approach that factors in the amount of effort required to use a particular operator.
9. Experts are often much better (faster and more accurate) problem solvers within their domain of expertise because they
   (a) have more experience with the typical problems in the domain.
   (b) are usually more intelligent than novices.
   (c) are able to focus on the underlying structure of the problem better than novices.
   (d) both (a) and (c)
   (e) Answers (a), (b), and (c) are all correct.

10. Bransford and Stein proposed the IDEAL framework of problem solving. *IDEAL* stands for:
    (a) Identify past solutions, Determine good strategies, Explore alternative methods, Always keep trying, Look back and learn
    (b) Inhibit surface features, Discover underlying structure, Explore possible solutions, Activate relevant knowledge, Learn from past mistakes
    (c) Identify potential representations, Decode chunked information, Examine past assumptions, Anticipate outcomes and act, Leap forward with intuition and insight
    (d) Interpret and comprehend, Define underlying assumptions, Elaborate, Activate relevant chunks, Learn from past mistakes
    (e) Identify problems, Define goals, Explore strategies, Anticipate outcomes and act, and Look back and learn

 Key Terms

Algorithm 280
Analogical transfer 277
Functional fixedness 272
Heuristic 280
Hill-climbing strategy 282
IDEAL framework 288
Ill-defined problem 269
Insight 275
Means-ends strategy 281
Mental set 277
Well-defined problem 269
Working-backward strategy 282

 Stop and Think Answers

11.1. Make a list of some of the problems you have already faced today.

Answers will vary.

11.2. For each problem in Stop and Think 11.1, identify the initial and goal states and how you went about solving the problem.

Answers will vary.

11.3. Which of the problems in Stop and Think 11.1 would you classify as well-defined and which as ill-defined? What characteristics of the problems led you to classify them in that way?

Answers will vary.

11.4 Consider the following problem. You have a jug of apple juice and a container of water. After putting both the apple juice and the water into a large pitcher, the apple juice and water remain separate. How does this happen?

Answers will vary.

11.5. As you consider potential solutions to the problem in Stop and Think 11.4, think about how you mentally represent it. What assumptions about the problem does your mental representation lead you to make?

Answers will vary.

11.6. A solution to the problem in Stop and Think 11.4 is that the water is frozen in the form of ice cubes. Do you think that you would have thought of the solution if the problem had stated "a tray of water" instead of a "container"?

Answers will vary, but this changed wording may have led to a solution more frequently.

11.7. Think about some of the problems you encounter in your own life. What are some situations where you try to solve them through trial and error? Are there ways in which these different situations are similar?

Answers will vary.

11.8. Are there other problems that you'd never consider trying to use trial and error to solve? Why would trial and error not work well in these situations?

Answers will vary.

11.9. Have you ever experienced that "aha" feeling when solving a problem? If you can remember what the problem and your solution was, do you think it was the result of changing the way you represented the problem?

Answers will vary.

11.10. Consider the following problem. The local baseball team holds tryouts for new pitchers and catchers. They invited sixteen players at each position to try out for the team. On the day of the tryouts, the weather is windy, so the coaches decide to have all of the players try out at the same time. However, two of the catchers have to cancel at the last moment. Can the coaches pair up the remaining players and have them all try out at the same time? Does this problem remind you of any of the problems earlier in the chapter?

This is similar to the dominoes checkerboard problem.

11.11. Compare the underlying structure of the baseball player problem in Stop and Think 11.10 and the checkerboard and dominos problem (see Figures 11.4 and 11.5). List the problem statement, desired goal, problem constraints, and solution for each. Would you consider the two problems to be analogous?

Problem statement: Missing two catchers out of sixteen and want to pair up pitchers and catchers

Desired goal: Pairing up the remaining players

Problem constraints: Each pair must contain a pitcher and catcher

Solution: You cannot pair up the remaining players and have each pair consist of one catcher and one pitcher.

The problems are analogous.

11.12. Think back to how you tried to solve the Sudoku problem in Figure 11.1. How did you decide on your first move? Did you focus on the overall solution to the problem, or did you identify a subgoal to try to solve?

Answers will vary.

11.13. Think about the problem-solving strategies described in this section. Can you think of some examples from your own life where you used these strategies to solve a problem?

Answers will vary.

11.14. Imagine that the GPS function on your phone is not working and you are driving to Disney World. What cognitive processes are you likely to rely on as you navigate your trip?

Answers will vary, but some possibilities are using working memory to keep track of where you are in reality and the position on the map, imagining the route in order to locate it on the map, and using retrieval from long-term memory to locate the appropriate map to use (e.g., Disney World is in Florida; where did you put the map of Florida?).

11.15. Think back to when you were trying to do the Sudoku problem in Figure 11.1. Where were you focusing your attention as you were considering options? Do you find it easier to write down options, or do you try to keep them in memory?

Answers will vary.

Student Study Site

Sharpen your skills with SAGE edge at **edge.sagepub.com/mcbridecp**

SAGE edge for students provides a personalized approach to help you accomplish your coursework goals in an easy-to-use learning environment.

Go to edge.sagepub.com/mcbridecp for additional exercises and web resources. Select Chapter 11, Problem Solving, for chapter-specific resources. All of the links listed in the margins of this chapter are accessible via this site.

Sudoku

The way Texas went
was in his hands–
and his six-guns
set it straight!
RANDOLPH
SCOTT
WARNER BROS.
'FORT WORTH'
TECHNICOLOR
DAVID BRIAN · PHYLLIS THAXTER
PALACE

Reasoning and Decision Making

Questions to Consider

- How logical are the conclusions you draw?
- Why are some things harder to reason about than others?
- How and when do we make inferences about causal relations?
- What steps do we go through when we make decisions?
- Do we always make the best choices?

Introduction: A Night at the Movies

Suppose it is one of those days when you are running late. You race back to your dorm room because you are supposed to be heading out to a movie with your roommate. You arrive to find that your roommate isn't there. You call your roommate, but she doesn't answer. You aren't sure what to do. Did she leave without you? Should you try to catch up with her at the theater? Or is she running late too? It seems out of character that your roommate would have left without you, but it is also atypical that she would be running late. You reason that if she is not there, then she must have gone to the movie without you. Looking around the room for clues you notice that a movie showtimes webpage is loaded up on the computer. The showing that you had planned to attend at the Omnimax is listed as sold out. There is a later showing at that same theater, but there is also an earlier showing of the movie at the Palace Theater. Should you wait for your roommate and go see the later showing, or do you leave now and head to the Palace? After some consideration, you reason that your roommate probably saw that the show was sold out and that you were running late, so she decided to head to the other theater to get tickets while they were still available. With this in mind, you grab your coat and head out, hoping to catch up with your roommate at the Palace.

Much of our everyday thinking is made up of reasoning and decision making. Generally we feel that our reasoning processes are logical (we come to the right conclusions) and that our decisions are sound (we make the right choices). However, it turns out that our thinking may not follow the standards of formal logical systems. Under what conditions do we act logically, and when do we deviate? This chapter reviews the theories and research behind how we reason about things like what your roommate probably did and which movie theater you decide to go to.

Our reasoning processes are what allow us to evaluate arguments and reach a conclusion. Cognitive psychologists and philosophers typically distinguish between two broad types of reasoning: deductive and inductive reasoning. **Deductive reasoning** *is often described as making arguments from general information to more specific information. For example, if we know that Vulcans are logical and Spock is a Vulcan, we can conclude that Spock is logical. In contrast,* **inductive reasoning** *is argumentation from specific instances to more general relationships. For example, in "A Scandal in Bohemia" Sherlock Holmes reasons that Dr. Watson had recently been caught in a rainstorm based on his observation of his shoes. Holmes reasoned that several parallel cuts on the leather must have resulted from careless scraping of mud from the sole and that the mud resulted from a recent torrential rainstorm. This series of reasoning is an example of inductive reasoning (despite the fact that Holmes usually described it as "simple deduction"). Most of us probably think of ourselves as rational and logical. However, the fact that we think of fictional characters such as Star Trek's Mr. Spock and Sherlock Holmes as extraordinarily logical in their thinking suggests that we are aware that we don't always follow the rules of logic.*

The Structure of Reason

Deductive reasoning: making and evaluating arguments from general information to specific information

Inductive reasoning: making and evaluating arguments from specific information to general information

Deductive Reasoning

Deductive reasoning is the making and evaluation of arguments following a logical set of rules or principles. Generally two types of reasoning have been the focus of philosophical and psychological investigation: syllogistic and conditional reasoning. The following sections briefly describe these two types of reasoning.

Photo 12.1 Logical thinkers Spock and Sherlock Holmes.

Syllogistic Reasoning

Aristotle developed the logical rules of **syllogistic reasoning**. Syllogistic reasoning is a process by which a conclusion follows necessarily from a series of premises (statements). If the premises are true, then by the rules of deduction, the conclusion must be true as well. This is referred to as the deductive validity of the argument. In logical arguments, syllogisms often take the following form:

All A's are B's. (first premise)

All B's are C's. (second premise)

All A's are C's. (conclusion)

The *All* is a quantifier. Other quantifiers include words like *no*, *some*, *some are not*, and *many*. The A's, B's, and C's are things in the world. Let's look at a concrete example.

All ants are insects.

All insects are animals.

All ants are animals.

The statement that "all ants are animals" is a valid conclusion that results from applying the rules of logic. My son recently used this type of logic to decide he didn't like butterflies, which he had liked prior to thinking this through. After a scary experience with flying insects (a ride at Disney World), he decided that "flying insects are scary." After encountering a butterfly in the backyard, he realized that "butterflies are flying insects. Therefore, butterflies are scary." And he has disliked them ever since.

The next question you might ask is how often we reason using these logical rules. Researchers have typically used straightforward methods to assess this question (e.g., Ford, 1994; Johnson-Laird, 2006; Johnson-Laird & Steedman, 1978; Roberts, Newstead, & Griggs, 2001). Typically participants are presented with the premises and asked to produce the logical conclusion. Other times they are asked to select the valid conclusions among a set of possible conclusions or given a single conclusion and asked to decide whether it is valid. Sometimes the syllogisms are presented in systematically varied formats (e.g., verbally or visually, with or without figures). In some studies participants are asked to talk aloud about why they came to their conclusions. While each method yields slightly different results, an overall, consistent conclusion can be reached: We are often not very good at following the rules of logic.

Syllogisms Activity

Consider the syllogisms in Table 12.1. For each one determine whether the argument is valid. What did you conclude for the first one in (a)? If you decided that the conclusion follows logically from the premises, then you are in agreement with most people. The

Syllogistic reasoning: a process by which a conclusion follows necessarily from a series of statements

Table 12.1 For Each Syllogism, Try to Determine Whether the Logical Conclusion Is Valid

(a) All beagles are dogs.
All beagles are mammals.
All dogs are mammals.

(b) All beagles are dogs.
All beagles are mammals.
Some mammals are dogs.

(c) No elephants are insects.
All insects are animals.
Some animals are not elephants.

conclusion that "all dogs are mammals" feels right. It fits with our world knowledge about dogs, and both of the premises were *all* statements. However, this argument is logically invalid. The conclusion that "all dogs are mammals" does not logically follow from the two premises. The second example in (b) is the same pairing of the premises but with a different conclusion. What did you conclude about this argument? This one is a valid argument. However, when given this pairing of premises, people rarely give this conclusion (or the other valid conclusion "Some dogs are mammals"). The third argument in (c) is valid as well. People typically find the third argument difficult to evaluate. When just given the premises, people often conclude that there is no valid logical argument.

The research suggests several factors impact how likely we are to correctly follow the rules of logic (e.g., Wilkins, 1928). One factor is the phrasing of the premises. Not all premises and conclusions are equally easy to reason about. Typically we find that arguments that include negations (*no* and *not*) are more difficult, as in (c). Arguments with *some* are typically harder than those with *all*. Another factor is how people understand the language used in the premises. There is a difference between the logical use of *some* and how we typically use *some* in our day-to-day language. Consider the conclusion in example (b). In day-to-day language, "some mammals are dogs" is typically understood as meaning "some mammals are dogs and some are not dogs." In logical terms, "some mammals are dogs" should be interpreted as "at least one mammal is a dog, but there may or may not be other mammals that are not dogs." Another factor is the content of the arguments (what the A's, B's, and C's are). For example, many people accept the argument in (a) as valid, when logically it is not. This is in part due to the fact that the conclusion "All dogs are mammals" is consistent with what we know about dogs. However, this knowledge is irrelevant for the logic rules; what the A's, B's, and C's are shouldn't matter. When we reason, we are influenced by the content of what we are reasoning about. Typically we are less likely to accept something that goes against our initial assumptions and are more likely to accept something consistent with our beliefs.

Monty Python on Deductive Reasoning

Conditional Reasoning

Conditional reasoning (propositional reasoning): a process by which a conclusion follows from conditional statements ("if, then" statements)

Conditional reasoning has a similar formal structure with the inclusion of connective words like *if* and *then* as part of the first premise (other connective words include *and*, *or*, and *not*, but for simplicity these are not discussed here). Conditional reasoning is sometimes referred to as propositional reasoning because of the connective words in propositional statements. Propositional statements are those that are either true or false (see Chapter 9 for a discussion of propositional representations in language). In logical arguments, they are often stated in a form similar to that used for syllogisms.

If *p* then *q* (major premise)

p (minor premise)

? (conclusion)

The major premise consists of the antecedent (*p*) and the consequent (*q*). The valid conclusion in this argument is "q."

Some conditional reasoning was involved in the movie scenario presented at the beginning of the chapter. You thought through some propositional statements in making your decision: If I wait for my roommate and she's gone to the earlier show at the Palace, I will miss the movie. If I go to the Palace and she's gone out to eat before heading to the later show, I will miss dinner and go to the wrong theater. Considering these premises helped you think about the consequences of your decision in each case.

Let's look at the concrete examples in Table 12.2. For each argument, decide whether you think the conclusion is valid. The first argument in (a) is often referred to as *modus ponens*. It is a valid argument and most people find it fairly straightforward. The second argument in (b) is called *modus tollens* and is also valid. Typically people find these arguments more difficult. What did you think about the third and fourth arguments in (c) and (d)? It turns out that both are invalid arguments (often called fallacies). The key is in the major premise "If it is sunny outside, then I will walk to class." This doesn't say anything about what I will do if it isn't sunny; I might still choose to walk to class. So in (c), the minor premise tells us that it is not sunny, but we don't have information about whether we will walk or not. The reverse is true in (d). Given that I might walk to class rain or shine, knowing that I walked to class doesn't tell me what the weather was like.

Conditional Arguments Activity

One of the most popular tasks researchers have used to examine this kind of reasoning is the four-card task developed by Wason (1968). Figure 12.1 illustrates this task.

Table 12.2 For Each of the Conditional Arguments, Try to Determine Whether the Logical Conclusion Is Valid

(a) If it is sunny outside, then I will walk to class.
It is sunny outside.
I will walk to class.

(b) If it is sunny outside, then I will walk to class.
I will not walk to class.
It is not sunny outside.

(c) If it is sunny outside, then I will walk to class.
It is not sunny outside.
I will not walk to class.

(d) If it is sunny outside, then I will walk to class.
I will walk to class.
It is sunny outside.

Wason 4-Card Task Activity

Imagine that you are presented with four double-sided cards (each with a letter on one side and a number on the other side) and the following claim: If a card has a vowel on one side, then it has an even number on the other side. You are allowed to turn over two cards to test whether the claim is true. Go ahead and give it a try. Which two cards would you turn over to test the claim? The solution and logical rationale to this problem are shown in Figure 12.2. If we represent the claim as the major premise of a conditional argument, we get the following:

If a card has a vowel (p), then it has an even number on the other side (q).

We should select the cards that correspond to the minor premises in the two valid arguments. In other words, we need to look for evidence like that in the (a) and (b) arguments. This corresponds to the *A* and *7* cards. Don't worry if you didn't get the right answer; less than 10 percent of people pick both of these cards (Oaksford & Chater, 1994; Klauer, Stahl & Erdfelder, 2007; Wason & Johnson-Laird, 1972). Let's quickly walk through the logic. We want to turn over any cards with vowels (p). If we turn over the *A* card and it has an odd number, then we know the claim is invalid. Most people do select this card, but it is not enough to fully test the claim. We also need to turn over any card that corresponds to "not q." That would be any card that doesn't have an even number—in this case the *7* card. If that card has a vowel on the other side, then we also know the claim is invalid. Turning over the *D* or *4* card doesn't help us. Whether the number on the other side of the *D* card is odd or even says nothing about the claim because *D* isn't a vowel. Turning over the *4* doesn't help because the letter on the other side doesn't matter (this is the second most common card people select). If it is a vowel, it is consistent with the claim, but if it is a consonant, that's okay too. The claim doesn't say anything about consonants, so finding an even number on the card with a consonant doesn't violate the claim.

As was the case with the earlier syllogisms, the rules of logic should apply regardless of the context. You probably had trouble with the version of Wason's four-card task presented in Figure 12.1. However, if we change the context of the argument, it can have an impact on how we reason about it. Wason and Shapiro (1971) gave a version of the task within a traveling context. Imagine that the cards have a location on one side and a method of travel on the other (see Figure 12.3). The claim to be tested is "Every time I go to Chicago I take the train." Which cards should you turn over to test this claim? Most people find this version of the task easier. You should turn over the Chicago card but not the New York City card (it doesn't matter how you got to New York). Your

Figure 12.1 Wason's (1968) Four-Card Task

"If a card has a vowel on one side, then it has an even number on the other side."
If we can only turn over two cards, how can we test the validity of this statement?

Figure 12.2 Solution to Wason's (1968) Four-Card Task

"If a card has a vowel on one side, then it has an even number on the other side."
If we can only turn over two cards, how can we test the validity of this statement?

Assume p = a card has a vowel on one side
Assume q = a card has an even number on the other side

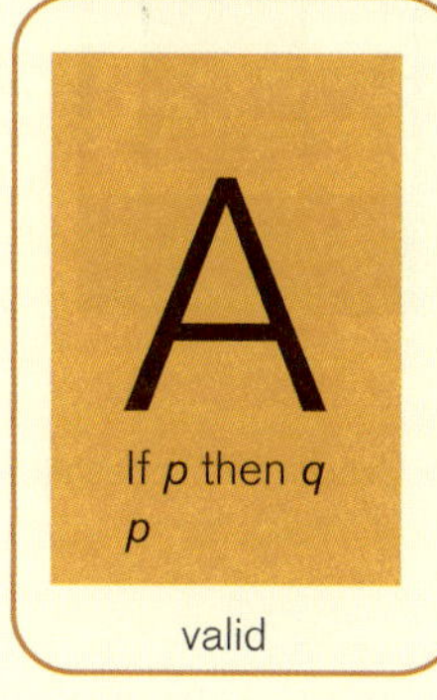

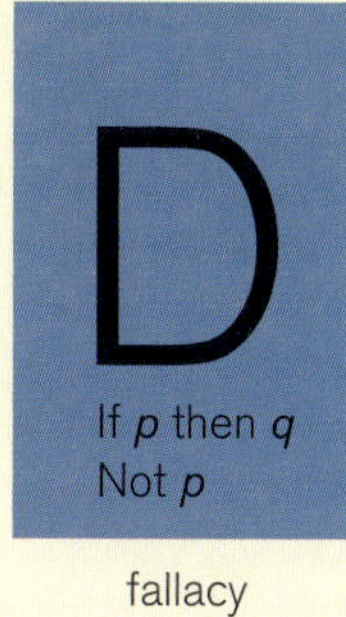

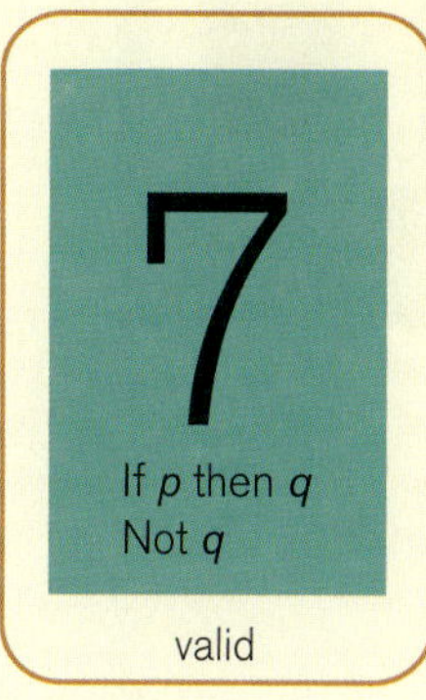

second card should be the plane card. If the other side has Chicago on it, then that violates the argument (you got to Chicago via a method other than the train). The train card just tells you where you went by train; it could be Chicago, but it could also be somewhere else. Again, it doesn't matter what is on the other side of the train card. Griggs and Cox (1982) had participants imagine that they were a police officer assigned to enforce a law requiring those who drink alcohol to be at least twenty-one years of age. The cards represent different patrons in a bar (see Figure 12.4). One side of the card lists what a person is drinking and the other side lists the person's age. Which patrons should the police officer check? (After you've made your guesses, check Figure 12.5 for the answer.) Griggs and Cox's participants had little trouble recognizing that there was no point in checking the person drinking soda or the person who was over twenty-one. Over 75 percent of their participants made the correct card choices.

Adapted Wason 4-Card Task Activity

Figure 12.3 Travel Version of Wason's Four-Card Task

"Every time I go to Chicago, I take the train"
If we can only turn over two cards, how can we test the validity of this statement?

Photos: *Chicago:* Digital Vision/Photodisc/Thinkstock; *New York:* Creatas Images/Creatas/Thinkstock; *train:* Stockbyte/Stockbyte/Thinkstock; *plane:* Jupiterimages/Photos.com/Thinkstock

Figure 12.4 Contextualized Version of Wason's Four-Card Task

"If a person is drinking a beer, then the person must be over 21 years of age."
If we can only turn over two cards, how can we test the validity of this statement?

Photos: *soda:* ITStock Free/Polka Dot/Thinkstock; *woman:* Ralf Nau/Digital Vision/Thinkstock; *man:* Goodshoot RF/Goodshoot/Thinkstock; *beer:* Thomas Northcut/Photodisc/Thinkstock

Research like this demonstrates that while we often aren't good at logical reasoning, we do use it in some contexts. The following section briefly reviews some of the theoretical approaches proposed to explain how and when we reason logically, why we find some arguments more difficult than others, and why we make particular errors.

Deductive-Reasoning Approaches

Generally, deductive reasoning involves understanding and representing the premises, combining these representations, and drawing a conclusion. Many theories have been proposed to explain how we deductively reason. Roberts (2005) classifies these into three general approaches: conclusion identification, representation explanations, and surface (or heuristic) approaches.

Conclusion Interpretation Approaches

These approaches propose that errors arise from general biases against making particular conclusions (e.g., Dickstein, 1981; Revlis, 1975; Roberts & Sykes, 2005). For example, people may be reluctant to make "no valid conclusion" responses because they feel that this is an uninformative conclusion. Another error may result because the order of the terms can be reversed ("called conversion") in some premises but not in others. For example, "Some ants are insects" and "Some insects are ants" are logically equivalent. However, "All ants are insects" and "All insects are ants" are not.

Representation-Explanation Approaches

Theories of this type focus on how we represent the arguments. The difficulty of an argument and the likelihood of making an error are the result of either incomplete information or incorrect representation of the argument. If your idea that your roommate would not want to exclude you is not correct (i.e., maybe she was really hungry and decided getting dinner before the movie was more important than making sure you had dinner with her), then your reasoning that she had gone to the earlier movie may be incorrect because you did not accurately represent your roommate's current priorities in your mind as you thought through the problem of which movie theater you should go to in order to meet up with her. Reasoning that requires complex chains of rules places demands on our working memory. The higher the demands, the more difficult the reasoning. Real-world problems, like that of our movie example, typically involve much uncertainty and incomplete information in which it is difficult, if not impossible, to think through all possible reasoning steps. One of the major differences across different theories is the kind of representation that is assumed.

Mental logic theories (e.g., Braine, 1978; Rips, 1994) propose that our deductive reasoning proceeds by applying a set of rules. Some of these theories propose context-free (so what the argument is about doesn't matter) rules that operate on propositional representations of the premises. Propositional representations are statements that are either true or false (see Chapters 9 and 10 for more discussion of propositions). Other theories propose that the context of the rules does matter. Cheng and Holyoak (1985) proposed that we reason using sets of rules defined with respect to particular goals (e.g., permissions, obligations, and causation) learned through ordinary day-to-day experiences. In contrast, Cosmides (1989) has argued that we have evolved to reason using rules related to social exchanges. For example, we may be born knowing a rule along the lines of "if I do something for you, then you do something for me." In other words, our reasoning is based on a kind of benefit-cost rule. However, not all approaches are based on applying mental rules.

Stop and Think

12.1. Are the arguments discussed in the Conditional Reasoning section representative of the kinds of arguments you face in your day-to-day experience? If not, how are they different?

12.2. Consider the following argument: All Introduction to Psychology courses are taught in large sections, and all large-section courses use multiple-choice exams. Therefore my Introduction to Psychology course will use multiple-choice exams. Is this a valid argument? Do you think it follows the "rules of logic"? Would you change your mind if you learned that the section of your course is being taught by a new professor?

12.3. Consider the following argument: If I study every term on the review sheet, then I will get an A on the exam. I studied hard, therefore I will get an A. Are these valid arguments? Do you think that they follow the "rules of logic"?

12.4. Do you generally consider yourself a "logical thinker"? When you reason about things, do you usually think through all aspects of an argument, or do you usually focus on just a few?

One of the most influential theories of reasoning was proposed by Philip Johnson-Laird and his colleagues (e.g., Johnson-Laird, 2001). This theory proposes that reasoning

Figure 12.5 Solution to the Contextualized Version of Wason's Four-Card Task

"If a person is drinking a beer, then the person must be over 21 years of age."
If we can only turn over two cards, how can we test the validity of this statement?

Assume p = a person is drinking a beer
Assume q = a person must be over 21 years of age

If *p* then *q*
Not *p*
fallacy

If *p* then *q*
q
fallacy

If *p* then *q*
Not *q*
valid

If *p* then *q*
p
valid

Photos: *soda:* ITStock Free/Polka Dot/Thinkstock; *woman:* Ralf Nau/Digital Vision/Thinkstock; *man:* Goodshoot RF/Goodshoot/Thinkstock; *beer:* Thomas Northcut/Photodisc/Thinkstock

proceeds through three stages. The first stage is model construction of the premises by building mental models of the world described by the premises. A mental model is essentially a simulation of the spatial relations, events, and processes. For example, Figure 12.6 shows the possible worlds described by the four basic premises we discussed earlier. Notice that many of the premises correspond to multiple mental models of the world. For example, the top left corner of Figure 12.6 shows the situations described by the premise "All ants are insects." It could be that ants are a subset of insects, or it could be that ants make up the entire set of things that are insects. Both are logical possibilities. The second stage of the model is conclusion-formulation. In this stage the mental models of premises are integrated such that consistent models are conjoined and inconsistent ones are discarded. Figure 12.7 depicts this for the argument "All ants are insects" and "All insects are animals." There are two mental models for each of the premises. Combining each of these results in four possible integrated models. The final stage is the conclusion-validation stage. In this stage we look for models that would falsify the conclusion. In our example, the conclusion is about the relationship between ants and animals, so we can simplify the mental models by removing the information about insects. What remains are two mental models about ants and animals. Both are consistent with the conclusion premise, so we can conclude that this is a valid argument. Essentially, we reason that an argument is valid unless we identify a mental model that falsifies it.

The model predicts that working-memory limitations (see Chapter 5 for further discussion of working memory) interact with the reasoning processes. The more mental models required to evaluate the argument, the more difficult and error prone our reasoning is because we cannot consider all of the models at one time. This exceeds our working-memory limit. For example, the premise "Some ants are insects" has four

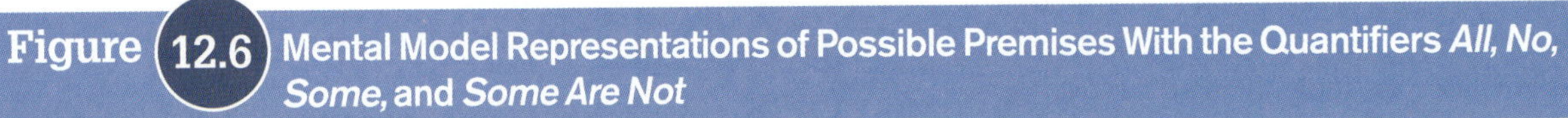

Figure 12.6 Mental Model Representations of Possible Premises With the Quantifiers *All, No, Some,* and *Some Are Not*

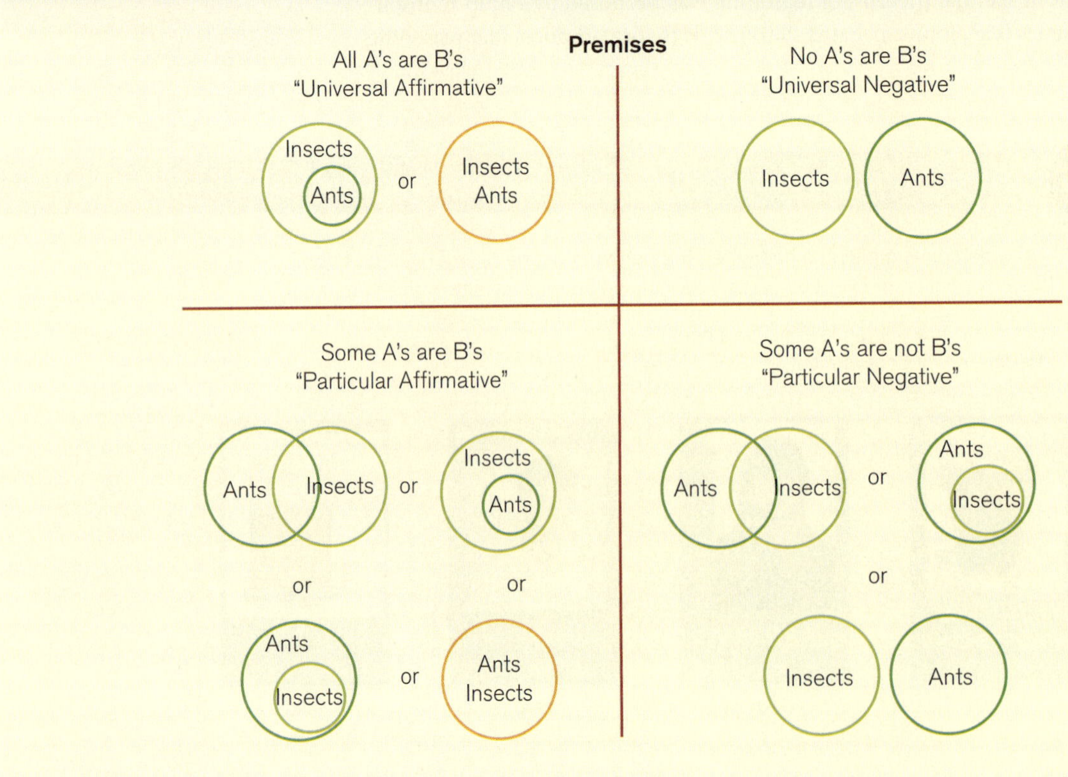

The labeled circles represent the set of ants and set of insects.

Figure 12.7 Mental Models of the Combination of the Premises "All Ants Are Insects" and "All Insects Are Animals" and the Logical Conclusion "All Ants Are Insects"

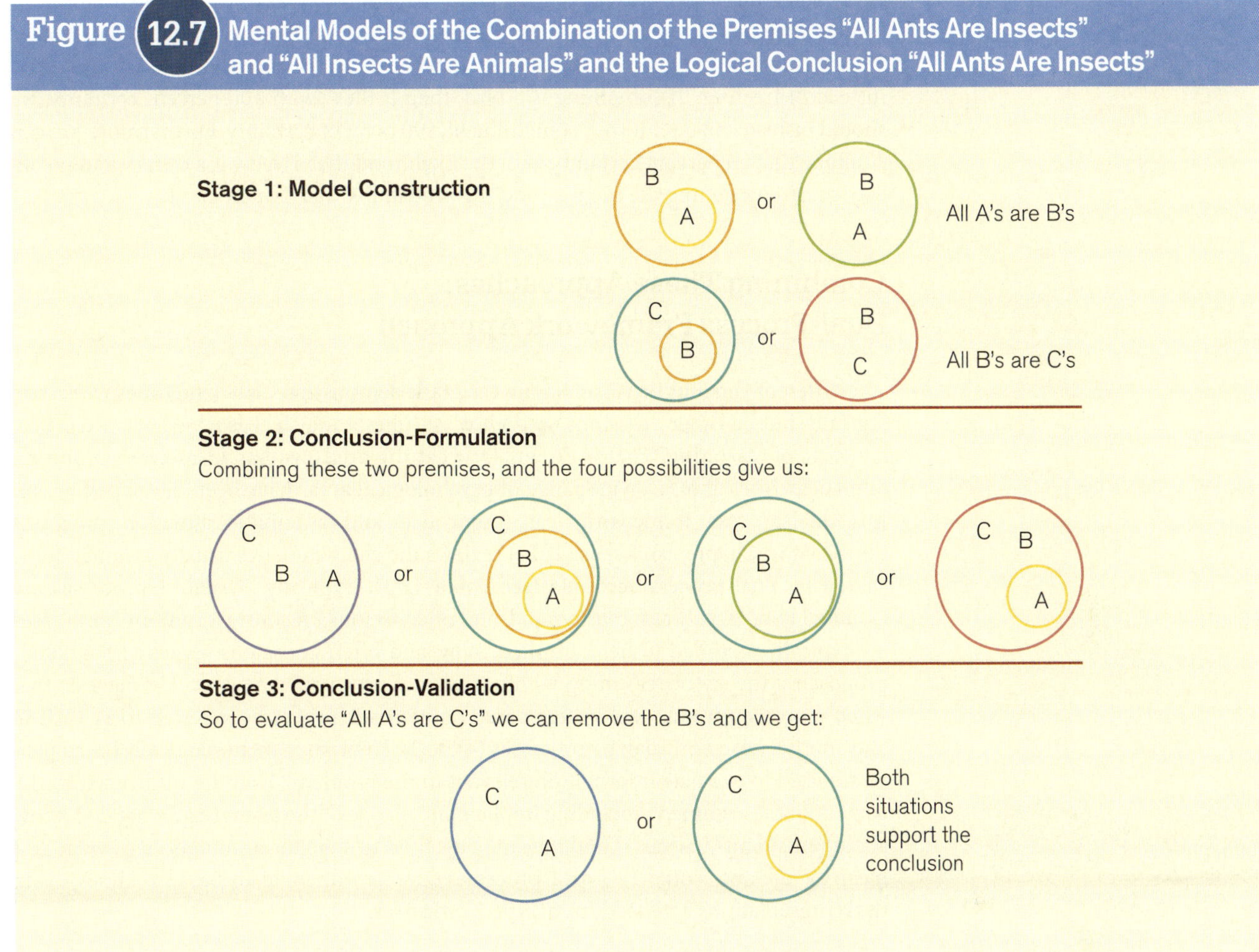

mental models to consider. If we were to combine it with "Some insects are animals," which also has four mental models, we would have sixteen integrated models to consider. If we don't consider all of the models, we may miss the critical one(s) that falsifies the premise in the conclusion.

Surface Approaches

Surface approaches propose that reasoning relies primarily on general heuristics focused on the surface properties of the quantifiers in the argument (e.g., Wetherick & Gilhooly, 1990; Woodworth & Sells, 1935) rather than on reasoning analytically. For example, if the argument contains premises about universals (*all* and *no*), then the conclusion probably is a universal. Or if the argument contains a negative premise (*no* or *some . . . not*), then the conclusion will be negative.

Chater and Oaksford (1999) proposed the probability heuristics model. Their proposal is that everyday reasoning is not based on logic but rather on probability. Rather than treating the premises as statements of truth, the probability heuristics model analyzes the probability of the premises and the strength of the argument. Consider the probability of something being an ant given the premise "All ants are insects." There is a 100 percent chance that something is an insect, given that it is an ant. Similarly, if the premise is "No ants are insects," there is a 0 percent chance that something is an insect given that it is an ant. For the other two premises (*some* and *some . . . not*) the probability will be somewhere from 0 percent to 100 percent. However, in everyday life we rarely encounter things with 100 percent certainty. Chater and Oaksford use the example "If something is a bird, then it flies" and "Tweety is a bird" so "Tweety must fly." But what if Tweety is an ostrich? Should you still infer that she flies? The model proposes that should instead of treating "If something is a bird, then it flies" with 100 percent certainty, we should instead consider it with something like 90 percent certainty. Furthermore, we can combine that 90 percent certainty with the likelihood that Tweety is a canary and not an ostrich, strengthening the premise and the probability that Tweety can fly.

Combining These Approaches: Dual-Process Framework Approach

The different versions of Wason's four-card task demonstrate that sometimes we reason logically, but on other occasions we do not. At times it may feel as if we have two different ways of reasoning. That is essentially what the **dual-process framework** proposes. Similar theories across a wide range of psychological areas have been developed within this dual-process framework (e.g., controlled and automatic attention processes described in Chapter 4). Evans (2012) reviews the characteristics usually assumed to be shared by dual-process accounts (see Table 12.3). Typically, System 1 processes are assumed to be largely automatic, rapid, and unconscious. In contrast, System 2 processes are typically assumed to be controlled, slow, and often conscious. Evans (1984, 2006) proposed a theory of reasoning within this dual-process framework. He suggests that when we reason we use one system based on heuristic processes (referred to as Type 1) and another based on analytic processes (Type 2). Heuristics are nonlogically based processes used to evaluate information relevant to the problem. They are influenced by the content of the argument, including implicit knowledge of the terms (e.g., what do I know about "ants" and "insects"?) and the language used to state the argument (e.g., what do I mean by "all" and "some"?). Type 2 processes operate with logically based analyses, using the representations activated from Type 1 processes.

Table 12.3 Generally Accepted Characteristics of Dual-Process Theories of Cognition

SYSTEM 1	SYSTEM 2
Unconscious, preconscious	Conscious
Rapid	Slow
Automatic	Controlled
Low effort	High effort
High capacity	Low capacity
Associative	Rule based
Intuitive	Deliberative
Contextualized	Abstract
Cognitive biases	Normative reasoning
Independent of cognitive capacity	Correlated with individual differences

SOURCE: Evans, J. St. B. T. (2012). Questions and challenges to the new psychology of reasoning. *Thinking & Reasoning, 18*(1), 5–31.

Dual-process framework: the idea that cognitive tasks can be performed using two separate and distinct processes

Inductive Reasoning

Stop and Think

12.5. When you make reasoned arguments, what sort of representations do you think you use? Does it feel like you are using something like those proposed by the mental logic or the mental models approach?

12.6. Do you think the approach you take when reasoning depends on what you are reasoning about?

Deductive reasoning has been the focus of much of the research on how we reason. However, deductive reasoning is about absolute truth, which is rare in our day-to-day lives. On the other hand, inductive reasoning examines the likelihood of a conclusion being true, rather than its absolute truth. This is something we do often in everyday reasoning (Feeney & Heit, 2007). There are many forms of inductive reasoning, some of which are reviewed in this section. What ties them together as a cohesive set is that they involve reasoning from specific data (based on both observation and knowledge) to broader generalizations. A result of these is the generation of new information. For example, think back to the story the chapter opened with. You looked for clues, and based on these clues, you reasoned that your roommate must have seen that the show was sold out and decided to go to another theater without you. This is all new information you have generated, not based on formal rules of deductive logic but rather on inductive reasoning processes. The following section discusses several types of inductive reasoning. Two types—analogical reasoning and category induction—are discussed in detail elsewhere in the textbook, so our discussion about these here is relatively brief.

Types of Inductive Reasoning

Analogical Reasoning

We use analogies often. In our daily lives they may take a form similar to Forrest Gump's "Life is like a box of chocolates, you never know what you're going to get." You have probably encountered more formal versions of analogical reasoning tasks on standardized tests (Rumelhart & Abrahamson, 1973; Sternberg, 1997). They typically look like the following example:

> A tree is to forest as a soldier is to __________
>
> (a) general (b) army (c) warfare

Analogical reasoning is the process of using the structure of one conceptual domain to interpret another domain. Reasoning in this example first involves recognizing the part-whole structural relationship between *tree* and *forest*. Then that structural relationship is mapped onto the second part of the argument such that *soldier* fits the "part" and the choice is to identify the best option for the "whole." In this case it should be (b) *army*. This process of analogical transfer is discussed in greater detail in Chapter 11.

Category Induction

Being able to organize and recognize a group of things as members of the same category is an important part of our cognitive system (see Chapter 10). If we see something new and can categorize it, then we can infer many properties of that thing. For example, if we are walking through the woods and we see a blue object on a branch making tweeting noises, we will probably categorize it as a bird. When we make this categorization, we will infer that the "bird" has properties common to other birds, like having feathers and the ability to fly. The inference of these properties is a kind of inductive reasoning: birds have feathers and can fly, this blue object is a bird, so the blue object is a bird and has feathers and can fly. Rips (1975) and others have demonstrated that we also reason in a similar way across categories. For example, suppose we are told that sparrows have a disease. Then we are asked how likely it is that robins and squirrels living in the same area might have the same disease. We make predictions about the likelihood that they have the disease using inductive reasoning. This research is discussed in detail in Chapter 10.

Causal Reasoning

Assessing Our Confidence

One of our fundamental human behaviors is to attempt to understand how the world around us works. We generally believe in a universe where there is cause and effect. In other words, things happen for a reason. Generally, causal reasoning infers cause-and-effect relationships between two events that occur together either in space or time. If we know the cause-and-effect relationships between events, then we can make predictions about, or even control, our environments. For example, suppose that one day you wake up feeling like you are coming down with a cold. You think back and remember that your friend accidentally sneezed on you the previous evening, and you come to the conclusion that his sneeze caused you to get sick (see Photo 12.2). In the future, if your friend is sick, you decide to avoid him until he gets better. Research suggests two factors are important when we draw causal conclusions: identifying the covariation between the two events and believing that there is a mechanism for the causal relationship. In our example, the sneezing event happened in close temporal proximity ("the previous evening"), and it preceded your feeling sick. This corresponds to the covariation aspect of the situation—how often the two events co-occur. Your causal belief may further include beliefs that germs are transmitted from one person to another and that cold symptoms are the body's reaction to germs (i.e., the cold virus).

Co-occurrence is necessary for one thing to cause another. However, many things covary together. We also should consider how often events do not co-occur. For example, are there times when somebody sneezes on us and we don't get sick? Or times when we get a cold without somebody sneezing on us? Cheng and Novick (1992) proposed a model in which our causal reasoning is based on these probabilities. The essential idea of the model is that the strength of our causal belief is a function of the difference between the probabilities of an event happening (e.g., getting a cold) with and without the causal event (e.g., being sneezed on and not being sneezed on).

Tom Le Goff/Photodisc/Thinkstock

Photo 12.2 Causal reasoning: If you get a cold after your friend sneezes on you, do you blame your friend?

However, as you may remember from Chapter 1, correlation is not the same as causation. For one thing to cause another thing, there must be a mechanism that connects the two processes (germs, in our example). Beliefs about the mechanisms that underlie the causal relationship are also important factors in our causal reasoning processes. This was demonstrated in a study conducted by Fugelsang, Thompson, and Dunbar (2006). They presented participants with brief stories containing an event and a possible cause of the event. Participants were asked to rate the likelihood that the cause was responsible for the effect. Across several experiments the researchers manipulated the degree of covariation between the cause and event, the believability of the causal power linking the cause and event, and the familiarity and imageability of the causal mechanisms. For example, consider their causal story about slippery roads. All versions started with "Imagine that you are a researcher for the ministry of transportation who is trying to determine the cause of slippery roads in townships." This was then followed by one of four potential causal hypotheses that varied with respect to different factors.

High belief and high covariation: "You have a hypothesis that the slippery roads may be due to ice storms."

Low belief and high covariation: "You have a hypothesis that the slippery roads may be due to slippery sidewalks."

High belief and low covariation: "You have a hypothesis that the slippery roads may be due to rainfall."

Low belief and low covariation: "You have a hypothesis that the slippery roads may be due to excessive traffic."

Participants were asked to rate their beliefs about the causal powers in the stories. Their results indicated that all of these factors were strongly associated with the strength of the inferred causal relationship. Furthermore, Cummins (1995) demonstrated that familiarity of alternative causal mechanisms also plays a role. For example, you know that germs can also be transmitted through touch, and yesterday you also used a public drinking fountain. Recalling this potential alternative explanation may lead you to adjust the strength of your belief about your friend's sneeze as the cause of your cold.

Photo 12.3 Which type of butter makes the better-tasting cookies? Experimenting with different brands tests the causal relationship between butter types and cookie taste.

As explained in Chapter 1, one of the best ways to establish causal relationships is by doing experiments. If we systematically manipulate a potential causal variable (independent variable) and observe what changes occur to the following event (dependent variable), then we have good data from which to make conclusions about causal relationships. While systematic manipulation of variables to test for cause and effect is the bread and butter of the scientific method, Sloman (2005) argues that it may also play a role in our day-to-day reasoning. We develop and update our causal models through both observing particular covariations and intervention with the causes and events.

For example, I recently baked a batch of cookies and discovered that they weren't as good as I had hoped (see Photo 12.3). I wasn't sure what was wrong, but I suspected that it was the generic brand of butter that I had used. So I tried making the same recipe, except this time I used a more expensive brand-named butter. The cookies turned out better, and I concluded that the generic butter was likely the problem in the first batch. In this situation, I manipulated the variable (butter type) and observed whether changes occurred in my measure of interest (how the cookies tasted). This allowed me to change my causal model about things that affected how the cookies tasted. In particular, I eliminated other potential causes of the bad taste (e.g., the bad taste wasn't because the milk was old).

Hypothesis Testing

Suppose somebody gave you this sequence of numbers: 2, 4, 6. Your task is to give the rule that makes up this sequence.

Hypothesis Testing Activity

What do you think the rule is? Without more information it is difficult to say. Let's further suppose that you cannot ask questions about the rule but may come up with other sequences of three numbers and ask whether they follow the rule as well. This was the task developed by Peter Wason (1960; Wason & Johnson-Laird, 1972), and it has been the subject of extensive study. We can think of the rules you come up with as hypotheses, and the triplets you test are experiments to test the hypotheses. Suppose you think that the rule is "even numbers" and ask about 8, 10, 12. Here the answer is "Yes, these follow the rule"; however, when you suggest your even-numbers rule the researcher says "No, that's not the rule." Maybe the rule is "start with a number and add 2 to get the next." So you may try the sequence 3, 5, 7. Again you get a "Yes, these follow the rule" response but "No, that's not the rule." The correct rule is a very general one:

"List numbers smallest to largest." Only 21 percent of Wason's participants correctly arrived at this conclusion on their first try, over 50 percent made at least one mistake, and the remaining 29 percent never found the correct rule.

Wason had his participants talk aloud while reasoning. He identified three general strategies his participants used. Sometimes they generated triplets designed to confirm their hypothesis (verification). On other occasions they generated triplets inconsistent with their hypothesis (falsification). The third strategy was to consider other variations of their hypothesis. If you stick to the first strategy, looking for evidence that confirms your theory, then you are falling prey to a confirmation bias. We often put far too much weight on evidence that is consistent with our hypotheses and far too little weight on evidence against them. Participants who follow the second strategy (falsification) are much more likely to arrive at the correct rule.

One way to facilitate performance on this task was investigated by Tweney et al. (1980). Instead of classifying the triplets their participants generated as yes or no, they were instead classified as belonging to one of two rules (e.g., "There are two rules: Med and Dax. The sequence 2, 4, 6 follows the Dax rule"). Performance increased dramatically, with 60 percent of participants correctly stating the rule on their first attempt. Having two rules to consider may have reduced the confirmation bias, encouraging their participants to consider multiple hypotheses, rather than focusing on verifying a single hypothesis (Mynatt, Doherty, & Dragan, 1993).

Counterfactual Thinking

Inductive reasoning also includes our ability to reason about things that could have happened but haven't. These typically take the form of "what if" and "if only" sentences. For example, suppose that you didn't do as well on your last calculus exam, but you believe you would have done better on your exam if only you had studied for an additional hour. Counterfactual thinking is used in conjunction with many other types of reasoning (Byrne, 2002). Examples include searching for counterexamples when evaluating hypotheses or when reasoning about causal relationships (especially after bad outcomes, like doing poorly on a test) and providing the building blocks for creative combinations of categories.

Stop and Think

12.7. Try to think of an example of causal reasoning you did today. How strong is the covariation between the cause and effect events? Did you consider both how often they did not co-occur as well as how often they did?

12.8. Considering the same example that you came up with in Stop and Think 12.7, did you consider alternative hypotheses about the causal effect? Did you engage in counterfactual thinking and ask yourself "What if I had done something else instead?" How does thinking about alternative causes and "what ifs" impact your causal reasoning?

Everyday Reasoning

At this point you may be asking yourself whether the formal reasoning tasks used in the laboratory are the same as the reasoning we do in our daily lives. Galotti (1989, 2002) identified many potential differences between reasoning in the laboratory and reasoning in our day-to-day lives. The main differences are presented in Table 12.4. In many respects the question is similar to the distinction made between well-defined and ill-defined problems described in Chapter 11. Laboratory problems tend to be well-defined, with clear premises supplied, a single correct answer, and arguments that are evaluated because the researchers ask you to evaluate them. In contrast, the arguments we evaluate on a day-to-day basis are typically much less defined. It isn't always easy to know what the premises are. The arguments are typically personally relevant, perhaps aimed at achieving a particular goal or outcome. And there isn't always a single clear solution. In fact, there may be several possible answers that vary in quality.

Cost-Benefit Reasoning in Everyday Life

Table 12.4 Differences Between Formal and Everyday Reasoning

FORMAL LABORATORY REASONING TASKS	EVERYDAY REASONING TASKS
All premises are supplied.	Some premises are implicit, and some are not supplied at all.
Problems are self-contained.	Problems are not self-contained.
There is typically one correct answer.	There are typically several possible answers that vary in quality.
Established methods of inference that apply to the problem often exist.	There are rarely established procedures for solving the problem.
It is typically unambiguous when the problem is solved.	It is often unclear whether the current "best" solution is good enough.
The content of the problem is often of limited academic interest.	The content of the problem has potentially personal relevance.
Problems are solved for their own sake.	Problems are often solved as a means of achieving other goals.

SOURCE: Galotti, K. M. (1989). Approaches to studying formal and everyday reasoning. *Psychological Bulletin, 105*, 331–351.

Think back to the reasoning in our opening movie story. Reasoning "If she is not here, then she must have gone to the movie without me" probably feels different from "If Charlie is a basketball player, then he is tall. Charlie is a basketball player." Because of these differences, everyday reasoning is more subtle and complex than most of the formal reasoning tasks studied in the lab. Research that examines the relationship between the two is still relatively new. One consistent finding is that everyday reasoning is subject to biases, many of which arise because of the use of heuristics. We discuss some of these heuristics in our review of decision making in the following section.

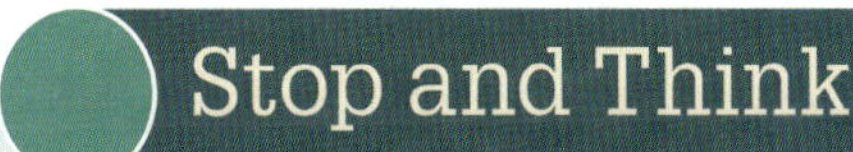

12.9. Think back to how you reasoned through the various versions of the four-card problems. How did the reasoning you used to answer those questions compare to how you reason about things in your day-to-day life?

Making Decisions

Making decisions is about assessing and making choices between different options. In our opening story we were trying to decide what to do, whether to wait for our roommate or go to the movie without her. Furthermore, if we do decide to go to the movie, to which theater should we go? Our days are filled with decisions, some big (e.g., "What do I want to do with my life after I graduate?" "Which house should I buy?") and others small ("Should I order a peanut butter and jelly sandwich for lunch?" "Paper or plastic?"). As was the case with your self-assessment about your reasoning abilities, you probably feel like you make the best logical decisions you can. But, as was the case with reasoning, we make our decisions within our cognitive system and are subject to the limitations of that system. This section reviews theories and research about how we make decisions.

A General Model of Decision Making

The Art of Choosing

Galotti (2002) describes a general model of decision making made up of five phases. The model closely resembles the general model of problem solving outlined in Chapter 11.

Setting goals. Goals are mental representations of desired states of affairs. Good decisions are those that get us closer to our goals. Goals are the targets we aim for. The recognition of a disparity between the current state of affairs and the goal is often a strong motivator, driving us into action to reduce the difference. As mentioned, goals differ in many ways: some are big, some are small; some are about things right now, others are things to do later; some are simple, others are complex. Big goals may need to be broken into smaller subgoals. Goals may also change along the way. Sometimes the process of trying to achieve your goals leads to a reassessment of and possibly a revision of your goals. Once our goals are set, then we begin to consider what options we may have available to us to achieve those goals.

In our movie story, your goal is to see a particular movie with your roommate. This goal may have been derived individually (e.g., you each saw a trailer for the movie and decided independently that you wanted to see it) or jointly (e.g., the desire to see the movie arose from a conversation about common interests). After realizing that your roommate may have already left, you need to weigh your options. Is it more important to find out where your roommate is so that you can see the movie together? Or is your desire to see the film more important than the goal of seeing it with your roommate? Is there enough time for you to get to the Palace, or should you wait a little longer and stick with the original plan to see the movie at the Omnimax? These options are tied up with the goals you set.

Gathering information. Once you have set your goals, then you need to acquire information needed to make the decision. This information includes your options, the likelihood of the different outcomes, and the criteria you use to make the decision. Consider the movie example again. If you go to the Palace Theater you should be able to see the movie, but your roommate may not be there. The same is true for the showing at the Omnimax. One piece of information you may want to consider is how likely you are to meet your roommate at each theater (and remember that there is also the possibility that she may be running late, too). However, as we will see later in the chapter, we gather more than just information about probabilities and options. The structure and limitations of our cognitive systems have a large impact on the information we use to make decisions.

Reasoning and Decision Making

Structuring the decision. Once we have our goals and have assembled our information, we need to organize the information in a way that will be useful for making the decision. Consider the common practice of making a list of pros and cons. Suppose that you are trying to decide whether to buy a desktop or laptop computer. Under the pros column for the laptop you list features like portability, great Wi-Fi on campus, and cool looks. Under cons, you list small screen and hard drive and risk of dropping it or having it stolen. The purpose of this exercise is to arrange the information you think is relevant to make the decision easier.

Prisoner's Dilemma Experiment

Making a final choice. After collecting the information and organizing it to make comparisons, it is time to actually choose an option. This isn't always an easy task. Often there is no one obvious choice. When we make decisions, we usually make our selections based on information loaded with uncertainty. Once again, think back to our opening story. You are trying to decide what to do and which theater to go to, not knowing where your roommate is. Without knowing this information, how do you make the decision? The sections to follow briefly describe some of the theories proposed to account for how we make decisions.

Evaluation. This last stage is often overlooked. Indeed, there is relatively little research that examines this final phase. The general attitude is that if the decision has been made, then it is time to move on. However, remember that we make many decisions every day. An important part of our cognitive processes is that we have a memory system. Our past decisions impact later decisions. So interpreting our choices and evaluating what went right or wrong are important aspects of decision making.

Ideal Decision Making: A Normative Model

We start by describing an idealized model of how we make decisions. Our first step is to break the decision down into all of the independent criteria. Next we need to weigh each criterion according to how important it is to the decision. Then we need to list all of the options and rate each option according to the list of criteria. The option with the highest score wins and that's the decision we make. Let's return to our computer buying example. Figure 12.8 illustrates how the idealized model might work. The first column lists the criteria that you want to consider. The second ranks them in terms of their importance. The next columns list the relevant features of each of the computer options. The numbers in parentheses represent the quantitative value of these features (1= high/good; 3s and 4s = low/poor). To determine which option is the best choice we can multiply the computers' scores by the weight of the criteria and then add up the scores. For the first laptop we get $(4 \times 1) + (3 \times 3) + (5 \times 2) + (2 \times 1) + (7 \times 2) + (8 \times 1) + (1 \times 4) + (6 \times 3) = 69$. We've set things up so that the lowest combined score is our choice. However, as we will see, decision making is rarely as straightforward as this ideal model suggests.

Heuristics and Biases

Heuristics are essentially mental shortcuts that we use to reduce the processing burden on our cognitive systems. They are typically faster, require fewer resources, and generally give the right answer. However, heuristics usually work by ignoring some information, which at times may result in making errors or biased conclusions. The list of heuristics we use when collecting and assembling information for decision making is too long to review here, so we limit our review to three heuristics (Kahneman, 2011).

Stop and Think

12.10. Think back to the last time you made a major purchase or decision (e.g., buying a car, renting a particular apartment, deciding what to major in). What factors did you consider when you made that decision? What kind of information did you gather? How did you combine that information to arrive at your decision?

12.11. Think back to a relatively minor decision (e.g., what to eat for breakfast, what to wear today). What factors did you consider when you made that decision? What kind of information did you gather? How did you combine that information to arrive at your decision?

12.12. How do the decision processes differ between your answers in Stop and Think 12.10 and 12.11?

Representativeness Bias

Read through the following description of Tom W created by Daniel Kahneman and Amos Tversky (Kahneman & Tversky, 1973, p. 238).

> Tom W is of high intelligence, although lacking in true creativity. He has a need for order and clarity, and for neat and tidy systems in which every detail finds its appropriate place. His writing is rather dull and mechanical, occasionally enlivened by somewhat corny puns and flashes of imagination of the sci-fi type. He has a strong drive for competence. He seems to have little feel and little sympathy for other people, and does not enjoy interacting with others. Self-centered, he nonetheless has a deep moral sense.

Tom's Job Activity

Figure 12.8 Making a Decision About Which Computer to Buy

Criteria	Importance	Laptops		Desktops	
Portability	4	High (1)	High (1)	Low (3)	Low (3)
Computation power	3	2.8 GHz (3)	2.4 GHz (4)	3.2 GHz (1)	3.1 GHz (2)
Hard disk space	5	250 GB (2)	150 GB (3)	500 GB (1)	500 GB (1)
Work potential	2	High (1)	High (1)	High (1)	High (1)
Gaming potential	7	Okay (2)	Okay (2)	High (1)	High (1)
"Coolness"	8	High (1)	Low (3)	Okay (2)	Okay (2)
Price	1	$1,200 (4)	$950 (1)	$1,100 (3)	$999 (2)
Screen size	6	17"(3)	15"(4)	27"(1)	19" (2)
		69	93	54	62

Computer Options

Importance is ranked from 1 to 8, representing the weighting of the different criteria. The numbers in parentheses represent a quantitative value for how each computer ranks on each criterion. The numbers at the bottom of the table are the combined scores computed by multiplying the scores by the weighting and then adding these numbers together. The highlighted number is the lowest combined score, so it is the computer of choice.

Computer photos: Ryan McVay/Photodisc/Thinkstock

Representativeness Heuristic Demonstration

Representativeness bias: a bias in reasoning where stereotypes are relied on to make judgments and solve problems

Now consider the following professions: computer science, engineering, business administration, law, education, and social science. Rank in order, from 1 to 5, the likelihood that Tom W is a graduate student in one of these fields (1 = most likely, 5 = least likely). If you are like most people, you probably ranked computer science and engineering high on your list and education and social science low. However, computer science and engineering typically have many fewer students than education and social sciences fields. Given the relative size of the fields, it would be better to predict that Tom was a student in the larger fields. Instead, you probably picked up on some of the characteristics of Tom (e.g., likes sci-fi and corny puns, is neat and tidy, and doesn't generally interact with others) and identified these characteristics as ones you associate with your stereotype of computer scientists and engineers. This is referred to as the **representativeness bias**. There may be some truth in stereotypes. The predictions that follow from the hypothesis may turn out to be correct. However, sometimes they are wrong. In Tom's case these features say relatively little about what field of study Tom may be in and thus should not be as important a factor in the decision as information like the size of the field.

Availability Bias

Recall that part of the decision-making process is to assemble information relevant to the choice that has to be made. In an ideal world we would have access to all of the necessary information. However, that is typically not the case. Consider our computer buying example. Suppose that when we are doing our research, we find that the computer store website is incomplete and that some of the information for some of the computer options isn't available. This lack of information will impact your ability to make a choice. Much of the time the information we use to make decisions comes from our own memory. As discussed in detail in Chapter 7, memory retrieval is far from perfect.

Availability Heuristic Demonstration

Tversky and Kahneman (1973) demonstrated that the ease with which we are able to retrieve information from memory has a large impact on our decision making. This is called the **availability bias**. For example, which do you think is more common in English: words that start with the letter *L* or words in which *L* is the third letter? It turns out that there are many more words in which *L* is the third letter, but it is much more difficult to think of examples of these words compared to thinking of words that begin with *L*. This is most likely related to how we organize words in our mental lexicon (see Chapter 9 for more discussion of the mental lexicon). Similar results have been found for other factors that influence how easily something is retrieved from memory (e.g., recent items, primed items, more vivid items). Findings like these suggest that the ease or difficulty of retrieval of information provides a metric for how likely an event is. This, in turn, can impact the decisions and choices we make. My son believes that all dogs will steal his food because his dog often tries to steal his food. He is using the availability bias to draw a conclusion about dogs that is not always accurate.

Framing Effects Exercise

Framing Bias

Let's return to our movie theater example and add a little more to the story. When you arrive at the theater box office and get your wallet out to pay for the $10 ticket, you realize that somewhere along the way you lost a $10 bill. You still have enough money to pay for the ticket. What would you do? Would you buy a ticket to see the show? Most people say that they would (Tversky & Kahneman, 1981). Let's change the story a bit. Instead, imagine that you get to the theater, buy your $10 ticket, and quickly run back to your car to make sure that you had locked it. When you return to the theater and attempt to enter, you suddenly realize that you lost your ticket. You still have enough money to pay for another ticket. What would you do in this case? In this case just over half of people say that they would not pay for another ticket. In both story continuations you are out $10, either for a lost ticket or a lost bill. So why do people usually make different choices in these two contexts?

Tversky and Kahneman argue that it is because we frame the problems differently (called the **framing bias**). In the second situation, we mentally represent the cost of going to the movie as $20, which seems to be excessive. In contrast, even though the total amount of money that has left our wallet that night is $20, we typically only associate $10 of it as related to the cost

Availability bias: bias in reasoning where examples easily brought to mind are relied on to make judgments and solve problems

Framing bias: a bias in reasoning where the context in which a problem is presented influences our judgment

Stop and Think

12.13. Suppose that you are trying to decide whether to get renter's insurance. You recently read a report in the paper that crime rates across the nation are at an all-time low. However, two of your friends recently had their apartment robbed. You go ahead and decide to pay for the insurance. Do you think that your choice may have been biased?

12.14. Can you think of any real-life decisions you have made that may have been the result of framing? If you were to be in the same situation again, do you think you would make the same decision?

of seeing the movie. This demonstrates that how we frame the information we use to make a decision also impacts the choices we end up making.

Descriptive Decision-Making Approaches

The use of heuristics, like those just presented, demonstrates that we are impacted by our cognitive architecture when collecting information relevant to our decision. Our cognitive processes also impact how we structure the decision and make the final choice. Think back to the model of decision making we described for the computer buying example. That process probably seems somewhat complex, and you may wonder whether you really go through all of that for all of your decisions. Remember that that process is a model of decision making under ideal conditions, without consideration of potentially limiting constraints as to the context or our cognitive processes. Research suggests that we use many different decision-making strategies depending on the situational context. We now consider a few of these.

Tversky (1972) described the elimination-by-aspects strategy. When we use this strategy, we dramatically limit the number of criteria we consider, by first considering only the most important. If this criterion is sufficient to make our choice, then we do so. If it is not, then we move to the next most important. In our computer buying example (see Figure 12.8), price is listed as the most important criterion. If we use the elimination-by-aspects strategy, we could focus on the prices of the computers and would probably end up selecting the pink laptop because it is the least expensive.

Another strategy we may use is to focus on the criteria that are easy to evaluate (Hsee, 2000). This can be especially true if you are considering the criteria alone, without information about the range and reference point. For example, it is fairly easy to imagine the difference between different screen sizes. However, for a feature like computational power it may be difficult to know how to interpret the differences: Is a jump from 3.1 to 3.2 GHz important enough to consider? The criteria "work" and "gaming" are potentially even more difficult to evaluate. So the strategy of ignoring difficult criteria in favor of those that are easy may result in making a misguided decision.

We also consider our past experiences when we make decisions. Suppose that the last computer you owned was made by the same company as one of the desktops you are considering. If you had problems with that earlier computer, that may lead you to avoid buying the same brand again. On the other hand, if you thought your last computer was great, you may have a preference for that brand that goes above and beyond the specific criteria listed. Clearly the consequences of past decisions may impact how you make your current choice.

Cognitive psychologists are not the only researchers who study decision making. Decision making is so central to our daily lives; understanding how and why we make decisions is of interest and importance in many areas. For example, people who sell us products are quite aware that our decision making is not always logical. Let's extend our opening movie story one last time. Suppose that we get into the theater and have time to buy some refreshments. We get to the counter and ask for a medium drink and popcorn. Rather than just give you what you ordered straight away, they instead make the following offer: "Would you like to make those both a large for just $1 more?" Given that the small is $3 and the medium is $5, getting a large for only $1 more may seem like a bargain that is too good to pass up, even though you don't really want the large popcorn and drink. This is a version of the "decoy effect." If we were only given the choice between the small and large popcorns, then we probably wouldn't have really considered the large one. However, the presence of the medium size, priced close to the large size, dramatically increases how often we select the large popcorn. The medium size is presented primarily as a decoy, looking like a poor choice when compared to the larger size and increasing the attractiveness of the large popcorn.

Prospect Theory

Kahneman and Tversky (1979) explained many of the heuristics and biases within a framework they called prospect theory. They noted that the biases in people's decision making often resulted from the fact that we do not treat gains and losses equally. Generally we treat losses as more important than gains (loss aversion). In other words, losing $100 is much more impactful than gaining $100. Additionally, the framework assumes diminishing returns; a gain or loss of $100 matters a lot if we have a balance of $1,000 in our account, but it matters very little if we have a balance of $100,000 in our account. Even though the change is $100 in both cases, the reference point impacts that $100. The theory also proposes that people tend to overweight low-probability outcomes and underweight high-probability outcomes (e.g., the odds of getting in an automobile accident are much higher than the odds of being in an airplane crash; however, more people fear flying than driving). This framework has been used to explain a wide variety of apparently irrational decisions. For example, businesses typically take little risk offering money-back guarantees because once people have a product, giving it up (a loss) is considered more aversive than the benefit of getting the money back (a gain).

Stockbyte/Stockbyte/Thinkstock

Photo 12.4 The decoy effect: If we are given the choice of a small for $3, medium for $5, and large for $6, we will select the large more often than if the medium size was not an option.

Dual-Process Framework

Prospect Theory in Street Magic

The finding that our choices often don't seem to follow logical, analytical models of decision making doesn't mean that we can't make decisions that way. It does, however, suggest that we can make decisions many different ways. The dual-process framework, discussed earlier in this chapter for reasoning, has also been proposed to explain why we may reason differently at different times (e.g., Evans, 2008; Kahneman, 2011).

Wilson and Schooler (1991) selected five varieties of jams that had been independently rated by experts for quality. The jams they selected ranged from the top-ranked jam down to one of the worst. In one condition they asked college students to taste the jams, think about what they liked and didn't like about them, and then to rate the jams for taste. The students' ratings looked very different from those of the experts. In another condition, with a different set of tasters, the researchers asked them to taste the jams, answer some questions about why they selected their major, and then rate the jams. The key difference between the conditions was that the raters in the second condition didn't think about why they liked or disliked the jams. Their ratings closely matched those of the experts. Within the dual-process approach, these results are interpreted as reflecting decisions made using two different decision-making systems. When asked to think deliberately and analytically about why they made their judgments about jams, the tasters engaged their System 2 thinking. When asked just to make preference ratings without thinking about the reasoning behind those ratings, the tasters used their System 1 thinking.

This means that how we make decisions in everyday situations can vary depending on what we think about in making those decisions. Dijksterhuis (2004; Dijksterhuis & Nordgren, 2006) has suggested that System 1 thinking that is more automatic and unconscious can result in better reasoning. In one of his studies, subjects were asked to consider apartments or roommates from a list. Alternatives were presented with both the pros and cons of each one. The alternatives were designed by the researchers to have one best option and one worst option based on the number of relative pros and cons. Subjects then made

Dual-Process Theories of Higher Cognition

Daniel Kahneman: Thinking, Fast and Slow

decisions (directly or through rating the alternatives) immediately after alternatives were presented, after a few minutes of conscious thought about the decision, or after completing a distractor task that allowed them to consider alternatives unconsciously (but not consciously). In all of the experiments, subjects who were in the unconscious consideration condition made the best decisions (i.e., chose the "best" alternatives more often or rated them most highly). These results suggest that everyday reasoning may be better when it involves more unconscious processes than conscious, deliberate thought.

Neuroscience of Decision Making

Future Advances in Theories of Reasoning and Decision Making

Understanding how we reason and make decisions under uncertainty is of interest not only to cognitive psychologists. One of the newly emerging multidisciplinary approaches has brought psychologists, neuroscientists, and economists together to develop the field of neuroeconomics (Loewenstein, Rick, & Cohen, 2008; Rustichini, 2009; Sanfey, Loewenstein, McClure, & Cohen, 2006). Researchers in this field are attempting to develop theories about the neural circuitry that underlies our reasoning and decision-making behaviors. However, these behaviors are extremely complex, involving interactions between systems of memory, knowledge representation, language, attention, and perception. Our understanding of the underlying neural circuitry is still in the very early stages, and many researchers recommend caution in using neuroscience findings to interpret theoretical claims (e.g., Del Pinal & Nathan, 2013; Goel, 2007; Henson, 2005, 2006; Poldrack, 2006; Rick, 2011). There is likely no single, unitary reasoning or decision-making system in the brain but instead distributed systems that dynamically respond to particular task demands and environmental cues (Goel, 2007).

How We Decide

Consider, for example, some of the research examining the neuroscience of heuristics and biases. De Neys, Vartanian, and Goel (2007) created scenarios designed to result in conflicts between our probabilistic and heuristic ways of processing (similar to the Tom W story presented earlier in the chapter). Participants were presented brief descriptions of studies and information about a person in the studies. Their task was to choose between two possibilities about that person based on the given information. In addition to recording their participants' behavioral responses, the authors used fMRI to record brain activity of their participants as they performed the task. Table 12.5 presents examples of the four conditions used in the study. The story in the incongruent condition pits base-rate cues (5 engineers and 995 lawyers) against stereotypical cues (no interest in politics, conservative, likes math puzzles). The other three story types were control conditions. In the congruent control condition, one of the answers was consistent with both the base-rate and stereotype information. In the neutral control, there was no stereotypical information in the story, so it was expected that the base-rate information would cue the answer. In the final control, the base-rate information was the same for both groups (e.g., 500 people in each group), so it was expected that participants would base their responses on heuristic information.

Iowa Gambling Task Demonstration

The behavioral results are presented in Figure 12.9. As expected, across the three control conditions participants used the base-rate and stereotypic cues from the stories to make the correct decisions most of the time. In the incongruent condition they sometimes used base-rate information and sometimes used stereotypic information. The authors examined the participants' fMRI data in the right lateral prefrontal cortex (RLPFC; a region involved in response inhibition) and the anterior cingulate cortex (ACC; a region involved in conflict detection). The results indicated that when participants in the incongruent condition responded with base-rate cued answers, there was increased activation in the RLPFC reflecting the inhibition of a stereotype-based response. This activation was not present when they made a stereotype-based response. Additionally, the ACC was activated both when making stereotypic and base-rate responses, indicating that the participants were detecting their bias regardless of which response they gave. The ACC did not show activation across the control conditions where there were no conflicting responses. The

Table 12.5 Examples of Stimuli Used in the De Neys et al. (2008) Study

Incongruent

Study with 5 engineers and 995 lawyers.

Jack is 45 and has four children. He shows no interest in political and social issues and is generally conservative. He likes sailing and mathematical puzzles.

What is most likely?

a. Jack is an engineer. (stereotype cued)
b. Jack is a lawyer. (base-rate cued)

Congruent Control

Study with 5 Swedish people and 995 Italians

Marco is 16. He loves to play soccer with his friends, after which they all go out for pizza or to someone's house for homemade pasta.

What is most likely?

a. Marco is Swedish.
b. Marco is Italian. (base-rate and stereotype cued)

Neutral Control

Study with 5 people who campaigned for Bush and 995 who campaigned for Kerry.

Jim is 5 foot 8 inches tall, has black hair, and is the father of two young girls. He drives a yellow van that is completely covered with posters.

What is most likely?

a. Jim campaigned for Bush.
b. Jim campaigned for Kerry. (base-rate cued)

Heuristic Control

Study with 500 forty-year-olds and 500 seventeen-year-olds.

Rylan lives in Buffalo. He hangs out with his buddies every day and likes watching MTV. He is a big Korn fan and is saving to buy his own car.

What is most likely?

a. Rylan is forty.
b. Rylan is seventeen. (stereotype cued)

Figure 12.9 The Behavioral Results of the Decisions Made in the De Neys et al. (2008) Study

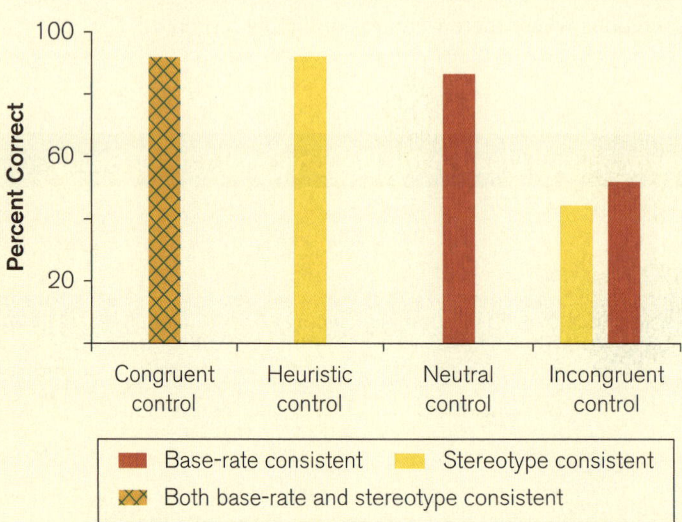

For the congruent control condition, correct answers were consistent with both base-rate and stereotypic cues. For the heuristic control condition, correct answers were consistent with stereotypic cues. For the neutral control condition, correct answers were consistent with base-rate consistent information. For the incongruent conditions, both answers were considered correct—one reflected the stereotypic cues, the other the base-rate cues.

authors interpreted these results as indicating that the bias of the representativeness heuristic results not from a failure to recognize conflicting information but from a failure to inhibit making stereotypic responses.

While our understanding of the massively complex underlying neural circuits involved in our reasoning and decision making is still in the very early stages, the multidisciplinary collaborative approaches that bring cognitive psychologists, economists, and neuroscientists together hold a bright promise. The integration of the insights, methods, and theories of the diverse disciplines is quickly advancing our level of understanding of how we reason and make decisions.

THINKING ABOUT RESEARCH

As you read the following summary of a research study in psychology, think about the following questions:

1. What kind of reasoning is being examined in this study?
2. What are the independent variables in this study?
3. What are the dependent variables in this study?

4. What alternative explanations can you come up with to explain the results of this study?

Study Reference

De Neys, W. (2006). Dual processing in reasoning: Two systems but one reasoner. *Psychological Science, 17*(5), 428–433.

Purpose of the study: The research was designed to examine the impact of working-memory capacity on syllogistic reasoning. The dual-process description of reasoning was tested using a task where cognitive load was manipulated.

Method of the study: Participants were asked to evaluate syllogistic arguments such as the following:

Figure 12.10 Results of the DeNeys (2006) Study. Reasoning Performance for High-, Medium-, and Low-Span Participants as a Function of Cognitive Load and Belief Consistency

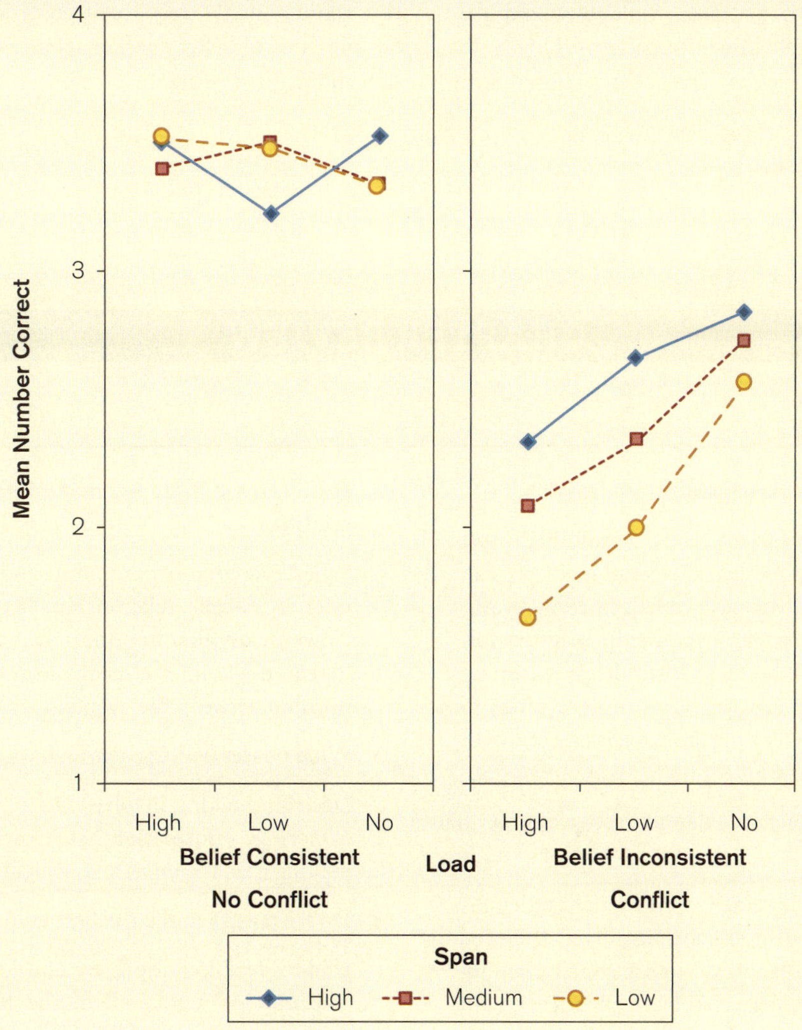

SOURCE: Figure 2, De Neys, W. (2006). Dual processing in reasoning: Two systems but one reasoner. *Psychological Science, 17*(5), 428–433.

(Continued)

(Continued)

All fruits can be eaten.

Hamburgers can be eaten.

Therefore, hamburgers are fruit.

They answered either that the conclusion follows or does not follow logically from the premises. Some of the problems had logically consistent conclusions that were in conflict with common beliefs; others had valid conclusions that were consistent with beliefs. To manipulate cognitive load, participants were also tested in a dot memory task. This task consisted of briefly presenting the participants with dot patterns and asking the participants to reproduce the patterns. High-load dot patterns had complex four-dot patterns, while low-load patterns consisted of simple three-dot patterns. Finally, the participants' working-memory spans were assessed using a word list recall task while performing simple math problems.

Results of the study: The results are presented in Figure 12.10. In the belief-consistent conditions, there were no differences between working-memory span and cognitive load. In contrast, when the conclusions conflicted with belief, there was an effect of cognitive load: As load increased, reasoning performance decreased.

Conclusions of the study: The author concluded that the results support a dual-process model of reasoning. In the absence of belief conflict, reasoning is performed through automatic, resource-free processing. However, the presence of belief conflict requires slower, resource-demanding processing.

CHAPTER REVIEW

Summary

- **How logical are the conclusions you draw?**

  Aristotle and other ancient Greeks established most of what we consider the formal rules of logic. We can use these rules to draw logical conclusions and evaluate formal arguments. However, we don't always follow these formal rules of logic. Instead, our reasoning behavior reflects the cognitive processes we use to reason and is affected by the limitations and biases of these processes.

- **Why are some things harder to reason about than others?**

  The rules of deductive logic are generally independent of the content of arguments. However, often the contents of the arguments do impact our reasoning because of the knowledge about and experience with those contents. Sometimes that knowledge and experience facilitate our reasoning, but in other situations it may interfere. Everyday reasoning is often more difficult because the arguments are often less clearly defined than typical formal arguments.

- **How and when do we make inferences about causal relations?**

  When events co-occur in time and/or space, we often infer a causal relationship between the events. However, another important factor is whether or not we can easily infer a mechanism for the causal relationship between the events.

- **What phases do we go through when we make decisions?**

  Decision making involves five phases: setting goals, gathering information, structuring the decision, making a final choice, and evaluation of the process.

- **Do we always make the best choices?**

  Under ideal conditions we consider all of the available options across all of the relevant conditions when we make decisions. However, often the conditions are not ideal. Because we make decisions using our cognitive processes, our decisions are constrained by those processes. We often use heuristic shortcuts to reduce cognitive demands.

Chapter Quiz

1. Using logical rules about the validity of an argument that draws a conclusion based on general information is an example of
   (a) representational reasoning.
   (b) deductive reasoning.
   (c) inductive reasoning.
   (d) analogical reasoning.
2. Drawing a conclusion about general properties based on specific data information is an example of
   (a) representational reasoning.
   (b) deductive reasoning.
   (c) inductive reasoning.
   (d) analogical reasoning.
3. Drawing conclusions by using the structure of one conceptual domain to interpret another domain is an example of
   (a) representational reasoning.
   (b) deductive reasoning.
   (c) intuitive reasoning.
   (d) analogical reasoning.
4. An example of a counterfactual reasoning problem is the following:
   (a) If all fire trucks are red, and my truck is red, then my truck is a fire truck.
   (b) If I had decided to become a firefighter instead of professor, then I would be in better physical condition.
   (c) If there are five firefighters and seven police officers in a room and two people walk out of the room, what is the probability that one is a firefighter and the other is a police officer?
   (d) Firefighter is to water hose as police officer is to __________?
5. Galotti describes decision making as consisting of which five phases?
   (a) setting goals, gathering information, structuring the decision, making a final choice, evaluation
   (b) identifying the purpose, determining the representation, estimating probabilities, adjusting expectations, learning from past mistakes
   (c) understanding the premise, building mental models, combining mental models, ruling out invalid combinations, evaluating the final model
   (d) identifying representative choices, retrieving available resources, framing the decision, applying heuristics, evaluation
6. Wilson and Schooler's jam experiment demonstrated that
   (a) students and expert tasters never show the same pattern of preferences.
   (b) students and expert tasters always show the same pattern of preferences.
   (c) students and expert tasters sometimes show the same pattern of preferences.
   (d) magazines that report the opinion of experts have no value for our everyday decisions.
7. What are the possible mental models for the statement "Some cars are Fords"?
8. When considering whether two events are related to one another causally, what factors should you consider?
9. Explain the elimination-by-aspects strategy for making decisions.
10. Using stereotypes to make decisions about people is likely to involve the use of what heuristic?

Key Terms

Availability bias 317
Conditional reasoning (propositional reasoning) 300
Deductive reasoning 298
Dual-process framework 308
Framing bias 317
Inductive reasoning 298
Representativeness bias 316
Syllogistic reasoning 299

Stop and Think Answers

12.1. Are the arguments discussed in the Conditional Reasoning section representative of the kinds of arguments you face in your day-to-day experience? If not, how are they different?

Answers will vary.

12.2. Consider the following argument: All Introduction to Psychology courses are taught in large sections, and all large-section courses use multiple-choice exams. Therefore my Introduction to Psychology course will use multiple-choice exams. Is this a valid argument? Do you think it follows the "rules of logic"? Would you change your mind if you learn that the section of your course is being taught by a new professor?

The argument is valid because the conclusion follows from the rules of deductive logic. Answers will vary, but many people change their answer if they think there is a chance that a "new professor" might not use a multiple-choice exam. If they do this, they are challenging the truth of the premises rather than the validity of the argument.

12.3. Consider the following argument: If I study every term on the review sheet, then I will get an A on the exam. I studied hard, therefore I will get an A. Are these valid arguments? Do you think that they follow the "rules of logic"?

Notice that the first part included "If I study every term on the review sheet," but the given information in the second part is "I studied hard." While these two may be related, they are not equivalent, so this is not a valid argument.

12.4. Do you generally consider yourself a "logical thinker"? When you reason about things, do you usually think through all aspects of an argument, or do you usually focus on just a few?

Answers will vary.

12.5. When you make reasoned arguments, what sort of representations do you think you use? Does it feel like you are using something like those proposed by the mental logic or the mental models approach?

Answers will vary.

12.6. Do you think the approach you take when reasoning depends on what you are reasoning about?

Answers will vary.

12.7. Try to think of an example of causal reasoning you did today. How strong is the covariation between the cause and effect events? Did you consider both how often they did not co-occur as well as how often that they did?

Answers will vary.

12.8. Considering the same example that you came up with in Stop and Think 12.7, did you consider alternative hypotheses about the causal effect? Did you engage in counterfactual thinking and ask yourself "What if I had done something else instead?" How does thinking about alternative causes and "what ifs" impact your causal reasoning?

Answers will vary.

12.9. Think back to how you reasoned through the various versions of the four-card problems. How did the reasoning you used to answer those questions compare to how you reason about things in your day-to-day life?

Answers will vary.

12.10. Think back to the last time you made a major purchase or decision (e.g., buying a car, renting a particular apartment, deciding what to major in). What factors did you consider when you made that decision? What kind of information did you gather? How did you combine that information to arrive at your decision?

Answers will vary.

12.11. Think back to a relatively minor decision (e.g., what to eat for breakfast, what to wear today). What factors did you consider when you made that decision? What kind of information did you gather? How did you combine that information to arrive at your decision?

Answers will vary.

12.12. How do the decision processes differ between your answers in Stop and Think 12.10 and 12.11?

Answers will vary.

12.13. Suppose that you are trying to decide whether to get renter's insurance. You recently read a report in the paper that crime rates across the nation are at an all-time low. However, two of your friends recently had their apartment robbed. You go ahead and decide to pay for the insurance. Do you think that your choice may have been biased?

Answers will vary, but the availability heuristic is likely to have influenced the decision.

12.14. Can you think of any real-life decisions you have made that may have been the result of framing? If you were to be in the same situation again, do you think you would make the same decision?

Answers will vary.

Student Study Site

Sharpen your skills with SAGE edge at **edge.sagepub.com/mcbridecp**

SAGE edge for students provides a personalized approach to help you accomplish your coursework goals in an easy-to-use learning environment.

Go to edge.sagepub.com/mcbridecp for additional exercises and web resources. Select Chapter 12, Reasoning and Decision Making, for chapter-specific resources. All of the links listed in the margins of this chapter are accessible via this site.

Glossary

Abstract imagery: an image of an environment based on an overview of the environment

Affordances: behaviors that are possible in a given environment

Algorithm: a prescribed problem-solving strategy that always leads to the correct solution in problems with a single correct solution

Amnesia: a memory deficit due to a brain lesion or deterioration

Analogical transfer: using the same solution for two problems with the same underlying structure

Anaphoric inference: using a pronoun to refer to something in a previous sentence

Anterograde amnesia: a memory deficit for information or experiences encountered after a brain lesion

Automatic processing: processing that is not controlled and does not tax cognitive resources

Availability bias: bias in reasoning where examples easily brought to mind are relied on to make judgments and solve problems

Axon: an extension from the neuron nucleus where an electrical impulse in the neuron occurs

Basic-level concept: level of concept hierarchy where common objects (e.g., dog) reside

Behaviorist: one who adheres to the perspective in psychology that focuses on observable behaviors

Biological perspective: perspective in psychology that describes cognition according to the mechanisms of the brain

Bizarreness effect: result showing that memory for unusual images is superior to memory for typical images

Bottom-up processing: understanding the environment through basic feature identification and processing

Broca's aphasia: a deficit in language production

Case study: a research study that focuses on intensive analyses of a single individual or more broadly on a single observation unit

Categorical perception: an issue in language comprehension due to the categorization of phonemes

Central executive: the part of the working-memory system that controls the flow of information within the system and into long-term memory

Childhood amnesia (infantile amnesia): a phenomenon where many episodic memories of early childhood are inaccessible in later life

Chunking: a process of organizing information that allows more items to be stored in memory

Coarticulation: an issue in language comprehension due to the overlapping of sounds in spoken language

Cocktail party effect: an effect of attention where one's focus changes abruptly due to a salient stimulus (such as one's name) in the environment

Cognitive economy: the idea that concept information is stored at the most efficient level of the hierarchy

Concreteness effect: a result showing that memory for concrete concepts is superior to memory for abstract concepts

Conditional reasoning (propositional reasoning): a process by which a conclusion follows from conditional statements ("if, then" statements)

Consolidation: neural process by which memories are strengthened and more permanently stored in the brain

Controlled processing: processing due to an intention that consumes cognitive resources

Correlational study: a research study that examines relationships between measured variables

Deductive reasoning: making and evaluating arguments from general information to specific information

Deep processing: encoding information according to its meaning

Deep structure: the meaning of a sentence

Dendrites: extensions from neurons that receive chemical messages (neurotransmitters) from other neurons

Dependent variable: the behavior that is measured in a research study

Determinism: the principle that behaviors have underlying causes and that understanding involves identification of what these causes are and how they are related to the behavior of interest

Distal stimulus: stimulus in the environment

Dorsal pathway: the pathway in the brain that processes "where" information about the environment

DRM procedure (Deese-Roediger-McDermott procedure): research methodology that experimentally creates false memories for theme items that are not presented as part of a list of related items

Dual-process framework: the idea that cognitive tasks can be performed using two separate and distinct processes

Dual-task method: a research procedure where subjects are given two tasks to perform at once—to compare with performance on one task alone—to examine interference due to the second task

Elaborative encoding: processing of information according to its meaning to allow for longer storage in memory

Electroencephalography (EEG): a brain recording technique that records the activity of large sections of neurons from different areas of the scalp

Embodied cognition: a perspective in psychology that cognition serves for bodily interaction with the environment

Empiricism: the principle that the key to understanding new things is through systematic observation

Encoding: the process of inputting information into memory

Encoding specificity principle: the idea that memory is best when the circumstances of encoding and retrieval are matched

Episodic buffer: the part of the working-memory system that holds episodic memories as an overflow for the phonological loop and visuospatial sketchpad

Episodic memory: memory for a specific episode or experience in one's life

Exemplar approach: the idea that concepts are represented based on exemplars of the category that one has experienced previously

Experimental study: a research study that examines causal relationships between variables

Framing bias: a bias in reasoning where the context in which a problem is presented influences our judgment

Functional magnetic resonance imaging (fMRI): an MRI technique that images brain activity during a task

Functional fixedness: focusing on how things are typically used and ignoring other potential uses in solving a problem

Gestalt psychology: a perspective in psychology that focuses on how organizational principles allow us to perceive and understand the environment

Heuristic: a problem-solving strategy that does not always lead to the correct solution

Hill-climbing strategy: a problem solving strategy that involves continuous steps toward the goal state

Hippocampus: the area of the brain important for memory encoding and retrieval

IDEAL framework: a step-by-step description of problem-solving processes

Ill-defined problem: a problem that lacks a clearly defined goal state and constraints

Implicit memory: procedural memory that alters performance based on previous experiences

Inattentional blindness (also change blindness): failure to notice a change in the environment

Independent variable: a factor in an experiment that is manipulated by the researcher (e.g., randomly assigning subjects to a group in the experiment)

Inductive reasoning: making and evaluating arguments from specific information to general information

Insight: suddenly realizing the solution to a problem

Invariance problem: an issue in language comprehension due to variation in how phonemes are produced

Level-of-processing effect: an effect showing better memory for information encoded with deep processing than with shallow processing

Long-term memory: long-term (i.e., lifetime) storage of memory after some elaborative processing has occurred

Magnetic resonance imaging (MRI): a technique to image the internal portions of the body using the magnetic fields present in the cells

Magnetoencephalography (MEG): a brain recording technique that records activity of large sections of neurons from different areas of the scalp using a large magnet that is placed over the head

Means-ends strategy: a problem-solving strategy that involves repeated comparisons between the current state and the goal state

Mental set: a tendency to use the same set of solutions to solve similar problems

Method of loci: a memory aid where images of to-be-remembered information are created with locations along a familiar route or place

Misinformation effect: a memory result where subjects have false memories for an event based on suggestive information provided by others

Mnemonics: memory techniques that aid memory performance

Morphemes: the smallest units of a language that contain meaning

Motor imagery: a mental representation of motor movements

Neuron: the basic cell of the brain

Parsimony: the principle of preferring simple explanations over more complex ones

Partial-report method: a research procedure where subjects are asked to report only a portion of the information presented

Pegword mnemonic: a memory aid where ordinal words (e.g., one, two) are rhymed with pegwords (e.g., bun, shoe) to create images of pegwords and to-be-remembered items interacting

Phonemes: distinct sound units that comprise a language

Phoneme restoration effect: the use of top-down processing to comprehend fragmented language

Phonological loop: the part of the working-memory system that holds auditory codes of information

Picture superiority effect: a result showing that memory for pictures is superior to memory for words of the same concepts

Plaques: bundles of protein that develop in the synapse, characteristic of Alzheimer's disease

Positron emission tomography (PET): a technique that images neuron activity in the brain through radioactive markers in the bloodstream

Pragmatics: the examination of how language is used in particular contexts

Primacy effect: an effect in memory showing the best memory for information encoded first

Principle of Pragnanz: an organizational principle that allows for the simplest interpretation of the environment

Proactive interference: when old information interferes with the storage or retrieval of new information

Procedural memory: memory for a skill or procedure

Propositional representation: the idea that visual information is represented nonspatially in the mind

Prospective memory: memory for future intentions

Prototype approach: the idea that concepts are represented based on a typical (common) instance of that concept

Proximal stimulus: stimulus as it is represented in the mind

Recency effect: an effect in memory showing the best memory for information encoded last

Representationalist: one who adheres to the perspective in psychology that concepts can be represented in the mind

Representativeness bias: a bias in reasoning where stereotypes are relied on to make judgments and solve problems

Retrieval: the process of outputting information from memory

Retroactive interference: when new information interferes with the storage or retrieval of old information

Retrograde amnesia: a memory deficit for information learned or experiences encountered before a brain lesion

Scenographic imagery: the image of an environment based on landmarks encountered in that environment along a navigated route

Schema: the general knowledge structure for an event or situation

Scientific method: a method of gaining knowledge in a field that relies on observations of phenomena that allows for tests of hypotheses about those phenomena

Semantic memory: memory for facts or knowledge

Semantics: meaning contained within language

Sensory memory: the very short-term memory storage of unprocessed sensory information

Sensory system: a system that receives and processes input from stimuli in the environment

Serial position curve: an effect in memory showing the best memory for information encoded at the beginning and end of an encoding session

Shadowing task: a research procedure where subjects are asked to repeat (i.e., shadow) a message heard over headphones

Shallow processing: encoding information according to its surface features

Short-term memory: the short-term storage of memory with minimal processing that is forgotten quickly without elaborative processing

Simon effect: interference in response due to inconsistency between the response and the stimulus

Single-cell recording: a brain activity recording technique that records activity from a single neuron or small group of neurons in the brain

Spacing effect: an effect showing better memory when information is studied in smaller units over time instead of all at once, as in cramming

Spatial representation: the idea that visual information is represented in analog form in the mind

Storage: the process of storing information in memory

Stroop task: a research procedure where subjects are asked to name the color of printed words where some words are color words that conflict with the print color showing interference in the naming task

Subordinate concept: the level of concept hierarchy where specific exemplars of a basic-level concept (e.g., husky) reside

Superordinate concept: the level of concept hierarchy where general categories of the basic-level concepts (e.g., mammal) reside

Surface structure: the order of words presented in a sentence

Syllogistic reasoning: a process by which a conclusion follows necessarily from a series of statements

Synapse: a space between neurons where neurotransmitters are released and received

Syntactic parsing: building the syntactic structure of a sentence

Syntax: the rules structure of a language

Tangles: protein fibers that develop in a neuron's nucleus characteristic of Alzheimer's disease

Testability: the principle that theories must be stated in ways that allow them to be evaluated through observation

Testing effect: an effect in memory showing better memory for information that has been tested in the retention interval as compared with other encoding of the information

Theory of unconscious inference: the idea that we make unconscious inferences about the world when we perceive it

Top-down processing: understanding the environment through global knowledge of the environment and its principles

Transcranial direct current stimulation (tDCS): a method of temporarily stimulating or suppressing neurons using an electrical current

Transcranial magnetic stimulation (TMS): a method of temporarily stimulating or suppressing neurons using a magnetic field

Transfer-appropriate processing: an effect in memory showing that matches in processing between encoding and retrieval improve memory

Typicality effect: a result where more common members of a category show a processing advantage

Ventral pathway: the pathway in the brain that processes "what" information about the environment

Visuospatial sketchpad: the part of the working-memory system that holds visual and spatial codes of information

Well-defined problem: a problem that has a clearly defined goal state and constraints

Wernicke's aphasia: a deficit in language comprehension

Working-backward strategy: a problem-solving strategy that involves beginning with the goal state and working back to the initial state

Working memory: processing a unit of information that is the current focus of attention

References

Abrams, R. A., & Balota, D. A. (1991). Mental chronometry: Beyond reaction time. *Psychological Science, 2*, 153–157.

Abu-Obeid, N. (1998). Abstract and scenographic imagery: The effect of environmental form on wayfinding. *Journal of Environmental Psychology, 18*, 159–173.

Aitchison, J. (2003). *Words in the mind: An introduction to the mental lexicon* (3rd ed.). Oxford, UK: Blackwell.

Allen, S. W., & Brooks, L. R. (1991). Specializing the operation of an explicit rule. *Journal of Experimental Psychology: General, 120*, 3–19.

Altmann, G. T. M. (1998). Ambiguity in sentence processing. *Trends in Cognitive Sciences*, 2, 146–152.

Amit, E., & Greene, J. D. (2012). You see, the ends don't justify the means: Visual imagery and moral judgment. *Psychological Science, 23*, 861–868.

Anderson, J. R. (1976). *Language, memory, and associative memory*. Washington, DC: Hemisphere Press.

Anderson, J. R., & Bower, G. H. (1973). *Human associative memory*. Washington, DC: Winson.

Anglin, J. M. (1977). *Word, object and conceptual development*. New York: Norton.

Arnold, J. E., Eisenband, J. G., Brown-Schmidt, S., & Trueswell, J. C. (2000). The rapid use of gender information: Evidence of the time course of pronoun resolution from eye tracking. *Cognition, 76*, B13–B26.

Atkinson, R. C., & Shiffrin, R. M. (1968). Human memory: A proposed system and its control processes. In K. W. Spence & J. T. Spence (Eds.), *The psychology of learning and motivation: Advances in research and theory* (Vol. 2, pp. 89–195). New York: Academic Press.

Baars, B. J. (2007). Attention and consciousness. In B. J. Baars & N. M. Gage (Eds.), *Cognition, brain, and consciousness: Introduction to cognitive neuroscience*. San Diego, CA: Academic Press.

Baddeley, A. D. (1992). Working memory. *Science, 255*, 556–559.

Baddeley, A. D. (1998). Recent developments in working memory. *Current Opinion in Neurobiology, 8*, 234–238.

Baddeley, A. D. (2000). The episodic buffer: A new component of working memory? *Trends in Cognitive Sciences, 4*, 417–423.

Baddeley, A. D. (2012). Working memory: Theories, models, and controversies. *Annual Review of Psychology, 63*, 1–29.

Baddeley, A. D., & Hitch, G. J. (1974). Working memory. In G. H. Bower (Ed.), *The psychology of learning and motivation: Advances in research and theory* (Vol. 8, pp. 47–89). New York: Academic Press.

Baddeley, A. D., Hitch, G. J., & Allen, R. J. (2009). Working memory and binding in sentence recall. *Journal of Memory and Language, 61*, 438–456.

Baddeley, A. D., Lewis, V., & Vallar, G. (1984). Exploring the articulatory loop. *Quarterly Journal of Experimental Psychology, 36A*, 233–252.

Baddeley, A. D., Thompson, N., & Buchanan, M. (1975). Word length and the structure of short-term memory. *Journal of Verbal Learning and Verbal Behavior, 14*, 575–589.

Bahrick, H. P. (1984). Semantic memory content in permastore: Fifty years of memory for Spanish learned in school. *Journal of Experimental Psychology: General, 113*, 1–29.

Balota, D. A. (1990). The role of meaning in word processing. In D. A. Balota, G. Flores D'Arcais, & K. Rayner (Eds.), *Comprehension processes in reading* (pp. 9–32). Hillsdale, NJ: Lawrence Erlbaum.

Balota, D. A., & Chumbley, J. I. (1984). Are lexical decisions a good measure of lexical access? The role of word frequency in the neglected decision stage. *Journal of Experimental Psychology: Human Perception and Performance, 10*, 340–357.

Banaji, M. R., & Greenwald, A. G. (1994). Implicit stereotyping in judgements of fame. *Journal of Personality and Social Psychology, 68*, 181–198.

Barron, E., Riby, L. M., Greer, J., & Smallwood, J. (2011). Absorbed in thought: The effect of mind wandering on the processing of relevant and irrelevant events. *Psychological Science, 22*, 596–601.

Barsalou, L. W. (1985). Ideals, central tendency, and frequency of instantiation as determinants of graded structure in categories. *Journal of Experimental Psychology: Learning, Memory, and Cognition, 11*, 629–654.

Barsalou, L. W. (2008). Grounded cognition. *Annual Review of Psychology, 59*, 617–645.

Barsalou, L. W. (2010). Grounded cognition: Past, present, and future. *Topics in Cognitive Science, 2*, 716–724.

Bartlett, F. C. (1932). *Remembering: A study in experimental and social psychology*. Cambridge, UK: Cambridge University Press.

Batteli, L., Pascual-Leone, A., & Cavanagh, P. (2007). The "when" pathway of the right parietal lobe. *Trends in Cognitive Sciences, 11*, 204–210.

Beall, A. C., & Loomis, J. M. (1997) Optic flow and visual analysis of the base-to-final turn. *International Journal of Aviation Psychology, 7*, 201–223.

Belleville, S., Clément, F., Mellah, S., Gilbert, B., Fontaine, F., & Gauthier, S. (2011). Training-related brain plasticity in subjects at risk of developing Alzheimer's disease. *Brain, 134*, 1623–1634.

Bergelson, E., & Swingley, D. (2012). At 6-9 months, human infants know the meanings of many common nouns. *Proceedings of the National Academy of Sciences, 109*, 3253–3258.

Berlin, B. (1992). *Ethnobiological classification. Principles of categorization of plants and animals in traditional societies.* Princeton, NJ: Princeton University Press.

Biederman, I. (1987). Recognition-by-components: A theory of human image understanding. *Psychological Review, 94,* 115–147.

Bilalic, M., McLeod, P., & Gobet, F. (2008). Why good thoughts block better ones: The mechanism of the pernicious Einstellung (set) effect. *Cognition, 108,* 652–661.

Bjork, R. A., & Bjork, E. L. (1992). A new theory of disuse and an old theory of stimulus fluctuation. In A. Healy, S. Kosslyn, & R. Shiffrin (Eds.), *From learning processes to cognitive processes: Essays in honor of William K. Estes* (Vol. 2, pp. 35–67). Hillsdale, NJ: Erlbaum.

Bjork, R. A., & Whitten, W. B. (1974). Recency-sensitive retrieval processes in long-term free recall. *Cognitive Psychology, 6,* 173–189.

Blaxton, T. A. (1989). Investigating dissociations among memory measures: Support for a transfer appropriate processing framework. *Journal of Experimental Psychology: Learning, Memory, and Cognition, 15,* 657–668.

Bock, J. K. (1996). Language production: Methods and methodologies. *Psychonomic Bulletin and Review, 34,* 395–421.

Bock, J. K., & Eberhard, K. M. (1993). Meaning, sound, and syntax in English number agreement. *Language & Cognitive Processes, 8,* 57–99.

Bock, J. K., & Miller, C. A. (1991). Broken agreement. *Cognitive Psychology, 23,* 45–93.

Böckler, A., van der Wel, P. R. D., & Welsh, T. N. (2014). Catching eyes: Effects of social and nonsocial cues on attention capture. *Psychological Science, 25,* 720–727.

Borchers, S., Christensen, A., Ziegler, L., & Himelbach, M. (2010). Visual action control does not rely on strangers: Effects of pictorial cues under monocular and binocular vision. *Neuropsychologia, 49,* 556–563.

Bowden, E. M., Jung-Beeman M., Fleck, J., & Kounios J. (2005). New approaches to demystifying insight. *Trends in Cognitive Sciences, 9,* 322–328.

Braine, M. D. S. (1978). On the relation between the natural logic of reasoning and standard logic. *Psychological Review, 85,* 1–21.

Brainerd, C. J., & Reyna, V. F. (1998). Fuzzy-trace theory and children's false memories. *Journal of Experimental Child Psychology, 71,* 81–129.

Brandone, A. C., Pence, K. L., Golinkoff, R. M., & Hirsh-Pasek, K. (2007). Action speaks louder than words: Young children differentially weight perceptual, social, and linguistic cues to learn verbs. *Child Development, 78,* 1322–1342.

Branigan, H. P., Pickering, M. J., & Cleland, A. A. (1999). Syntactic priming in written production: Evidence for rapid decay. *Psychonomic Bulletin & Review, 6,* 635–640.

Bransford, J. D., & Johnson, M. K. (1972). Contextual prerequisites for understanding: Some investigations of comprehension and recall. *Journal of Verbal Learning and Verbal Behavior, 11,* 717–726.

Bransford, J. D., & Stein, B. S. (1993). *The ideal problem solver: A guide for improving thinking, learning, and creativity* (2nd ed.). New York: W. H. Freeman.

Brewer, M. B., Dull, V., & Lui, L. (1981). Perceptions of the elderly: Stereotypes as prototypes. *Journal of Personality and Social Psychology, 41,* 656–670.

Brewer, W. F., & Treyens, J. C. (1981). Role of schemata in memory for places. *Cognitive Psychology, 13,* 207–230.

Broadbent, D. E. (1958). *Perception and communication.* London: Pergamon Press.

Broca, P. (1861). Remarques sur le siége de la faculté. de la parole articulé, suivies d'une observation d'aphémie (perte de parole). *Bulletin de la Société d'Anatomie* (Paris), *36,* 330–357.

Brooks, L. R. (1968). Spatial and verbal components of the act of recall. *Canadian Journal of Psychology, 22,* 349–368.

Brown, J. (1958). Some tests of the decay theory of immediate memory. *Quarterly Journal of Experimental Psychology, 10,* 12–21.

Brown, R. (1958). *Words and things.* Glencoe, IL: Free Press.

Bullock, T. H. (1961). *Four notes for discussion.* Cambridge, MA: MIT Press.

Byrne, R. M. J. (2002). Mental models and counterfactual thinking. *Trends in Cognitive Sciences, 6,* 405–445.

Calvo-Merino, B., Glaser, D. E., Grèzes, J., Passingham, R. E., & Haggard, P. (2005). Action observation and acquired motor skills: An fMRI study with expert dancers. *Cerebral Cortex, 15,* 1243–1249.

Campo, N. S., Gregory, A. H., & Fisher, R. (2012). Interviewing behaviors in police investigators: A field study of a current U.S. sample. *Psychology, Crime, and Law, 18,* 359–375.

Carey, S. (1985). *Conceptual change in childhood.* Cambridge, MA: MIT Press.

Castel, A. D., McCabe, D. P., Roediger, H. L., III, & Heitman, J. L. (2007). The dark side of expertise: Domain-specific memory errors. *Psychological Science, 18,* 3–5.

Chase, W. G., & Simon, H. A. (1973). The mind's eye in chess. In W. G. Chase (Ed.), *Visual information processing* (pp. 215–281). New York: Academic Press.

Chater, N., & Oaksford, M. R. (1999). The probability heuristics model of syllogistic reasoning. *Cognitive Psychology, 38,* 191–258.

Chein, J. M., & Weisberg, R. W. (2014). Working memory and insight in verbal problems: Analysis of compound and remote associates. *Memory & Cognition, 42,* 67–83.

Cheng, P. W., & Holyoak, K. J. (1985). Pragmatic reasoning schemas. *Cognitive Psychology, 17,* 391–416.

Cheng, P. W., & Novick, L. R. (1992). Covariation in natural causal induction. *Psychological Review, 99,* 365–382.

Cherry, E. C. (1953). Some experiments on the recognition of speech, with one and with two ears. *Journal of the Acoustical Society of America, 25,* 975–979.

Chi, M. T. H. (2006). Two approaches to the study of experts' characteristics. In K. A. Ericsson, N. Charness, P. J. Feltovich, & R. R. Hoffman (Eds.), *The Cambridge handbook of expertise and expert performance* (pp. 21–30). Cambridge, UK: Cambridge University Press.

Chi, M. T. H., Feltovich, P. J., & Glaser, R. (1981). Categorization and representation of physics problems by experts and novices. *Cognitive Science, 5,* 121–152.

Chi, R. P., & Snyder, A. W. (2011). Facilitate insight by non-invasive brain stimulation, *PLoS One, 6,* 181–197.

Chi, R. P., & Snyder, A. W. (2012). Brain stimulation enables the solution of an inherently difficult problem. *Neuroscience Letters, 515*, 121–124.

Chomsky, N. (1957). *Syntactic structures.* The Hague: Mouton.

Chomsky. N. (1959). A review of Skinner's Verbal Behavior. *Language, 35*, 26–58.

Chomsky, N. (1965). *Aspects of the theory of syntax.* Cambridge, MA: MIT Press.

Chronicle, E. P., Ormerod, T. C., & MacGregor, J. N. (2001). When insight just won't come: The failure of visual cues in the nine-dot problem. *Quarterly Journal of Experimental Psychology: Human Experimental Psychology, 54*(A), 903–919.

Clark, H. H. (1996). *Using language.* Cambridge, UK: Cambridge University Press.

Clifasefi, S. L., Bernstein, D. M., Mantonakis, A., & Loftus, E. F. (2013). "Queasy does it": False alcohol beliefs and memories may lead to diminished alcohol preferences. *Acta Psychologica, 143*, 14–19.

Coane, J. H., & McBride, D. M. (2006). The role of test structure in creating false memories. *Memory & Cognition, 34*, 1026–1036.

Cohen, B., & Murphy, G. L. (1984). Models of concepts. *Cognitive Science, 8*, 27–58.

Cohen, G., & Faulkner, D. (1989). Age differences in source forgetting: Effects on reality monitoring and eyewitness testimony. *Psychology and Aging, 4*, 10–17.

Colbert, J. M., & McBride, D. M. (2007). Comparing decay rates for accurate and false memories in the DRM paradigm. *Memory & Cognition, 35*, 1600–1609.

Collins, A. M., & Loftus, E. F. (1975). A spreading-activation theory of semantic processing. *Psychological Review, 82*, 407–428.

Collins, A. M., & Quillian, M. R. (1969). Retrieval time from semantic memory. *Journal of Verbal Learning and Verbal Behavior, 8*, 241–248.

Conrad, R. (1964). Acoustic confusion in immediate memory. *British Journal of Psychology, 55*, 75–84.

Conway, A. R. A., Cowan, N., & Bunting, M. F. (2001). The cocktail party phenomenon revisited: The importance of working memory capacity. *Psychonomic Bulletin & Review, 8*, 331–335.

Corballis, M. C. (2010). Mirror neurons and the evolution of language. *Brain and Language, 112*, 25–35.

Cosmides, L. (1989). The logic of social exchange: Has natural selection shaped how humans reason? Studies with the Wason selection task. *Cognition, 31*, 187–316.

Cowan, N. (1988). Evolving conceptions of memory storage, selective attention, and their mutual constraints within the human information processing system. *Psychological Bulletin, 104*, 163–191.

Cowan, N. (1999). An embedded-processes model of working memory. In A. Miyake & P. Shah (Eds.), *Models of working memory: Mechanisms of active maintenance and executive control* (pp. 62–101). Cambridge, UK: Cambridge University Press.

Cowan, N. (2001). The magical number 4 in short-term memory: A reconsideration of mental storage capacity. *Behavioral and Brain Sciences, 24*, 87–185.

Cox, C. S., Chee, E., Chase, G. A., Baumgardner, T. L., Schuerholz, L. J., Reader, M. J., et al. (1997). Reading proficiency affects the construct validity of the Stroop Test Interference Score. *Clinical Neuropsychologist, 11*, 105–110.

Craik, F. I. M., & Tulving, E. (1975). Depth of processing and the retention of words in episodic memory. *Journal of Experimental Psychology: General, 104*, 268–294.

Cree, G. S., McRae, K., & McNorgan, C. (1999). An attractor model of lexical conceptual processing: Simulating semantic priming. *Cognitive Science, 23*, 371–414.

Cruse, D. A. (1977). The pragmatics of lexical specificity. *Journal of Linguistics, 11*, 153–164.

Cummins, D. D. (1995). Naïve theories and causal deduction. *Memory & Cognition, 23*, 646–658.

Cutting, C. J., & Ferreira, V. S. (1999). Semantic and phonological information flow in the production lexicon. *Journal of Experimental Psychology: Learning, Memory, and Cognition, 25*, 318–344.

Damian, M. F., & Martin, R. C. (1999). Semantic and phonological factors interact in single word production. *Journal of Experimental Psychology: Learning, Memory, and Cognition, 25*, 345–361.

Darwin, C. T., Turvey, M. T., & Crowder, R. G. (1974). An auditory analogue of the Sperling partial report procedure: Evidence for brief auditory storage. *Cognitive Psychology, 3*, 255–267.

Davidson, J. E. (1995). The suddenness of insight. In R. J. Sternberg & J. E. Davidson (Eds.), *The nature of insight* (pp. 125–155). Cambridge, MA: MIT Press.

Davidson, J. E., & Sternberg, R. J. (1986). What is insight? *Educational Horizons, 64*, 177–179.

de Groot, A. D. (1966). Perception and memory versus thought: Some old ideas and recent findings. In B. Kleinmuntz (Ed.), *Problem solving: Research, method and theory* (pp. 19–50). New York: John Wiley & Sons.

De Neys, W. (2006). Dual processing in reasoning: Two systems but one reasoner. *Psychological Science, 17*(5), 428–433.

De Neys, W., Vartanian, O., & Goel, V. (2008). Smarter than we think: When our brains detect that we are biased. *Psychological Science, 19*, 483–489.

DeCasper, A. J., Lecanuet, J.-P., Busnel, M. C., Granier-Deferre, C., & Maugeais, R. (1994). Fetal reactions to recurrent maternal speech. *Infant Behaviour and Development, 17*(2), 159–164.

Decety, J., & Grèzes, J. (2006). The power of simulation: Imagining one's own and other's behavior. *Brain Research, 24*, 4–14.

Deese, J. (1950). On the prediction of occurrence of particular verbal intrusions in immediate recall. *Journal of Experimental Psychology, 58*, 17–22.

Del Pinal, G., & Nathan, M. J. (2013). There and up again: On the uses and misuses of neuroimaging in psychology. *Cognitive Neuropsychology, 30*, 233–252.

Dell, G. S. (1986). A spreading-activation theory of retrieval in sentence production. *Psychological Review, 93*, 283–321.

Demers, R. A. (1988). Linguistics and animal communication. In F. J. Newmeyer (Ed.), *Linguistics: The Cambridge survey* (pp. 314–335). New York: Cambridge University Press.

Devine, P. G. (1989). Stereotypes and prejudice: Their automatic and controlled components. *Journal of Personality and Social Psychology, 56*, 5–18.

Dewey, J. (1910). *How we think*. Boston: Heath.

Dickstein, L. S. (1981). Conversion and possibility in syllogistic reasoning. *Bulletin of the Psychonomic Society, 18*, 229–232.

Dijksterhuis, A. (2004). Think different: The merits of unconscious thought in preference development and decision making. *Journal of Personality and Social Psychology, 87*, 586–598.

Dijksterhuis, A., & Nordgren, L. F. (2006). A theory of unconscious thought. *Perspectives on Psychological Science, 1*, 95–109.

Dominey, P. F., & Dodane, C. (2004). Indeterminacy in language acquisition: The role of child directed speech and joint attention. *Journal of Neurolinguistics, 17*, 121–145.

Donders, F. C. (1969). On the speed of mental processes. *Acta Psychologica, 30*, 412–431. [Translation of Die Schnelligkeit psychischer Processe, first published in 1868.]

Dronkers, N. F., Plaisant, O., Iba-Zizen, M. T., & Cabanis, E. A. (2007). Paul Broca's historic cases: High resolution MR imaging of the brains of Leborgne and Lelong. *Brain, 130*, 1432–1441.

Duncker, K. (1945). On problem solving. *Psychological Monographs, 58*(5), i–113.

Düzel, E., Yonelinas, A. P., Mangun, G. R., Heinz, H-J., & Tulving, E. (1997). Event-related brain potential correlates of two states of conscious awareness in memory. *Proceedings of the National Academy of Sciences, 94*, 5973–5978.

Eagle, M., & Leiter, E. (1964). Recall and recognition in intentional and incidental learning. *Journal of Experimental Psychology, 68*, 58–63.

Ebbinghaus, H. (1885). *Memory: A contribution to experimental psychology*. Translated by H. A. Ruger & C. E. Bussenius (1913). New York: Teachers College, Columbia University.

Eich, E. (1995). Searching for mood dependent memory. *Psychological Science, 6*, 67–75.

Eimas, P. D., Siqueland, E. R., Jusczyk, P., & Vigorito, J. (1971). Speech perception in infants. *Science, 171*, 303–306.

Einstein, G. O., & McDaniel, M. A. (1990). Normal aging and prospective memory. *Journal of Experimental Psychology: Learning, Memory, and Cognition, 16*, 717–726.

Einstein, G. O., McDaniel, M. A., Thomas, R., Mayfield, S., Shank, H., Morrisette, N., et al. (2005). Multiple processes in prospective memory retrieval: Factors determining monitoring versus spontaneous retrieval. *Journal of Experimental Psychology: General, 134*, 327–342.

Ellis, N. C., & Hennelly, R. A. (1980). A bilingual word-length effect: Implications for intelligence testing and the relative ease of mental calculation in Welsh and English. *British Journal of Psychology, 71*, 43–51.

Emberson, L. L., Lupyan, G., Goldstein, M. H., & Spivey, M. J. (2010). Overheard cell-phone conversations: When less speech is more distracting. *Psychological Science, 21*, 1383–1388.

Epstein, M. L. (1980). The relationship of mental imagery and mental rehearsal to performance of a motor task. *Journal of Sport & Exercise Psychology, 2*, 211–220.

Erard, M. (2007). *Um. . .: Slips, stumbles, and verbal blunders, and what they mean*. New York: Random House.

Erickson, K. I., Voss, M. W., Prakash, R. S., Basak, C., Szabo, A., Chaddock, L., et al. (2011). Exercise training increases size of hippocampus and improves memory. *Proceedings of the National Academy of Sciences, 108*, 3017–3022.

Evans, J. St. B. T. (1984). Heuristic and analytic processes in reasoning. *British Journal of Psychology, 75*, 451–468.

Evans, J. St. B. T. (2006). The heuristic-analytic theory of reasoning: Extension and evaluation. *Psychonomic Bulletin and Review, 13*, 378–395.

Evans, J. St. B. T. (2008). Dual-process accounts of reasoning, judgment, and social cognition. *Annual Review of Psychology, 59*, 255–278.

Evans, J. St. B. T. (2012). Questions and challenges to the new psychology of reasoning. *Thinking & Reasoning, 18*(1), 5–31.

Fajen, B., Riley, M., & Turvey, M. (2009). Information, affordances, and the control of action in sport. *Journal of Sport Psychology, 40*(1), 79–107.

Feeney, A., & Heit, E. (2007). *Inductive reasoning: Experimental, developmental and computational approaches*. Cambridge, UK: Cambridge University Press.

Fernandez-Duque, D., & Johnson, M. L. (1999). Attention metaphors: How metaphors guide the cognitive psychology of attention. *Cognitive Science, 23*, 83–116.

Fiebelkorn, I. C., Foxe, J. J., Schwartz, T. H., & Molholm, S. (2010). Staying within the lines: The formation of visuospatial boundaries influences multisensory feature integration. *European Journal of Neuroscience, 31*, 1737–1743.

Foer, J. (2011). *Moonwalking with Einstein: The art and science of remembering everything*. New York: Penguin Press.

Foley, J. E., & Cohen, A. J. (1984). Mental mapping of megastructure. *Canadian Journal of Psychology, 38*, 440–453.

Ford, M. (1994). Two modes of representation and problem solution in syllogistic reasoning. *Cognition, 54*, 1–71.

Fouts, R. S., Fouts, D. H., & Van Canfort, T. E. (1989). The infant Loulis learns signs from cross-fostered chimpanzees. In R. A. Gardner, B. T. Gardner, & T. E. Van Cantfort (Eds.), *Teaching sign language to chimpanzees*. Albany: State University of New York Press.

Fox Tree, J. E. (2001). Listeners' uses of um and uh in speech comprehension. *Memory & Cognition, 29*(2), 320–326.

Francis, W. S. (2005). Bilingual semantic and conceptual representation. In J. F. Kroll & A. M. B. de Groot (Eds.), *Handbook of bilingualism: Psycholinguistic approaches* (pp. 251–267). New York: Oxford University Press.

Frazier, L. (1987). Sentence processing: A tutorial review. In M. Coltheart (Ed.), *Attention and performance: Vol. XII. The psychology of reading* (pp. 559–586). Hillsdale, NJ: Erlbaum.

Frazier, L., & Fodor, J. D. (1978). The sausage machine: A new two-stage parsing model. *Cognition, 6*, 291–325.

Fromkin, V. A. (1971). The non-anomalous nature of anomalous utterances. *Language, 47*, 27–52.

Fugelsang, J. A., Thompson, V. A., & Dunbar, K. N. (2006). Examining the representation of causal knowledge. *Thinking & Reasoning, 12*, 1–30.

Gallo, D. A. (2010). False memories and fantastic beliefs: 15 years of the DRM illusion. *Memory & Cognition, 38*, 833–848.

Galotti, K. M. (1989). Approaches to studying formal and everyday reasoning. *Psychological Bulletin, 105*, 331–351.

Galotti, K. M. (2002). *Making decisions that matter: How people face important life choices.* Mahwah, NJ: Erlbaum.

Ganel, T., Tanzer, M., & Goodale, M. A. (2008). A double dissociation between action and perception in the context of visual illusions: Opposite effects of real and illusory size. *Psychological Science, 19*, 221–225.

Gardner, R. A., & Gardner, B. T. (1969). Teaching sign language to a chimpanzee. *Science, 165*, 664–672.

Garrett, M. F. (1975). The analysis of sentence production. In G. H. Bower (Ed.), *The psychology of learning and motivation* (Vol. 9). New York: Academic Press.

Garrett, M. F. (1988). Processes in language production. In F. J. Nieuwmeyer (Ed.), *Linguistics: The Cambridge survey. Vol. III. Biological and psychological aspects of language* (pp. 69–96). Cambridge, MA: Harvard University Press.

Garrod, S., & Anderson, A. (1987). Saying what you mean in dialogue: A study in conceptual and semantic co-ordination. *Cognition, 27*, 181–218.

Garrod, S., & Pickering, M. J. (2004). Why is conversation so easy? *Trends in Cognitive Sciences, 8*, 8–11.

Garrod, S., & Sanford, A. J. (1977). Interpreting anaphoric relations: The integration of semantic information while reading. *Journal of Verbal Learning and Verbal Behavior, 16*, 77–90.

Geiselman, R. E., Fisher, R. P., MacKinnon, D. P., & Holland, H. L. (1986). Enhancement of eyewitness memory with the cognitive interview. *American Journal of Psychology, 99*, 385–401.

Gentner, T. Q., Fenn, K. M., Margoliash, D., & Nusbaum, H. C. (2006). Recursive syntactic pattern learning by songbirds. *Nature, 440*, 1204–1207.

Gernsbacher, M. A., & Kaschak, M. P. (2003). Neuroimaging studies of language production and comprehension. *Annual Review of Psychology, 54*, 91–114.

Gibson, E., & Pearlmutter, N. J. (1998). Constraints on sentence comprehension. *Trends in Cognitive Sciences, 2*(7), 262–268.

Gibson, J. J. (1979). *Ecological approach to visual perception.* Boston: Houghton Mifflin.

Gick, M. L., & Holyoak, K. J. (1980). Analogical problem solving. *Cognitive Psychology, 12*, 306–355.

Glanzer, M., & Cunitz, A. R. (1966). Two storage mechanisms in free recall. *Journal of Verbal Learning and Verbal Behavior, 5*, 351–360.

Glenberg, A. M., & Kaschak, M. P. (2002). Grounding language in action. *Psychonomic Bulletin & Review, 9*, 558–565.

Gobet, F., & Simon, H. A. (1996). The roles of recognition processes and look-ahead search in time-constrained expert problem solving: Evidence from grand-master-level chess. *Psychological Science, 7*, 52–55.

Godden, D. R., & Baddeley, A. D. (1975). Context-dependent memory in two natural environments: On land and underwater. *British Journal of Psychology, 66*, 325–331.

Goel, V. (2007). Anatomy of deductive reasoning. *Trends in Cognitive Sciences, 11*, 435–441.

Goel, V. (2010). Neural basis of thinking: Laboratory problems versus real-world problems. *WIREs Cognitive Science, 1*, 613–621.

Golinkoff, R. M., Mervis, C. B., & Hirsh-Pasek, K. (1994). Early object labels: The case for a developmental lexical principles framework. *Journal of Child Language, 21*, 125–155.

Gosche, K. M., Mortimer, J. A., Smith, C. D., Markesbery, W. R., & Snowdon, D. A. (2002). An automated technique for measuring hippocampal volumes from MR imaging studies. *American Journal of Neuroradiology, 22*, 1686–1689.

Grant, E. R., & Spivey, M. J. (2003). Eye movements and problem solving: Guiding attention guides thought. *Psychological Science, 14*(5), 462–466.

Grice, H. P. (1989). *Studies in the way of words.* Cambridge, MA: Harvard University Press.

Griffin, Z. M. (2004). Why look? Reasons for eye movements related to language production. In J. M. Henderson & F. Ferreira (Eds.), *The interface of language, vision, and action: Eye movements and the visual world* (pp. 213–248). New York: Psychology Press.

Griggs, R. A., & Cox, J. R. (1982). The elusive thematic-materials effect in Wason's selection task. *British Journal of Psychology, 73*, 407–420.

Grill-Spector, K. (2008). What has fMRI taught us about object recognition? In S. J. Dickinson, A. Leonardis, B. Schiele, & M. J. Tarr (Eds.), *Object categorization: Computer and human vision perspectives* (pp. 102–128). Cambridge, UK: Cambridge University Press.

Gross, C. G. (2002). Genealogy of the "grandmother cell." *Neuroscientist, 8*, 512–518.

Haider, H., & Frensch, P. A. (1999). Eye movement during skill acquisition: More evidence for the information-reduction hypothesis. *Journal of Experimental Psychology: Learning, Memory, and Cognition, 25*(1), 172–190.

Hampton, J. A. (1979). Polymorphous concepts in semantic memory. *Journal of Verbal Learning and Verbal Behavior, 18*, 441–461.

Hampton, J. A. (1982). A demonstration of intransitivity in natural categories. *Cognition, 12*, 151–164.

Hampton, J. A. (1997). Associative and similarity-based processes in categorization decisions. *Memory & Cognition, 25*, 625–640.

Hanson, V. I. (1990). Recall of order information by deaf signers: Phonetic coding in temporal order recall. *Memory & Cognition, 18*, 604–610.

Harlow, J. M. (1868/1993). Recovery from the passage of an iron bar through the head. *History of Psychiatry, 4*, 274–281.

Hart, B., & Risley, T. (1995). *Meaningful differences in the everyday experience of young American children*. Baltimore: Brookes.

Hashtroudi, S., Johnson, M. K., & Chrosniak, L. D. (1990). Aging and qualitative characteristics of memories for perceived and imagined complex events. *Psychology and Aging, 5*, 119–126.

Hauk, O., Johnsrude, I., & Pulvermüller, F. (2004). Somatotopic representation of action words in human motor and premotor cortex. *Neuron, 41*, 301–307.

Hauser, M. D., Chomsky, N., & Fitch, W. T. (2002). The faculty of language: What is it, who has it, and how did it evolve? *Science, 298*, 1569–1579.

Healy, A. F. (1974). Separating item from order information in short-term memory. *Journal of Verbal Learning and Verbal Behavior, 13*, 644–655.

Hegarty, M. (1992). Mental animation: Inferring movement from static displays of mechanical systems. *Journal of Experimental Psychology: Learning, Memory, and Cognition, 18*, 1084–1102.

Hegarty, M. (2004). Dynamic visualizations and learning: Getting to the difficult questions. *Learning and Instruction, 14*, 343–351.

Heit, E., & Rubinstein, J. (1994). Similarity and property effects in inductive reasoning. *Journal of Experimental Psychology: Learning, Memory, and Cognition, 20*, 411–422.

Henson, R. (2005). What can functional neuroimaging tell the experimental psychologist? *Quarterly Journal of Experimental Psychology, 58*, 193–234.

Henson, R. (2006). Forward inference using functional neuroimaging: Dissociations versus associations. *Trends in Cognitive Sciences, 10*, 64–69.

Higuchi, T., Murai, G., Kijima, A., Seya, Y., Wagman, J. B., & Imanaka, K. (2011). Athletic experience influences shoulder rotations when running through apertures. *Human Movement Science, 30*, 534–549.

Hilton, J. L., & von Hippel, W. (1996). Stereotypes. *Annual Review of Psychology, 47*, 237–271.

Hilts, P. J. (1996). *Memory's ghost: The nature of memory and the strange tale of Mr. M.* New York: Simon & Schuster.

Hirsh-Pasek, K., Golinkoff, R. M., & Hollich, G. (2000). An emergentist coalition model for word learning: Mapping words to objects is a product of the interaction of multiple cues. In R. M. Golinkoff, K. Hirsh-Pasek, L. Bloom, L. B. Smith, A. L. Woodard, N. Akhtar, et al. (Eds.), *Becoming a word learner: A debate on lexical acquisition* (pp. 179–186). New York: Oxford University Press.

Hockett, C. (1960). The origin of speech. *Scientific American, 203*, 88–111.

Hollich, G., Hirsh-Pasek, K., & Golinkoff, R. M. (with Hennon, E., Chung, H. L., Rocroi, C., Brand, R. J., & Brown, E.). (2000). Breaking the language barrier: An emergentist coalition model for the origins of word learning. *Monographs of the Society for Research in Child Development, 65*, (3, Serial No. 262).

Holyoak, K. J., & Koh, K. (1987). Surface and structural similarity in analogical transfer. *Memory & Cognition, 15*, 332–340.

Hommel, B. (1993). The role of attention for the Simon effect. *Psychological Research, 55*, 208–222.

Hsee, C. K. (2000). Attribute evaluability: Its implications for joint–separate evaluation reversals and beyond. In D. Kahneman & A. Tversky (Eds.), *Choices, values, and frames* (pp. 543–563). Cambridge, UK: Cambridge University Press.

Hubel, D. H., & Weisel, T. N. (1959). Receptive fields of single neurons in the cat's striate cortex. *Journal of Physiology, 148*, 574–591.

Huettig, F., & Hartsuiker, R. J. (2010). Listening to yourself is like listening to others: External, but not internal, verbal self-monitoring is based on speech perception. *Language and Cognitive Processes, 25*(3), 347–374.

Hulme, C., Thompson, N., Muir, C., & Lawrence, A. (1984). Speech rate and the development of short-term memory span. *Journal of Experimental Child Psychology, 38*, 241–253.

Humphrey, K. H., & Bock, J. K. (2005). Notional number agreement in English. *Psychonomic Bulletin & Review, 12*(4), 689–695.

Isarida, T., Isarida, T. K., & Sakai, T. (2012). *Memory & Cognition, 40*, 1225–1235.

Iverson, P., Kuhl, P. K., Akahane-Yamada, R., Diesch, E., Tohkura, Y., Kettermann, A., et al. (2003). A perceptual interference account of acquisition difficulties for non-native phonemes. *Cognition, 87*, B47–B57.

Jackendoff, R. (1994). *Patterns in the mind: Language and human nature*. New York: Basic Books.

Jackendoff, R. (2010). *Meaning and the lexicon: The parallel architecture, 1975–2010*. Oxford, UK: Oxford University Press.

Jacoby, L. L., Woloshyn, V., & Kelley, C. (1989). Being famous without being recognized: Unconscious influences of memory produced by dividing attention. *Journal of Experimental Psychology: General, 118*, 115–125.

James, W. (1890). *The principles of psychology* (Vol. 1). New York: Henry Holt.

Jeannerod, M. (1995). Mental imagery in the motor cortex. *Neuropsychologia, 33*, 1419–1432.

Jenkins, J. B., & Dallenbach, K. M. (1924). Oblivescence during sleep and waking. *American Journal of Psychology, 35*, 605–612.

Johnson-Laird, P. N. (1983). *Mental models*. Cambridge, UK: Cambridge University Press.

Johnson-Laird, P. N. (2001). Mental models and deduction. *Trends in Cognitive Sciences, 5*(10), 434–442.

Johnson-Laird, P. N. (2006). *How we reason*. Oxford, UK: Oxford University Press.

Johnson-Laird, P. N., & Steedman, M. J. (1978). The psychology of syllogisms. *Cognitive Psychology, 10*, 64–99.

Jonides, J., Lewis, R. L., Nee, D. E., Lustig, C. A., Berman, M. G., & Moore, K. S. (2008). The mind and brain of short-term memory. *Annual Review of Psychology, 59*, 193–224.

Jung-Beeman, M., Bowden, E. M., Haberman, J., Frymiare, J. L., Armabel-Lui, S., Greenblatt, R., et al. (2004). Neural activity when people solve verbal problems with insight. *PLoS Biology, 2*, 500–510.

Kahana, M. J., & Loftus, G. (1999). Response time versus accuracy in human memory. In R. J. Sternberg (Ed.), *The nature of cognition* (pp. 323–384). Cambridge, MA: MIT Press.

Kahneman, D. (1973). *Attention and effort*. Englewood Cliffs, NJ: Prentice Hall.

Kahneman, D. (2011). *Thinking, fast and slow*. New York: Farrar, Straus & Giroux.

Kahneman, D., & Tversky, A. (1973). On the psychology of prediction. *Psychological Review, 80*, 237–251.

Kahneman, D., & Tversky, A. (1979). Prospect theory: An analysis of decision under risk. *Econometrica, 47*, 263–292.

Kaplan, C. A., & Simon, H. A. (1990). In search of insight. *Cognitive Psychology, 22*, 374–419.

Karpicke, J. D., & Blunt, J. R. (2011). Retrieval practice produces more learning than elaborative studying with concept mapping. *Science, 331*, 772–775.

Keil, F. C. (1989). *Concepts, kinds, and cognitive development*. Cambridge, MA: MIT Press.

Kelly, M. H., Bock, J. K., & Keil, F. C. (1986). Prototypicality in a linguistic context: Effects on sentence structure. *Journal of Memory and Language, 25*, 59–74.

Keppel, G., & Underwood, B. J. (1962). Proactive inhibition in short-term retention of single items. *Journal of Verbal Learning and Verbal Behavior, 1*, 153–161.

Kershaw, T. C., & Ohlsson, S. (2004). Multiple causes of difficulty in insight: The case of the nine-dot problem. *Journal of Experimental Psychology: Learning, Memory, and Cognition, 30*, 3–13.

Kiefer, M., & Pulvermüller, F. (2012). Conceptual representations in mind and brain: Theoretical developments, current evidence and future directions. *Cortex, 48*, 805–825.

Kinsbourne, M., & George, J. (1974). The mechanism of the word-frequency effect on recognition memory. *Journal of Verbal Learning and Verbal Behavior, 13*, 63–69.

Klatzky, R. L., McCloskey, B., Doherty, S., Pellegrino, J., & Smith, T. (1987). Knowledge about hand movements and knowledge about objects. *Journal of Motor Behavior, 19*, 187–213.

Klatzky, R. L., Pellegrino, J., McCloskey, B., & Doherty, S. (1989). Can you squeeze a tomato? The role of motor representations in semantic sensibility judgments. *Journal of Memory and Language, 28*, 56–77.

Klauer, K. C., Stahl, C., & Erdfelder, E. (2007). The abstract selection task: New data and an almost comprehensive model. *Journal of Experimental Psychology: Learning, Memory, and Cognition, 33*, 680–703.

Knoblich, G., Ohlsson, S., Haider, H., & Rhenius, D. (1999). Constraint relaxation and chunk decomposition in insight problem solving. *Journal of Experimental Psychology: Learning, Memory, and Cognition, 25*, 1534–1555.

Knoblich, G., Ohlsson, S., & Raney, E. G. (2001). An eye movement study of insight problem solving. *Memory & Cognition, 29*, 1000–1009.

Köhler, W. (1959). Gestalt psychology today. *American Psychologist, 14*, 727–734.

Kosslyn, S. M. (1973). Scanning visual images. *Perception & Psychophysics, 14*, 90–94.

Kosslyn, S. M., Alpert, N. M., Thompson, W. L., Maljkovic, V., Weise, S. B., Chabris, C. F., et al. (1993). Visual mental imagery activates topographically organized visual cortex: PET investigations. *Journal of Cognitive Neuroscience, 5*, 263–287.

Kosslyn, S. M., Ball, T. M., & Reiser, B. J. (1978). Visual images preserve metric spatial information: Evidence from studies of image scanning. *Journal of Experimental Psychology: Human Perception and Performance, 4*, 47–60.

Kosslyn, S. M., Ganis, G., & Thompson, W. L. (2006). Mental imagery and the human brain. In Q. Jin, M. R. Rosenzweig, G. d'Ydewalle, H. Zhang, H-C. Chen, & K. Zhang (Eds.), *Progress in psychological science around the world: Neural, cognitive, and developmental issues* (Vol. 1, pp. 195–209). New York: Psychology Press.

Kosslyn, S. M., Thompson, W. L., Kim, I. J., & Alpert, N. M. (1995). Topographical representations of mental images in primary visual cortex. *Nature, 378*, 496–498.

Kounios, J., & Beeman, M. (2009). The aha! moment: The cognitive neuroscience of insight. *Current Directions in Psychological Science, 18*, 210–216.

Kuhl, P. K., Stevens, E., Hayashi, A., Deguchi, T., Kiritani, S., & Iverson, P. (2006). Infants show facilitation for native language phonetic perception between 6 and 12 months. *Developmental Science, 9*, 13–21.

Kvavilashvili, L., Kornbrot, D., Mash, V., Cockburn, J., & Milne, A. (2009). Differential effects of age on prospective and retrospective memory tasks in young, young-old, and old-old adults. *Memory, 17*, 180–196.

LaBerge, D. (1983). Spatial extent of attention to letters and words. *Journal of Experimental Psychology: Human Perception and Performance, 9*, 371–379.

LaBerge, D., & Brown, V. (1986). Variations in size of the visual field in which targets are presented: An attentional range effect. *Perception & Psychophysics, 40*, 188–200.

LaBerge, D., Carlson, R. L., Williams, J. K., & Bunney, B. G. (1997). Shifting attention in visual space: Tests of moving-spotlight models versus an activity-distribution model. *Journal of Experimental Psychology: Human Perception and Performance, 23*, 1380–1392.

Lakoff, G. (1987). *Women, fire, and dangerous things*. Chicago: University of Chicago Press.

Larkin, J. H., & Simon, H. A. (1987). Why a diagram is (sometimes) worth ten thousand words. *Cognitive Science, 11*, 65–100.

Lashley, K. S. (1951). The problem of serial order in behavior. In L. A. Jeffress (Ed.), *Cerebral mechanisms in behavior* (pp.112–136). New York: Wiley.

Lassaline, M. E. (1996). Structural alignment in induction and similarity. *Journal of Experimental Psychology: Learning, Memory, and Cognition, 22*, 754–770.

LePort, A. K. R., Mattfeld, A. T., Dickinson-Anson, H., Fallon, J. H., Stark, C. E. L., Kruggel, F., et al. (2012). Behavioral and neuroanatomical investigation of highly superior autobiographical memory (HSAM). *Neurobiology of Learning and Memory, 98*, 78–92.

Lesgold, A., Rubinson, H., Feltovich, P., Glaser, R., Klopfer, D., & Wang, Y. (1988). Expertise in a complex skill: Diagnosing X-ray pictures. In M. T. H. Chi, R. Glaser, & M. J. Farr

(Eds.), *The nature of expertise* (pp. 311–342). Hillsdale, NJ: Erlbaum.

Levelt, W. J. M. (1983). Monitoring and self-repair in speech. *Cognition, 14*, 41–104.

Levelt, W. J. M. (1989). *Speaking: From intention to articulation*. Cambridge, MA: MIT Press.

Levelt, W. J. M. (2012). *A history of psycholinguistics: The pre-Chomskyan era*. Oxford, UK: Oxford University Press.

Liberman, A. M., Harris, K. S., Eimas, P., Lisker, L., & Bastian, J. (1961). An effect of learning on speech perception: The discrimination of durations of silence with and without phonemic significance. *Audiology and Speech-Language Pathology, 53*, 175–195.

Liberman, A. M., Harris, K. S., Hoffman, H. S., & Griffith, B. C. (1957). The discrimination of speech sounds within and across phoneme boundaries. *Journal of Experimental Psychology, 54*, 358–368.

Liberman, P. (1984). *The biology and evolution of language*. Cambridge, MA: Harvard University Press.

Libet, B. (1985). Unconscious cerebral initiative and the role of conscious will in voluntary action. *Behavioral and Brain Sciences, 8*, 529–566.

Lin, E. L., & Murphy, G. (1997). Effects of background knowledge on object categorization and part detection. *Journal of Experimental Psychology: Human Perception and Performance, 23*(4), 1153–1169.

Lindsay, D. S. (1990). Misleading suggestions can impair eyewitnesses' ability to remember event details. *Journal of Experimental Psychology: Learning, Memory, and Cognition, 16*, 1077–1083.

Loewenstein, G., Rick, S., & Cohen, J. D. (2008). Neuroeconomics. *Annual Review of Psychology, 59*, 647–672.

Loftus, E. F. (1993). The reality of repressed memories. *American Psychologist, 48*, 518–537.

Loftus, E. F. (2005). Planting misinformation in the human mind: A 30-year investigation of the malleability of memory. *Learning & Memory, 12*, 361–366.

Loftus, E. F., & Palmer, J. C. (1974). Reconstruction of the automobile destruction: An example of the interaction between language and memory. *Journal of Verbal Learning and Verbal Behavior, 13*, 585–589.

Logan, G. D. (1988). Toward an instance theory of automatization. *Psychological Review, 95*, 492–527.

Logan, G. D. (1990). Repetition priming and automaticity: Common underlying mechanisms? *Cognitive Psychology, 22*, 1–35.

Logan, G. D. (1992). Shapes of reaction-time distributions and shapes of learning curves: A test of the instance theory of automaticity. *Journal of Experimental Psychology: Learning, Memory, and Cognition, 18*, 883–914.

Luo, J., & Knoblich, G. (2007). Studying insight problem solving with neuroscientific methods. *Methods, 42*, 77–86.

Lu, Z-L., Neuse, J., Madigan, S., & Dosher, B. A. (2005). Fast decay of iconic memory in observers with mild cognitive impairment. *Proceedings of the National Academy of Sciences, 102*, 1797–1802.

Lu, Z-L., Williamson, S. J., & Kaufman, L. (1992a). Human auditory primary and association cortex have differing lifetimes for activation traces. *Brain Research, 572*, 236–241.

Lu, Z.-L., Williamson, S. J., & Kaufman, L. (1992b). Behavioral lifetime of human auditory sensory memory predicted by physiological measures. *Science, 258*, 1668–1670.

Luchins, A. S. (1942). Mechanization in problem solving: The effect of Einstellung. *Psychological Monographs, 54*(6), 95.

Luo, J., & Knoblich, G. (2007). Studying insight problem solving with neuroscientific methods. *Methods, 42*, 77–86.

MacGregor, J. N., Ormerod, T. C., & Chronicle, E. P. (2001). Information processing and insight: A process model of performance on the nine dot and related problems. *Journal of Experimental Psychology: Learning, Memory, & Cognition, 27*, 176–201.

Mack, M. L., Preston, A. R., & Love, B. C. (2013). Decoding the brain's algorithm for categorization from its neural implementation. *Current Biology, 23*, 2023–2027.

Macrae, C. N., Bodenhausen, G. V., & Milne, A. B. (1995). The dissection of selection in person perception: Inhibitory processes in social stereotyping. *Journal of Personality and Social Psychology, 69*, 397–407.

Macrae, C. N., Milne, A. B., & Bodenhausen, G. V. (1994). Stereotypes as energy-saving devices: A peek inside the cognitive toolbox. *Journal of Personality and Social Psychology, 66*, 37–47.

Mahler, J., Jusczyk, P., Lambertz, G., Halsted, N., Bertoncini, J., & Amiel-Tison, C. (1988). A precursor of language acquisition in young infants. *Cognition, 29*, 143–178.

Mahon, B. Z., & Caramazza, A. (2009). Concepts and categories: A cognitive neuropsychological perspective. *Annual Review of Psychology, 60*, 27–51.

Maier, N. R. F. (1930). Reasoning in humans: I. On direction. *Journal of Comparative Psychology, 10*, 115–143.

Maier, N. R. F. (1931). Reasoning in humans: II. The solution of a problem and its appearance in consciousness. *Journal of Comparative Psychology, 12*, 181–194.

Malcolm, G. L., Nuthmann, A., & Schyns, P. G. (2014). Beyond gist: Strategic and incremental information accumulation for scene categorization. *Psychological Science, 25*, 1087–1097.

Malek, E. A., & Wagman, J. B. (2008). Kinetic potential influences visual and remote haptic perception of affordances for standing on an inclined surface. *Quarterly Journal of Experimental Psychology, 61*, 1813–1826.

Malt, B. C. (1989). An on-line investigation of prototype and exemplar strategies in classification. *Journal of Experimental Psychology: Learning, Memory, and Cognition, 15*(4), 539–555.

Markman, A. B., & Wisniewski, E. J. (1997). Similar and different: The differentiation of basic-level categories. *Journal of Experimental Psychology: Learning, Memory, and Cognition, 23*, 54–70.

Markman, E. M. (1989). *Categorization and naming in children: Problems of induction*. Cambridge, MA: MIT Press.

Martin A. (2007). The representation of object concepts in the brain. *Annual Review of Psychology, 58*, 25–45.

Martin, K. A., Moritz, S. E., & Hall, C. R. (1999). Imagery use in sport: A literature review and applied model. *Sport Psychologist, 13*, 245–268.

Mayberry, E. J., Sage, K., & Lambon Ralph, M. A. (2011). At the edge of semantic space: The breakdown of coherent concepts in semantic dementia is constrained by typicality and severity but not modality. *Journal of Cognitive Neuroscience, 23*, 2240–2251.

McBeath, M. K., Shaffer, D. M., & Kaiser, M. K. (1995). How baseball outfielders determine where to run to catch fly balls. *Science, 268*, 569–573.

McBride, D. M., Beckner, J. K., & Abney, D. H. (2011). Effects of delay of prospective memory cues in an ongoing task on prospective memory performance. *Memory & Cognition, 39*, 1222–1231.

McClelland, J. L. (1999). Cognitive modeling, connectionist. In R. A. Wilson & F. Keil (Eds.), *The MIT encyclopedia of the cognitive sciences* (pp. 137–139). Cambridge, MA: MIT Press.

McClelland, J. L., & Rumelhart, D. E. (1981). An interactive activation model of context effects in letter perception: Part 1. An account of basic findings. *Psychological Review, 88*, 375–407.

McCloskey, M. E., & Glucksberg, S. (1978). Natural categories: Well defined or fuzzy sets? *Memory & Cognition, 6*, 462–472.

McDaniel, M. A., & Einstein, G. O. (1986). Bizarre imagery as an effective aid: The importance of distinctiveness. *Journal of Experimental Psychology: Learning, Memory, and Cognition, 12*, 54–65.

McDaniel, M. A., Einstein, G. O., DeLosh, E. L., May, C. P., & Brady, P. (1995). The bizarreness effect: It's not surprising, it's complex. *Journal of Experimental Psychology: Learning, Memory, and Cognition, 21*, 422–435.

McDaniel, M. A., LaMontagne, P., Beck, S. M., Scullin, M. K., & Braver, T. S. (2013). Dissociable neural routes to successful prospective memory. *Psychological Science, 24*, 1791–1800.

McGaugh, J. L. (2000). Memory: A century of consolidation. *Science, 287*, 248–251.

McIntosh, R. D., & Lashley, G. (2008). Matching boxes: Familiar size influences action programming. *Neuropsychologia, 46*, 2441–2444.

McKoon, G., & Ratcliff, R. (1992). Spreading activation versus compound cue accounts of priming: Mediated priming revisited. *Journal of Experimental Psychology: Learning, Memory, and Cognition, 18*, 1155–1172.

Medin, D. L., Lynch, E. B., Coley, J. D., & Atran, S. (1997). Categorization and reasoning among tree experts: Do all roads lead to Rome? *Cognitive Psychology, 32*, 49–96.

Medin, D. L., & Schaffer, M. (1978). A context theory of classification learning. *Psychological Review, 85*, 207–238.

Meier, B., & Graf, P. (2000). Transfer appropriate processing for prospective memory tests. *Applied Cognitive Psychology, 14*, S11–S27.

Meints, K., Plunkett, K., & Harris, P. L. (1999). When does an ostrich become a bird? The role of typicality in early word comprehension. *Developmental Psychology, 35*, 1072–1078.

Melton, A. W. (1970). The situation with respect to the spacing of repetitions and memory. *Journal of Verbal Learning and Verbal Behavior, 9*, 596–606.

Memon, A., Meissner, C. A., & Fraser, J. (2010). The cognitive interview: A meta-analytic review and study space analysis of the past 25 years. *Psychology, Public Policy, and Law, 16*, 340–372.

Mervis, C. B., Catlin, J., & Rosch, E. (1976). Relationships among goodness-of-example, category norms, and word frequency. *Bulletin of the Psychonomic Society, 7*, 283–294.

Metcalfe, J. A., & Wiebe, D. (1987). Intuition in insight and noninsight problem solving. *Memory & Cognition, 15*, 238–246.

Meyer, D. E., & Schvaneveldt, R. W. (1971). Facilitation in recognizing pairs of words: Evidence of a dependence between retrieval operations. *Journal of Experimental Psychology, 90*, 227–234.

Meyer, D. E., Osman, A. M., Irwin, D. E., & Yantis, S. (1988). Modern mental chronometry. *Biological Psychology, 26*, 3–67.

Miller, G. A. (1951). *Language and communication*. New York: McGraw-Hill.

Miller, G. A. (1956). The magical number seven, plus or minus two: Some limits on our capacity for processing information. *Psychological Review, 63*, 81–97.

Milner, A. D., & Goodale, M. A. (2008). Two visual streams re-viewed. *Neuropsychologia, 46*, 774–785.

Mintzer, M. Z., & Snodgrass, J. G. (1999). The picture superiority effect: Support for the distinctiveness model. *American Journal of Psychology, 112*, 113–146.

Mitchell, T. M., Shinkareva, S. V., Carlson, A., Chang, K-M., Malave, V. L., Mason, R. A., et al. (2008). Predicting human brain activity associated with the meanings of nouns. *Science, 320*, 1191–1195.

Monsell, S. (1991). The nature and locus of word frequency effects in reading. In D. Besner & G. W. Humphreys (Eds.), *Basic processes in reading: Visual word recognition* (pp. 148–197). Hillsdale, NJ: Erlbaum.

Moray, N. (1959). Attention in dichotic listening: Affective cues and the influence of instructions. *Quarterly Journal of Experimental Psychology, 11*, 56–60.

Moreno, F. J., Reina, R., Luis, V., & Sabido, R. (2002). Visual search strategies in experienced and inexperienced gymnastic coaches. *Perceptual and Motor Skills, 95*, 901–902.

Morris, C. D., Bransford, J. D., & Franks, J. J. (1977). Levels of processing versus transfer appropriate processing. *Journal of Verbal Learning and Verbal Behavior, 16*, 519–533.

Moscovitch, M., Chein, J. M., Talmi, D., & Cohn, M. (2007). Learning and memory. In B. J. Baars & N. M. Gage (Eds.), *Cognition, brain, and consciousness: Introduction to cognitive neuroscience*. San Diego, CA: Academic Press.

Moulton, S. T., & Kosslyn, S. M. (2009). Imagining predictions: Mental imagery and mental emulation. *Philosophical Transactions of the Royal Society B, 364*, 1273–1280.

Mulligan, N. M. (2012). Differentiating between conceptual implicit and explicit memory: A crossed double dissociation between category-exemplar production and category-cued recall. *Psychological Science, 23*, 404–406.

Murphy, G. L. (2002). *The big book of concepts*. Cambridge, MA: MIT Press.

Murphy, G. L., & Brownell, H. H. (1985).Category differentiation in object recognition: Typicality constraints on the basic category advantage. *Journal of Experimental Psychology: Learning, Memory, and Cognition, 11*, 70–84.

Murphy, G. L., Hampton, J. A., & Milovanovic, G. S. (2012). Semantic memory redux: An experimental test of hierarchical category representation. *Journal of Memory and Language, 67*, 521–539.

Murphy, G. L., & Lassaline, M. E. (1997). Hierarchical structure in concepts and the basic level of categorization. In K. Lamberts & D. Shanks (Eds.), *Knowledge, concepts, and categories* (pp. 93–131). London: Psychology Press.

Murphy, G. L., & Medin, D. L. (1985). The role of theories in conceptual coherence. *Psychological Review, 92*, 289–316.

Murphy, G. L., & Ross, B. H. (2005). Two faces of typicality in category-based induction. *Cognition, 95*, 175–200.

Murphy, G. L., & Wright, J. C. (1984). Changes in conceptual structure with expertise: Differences between real-world experts and novices. *Journal of Experimental Psychology: Learning, Memory and Cognition, 10*, 144–155.

Mynatt, C. R., Doherty, M. E., & Dragan, W. (1993). Information relevance, working memory, and the consideration of alternatives. *Quarterly Journal of Experimental Psychology, 46A*, 759–778.

Nairne, J. S., & Neath, I. (2013). Sensory and working memory. In A. F. Healy & R. W. Proctor (Eds.), *Comprehensive handbook of psychology* (2nd ed.), *Vol. 4: Experimental psychology* (pp. 419–445). New York: Wiley.

Nairne, J. S., & Pandeirada, J. N. S. (2008). Adaptive memory: Remembering with a stone-age brain. *Current Directions in Psychological Science, 17*, 239–243.

Nairne, J. S., Van Arsdall, J. E., Pandeirada, J. N. S., Cogdill, M., & LeBreton, J. M. (2013). Adaptive memory: The mnemonic value of animacy. *Psychological Science, 24*, 2099–2105.

Naveh-Benjamin, M., & Ayres, T. J. (1986). Digit span, reading rate, and linguistic relativity. *Quarterly Journal of Experimental Psychology, 38A*, 739–751.

Neath, I., & Knoedler, A. J. (1994). Distinctiveness and serial position effects in recognition and sentence processing. *Journal of Memory and Language, 33*, 776–795.

Neisser, U. (1967). *Cognitive psychology*. New York: Appleton-Century-Crofts.

Nelson, D. L., Kitto, K., Galea, D., McEvoy, C. L., & Bruza, P. D. (2013). How activation, entanglement, and searching a semantic network contribute to event memory. *Memory & Cognition, 41*, 797–819.

Newell, A., & Simon, H. (1972). *Human problem solving*. Englewood Cliffs, NJ: Prentice-Hall.

Newsome, W. T., Britten, K. H., & Movshon, J. A. (1989). Neuronal correlates of a perceptual decision. *Nature, 341*, 52–54.

Nicoletti, R., & Umiltá, C. (1989). Splitting visual space with attention. *Journal of Experimental Psychology: Human Perception and Performance, 15*, 164–169.

Norman, D., & Shallice, T. (1986). Attention to action: Willed and automatic control of behavior. In R. Davidson, R. G. Schwartz, & D. Shapiro (Eds.), *Consciousness and self-regulation: Advances in research and theory* (pp. 1–18). New York: Plenum Press.

Noveck, I. A., & Reboul, A. (2008). Experimental pragmatics: A Gricean turn in the study of language. *Trends in Cognitive Sciences, 12*(11), 425–431.

Novick, L. R. (1988). Analogical transfer, problem similarity, and expertise. *Journal of Experimental Psychology: Learning, Memory, and Cognition, 14*(3), 510–520.

Nozari, N., Dell, G. S., & Schwartz, M. F. (2011). Is comprehension necessary for error detection? A conflict-based account of monitoring in speech production. *Cognitive Psychology, 63*, 1–33.

Oaksford, M. R., & Chater, N. (1994). A rational analysis of the selection task as optimal data selection. *Psychological Review, 101*, 608–631.

Ohlsson, S. (1992). Information-processing models of insight and related phenomena. In M. T. Keane & K. J. Gilhooly (Eds.), *Advances in the psychology of thinking* (Vol. 1, pp. 1–44). New York: Harvester/Wheatsheaf.

Oyama, T., Simizu, M., & Tozawa, J. (1999). Effects of similarity on apparent motion and perceptual grouping. *Perception, 28*, 739–748.

Padgitt, A. J., & Hund, A. M. (2012). How good are these directions? Determining direction quality and wayfinding efficiency. *Journal of Environmental Psychology, 32*, 164–172.

Paivio, A. (1975). Coding distinctions and repetition effects in memory. In G. H. Bower (Ed.), *The psychology of learning and motivation* (Vol. 9, pp. 179–215). New York: Academic Press.

Paivio, A. (1986). *Mental representations: A dual coding approach*. New York: Oxford University Press.

Paivio, A. (1991). Dual coding theory: Retrospect and current status. *Canadian Journal of Psychology, 45*, 255–287.

Paivio, A. (1995). Imagery and memory. In M. S. Gazzaniga (Ed.), *The cognitive neurosciences* (pp. 977–986). Cambridge, MA: MIT Press.

Paivio, A., & Csapo, K. (1973). Picture superiority in free recall: Imagery or dual coding? *Cognitive Psychology, 5*, 176–206.

Paivio, A., & Madigan, S. A. (1968). Imagery and association value in paired-associate learning. *Journal of Experimental Psychology, 76*, 35–39.

Parker, E. S., Cahill, L., & McGaugh, J. L. (2006). A case of unusual autobiographical remembering. *Neurocase, 12*, 35–49.

Patterson, K., Nestor, P. J., & Rogers, T. T. (2007). Where do you know what you know? The representation of semantic knowledge in the human brain. *Nature Reviews: Neuroscience, 8*, 976–987.

Pavlenko, A. (1999). New approaches to concepts in bilingual memory. Bilingualism: *Language & Cognition, 2*, 209–230.

Payne, D. G., Elie, C. J., Blackwell, J. M., & Neuschatz, J. S. (1996). Memory illusions: Recalling, recognizing, and recollecting events that never occurred. *Journal of Memory and Language, 35*, 261–285.

Pepperberg, I. M. (2009). *The Alex studies: Cognitive and communicative abilities of grey parrots*. Cambridge, MA: Harvard University Press.

Peterson, L. R., & Johnson, S. T. (1971). Some effects of minimizing articulation on short-term retention. *Journal of Verbal Learning and Verbal Behavior, 10*, 346–354.

Peterson, L. R., & Peterson, M. J. (1959). Short-term retention of individual verbal items. *Journal of Experimental Psychology, 58*, 193–198.

Peterson, R. R., & Savoy, P. (1998). Lexical selection and phonological encoding during language production: Evidence for cascaded processing. *Journal of Experimental Psychology: Learning, Memory, and Cognition, 24*, 539–557.

Pilley, J. W., & Reid, A. K. (2011). Border collie comprehends object names as verbal referents. *Behavioural Processes, 86*, 184–195.

Pinker, S., & Kosslyn, S. M. (1978). The representation and manipulation of three-dimensional space in mental images. *Journal of Mental Imagery, 2*, 69–83.

Poldrack, R. A. (2006). Can cognitive processes be inferred from neuroimaging data? *Trends in Cognitive Sciences, 10*, 59–63.

Polya, G. (1957). *How to solve it.* Princeton, NJ: Princeton University Press.

Pomerantz, J. R., & Portillo, M. C. (2012). Grouping and emergent features in vision: Toward a theory of basic Gestalts. *Journal of Experimental Psychology: Human Perception and Performance, 37*, 1331–1349.

Pongrácz, P., Molnár, C., & Miklósi, Á. (2006). Acoustic parameters of dog barks carry emotional information for humans. *Applied Animal Behaviour Science, 100*, 228–240.

Posner, M. I. (2005). Timing in the brain: Mental chronometry as a tool in neuroscience. *PLoS Biology, 3*, 204–206.

Premack, A. J., & Premack, D. (1972). Teaching language to an ape. *Scientific American, 227*, 92–99.

Premack, D. (1988). Minds with and without language. In L. Weiskrantz (Ed.), *Thought without language* (pp. 46–65). New York: Oxford University Press.

Pretz, J. E., Naples, A. J., & Sternberg, R. J. (2003). Recognizing, defining, and representing problems. In J. E. Davidson & R. J. Sternberg (Eds.), *The psychology of problem solving* (pp. 3–30). New York: Cambridge University Press.

Proffitt, D. R., Stefanucci, J., Banton, T., & Epstein, W. (2003). The role of effort in perceiving distance. *Psychological Science, 14*, 106–112.

Pruden, S. M., Hirsh-Pasek, K., Golinkoff, R. M., & Hennon, E. A. (2006). The birth of words: Ten-month-olds learn words through perceptual salience. *Child Development, 77*, 266–280.

Pulvermüller, F. (2010a). Brain embodiment of syntax and grammar: Disrete combinatorial mechanisms spelt out in neural circuits. *Brain & Language, 112*, 167–179.

Pulvermüller, F. (2010b). Brain language research: Where is the progress? *Biolinguistics, 4*, 255–288.

Pylyshyn, Z. W. (1973). What the mind's eye tells the mind's brain: A critique of mental imagery. *Psychological Bulletin, 80*, 1–24.

Pylyshyn, Z. W. (1981). The imagery debate: Analogue media versus tacit knowledge. *Psychological Review, 87*, 16–45.

Pylyshyn, Z. W. (2002). Mental imagery: In search of a theory. *Behavioral and Brain Sciences, 25*, 157–238.

Pylyshyn, Z. W. (2003). Return of the mental image: Are there pictures in the brain? *Trends in Cognitive Sciences, 7*, 113–118.

Quinn, J. G., & McConnell, J. (1996). Irrelevant pictures in working memory. *Quarterly Journal of Experimental Psychology, 49A*, 200–215.

Quiroga, R. Q., Reddy, L., Kreiman, G., Koch, C., & Fried, I. (2005). Invariant visual representation by single neurons in the human brain. *Nature, 23*, 1102–1107.

Ramos, D., & Ades, C. (2012). Two-item sentence comprehension by a dog (Canis familiaris). *PLOS One, 7*(2): e29689.

Rayner, K., Carlson, M., & Frazier, L. (1983). The interaction of syntax and semantics during sentence processing: Eye movements in the analysis of semantically biased sentences. *Journal of Verbal Learning and Verbal Behavior, 22*, 358–374.

Rayner, K., & Duffy, S. A. (1986). Lexical complexity and fixation times in reading: Effects of word frequency, verb complexity, and lexical ambiguity. *Memory & Cognition, 14*, 191–201.

Reicher, G. M. (1969). Perceptual recognition as a function of meaningfulness of stimulus material. *Journal of Experimental Psychology, 81*, 275–280.

Reingold, E. M., Charness, N., Pomplun, M., & Stampe, D. M. (2001). Visual span in expert chess players: Evidence from eye movements. *Psychological Science, 12*(1), 48–55.

Revlis, R. (1975). Syllogistic reasoning: Logical decisions from a complex data base. In R. J. Falmagne (Ed.), *Reasoning: Representation and process.* New York: John Wiley & Sons.

Richardson, D. C., & Dale, R. (2005). Looking to understand: The coupling between speakers' and listeners' eye movements and its relationship to discourse comprehension. *Cognitive Science, 29*, 1045–1060.

Richardson, D. C., & Spivey, M. J. (2000). Representation, space and Hollywood Squares: Looking at things that aren't there anymore. *Cognition, 76*, 269–295.

Richmond, J., & Nelson, C. A. (2007). Accounting for change in declarative memory: A cognitive neuroscience perspective. *Developmental Review, 27*, 349–373.

Rick, S. (2011). Losses, gains, and brains: Neuroeconomics can help to answer open questions about loss aversion. *Journal of Consumer Psychology, 21*, 453–463.

Rips, L. J. (1975). Inductive judgments about natural categories. *Journal of Verbal Learning and Verbal Behavior, 14*, 665–681.

Rips, L. J. (1989). Similarity, typicality, and categorization. In S. Vosniadou & A. Ortony (Eds.), *Similarity and analogical reasoning* (pp. 21–59). Cambridge, UK: Cambridge University Press.

Rips, L. J. (1994). *The psychology of proof.* Cambridge, MA: MIT Press.

Rips, L. J., Shoben, E. J., & Smith, E. E. (1973). Semantic distance and the verification of semantic relations. *Journal of Verbal Learning and Verbal Behavior, 12*, 1–20.

Rizzolatti, G., Fadiga, L., Gallese, V., & Fogassi, L. (1996). Premotor cortex and the recognition of motor actions. *Cognitive Brain Research, 3*, 131–141.

Rizzolatti, G., & Craighero, L. (2004). The mirror-neuron system. *Annual Review of Neuroscience, 27*, 169–192.

Roberts, M. J. (2005). Expanding the universe of categorical syllogisms: A challenge for reasoning researchers. *Behavior Research Methods, 37*, 560–580.

Roberts, M. J., Newstead, S. E., & Griggs, R. S. (2001). Quantifier interpretation and syllogistic reasoning. *Thinking & Reasoning, 7*, 173–204.

Roberts, M. J., & Sykes, E. D. A. (2005). Categorical reasoning from multiple premises. *Quarterly Journal of Experimental Psychology, 58A*, 333–376.

Roediger, H. L. III (1990). Implicit memory: Retention without remembering. *American Psychologist, 45*, 1043–1056.

Roediger, H. L. III, & Karpicke, J. D. (2006a). Test enhanced learning: Taking memory tests improves long-term retention. *Psychological Science, 17*, 249–255.

Roediger, H. L. III, & Karpicke, J. D. (2006b). The power of testing memory: Basic research and implications for educational practice. *Perspectives on Psychological Science, 1*, 181–210.

Roediger, H. L. III, & McDermott, K. B. (1995). Creating false memories: Remembering words not presented in lists. *Journal of Experimental Psychology: Learning, Memory, and Cognition, 21*, 803–814.

Roediger, H. L. III, & Pyc, M. A. (2012). Inexpensive techniques to improve education: Applying cognitive psychology to enhance educational practice. *Journal of Applied Research in Memory and Cognition, 1*, 242–248.

Rogers, T., & McClelland, J. (2004). *Semantic cognition: A parallel distributed processing approach*. Cambridge, MA: MIT Press.

Rorden, C., & Karnath, H. O. (2004). Using human brain lesions to infer function: A relic from a past era in the fMRI age? *Nature Reviews, 5*, 813–819.

Rosch, E. (1978). Principles of categorization. In E. Rosch & B. B. Lloyd (Eds.), *Cognition and categorization* (pp. 27–48). Hillsdale, NJ: Erlbaum.

Rosch, E., & Mervis, C. B. (1975). Family resemblance: Studies in the internal structure of categories. *Cognitive Psychology, 7*, 573–605.

Rosch, E., Mervis, C. B., Gray, W., Johnson, D., & Boyes-Braem, P. (1976). Basic objects in natural categories. *Cognitive Psychology, 8*, 382–439.

Rosenbaum, D. A. (2012). The tiger on your tail: Choosing between temporally extended behaviors. *Psychological Science, 23*, 855–860.

Rosenbaum, D. A., Brach, M., & Semenov, A. (2011). Behavioral ecology meets motor behavior: Choosing between walking and reaching paths. *Journal of Motor Behavior, 43*, 131–136.

Ross, B. H. (1984). Remindings and their effects in learning a cognitive skill. *Cognitive Psychology, 16*, 371–416.

Ross, B. H. (1989). Distinguishing types of superficial similarities: Different effects on the access and use of earlier problems. *Journal of Experimental Psychology: Learning, Memory, and Cognition, 15*, 456–468.

Ross, B. H., & Kilbane, M. C. (1997). Effects of principle explanation and superficial similarity on analogical mapping in problem solving. *Journal of Experimental Psychology: Learning, Memory, and Cognition, 23*, 427–440.

Rumelhart, D. E., & Abrahamson, A. A. (1973). Toward a theory of analogical reasoning. *Cognitive Psychology, 5*, 1–28.

Rumelhart, D. E., & Norman, D. A. (1988). Representation in memory. In R. C. Atkinson, R. J. Herrnstein, G. Lindzey, & R. D. Luce (Eds.), *Stevens' handbook of experimental psychology* (2nd ed., pp. 511–587). New York: Wiley.

Rustichini, A. (2009). Neuroeconomics: What have we found, and what should we search for. *Current Opinion on Neurobiology, 19*, 672–677.

Sach, A. T., Kohler, A., Bestmann, S., Linden, D. E. J., Dechent, O., Goebel, R., et al. (2007). Imaging the brain activity changes underlying impaired visuospatial judgments: Simultaneous fMRI, TMS, and behavioral studies. *Cerebral Cortex, 17*, 2841–2852.

Sacks, O. (1990). *The man who mistook his wife for a hat*. New York: Harper Perennial.

Salomon, M. M., Magliano, J. P., & Radvansky, G. A. (2013). Verb aspect and problem solving. *Cognition, 128*, 134–139.

Sanfey, A. G., Loewenstein, G., McClure, S. M., & Cohen, J. D. (2006). Neuroeconomics: Cross-currents in research on decision-making. *Trends in Cognitive Sciences, 10*, 108–116.

Savage-Rumbaugh, E. S., Murphy, J., Sevcik, R. A., Brakke, K. E., Williams, S. L, & Rumbaugh, D. M. (1993). Language comprehension in ape and child. *Monographs of the Society for Research in Child Development, 233*, 1–252.

Schacter, D. L. (2002). *The seven sins of memory: How the mind forgets and remembers*. New York: Houghton Mifflin Harcourt.

Schiller, P. H. (1966). Developmental study of color-word interference. *Journal of Experimental Psychology, 72*, 105–108.

Schneider, W., & Shiffrin, R. M. (1977). Controlled and automatic human information processing: I. Detection, search, and attention. *Psychological Review, 84*, 1–66.

Schriefers, H., Meyer, A. S., & Levelt, W. J. M. (1990). Exploring the time course of lexical access in speech production: Picture-word interference studies. *Journal of Memory and Language, 29*, 86–102.

Schurger, A., Sitt, J. D., & Dehaene, S. (2012). An accumulator model for spontaneous neural activity prior to self-initiated movement. *Proceedings of the National Academy of Sciences, 109*, E2904–E2913.

Schwarzkopf, D. S., Song, C., & Rees, G. (2011). The surface area of human V1 predicts the subjective experience of object size. *Nature Neuroscience, 14*, 28–30.

Scott, C. L., Harris, R. J., & Rothe, A. R. (2001). Embodied cognition through improvisation improves memory for a dramatic monologue. *Discourse Processes, 31*, 293–305.

Scullin, M. K., & McDaniel, M. A. (2010). Remembering to execute a goal: Sleep on it! *Psychological Science, 21*, 1028–1035.

Segaert, K., Menenti, L., Weber, K., Petersson, K. M., & Hagoort, P. (2012). Shared syntax in language production and language comprehension: An fMRI study. *Cerebral Cortex, 22*, 1662–1670.

Sellen, A. J., Louie, G., Harris, G. E., & Wilkins, A. J. (1997). What brings attention to mind? An in situ study of prospective memory. *Memory, 5*, 483–507.

Shaffer, D. M., Krauchunas, S. M., Eddy, M., & McBeath, M. K. (2004). How dogs navigate to catch Frisbees. *Psychological Science, 15*, 437–441.

Shepard, R. N., & Metzler, J. (1971). Mental rotation of three-dimensional objects. *Science, 171*, 701–703.

Shiffrin, R. M., & Schneider, W. (1977). Controlled and automatic human information processing: II. Perceptual learning, automatic attending, and a general theory. *Psychological Review, 84*, 127–190.

Simon, H. A. (1974). How big is a chunk? *Science, 183*, 482–488.

Simon, J. R. (1969). Reactions toward the source of stimulation. *Journal of Experimental Psychology, 81*, 174–176.

Simon, J. R., & Rudell, A. P. (1967). Auditory S-R compatibility: The effect of an irrelevant cue on information processing. *Journal of Applied Psychology, 51*, 300–304.

Simon, J. R., & Wolf, J. R. (1963). Choice reaction time as a function of angular stimulus-response correspondence and age. *Ergonomics, 6*, 99–105.

Simons, D. J., & Chabris, C. F. (1999). Gorillas in our midst: Sustained inattentional blindness for dynamic events. *Perception, 28*, 1059–1074.

Simons, D. J., & Levin, D. T. (1998). Failure to detect changes to people during a real-world interaction. *Psychonomic Bulletin & Review, 5*, 644–649.

Simpson, G. B., & Burgess, C. (1985). Activation and selection processes in the recognition of ambiguous words. *Journal of Experimental Psychology: Human Perception and Performance, 11*(1), 28–39.

Sinclair, R. J., & Burton, H. (1996). Discrimination of vibrotactile frequencies in a delayed pair comparison task. *Perception & Psychophysics, 58*, 680–692.

Singer, M. (1994). Discourse inference processes. In M. A. Gernsbacher (Ed.), *Handbook of psycholinguistics* (pp. 479–515). San Diego, CA: Academic Press.

Sinha, I., & Smith, M. F. (2000). Consumers' perceptions of promotional framing of price. *Psychology & Marketing, 17*, 257–275.

Skinner, B. F. (1957). *Verbal behavior*. New York: Appleton-Century-Crofts.

Sloman, S. A. (2005). *Causal models*. Oxford, UK: Oxford University Press.

Slotnick, S. D., Thompson, W. L., & Kosslyn, S. M. (2012). Visual memory and visual mental imagery recruit common control and sensory regions of the brain. *Cognitive Neuroscience, 3*, 14–20.

Sloutsky, V. M., Kloos, H., & Fisher, A. V. (2007). When looks are everything: Appearance similarity versus kind information in early induction. *Psychological Science, 18*, 179–185.

Smith, E. E., & Osherson, D. N. (1984). Conceptual combination with prototype concepts. *Cognitive Science, 8*, 357–361.

Smith, E. E., Osherson, D. N., Rips, L. J., & Keane, M. (1988). Combining prototypes: A selective modification model. *Cognitive Science, 12*, 485–527.

Smith, E. E., Rips, L. J., & Shoben, E. J. (1974). Semantic memory and psychological semantics. In G. H. Bower (Ed.), *The psychology of learning and motivation* (Vol. 8, pp. 1–45). New York: Academic Press.

Smith, J. D., & Minda, J. P. (2000). Thirty categorization results in search of a model. *Journal of Experimental Psychology: Learning, Memory, and Cognition, 26*, 3–27.

Smith, S. M., & Vela, E. (2001). Environmental context-dependent memory: A review and meta-analysis. *Psychonomic Bulletin & Review, 8*, 203–220.

Snodgrass, J. G., & McClure, P. (1975). Storage and retrieval properties of dual codes for pictures and words in recognition memory. *Journal of Experimental Psychology: Human Learning and Memory, 1*, 521–529.

Snow, C. E. (1977). The development of conversation between mothers and babies. *Journal of Child Language, 4*, 1–22.

Sperling, G. (1960). The information available in brief visual presentations. *Psychological Monographs, 74*(498), 1–29.

Squire, L. R. (2004). Memory systems of the brain: A brief history and current perspective. *Neurobiology of Learning and Memory, 82*, 171–177.

Squire, L. R. (2009). The legacy of patient H. M. for neuroscience. *Neuron, 61*, 6–9.

Stark, C. E. L., Okado, Y., & Loftus, E. F. (2010). Imaging the reconstruction of true and false memories using sensory reactivation and the misinformation paradigm. *Learning and Memory, 17*, 485–488.

Steblay, N. M., Dysart, J., Fulero, S., & Lindsay, R. C. L. (2001). Eyewitness accuracy rates in sequential and simultaneous lineup presentations: A meta-analytic comparison. *Law and Human Behavior, 25*, 459–474.

Sternberg, R. J. (1997). *Thinking styles*. Cambridge, UK: Cambridge University Press.

Stickgold, R., Hobson, J. A., Fosse, H. R., & Fosse, M. (2001). Sleep, learning, and dreams: Off-line memory processing. *Science, 294*, 1052–1057.

Strayer, D. L., & Johnston, W. A. (2001). Driven to distraction: Dual-task studies of simulated driving and conversing on a cellular telephone. *Psychological Science, 12*, 462–466.

Stroop, J. R. (1935). Studies of interferences in serial verbal reactions. *Journal of Experimental Psychology, 18*, 643–662.

Swinney, D. (1979). Lexical access during sentence comprehension: (Re)-consideration of context effects. *Journal of Verbal Learning and Verbal Behavior, 18*, 645–659.

Talarico, J. M., & Rubin, D. C. (2003). Confidence, not consistency, characterizes flashbulb memories. *Psychological Science, 14*, 455–461.

Tanaka, J. W., & Taylor, M. (1991). Object categories and expertise: Is the basic level in the eye of the beholder? *Cognitive Psychology, 23*, 457–482.

Taraban, R., & McClelland, J. L. (1988). Constituent attachment and thematic role assignment in sentence processing: Influences of content-based expectations. *Journal of Memory and Language, 27*, 597–632.

Terrace, H. S., Pettito, L. A., Sanders, R. J., & Bever, T. G. (1979). Can apes create a sentence? *Science, 206*, 891–902.

Thaler, R. H. (1985). Mental accounting matters. *Journal of Behavioral Decision Making, 12*, 183–206.

Thomas, A. K., & Loftus, E. F. (2002). Creating bizarre false memories through imagination. *Memory & Cognition, 30*, 423–431.

Thomas, L. E. (2013). Spatial working memory is necessary for actions to guide thought. *Journal of Learning, Memory, and Cognition, 39*(6), 1974–1981.

Thompson-Schill, S. L. (2003). Neuroimaging studies of semantic memory: Inferring "how" from "where." *Neuropsychologia, 41*, 280–292.

Thorndike, E. L. (1898). *Animal intelligence.* New York: Macmillan.

Treisman, A. M. (1960). Contextual cues in selective listening. *Quarterly Journal of Experimental Psychology, 12,* 242–248.

Treisman, A. M. (1961). *Attention and speech.* Unpublished dissertation. Oxford University.

Treisman, A. M. (1964). Monitoring and storage of irrelevant messages in selective attention. *Journal of Verbal Learning and Verbal Behavior, 3,* 449–459.

Treisman, A. M., & Gelade, G. (1980). A feature integration theory of attention. *Cognitive Psychology, 12,* 97–136.

Treisman, A. M., Sykes, M., & Gelade, G. (1977). Selective attention and stimulus integration. In S. Dornic (Ed.), *Attention and performance IV* (pp. 333–361). Hillsdale, NJ: Lawrence Erlbaum.

Turvey, M. T., Brick, P., & Osborn, J. (1970). Proactive interference in short-term memory as a function of prior-item retention interval. *Quarterly Journal of Experimental Psychology, 22,* 142–147.

Tversky, A. (1972). Elimination by aspects: A theory of choice. *Psychological Review, 79,* 281–299.

Tversky, A., & Kahneman, D. (1973). Availability: A heuristic for judging frequency and probability. *Cognitive Psychology, 5,* 207–232.

Tversky, A., & Kahneman, D. (1981). The framing of decisions and the psychology of choice. *Science, 211,* 453–458.

Tweney, R. D., Doherty, M. E., Worner, W. J., Pliske, D. B., Mynatt, C. R., Gross, K. A., et al. (1980). Strategies of rule discovery in an inference task. *Quarterly Journal of Experimental Psychology, 32,* 109–123.

VanDenBroek, P., Lorch, R. F., Linderholm, T., & Gustafson, M. (2001). The effects of readers' goals on inference generation and memory for texts. *Memory & Cognition, 29*(8), 1081–1087.

Vigliocco, G., Antonini, T., & Garrett, M. F. (1997). Grammatical gender is on the tip of Italian tongues. *Psychological Science,* 8, 314–317.

Vigliocco, G., & Harsuiker, R. (2002). The interplay of meaning, sound, and syntax in sentence production. *Psychological Bulletin, 128*(3), 442–472.

von Frisch, K. (1967). *The dance language and orientation of bees.* Cambridge, MA: Harvard University Press.

von Helmholtz, H. L. F. (1850/1853). Uber die methoden, kleinste Zeittheile zu messen, und ihre Anwendung fur physiologische Zwecked. Original work translated in *Philosophical Magazine,* 1853, 6 (Section 4), 313–325.

Wagemans, J., Elder, J. H., Kubovy, M., Palmer, S. E., Peterson, M. A., Singh, M., et al. (2012). A century of Gestalt psychology in visual perception: I. Perceptual grouping and figure-ground organization, *Psychological Bulletin, 138,* 1172–1217.

Wallas, G. (1926). *The art of thought.* New York: Harcourt, Brace.

Warren, R. M. (1970). Perceptual restoration of missing speech sounds. *Science, 167,* 392–393.

Warrington, E. K. (1975). The selective impairment of semantic memory. *Quarterly Journal of Experimental Psychology, 27,* 635–657.

Warrington, E. K., & Weiskrantz, L. (1968). A new method for testing long-term retention with special reference to amnesic patients. *Nature, 217,* 972–974.

Warrington, E. K., & Weiskrantz, L. (1970). Amnesic syndrome: Consolidation or retrieval. *Nature, 228,* 628–630.

Warrington, E. K., & Weiskrantz, L. (1974). The effect of prior learning on subsequent retention in amnesic patients. *Neuropsychologia, 12,* 419–428.

Wason, P. C. (1960). On the failure to eliminate hypotheses in a conceptual task. *Quarterly Journal of Experimental Psychology, 12,* 129–140

Wason, P. C. (1968). Reasoning about a rule. *Quarterly Journal of Experimental Psychology, 20,* 273–281.

Wason, P. C., & Johnson-Laird, P. N. (1972). *Psychology of reasoning: Structure and content.* London: Batsford.

Wason, P. C., & Shapiro, D. A. (1971). Natural and contrived experience in a reasoning problem. *Quarterly Journal of Experimental Psychology, 23,* 63–71.

Waugh, N. C., & Norman, D. A. (1965). Primary memory. *Psychological Review, 72,* 89–104.

Weisberg, R. W. (1988). Problem solving and creativity. In R. J. Sternberg (Ed.), *The nature of creativity: Contemporary psychological perspectives* (pp. 148–176). New York: Cambridge University Press.

Weisberg, R. W., & Alba, J. W. (1981). An examination of the alleged role of "fixation" in the solution of "insight" problems. *Journal of Experimental Psychology: General, 110,* 169–192.

Wells, G. L., & Bradfield, A. L. (1998). "Good, you identified the suspect": Feedback to eyewitnesses distorts their reports of the witnessing experience. *Journal of Applied Psychology, 83,* 360–376.

Wells, G. L., Small, M., Penrod, S., Malpass, R. S., Fulero, S. M., & Brimacombe, C. A. E. (1998). Eyewitness identification procedures: Recommendations for lineups and photo spreads. *Law and Human Behavior, 22,* 1–39.

Wernicke, C. (1874). The symptom complex of aphasia. Reprinted in English in *Proceedings of the Boston Colloquium for the Philosophy of Science, 4,* 34–97.

Wertheimer, M. (1959). *Productive thinking* (Enlarged ed.). New York: Harper and Brothers. (Original work published 1945)

Wetherick, N. E., & Gilhooly, K. J. (1990). Syllogistic reasoning: Effects of premise order. In K. Gilhooly, M. Keane, R. Logie, & G. Erdos (Eds.), *Lines of thinking: Reflections on the psychology of thought* (Vol. 1, pp. 99–108). Chichester, UK: John Wiley & Sons.

Wickens, D. D. (1970). Encoding categories of words: An empirical approach to meaning. *Psychological Review, 77,* 1–15.

Wiley, J., & Jarosz, A. F. (2012). Working memory capacity, attentional focus, and problem solving. *Current Directions in Psychological Science, 21*(4), 258–262.

Wilkins, M. C. (1928). The effect of changed material on ability to do formal syllogistic reasoning. *Archives of Psychology, 102*, 83.

Wilson, T. D., & Schooler, J. W. (1991). Thinking too much: Introspection can reduce the quality of preferences and decisions. *Attitudes and Social Cognition, 60*(2), 181–192.

Witt, J. K., Linkenauger, S. A., & Proffitt, D. R. (2012). Get me out of this slump! Visual illusions improve sports performance. *Psychological Science, 23*, 397–399.

Witt, J. K., & Proffitt, D. R. (2005). See the ball, hit the ball: Apparent ball size is correlated with batting average. *Psychological Science, 16*, 937–938.

Wittgenstein, L. (1953). *Philosophical investigations*. New York: Macmillan.

Wixted, J. T. (2004). The psychology of neuroscience and forgetting. *Annual Review of Psychology, 55*, 235–269.

Wixted, J. T. (2010). The role of retroactive interference and consolidation in everyday forgetting. In S. Della Sala (Ed.), *Forgetting* (pp. 285–312). East Sussex, UK: Psychology Press.

Wood, N., & Cowan, N. (1995). The cocktail party phenomenon revisited: How frequent are attention shifts to one's name in an irrelevant auditory channel? *Journal of Experimental Psychology: Human Perception and Performance, 21*, 255–260.

Woodworth, R. S. & Sells, S. B. (1935). An atmosphere effect in syllogistic reasoning. *Journal of Experimental Psychology, 18*, 451–460.

Zaretskaya, N., Anstis, S., & Bartels, A. (2013). Parietal cortex mediates conscious perception of illusory Gestalt. *Journal of Neuroscience, 33*, 523–531.

Zhang, G., & Simon, H. A. (1985). STM capacity for Chinese words and idioms: Chunking and acoustical loop hypotheses. *Memory & Cognition, 13*, 193–201.

Zu, B., Chen, C., Loftus, E. F., He, Q., Chen, C., Lei, X., et al. (2002). Brief exposure to misinformation can lead to long-term false memories. *Applied Cognitive Psychology, 26*, 301–307.

Zwaan, R. A., & Radvansky, G. A. (1998). Situation models in language comprehension and memory. *Psychological Bulletin, 123*, 162–185.

Zwaan, R. A., Stanfield, R. A., & Yaxley, R. H. (2002). Do language comprehenders routinely represent the shapes of objects? *Psychological Science, 13*, 168–171.

Author Index

Abney, D. H., 118
Abrahamson, A. A., 309
Abrams, R. A., 14
Abu-Obeid, N., 193
Aitchison, J., 212
Akahane-Yamada, R., 212
Alba, J. W., 275, 276
Allen, R. J., 112, 113
Allen, S. W., 247, 248, 249
Alpert, N. M., 28, 185
Altmann, G. T. M., 216
Amiel-Tison, C., 227
Amit, E., 197
Anderson, A., 226
Anderson, J. R., 254
Anglin, J. M., 253
Anstis, S., 53, 79, 80
Antonini, T., 223
Arnold, J. E., 217, 218
Atkinson, R. C., 98, 99
Atran, S., 260
Ayres, T. J., 112

Baars, B. J., 79
Baddeley, A. G., 108, 109, 111, 112, 113, 114, 137, 138, 139
Bahrick, H. P., 105
Ball, T. M., 183, 185
Balota, D. A., 14, 213
Banaji, M. R., 259
Banton, T., 15
Barron, E., 34, 35
Barsalou, L. W., 196, 244, 249, 252, 256
Bartels, A., 53, 79, 80
Bartlett, F., 13, 157
Basak, C., 173
Bastian, J., 212
Batteli, L., 60
Baumgardner, T. L., 85
Beall, A. C., 62
Beck, S. M., 37, 38
Beckner, , J. K., 118
Beeman, M., 286
Belleville, S., 173
Bergelson, E., 227
Berlin, B., 252
Berman, M. G., 114
Bernstein, D. M., 169
Bertoncini, J., 227
Bestmann, S., 32
Bever, T. G., 232
Biederman, I., 47
Bilalic, M., 277
Bjork, E. L., 135
Bjork, R. A., 134, 135
Blackwell, J. M., 161
Blaxton, T. A., 140
Blunt, J. R., 135
Bock, J. K., 221, 224, 243
Böckler, A., 88, 89, 90
Bodenhausen, G. V., 259
Borchers, S., 57
Bowden, E. M., 286
Bower, G. H., 254
Boynes-Braem, P., 253
Brach, M., 56, 58
Bradfield, A. L., 167
Brady, P., 144
Braine, M. D. S., 305
Brainerd, C. J., 163
Brakke, K. E., 232
Brandone, A. C., 229
Branigan, H. P., 226
Bransford, J. D., 140, 141, 157, 160, 268, 288
Braver, T. S., 37, 38
Brewer, M. B., 259
Brewer, W. F., 158
Brick, P., 105
Brimacombe, C. A. E., 167
Britten, K. H., 60
Broadbent, D. E., 71
Brooks, L. R., 104, 247, 248, 249
Brown, J., 103
Brown, R., 253
Brown, V., 75
Brownell, H. H., 253
Brown-Schmidt, S., 217, 218
Bruza, P. D., 254
Buchanan, M., 111, 112
Bullock, T. H., 47
Bunney, B. G., 75
Bunting, M. F., 72
Burgess, C., 215
Burton, H., 101
Busnel, M. C., 226
Byrne, R. M. J., 312

Cabanis, E. A., 210
Cahill, L., 144
Calvo-Merino, B., 60
Campo, N. S., 168
Caramazza, A., 256
Carey, S., 251
Carlson, A., 36
Carlson, M., 216, 217
Carlson, R. L., 75
Castel, A. D., 174, 175
Catlin, J., 243
Cavanagh, P., 60

Chabris, C. F., 28, 81
Chaddock, L., 173
Chang, K-M., 36
Charness, N., 287
Chase, G. A., 85
Chase, W. G., 287
Chater, N., 302, 307, 308
Chee, E., 85
Chein, J. M., 97, 107, 284
Chen, C., 165
Cheng, P. W., 305, 310
Cherry, E. C., 72
Chi, R. P., 276, 286, 287
Chomsky, N., 4, 210, 215, 228, 231
Christensen, A., 57
Chronicle, E. P., 276
Chrosniak, L. D., 168
Chumbley, J. I., 213
Clark, H. H., 225
Cleland, A. A., 226
Clément, F., 173
Clifasefi, S. L., 169
Coane, J. H., 163
Cockburn, J., 118
Cogdill, M., 146
Cohen, A. J., 193
Cohen, B., 250, 260
Cohen, G., 168
Cohen, J. D., 320
Cohn, M., 97, 107
Colbert, J. M., 162
Coley, J. D., 260
Collins, A. M., 254, 255
Conrad, R., 103
Conway, A. R. A., 72
Corballis, M. C., 231
Cosmides, L., 305
Cowan, N., 101, 102, 114
Cox, C. S., 85
Cox, J. R., 303
Craighero, L., 29
Craik, F. I. M., 131, 132
Cree, G. S., 252
Crowder, R. G., 101
Cruse, D. A., 253
Csapo, K., 186, 188
Cummins, D. D., 311
Cunitz, A. R., 134
Cutting, C. J., 223

Dale, R., 226
Dallenbach, K. M., 130
Damian, M. F., 223
Darwin, C. T., 101
Davidson, J. E., 275
de Groot, A. D., 287
De Neys, W., 320, 321, 322, 323
DeCasper, A. J., 226
Decety, J., 196
Dechent, O., 32
Deese, J., 160
Deguchi, T., 212
Dehaene, S., 36
Del Pinal, G., 320
Dell, G. S., 221, 222, 225
DeLosh, E. L., 144
Demers, R. A., 230
Devine, P. G., 259
Dewey, J., 268
Dickinson-Anson, H., 145
Dickstein, L. S., 304
Diesch, E., 212
Dijksterhuis, A., 319
Dodane, C., 227
Doherty, M. E., 312
Doherty, S., 193, 195
Dominey, P. F., 227
Donders, F., 13
Dosher, B. A., 101
Dragan, W., 312
Dronkers, N., 210
Duffy, S. A., 215
Dull, V., 259
Dunbar, K. N., 310
Duncker, K., 274, 275, 277
Düzel, E., 28, 30, 162
Dysart, J., 167

Eagle, M., 116
Ebbinghaus, H., 128
Eberhard, K. M., 224
Eddy, M., 62
Eich, E., 139
Eimas, P. D., 212
Einstein, G. O., 118, 144, 188, 189
Eisenband, J. G., 217, 218
Elder, J. H., 51, 60
Elie, C. J., 161
Ellis, N. C., 112
Emberson, L. L., 233
Epstein, M. L., 195, 196
Epstein, W., 15
Erard, M., 221
Erdfelder, E., 302
Erickson, K. L, 173
Evans, J. St. B. T., 308, 319

Fadiga, L., 29, 57
Fajen, B., 54
Fallon, J. H., 145
Faulkner, D., 168
Feeney, A., 309
Feltovich, P. J., 287
Fenn, K. M., 231
Fernandez-Duque, D., 71, 73
Ferreira, V. S., 223
Fiebelkorn, I. C., 53, 79
Fisher, A. V., 261, 262
Fisher, R., 168
Fisher, R. P., 167

Fitch, W. T., 231
Fleck, J., 286
Fodor, J. D., 216
Foer, J., 128, 144, 182, 189
Fogassi, L., 29, 57
Foley, J. E., 193
Fontaine, F., 173
Ford, M., 299
Fosse, H. R., 129
Fosse, M., 129
Fouts, D. H., 232
Fouts, R. S., 232
Fox Tree, J. E., 225
Foxe, J. J., 53, 79
Francis, W. S., 208
Franks, J. J., 140, 141
Fraser, J., 167, 168
Frazier, L., 216, 217
Frensch, P. A., 287
Fried, I., 29
Fromkin, V. A., 221
Fugelsang, J. A., 310
Fulero, S. M., 167

Galea, D., 254
Gallese, V., 29, 57
Gallo, D. A., 163
Galotti, K. M., 33, 48, 312, 314
Ganel, T., 57
Ganis, G., 183, 185
Gardner, B. T., 232
Gardner, R. A., 232
Garrett, M. F., 221, 223
Garrod, S., 225, 226, 243
Gauthier, S., 173
Geiselman, R. E., 167
Gelade, G., 73, 77, 78, 86
Gentner, T. Q., 231
George, J., 117
Gernsbacher, M. A., 28
Gibson, E., 216
Gibson, J., 54
Gick, M. L., 277, 278, 279
Gilbert, B., 173
Gilhooly, K. J., 307
Glanzer, M., 134
Glaser, D. E., 60
Glaser, R., 287
Glenberg, A. M., 219
Glucksberg, S., 242
Gobet, F., 277, 288
Godden, D. R., 137, 138, 139
Goebel, R., 32
Goel, V., 269, 320, 321, 322
Goldstein, M. H., 233
Golinkoff, R. M., 228, 229
Goodale, M. A., 56, 57
Gosche, K. M., 173
Graf, P., 137, 141, 142
Granier-Deferre, C., 226
Grant, E. R., 283, 289, 290
Gray, W., 253
Greene, J. D., 197
Greenwald, A. G., 259
Greer, J., 34, 35
Gregory, A. H., 168
Grèzes, J., 60, 196
Grice, P., 208
Griffin, Z. M., 225
Griffith, B. C., 212
Griggs, R. A., 303
Griggs, R. S., 299
Grill-Spector, K., 36
Gross, C. G., 29
Gross, K. A., 312
Gustafson, M., 218

Haggard, P., 60
Hagoort, P., 35
Haider, H., 275, 284, 285, 287
Hall, C. R., 196
Halsted, N., 227
Hampton, J. A., 244, 254, 255
Hanson, V. I., 103
Harlow, J. M., 23
Harris, G. E., 118
Harris, K. S., 212
Harris, P. L., 243
Harris, R. J., 6
Harsuiker, R., 225
Hart, B., 227
Hartsuiker, R. J., 225
Hashtroudi, S., 168
Hauk, O., 219, 220
Hauri, P., 30
Hauser, M. D., 231
Hayashi, A., 212
He, Q., 165
Healy, A. F., 103
Hegarty, M., 191, 192
Heinz, H-J., 28, 30, 162
Heit, E., 258, 309
Heitman, J. L., 174, 175
Hennelly, R. A., 112
Hennon, E. A., 228
Henson, R., 320
Higuchi, T., 6
Hilton, J. L., 259
Hilts, P. J., 24
Himelbach, M., 57
Hirsh-Pasek, K., 228, 229
Hitch, G. J., 108, 112, 113
Hobson, J. A., 129
Hockett, C., 230
Hoffman, H. S., 212
Holland, H. L., 167
Hollich, G., 228, 229
Holyoak, K. J., 277, 278, 279, 305
Hommel, B., 82
Hsee, C. K., 318

Hubel, D. H., 47
Huettig, F., 225
Hulme, C., 112
Humphrey, K. H., 224
Hund, A. M., 193

Iba-Zizen, M., 210
Imanaka, K., 6
Irwin, D. E., 14
Isarida, T., 138
Isarida, T. K., 138
Iverson, P., 212

Jackendoff, R., 208
Jacoby, L. L., 117
James, W., 70
Jarosz, A. F., 283
Jeannerod, M., 195
Jenkins, J. B., 130
Johnson, D., 253
Johnson, M. K., 157, 160, 168
Johnson, M. L., 71, 73
Johnson, S. T., 111
Johnson-Laird, P. N., 218, 299, 305, 311
Johnsrude, I., 219, 220
Johnston, W. A., 76, 77, 85
Jonides, J., 114
Jung-Beeman, M., 286
Jusczyk, P., 212, 227

Kahana, M. J., 14
Kahneman, D., 76, 315, 317, 319
Kaiser, M. K., 62
Kaplan, C. A., 275
Karnath, H. O., 23
Karpicke, J. D., 135
Kaschak, M. P., 28, 219
Kaufman, L., 101
Keane, M., 260
Keil, F. C., 243, 251
Kelley, C., 117
Kelly, M. H., 243
Keppel, G., 104
Kershaw, T. C., 276
Kettermann, A., 212
Kijima, A., 6
Kilbane, M. C., 279
Kim, I. J., 185
Kinsbourne, M., 117
Kiritani, S., 212
Kitto, K., 254
Klatzky, R. L., 193, 195
Klauer, K. C., 302
Kloos, H., 261, 262
Klopfer, D., 287
Knoblich, G., 36, 275, 284, 285
Knoedler, A. J., 105
Koch, C., 29
Koh, K., 279
Kohler, A., 32
Köhler, W., 274
Kornbrot, D., 118
Kosslyn, S. M., 28, 183, 184, 185, 191
Kounios, J., 286
Krauchunas, S. M., 62
Kreiman, G., 29
Kruggel, F., 145
Kubovy, M., 51, 60
Kuhl, P. K., 212
Kvavilashvili, L., 118

LaBerge, D., 74, 75
Lambertz, G., 227
Lambon Ralph, M. A., 244
LaMontagne, P., 37, 38
Larkin, J. H., 283
Lashley, G., 57
Lashley, K., 210
Lassaline, M. E., 253, 258
Lawrence, A., 112
LeBreton, J. M., 146
Lecanuet, J.-P., 226
Lei, X., 165
Leiter, E., 116
LePort, A. K. R., 145
Lesgold, A., 287
Levelt, W. J. M., 210, 221, 223, 224, 225
Levin, D. T., 81
Lewis, R. I., 114
Lewis, V., 111
Liberman, A. M., 212
Liberman, P., 231
Libet, B., 36
Lin, E. L., 250, 251
Linden, D. E. J., 32
Linderholm, T., 218
Lindsay, D. S., 165, 166
Lindsay, R. C. L., 167
Linkenauger, S. A., 56, 57, 58, 59
Lisker, L., 212
Loftus, E., 164, 165, 166, 168, 169, 190, 254
Loftus, G., 14
Logan, G. D., 87
Loomis, J. M., 62
Lorch, R. F., 218
Louie, G., 118
Love, B. C., 248
Lowenstein, G., 320
Lu, Z.-L., 101
Luchins, A. S., 276
Lui, L., 259
Luis, V., 287
Luo, J., 36, 285
Lupyan, G., 233
Lustig, C. A., 114
Lynch, E. B., 260

MacGregor, J. N., 276
Mack, M. L., 248
MacKinnon, D. P., 167

Macrae, C. N., 259
Madigan, S., 101
Madigan, S. A., 188
Magliano, J. P., 283
Mahler, J., 227
Mahon, B. Z., 256
Maier, N. R. F., 272, 275, 276
Malave, V. L., 36
Malcolm, G. L., 62, 63
Malek, E. A., 56
Maljkovic, V., 28
Malpass, R. S., 167
Malt, B. C., 249
Mangun, G. R., 28, 30, 162
Mantonakis, A., 169
Margoliash, D., 231
Markesbery, W. R., 173
Markman, A. B., 253
Martin, A., 196
Martin, R. C., 223
Mash, V., 118
Mason, R. A., 36
Mattfield, A. T., 145
Maugeais, R., 226
May, C. P., 144
Mayberry, E. J., 244
Mayfield, S., 118
McBeath, M. K., 62
McBride, D. M., 118, 162, 163
McCabe, D. P., 174, 175
McClelland, J. L., 7, 216, 252, 254
McCloskey, B., 193, 195
McCloskey, M. E., 242
McClure, P., 187
McClure, S. M., 320
McConnell, J., 109, 110
McDaniel, M. A., 37, 38, 118, 119, 120, 144, 188, 189
McDermott, K. B., 106, 160, 162, 163
McEvoy, C. L., 254
McGaugh, J. L., 144
McIntosh, R. D., 57
McKoon, G., 218
McLeod, P., 277
McNorgan, C., 252
McRae, K., 252
Medin, D. L., 246, 250, 260
Meier, B., 137, 141, 142
Meints, K., 243
Meissner, C. A., 167, 168
Mellah, S., 173
Melton, A. W., 131, 132
Memon, A., 167, 168
Menenti, L., 35
Mervis, C. B., 242, 243, 244, 249, 253
Metcalfe, J. A., 275
Metzler, J., 110, 111, 184
Meyer, A. S., 223, 224
Meyer, D. E., 14, 214
Miklósi, Á., 231
Miller, C. A., 224
Miller, G. A., 102, 210
Milne, A. B., 118, 259
Milner, A. D., 56
Milovanovic, G. S., 255
Minda, J. P., 252
Mintzer, M. Z., 189
Mitchell, T. M., 36
Molholm, S., 53, 79
Molnár, C., 231
Monsell, S., 213
Moore, K. S., 114
Moray, N., 72
Moreno, F. J., 287
Moritz, S. E., 196
Morris, C. D., 140, 141
Morrisette, N., 118
Mortimer, J. A., 173
Moscovitch, M., 97, 107
Moulton, S. T., 191
Movshon, J. A., 60
Muir, C., 112
Mulligan, N. M., 137
Murai, G., 6
Murphy, G. L., 240, 249, 250, 251, 253, 255, 258, 259, 260
Murphy, J., 232
Mynatt, C. R., 312

Nairne, J. S., 102, 104, 112, 146, 152
Naples, A. J., 268
Nathan, M. J., 320
Naveh-Benjamin, M., 112
Neath, I., 102, 104, 105, 112
Nee. D. E., 114
Neisser, Ulric, 4
Nelson, C. A., 173
Nelson, D. L., 254
Nestor, P. J., 256, 257
Neuschatz, J. S., 161
Neuse, J., 101
Newell, A., 280, 281
Newsome, W. T., 60
Newstead, S. E., 299
Nicoletti, R., 82, 83
Nordgren, L. F., 319
Norman, D., 114
Norman, D. A., 5, 103
Noveck, I. A., 208
Novick, L. R., 279, 287, 310
Nozari, N., 225
Nusbaum, H. C., 231
Nuthmann, A., 62, 63

Oaksford, M., 302, 307, 308
Ohlsson, S., 275, 276, 283, 284, 285
Okado, Y., 165, 166
Ormerod, T. C., 276
Osborn, J., 105
Osherson, D. N., 260
Osman, A. M., 14
Oyama, T., 61

Padgitt, A. J., 193
Paivio, A., 186, 188
Palmer, J., 164, 165, 166
Palmer, S. E., 51, 60
Pandeirada, J. N. S., 146, 152
Parker, E. S., 144
Pascual-Leone, A., 60
Passingham, R. E., 60
Patterson, K., 256, 257
Pavlenko, A., 208
Payne, D. G., 161
Pearlmutter, M. J., 216
Pellegrino, J., 193, 195
Pence, K. L., 229
Penrod, S., 167
Peterson, L. R., 103, 104, 111
Peterson, M. A., 51, 60
Peterson, M. J., 103, 104
Peterson, R. R., 223
Petersson, K. M., 35
Pettito, L. A., 232
Pickering, M. J., 225, 226
Pilley, J. W., 232
Pinker, S., 184
Plaisant, O., 210
Pliske, D. B., 312
Plunkett, K., 243
Poldrack, R. A., 320
Polya, G., 268
Pomerantz, J. R., 53
Pomplun, M., 287
Pongrácz, P., 231
Portillo, M. C., 53
Posner, M. I., 14
Prakash, R. S., 173
Premack, A. J., 232
Premack, D., 232
Preston, A. R., 248
Pretz, J. E., 268
Proffitt, D. R., 15, 56, 57, 58, 59
Pruden, S. M., 228
Pulvermüller, F., 28, 35, 219, 220
Pyc, M. A., 135, 136
Pylyshyn, Z. W., 184, 185

Quillian, M. R., 254, 255
Quinn, J. G., 109, 110
Quiroga, R. Q., 29

Radvansky, G. A., 218, 283
Ramos, D., 232
Raney, E. G., 285
Ratcliff, R., 218
Rayner, K., 215, 216, 217
Reader, M. J., 85
Reboul, A., 208
Reddy, L., 29
Rees, G., 49
Reicher, G. M., 212
Reid, A. K., 232
Reina, R., 287
Reingold, E. M., 287
Reiser, B. J., 183, 185
Revlis, R., 304
Reyna, V. F., 163
Rhenius, D., 275, 284, 285
Riby, L. M., 34, 35
Richardson, D. C., 6, 226
Richmond, J., 173
Rick, S., 320
Riley, M., 54
Rips, L. J., 243, 244, 251, 254, 258, 260, 305, 310
Risley, T., 227
Rizzolatti, G., 29, 57
Roberts, M. J., 299, 304
Robinson, H., 287
Roediger, H. L., III, 106, 135, 136, 140, 160, 162, 163, 174, 175
Rogers, T. T., 252, 256, 257
Rorden, C., 23
Rosch, E., 242, 243, 244, 249, 253
Rosenbaum, D., 55, 56, 58
Ross, B. H., 258, 279
Rothe, A. R., 6
Rubin, D. C., 106
Rubinstein, J., 258
Rudell, A. P., 82
Rumbaugh, D. M., 232
Rumelhart, D. E., 5, 254, 309
Rustichini, A., 320

Sabido, R., 287
Sach, A. T., 32
Sacks, O., 23
Sage, K., 244
Sakai, T., 138
Salomon, M. M., 283
Sanders, R. J., 232
Sanfey, A. G., 320
Sanford, A. J., 243
Savage-Rumbaugh, E. S., 232
Savoy, P., 223
Schacter, D., 153, 154, 156, 175
Schaffer, M., 246
Schiller, P. H., 85
Schneider, W., 85, 86, 87
Schooler, J. W., 319
Schriefers, H., 223, 224
Schuerholz, L. J., 85
Schurger, A., 36
Schvaneveldt, R. W., 14, 214
Schwartz, M. F., 225
Schwartz, T. H., 53, 79
Schwarzkopf, D. S., 49
Schyns, P. G., 62, 63
Scott, C. L., 6
Scullin, M. K., 37, 38, 119
Segaert, K., 35
Sellen, A. J., 118
Sells, S. B., 307

Semenov, A., 56, 58
Sevcik, R. A., 232
Seya, Y., 6
Shaffer, D. M., 62
Shallice, T., 114
Shank, H., 118
Shapiro, D. A., 302
Shepard, R. N., 110, 111, 184
Shiffrin, R. M., 85, 86, 87, 98, 99
Shinkareva, S. V., 36
Shoben, E. J., 243, 244, 254
Simizu, M., 61
Simon, H. A., 103, 275, 280, 281, 283, 287, 288
Simon, J. R., 82
Simons, D., 81
Simpson, G. B., 215
Sinclair, R. J., 101
Singer, M., 218
Singh, M., 51, 60
Sinha, I., 8
Siqueland, E. R., 212
Sitt, J. D., 36
Skinner, B. F., 3, 209, 228
Sloman, S. A., 311
Slotnick, S. D., 185
Sloutsky, V. M., 261, 262
Small, M., 167
Smallwood, J., 34, 35
Smith, C. D., 173
Smith, E. E., 243, 244, 254, 260
Smith, J. D., 252
Smith, M. F., 8
Smith, S. M., 138
Smith, T., 193, 195
Snodgrass, J. G., 187, 189
Snow, C. E., 227
Snowdon, D. A., 173
Snyder, A. W., 276, 286
Song, C., 49
Sperling, G., 99, 100, 101
Spivey, M. J., 6, 233, 283, 289, 290
Squire, L. R., 9, 107
Stahl, C., 302
Stampe, D. M., 287
Stanfield, R. A., 219
Stark, C. E. L., 145, 165, 166
Steblay, N. M., 167
Steedman, M. J., 299
Stefanucci, J., 15
Stein, B. S., 268, 288
Sternberg, R. J., 268, 275, 309
Stevens, E., 212
Stickgold, R., 129
Strayer, D. L., 76, 77, 85
Stroop, J. R., 83
Swingley, D., 227
Swinney, D., 214
Sykes, E. D. A., 304
Sykes, M., 77
Szabo, A., 173

Talarico, J. M., 106
Talmi, D., 97, 107
Tanaka, J. W., 253, 259
Tanzer, M., 57
Taraban, R., 216
Taylor, M., 253, 259
Terrace, H. S., 232
Thaler, R. H., 8
Thomas, A. K., 168
Thomas, L. E., 284
Thomas, R., 118
Thompson, N., 111, 112
Thompson, V. A., 310
Thompson, W. L., 28, 183, 185
Thompson-Schill, S. L., 256
Thorndike, E. L., 274
Tohkura, Y., 212
Tozawa, J., 61
Treisman, A. M., 73, 74, 77, 78, 86
Treyens, J. C., 158
Trueswell, J. C., 217, 218
Tulving, E., 28, 30, 131, 132, 162
Turvey, M., 54, 101, 105
Tversky, A., 315, 317, 318, 319
Tweney, R. D., 312

Umiltá, C., 82, 83
Underwood, B. J., 104

Vallar, G., 111
Van Arsdall, J. E., 146
Van Canfort, T. E., 232
van der Wel, P. R. D., 88, 89, 90
VanDenBroek, P., 218
Vartanian, O., 320, 321, 322
Vela, E., 138
Vigliocco, G., 223, 225
Vigorito, J., 212
von Frisch, K., 231
von Helmholtz, H., 12
von Hippel, W., 259
Voss, M. W., 173

Wagemans, J., 51, 60
Wagman, J. B., 6, 56
Wallas, G., 268
Wang, Y., 287
Warren, R., 212
Warrington, E. K., 107, 171, 256
Wason, P. C., 301, 302, 303, 308, 311
Wassermann, E., 30
Waugh, N. C., 103
Weber, K., 35
Weisberg, R. W., 275, 276, 284
Weise, S. B., 28
Weisel, T. N., 47
Weiskrantz, L., 107, 171
Wells, G. L., 167
Welsh, T. N., 88, 89, 90
Wernicke, K., 209

Wertheimer, M., 275
Wetherick, N. E., 307
Whitten, W. B., 134
Wickens, D. D., 104
Wiebe, D., 275
Wiley, J., 283
Wilkins, A. J., 118
Wilkins, M. C., 300
Williams, J. K., 75
Williams, S. L., 232
Williamson, S. J., 101
Wilson, T. D., 319
Wisniewski, E. J., 253
Witt, J. K., 56, 57, 58, 59
Wittgenstein, L., 241
Wixted, J. T., 129, 130
Wolf, J. R., 82
Woloshyn, V., 117
Wood, N., 72
Woodworth, R. S., 307
Worner, W. J., 312
Wright, J. C., 259

Yantis, S., 14
Yaxley, R. H., 219
Yonelinas, A. P., 28, 30, 162

Zaretskaya, N., 53, 79, 80
Zhang, G., 103
Ziegler, L., 57
Zu, B., 165
Zwaan, R. A., 218, 219

Subject Index

Accuracy measurements, 13
Alignment theory, 225–226
Alzheimer's disease, 172–173, 172 (figure)
American Sign Language, 232
Amnesia
  Alzheimer's disease, 172–173, 172 (figure)
  in childhood, 173
  implicit memory and, 170–171
  types of, 24, 169–170, 170 (figure)
Analogical transfer strategy, 277–279, 278 (table), 287, 309
Animals and communication, 230–232
Aphasia, 23, 209
Attention
  automatic and controlled processing, 84–88
  cocktail party effect, 72–73
  dual-task method of, 76–77, 77 (figure)
  eye contact and motion, 88–90 (box)
  feature-integration model of, 77–80, 78 (figure), 79 (figure)
  inattentional or change blindness, 81
  as information filter, 71–73, 71 (figure), 74 (figure)
  memory and, 84–88, 113–114
  as mental capacity, 76–77
  shadowing task, 71–72, 72 (figure), 73
  Simon effect, 81–83, 82 (figure)
  spotlight model of, 74–75, 75 (figures)
  Stroop task, 83–84, 84 (figure)
Attenuation theory of attention, 73, 74 (figure)
Automaticity, theory of, 87–88
Axon, 25

Baddeley, Alan, 108–114
Baddeley's model of working memory
  central executive, 113–114
  episodic buffer, 112–113
  overview, 109 (figure)
  phonological loop, 110–112
  visuospatial sketchpad, 108–110
Bartlett, Frederic, 13, 157
Behavior and brain activity, 36–37
Behaviorist perspective, 3
Bell, Andi, 128
Bias, types of, 315–318
The Big Book of Concepts (Murphy), 240
Biological perspective of cognition, overview of, 6–7
Bizareness effect, 188–189, 188 (table)
Bottom-up processing, 46–48, 47 (figure)
Brain function
  behaviors and, 36–37
  brain imaging techniques, 14, 32–36
  cognitive ability and, 24, 35–36, 97
  concept organization, 254–256, 257 (figure)
  diagram of, 27 (figure)
  emotional regulation, 23
  language ability and, 23, 209
  measures of, 29–32
  memory and, 24, 28, 97
  mind-body problem, 36–37
  nervous system and, 25–28
  object identification and, 23–24
  object recognition and location ability, 56–57, 59 (figure)
  recording techniques, 33–36, 57
  in sensory system, 44–46
Broca, Paul, 23, 209
Broca's aphasia, 23, 24 (figure), 209

Case study methodology, 8–9
Category induction, 258, 261–263 (box), 309–310
  See also Concepts; Inductive reasoning
Causal reasoning, 310–311
Central executive. 113–114
  See also Memory; Working memory
Change blindness, 81
Chomsky, Noam, 3–4, 4 (photo), 210
Chunking of information, 102
Cocktail party effect, 72–73
Cognition
  automatic and controlled processing, 84–88
  computer model of, 5–6
  concept organization, 254–256, 257 (figure)
  connectionist models of, 7
  definition of, 2
  embodied, 6
  imagery and, 182–183, 190–193
  See also Brain function; Concepts; Problem solving
Cognitive economy, 254
Cognitive neuroscience
  brain function and cognitive processes, findings on, 35–36
  clinical case studies in, 22–24
  concepts, approaches to, 255–256
  and decision making, research on, 320–322, 321 (table)
  measures in, 29–36
  and memory processes, 97
  mind-body debate, 36–37
Cognitive psychology
  biological perspective, 6–7
  definitions of, 2–3
  embodied cognition perspective, 6
  historical development of, 3–5
  measures used in, 12–15, 29–36
  representationalism, 5–6
Communication. *See* Language
Concepts
  basic level, 253–254
  category induction, 258, 261–263 (box)
  as definitions, 241–244
  exemplar approach to, 246–249
  expertise and, 259–260
  feature comparison approaches, 255

hierarchy of, 252, 253 (figure), 254, 255 (figure), 259–260
memory and, 246–247, 254–256
neuroscience approaches, 255–256
as perceptions, 252
prototype approach to, 244–245
stereotypes, 258–259
stored-network approaches to, 254, 255 (figure)
typicality effects, 242–244, 246, 255
world knowledge approach to, 249–251
Concreteness effect, 187–188
Conditional reasoning, 300–304, 301 (table)
Consolidation, 129
Correlational studies, 9–10
Cotton, Ronald, 152, 153, 155
Counterfactual thinking, 312

Decision making
availability bias, 317
dual-process framework in, 319–320, 322–324 (box)
elimination-by-aspects strategy, 318
framing bias in, 317–318
general model of, 314–315
idealized model of, 315, 316 (figure)
past experience consideration in, 318
prospect theory, 319
representativeness bias in, 315–317
See also Deductive reasoning; Inductive reasoning
Deductive reasoning
conclusion interpretation approaches, 304
conditional reasoning, 300–304, 301 (table)
dual-process framework, 308, 308 (table), 319–320, 322–324 (box)
four-card task and, 301–302, 302 (figure), 303 (figures), 304 (figure)
representation-explanation approaches, 304–307, 306 (figure), 307 (figure)
surface approaches, 307–308
syllogistic reasoning, 299–300, 300 (table)
See also Decision making; Inductive reasoning
Dementia, 255–256
Dendrites, 25
Dependent variable, 8, 9–12
Determinism, 7
Distal stimulus, 46
Donders, Franciscus, 13
Dorsal pathway/stream, 57, 59 (figure)
DRM procedure for false memories, 160–163, 161 (figure)
Dual-process framework of reasoning, 308, 308 (table), 319–320, 322–324 (box)
Dual-task method of attention, 76–77, 77 (figure)

Ebbinghaus, Hermann, 3
Ebbinghaus illusion, 56, 58 (figure)
Electroencephalography (EEG), 29–30, 29 (photo), 30 (figure), 34
Embodied cognition, 6
Empiricism, 7
Encoding process in memory
levels of processing, 131–132
overview, 97, 98 (figure)
retrieval process interactions, 137–143
serial position curve, 133–135
spacing effects, 132–133
Encoding specificity principle, 137
Episodic buffer, 108, 112–113
See also Memory; Working memory
Episodic memory, 106
Experimental studies, 10–12

Foer, Joshua, 128, 144
Framing bias, 317–318
Functional magnetic resonance imaging (fMRI), 32–33, 33 (figure)
Fuzzy trace theory, 163

Gage, Phineas, 23
Gestalt approaches to problem solving
analogical transfer, 277–279, 278 (table)
insight, 275–276
mental set, 276–277
Gestalt principles and perception
closure, 52, 52 (figure)
good continuation, 50 (photo), 52, 53 (photo)
principle of Pragnanz, 52–53, 54 (photos)
proximity, 51–52, 52 (photo)
similarity, 51, 52 (photo)

H. M. (Henry Molaison), 8–9, 24, 169–170
Hypothesis testing, 311–312

IDEAL framework for problem solving, 288
Illusions, 48–50, 49 (photo), 58 (figure)
Imagery
bizarreness effect, 188–189, 188 (table)
cognition and, 182–183
concreteness effect, 187–188
false memories and, 190
judgment and, 197–198 (box)
mnemonics and, 189–190
nonvisual, 193–197
picture superiority effect, 186–187
problem solving and, 191–193
spatial and propositional representation, 183–186
wayfinding and, 193, 194–195 (figure)
Implicit memory, 117
Inattentional blindness, 81
Independent variable, 8, 9–12
Inductive reasoning
analogical reasoning, 277–279, 309
category induction, 258, 261–263 (box), 309–310
causal reasoning, 310–311
counterfactual thinking, 312
hypothesis testing, 311–312
See also Decision making; Deductive reasoning

James, William, 70

Knowledge. *See* Concepts; Language

Language
animal comprehension of, 230–232
aphasia, 23, 209

characteristics of human communication, 230–231, 230 (table)
development of, 226–229
dialogue, 225–226, 232–233 (box)
inferences in, 217–219
lexical recognition, 213–215, 214 (figure), 215 (figure)
perception, 211–212
processing, 209–210
production, 220–225
speech errors, 221, 222 (table)
structure of, 205–209
syntactic analysis, 215–217
Level-of-processing effect in memory, 131
Logic theories, 305
Long-term memory
animate objects and, 145–146 (box)
encoding effects, 131–135, 137–143
implicit, 117
prospective, 117–118
recall tasks, 115–117, 133–135
recognition tasks, 115–117
retrieval process, 135–143, 143 (table)
types of, 106–107
See also Memory

Magnetic resonance imaging (MRI), 32, 32 (photo)
Magnetoencephalography (MEG), 31
Measurements
accuracy of, 13
brain imaging techniques, 32–36, 32 (photo), 33 (photo)
brain visualization measures, 14
electroencephalography (EEG), 29–30, 29 (photo), 30 (figure), 34
magnetoencephalography (MEG), 31
response time, 13–14
single-cell recording, 29, 29 (figure), 34
transcranial direct current stimulation (tDCS), 32, 276
transcranial magnetic stimulation (TMS), 31–32, 31 (figure)
Memory
amnesia, 169–173
attention and, 84–88, 113–114
autobiographical, 144–145
Baddeley's model of working memory, 108–114, 109 (figure)
brain function and, 24, 28
concepts and, 246–247, 254–256
in deductive reasoning, 305–307
encoding process in, 97, 98 (figure), 131–135, 137–143
environmental context effects, 137–138
episodic, 106
errors (*See* Memory errors)
expertise-related information and, 174–175 (box)
false memory creation, 160–163, 161 (figure), 190
forgetting, causes of, 127–130, 154
imagery and, 186–190
implicit, 117
long-term memory (overview), 105–107
mnemonic techniques, 128, 143–144, 189–190
modal model of (overview), 97–98, 99 (figure)
mood-dependent effects, 139, 140 (figure)
problem solving and, 287
procedural, 107
prospective, 37–38 (box), 117–118
recall tasks, 115–117, 133–135, 134 (figure)
recognition tasks, 115–117
reconstruction of, 157–160
retrieval process, 97, 98 (figure), 135–143, 143 (table)
semantic, 107, 254, 255
sensory, 99–101, 100 (figure)
short-term memory, 101–105, 104 (figure), 105 (figure)
and sleep, 119–120 (box)
storage process, 97, 98 (figure)
transfer-appropriate processing, 140
See also Long-term memory; Working memory
Memory errors
absentmindedness, 154
bias, 156
blocking, 154–155
DRM procedure and, 160–163, 161 (figure)
in eyewitness accounts, 164–168
persistence, 156
reconstruction and, 157–160
source misattribution, 155
suggestibility, 155–156
transience, 154
Mind-body problem, 36–37
Misinformation effect on memory, 164
Mnemonic techniques, 128, 143–144, 189–190
Modal model of memory, 97–107, 99 (figure)
See also Memory
Molaison, Henry (H. M.), 8–9, 24, 169–170
Moonwalking with Einstein (Foer), 128
Morphemes, 206
Motor imagery, 196
Murphy, Gregory, 240

Neisser, Ulric, 4, 4 (photo)
Nervous system, 25–29, 25 (figure), 26 (figures), 27 (figure)
Neuroeconomics, 320
Neuron cells, 25–29, 25 (figure), 26 (figures), 27 (figure)
Neuroscience. *See* Cognitive neuroscience

Object agnosia, 23–24
Observation
in correlational studies, 10
systematic, 7

Parsimony, 8
Partial report method, 99–100, 100 (figure)
Perception
attention influences on, 80–84
bottom-up processing and, 46–48, 47 (figure)
Gestalt approaches to, 50–54, 51 (table), 61
motion, 60–62
perception/action approach, 54–57, 62
top-down processing and, 48–50, 49 (figure), 49 (photo)
unconscious inference, theory of, 50, 50 (photo)
visual, 48–50, 56–57
See also Attention; Gestalt principles and perception
Perceptual loop, 225
Phineas Gage case study, 23
Phonemes, 205–206, 212

Phonological loop, 110–112
  See also Memory; Working memory
Picture superiority effect, 186–187
Ponzo illusion, 49, 49 (photo), 57
Positron emission tomography (PET), 32, 33 (photo)
Pragmatics, 208–209
Principle of Pragnanz, 52–53, 54 (photos)
Problem solving
  functional fixedness, 272–273
  Gestalt approaches to, 274–279, 278 (table)
  hill-climbing strategy, 282
  IDEAL framework for, 288
  ill-defined problems, 269
  improvement strategies, 286–288
  knowledge organization examples, 270, 270 (figure), 271–272 (figures)
  matchstick math problem examples, 284–286, 285 (figure), 286 (figure)
  means-ends strategy, 281–282
  memory and, 287
  mental resources for, 283–286
  Sudoku puzzles and, 268, 269, 269 (figure), 283–284, 284 (figure), 288 (figure)
  Tower of Hanoi problem, 280–283, 281 (figure), 282 (figure)
  trial-and-error approaches to, 274
  well-defined problems, 269
  working-backward strategy, 282–283
  See also Decision making
Procedural memory, 107
Propositional representation of mental images, 184–185
Prospective memory tasks, 117–118
Proximal stimulus, 46

Reasoning, everyday, 312–313, 313 (table)
  See also Decision making; Deductive reasoning; Inductive reasoning
Recall tasks, 115–117, 133–135, 134 (figure)
Representationalist perspective of cognition, overview of, 5–6
Representativeness bias, 315–317
Research methods
  case studies, 8–9
  correlational studies, 9–10
  experimental studies, 10–12
  scientific method, 7–8
Research study examples
  on attention, 88–90 (box)
  on category induction, 261–263 (box)
  on complex scene interpretations, 62–64 (box)
  on dialogues, 232–233 (box)
  on dual-process framework, 322–324 (box)
  on long-term memory retrieval, 145–146 (box)
  on memory and expertise-related information, 174–175 (box)
  on memory and sleep, 119–120 (box)
  on physical effort effects on distance judgments, 15–16 (box)
  on problem solving, 289–291 (box)
  on prospective memory, 37–38 (box)
  on visual imagery and moral judgment, 197–198 (box)
Response time as measure, 13–14
Retrieval process
  encoding specificity principle, 137–143
  overview, 97, 98 (figure), 143 (table)
  testing effect, 135–137
  See also Memory
Retroactive interference, 103
Rosch, Eleanor, 244

Sacks, Oliver, 23–24
Scientific method, core principles of, 7–8
Semantic memory, 106, 254
Semantics, 208, 214, 223–225
Sensory memory, 99–101, 100 (figure)
Sensory system
  functions of, 46
  parts of, 44–45, 45 (figure)
  See also Perception
Serial position curve of recall, 133–135, 134 (figure)
The Seven Sins of Memory (Schacter), 153
Shadowing task, 71–72, 72 (figure)
Short-term memory
  capacity of, 102
  chunking of information, 102
  decay theory, 103, 105 (figure)
  duration of, 103–105
  proactive interference, 104, 105 (figure)
  retroactive interference, 103, 105 (figure)
  working memory and, 102, 107–108
  See also Memory
Sign language, 232
Simon effect, 81–83, 82 (figure)
Single-cell recording, 29, 29 (figure), 57
Skinner, B. F., 3, 209
Sleep and effect on memory, 119–120 (box)
Spatial representation of images, 183–184
Spacing effect in memory, 132–133, 133 (figure)
Stereotypes, 258–259
Storage and memory, 97, 98 (figure)
Stroop task, 83–84, 84 (figure)
Sudoku puzzles, 268, 269, 269 (figure), 283–284, 284 (figure), 288 (figure)
Syllogistic reasoning, 299–300, 300 (table)
Synapse, 25
Synatic Structures (Chomsky), 210
Syntax, 206–207, 215–217, 223–225

Testability, 7–8
Thompson, Jennifer, 152, 155
Top-down processing, 48–50, 49 (figure)
Tower of Hanoi problem, 280–283, 281 (figure), 282 (figure)
Transcranial direct current stimulation (tDCS), 32, 276
Transcranial magnetic stimulation (TMS), 31–32, 31 (figure)
Transfer-appropriate processing effects, 140–142
Typicality effect, 242–244, 255

Unconscious inference, theory of, 50, 50 (photo)

Ventral pathway/stream, 56–57, 59 (figure)
Verbal Behavior (Skinner), 209
Visual imagery. *See* Imagery
Visuospatial sketchpad, 108–110, 110 (figure)
  See also Memory; Working memory
von Helmholtz, Herman, 12

Wason, Peter, 301–302, 311–312
Wearing, Clive, 96, 102, 107
Wernicke, Karl, 23, 209
Wernicke's aphasia, 23, 24 (figure), 209
Wittgenstein, Ludwig, 241, 241 (photo)
Working memory
  attention and, 113–114
  central executive, 113–114
  description of, 107–108
  episodic buffer, 112–113
  phonological loop, 110–112
  visuospatial sketchpad, 108–110
Wundt, Wilhelm, 3

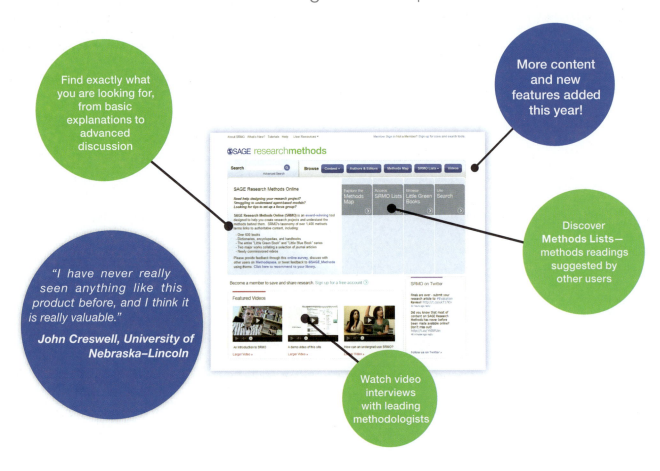

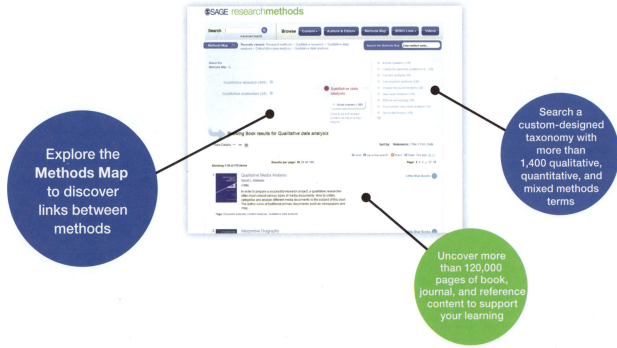